"(The [General] Reader) can read *Love and Death in the American Novel* for his pleasure alone—indeed, I know of few works of criticism that are so likely to involve the reader whose interest in literature is not of a professional kind . . . it amounts to a general cultural history of the nation."
—Lionel Trilling

"Anyone concerned with the understanding of American literature and American morals will have to take it into account."
—George Steiner, *The Reporter*

"A powerful achievement."
—*Times Literary Supplement*

"It is, in truth, one of the very few important assessments of our culture to appear since the publication twenty years ago of Matthiessen's *American Renaissance*."
—Benjamin DeMott, *Commentary*

Leslie A. Fiedler

A SCARBOROUGH BOOK

🄱 STEIN AND DAY/*Publishers*/New York

LOVE AND

DEATH

IN THE

AMERICAN

NOVEL

REVISED EDITION

THIRD SCARBOROUGH BOOKS EDITION, 1982

Revised edition first published in 1966
First edition published in 1960
Copyright © 1960 and 1966 by Leslie A. Fiedler
Library of Congress Catalog No. 66-14948
All rights reserved
Printed in the United States of America
Stein and Day/*Publishers*/Scarborough House,
Briarcliff Manor, New York 10510
ISBN 0-8128-1799-0

IN MEMORY

OF

WILLIAM

ELLERY

LEONARD

PREFACE

TO THE SECOND EDITION

REREADING *Love and Death in the American Novel* ten years after the moment at which I first began to set it down, I have been delighted and astonished to discover that I still believe what it says. The voice which speaks in its pages I no longer recognize as quite my own, but I find it a sympathetic one—for all its exclamatory and insistent tone. Like others, I have now grown so used to what was new and daring in its theses once, that I am sometimes annoyed at how hard it presses or how pleased it seems with its own insights. "But we all accept these contentions," I am tempted to cry. "This is where we now begin." Yet for old times' sake, I have not willingly surrendered more than a few exclamation points, strategic capitalizations, or italicized words.

In preparing a new edition I have, therefore, not tampered with the language or the style of the original, only everywhere pruned and condensed, out of a sense that the first version was somehow too thickly allusive, with too many asides, too intent on overwhelming the sceptical to suit the needs of readers a decade later.

I have, moreover, worked back into the main body of the text certain detailed analyses of *The Scarlet Letter, Moby Dick,* and *Huckleberry Finn,* originally consigned to a kind of appendix called "Accommodation and Transcendence." I have done this first of all because I believe that is where they best fit, but also because I have a hunch that some readers of the earlier edition never reached them at all—and they are of critical importance to the total meaning of my book.

That book as now revised seems to me a more shapely and for that reason a clearer one—one in which, for instance, the balance between psychological and sociological insights essential to my approach is more readily perceived; and the relation of both to the books I best love more cogently exposed. And especially, I hope, even the most casual reader will be able this time around to recognize the sense in which *Love and Death* can be read not as a conventional scholarly book—or an eccentric one—but a kind of gothic novel (complete with touches of black humor) whose subject is the American experience as recorded in our classic fiction. Our most serious as well as our funniest writers have found the gothic mode an apt one for telling the truth about the quality of our life; and I should, therefore, have been ashamed not to try to use it for my own purposes.

Despite all these safeguards, however, I discover that my excisions and re-arrangements have given a new pattern and rhythm and pace to a statement unaltered in substance and only slightly modified in tone. If *Love and Death* is a more spare and elegant book this time around, it is because it can afford to be a less forensic, even a less formidable one.

It has survived into a new literary era and will, I trust, continue to flourish in a new cultural climate, which, indeed it may have helped to create. The year 1960 is not very far behind us; but certain kinds of criticism still practiced and admired then—the last examples of the new genteel tradition, with its emphasis on textual analysis, its contempt for general ideas, and its fear of popular culture—now strike us as irrelevant and remote. It is my sense of the continuing relevance and immediacy of this study which has impelled me to recast and re-issue it. It is my hope that to new readers and old, it will seem still as lively and in the best sense of the word, as vulgar as ever.

LESLIE A. FIEDLER
Buffalo, New York
January, 1966

PREFACE

TO THE FIRST EDITION

THE CAUTIOUS READER, approaching a book as thick and complex as this, has every right to expect some prefatory word from the author about what he is after, what he thinks he has done; and the author (if he is I, at least) is delighted to explain himself, to welcome the kind of audience he has all along desired, and to warn off the unsympathetic. This is not, in the customarily accepted sense of the word, an academic or scholarly book, though it is indebted throughout to works of scholarship. The lack of footnotes and formal bibliography will advise the wary that I have sought everywhere the kind of validity which depends not on faithfulness to "fact" but on insight and sensitivity to nuance. I do not mean, of course, that I have despised accuracy (within the limits of my approach and temperament I have sought it) but that I have tried to produce a literary rather than a scientific work, a labor of love rather than one of patience.

I have not, however, written what is most often meant these days by a "critical" study, mere textual analysis, ahistorical, anti-biographical: the kind of guide for courses in higher remedial reading which an age of lapsing literacy perhaps demands, but which it is somewhat craven to supply. There are, to be sure, many full-scale readings of novels included in these pages: lengthy analyses of *Moby Dick, The Scarlet Letter,* and *Huckleberry Finn,* and shorter ones of books ranging from *Edgar Huntly* and *The Last of the Mohicans* through *Uncle Tom's Cabin* and *The Monks of Monk Hall* to *The Victim.* But nowhere is it suggested that such résumés are the key to the essential work of art, whatever that catch phrase may still mean; and they are everywhere embedded in a context of more general or theoretical explications.

The experience of a work of art is, as everyone seems willing to grant without pondering the implications, unique and untranslatable; to suggest that one has captured it in an analysis is, therefore, to falsify and mislead. The best criticism can hope to do is to set the work in as many illuminating contexts as possible: the context of the genre to which it belongs, of the whole body of work of its author, of the life of that author and of his times. In this sense, it becomes clear that the "text" is merely one of the contexts of a piece of literature, its lexical or verbal one, no more or less important than the sociological, psychological, historical, anthropological or generic. The contextual critic desires only to *locate* the work of art, to point toward the place where his contextual circles overlap, the place in which the work exists in all its ambiguity and plenitude.

Ideally, of course, an object of critical attention should be set in *all* its relevant contexts; but this is the never-completed communal task of criticism as a continuing institution, and no one critic is able to do more than a small part of the whole job. With both the goals and limitations of contextual criticism in mind, I have attempted in the present study to emphasize the neglected contexts of American fiction, largely depth-psychological and anthropological, but sociological and formal as well. Certain other approaches and insights, well-established in textbooks and in the classroom, I have not touched on at all, assuming them to exist in the minds of anyone who would be led to read this book. My own contributions I consider not as alternative to standard ways of reading but as complementary to them; I find no greater pleasure than in reminding myself that my interpretations are as partial as those which bore me the most. I trust that in the end my own insights will, without themselves coming to seem dishearteningly satisfactory, make more established ways of understanding our fiction appear pat and inadequate.

Nothing (I know, as all writers suspect and any teacher is aware) will drive some readers back from the certainties of textbook explanations to the difficulties of the work of art itself; but others, less resolutely insensitive, will, I hope, be troubled enough by suggestions of new possibilities in old works, so that (whether ultimately they accept my views or not) they will never again be able

to half-read *Huckleberry Finn* or *The Last of the Mohicans* in the
the state of torpor they have taken for cultural security. American
literature is distinguished by the number of dangerous and disturbing books in its canon—and American scholarship by its ability to
conceal this fact. To redeem our great books from the commentar-
ies on them is one of the chief functions of this study.

I have, in general, tried to demonstrate that the American novel
has a character and fate different from the novel in France, Germany, even Russia. That there are resemblances, too, the very use
of the common term for the genre makes evident; but such resemblances are not my primary concern. In order to make clear the
divergence of our own novelistic tradition from the continental ones
(and of our own life from life in Europe), I have found it useful to
concentrate on the themes of love and death as treated by our
major writers—and especially on the duplicity with which those
themes are handled in the United States. My treatment is, therefore, thematic rather than strictly historical, selective rather than
exhaustive. Though the time span covered in my essay extends
from 1789 to 1959, I have not pretended to deal with all the remembered novelists of those years. Particularly in the more recent
period, I have ignored certain fictionists, highly regarded in some
quarters, who do not share what I believe to be the major concerns
of our tradition. I have not, however, failed to treat any writer
whom I consider to be of first rank merely because he has had the
ill grace to be un-symptomatic or eccentric; in no case have I deliberately sacrificed considerations of value to the pursuit of my
themes. Nonetheless, certain partisan readers will doubtless resent
the passing mention or the total silence accorded such novelists as
William Dean Howells, Sinclair Lewis, John Dos Passos, or
Thomas Wolfe. I can only hope that they will find appropriate
compensation in my concern with figures often scanted despite
their real merits: William Hill Brown, George Lippard, Oliver
Wendell Holmes, Nathanael West, and Wright Morris.

My desire to define what is peculiarly American in our books has
made it necessary for me to approach our literature from a com-
paratist point of view; and I have not hesitated to include rather
detailed readings of books by Samuel Richardson, Walter Scott,
and M. G. Lewis, books which provided prototypes for our own
earliest attempts in the various sub-forms of the novel. To discuss
literature in the United States without reference to contemporary
developments in Europe, seems to me as futile as discussing it

without a consideration of the way in which the very concept of literature and the theme of love were re-born together in the West at the end of the Middle Ages. That such a consideration demands certain general theories about art and the human mind has stimulated rather than dismayed me; and the forewarned reader should be no more dismayed when he comes upon a rather full examination of the rise of courtly-love poetry at the end of the eleventh century, or of the novel and the Sentimental Love Religion in the mid-eighteenth.

I have learned painfully that without such a pre-discussion before him, any but the most sophisticated reader is likely to misunderstand some of my specific observations on our literature and ourselves—my theory, for instance, about the relationship between sentimental life in America and the archetypal image, found in our favorite books, in which a white and a colored American male flee from civilization into each other's arms. Certainly, my earliest formulation of this theory in "Come Back to the Raft Ag'in, Huck Honey" has met with a shocked and, I suspect, partly willful incomprehension. I have been accused of impiety, grossness, a contempt for the classics of childhood, even of a disturbing influence on private lives. I trust that the full development of my contentions in these pages will obviate at least the simpler kinds of misunderstanding, and that my additional comments on the importance in our literature of brother-sister incest and necrophilia will not stir up new protests of a similar kind.

I do not relish the role of a private eye making courtroom revelations, but it is one into which some of our writers have, not without malice, forced the critic. Walt Whitman, who finally gives so much away, makes this point clear:

For it is not for what I have put into it that I have written this
    book,
Nor is it by reading it you will acquire it . . .
For all is useless without that which you may guess at many
    times and not hit, that which I hinted at . . .

The failure of the American fictionist to deal with adult heterosexual love and his consequent obsession with death, incest and innocent homosexuality are not merely matters of historical interest or literary relevance. They affect the lives we lead from day to day and influence the writers in whom the consciousness of our plight is given clarity and form. Paul Bowles, writing highbrow terror-fiction in the middle of the twentieth century, cannot escape the limitations that plagued Charles Brockden Brown at the beginning of the eighteenth; and Saul Bellow, composing a homoerotic *Tarzan of the Apes* in *Henderson the Rain King,* is back on the raft with Mark Twain. There is a pattern imposed both by the writers of our past and the very conditions of life in the United States from which no American novelist can escape, no matter what philosophy he consciously adopts or what theme he thinks he pursues. In Parts One and Two of this study, I have traced in some detail the emergence and development of this pattern; and in Part Three, I have tried to show how our three greatest novelists, each once and once only, made of the pattern they could not evade literature of the first excellence.

Though this is finally a very personal book, in which I attempt to say with my own voice out of my own face (all masks abandoned) what I have found to be some major meanings of our literature and our culture, it does not spring to life unbegotten, unaffiliated and unsponsored. In one sense, it has been essentially present from the moment that I read aloud to two of my sons (then five and seven) for their first time *Huckleberry Finn,* and saw all at once what it has taken me so long to get down. In another, it has taken shape slowly through a lifetime of reading and seven years or more of concentrated labor. My first obligation, then, is to Mark Twain and to my children; my second, much harder to document, to all the texts on which I comment, to hundreds of critical and scholarly books, most of which I do not mention—as well as to certain fugitive remarks and by-the-way observations, sowed by friends and enemies in conversations I no longer quite remember.

Four major sources of indebtedness I feel moved to acknowledge here, though in all four I have so grossly adapted, so shamelessly distorted certain original insights that their authors may well find my acknowledgments presumptuous, even offensive. The first is C. S. Lewis, whose *The Allegory of Love* taught me at the age of eighteen the sense in which love is an invention and the poets its inventors. His book has left me ever since wrestling with the problem of the psychic break-through that at the same moment introduced into a patriarchal world the worship of women and into a Christian one the cult of art. Other insights into this problem I have found in Denis de Rougement—and in the Provençal poets with whom both the latter and Lewis deal; but my introduction to a fertile and fascinating area I owe primarily to *The Allegory of Love*.

Similarly, certain Marxian critics had made clear to me before I was twenty what otherwise might have remained too obvious for me to see: that the class-relations of a culture help determine the shape of its deepest communal fantasies, the obsessive concerns of its literature. Without clues from such analysts, I do not think I could have understood, for instance, the genesis of the radical shift in the nature of the villain as portrayed in European and American gothic fiction—and the ideological revolution which that shift projects. Yet the substitution of the Indian for the Inquisitor, the symbol of untamed nature for that of corrupt civilization, as horror and threat, bodies forth certain essential meanings of Poe and Hawthorne, and underlies certain intolerable contradictions in Melville and Twain. In light of my debt to Marxist thought, it seems fair enough that the first statement of one of the key notions of this book should have appeared in *Partisan Review,* American heir—for a while at least—to the Marxian critical approach.

To Freud and his followers, and also to Carl Jung, I owe a similar debt. Readers familiar with orthodox Freudianism and Jungian revisionism will recognize the sources of much of my basic vocabulary; I cannot imagine myself beginning the kind of investigation I have undertaken without the concepts of the conscious and the unconscious, the Oedipus complex, the archetypes, etc. Only my awareness of how syncretically I have yoked together and how cavalierly I have transformed my borrowings prevents my making more specific acknowledgments. Quite appropriately, I was able to develop some of the leading arguments in this book in the Freud Memorial Lecture for 1956, given before the Philadelphia Association for Psychoanalysis, for which opportunity I owe thanks especially to Dr. Paul Sloane and Robert Waelder.

Of all the literary critics who have written about American books, the one who has seemed to me closest to the truth, even at those points where I finally disagree with him, and who has brought to his subject an appropriate passion and style, is, of course, D. H. Lawrence. His *Studies in Classic American Literature* attempted for the first time the kind of explication which does not betray the complexity or perilousness of its theme; and in the pages of that little book I found confirmation of my own suspicions that it is duplicity and outrageousness which determine the quality of those American books ordinarily consigned to the children's shelf in the library. Only Melville himself, in his published remarks on Hawthorne, more precisely identified the nature of the American novel.

Such acknowledgments as these, however, only begin to indicate the sources on which I have drawn for a book that was not wholly written in the privacy of my study, but which found its shape in the classroom and on the lecture platform. Especially fruitful were: my classes at what is now the Indiana School of Letters in 1952 and 1954; my lectures in Rome, Bologna, and Venice as a Fulbright Fellow between the fall of 1951 and the summer of 1953; my platform appearances before college and professional groups all up and down the United States in the last five or six years; and especially the Christian Gauss Seminars at Princeton in 1957, during which I worked out almost all of Part Three of this study.* I cannot enumerate all of those to whom I am grateful for making these occasions possible and lively (I do not even remember the name of the figure who remains most vivid in my mind—the questioner at one lecture, so appalled by the enormity of what I had to say about the relationship of Queequeg and Ishmael, that he accused me of having stolen his raincoat!), but I should like to name a few: Mario Praz, Agostino Lombardo, Carlo Izzo, Gabriele Baldini, John Crowe Ransom, James Cox, R. P. Blackmur, and E. B. O. Borgerhoff. Easiest to forget and hardest to thank, because they have provided the very atmosphere in which I live, are my colleagues and students at Montana State University—who have sustained me by their affection and trust for nearly twenty years. All the others will forgive me, I know, if I name only H. G. Merriam and Edmund Freeman.

My deepest debt goes back beyond any of these to the time during which I was a graduate student of William Ellery Leonard, a great and, I hope, unforgotten teacher, as well as a rebel, poet, translator, and essayist. It was he who first not merely told but showed me—showed in the rich, tragic quality of his own being as well as by the excitement that he engendered in the classroom—that literature is more than what one learns to read in schools and libraries, more even than a grace of life; that it is the record of those elusive moments at which life is alone fully itself, fulfilled in

---

* All the content of Part Three of the first edition has been incorporated in other sections in the present edition.

consciousness and form. No one who has been his student can regard literary criticism as anything less than an act of total moral engagement, in which tact, patience, insolence, and piety consort strangely but satisfactorily together; nor can anyone who once listened to him believe that the truth one tries to tell about literature is finally different from the truth one tries to tell about the indignities and rewards of being the kind of man one is—an American, let's say, in the second half of the twentieth century, learning to read his country's books.

LESLIE A. FIEDLER

Missoula, Montana
13 October 1959

CONTENTS

PART TWO: ACHIEVEMENT
AND FRUSTRATION

LOVE AND

DEATH

IN THE

AMERICAN

NOVEL

PART ONE

PROTOTYPES
AND
EARLY
ADAPTATIONS

1

THE NOVEL AND AMERICA

BETWEEN THE NOVEL and America there are peculiar and intimate connections. A new literary form and a new society, their beginnings coincide with the beginnings of the modern era and, indeed, help to define it. We are living not only in the Age of America but also in the Age of the Novel, at a moment when the literature of a country without a first-rate verse epic or a memorable verse tragedy has become the model of half the world.

We have known for a long time, of course, that our national literary reputation depends largely upon the achievement of our novelists. The classical poetic genres revived by the Renaissance had lost their relevance to contemporary life before America entered the cultural scene; and even the lyric has provided us with occasions for few, and limited, triumphs. Not only in the United States, though pre-eminently there, literature has become for most readers quite simply prose fiction; and our endemic fantasy of writing "the Great American Novel" is only a local instance of a more general obsession. The notions of greatness once associated with the heroic poem have been transferred to the novel; and the shift is a part of that "Americanization of culture" which some European intellectuals continue ritually to deplore.

But is there, as certain continental critics have insisted, an "American novel," a specific sub-variety of the form? If we turn to these critics for a definition, we come on such terms as "neo-realist," "hard-boiled," "naive," and "anti-traditional"—terms derived from a standard view of America as an "anti-culture," an eternally maintained preserve of primitivism. This view (notoriously exemplified by André Gide) ends by finding in Dashiell Hammett the same values as in William Faulkner, and is more a symptom of European cultural malaise than a useful critical distinction. It is tempting to insist on the pat rebuttal that, far from being an anti-culture, we are merely a branch of Western culture; and that there is no "American novel," only local variants of standard European kinds of fiction: American sentimental, American gothic, American historical romance, etc. Certainly no single sub-genre of the novel was invented in the United States. Yet the peculiarities of our variants seem more interesting and important than their resemblances to the parent forms.

There is a real sense in which our prose fiction is immediately distinguishable from that of Europe, though this is a fact that is difficult for Americans to confess. In this sense, our novels seem not primitive, perhaps, but innocent, unfallen in a disturbing way, almost juvenile. The great works of American fiction are notoriously at home in the children's section of the library, their level of sentimentality precisely that of a pre-adolescent. This is part of what we mean when we talk about the incapacity of the American novelist to develop; in a compulsive way he returns to a limited world of experience, usually associated with his childhood, writing the same book over and over again until he lapses into silence or self-parody.

Merely finding a language, learning to talk in a land where there are no conventions of conversation, no special class idioms and no dialogue between classes, no continuing literary language—this exhausts the American writer. He is forever *beginning*, saying for the first time (without real tradition there can never be a second time) what it is like to stand alone before nature, or in a city as appallingly lonely as any virgin forest. He faces, moreover, another problem, which has resulted in a failure of feeling and imagination perceptible at the heart of even our most notable works. Our great novelists, though experts on indignity and assault, on loneliness and terror, tend to avoid treating the passionate encounter of a man and woman, which we expect at the center of a novel. Indeed, they rather shy away from permitting in their fictions the presence of any full-fledged, mature women, giving us instead monsters of virtue or bitchery, symbols of the rejection or fear of sexuality.

To be sure, the theme of "love" in so simple a sense is by no means necessary to all works of art. In the *Iliad,* for instance, and in much Greek tragedy, it is conspicuously absent; and in the heroic literature of the Middle Ages, it is peripheral where it exists at all. The *"belle Aude"* of the *Chanson de Roland* is a supernumerary, and the only female we remember from *Beowulf* is a terror emerging from the darkness at the bottom of the waters. The world of the epic is a world of war, and its reigning sentimental relationship is the loyalty of comrades in arms; but by the eighteenth century the notion of a heroic poem without romance had come to seem intolerable. The last pseudo-epics of the baroque had been obsessed with the subject of love, and the rococo had continued to elaborate that theme. Shakespeare himself appeared to the English Augustans too little concerned with the "reigning passion" to be quite interesting without revision. Why, after all, should Cordelia not survive to marry Edgar, they demanded of themselves—and they rewrote *King Lear* to prove that she should.

The novel, however, was precisely the product of the sentimentalizing taste of the eighteenth century; and a continuing tradition of prose fiction did not begin until the love affair of Lovelace and Clarissa (a demythicized Don Juan and a secularized goddess of Christian love) had been imagined. The subject par excellence of the novel is love or, more precisely—in its beginnings at least—seduction and marriage; and in France, Italy, Germany, and Russia, even in England, spiritually so close to America, love in one form or another has remained the novel's central theme, as necessary and as expected as battle in Homer or revenge in the Renaissance drama. But our great Romantic *Unroman,* our typical anti-novel, is the womanless *Moby Dick.*

Where is our *Madame Bovary,* our *Anna Karenina,* our *Pride and Prejudice* or *Vanity Fair?* Among our classic novels, at least those before Henry James, who stands so oddly between our own traditions and the European ones we rejected or recast, the best attempt at dealing with love is *The Scarlet Letter,* in which the physical consummation of adultery has occurred and all passion burned away before the novel proper begins. For the rest, there are *Moby Dick* and *Huckleberry Finn, The Last of the Mohicans, The Red Badge of Courage,* the stories of Edgar Allan Poe—books that turn from society to nature or nightmare out of a desperate need to avoid the facts of wooing, marriage, and child-bearing.

The figure of Rip Van Winkle presides over the birth of the

American imagination; and it is fitting that our first successful homegrown legend should memorialize, however playfully, the flight of the dreamer from the drab duties of home and town toward the good companions and the magic keg of Holland's gin. Ever since, the typical male protagonist of our fiction has been a man on the run, harried into the forest and out to sea, down the river or into combat—anywhere to avoid "civilization," which is to say, the confrontation of a man and woman which leads to the fall to sex, marriage, and responsibility.

Rip's world is not only asexual, however, it is terrible: a world of fear and loneliness, a haunted world; and the American novel is pre-eminently a novel of terror. To "light out for the territory" or seek refuge in the forest seems easy and tempting from the vantage point of a chafing and restrictive home; but civilization once disavowed and Christianity disowned, the bulwark of woman left behind, the wanderer feels himself without protection, more motherless child than free man. To be sure, there is a substitute for wife or mother presumably waiting in the green heart of nature: the natural man, the good companion, pagan and un-ashamed—Queequeg or Chingachgook or Nigger Jim. But the figure of the natural man is ambiguous, a dream and a nightmare at once. The other face of Chingachgook is Injun Joe, the killer in the graveyard and the haunter of caves; Nigger Jim is also the Babo of Melville's "Benito Cereno," the humble servant whose name means "papa" holding the razor to his master's throat; and finally the dark-skinned companion becomes the "Black Man," which is a traditional American name for the Devil himself.

The enemy of society on the run toward "freedom" is also the pariah in flight from his guilt, the guilt of that very flight; and new phantoms arise to haunt him at every step. American literature likes to pretend, of course, that its bugaboos are all finally jokes: the headless horseman a hoax, every manifestation of the super-natural capable of rational explanation on the last page—but we are never quite convinced. *Huckleberry Finn,* that euphoric boys' book, begins with its protagonist holding off at gun point his father driven half mad by the D.T.'s and ends (after a lynching, a dis-interment, and a series of violent deaths relieved by such humor-ous incidents as soaking a dog in kerosene and setting him on fire) with the revelation of that father's sordid death. Nothing is spared; Pap, horrible enough in life, is found murdered brutally, aban-doned to float down the river in a decaying house scrawled with obscenities. But it is all "humor," of course, a last desperate attempt to convince us of the innocence of violence, the good clean fun of horror. Our literature as a whole at times seems a chamber of horrors disguised as an amusement park "fun house," where we pay to play at terror and are confronted in the innermost chamber with a series of inter-reflecting mirrors which present us with a thousand versions of our own face.

In our most enduring books, the cheapjack machinery of the gothic novel is called on to represent the hidden blackness of the human soul and human society. No wonder our authors mock themselves as they use such devices; no wonder Mistress Hibbins in *The Scarlet Letter* and Fedallah in *Moby Dick* are treated half jocularly, half melodramatically, though each represents in his book the Faustian pact, the bargain with the Devil, which our authors have always felt as the essence of the American experience. However shoddily or ironically treated, horror is essential to our literature. It is not merely a matter of terror filling the vacuum left by the suppression of sex in our novels, of Thanatos standing in for Eros. Through these gothic images are projected certain obsessive concerns of our national life: the ambiguity of our relationship with Indian and Negro, the ambiguity of our encounter with nature, the guilt of the revolutionist who feels himself a parricide—and, not least of all, the uneasiness of the writer who cannot help believing that the very act of composing a book is Satanic revolt. "Hell-fired," Hawthorne called *The Scarlet Letter,* and Melville thought his own *Moby Dick* a "wicked book."

The American writer inhabits a country at once the dream of Europe and a fact of history; he lives on the last horizon of an endlessly retreating vision of innocence—on the "frontier," which is to say, the margin where the theory of original goodness and the fact of original sin come face to face. To express this "blackness ten times black" and to live by it in a society in which, since the decline of orthodox Puritanism, optimism has become the chief effective religion, is a complex and difficult task.

It was to the novel that the American writer turned most naturally, as the only *popular* form of sufficient magnitude for his vision. He was, perhaps, not sufficiently sophisticated to realize that such learned forms as epic and tragedy had already outlived their usefulness; but, working out of a cultural background at best sketchy and unsure, he felt insecure before them. His obligations urged him in the direction of tragedy, but traditional verse tragedy was forbidden him; indeed, a chief technical problem for American novelists has been the adaptation of nontragic forms to tragic ends. How could the dark vision of the American—his obsession with violence and his embarrassment before love—be expressed in the sentimental novel of analysis as developed by Samuel Richardson or the historical romance as practiced by Sir Walter Scott? These sub-genres of fiction, invented to satisfy the emotional needs of a merchant class in search of dignity or a Tory squirearchy consumed by nostalgia, could only by the most desperate expedients be tailored to fit American necessities. Throughout their writing lives, such writers as Charles Brockden Brown and James Fenimore Cooper devoted (with varying degrees of self-consciousness) all their ingenuity to this task, yet neither Brown nor Cooper finally proved capable of achieving high art; and the literary types invented by both have fallen since into the hands of mere entertainers—that is, novelists able and willing to attempt anything *except* the projection of the dark vision of America we have been describing. The Fielding novel, on the other hand, the pseudo-Shakespearean "comic epic" with its broad canvas, its emphasis upon reversals and recognitions, and its robust masculine sentimentality, turned out, oddly enough, to have no relevance to the American scene; in the United States it has remained an exotic, eternally being discovered by the widest audience and raised to best-sellerdom in its latest imported form, but seldom home-produced for home consumption.

It is the gothic form that has been most fruitful in the hands of our best writers: the gothic *symbolically* understood, its machinery and décor translated into metaphors for a terror psychological, social, and metaphysical. Yet even treated as symbols, the machinery and décor of the gothic have continued to seem vulgar and contrived; symbolic gothicism threatens always to dissolve into its components, abstract morality and shoddy theater. A recurrent problem of our fiction has been the need of our novelists to find a mode of projecting their conflicts which would contain all the dusky horror of gothic romance and yet be palatable to discriminating readers, palatable first of all to themselves.

Such a mode can, of course, not be subsumed among any of those called "realism." Our fiction is essentially and at its best nonrealistic, even anti-realistic; long before *symbolisme* had been invented in France and exported to America, there was a full-fledged native tradition of symbolism. That tradition was born of the profound contradictions of our national life and sustained by the inheritance from Puritanism of a "typical" (even allegorical) way of regarding the sensible world—not as an ultimate reality but as a system of signs to be deciphered. For too long, historians of American fiction have mistakenly tried to impose on the course of a brief literary history a notion of artistic "progress" imported from France or, more precisely perhaps, from certain French literary critics.

But the moment at which Flaubert was dreaming *Madame Bovary* was the moment when Melville was finding *Moby Dick,* and considered as a "realistic" novel the latter is a scandalous botch. To speak of a counter-tradition to the novel, of the tradition of "the romance" as a force in our literature, is merely to repeat the rationalizations of our writers themselves; it is certainly to fail to be *specific* enough for real understanding. Our fiction is not merely in flight from the physical data of the actual world, in search of a (sexless and dim) Ideal; from Charles Brockden Brown to William Faulkner or Eudora Welty, Paul Bowles or John Hawkes, it is, bewilderingly and embarrassingly, a gothic fiction, nonrealistic and negative, sadist and melodramatic—a literature of darkness and the grotesque in a land of light and affirmation.

Moreover—and the final paradox is necessary to the full complexity of the case—our classic literature is a literature of horror for boys. Truly shocking, frankly obscene authors we do not possess; Edgar Allan Poe is our closest approximation, a child playing at what Baudelaire was to live. A Baudelaire, a Marquis de Sade, a "Monk" Lewis, even a John Cleland was inconceivable in the United States.* Our flowers of evil are culled for the small girl's bouquet, our novels of terror (*Moby Dick, The Scarlet Letter, Huckleberry Finn,* the tales of Poe) are placed on the approved

---

* In recent years the situation appears to have altered radically—perhaps, in part, because the taste of boys has changed, as the "latency period," which Freud thought immutable, tends to be abolished. At any rate, the line between "pornography" and respectable literature has blurred; and certain traditional themes of American literature—the love of white and colored males, for instance, and the vilification of women—are rendered with explicit sexual detail. Indeed, such detail becomes required rather than forbidden as American puritanism learns to stand on its head. It is a long way from James Fenimore Cooper to James Baldwin, or from Herman Melville to Norman Mailer; but even if our dreams have become more frankly erotic, the American *eros* has not really changed. We continue to dream the female dead, and ourselves in the arms of our dusky male lovers.

book lists of Parents' Committees who nervously fuss over the latest comic books. If such censors do not flinch at necrophilia or shudder over the book whose secret motto is "I baptise you not in the name of the Father . . . but of the Devil," or fear the juvenile whose hero at his greatest moment cries out, "All right, I'll *go* to Hell," it is only another irony of life in a land where the writers believe in hell and the official guardians of morality do not.

Yet our authors are as responsible as the P.T.A.'s for the confusion about the true nature of their books; though they may have whispered their secret to friends, or confessed it in private letters, in their actual works they assumed what camouflage prudence dictated. They *wanted* to be misunderstood. *Huckleberry Finn* is only the supreme instance of a subterfuge typical of our classic novelists. To this very day, it is heresy in some quarters to insist that this is not finally the jolliest, the *cleanest* of books; Twain's ironical warning to significance hunters, posted just before the title page, is taken quite literally, and the irreverent critic who explicates the book's levels of terror and evasion is regarded as a busybody and scandalmonger. Why, one is driven to ask, why the distortion and why the ignorance?

Perhaps the whole odd shape of American fiction arises simply (as simplifying Europeans are always ready to assure us) because there is no real sexuality in American life and therefore there cannot very well be any in American art. What we cannot achieve in our relations with each other it would be vain to ask our writers to portray or even our critics to miss. Certainly many of our novelists have themselves believed, or pretended to believe, this. Through *The Scarlet Letter,* there is a constant mournful undercurrent, a series of asides in which Hawthorne deplores the sexual diminution of American women. Mark Twain in *1601* somewhat similarly contrasts the vigor of Elizabethan Englishwomen with their American descendants; contrasting the sexual utopia of precolonial England with a fallen America where the men copulate "but once in seven yeeres"; and his pornographic sketch ends on the comic-pathetic image of an old man's impotent lust that "would not stand again." Such pseudo-nostalgia cannot be taken too seriously, however; it may, indeed, be the projection of mere personal weakness and fantasy. Certainly, outside their books, Hawthorne and Twain seem to have fled rather than sought the imaginary full-breasted, fully sexed woman from whom American ladies had presumably declined. Both married, late in life, pale hypochondriac spinsters, intellectual invalids—as if to assert publicly that they sought in marriage not sex but culture.

Such considerations leave us trapped in the chicken-egg dilemma. How can one say whether the quality of passion in American life suffers because of a failure of the writer's imagination or vice versa? What is called "love" in literature is a rationalization, a way of coming to terms with the relationship between man and woman that does justice, on the one hand, to certain biological drives and, on the other, to certain generally accepted conventions of tenderness and courtesy; and literature, expressing and defining those conventions, tends to influence "real life" more than such life influences it. For better or for worse and for whatever reasons, the American novel is different from its European prototypes, and one of its essential differences arises from its chary treatment of woman and of sex.

To write, then, about the American novel is to write about the fate of certain European genres in a world of alien experience. It is not only a world where courtship and marriage have suffered a profound change, but also one in the process of losing the traditional distinctions of class; a world without a significant history or a substantial past; a world which had left behind the terror of Europe not for the innocence it dreamed of, but for new and special guilts associated with the rape of nature and the exploitation of dark-skinned people; a world doomed to play out the imaginary childhood of Europe. The American novel is only *finally* American; its appearance is an event in the history of the European spirit—as, indeed, is the very invention of America itself.

I I

Though it is necessary, in understanding the fate of the American novel, to understand what European prototypes were available when American literature began, as well as which ones flourished and which ones disappeared on our soil, it is even more important to understand the meaning of that moment in the mid-eighteenth century which gave birth to Jeffersonian democracy and Richardsonian sentimentality alike: to the myth of revolution and the myth of seduction. When Charles Brockden Brown, the first professional American author, sent a copy of his *Wieland* to Thomas Jefferson in 1798, he must, beneath his modest disclaimers, have

had some sense of his and the President's kinship as revolutionaries. "I am therefore obliged to hope," Brown wrote, "that . . .
the train of eloquent and judicious reasoning . . . will be regarded
by Thomas Jefferson with as much respect as . . . me." But if
Jefferson ever found the time to read Brown's novel, he left no
record; we know only that he expressed general approval of
"works of the imagination" as being able, more than history, to
"possess virtue in the best and vice in the worst forms possible."
It is a chillingly rational approach to art and a perhaps sufficient
indication of the hopelessness of Brown's attempting in those
sensible years to live by his writing.

Yet despite the fact that no professional novelist of real seriousness was to find a supporting public in America for twenty-five or
thirty years more, Brown's instincts had not deceived him. He and
Jefferson *were* engaged in a common enterprise; the novel and
America did not come into existence at the same time by accident. They are the two great inventions of the bourgeois, Protestant mind at the moment when it stood, on the one hand, between
Rationalism and Sentimentalism, and on the other, between the
drive for economic power and the need for cultural autonomy.
The series of events which includes the American and the French
Revolutions, the invention of the novel, the rise of modern psychology, and the triumph of the lyric in poetry, adds up to a
psychic revolution as well as a social one. This revolution, viewed
as an overturning of ideas and artistic forms, has traditionally been
called "Romantic"; but the term is paralyzingly narrow, defining
too little too precisely, and leading to further pointless distinctions
between Romanticism proper, pre-Romanticism, *Sturm und Drang,*
Sentimentalism, *Symbolisme,* etc. It seems preferable to call the
whole continuing, complex event simply "the Break-through," thus
emphasizing the dramatic entry of a new voice into the dialogue
of Western man with his various selves.

The Break-through is characterized not only by the separation
of psychology from philosophy, the displacement of the traditional
leading genres by the personal lyric and analytic prose fiction
(with the consequent subordination of plot to character); it is
also marked by the promulgation of a theory of revolution as a
good in itself and, most notably perhaps, by a new concept of
inwardness. One is almost tempted to say, by the invention of a
new kind of self, a new level of mind; for what has been happen-
ing since the eighteenth century seems more like the development

of a new organ than the mere finding of a new way to describe old experience.

It was Diderot who represented a first real awareness that man is *double* to the final depths of his soul, the prey of conflicting psyches both equally himself. The conflict had, of course, always been felt, but had traditionally been described as occurring between man and devil, or flesh and spirit; that the parties to the dispute are both man and spirit was a revolutionary suggestion. In his demi-novel, *Rameau's Nephew,* Diderot projected the conflicting divisions within man's mind as the philosopher and the parasite, the rationalist and the underground man, debating endlessly the cause of the head versus that of the gut. And in his pornographic *Bijoux Indiscrets,* he proposed another version of the same dialogue: the enchanted (and indiscreet) genitals speak the truth which the mouth will not avow, thus comprising an allegorical defense of pornography in the guise of a pornographic work. In the same year in which Richardson's sentimental novel *Clarissa* was published, John Cleland's long-lived dirty book *The Memoirs of Fanny Hill* was making a stir. Pornography and obscenity are, indeed, hallmarks of the age of the Break-through. Not only pious novels but titillating ones show the emergence of the underground emotions (of what the period itself euphemistically called "the heart") into high culture. Quite as influential as Diderot (or Richardson or Rousseau) in the *bouleversement* of the eighteenth century is the Marquis de Sade, who stands almost emblematically at the crossroads of depth psychology and revolution.

Not only did de Sade shed new light on the ambivalence of the inner mind, revealing the true darkness and terror implicit in the drive which the neo-classical age (revolting against Christian notions of sin) had been content to celebrate as simple "pleasure" or polite "gallantry"; he may even have caused that symbolic storming of an almost empty prison with which the Fernch Revolution begins. Himself a prisoner in the *Tour de la liberté* of the Bastille, de Sade, through an improvised loudspeaker made of a tube and funnel, screamed to bystanders to rescue his fellow inmates who were having their throats cut—and scattered hand-written leaflets complaining about jail conditions to the crowd he attracted. On July 3, 1789, he was finally transferred elsewhere to insure "the safety of the building," but not before he had started to write *Justine, or the Misfortunes of Virtue,* that perverse offshoot of the Richardsonian novel, and had thus begun to create the first example of revolutionary pornography.

In the Marquis de Sade, the Break-through found its most stringent and spectacular spokesman: the condemned man judging his judges, the pervert mocking the normal, the advocate of destruction and death sneering at the defenders of love and life; but his *reductio* follows logically enough from assumptions shared by Jefferson and Rousseau, Richardson and Saint-Just. Whatever has been suspect, outcast, and denied is postulated as the source of good. Before the Break-through, no one, Christian or Humanist, had doubted the inferiority of passion to reason, of impulse to law; and though it is possible sophistically to justify all eighteenth-century reversals by quoting the verse which says the last shall be the first, Christianity is dead from the moment such a justification is made. The Break-through is profoundly anti-Christian though it is not always willing to appear so. There is a brief age of transition when the Enlightenment and Sentimentalism exist side by side, when it is still possible to pretend that true reason and true feeling, the urgings of passion and the dictates of virtue are identical—and that all are alike manifestations of the orthodox God. But Sentimentalism yields quickly to the full Romantic revolt; in a matter of months, Don Juan, enemy of Heaven and the family, has been transformed from villain to hero; and before the process is finished, audiences have learned to weep for Shylock rather than laugh him from the stage. The legendary rebels and outcasts, Prometheus and Cain, Judas and the Wandering Jew, Faust and Lucifer himself are one by one redeemed. The parricide becomes an object of veneration and tourists (among them that good American abroad, Herman Melville) carry home as an icon Guido's picture of Beatrice Cenci, slayer of her father!

The process is continuous and nearly universal. Even the values of language change: "gothic" passes from a term of contempt to one of description and then of praise, while "baroque" makes more slowly the same transition; meanwhile terms once used honorifically to describe desired traits—"condescension," for example—become indicators of disapproval. The child is glorified over the man, the peasant over the courtier, the dark man over the white, the rude ballad over the polished sonnet, the weeper over the thinker, colony over mother country; the commoner over the king—nature over culture. At first, all this is a game: the ladies of the court in pastoral dress swing high into the air to show their legs with a self-consciousness quite unlike the abandon of children to which they are pretending. But in a little while, Jean-Jacques Rousseau has fainted on the road to Vincennes and awakened to find his waistcoat soaked with tears; and it is suddenly all in earnest. Whatever was down is now up, as the under-mind heaves up out of the darkness; barricades are erected and the novel becomes the reigning form; the Jew walks openly out of the ghetto, and otherwise sensible men hang on their walls pictures of trees and cattle. The conjunctions are comic in their unexpectedness and variety.

It is hard to say what was cause and what effect in the complex upheaval; everything seems the symptom of everything else. Yet deep within the nexus of causes (gods must die for new genres to be born) was that "death of God" that has not yet ceased to trouble our peace. Somewhere near the beginning of the eighteenth century, Christianity (more precisely, perhaps, that desper-ate compromise of the late Middle Ages and early Renaissance, Christian Humanism) began to wear out. It was not merely, or even primarily, a matter of the destruction of the political and social power of one Church or another, much less of the lapse of economic control by the priests. The divisions within Christen-dom surely contributed to the final collapse, but they are perhaps better regarded as manifestations than as causes of the insecurity over dogma that was at work deep within. Institutionalized Chris-tianity at any rate began to crumble when its mythology no longer proved capable of controlling and revivifying the imagination of Europe.

The darker motive forces of the psyche refused any longer to accept the names and ranks by which they had been demeaned for almost two thousand years; once worshiped as "gods," they had been made demons by fiat, but now they stirred again in discon-tent. Especially the Great Mother—cast down by the most patri-archal of all religions (to the Hebrews, she was Lilith, the bride of darkness), ambiguously redeemed as the Blessed Virgin and denied once more by a Hebraizing Protestantism—clamored to be honored once more. The very distinction between God and Devil, on which the psychic balance of Europe had for so long been staked, was threatened. It did not matter that some people (chiefly women) continued to go to church, or even that there were re-vivals within the framework of surviving sects; fewer and fewer men lived by the legends of the church, and the images of saints represented not living myths but "mythology" in a literary sense.

The effect of the growing awareness (an awareness, to be sure, at first shared by only a handful of advanced thinkers) of this cosmic catastrophe was double: a sense of exhilaration and a spasm of terror, to which correspond the two initial and overlapping stages of the Break-through. There was first of all the conviction of the Age of Reason and its spokesmen, the *philosophes,* gravediggers of the Christian God, that they—and all of mankind—were at last *free,* free of the superstition and ignorance so long sponsored by the priests for their own selfish ends. Those demons into which the early Christian apologists had translated the gods of antiquity seemed to the *philosophes* idle inventions of the Church itself: bugaboos to scare the pious into unquestioning subservience. Even the Christian God seemed to them such a contrivance, demonic and irrational. In the imagined universe presided over by their own "Author of Creation," there could be no place for mystery or blackness. Once *"l'infâme,"* the scandalous Church, had been crushed, all monsters would be eliminated forever, and man could take up his long, baffled march toward perfection in a sweet, sunlit, orderly world. Just such a vision, however modified by circumstance, moved the Deist intellectuals who founded America, especially that Thomas Jefferson to whom C. B. Brown, himself a follower of the *philosophes,* proffered his gothic novel.

Insofar as America is legendary, a fact of the imagination as well as one of history, it has been shaped by the ideals of the Age of Reason. To be sure, the European mind had dreamed for centuries before the Enlightenment of an absolute West: Atlantis, Ultima Thule, the Western Isles—a place of refuge beyond the seas, to which the hero retreats to await rebirth, a source of new life in the direction of the setting sun which seems to stand for death. Dante, however, on the very brink of an age which was to turn the dream into the actualities of exploration, had prophetically sent to destruction in the West, Ulysses, the archetypal explorer. The direction of his westward journey through the great sea is identified with the sinister left hand; and Ulysses himself comes to stand for man's refusal to accept the simple limits of traditional duty; "not the sweetness of having a son, nor the pious claim of an old father, nor the licit love that should have made Penelope rejoice could quench in me the burning to

become familiar with the vice of men and men's valor." It is a
fitting enough epigraph to represent that lust for experience which
made America. There is, indeed, something blasphemous in the
very act by which America was established, a gesture of defiance
that began with the symbolic breaching of the pillars of Hercules,
long considered the divine signs of limit.

To be sure, the poets of later Catholicism made an effort to
recast the dream of America in terms viable for their Counter-
Reformation imaginations, to forge a myth that would subserve
new political exigencies. It is, however, the Enlightenment's vision
of America rather than that of the Church that was written into
our documents and has become the substance of our deepest
sense of ourselves and our destiny. If North America had remained
Latin, the story might have been different; but Jefferson himself
presided over the purchase of the Louisiana Territory, which
settled that question once and for all. History sometimes provides
suitable symbolic occasions, and surely one of them is the scene
that finds Jefferson and Napoleon, twin heirs of the Age of
Reason, preparing the way for Lewis and Clark, that is to say,
for the first actors in our own drama of a perpetually retreating
West. Napoleon, it must be remembered, was the sponsor of the
painter David and Jefferson the planner of Monticello; good neo-
classicists both, they place the American myth firmly in the
classicizing, neo-Roman tradition of the late eighteenth century.
The New World is, of course, in one sense an older one than
Europe, a preserve of the primitive, last refuge of antique virtue;
indeed, the writers and artists of the Empire period could never
quite tell the difference between Americans, red or white, and the
inhabitants of the Roman Republic. The face of Washington, as
rendered in bronze by Houdon, is that of the noblest Roman of
them all, or, in Byron's phrase (already a cliché), "the Cincin-
natus of the West."

But America is not exclusively the product of Reason—not
even in the area of legend. Behind its neo-classical façade, ours is
a nation sustained by a sentimental and Romantic dream, the
dream of an escape from culture and a renewal of youth. Beside
the *philosophes,* with whom he seemed at first to accord so well
that they scarcely knew he was their profoundest enemy, stands
Rousseau. It is his compelling vision of a society uncompromised
by culture that has left the deepest impress on the American mind.
The heirs of Rousseau are Chateaubriand and Cooper, after

whom the world of togas and marble brows and antique heroism is replaced by the sylvan scene, across which the melancholy refugee plods in search of the mysterious Niagara, or where Natty Bumppo, buckskinned savior, leans on his long rifle and listens for the sound of a cracking twig. The bronze face of a bewigged Washington gives way to the image of young Abe splitting logs in a Kentucky clearing.

The dream of the Republic is quite a different thing from that of the Revolution. The vision of blood and fire as ritual purification, the need to cast down what is up, to degrade the immemorial images of authority, to impose equality as the ultimate orthodoxy—these came from the *Encyclopédie,* perhaps, as abstract ideas; but the spirit in which they were lived was that of full-blown Romanticism. The Revolution of 1789 (for which ours was an ideological dress rehearsal) may have set up David as its official interpreter, but it left the world to Delacroix; and though it enthroned Reason as its goddess, it prepared for a more unruly Muse.

In Sentimentalism, the Age of Reason dissolves in a debauch of tearfulness; sensibility, seduction, and suicide haunt its art even before ghosts and graveyards take over—strange images of darkness to usher in an era of freedom from fear. And beneath them lurks the realization that the "tyranny of superstition," far from being the fabrication of a Machiavellian priesthood, was a projection of a profound inner insecurity and guilt, a hidden world of nightmare not abolished by manifestos or restrained by barricades. The final horrors, as modern society has come to realize, are neither gods nor demons, but intimate aspects of our own minds.

2

THE NOVEL'S AUDIENCE AND THE SENTIMENTAL LOVE RELIGION

IT SHOULD BE QUITE CLEAR at this point that the word "novel" is being used here not to mean any long prose fiction, but to designate specifically the "modern" or "bourgeois" novel, that is to say, the kind of book first written in the second quarter of the eighteenth century by men like Richardson or Prévost or Marivaux. Such a definition excludes not only the long fictions of the Hellenistic period, but also the Mannerist proto-novels of the later sixteenth century as the *Arcadia,* Lyly's *Euphues,* even so great a work as *Don Quixote.* Though the latter, unlike most prose fictions contemporary with it, is still read for pleasure, and though its influence is occasionally felt still in modern fiction, it institutes no continuing tradition, but stands looking backward toward those romances of chivalry which it was intended to mock. Similarly, baroque fictions like the *Cléopatre* of La Calprenède or Mlle. de Scudéry's *Le Grand Cyrus* remain outside the main line of descent; meant to dazzle with their richness an aristocratic audience and dedicated to the revival of courtly love, they seemed alien to the class of readers for whom the modern novel was produced. Even Madame de Lafayette's subtle and subdued attack on *l'amour courtois,* in her *Princesse de Clèves,* does not break out of the limits of the courtly baroque; and a character in a Richardson novel typically found her heroine "silly."

When the novel proper was finally born, it pretended—at least in the hands of Richardson and his followers—to serve verisimilitude first of all: to deal with the truth of daily existence. In the

39

language of eighteenth-century genre criticism, it was classified not as legend or epic (despite Fielding's attempt to justify his own practice in epic terms) but as "fictional history." The Richardsonian novel has a mythology to be sure, but it is an unavowed, a secret one, rediscovered in the depths of the human heart, at the center of what the Marquis de Sade described as "nature's maze," where the monstrous and the heroic eternally abide. Even the gothic novel seeks its "magic and phantasmagoria" not so much in traditional story as in contemporary nightmare—projecting the same terrors which Richardson treated in terms of psychological motivation and social conflict.

The turning of the modern novel from mythology to psychology, from a body of communal story to the mind of the individual is an enterprise typical of our times. Indeed, only in the sub-mind of a dreaming man can we discover images common to everyone in our multifarious culture; and these images, though not traditional mythology, are myth in the profoundest sense of the word. The novel has, in the course of its search for inwardness, managed to save the mythic in an age of prose and science. This Diderot, Encyclopedist and advocate of reason, perceived in reading *Clarissa,* greatest of the novels of the high priest of sentimentalism, Samuel Richardson. Of Richardson, Diderot observes: "It is he who carries the torch to the back of the cave. . . . He blows upon the glorious phantom who presents himself at the entrance of the cave; and the hideous Moor whom he was masking reveals himself." Surely, "the hideous Moor" is a striking symbol of the demonic in ourselves, which the Enlightenment inadvertently discovered in its quest for light.

Born in a time of rationalism, the novel breaks through the rational, representing one facet of that strange revolt against the Enlightenment bred within the Enlightenment itself. "The Dream of Reason breeds monsters," Goya inscribed as a rubric on his *Caprichos,* and precisely those monsters the bourgeois novel describes. But the novel not only attacks the sovereignty of reason, it challenges the primacy of ideas. On the one hand, it opposes to the idea the fact, and moves in the direction of realism; on the other hand it holds up against the idea feeling, and tends toward sentimentalism.

The irrational essence of the novel is revealed by the very nature of its form, a form without a theory. It was born by accident, as it were, out of an odd mating of allegory with the plot structure of sensational drama, and of the letter book with prose history or scandalmongering. It is a genre that still defies an Aristotelian definition, a kind contrived when all the kinds had already been classified and arranged, an unforeseen and disruptive stranger. Its very name was used in earlier times as a term of deprecation, as if the genre were essentially disreputable. For traditional critics in the eighteenth century, it appeared to be essentially sub-literature and any attempt to distinguish between serious fiction and trash seemed to them as absurd as a similar distinction among comic books would seem now.

It was not until the appearance of *Madame Bovary* in France, or James's *The Art of Fiction* in England, that the novel seemed even discussable as art; until then (and to some degree to this very day), prose fiction was left in the hands of improvisors and amateurs, who were expected to proffer their untidiness and lack of self-consciousness as their very credentials.

Called for by no one in authority, condemned with equal fervor by critics and clergy, why did this hybrid form come into existence at all? And how has it managed, against all prevision, to replace the traditional poetic forms as the reigning genre of the West? It is well known that the novel succeeded, in the first instance, because it managed to satisfy a new group of readers, to whose cultural aspirations and spiritual needs it responded with peculiar aptness. This new audience was middle-class, Protestant, and urban, which is to say, uncertain of its status and alienated from older folk literature. It was the first body of readers in Europe to stand outside the gentlemanly value-system invented in the Renaissance and sponsored by court, salon, and school, the first "mass public." The Bible should have supplied this public with all the "literature" it needed; but its members lived at a time when for all but the most devout religion no longer dominated the imagination, having become observance only rather than life itself. At this group—not at its devoted center, but its less pious periphery—the novel was aimed.

The new group of readers was a large one, the largest in history, and it grew steadily on into the nineteenth century until it had established publishing as the first mass-production industry in the world; but its members were imperfectly educated—progressively less well educated, some would argue, the larger their number grew. Before the rise of the bourgeoisie, literacy was not considered something valuable in itself, but merely one of a desirable set of skills, values, and traditions. When a man learned to read at all, he acquired, with the mechanical art of spelling out words, certain standards; but with the final victories of the new class, literacy became a political demand and a sign of status, like suffrage or the right to carry weapons. As a crowning privilege, a final token of recognition, the bourgeoisie asked to enter into the culture of the ruling classes, to be permitted to read and write on the highest levels. In the Augustan literature of England, one finds the first fruits of this privilege in a literature in which common sense and a respect for antiquity exist side by side.

But traditional literature, even in its accommodated Augustan form, did not satisfy the hunger of the majority of the new social group; and certainly the masculine wit of eighteenth-century verse and essay seemed more at home in the coffee house than in the boudoir, where the middle classes tended to believe books were properly to be consumed. The merchant was unwilling to spend much of his time (which he never forgot was money) on the trivialities of art; such pursuits seemed to him more proper for the female members of his family—for his wife or, more particularly, his daughter, not yet burdened with the cares of running a household. The moment at which the novel took hold coincides with the moment of the sexual division of labor which left business to the male, the arts to the female—thus laying up for the future the perils of Bovaryism, on the one hand, and on the other, the dictatorship of "what the young girl wants" or, perhaps better, what her father thinks she *should* want. In light of the novel's predominantly feminine audience, it is scarcely surprising that its ideal theme should be love and marriage, and that its ideal protagonist should be a woman—no grand lady, but some girl, passionate and pure, and known only by her first name: Clarissa, Pamela, Charlotte, Emma, Julie.

Traditional literature in verse was certainly not attractive to them. It was, quite simply, too difficult—not only in diction and metaphor, but also, perhaps especially, in its involvement with codes and conventions belonging to a life alien and incomprehensible to them. The concept of honor, for instance, and the adulterous codes of courtly love, were strange and abhorrent to the bourgeois mind. It was to take much time and a long growth in self-confidence before any spokesman for the new group dared commit to print such a wholesale condemnation of "aristocratic literature" as that Tolstoy (himself an aristocrat!) expressed in

What is Art? But his apparent paradoxes had long been common-places of the middle-class Protestant mind, which had in the interim been carrying on an underground warfare against high culture, with the best-selling novel as a chief weapon. The novel, though it is many other things and has been captured for their own purposes by serious artists, was the first of a series of inventions devised by mass culture for giving the illusion of reading while requiring, less and less rigorously, its practice—a series that has come by now to include the book digest, the picture magazine, the comic-book, movies, television, etc.

As practical men, the new middle classes found literature frivolous; as pious ones, they found it idolatrous; as class-conscious citizens, they felt it too committed to court and salon. Yet they could not live without it; a lust for images of their own lives, projections of their own dreams and nightmares moved them obscurely. They demanded a form that would be really their own, a mass-produced commodity to be bought or rented in the marketplace like other goods, a thick and substantial item to be placed on the table with other evidences of their wealth and taste. The novel is the first large-scale example of "mass art." It is quite different from "folk art," with its hand-made appearance and its air of knowing its place, for folk art is rooted in the country and in agriculture; it changes slowly and almost imperceptibly, its chief appeal being its resemblance to what has come before. "Mass art," on the other hand, is urban art, changing with the rapid changes of fashion, and seeming as much the product of new advances in technique as of any profound shift in the imagination. Like other mass-produced products, it tends to drive out of existence craft objects, which cannot survive the class structures which demand them and the class-consciousness which defines their consumers. Just as the spectacular rise of the novel is inconceivable without the perfection of printing, its final victory is inconceivable without the invention of the circulating library; mass-produced, it is also mass-circulated like any commodity in an expanding mercantile economy.

Not intended for recitation or performance in the fields or at the courts like verse, not intended for public production like drama, the novel belongs to an era when literature came to be thought of as something enjoyed in loneliness. The family reading aloud in the patriarchal parlor for a time challenged but could not really destroy the concept of reading as a retreat to privacy—in the closet, the boudoir, the toilet, last of refuges, the point is the same. Literature, which had originally served to enhance the sense of community, bringing shoulder to shoulder a representative audience, before the storyteller or at the open-air tragic festival, now served only to make possible the simultaneous solitude of thousands of readers. Mass production and lonely consumption—these are the hallmarks of a new age. The process that had begun with the move into an indoor, darkened theater reached its climax in the novel, that private theater in the innermost darkness of the individual mind.

The form of the novel was, however, not only determined by the conception of art as a commodity for private consumption; it was a result also of the hypocrisy of the bourgeoisie in the presence of art, and is for this reason the art form least like art. Prose was, of course, less suspect than verse to the "no-nonsense" middle-class mind; and the novel from its beginnings was intended to seem closer to the chronicles and news accounts which its readers trusted than to poetry which they feared. The novel is fiction pretending to be truth, the marvelous pretending to be the probable. One can scarcely open an early example of the genre without finding in the body of the work a condemnation of "novels," i.e., all *other* novels, and on the title page the claim "founded in truth" or "a tale of truth." It is well to remember that the "realism" that distinguishes the novel from the start is rooted in this kind of double-dealing.

Though the novel marks the entrance of the libido onto the stage of European art, in it the libido enters with eyes cast down and hands clasped—in the white garments of a maiden. Richardson speaks in the same breath of himself as an artistic innovator and religious reformer, boasting that he has helped establish "A new species of writing, that might possibly turn young people into a source of reading different from the pomp and parade of Romance writing, and dismissing the improbable and marvelous with which novels generally abound, might tend to promote the cause of religion and virtue." "The improbable and marvelous" are not, of course, necessarily opposed to "religion and virtue"; in the seventeenth century they were, indeed, exploited in behalf of such ends by the more lavish artist-propagandists of the Counter-Reformation. The novel is, however, essentially a Protestant genre, and begins, in effect, by removing the gilded crosses, the polychrome marbles, and the stained glass from the house of fiction. It is, perhaps, better to think of Richardson's stylistic reform as "puritan" rather than "realistic" in any modern sense of the world. For him, mere faithfulness to the world of appearances must be defended in terms of its usefulness in promoting true piety as defined by scripture.

But there is still to be examined a third level of duplicity in the novel: beyond its representing the marvelous as the ordinary and passionate impulse as Christian piety, it also represents entertainment pretending to be a sermon (or alternately, a sermon pretending to be entertainment). "To promote the cause of religion and virtue," Richardson designated as the end of fiction, and his followers took up the same strain: "to inspire the FEMALE MIND with a principle of SELF COMPLACENCY and to promote the ECONOMY of HUMAN LIFE", to "win the mind to Sentiment and Truth." On its most obvious level, the novel was a kind of conduct book for the daughters of the bourgeoisie, aimed at teaching obedience to parents and wariness before potential seducers; and dedicated therefore to the same brand of poetic justice as that advocated by Thomas Jefferson. Not only did the bourgeois novelist seek to "present virtue in the best & vice in the worst forms possible"; he was also dedicated to showing vice punished and virtue rewarded as they are uncomfortably not in history.

The earliest novelists (particularly in America) were eternally aware of the voices from pulpit and press that cried out against the novel as "one great engine in the hands of the fiend of darkness," a charge whose validity they were willing to grant for all fiction but their own; and they strove to silence their critics by embodying in their work the practical morality of the class they served. Over and over they expressed the conviction of their readers that success is, if not salvation itself, at least its sign; and that virtue must be rewarded here and now, certainly in the final chapters of a book. But beside virtue and truth, the early novel enshrines "sentiment"; beside Christianity, it honors the Sentimental Love Religion, which was hopelessly confused in its pages with orthodoxy.

Though the novel merely seemed to serve the thin, rigid Protestantism that threatened it, it paid allegiance in fact to that secret religion of the bourgeoisie in which tears are considered a truer service of God than prayers, the Pure Young Girl replaces Christ as the savior, marriage becomes the equivalent of bliss eternal, and the Seducer is the only Devil. The Sentimental Love Religion demands of its adherents that they be unaware of the implications of their faith; and there are, therefore, no official scriptures of the new religion. Not even half-playfully formulated as were the conventions of courtly love by Andreas Capellanus, the codes of sentimental love were set forth only implicitly in the stereotyped characters and plots demanded of the novelists of the age. In this respect, they were much like our own latter-day romantic myths, which persist unexamined and only half-recognized in ladies' magazines and popular movies. The presence of such unconfessed dogmas and their appropriate mythologies is manifested chiefly in the extraordinary success of certain books—books which pretend to be novels, but are in fact secret scriptures. Best-sellers are by and large holy books, and the age of the best-seller is an age unable to confess its true religion except in terms of commodity fiction.

Certain elements of the underground faith of the eighteenth century have come to seem to us absurd; but we live still in the Age of the Novel (and of the cinema which is its child), so that no matter how vulgarized the sentimental myth may have become, no matter how smugly we snicker at it, we are somehow still its victims and beneficiaries. Certainly, there is no one in our world to whom the phrase "They lived happily ever after" is meaningless or unclear; for us the "happy ending" is defined once and for all: after many trials, the sacred marriage! Our secure sense of what happiness means in this context has nothing to do with what we *know* about divorce statistics or the possibilities of successful adjustment in marriage; it is a mythological rather than a factual statement.

The mythology it represents is, however, far from eternal. To Augustine or Dante, Sophocles or Plato, to the author of *Beowulf* or of the *Chanson de Roland,* the tag "they lived happily ever after" would by no means have had the meaning it has for us. Plato would not even have identified the "they" as male and female; while neither he nor Augustine would have conceived ultimate bliss as a joining of flesh with flesh, no matter how fully sanctified by ritual and custom. Even for Dante, real happiness would have meant the final turning of the lover and the beloved from each other to God, from the creature to the Creator. The belief in love between man and woman as the supreme happiness is neither a classical concept nor a Christian one; it finds certain parallels in the New Comedy of Menander or Plautus and Terence and in the Alexandrian romances; but the concept of the Pure Maiden is strange to the earlier prototypes—and one would have thought that the coming of Christianity (with its basic view of woman as temptress) would have discouraged rather than fostered such sentimental idolatry.

II

What, then, is the source of the convention of sentimental love? To be understood at all, it must be seen as part of a continuous process whose end is not yet in sight. It stands between the codes of courtly love, on the one hand, and recent Romantic defenses of passion as the end of life, on the other. Though in its eighteenth-century sentimental form it postulates marriage as salvation, this is only a parochial development (Protestant, chiefly Anglo-Saxon) of a larger theory of love between the sexes as the fountainhead of virtue and joy. There are two major moments in the process: the Catholic, aristocratic, Mediterranean moment and the Protestant, bourgeois, Atlantic moment. Both are associated with the birth of new, apparently secular literary forms, which are in fact the disguised scriptures of unofficial religions. The wave that begins in Provence in the waning years of the eleventh century and turns from the sacred language of Latin to the vernacular re-invents the lyric and regards the *canzone* as the great literary form. The second wave, which starts somewhere just before the middle of the eighteenth century in England, disavows traditional verse forms in favor of prose and elevates the novel to the supreme place among literary genres.

Both represent the inruption of the female principle into a patriarchal world, a revenge of the (officially rejected) Great Mother. Certainly in each, there is a symbolic installation of Woman, half in play, half in ritual earnest, in positions of reverence and power quite out of accord with her actual status—or her theoretical place according to Christian orthodoxy. It is striking that the characteristic modern literary forms (as opposed to those genres archaeologically revived from the study of the ancients) begin only in conjunction with such revivals of the dethroned Aphrodite, who is also the Muse of antiquity; and conversely, that such inruptions of the female principle demand a break with traditional forms and language. Though Adelbert the Archbishop of Tours could write in Latin to Adele, the daughter of William the Conqueror: "He is useless and vile who confounds your worth with other mortals. For sure you will always be the first of the other Goddesses," he is only indulging in a Humanist exercise. It was not the language of the Church and the revival of learning but the mother tongue that was necessary to produce *amour courtois,* as prose was necessary (when women ceased to respond to verse) to the birth of the Sentimental Love Religion.

No genuine archetypal figure from the mythologies of the past ever dies, no matter how reviled and bedeviled; thrust down as divinity, it will emerge as sentiment or hysteria or madness. In primitive Christianity, however, as in the Judaism of the Old Testament, the Great Mother had been viewed as abomination, the idol of the Canaanites. She persists only as the Bride of Darkness, the flesh of the sow, the whore of Babylon; and even Mother Eve is conceived of primarily as the source through which evil entered the world.

The huge, warm, enveloping darkness of unconscious life, the blind source of passion and reproduction and death, takes form as the triple Goddess and is worshiped in the ancient world by men content to be eternal sons. The Lord of Hosts of Christian and Jew represents an utterly different principle, one who can never be enthroned side by side with the Mother, as in Greece after the defeat of the matriarchy, but who insists upon reigning by himself, in a splendor so lonely and abstract that the ancient world thought him no god at all—merely *nothing!* Without some rebellion against the female blackness, there can be, of course, no civilization, no science, no law, no proper consciousness at all; but denied utterly, that blackness returns as nightmare or as art, in the witch cult or in Romantic literature to undermine everything built in its despite.

With the rebirth of secular literature in Provence there appears a strange new concept of sexual passion *—not as the (simple but rather degrading) pleasure it seemed to Ovid, nor as the madness of middle-aged mothers it seemed to Euripides, nor as the terrible burning it seemed to St. Paul, but as the supreme end of life: the subject par excellence of art, the pivot of polite society, the school of virtue. The center of courtly love is the convention of the inferiority of the lover to his mistress—or, more properly, to the Mistress, that physically undefined, faceless and history-less goddess, cruel, remote, and desirable. In a society where, by law and

---

* Certain academic types have in our time attempted to demonstrate that courtly love never existed at all. But there have always been such blasphemers, for whom the myth by which Dante and Chaucer and Spenser lived and dreamed has seemed an insufficient and unreliable truth.

custom, women were disposed of at the will of their fathers and husbands, where it would have been considered a lack of manliness not to rape an unprotected lower-class female, and where the Church insisted upon the submission of wives to husbands and preached the essential unchastity of all women—in such a society, the lover pretended the most abject humility before an idealized beloved, submitted to her most outrageous whims without regard to dignity and in the teeth of reason.

There may have been, as some of the earlier writers on the subject suggest, a social basis for this astonishing pose, i.e., the situation, not uncommon in Provence, in which landless knights dependent for their very existence on the idle lady of the castle played out in verse and song endless, humble flirtations. But William of Poitou, with whom courtly love poetry as we know it begins, was a king, not a dependent knight. He is a strange double-faced figure: the author of phallic poems full of male arrogance ("and so I screwed them eighteen times so hard I broke my belt and armor") and contempt for women, and, at the same time, the first of the poets of domnei—the service of ladies. The relationship of lover to lady is expressed in feudal terms (as, indeed, the relationship of man to God was contemporaneously expressed) because this was for the time the natural language of subordination. The lover is his beloved's "man"; he owes her "service"; she is even sometimes addressed as *"midons,"* not "my lady" but, literally, "my lord."

That final epithet strikes, however, a disconcerting note, poses problems not easily explicable even in terms of feudal usage. If on the one hand the code of courtly love blurs oddly into heresy, the last major flare-up of Manichaean dualism in Europe, on the other, it even more strangely merges with homosexuality. Indeed, one senses from the start in the verse of courtly love a desire to mitigate by ritualized and elegant foreplay a final consummation felt as brutal, or else a desire to avoid entirely any degrading conjunction with female flesh. It is wrong, I think, to believe with Denis de Rougemont (in his *Love in the Western World*) that the troubadours were secret sharers in the Albigensian heresy; they were heretics of another order—not secret but *unconscious* self-castrators. For surely their exaggerated worship of the lady unmanned them successfully enough to have pleased any of the world-denying Cathari among the Albigensians.

In any case, the service of love, beginning with an abject surrender of the will to an arbitrary lady, passes readily into an abysmal sort of masochism, and ends with the appearance of certain symptoms which would nowadays be taken to indicate a break-down, and which would once have been read as signs of demonic possession: sleeplessness, hot flashes and chills, loss of appetite and a consequent wasting away, obsessive preoccupation with the beloved, inability to perform ordinary duties or even to keep one's clothing in repair, melancholy, anxiety spells, etc., etc. No wonder some students of the literature are tempted to read these symptoms as encoded ritual, to protest that so much torment so solemnly endured cannot be caused by the mere issue of sleeping with a woman, while others have insisted that the lover is not in love with the lady at all, but with suffering itself—ultimately with death.

There is a kind of truth in both these contentions. It is not prob-able that the poets of Provence (however close their personal ties to the Albigensian heretics) were writing about the forbidden religion taught by the Cathari; though there may have been an occasional secret believer who *used* the praise of Woman as a screen for his beliefs. The religion of the poets of courtly love is no more the Albigensian heresy than it is Christianity, despite the figures they borrowed from the ritual of the latter creed, their habit of referring to "martyrs" and "saints" and "relics" of love. Indeed, trifling with sacred terminology is a kind of blasphemy which be-comes balder and balder, culminating in the pornographers of the eighteenth century, one of whom describes the male orgasm as "a sacrifice poured out upon the altar of Nature." The God of the troubadours is not the *Amor* of fearful aspect that they borrowed from classic mythology; he is only another sort of window-dress-ing. Their deity is the lady, the female principle, the White God-dess, never really deposed in the Mediterranean basin, though for a thousand years driven underground.

The dissatisfaction with the overwhelming paternalism of feudal Christianity, which led to the specifically religious protest of Albi-gensianism, also lay behind the aesthetic revolution of the trouba-dours. Courtly love developed in a society no longer content with pious asceticism and simple-minded codes of combat loyalty, but unwilling to submit to the money values of the wealthy merchants just then flourishing in southern France. Against the worship of money the poets of Provence quite freely inveigh; against the ideals of the Church they do not dare to speak candidly, though Christ as well as mammon is inimical to the world they dream. What they desire is a secular utopia of "courtesy," where the free dialogue between male and female is endlessly varied with pretty compliments and parlor games and songs. They invoke the Great Goddess primarily as a Muse, a civilizing Muse who will preside over the rebirth of the lyric and the reform of manners. But even the manners to which they aspire deny the orthodox belief that "the extinction of humanity would be preferable to propagating it by sexual intercourse" or that "the man who loves his own wife too passionately is an adulterer."

The Christianity which promulgated such harsh doctrines had quite simply failed to make possible an accord between man's passionate impulses and his ego-ideals. The celibacy of the clergy was notoriously more theoretical than actual; and the lay Christian seemed doomed forever to shuttle between riots of self-indulgence and orgies of maudlin repentance. A new concept of salvation was demanded that would take into account the dark surge of sexual desire: the helplessness of the male before the female and the serpent to whom she listens. Salvation according to the female principle is called *"joia,"* an ambiguous term meaning both the simple pleasure of physical consummation (what the Italians even now call *"piacere"*) and the satisfaction of loving, with or without consummation. The love mythology of Europe is attracted, on the one hand, to this ideal of love as the *gai saber,* the education of the soul to courtesy through joy; but on the other is drawn toward the *Liebestod,* the sense that only death is the true *princesse lointaine,* the absolute Bride. Love as joy and love as death; from its very beginnings courtly love looks in both directions.

The themes of self-punishment and self-destruction are inseparable (in the West at least) from the worship of the Female, who represents the dissolution of consciousness as well as poetic vision, the blackness of extinction as well as that of ecstasy. "The horseleech's two daughters: give and give." Submission to the Mother, moreover, is felt as a betrayal of the Father, as the priests of Christianity are only too willing to remind the poets, who, more often than not, end by recanting all their lovely praises of love when the church bell tolls them home. The conviction of guilt associated with the new concept of love is projected in its adulterous form, with the strategic substitution of the secondary triangle husband-wife-lover for the primary one father-mother-son. The sense of Oedipal guilt is surely one source of the taboo of silence; this is the secret that cannot be told, but which is forever betrayed by the *trichador,* the dark double of the lover who exposes him to the husband-father, who is also the Christian God. Poor husband, he is the surrogate for all the self-reproach of a poet leaving the orthodox ego-system of the Church for the plunge into the unconscious! Yet he is a real husband, too, for courtly love is life as well as myth; and the archetype becomes the mere poetry of the seducer, the poetry finally bedroom farce.

In the mythicized life of the troubadour Guillem de Cabestanh, we can read in archetypal form the nightmare of the lover, his guilt-ridden fantasy of the punishment which is a final ecstasy, and which he desires as much as he fears: "and he [the husband] killed him [the lover]; and had his heart drawn out of his body and his head cut off . . . and he had the heart roasted and seasoned with pepper and had it given to his wife [the beloved] to eat. And when the lady had eaten it, Raimons de Castel Rossillo said to her, 'Do you know what you have eaten?' and she said, 'No. Except that it was a most tasty and delicious dish' . . . and he told her it was the heart of El Guillem de Cabestanh . . . and when she came to herself she said, 'My lord, you have indeed given me so fine a dish that I shall never eat another . . .' and so she died."

In our society, at any rate, the archetypes of the Love Religion in its first phase are all adulterous: Paolo and Francesca, Tristan and Iseult, Lancelot and Guinevere. Indeed, the love of the troubadours is as naturally adulterous as the songs that express it are vernacular; it is to an alliance without benefit of clergy with a woman and not a girl that they aspire. One must be wary of the troubadours' own explanations of why marriage is the enemy of love; they serve to conceal the fact that the beloved *must* be married—but to someone other than her lover; she must, in short, be like a mother: remote, superior, unattainable, or at least attainable only with the sense of breaking the deepest taboo. No wonder the lover desires almost as much not to possess her as to possess her: "He knows little or nothing of *dompnei* [the Woman cult] who desires to have his *donz* [master-mistress] completely."

To comprehend the power of courtly love, the unforeseen effect this pass-time for idle courtiers has had on the soul of the West, is to become aware of the sense in which it is a true counter-religion to Christianity. Between its elevation of the lady to a kind of Godhead and the Christian teaching that such adulation is idolatry or worse there can be no compromise. Certain latter-day Christian apologists (notably Charles Williams) have tried to redeem in mystical terms the identification of love of woman and love of

God; and such apologists certainly had forerunners as early as Botticelli, who represented Venus rising from the sea in terms of an iconography previously used only for the baptism of Christ— thus equating *amor* and *caritas,* passion and charity. More typical, however, are the words of Andreas Capellanus, who in the final pages of his handbook for the courts of love recanted in classic form: "No man through any good deeds can please God so long as he serves in the service of love." This is the irreconcilable Christian answer to the assertion of the troubadour Bernard de Ventadour: *"nuls om ses amor re no vau."* No man is worth anything without love!

Insofar as courtly love represented a general break-through of the mother image into the under-mind of Europe, the Catholic Church was able to deal with it in its immemorial way, absorbing it into the cult of the Virgin. Ben Jonson once remarked of Donne's *Anniversarie,* "that it said of a mortal woman what should only have been said of the Blessed Virgin"; and the criticism suggests the solution: to substitute the Virgin for the secular madonna of the typical love poem. After all, Mariolatry and courtly love are both aspects of the same psychic revolution, that resurgence of the Female which, toward the close of the Middle Ages, left its impress everywhere, even on the chessboard, where the queen appears for the first time as the all-powerful piece. It was certainly less difficult for the Church to assimilate the courtly Woman cult to the adoration of the Virgin than it had been to syncretize the scriptural legends of the Mother of God with the folktales which attributed to her the role of Aphrodite. In the *Golden Legend* itself, Mary figures as the Great Goddess, lying in bed beside unworthy husbands while their wives steal out to their lovers, or presiding over the births of illegitimate children.

Insofar, however, as courtly love attempted to celebrate the love of man and woman as a source of grace, a rival to the love of God, it was attacked bitterly by the Church; and what poet pledged to courtly values could doubt, so long as he remained a Christian, that his soul was in jeopardy? What could he do? On the one hand, he could live as most men have in the last two thousand years, by compartmentalizing his allegiances. Even as in our time men can serve money or the state, pushing off repentance to a deathbed scene, so then some served Woman until the failure of animal vigor left them nothing but the pleasures of recantation. Others tried to have it both ways at once by idealizing, which is to say, de-carnalizing love; but this was likely to leave them with the conflict compounded rather than resolved. The idealized codes of love demanded the pure worship of the mistress; the flesh required sexual satisfaction; the love of God demanded the renunciation of both. The love of another man's wife remained adulterous whether consummated in the flesh or not; and superadding a pseudo-religious note merely complicated the original sin with an overlay of idolatry. What began in the self-consciousness of the poets as a playful parody of Christianity, ends as a full-fledged counter-religion, complete with ritual and metaphysics.

It was the Italians who completed the "sanctification" of passion. From Frederic II of Sicily, who learned from the Arabs to keep a harem and from the Provençals to sing the praise of women, the tradition was carried on to the *Vita Nuova* of Dante, where what had already been transformed from passion to art becomes theology. For every man, Dante suggests, there is somewhere a woman who is his personal mediator, a "miraculous" avenue to salvation. The name "Beatrice" provides tempting opportunities for puns on "she who beatifies"; and Dante cannot resist extending his quibbles until he has hinted that Beatrice is, in some mystical sense, Christ! At this point the Inquisition moved in to expurgate his little book. Beyond the mystical symbolism of the *Vita Nuova* lies the allegory of the *Comedy,* which makes of Beatrice Divine Theology, and the game is saved: not an actual woman but only that for which she stands is the source of salvation. It is a solution which leaves unresolved the contradiction with which it began; leaves to the soul of the West an institutionalized schizophrenia. So Petrarch, who followed Dante, after a lifetime of singing his passion can only disavow it in his old age. *"Vergogna e 'l frutto!"* Shame is the fruit!

In the Catholic south of Europe, the conflict of maternal and paternal, of lust and order, has *never* been resolved—only (somewhat cynically) compromised. The nominal victory has been awarded God the Father, but he remains invisible, while everywhere the Virgin with the Babe in her lap looks complacently down. The orthodox Trinity of Father, Son, and Holy Ghost has yielded in art and the popular imagination to the baroque trinity, derived ultimately from Venus, Vulcan, and Cupid, and still, despite the new names of Mary, Joseph, and Jesus, what it always was: an archetypal representation of cuckold, mother, and son, the last degradation of fatherhood. But the seventeenth century, which saw the triumph of the baroque trinity, witnessed also the last literary revival of courtly love, from which (progressively debased but still living) has been derived the cynical ritual of upper-class adultery.

Yet however vulgarized, the tradition of domnei has served in the South to maintain that sense of the reality and power of passion which gives to Mediterranean literature a dimension lacking in the North. In a world where the smallest boy screams "Horns!" as a conventional insult, the comedy of cuckoldry can never die; and where such comedy exists, its darker tragic counterpart is always waiting to be reborn. Indeed, from Stendhal to Flaubert, from Constant to Balzac and Zola, adulterous love defined the theme of the novel for the Mediterranean world. A critic like Denis de Rougement, brought up on continental fiction, can say almost without thinking what to an American is unthinkable: "To go by literature, adultery would seem to be the most notable occupation of both Europe and America. Few are the novels that fail to allude to it." One remembers William Dean Howells, realistic American novelist, who in forty novels did not treat adultery once; but this serves only to emphasize the truth of de Rougemont's contention for Europe.

On the other hand, where the Marian, Catholic tradition existed alone, the novel as a form never attained first importance. The heroic figure of the seducer, the pathetic figure of the seduced, and the comic figure of the deceived husband found their natural embodiment on the stage, especially in opera, which functioned as the novel of a resolutely illiterate South. The Don Juan archetype, in which we see the ambivalence of the European mind toward the courtly lover at the moment when his courtesy had come to seem merely the wiles of a seducer, was treated worthily by a novelist only once, and then by an Englishman, who calls him Lovelace and pretends he is not a myth at all. In Italy, the bourgeois novel came late and in imitation of foreign examples; in Spain its beginnings were even further delayed and less noteworthy; in Greece it has scarcely come into existence in our time. Though there has been a handful of first-rate novelists in the world of the Great Mother, there is no tradition of the novel, and few works that live in the imagination of Europe as great examples.

III

It was on the religious marches of Europe, where mother-directed Catholicism and father-centered Protestantism met, in France, Germany, and England, that the novel especially flourished; Rousseau moves typically back and forth between the two worlds of Catholicism and Protestantism, though finally his *sensibility* is as Protestant as that of Richardson or Goethe, the other founding fathers of the form. Committed to the Northern rejection of the Virgin, such men sought with special urgency to smuggle the mother principle back into their cultures. They were thus specially qualified to satisfy the secret hunger of the puritanical bourgeoisie, which demanded bootlegged madonnas; it was the function of the early novel to supply them. Here is another source of guilt, added to the original conflicts which underlie the origins of love in Europe. No wonder the early novelists carried forward in the new genre the theme of the *Liebestod* rather than of the *gai saber*. Tristan is their legendary hero rather than Don Juan, the sufferer rather than the seducer, whose sword serves as a barrier between him and his beloved rather than a weapon with which he hews his way to her side.

By the time of Rousseau's *Julie,* the pattern is set and in Goethe's *Werther* it inflames the imagination of the world: tears as the only orgasm possible to the languishing lover whose beloved is cut off from him by marriage or betrothment, disease or class or color—or, finally, by an incestuous degree of relationship. How many early novels (including the first one ever published in America) end with the discovery by the hero that the mistress for whom he has sighed is his sister! In the full flush of romantic candor, the long-kept secret is almost revealed in its nakedness; the desired bride is the sister, first surrogate for the mother—and the enemy is the father.

If, on the one hand, the triangle of wife-husband-lover becomes that of sister-father-brother, translated down toward its Oedipal base, on the other hand, it is interpreted upward into metaphysical abstractions. The forbidden bride becomes the Indeterminate, the Impossible itself; and it becomes difficult to know whether the lover is pursuing his sister or the horizon. In either case, however, the only consummation is death. "The grave's a fine and private place," the poet Andrew Marvell had naively observed, "but none, I think, do there embrace." He is, of course, egregiously wrong; in a score of sentimental novels (as well as in the tales of that supereminent necrophile Poe) the grave proves the only marriage bed; and the dust of those who cannot on earth embrace without guilt mingles innocently there. For death which punishes also forgives, which seems to sunder really joins. It is the night side of the Great Mother herself—a terrifying (but delicious) name for the lapsing of male consciousness into the female unknowing, from which it fell originally to pain and division and endless desire.

This tension out of which the European novel develops depends upon a delicate balance of Catholic and Protestant, aristocratic and bourgeois, North and South, which threatens to dissolve on the one side into Latin "gallantry," on the other, into Anglo-Saxon sentimentality. In one case, the suffering servitor becomes Don Juan; in the other, the *donna angelicata* becomes the Angel in the House; in one instance, *joia* becomes *piacere,* in the other it is converted into ever-after happiness. The beginning of the latter trend first became noticeable toward the end of the sixteenth century, when there appeared in England two simultaneous though quite opposed attempts to resolve the contradictions between courtly love and Christianity. The first is expressed in the *Sonnets* of Shakespeare (summarily in sonnet 144), the other in Spenser's *Faerie Queene* (especially in Books III and IV).

The Shakespearean solution was so extraordinary, so alien to officially accepted codes of bourgeois society, that it has scarcely been recognized at all. The resistance to the meaning of these "sugared" poems began as indifference (more than thirty years passed between the first and second editions), and developed with their growing popularity into outright expurgation, until in the seventeenth century certain embarrassingly male pronouns were quietly changed to the appropriate female forms, thus disguising the eccentric point of the sequence. A few lines from sonnet 144, however, put that point succinctly:

> Two loves I have, of comfort and despair,
> Which like two spirits do suggest me still;
> The better angel is a man right fair,
> The worser spirit a woman colour'd ill.
> To win me soon to hell, my female evil
> Tempteth my better angel from my side . . .

The theory of two loves, one angelic, the other diabolic, is at least a new way of stating the old problem, especially when these drives are directed respectively toward a fair youth (loved as purely as any Italian poet of the sweet new style longed for his lady) and the black woman (lusted after in self-hatred and disgust). But this means that sentimental salvation is attributed to the male, passionate damnation to the female. Shakespeare has used the form of the sonnet sequence, ordinarily dedicated to the service of ladies, to disavow domnei; and so successful is his subterfuge that men in willful ignorance have continued for generations to read to their mistresses Shakespeare's anti-feminist praises of the youth, for these are truly love poems of great tenderness. This obvious fact modern critics have tended to disregard in their concern with establishing the fact that Shakespeare did not actually have physical relations with boys. Apparently, such critics are not discomfited by the notion that the poet slept with women and considered it filthy, while chastely embracing an idealized male lover.

For Shakespeare himself, however, the system of two loves was not a satisfactory compromise, since the two loves tend to fall together; the youth desired as a symbol of innocent love, himself lusts for the female symbol of concupiscence, and there remains only the terrible cry, as old as Christianity itself: "Th' expense of spirit in a waste of shame/Is lust in action." The fable of the *Sonnets* describes the fate of the youth as he falls into the power of the Lady who "would corrupt my saint to be a devil." But the seed of corruption was already in him, already in the chaste relationship between him and the poet. There is no pure masculine principle, no male immune to the sinfulness represented by the Female; the fair youth having had a mother is tainted with evil from birth. Only the "man not born of woman," the motherless man, can break out of the trap of sin. The same kind of scholar who finds the *Sonnets* morally unexceptionable is shocked by, tries to expurgate as clearly un-Shakespearean, the speech in *Cymbeline* in which Posthumus Leonatus declares:

> Is there no way for men to be, but women
> Must be half-workers? We are all bastards,
> And that most venerable man which I
> Did call my father was I know not where
> When I was stamp'd . . .
>   Could I find out

The woman's part in me! For there's no motion
That tends to vice in man but I affirm
It is the woman's part. . . .

It is all of a piece, however: the dream of a pure, homoerotic love and the sense of panic before the terrible Female. Shakespeare's mind is possessed by the witch-stepmother figures out of Germanic legend; in *The Tempest,* his nearly final statement and one of his few original plays, the only mother evoked is that devil's dam, Sycorax, the "blue-eyed witch." Set against her is the *anima* figure of Miranda, daughter of the father, pledged to virginity as long as the play lasts, and permitted to marry in a union blessed by Circe but untainted by the intervention of Aphrodite or Eros:

> I met her Deity
> Cutting the clouds toward Paphos, and her son
> Dove-drawn with her. Here thought they to have done
> Some wanton charm upon this man and maid . . .
>   but in vain.
> Mars' hot minion is returned again;
> Her waspish-headed son has broke his arrows,
> Swears he will shoot no more . . .

It is the Protestant White Goddess who presides over Shakespeare's nearly sexless romance, the Great Mother stripped of her Satanic and aphrodisiac aspects.

Here his solution most nearly coincides with the Puritan synthesis of the *Faerie Queen.* Where the Mother of God is rejected as an image, the notion of love sanctified by marriage, of the wife as a secular madonna, takes over the special authority. It seems only natural to us (so fully are we the heirs of the Spenserian synthesis) that the passion which leads to virtue and *gentilesse* be felt by a man for a maiden and that it be sealed by marriage. June is for us a month as sacred as was May to the sighing, adulterous lovers of Provence, and the twin symbols of June, sentimentalized on a thousand cards of congratulation, are the bridal bouquet and the white veil symbolizing virginity. We must remember, however, that for medieval orthodoxy marriage did not make sex a holy thing; not until the sixteenth century was the marriage ceremony officially declared a sacrament. To marry rather than burn, to wed for the sake of progeny and companionship, these were standard and acceptable notions; but to identify the feeling which leads to and persists in marriage with the ennobling passion sung by the troubadours, this was a revolutionary step.

When the "virgin knight" Britomart in Book III of the *Faerie Queen* rescues Amorest from "the house of Busyrane,/Where Loves spoiles are exprest" and where an altar is erected to Dan Cupid *"Victor of the Gods,"* the end of courtly love is at hand. It is the British Protestant who first learns of that catastrophe; but the news soon spreads to the rest of the bourgeois world. The lover may kneel still before his mistress, but he kneels not to pledge himself to humility and secrecy, but to ask her hand, that is, to become not her servant but her master. The courtly conviction that love cannot exist in marriage is denied; and though the trappings of courtly service (plus the courtly belief in love as the fountainhead of virtue) persist, *amour courtois* is dead. It is instructive to compare the sentimental eroticism of Spenser's Northern romantic epic with the ironical sensuality of Ariosto's Southern *Orlando Furioso,* so closely linked to the former in form and versification. Ariosto's Angelica, who inspires no thought but rape even in the mind of the most ascetic and ancient monk, is also a product of the break-up of courtly love; but she marks the point at which domnei is modified by civilized laughter into the sensuality of the gentleman, while Spenser's Amoret memorializes the troubled search for a love that is also chastity, for an order of passion amenable to law.

Henceforth, in Anglo-Saxondom at least, the beloved who was the Muse of Europe's reborn lyric will be a respectable woman! Yet to make art of married bliss has proved impossible. In verse, the cult of the Wife ends up in so dull a piece of sentimentality as Coventry Patmore's *Angel in the House;* and even in the novel it produces at best the mild, Biedermeier effects of, say, the domestic scenes in *David Copperfield.* Quite early, the bourgeois sentimental novelists discovered that their proper subject was not marriage itself but what leads up to it: courtship, or its travesty, seduction. This subject Spenser was too learned to discover; he succeeded no more than Shakespeare in inventing abiding images for the new concept of love he foreshadowed.

He arrived on the scene too early, before the class whose aspirations he anticipated was securely enough placed to demand an art of its own. Between the values Spenser advocates and the form he employs, there is a deep contradiction. He looks backward—he is an archaizer not only in language—to the traditions of the metrical romance, an aristocratic amusement, intended for those idle and well-read enough to play with Arthurian or Carolingian mythology. Besides, Spenser's personal predilections were modified by the official cult of the Queen, that Gloriana-worship which, under Elizabeth I, usurped the traditions of domnei for political ends. For England, the Great Goddess had been made flesh. How different it was some two hundred and fifty years later, when Victoria assumed the throne but rejected the role of Gloriana in favor of that of the modest wife—and how poor Dickens howled through the streets of London, driven by her marriage into a frenzy that was only half play-acting. Between the late sixteenth and the early nineteenth century, a sentimental revolution had occurred, which Spenser could foresee but not begin, a revolution carried out in modest silence by the literary form that had in the meantime dethroned poetry—the modern or bourgeois novel.

3

RICHARDSON AND THE
TRAGEDY OF SEDUCTION

THE NOVEL PROPER could not be launched until some author imagined a prose narrative in which the Seducer and the Pure Maiden were brought face to face in a ritual combat destined to end in marriage or death; the form and its mythology were born together, in the works of Samuel Richardson, a melancholy and pious printer, who in 1740 became the first modern novelist almost by mistake. He wrote three large, tearful novels before he was through, *Pamela, Clarissa,* and *Sir Charles Grandison*—the first still read, at least in schools, but condescendingly (did not Fielding laugh it from the scene with *Shamela* and *Joseph Andrews?*), the other two now left to gather dust in libraries, though all Europe once wept over *Clarissa;* and Jane Austen, who could not bear the tragic tone of the greater work, learned her craft from *Grandison. Autres temps, autres moeurs.*

Pamela is the comedy of sentimental love, *Clarissa* the tragedy; *Grandison* is an afterword that added little new. It is *Clarissa* that counts for our purpose, not only because it is superior to its predecessor and successor—it is a study of the ambiguities of motivation unequaled until Proust—but because it is a product of mythopoeic power as well as art. In *Clarissa,* the mythology of the Sentimental Love Religion, the bourgeois *Liebestod* is defined once and for all; and the bare outline of its plot, its mythos, at least, should be familiar to anyone interested in the history of the novel.

Clarissa Harlowe is a dutiful daughter, the glory of her family, at once submissive and strong-willed, pious and intelligent, modest and beautiful. Harried by almost inexplicable hostility, by the hatred of a jealous brother (who wants to ruin her) and the bullying of a tyrannical father (who wants to marry her off to a wealthy, ugly old man), she is driven into the hands of Lovelace, who desires only to seduce her. Lovelace is a Machiavelli of the boudoir, a Don Juan who turns monomaniac before the unconquerable virtue of Clarissa, who loves him deeply but will not surrender to him on his terms. Lovelace is driven not by lust but by a desire for power and by perverted principle, for he is an "emancipated man" of his time, a rationalist and free-thinker who opposes marriage on theoretical grounds. He is also an aristocrat, handsome, courageous, endowed with all the charms of a disappearing class. Indeed, Richardson rendered so faithfully the strength of Lovelace's appeal that his hero-villain won the hearts of lady readers more completely than he could ever win Clarissa's.

The chief action of the book concerns Lovelace's attempts to reduce Clarissa to submission after she has fallen under his control. He subjects her to one indignity after another, finally tricking her into living in a brothel unawares, but he cannot sway her will; at last, in desperation he drugs and rapes her. That this is no victory he is painfully aware (Clarissa is not so sure; scrupulous beyond all reason, she suspects her deepest self of some secret complicity), for he desires the submission not of her body but her soul, and when he can gain her assent in no other way offers to marry her. His proposal Clarissa (staunchly backed by Richardson, despite a flood of letters from readers urging him to relent) will not accept, though she loves him still. Instead, she proceeds to die slowly and stubbornly of a broken heart, meanwhile designing and ordering her coffin and writing appropriate verses. Too late, her family repents, and at the end Lovelace is killed in a duel by his closest friend—not, however, before having a vision of Clarissa in heaven and himself in hell.

Practically everyone who knows the name of Richardson knows the meager plot of *Pamela:* how the virtuous lower class girl resists the advances of her employer's son and finally compels him to marry her. It is the first success story of the female bourgeois world, at once practical, prurient, and edifying—a thoroughgoing piece of *almost* unconscious duplicity, though quite charming all the same. The "almost" is the secret of Richardson's deepest appeal: he knows really what Pamela is after all along, knows her for the female Ben Franklin that she is, though he does not quite know how he knows it; this happy state of quasi-insight (he never falsifies the hidden motivations of his protagonists) he shares with his heroines and the readers who identify with them. *Clarissa* is, however, no second *Pamela;* for Richardson had the unexpected integrity to resist rewriting the successful formula he himself had invented. The piety and pornography remain in his second book (one is a reward for enduring the other), but the morality has matured, survived the temptation of the happy ending. The re-formed rake as repentant husband now strikes Richardson as a pretty doubtful kind of reward for virtue; and the acceptance of such a husband as pretty doubtful virtue. His insight into the complexities of the female mind has become terrifyingly acute; it takes an equally acute critic (Dr. Johnson was one!) to realize, for instance, that Clarissa, for all her undoubted goodness, somehow never *quite* manages to tell the *exact* truth. At this point, Richardson has truly carried the torch to the back of the cave.

Yet this book, equally impressive as myth and psychology, is unfortunately impossibly long and consequently (in a world grown even more indolent than harried) almost unread. C. F. McIntyre, translator and editor of Baudelaire's poems, could not in 1947 identify Lovelace; in explicating *"Danse macabre,"* he took the name for that of the Cavalier poet and ended in bewilderment. Similarly, a living authority on the American novel has written of *Clarissa* (with whose influence on our own books he had had to come to terms) that "it showed the sad end of a girl who failed to resist a man's blandishments before she got his wedding ring" and describes that heroine as "wicked"! The flippant tone is that required in some quarters of a sophisticated modern writing about the sentimental novel, and can be forgiven; but the critic's ignorance of the novel itself is unpardonable.

Against such latter-day misrepresentations, it must be insisted that Richardson succeeded in creating a heroine capable of satisfying the moral standards of almost everyone in his time from the most advanced Encyclopedist to the most philistine member of the middle class. Far from finding his *Clarissa* "wicked," all but the sternest of fathers exonerated it of any part in causing "female depravity"; and we even read of quite pious Christians permitting their daughters to read only "The Holy Bible and *Clarissa Harlowe.*" The novelist's more ardent female admirers described Richardson's printing press as an "altar" from which "hallowed incense" wafted forth, and referred to the pages of his books as "virgin sheets" that "no prostitution stains."

These seem oddly reverential terms for one who was, after all, secretly (perhaps even from himself) preparing that revolution of passion that was to reach its climax in Romanticism. Among the immediate heirs of Richardson were Rousseau and Goethe, not to mention Choderlos de Laclos and the Marquis de Sade. Yet there is something just all the same in the religious metaphors, for *Clarissa* was the first sacred book of the bourgeoisie, and if the church bells were tolled throughout England to signalize its heroine's death it is because that death was more than a literary event. Like the myth of the Crucifixion, the myth of Clarissa's immolation represents archetypally that victory which can only be wrung from defeat and which lifts up the heart in exultation above merely human notions of success and failure. But her story functions on other levels besides the final religious one; it manages, indeed, to symbolize all the chief aspirations of an entire class, aspirations of which its fable was in some cases their first consciousness. What Tristan had been for the aristocrat in love, Clarissa was for the bourgeoisie—a symbol of the self to which ordinary men in the midst of ordinary experience vainly aspire. Like a true archetype, she has not ceased to move us even now that we have ceased to read the work that first bodied her forth.

II

Perhaps even more clearly than Clarissa, Lovelace is an archetypal figure: just as Hamlet signifies finally only "hamletism" or Don Quixote "the quixotic," so Lovelace represents a complex that only his name fully defines. Baudelaire used that name without a capital in his *"Danse macabre,"* and defending the use of the lower case his French editor insisted, *"En somme, Lovelace est preseque un substantif de convention."* It is tempting to identify him simply as Don Juan, from whom, to be sure, he is somehow derived. Certainly, like the older archetype, Lovelace embodies contempt for religion, aristocratic charm, and an absolute, almost magical, ability to compel love; and like his predecessor, he is swordsman and libertine—dangerous thoughts in his head, a naked blade in his hand. The deaths of both figures are caused, at one remove or another, by duels, in that conflict of honor that is the traditional prerogative of the aristocrat in combat, just as seduction is his privilege in the area of passion. Both are caricatures of the courtly lover, whom they portray as a glib but essentially brutal sexual aggressor.

Don Juan, however, is essentially the impenitent; he can be damned but not persuaded, punished but not defeated. And the instrument of his damnation is the figure of the Father, that stone papa who stands for the patristic Church he has challenged. From Tirsa de Molina to Molière, Don Juan is unequivocally condemned, at least in the conscious judgments of the playwrights who evoke him; but he is the sole hero of the dramas through which he moves, and becomes easily (a mere change in acting technique will do the trick) the sympathetic rebel beloved by the Romantics. Lovelace, on the other hand, though equally courageous, equally irresistible in love, meets an opponent who is stronger than God—stronger, that is, than any religious scruple the seventeenth century had been able to set in the way of the principle of sexual conquest. The women who surround Don Juan in his legendary career blend into one another and the darkness out of which he emerges. Donna Ana, Donna Iñez, Donna Elvira, even taken together with all their wifely claims and oaths of holy chastity, do not add up to one Clarissa: a female principle equal and opposite to the male force of Don Juan. His legend projects the naked encounter of father and son (the women mere occasions), of the alienated individual and the society he defies. There is no mother figure to balance either, no symbol of nature or feeling strong enough to function as a principle of grace in a world completely given over to power and pleasure.

In the story of Lovelace, however, there is portrayed the meeting of an irresistible force and an immovable obstacle, that is to say, of Lovelace and Clarissa. Clarissa stands for a power not yet even conceived by the mind of seventeenth-century Italy or Spain, a power before which Lovelace can no longer function as the universal lover (with his vain mathematical boast: *mille e tre!*) but is transformed into the monogamous Seducer, the seducer who has found his life's work in a single woman. But monogamy, with whatever dishonorable intentions, leads finally to submission to the lady and repentance before her, if not before the God in whose name she speaks. It is tempting, indeed, to say that there is no God (certainly, no God the Father!) in the world of Richardson where His name is so often invoked. In his Manichaean world, there are only man and woman in eternal conflict; for the divine principle has been subsumed in the female even as the diabolic has been in the male.

Clarissa is, then, simply woman, but she is disconcertingly sexless in her bourgeois form—no symbol of insatiable passion or teeming fertility, but a savior, a mediator. She is the Persecuted Maiden, a projection of male guilt before the female treated as a mere sexual object; and she flees through two hundred years of fiction, hounded by father and lover, brother and fiancé: the heroine of all her sex, who applaud her example but are powerless to help her in her hour of need. She is feeling without passion, and her love climax is tears. She is a Protestant virgin, proper to a society that destroyed the splendid images of the Mother of God, but she is also the product of anti-metaphysical Sentimentalism, which found it easier to believe that the human could achieve divinity than that the divine could descend into the human. It is as Pure Maiden that she offers salvation, and upon her maintenance of that purity depends not only her own eternal bliss but that of the male who attempts to destroy it. Even more specifically she is the bourgeois Maiden, whose virginity is the emblem of the ethical purity of her class, the soul of a world whose body is money; and upon her triumph and fall the fate of that class symbolically depends.

Clarissa is, indeed, indistinguishable from her virginity. But that virginity, unlike the chastity advocated by the early Church, is not in itself an end, a supreme good; it is the sign that she has been tried and found worthy of fulfillment in marriage. If Clarissa as a maiden is the type of the savior, marriage is the symbol for the salvation she promises. Marriage alone, "marriage with a Good Woman," can save the depraved male; but such a marriage is of no effect unless woman brings intact to her wedding day the magic of her maidenhead. In a society where morality comes to be associated more and more exclusively with sexual continence, where being good is equated with being chaste, where love is happiness and marriage the fulfillment of love, there is a natural demand for "purity" in its most physical sense—for the unruptured hymen.

This is why in the bourgeois mind purity is associated only with the female; for the maidenhead of the male is too abstract to be believed in. It is not merely that only in a girl is virginity a fact provable in court; it is also that, for the middle-class mind, only femaleness has anything symbolically to do with purity. The final form of Protestantism is Puritanism, whose basic mode of perception is allegorical and to which the sexes are therefore emblems of salvation and damnation. To the mid-eighteenth-century bourgeois, the male is *per se* the tempter, and the female *per se* the savior; it is as simple as that.

Wherever, in any case, a sentimental world-view is substituted for a rationalist one, the male principle comes to seek the dark one, the female the light. Where, on the other hand, law is considered superior to impulse, reason to feeling, the symbolic Fall stories project a female tempter, or, at the very least, portray woman as the gate through which evil comes into the world. "The woman gave me and I did eat." The period of the male tempter is comparatively short in Europe, though long enough to have produced the Faust-Gretchen story as its supreme manifestation. Soon, however, the European writer and the American alike learn to distinguish between feminine and female, to split Woman into Dark Lady and Fair Maiden, savior and tempter, between whom the helpless male is eternally torn. The vampire who began as a male ghoul soon becomes the female "vamp" and the man her victim; but for a while at least, woman plays in the literature of the West the single role of victim-savior.

It must be noted finally that Clarissa represents not only the archetype become a fictional character, but also the fictional character projected as a moral paradigm. Life itself was required to provide examples no longer permitted to be painted on church windows. In the bourgeois world, particularly in its Anglo-Saxon reaches, every woman was expected to seem if not to be Clarissa; it was a burden, indeed, not cast off until the battles of the feminists had been fought and won. The imposition of the Clarissa-image on the young girl represents an insidious form of enslavement; all the idealizations of the female from the earliest days of courtly love had been in fact devices to deprive her of freedom and self-determination, but this last represents the final attempt to imprison woman within a myth of Woman. The demand that every woman act out the allegorical role of Womanhood is like the contemporary pressure on all Negroes to play The Negro; and the Clarissa image, when degraded from archetype to stereotype, is analogous to the current image of Uncle Tom.

Clarissa cannot exist without Lovelace any more than he without her; without him, she is a thematic abstraction awaiting a drama to embody it, a figure of speech in a sermon; without her he is only

Don Juan in the world of the bourgeoisie, that is to say, Lord Byron before the fact. Once mutually defined, their futures differ greatly; for Lovelace stands at the end of a tradition, Clarissa at the beginning.* From her descend directly Goethe's Charlotte and Gretchen, the Julie of Rousseau, Diderot's *La Religieuse,* the Justine of the Marquis de Sade, Melville's Lucy and Hawthorne's Hilda, even the Daisy Miller of Henry James. But Lovelace is quickly degraded into the stock villain of popular fiction and drama; it is hard to think of any later incarnation which approaches in scope or subtlety the vision of Richardson (perhaps the Valmont of *Les Liaisons Dangereuses*). Typically, he is converted into the masturbatory fantasy figure of bourgeois ladies: from the Montraville of Mrs. Rowson's *Charlotte Temple* to the Noel Airman of Herman Wouk's *Marjorie Morningstar.* In the gothic novel, he leads a somewhat more complex life, becoming the Byronic hero with burning eyes and a secret shame, and he is even improbably converted, via the Saint-Preux of Rousseau and the Young Werther of Goethe, into the image of the guilty artist in the middle-class world.

In the original Richardsonian forms, however, Lovelace and Clarissa are defined by their fatal encounter, that is to say, by the archetypal act of Seduction. In this relationship they stand alone; the characters who surround them, in Richardson's novel and in other early workings of the theme, serve only to maneuver them into isolation. Much later, when the myth has been completely profaned, deliberately burlesqued in comic strips and unwittingly parodied in movies, when Clarissa has become Belinda and Lovelace Rudolph Razzeltine, a third character is added: the blond, moose-jawed, clean-living Hairbreadth Harry, who arrives in the nick of time to snatch Belinda from the revolving saw or the approaching train. This is a perversion of the legend, necessitated by the habit (particularly strong in nineteenth-century America) of thinking of Woman as weakness rather than strength, thus standing the Clarissa-archetype on its head. The original point was, of course, that Clarissa needed the intervention of no hero to save either herself or Lovelace; for she was conceived as spirit, and spirit as the only force capable of defeating evil. But evil par excellence was seduction, that "fate worse than death" whose conventional description now cues only the undergraduate's guffaw. The

* Though sociologically defined as belonging to just about the same level of society, they are mythologically presented as aristocrat and *bourgeoise.*

melodramatic phrases, "Unhand me, you villain" and "At last you are in my power," whose very success made them ridiculous, are, it must be admitted, the invention of Richardson, who in two books created once and for all the standard language of the drama of seduction: comically in *Pamela,* in which the seducer fails; tragically in *Clarissa,* in which to one degree or another the seducer succeeds.

Seduction is at best a slippery concept, applying as it does to an act halfway between legitimate persuasion and rape, to which moral indignation can respond but which the law cannot define. Implicit in it is a belief in the weakness of women in the hands of men that directly contradicts the heroic feminist myth which emerges from its literature. Several generations of insistence upon the equality of the sexes has made the term all but meaningless to many moderns; and our "sexual emancipation" has made it hard for us to share the pity and horror with which a whole society once contemplated the Fallen Woman. The plaintive lines of Goldsmith, which reflect faithfully the sentimentality of Richardson,

> When lovely woman stoops to folly,
>   And finds too late that men betray,
> What charm can soothe her melancholy?
>   What art can wash her tears away?

> The only art her guilt to cover,
>   To hide her shame from ev'ry eye,
> To give repentance to her lover,
>   And wring his bosom is—to die.

become the rueful travesty of T. S. Eliot:

> When lovely woman stoops to folly and
> Paces about her room again, alone,
> She smooths her hair with automatic hand,
> And puts a record on the gramophone.

The old notions of seduction and virginity are not yet dead, however, on a less sophisticated level; until a very few years before the writing of Eliot's *The Waste Land,* in which Lovelace has become "the young man carbuncular" and Clarissa "the typist home at teatime," *Charlotte Temple,* a novel of seduction written in

1791, was being reprinted and widely sold in the United States; while in 1955, the revived seduction theme in all its pristine naïveté could make of *Marjorie Morningstar* a best-seller and of its protagonist a national heroine.

Behind the seduction theme lies the bourgeois redefinition of all morality in terms of sexual purity. If the Pure Maiden is the savior, alone capable of converting male rationality (which threatens to become free-thinking) to faith, and male sexuality (which threatens to become animal aggression) to tenderness, and if marriage is the holy state itself, then seduction is truly blasphemy: the denial of the savior and of salvation. Even worse, it is the sin of Judas, "betrayal with a kiss"!

The theme of seduction stands for more than blasphemy, however; it also represents a view of the sexual encounter as a battle. It is, indeed, as Denis de Rougement has observed, a special accomplishment of the modern age to have made of war a passion; and the same age has made of passion a war. The head-on collision of Pamela and Mr. B. or of Clarissa and Lovelace represents, perhaps first of all, the notion of love as the war of the sexes: an almost irreconcilable struggle between the male, who desires sexual satisfaction without marriage, and the female, who desires marriage if not without sex, at least with as little of it as possible. But this struggle is carried on in a world where all the socially powerful (i.e., the men) are arrayed solidly on one side, and all the socially powerless (i.e., the women) attempt to unite on the other —though, indeed, they cannot prevent occasional defections to the side of power.

Superficially, the literary war of the sexes reflects a psychological fact of bourgeois self-consciousness, institutionalized in bourgeois life; symbolically, it stands for a more complex sociological phenomenon: for class war in eighteenth-century England. Part of the appeal of the seduction novel rested surely on its presentation of the conflict of aristocracy and bourgeoisie within the confines of the boudoir. Typically, the Lovelace character is a nobleman, the girl he attempts to seduce of humbler stock. Sometimes, like Clarissa, she is rich and bourgeois, occasionally she is poor; and the seducer is sometimes given anti-democratic speeches, in which he scorns the notion of a marriage that will bring him neither profit or distinction. Against such cold class-consciousness and self-seeking are balanced the arguments of sentimentality: that it is the quality of the soul which counts, that the truest nobility is piety, etc., etc. In this sense, the novel is the long-delayed answer of the lower classes to the courtly *pastourelle,* the love debate of shepherdesses and nobleman, which ends typically with a tumbling in the grass. It is a protest, democratic and sentimental at once, against the courtly love codes and the sexual tyranny which they disguised. It rejects alike the conviction that love must be adulterous and the off-hand assumption that the lord of the manor has a right to take whatever girl of inferior rank is pleasing to him. On the one hand, the bourgeois novel insists that the pre-marital period is the proper time for love and legitimate marriage its only proper consummation; on the other, it asserts the sexual rights of its daughters as persons, capable of consent or refusal. But its protest against seduction is metaphorical as well as literal; through Richardson a whole class cries: We will be raped and bamboozled no more!

There is moreover an even deeper level at which the war of the sexes and classes is understood to represent a psychological division in the soul of man itself—and the conflict of ideologies which arises from this division. Lovelace and Clarissa are, as we have seen, the male principle and the female, Devil and savior, aristocracy and bourgeoisie; but they are also the head and the heart— what we would call now super-ego and (in somewhat expurgated form) id. Lovelace is above all things an intellectual—*philosophe* and libertine, Clarissa essentially a believer, however agile at apologetics—a sentimental Christian; Lovelace, that is to say, is a parody of the Enlightenment itself, Clarissa the idealization of all that lies beyond mere rationalism.* Richardson as a champion of the heart over the head, a secret enemy of Reason, is the philistines' Rousseau, the Jean-Jacques of the timid bourgeoisie. Like his French opposite number, he exacts from his reader the supreme tribute of tears. The triumphant fall of Clarissa, by releasing pity and melting the heart, becomes the instrument of salvation it recommends. Whoever weeps is saved; and all Europe wept at Clary's end, felt itself redeemed by self-knowledge as well as sympathy.

Yet though *Clarissa* is a sacred book and a treasure house of symbols dear to the rising bourgeoisie, it is by no means a book only valuable as scripture and symbol. It achieves its mythic reso-

---

* We must not be deceived by how well Clarissa talks; it is her feelings that count. She is a rationalizer of her heart's promptings, not a heartless rationalist.

nance without sacrificing verisimilitude, without ceasing to be a scrupulous portrayal of contemporary manners and modes of consciousness. Its very epistolary form, the presentation through letters not of action itself but of response to action, is not merely an amateur's way out, as some critics have thought, but the analyst's way in, a way of rendering inwardness with extraordinary immediacy. Indeed, after abandoning the letter convention, the novel did not achieve comparable subtlety and directness in the presentation of thought until the invention of stream-of-consciousness in the twentieth century. The creation of "character" in the full modern sense, that is, of fictional actors at once complexly motivated and consistent, highly individualized and typical—this is the essential achievement of Richardson's art.

To one brought up inside the view of the English novel that was universally accepted at the beginning of the present century, Richardson is hard to appreciate. Was his reputation not almost immediately deflated by the irony of Fielding? Did not readers move with relief from the fetid atmosphere of his airless boudoirs to the broad open-air vistas of the pseudo-Shakespearean novel of masculine protest? Did not ingenious plotting and fast action, good theater, replace the tedious revelation of the dark underside of the souls of young girls? Of course they did not; for the novel must continue to carry the torch to the back of the cave (whatever else it does in addition) or surrender its birthright, its essential function. Parody destroys nothing; it is only a reluctant and shamefaced way of honoring an example one is ashamed to acknowledge, and, for one too proud to attempt so popular a form as the novel without tongue in cheek, a way of becoming a novelist.

4

THE BOURGEOIS
SENTIMENTAL NOVEL
AND THE
FEMALE AUDIENCE

FIELDING, especially since the rejection of gentility has become an important touchstone in the academic world of the United States and new notions of sexual freedom have prevailed, has come to seem the true, tough-minded ancestor of "honest" fiction, the preferred father of the novel. The legendary contest with which modern fiction is supposed to have begun is the struggle between Pamela and Joseph Andrews, in which the sentimental sister is mocked to silence by her comic brother and the way is cleared for Tom Jones.

The preference of contemporary American critics for the Good Bad Boys of Fielding over the Good Good Girls of Richardson is a phenomenon some of whose causes will be made clear in the following discussion; but the critics' personal inclination is not of first importance. Nor does it matter in a total view of the American novel that to most of Europe, Fielding has always seemed of lesser importance than Richardson. Even Dr. Johnson's view of the matter can be shrugged aside as aberrant. After all, he was a man given over to prejudice and invective, one with the temerity to call Fielding a "blockhead," in the very interchange in which he insists, "Sir, there is more knowledge of the heart in one letter of Richardson's than in all *Tom Jones*." But the student of American letters must come to terms with the earliest American reactions to the author of *Clarissa*.

In 1790, Enos Hitchcock wrote, "His Clarissa has been considered by good judges, as the most finished model of female excellence which has ever been offered for their imitation," and Charles Brockden Brown puts into the mouth (or rather, in good Richardsonian fashion, onto the tip of the pen) of his heroine the following pledge of allegiance: "I am a disciple of that religion and philosophy of which the effects are to be seen in Clarissa. O best of men!" Though *Tom Jones* had to wait fifty-four years for an American edition, *Pamela* was published in Philadelphia only four years after its appearance in England. (The latter was the first book printed in America, naturally enough by Benjamin Franklin, who, though no friend of sentimental love—"use venery," he coolly recommended, "for health and offspring"—knew something about business.) The British fleet during the Revolution brought in *Clarissa* in eight-volume sets, and by 1800 there were twenty native imprints of Richardson in the United States, even illustrated and abridged versions of *Clarissa* and *Grandison*, "for the Instruction and Amusement of Children"!

For better or for worse, the values of the Sentimental Love Religion, inextricably bound up with the example of Richardson, entered into the American novel at the moment of its creation. There is scarcely a nineteenth-century book written by an American, whether avowedly in the analytical school that derives from *Pamela*, or in the gothic tradition out of Ann Radcliffe and "Monk" Lewis, or in the line of the historical romance as defined by Scott, which does not accept the standards of that code. These are the three chief strains of our earliest fiction, and, whatever other differences may separate them, they are at one in espousing "that religion and philosophy of which the effects are to be seen in Clarissa."

It is not enough, however, simply to say that Sentimentalism triumphed everywhere in our fiction; it must also be added that it proved almost everywhere a *blight*, a universal influence which was also a universal calamity. The Pure Young Maiden who derives from Clarissa and pre-empts the place of the heroine in our classic books is almost invariably a dull and embarrassing figure, a monster of virtue, her derivation a vulgarization and a falling off. The scarcely distinguishable ingenues of Cooper, the incredible Lucy over whom Melville drivels in *Pierre* (so shamelessly that his admirers have tried ever since to persuade themselves he was engaging in burlesque), Hawthorne's pale Priscilla and unbearably dovelike Hilda: these are the scandals of our literature. Indeed, it was their awareness of the inadequacy of such female characters (and their inability to imagine others) that led many of our authors to that strategy of evasion, that flight from society to nature, from the world of women to the haunts of womanless men, which sets our novel apart from that of the rest of the Western world.

Why did the Richardsonian example, elsewhere so fertile, prove so sterile in the United States? A tradition capable of supplying the love story for Part I of *Faust*, for *I Promessi Sposi*, or even for *The Heart of Midlothian* might well have been expected to inform works of equal merit in America. Why does the relationship of Heinrich and Gretchen (like that of Clarissa and Lovelace) still possess the imagination of the West, breeding new works of art, while that of Lucy and Pierre seems irrelevant and a little comic? The beginning of an explanation can be found in the fact that there is no real tradition of gallantry in America, no debased aristocratic codes of love against which the bourgeois belief can define itself; and consequently the tension and urgency which make dramatic the works of Richardson and Rousseau and Goethe are lacking. It is impossible to contrast domestic virtues with courtly ones in a country where there has never been a court, so that the essential Richardsonian conflict, which is also the dialectic of the form, is inevitably lost.

It is true, of course, that Richardson himself formally rejected adultery as a subject; and the struggle over the virtue of Clarissa has been moved from the arena of marriage to that of maidenhood. Yet where the figure of Don Juan persists, no matter in what disguise, the theme of adultery hides underground, as it were, awaiting a resurrection. In the novels of Richardson's most faithful followers, in the *Nouvelle Héloïse* of Rousseau or Goethe's *Werther*, published within twenty-five years of *Clarissa*, the old courtly theme reasserts itself: adultery, consummated or unconsummated, comes to stand beside seduction at the sentimental heart of these fictions; and when seduction itself loses not only its appeal but its very meaning, the European novel reverts completely to the oldest theme of Western secular literature. "Society requires that women have husbands," Denis de Rougemont remarks, "but in novels it is found necessary that they have lovers."

Not so in American fiction during its classical period, where except for Hawthorne's odd example, no major book confronts that major theme until the time of Henry James. Similarly, there existed in America no body of pornographic literature. But this cuts our bourgeois literature off from the device of borrowing the brutality and frankness of pornography on the grounds that opposing forces, in order to meet, even on a moral battleground, must adopt similar strategies. There is a real sense in which the novels of Richardson, at their Hogarthian strongest and most appealing, are "dirty books." It is no accident that *Fanny Hill,* that masterpiece of British pornography published in the same year as *Clarissa,* itself adopted—however cursorily—the letter form of *Pamela;* or that Diderot was the author of the *Bijoux Indiscrets,* an extended smutty joke, or that in his most Richardsonian novel, *La Religieuse,* he pursued sexual titillation even in the midst of moralizing and tears. Implicit in Diderot—and, though quite differently, also in Rousseau—are the seeds of the infamous *Justine,* the book the Marquis de Sade would never quite confess he had written, and of *Les Liaisons Dangereuses,* last of the great epistolary novels, which defined a delicate line between obscenity and art, inconceivable to the American mind.

The American novelist, then, was deprived of the privilege of defining his own middle-class values against a surviving tradition of gallantry or *gauloiserie.* Only in Puritanism could he discover an antithesis to his sentimental world-view, a source of tension to protect him from moral flaccidity. But before the novel proper was invented, Puritanism had begun to decay; indeed, the Sentimental Love Religion was itself, as we have seen, a by-product of the softening of Protestant rigor; and novels could not even have been printed if the church of the Pilgrims had not first relinquished its social control. The printing press came first to America, like so much else, in the service of God, and the first book published on our soil was *The Whole Book of Psalmes Faithfully Translated into English Metre.*

But the century that elapsed between the publication of the *Bay Psalm Book* in 1640 and that of the American edition of *Pamela* in 1744 saw the break-up of the political power of Puritanism in America, and the consequent slow transformation of Calvinist dogma into sentimental piety. By 1688, it was clear that no new settlement could restore the power destroyed by the Restoration of the Stuarts; and the hysterical hunt for a conspiracy of witches represents the loss of nerve among the elders of the church, a desperate attempt to identify some visible enemy who could be blamed for what time and history had done to their dream. The vision of a Protestant Commonwealth in the New World compromised and dissipated, they could find nothing better to do than hang old women and dogs. Worse, however, was to come; for in the final years of the eighteenth century and the first decades of the nineteenth (at precisely the moment when the American novel was being born), the old church was forced to endure a double-barreled attack. From without and within Calvinist doctrine was assailed: by the Deists who deserted the places of worship and by the "liberal Christians" (who were to call themselves in the end "Unitarians") who attempted to take them over. By the time the first American novel appeared, in the critical year of 1789, Calvinism was doomed, on the one hand, to be dissipated among a hundred frantic, life-denying sects, and on the other, to be gradually sapped away by "liberalism." The father-centered, ascetic, intellectual faith upon which America had been founded survived, by the time of William Hill Brown, the first native novelist, chiefly in the form of secularized feelings of guilt.

To those guilt-feelings the American novel paid tribute by attempting to justify its existence on moral grounds—declaring itself the servant of religion and especially the keeper of the consciences and the virginity of young girls. The original Puritan impulse had represented an extreme revulsion from Mariolatry, an absolute refusal to give the female principle its due. As late as Hawthorne (though perhaps later for him than for others not so obsessed with the Puritan past), the image for the ancestral faith is a paternal image: "Grave, bearded, sable-cloaked and steeple-crowned . . . with his Bible and his sword . . . ," and that image Hawthorne mythicized for us all in *The Scarlet Letter*.

By the time of Mark Twain, however, even the claims of the old faith are asserted only by women; it is woman who has become the guardian of morality and the embodiment of conscience, whether in the palatable form of the widow Douglas, "dismal regular and decent . . . in all her ways," yet able to "talk about Providence in a way to make a body's mouth water" and much given to weeping over "poor lost lambs"; or the more forbidding shape of Miss Watson, "a tolerable slim old maid with goggles on," addicted to telling squirming small boys "all about the bad place." "Crying" religion or "pecking" religion, Calvinist or sentimental, religion is thought of as exemplified by mother or aunt, the Puritan image of the bearded Progenitor gone once and for all.

The American had finally denied too many fathers to survive except as the fatherless man. The fatherland abandoned, the Pope rejected, the bishops denied, the king overthrown—only the mother remained as symbol of an authority that was one with love. What the original, archetypal American experience established as a pattern, the experience of the immigrant generations somehow repeats; for better or worse, the children of Slavic peasants, of German revolutionaries and Jewish scholars are become alike heirs of a handful of Englishmen who settled New England. "The individual rejection of the European father . . . every second-generation American had to perform . . . ," Geoffrey Gorer writes in *The American People;* "the making of an American demanded that the father should be rejected both as a model and as a source of authority. Father never knows best." The symbolic vacuum left by the deposition of the Father is filled by the figure of woman, as Maiden and Mother; and America remains still the only Christian country in which a major religious denomination was founded by a woman.

The American novel is both beneficiary and cause of this symbolic shift of allegiance. Its salvationist myths meet head-on the older Pauline notions of the female as tempter and marriage as a necessary evil. In the strongholds of Calvinism, it was taught that copulation of husband and wife on the Lord's day is especially sinful, which is to say, that the rite of marriage does not transform the sexual act into a sacramental one. Indeed, the distrust of sexuality is not denied by the sentimental code itself, which only combined it uneasily with a sense that not the lonely saint but the married man is the truest friend of God. The Sentimental Love Religion, which simultaneously disowns sex and glorifies woman, could not triumph until the traditional association of the fear of passion with a contempt for the female had fallen apart.

The myth of the Fall in the Garden was interpreted by the Puritan allegorist as it had been interpreted by Milton: once reason (represented by the male) has been lulled to sleep, feeling (represented by the female) is easily subverted by evil, and in turn easily subverts reason itself. This is, of course, almost precisely opposed to the deepest meaning of the sentimental myth of the Seducer and the Maiden; for that archetype projects the image not of passion seducing intellect, but of the head attempting to lead the heart astray. The anti-intellectualism of the sentimental code, its theory that simple feeling is closer to God's truth than educated intelligence, could exist only in the decline of Puritanism and is, indeed, a symptom of that decline.

More, however, is involved than this. The Sentimental Love Religion challenges the fundamental Calvinist belief in natural depravity; for it teaches that women, woman in general and some women in particular, are absolutely pure; and that their merely human purity can do Christ's work in the world: redeem corrupted souls from sin.

In America, especially, the use of women as symbols of piety and purity led to an unfortunate series of misunderstandings.* With no counter-tradition, cynical or idealizing, to challenge it, the sentimental view came to be accepted as quite *literally* true, was imposed upon actual woman as a required role and responded to by men as if it were a fact of life rather than of fancy. Even Hawthorne, who attempted valiantly to restore the anti-sentimental insights of Calvinism to secular thinking, stumbled here. Of his Hilda in *The Marble Faun,* whom he seems always on the tantalizing verge of turning into the Blessed Virgin, he remarks through his mouthpiece, the artist Kenyon: "Her womanhood is of the ethereal type, and incompatible with any shadow of darkness or evil." This comment Miriam, herself a nonethereal type, glosses further: "You are right . . . there are women of that ethereal type as you term it, and Hilda is one of them. She would die of her first wrong-doing—supposing for a moment that she would be capable of doing wrong."

One has only to imagine the incredulity of St. Paul or Augustine, Calvin or Cotton Mather before such a statement to realize how revolutionary it is in its implications. Any cynical phrase taken at random out of Rabelais is far closer to orthodox opinion on the subject: "When I say, *womankind,* I speak of a sex so frail, so variable, so changeable, so futile, inconstant and imperfect, that, in my opinion, *Nature* . . . did in a manner . . . stray exceedingly from that excellence of providential judgment by which she had created and formed all other things, when she built, framed and made up the woman."

Richardson himself did not for all his bland moralizing portray his heroines as so exempt from all sinfulness. Pamela is gifted with the sharpest of eyes for the main chance, and Clarissa, pattern of excellence that she is, has her weaknesses. It is not Puri-

---

* Even female Indians were regarded as dusky Pamelas. And it would be a shame not to mention in this connection the name of Pocahontas, who has been the inspiration of so many bad sentimental novels—as well as of so many debunking male travesties, culminating in John Barth's *The Sot-weed Factor* (1960).

tanism, which however pharisaical was not given to self-deceit, which creates the illusory image of female perfection, but the genteel oposition which sought to humanize the earlier faith. The very force which permits the appearance of the novel and welcomes its tearful philanthropy leads to a falsification of life (at least on the side of women) which emasculates the form. Whatever his opinion of sexual passion, no Puritan denied or was afraid to describe its omnipresence and power. And even as late as 1803, it was possible to devote one of the chief commencement addresses at Harvard to the subject of Seduction, a topic which by the end of the century had become taboo on all public occasions, and is, indeed, not even treated in the novels of a "realist" like William Dean Howells.

No Puritan divine would have been shocked as Thoreau was at the appearance of phallic forms in nature, for he would have expected no better. And none would have thought that the way to deal with sex was to ignore it, or to ban from literature the words by which it is customarily described; but the genteel impulse, confusing civilization and bowdlerization, chose to speak of dying as "passing over," of pregnancy as an "interesting condition," and of copulation not at all. Richardsonian Sentimentalism was degraded step by step to genteel sentimentalism, as the novel of seduction was deprived of its now unmentionable theme.

The Seducer was first demoted to the unworthy wooer, pressing his insulting suit, and then was eliminated completely, while the Clarissa character was reduced in age from maturity to early adolescence to childhood—so that her virtue might be tested and proved without the intrusion of sex. At the close of the eighteenth century, an abridged Clarissa was considered quite suitable fare for children; at the beginning of the nineteenth century, grown women felt safe from possible offense only with a juvenile: thrilled sedately as Ellen Ware faced down the insolent dry-goods salesman in Susan Warner's *The Wide, Wide World,* that child's book which became one of the great adult best-sellers of our history. The movement which produced so strange a development was the movement of warm-hearted reform that nurtured abolition, prohibition, anti-vivisection, and vegetarianism; that drove Mama to the Chautauqua lecture and Papa outdoors to smoke; that delivered pious America from the threat of damnation and the fear of the seducer. It was in short what its best friend and severest critic, Mark Twain, called "civilization."

II

Before the sentimental novel came to America, it had already been transformed by the heirs of Richardson in England; and it is through those heirs that the master was approached in the United States. Like all provincial literatures, the American began with a cultural lag, emulating long-lapsed styles of the center. It was not until 1789, nearly fifty years after the publication of *Pamela,* that our first home-grown sentimental novel appeared. The year 1789 marked the close of a long dull period of recapitulation in the literature of Europe; there was a sense that the masters had all departed, leaving no worthy successors. Fielding had died in 1754, Richardson in 1761, Sterne in 1770, and Smollett in 1771. The year of Richardson's death had seen the appearance of Rousseau's *Nouvelle Héloïse,* and Smollett's death had coincided with the publication of *Werther.*

On the continent as well as in England, the work of the great ground-breakers was over; and everywhere there was a sense that the old lines of development would have to be given a new turn or abandoned altogether. To be sure, a "new" literature was beginning in England at almost the same moment that the sentimental novel was being reborn in America. The main body of work of Mrs. Radcliffe began to appear in 1789, a series of novels which, with *The Monk* of M. G. Lewis, was to succeed in creating the "modern novel" of the declining eighteenth century —the gothic romance. This form, however, was not to reach America for another decade. Our first authors looked for examples to the continuing tradition of Richardson, and what they found was not particularly exciting.

The intended audience for Richardsonian fiction had been from the beginning largely if not exclusively feminine. The protagonists of his books had been, indeed, females in whom his readers could find a glorified image of themselves; but when women became the chief authors as well as the chief characters of the novel, a real change took place. Never before had there been an art form in whose production women played so predominant a part (except, perhaps, the late baroque romances of France), and whose modes and values they so decisively influenced that later male authors had (like Melville in *Pierre*) to imitate them in order to bid for their audiences. Before his death, Smollett had been driven to cry out that "that branch of business is now engrossed by female authors who publish merely for the propagation of virtue. . . ." "Merely for the propagation of virtue," he ironically defines their goal; but his metaphors, "branch of the business," "engrossed" indicate the other goal of such writers.

One essential contradiction of Puritanism, at least, survived to haunt the lady purveyors of genteel, sentimental fiction: the mutually incompatible injunctions to be "one deadhearted to the world" and to "bestir yourself for profit!" At any rate, the manufacture of novels is the first business in the modern world into which women were permitted to enter in large numbers, and in which, competing on an equal footing with males, they achieved financial success. If the birth of the novel is in one sense an episode in the rise of the bourgeoisie and in another an incident in the genteel reform of manners, it is also a critical moment in the emancipation of woman.

America was no exception in the trend toward female authorship; indeed, before the publication of Cooper's *Precaution* in 1820, one-third of all our novels had been written by women—and within that third were to be found almost all the early bestsellers. Past the middle of the same century, Hawthorne is still deploring the "d——d mob of scribbling women," who have pre-empted the audience for novels; while the books of Susanna Rowson, Harriet Beecher Stowe, and Susan Warner remain to this day the most popular American fiction of all time, rivaled only by such later products of female authors as *Gone With the Wind* and *Peyton Place*. It is difficult in the early stages to distinguish between the work of the British lady-epigones and the American ones; indeed, the authors sometimes moved back and forth between the old country and the new with an ease which distresses the classifier. Mrs. Susanna Rowson, author of the most reprinted of all American books, *Charlotte Temple,* was born in England and wrote her first three novels there; *Charlotte* itself was published in London three years before its appearance in New York. For the English, however, Mrs. Rowson is a minor figure in the decline of the Richardsonian novel, a belated supernumerary of the rank of the Miss Minifies or Mrs. Woodfins; for us, she is a pioneer! To be sure, such third-rate sentimentalists made some difference in the history of English taste—but for America they made *all* the difference.

What, then, was the nature of their achievement? What did the

Sentimental Love Religion and the novel of analysis become in their hands? It must be said first of all that the sentimental novel of analysis, once firmly in the hands of genteel females, ceased to be analytic at all. To observers as different in taste and ambitions (though all male!) as Diderot, the Marquis de Sade, and Dr. Johnson, it was clear from the start that the abiding value of Richardson's work lay in his knowledge of the intricacies of the female mind (or, as it was called then, the "heart"), and in his invention of a technique for rendering in all their complexity and evanescence moments of choice or equivocation within that "heart." Neither inwardness nor character, however, interested the scribbling ladies at all. They sought, however unconsciously, the mythical beneath the psychological—and rendered the myth in sub-literary or pre-literary form, degraded it to the stereotype. They preserved the letter form of Richardson's fiction with no feeling for what that device was intended to do: to redeem the novel's action from the historical past for the dramatic present. For them, it was simply the way novels were put together.

Integrated into carefully differentiated letters, rendered always through an actor in his story, Richardson's prosiest sermons have a point and an aesthetic function. They serve to define character and milieu with a truth quite independent of their own validity in terms of ethical systems. But introduced into third-person narrative, or only perfunctorily assigned to some interpolated mouthpiece of the author, they remain interesting only so long as they strike the reader as fresh or significant. Plot is, of course, another matter. Richardson is certainly no greater contriver of plots, but he does possess extraordinary mythopoeic powers—so that, though there is perfect justice in Samuel Johnson's rejoinder to one who found Richardson "very tedious": "Why, Sir, if you were to read Richardson for the story, your impatience would be so much fretted that you would hang yourself," there is much more to be said. It was, at any rate, precisely "the story" that the female Richardsonians sought to extricate and recreate, for they were aware, as Johnson was not, that even the bare bones of the seduction archetype had an import for the whole community beyond that of literature. The appeal of the seduction mythos is, however, limited in time; only for a little while was it able to appeal to an audience which included the learned as well as the scarcely literate. Yet even in reduced straits, it retains some vestige of its legendary power, and can at any moment achieve an unforeseen popular success.

The natural ease of Richardson's style concealed its technical virtuosity and led his imitators to believe, on the one hand, that anyone who could write letters could string them together into a book; and, on the other, to feel that artlessness was itself a Richardsonian quality: a natural adjunct of piety and a guarantee of the "truth" as well as the moral usefulness of a work which no sentimental Christian would concede was merely art. The lady Richardsonians were moreover not only the enemies of psychology and technique; they were also the sworn foes of candor. Though they clung for a long time to the seduction theme itself (they could think of no other core for a novel equally sure-fire in its appeal) and consequently never became quite pure enough to satisfy their even more genteel descendants, they expurgated the treatment of the encounter at the heart of their fiction, until they almost seemed to be writing in code. Richardson himself is not guiltless of euphemism in dealing with rape or devirgination or even childbirth, but he is able to write scenes such as that of the death of the bawd, Mrs. Sinclair ("Behold her, then, spreading the whole troubled bed with her huge quaggy carcase: her mill-post arms held up . . . her livid lips parched and working violently . . . her wide mouth . . . splitting her face, as it were two parts; and her huge tongue hideously rolling in it . . . her bellows-shaped and various coloured breasts ascending by turns to her chin, and descending out of sight, with the violence of her gaspings") with a forthrightness and vigor lost to his tradition after its capture by women.

As early as *The Hapless Orphan* (1793), American novelists were attempting to find sentimental substitutes for the struggle with the seducer; and before the process begun in the declining years of the eighteenth century was through, the treatment of seduction had been surrendered to literary radicals and semi-pornographers. *Charlotte Temple* itself, that first American monument to expurgated Richardsonianism, came at last to be thought of as a "dirty book," and was peddled in working-class districts (slightly amended and dressed in lurid covers) to young girls in search of literary titillation. It was a long way, however, from the first expurgations of the seduction theme to its final casting out; and before that rejection could be accomplished the genteel revolution had to run its full course.

Even more critical, perhaps, than the flight from art and candor, is the rejection of tragedy in the second-generation sentimental novel. The success of his attempt at a tragedy of seduction, in

Clarissa, is attested by the impossibility of summarizing the latter book in any pat formula. We have already noticed how misleading a modern, off-hand attempt to sum up its effect can be. Whatever *Clarissa* is, it is not an account of "the sad end of a girl who failed to resist a man's blandishments." For Richardson, the effects of violation are real and irrecoverable; Clarissa's devirgination has taken away her *mana* as Maiden-savior, and she is for him, a creature of his time, as "ruined" as if she had consented. She triumphs only (the Kierkegaardian terms suggest themselves inevitably) "by virtue of the absurd," because her creator has rejected for her the "aesthetic" solution of a "happy ending." The outward form of her victory is death.

Such a tragic conclusion (whose complexities, indeed, I have only begun to suggest) not only baffled Richardson's readers, who bombarded him with requests to relent and restore Clary to life and Lovelace, but shocked even Fielding, one of whose objections to Richardson was to his stubbornly dark vision of life; while so great a writer as Jane Austen could not, as we have noticed, accommodate to her world of wit and dialectic the grimness of *Clarissa.* If such distinguished, genial spirits faltered before the inexorable doom of Clarissa, no wonder the unintellectual imitators of Richardson were incapable of responding to the complex moral dilemma and the desperate triumph of this heroine. They wanted virtue rewarded and vice punished—virtue triumphant in indignity was for them a concept as dangerous as it was difficult.

Not that at first they avoided all "sad" endings; far from it! They had been taught by Sterne as well as by Richardson the lesson (which Goethe and Rousseau each expounded after his own taste) that only he who weeps is saved. It was a reigning doctrine in an age which saw sensibility compound sentimentality and which took tears for the truest testimony of good faith. Never had the lust of ladies for a "good cry" found such sage apologists. But the sentimental ending is not inevitably a tragic one; and for the pathos of *Clarissa* the followers of Richardson substituted a lesser pathos. Their novels, when they did not deal with the success of a worthy girl, complied in fact with the formula misread into their master: "the sad end of a girl who failed to resist a man's blandishments."

The seduced maiden, in such fictions, finds herself pregnant and abandoned by her lover, who has meanwhile fallen in love with a good woman and married. He is more often shown as negligent than cruel (the soft hearts of the genteel Richardsonians mitigating

Lovelace himself), sometimes even the victim of the deceits of a trusted friend. He finally discovers the plight of his abandoned love, but before he can arrive with help the traduced girl has found peace in suicide or has died giving birth under the most miserable of conditions—usually to a little girl. Not uncommonly, the author pleads at this point for understanding and sympathy toward the seducer's victim, pointing out that some humble life of usefulness might still remain for the ruined girl, but such authors scarcely ever can bring themselves to let her live, thus surrendering the tearful climax. Her death, however, is never proffered as the absolute end; there is always a hint that her suffering has redeemed her in the eyes of a benevolent Maker (the harsh, Puritan God had been deposed before such novels began to appear) and that her tears will be wiped away in heaven.

For those who did not find motive enough for tears in such suicides or childbed deaths, there was in reserve the child left by the dying mother to the protection of some kind female benefactor (always conveniently out of town at the critical moment). A not unusual fate for such illegitimate girls was to fall in love with the legitimate sons of their reformed fathers, learning only at the very altar the truth which condemned them to a single, melancholy, and useful life or a death by brain fever. Such flirtations with incest, however, betray the influence of the French novelist Prévost, and are the fruits of a hunger for "unnatural" sensationalism which goes beyond the decent bourgeois limits of Richardsonian pathos.

It took scores of years to persuade the great, genteel audience, male and female alike, that the "happy ending" was preferable to the tearful close. The death of Little Eva surely sold as many copies of *Uncle Tom's Cabin* as the fatal whipping of the pious slave; and Dickens could with the death of Little Nell stir up a public orgy of weeping in which we find it hard to believe. As the thrill of seduction was expurgated from popular fiction and the threat of rape removed, death was more and more demanded; the titillation provided once by peering through the keyhole at the nubile maiden struggling for her honor was, somewhat perversely, replaced by the ambiguous pleasure of standing over the snow-white deathbed of the virgin child.

Finally, melancholy becomes contraband in the polite world of woman's books, permitted when bootlegged in small amounts, but frowned on as "morbid" when overwhelmingly present. When the sentimental novel of seduction is reborn in the twentieth century as *Marjorie Morningstar,* Herman Wouk grants to his seduced heroine the happy ending of marriage—though he is still deeply enough committed to the genteel mystique of virginity to make it clear that her husband only accepts her as something maimed. Cheerfulness may at long last become obligatory in popular American fiction, but it has to fight hard against the allure of tearful melodrama, that *ersatz* of tragedy striving always to recapture the somber thrill that shook all of Europe when Clarissa died.

A further distortion of the Richardsonian prototype attempted to transform the seduction theme into a feminist attack upon the male, a symbolic castration of the oppressing sex. There had been present in Richardson from the first, of course, a view of the sexual encounter as warfare between man and woman, with the male in the role of the enemy. In his novels, however, the identification of the male with evil had been determined by the Sentimentalist's need to make the negative principle the "head," i.e., the intellectualism of the male. He felt obligated, moreover, in his portrayal of the class struggle to make the representative of the bourgeoisie a woman, since he would have regarded the marriage of an upper-class woman to a man from the lower classes—a duchess, let us say, to a footman—as degrading and a little ridiculous. To Englishmen, it has always seemed necessary only to change the sexes in the *Pamela* story in order to turn it into parody; and no one but a sentimental rebel and outsider like Rousseau dared treat seriously the aspiration of a Saint-Preux for his aristocratic pupil-mistress.

But Richardson, too, within his own cautious limits, was a revolutionary, his books the manifesto of a class struggling for dignity as well as power. In America, his class-determined fable had to be adapted to the needs of a society quite different from the one which had bred it. What was an American bourgeoisie to make of the opposition to Don Juanism so essential to the Sentimental Love Religion, or the sense in which virtue was identified with the social demands of a rising mercantile class? The scrupulosity with which Richardson in his novels balanced bourgeois-domestic virtues against courtly-gallant ones (not only in the persons of Pamela and Mr. B., but even in Clarissa and Lovelace, whose social origins are so much alike) was wasted on the reader who inhabited a world in which there were nothing but bourgeois-domestic values.

In America, therefore, which possessed no hereditary aristocracy and whose shifting class distinctions took no hold on the popular imagination, the class-war meanings of the sentimental novel are lost. This fact Oliver Wendell Holmes quite clearly saw and registered in the opening pages of his own sentimental novel *Elsie Venner:* "There is nothing in New England corresponding at all to the feudal aristocracies of the Old World. Whether it be owing to the stock from which we were derived . . . or the abrogation of the technical 'law of honor,' which draws a sharp line between the personally responsible class of 'gentlemen' and the unnamed multitude who are not expected to risk their lives for an abstraction— whatever be the cause, we have no such aristocracy here as that which grew up out of the military systems of the Middle Ages." Take the sword out of the hand of Lovelace-Don Juan and an essential part of his meaning has disappeared.

To be sure, there was some attempt in the United States to interlace the seduction story with reflections on the relations of rich and poor, and especially on the desire of young men to marry for money; but such moralizing seems perfunctory in the hands of all but such socialist novelists as George Lippard (who wrote in the mid-nineteenth century one of the most eccentric of all anti-seduction novels, *The Monks of Monk Hall*) or Theodore Dreiser (who made of the sentimental heroine the protagonist of books otherwise brutally realistic). It was a long time, however, before socialism penetrated deep enough into the American mind to make a modern version of the class-struggle novel possible; and meanwhile generation after generation of female sentimentalists contented themselves with portraying good Revolutionary colonial girls defending their honor against swaggering Redcoats, or Confederate lasses fighting the same fight against dashing Union officers, or last of all, the country girl upholding her honor against the city slicker. In this sense, the farmer's daughter and the traveling salesman of a thousand dirty jokes represent a last degradation (though a strange persistence, too) of the archetypal figures of Clarissa and Lovelace.

Such versions of the sexual conflict remain peripheral in our early novels, however; the center is elsewhere. In popular fiction produced in America by and for females, the seduction fable comes chiefly to stand for the war between the sexes and the defeat of the seducer (in such books he is finally conquered whether or not he initially prevails) as a symbol of the emasculation of American men. The Satanism of Lovelace is interpreted as standing for nothing more than the nature of maleness itself; while the divinity of Clarissa comes more than ever to signify the essential goodness of

women as such. Granted both such pat symbolism and the obligation to poetic justice, and it is clear that the sentimental novel in
the United States must end with the downfall of the male. From
Charlotte Temple to the latest daytime serial on radio or TV, the
legend of a moral struggle ending in the moral dominance of
woman informs the literature which makes the mass mind of
America. In this country the only class war is between the sexes!

Tearful extravaganzas in which the female is portrayed as pure
sentiment, the male as naked phallus proliferated endlessly. In the
end, even that intelligence for which the Lovelace figure originally
stood is travestied in favor of woman's "finer feelings"; though the
male is allowed still to spout "ideas," those ideas are revealed as
irrelevant to life and good sense, the babble of a bookish child. It
is easy enough, in a way, to understand why women should have
propagated and welcomed this mythical account of the qualities of
the sexes and of their relationship. What is baffling is why men,
too, should have accepted this travesty on their nature and role in
life; but they did, in fact, accept it, even repeating in their own
books the formulas of feminist sentimentality. Perhaps it seemed to
them, on one level of consciousness or another, a symbolic restitution for the injustices they had no intention of reforming—rather
like the wealthy Victorian's self-satisfied weeping over the plight
of the poor.

In the end, male and female arrived at a mutual pact, based on
guilt and resentment, to castrate father: to make him seem a
spoiled child rather than a sexual aggressor. The acceptance by the
male of the female image of him first as seducer and blackguard,
then (in America) as Bad Boy, follows naturally upon the female's
acceptance of the male's image of her as sexless savior and (in
America) eternal Mama; and perhaps, after all, the former travesty
is a revenge for the latter one, rather than for the social indignities
visited upon woman.

Whatever the social reality, in fiction certainly, instances of male
humiliation are endlessly multiplied. The first popular American
image of the Seducer, our own Lovelace, was Mrs. Rowson's
Montraville, who betrayed Charlotte Temple, and whom we meet
for the last time in *Lucy Temple* (also known as *Charlotte's
Daughter; or the Three Orphans*), "sunk upon the shoulder of his
wife, pale and almost lifeless" and learn "that he sometimes la-
bored under slight fits of insanity . . . indeed it is only by powerful
opiates that he obtains any, and by them alone the smallest exhila-

ration of spirits." Not merely as a seducer but as a father (in wedlock and out) Montraville is punished, forced to watch his children on the verge of an incestuous catastrophe bred by his sin and cowardice. Mrs. Rowson leaves her readers in no doubt as to the cause of the degradation of her seducer. "All blighted," she explains, "by once yielding to the impulse of guilty passions."

Hawthorne himself, so oppressed by the "female scribblers," was not averse to taking a leaf from their book. Dimmesdale moves through the final pages of *The Scarlet Letter* like one half dead, "his movements resembling the wavering effort of an infant with its mother's arms in view. . . ." And those "mother's arms" do in fact await him, stretched out by Hester whom he traduced. The pattern of Mrs. Rowson is repeated once more in *The Blithedale Romance.* "As they approached me," Hawthorne writes of his archetypal couple, "I observed in Hollingsworth's face a depressed and melancholy look, that seemed habitual; the powerfully built man showed a self-distrustful weakness, and a child-like or childish tendency to press closer, and closer still, to the side of the slender woman whose arm was within his." The ending is the same on the level of best-selling pseudo-piety: "scarcely a man," "infant," "child-like or childish," "sunk upon the shoulder of his wife." And the wife hovers over the broken male, not only with what Hawthorne describes as a "protective and watchful quality" —but also what he is acute and disingenuous enough to call a "veiled happiness." Hawthorne had begun by describing her as "as perilously situated as the maiden whom, in the old classical myths, people used to expose to a dragon": but she has triumphed over the dragon-father—her weakness is stronger than his strength. And she smiles now at being able to support what she has already unmanned. She has made of the resolutely masculine rebel against domestic conformity a dependent child.

Hollingsworth is, however, no seducer, but an advocate of reform, what Hawthorne calls "that steel engine of the Devil's contrivance, a philanthropist." He is, in short, what we would call a radical and an "intellectual," the dreamer of a utopian society incapable of loving his individual fellow men. He is only half the total (villainous) male principle of *The Blithedale Romance;* his alter ego is the dark and utterly damned hypnotist Westervelt, who also has tried to seduce the will of the veiled maiden, Priscilla. Together they add up to the original "libertine," free thinker, *and* trifler with women, the Don Juan archetype who survives unsplit though debased in more orthodox female fiction: as, for instance, the Baron de Launa, the "illuminated" (i.e., enlightened) Baron of Mrs. Sarah Sayward Barell Keating Wood, who published in 1800 a gothic-sentimental farrago called *Julia and the Illuminated Baron.*

Mrs. Wood is the prototype of the early American lady novelist in many senses, but in none more so than in her desire to have the best of all possible worlds. Eager to espouse the cause of women, she goes out of her way to introduce into her fictional action the actual living poetess, Mrs. Morton, "the darling of the muses"; but she is careful to make it clear that the female writer should not be a refugee from traditional female duties. At least of herself she asserts that "not one social, or one domestic duty, have ever been sacrificed or postponed by her pen." Desiring all the romantic associations of the European scene and having a declared "aversion to introducing living characters," Mrs. Wood sets her scene in France and Spain. Yet she cannot resist bringing one of her protagonists back to America to meet Mrs. Morton and to be rescued by the slaves of the "illustrious Washington." Most typically of all, she insists upon making her villain at once a nobleman (to trade on all the good bourgeois prejudice against a corrupt hereditary nobility) and a member of the Illuminati, that is, a secret Jacobin plotter (to take advantage of the genteel conservative reversion from the excesses of the French Revolution). The Baron de Launa is a fascinating transitional figure, a sort of composite bugaboo of middle-class timidity: half Don Juan and half Robespierre, a projection of the blackness of the past and of the threat of the future. The verse on the title page of Mrs. Wood's novel makes it quite clear that her chief fear is of the revolutionary conspirator; the aristocrat is a vestigial ghost.

> This volume to the reader's eye displays
> Th' infernal conduct of abandoned man;
> When French philosophy infects his ways,
> And pours contempt on Heav'n's eternal plan;
> Reversing order, truth, and ev'ry good,
> And whelming the world with ruin's awful flood.

The final effect of the kidnaping of the sentimental form and fable by women writers in a relatively classless society was to define in America from the very beginning an *anti-literature:* bourgeois, timid, not quite literate—and to identify this *ersatz* art with the values and aspirations of women. There is, after all, another distinction among social groups in America, logically separable from that of male and female, with which it tends to be confused, and that is the division between the "intellectual" and the unlettered or practical man in the street together with his home-loving wife. It is the "Brahmin caste," defined by Oliver Wendell Holmes as a "harmless, inoffensive, untitled aristocracy," which seems to the female novelists not at all harmless or inoffensive, but rather the prime source of villainy and seduction. From the Sanford of Mrs. Foster's *The Coquette* (reputed to have been drawn from the real-life character of Pierrepont Edwards) to Hawthorne's Dimmesdale, the traducers of women in our literature have tended to be drawn from Holmes's "race of scholars . . . in which aptitude for learning . . . [is] congenital and hereditary." Similar tendencies toward a timid, best-selling literature existed elsewhere, but were counterbalanced by great mediating figures like Rousseau or Goethe, who tickled at once the most genteel ladies and the Encyclopedists themselves—thus keeping together almost to the verge of our time the two audiences whose sundering has finally wounded literature everywhere.

In America, however, the late start of the novel and the lack of distinguished figures in its early years helped create simultaneously the genteel, sentimental, quasi-literate, female audience (female in sensibility whatever the nominal sex of the readers who composed it) and a product which satisfied it. *Against* this audience and in competition with the writing which satisfied it, our best fictionists from Charles Brockden Brown to Edgar Allan Poe to Hawthorne and Melville have felt it necessary to struggle for their integrity and their livelihoods. Though the interruption of the Scott-Cooper tradition of the novel serves later to conceal the fact for a little while, this profound split has always influenced the shape of our literature and is one still felt by practicing authors as an essential and crippling aspect of their situation. For better or for worse, the best-seller was invented in America (the flagrantly *bad* best-seller) before the serious successful novel.

III

Mrs. Rowson's *Charlotte Temple* is a book scarcely *written* at all, only in the most perfunctory manner told; yet it is the first book by an American to move American readers, and certain historians of the American novel, not themselves critics or readers of criticism, have praised it absurdly for its "basic sincerity and power," or its "simple vividness." To be sure, the popularity of *Charlotte* poses a real problem. Why a book which barely climbs above the lower limits of literacy, and which handles, without psychological acuteness or dramatic power, a handful of stereotyped characters in a situation already hopelessly banal by 1790, should have had more than two hundred editions and have survived among certain readers for a hundred and fifty years is a question that cannot be ignored. It is tempting to say that popular taste given the choice between a better and a worse book will inevitably choose the worse; but this is an anti-sentimental simplification no more helpful than its sentimental opposite number. Only certain bad books succeed, apparently not by the simple virtue of their badness, but because of the theme they have chosen to handle badly.

Mrs. Rowson's book apparently comprises something that is not literature, though it is published in the guise of literature. It is apparent at least that the appeal of *Charlotte* is based not upon form or characterization or insight or beauty of language, not even upon the simplest skills of composition, but upon the bare bones of plot, on what its readers would call quite simply "the story." That story, which it is almost impossible to retell without improving, represents in its essential form the myth or archetype of seduction as adapted to the needs of the American female audience. To Mrs. Rowson we must be grateful for having separated the archetype from its literary or pseudo-literary envelope, for having, as the scientists say, "isolated" it.

To be sure, there are some literary pretensions in Mrs. Rowson's approach—a certain self-consciousness which makes her pause occasionally to address the critic over the shoulder of the servant girl who is her ideal reader. "I hope, Sir," she remarks, addressing naturally the *male* caviler, "your prejudices are now removed in regard to the probability of my story? Oh, they are. Well, then, with your leave I will proceed." But her intended literary devices are most often as naively transparent as the pseudo-quotation from Shakespeare on her title page: "She was her parents' only joy/ They had but one—one darling child." This poor, limping verse she attributes hopefully to *Romeo and Juliet;* but though she was an actress and became a teacher, she has misremembered or simply faked.

Occasionally, she strives for a kind of Biedermeier decoration, visualizing a scene in terms of the most sentimental genre painting of her day: "we will have some cows, and you shall be queen of the dairy; in the morning, while I look after my garden, you shall take a basket on your arm, and sally forth to feed your poultry; and as they flutter round you in token of humble gratitude, your father shall smoke his pipe in a woodbine alcove. . . ." But aside from the old man with his pipe and the humbly grateful hens, nothing is visualized in the book. It is morality not art at which Mrs. Rowson consciously aims; and she desires, as she tells us disarmingly if ungrammatically, nothing more than to convince her readers "that I have not wrote a line that conveys a wrong idea to the head." She is, indeed, almost openly anti-literary in a defensive way, hinting that "trifling performances" like her own are to be preferred to "the most elegant, finished piece of literature whose tendency might deprave the heart or mislead the understanding." Her book at least is firmly committed to the notion "that vice, however prosperous in the beginning, in the end leads only to misery and shame."

There is no duplicity in *Charlotte Temple,* or at least, only the unwitting duplicity of the best-seller which confuses the wish with the fact, and presents the dreams of its readers as an account of real actions in the real world. It is a book no one could have faked, even its tender lingering over the details of vice which it presumably hates arising from an essential artlessness. As even its title declares, Mrs. Rowson's novel (called *Charlotte* in the English edition of 1791, *Charlotte Temple* in America in 1794) is completely a woman's book—a tale in which female suffering is portrayed from a female point of view in order to stir female sympathy; while vice and virtue are judged by female standards. Mrs. Rowson, who was in her life governess, lady novelist, actress, playwright, songwriter, and head of a girls' school, who had been forced by her husband's failure to make herself a career and forge by her own hard work a shield of respectability, stood unequivocally on the woman's side in that war of the sexes whose existence she would not for a moment have denied. Her title declares her allegiance, her conviction that she is one of the girls. The single first name (returning to the tradition of *Pamela*) suffices to describe what the book is about; and there is no ambitious subtitle to lead us up metaphysical blind alleys—only the conventional boast "A Tale of Truth." The facts related do, indeed, seem to be derived from the real-life experiences of a certain Charlotte Stanley, but Richardson had invented that person's life before she managed to live it.

The action of *Charlotte Temple* begins in England and passes to America, making England the place of Charlotte's innocence and the United States that of her repentance, with the ocean between the scene of her deflowering. She is buried in an American grave, where, her fall redeemed by death, she becomes an American Magdalene, a saint of love. Meanwhile, her seducer, who vainly offers his bosom and his sword to Charlotte's father at that very grave, returns to England. Mrs. Rowson, herself an immigrant, manages thus to tie together the fable of seduction and the story of immigration into the United States, creating a kind of sentimental myth of the relationship of the two countries—and thereby insuring the success of her book on this side of the water. Certainly, it was a failure in England, living its incredible posthumous life only here.

Charlotte is betrayed not only by the British officer, Montraville, but also by her French teacher, Mlle. La Rue, who persuades her to elope with her lover and actually runs away to America with her. Mlle. La Rue, who projects all the American fear of Latin perfidy, plays the Juliette to Charlotte's Justine: the one represents virtue traduced and defeated, the other vice cherished and rewarded; though, indeed, just before the book ends Mlle. La Rue is given—rather perfunctorily—her just deserts. Charlotte, after her sin, is overwhelmed with remorse and hounded by disaster. Cast off by Montraville, who marries a wealthy woman, deprived even of the conscience money he sends her by his companion Belcour, who thinks poverty will force her to become his mistress, and vilified as faithless by Belcour when he fails in his suit, Charlotte endures unremitting misery. Mlle. La Rue, on the other hand, profits by her calculated vice, finally marrying a prosperous and credulous merchant and living the life of comfortable, respectable New York society.

It is to her old teacher and false advisor that Charlotte turns in the most absurd of all the book's bathetic scenes, only to be forced out into the wintry storm, pregnant and destitute. "Here on my knees I conjure you to save me from perishing in the street. . . . O, for charity's sweet sake, this night let me be sheltered from the winter's piercing cold." But Mlle. La Rue, now Mrs. Crayton, is merciless. "Take her away . . . she will really frighten me into hysterics; take her away, I say, this instant." Charlotte finds shelter in the house of a servant of Mrs. Crayton, kinder than his mistress, but dies after bearing her child in a bare and drafty hovel. Her father arrives from England in time to witness her death and hear her plea that he protect her child; "She raised her eyes to heaven —and then closed them forever." There remains nothing more but the duel at the graveside between Montraville and his false friend, Belcour, in which the latter is killed; and, almost as an after-thought, the coming of Mlle. La Rue as a dying beggar to the door of Charlotte's parents.

It is the Richardsonian story as it has descended through the female line in its most banal form. In Mrs. Rowson's version, how-ever, it succeeded in projecting once and for all the American woman's image of herself as the long-suffering martyr of love—the inevitable victim of male brutality and lust. Not for nothing is Charlotte called "Temple"; she represents a cult object, a center of worship—and on her (supposed) tomb, the floral tribute of gen-erations of girls expressed their adoration of the Great Goddess whom they could venerate only if they believed her a "real" woman like themselves.

It is the nature of American scriptures to be vulgarizations of the holy texts from which they take their cues; and just as *The Book of Mormon* caricatures the Bible unawares, so *Charlotte Temple* is an unwitting travesty of *Clarissa Harlowe*. The sacred power is still there, but the subtlety and passion, the style and distinction have gone. What was mythic literature has become sub-literate myth.

Mrs. Rowson, who had little sense, of course, of the scriptural character of her best-selling book, tried to continue it in a sequel, as if it were an ordinary novel. *Lucy Temple,* however, lacked the archetypal appeal of the earlier volume; though (as we have noted earlier) it establishes the prototype of the repentant seducer, re-duced to trembling dependence and near idiocy. *Lucy Temple* deals with the fortunes of three unprotected girls, one of whom is seduced, tricked into a false marriage, stripped of all her posses-sions, while another marries a country parson who has come into considerable wealth. It is with the third orphan (Charlotte's daugh-ter, Lucy!) that the book is chiefly concerned, for her life exempli-fies the continuing evil bred by seduction. Lucy learns almost too late that her husband-to-be is her brother, legitimate son of the officer who had betrayed and abandoned Charlotte. The revelation comes to her in a moment of philanthropic indulgence, when to celebrate her coming wedding she has given a feast and distributed a hundred guineas to sixty of "the most respected poor" of the parish. The theme of brother-sister incest haunts the early American novel on its lower levels of literacy as well as on the higher—a nightmare from which our writers do not choose to awaken too soon, since it is one their readers are willing to pay to share.

Mrs. Rowson was too pious, however, to grant either her audience or herself a sentimental orgy of death; her Lucy makes a "perfect recovery," while her lover, instead of committing suicide, takes himself off to India. "She regarded him," Mrs. Rowson informs us, "as devoted to his country, herself as set apart for the holy cause of humanity." That "holy cause" she serves by becoming a teacher of "female children," and presiding as high priestess over a school-house indistinguishable from a temple: "a specimen —one might almost say, a model of Ionic architecture . . . with chaste white pillars and modest walls. . . ."

I V

The sentimental legend of seduction could not, in any case, be laughed out of existence. Not only did the editions of *Charlotte Temple* dizzyingly, incredibly proliferate, but other examples quickly appeared, some from the fertile pen of Mrs. Rowson herself, some from those of others. Hannah Foster's *The Coquette,* for instance, published in 1797, fictionalized a contemporary scandal (which may have involved Aaron Burr or, at least, the son of Jonathan Edwards) with only the most perfunctory attempt at disguise. The heroine, called in real life Elizabeth Whitman, is known in this book as Eliza Wharton; but her "real life" sentimental mishaps, like those of many well-read young ladies at the end of the eighteenth century, fall only too patly into the stereotypes of seduction derived from Richardson. Indeed, events can never provide for the imagination new sentimental plots, since sentiment is first imagined and only then lived. In society as well as in literature, the archetypal encounter of Lovelace and Clarissa was reported over and over—or at least imposed itself upon life in the perceiving mind—until that encounter, and its actors, had become stereotypes from which no American author could entirely escape.

Charles Brockden Brown, whose anti-bourgeois novels we shall examine in detail later, submitted to Richardson as enthusiastically as any of his female contemporaries. In a sketch for a sentimental novel which he abandoned, the so-called "Correspondence with Henrietta G." (taken by some critics—so confused do sentimental life and sentimental literature become—to be an actual exchange of letters entered in his journal), he entrusts what are surely his sentiments to one of his fictional correspondents: "I am a disciple of that religion and philosophy of which the effects are to be seen in the conduct of Clarissa. O best of men! Most eloquent of writers! It is from thy immortal production that I have imbibed the love of virtue; of moral harmony and beauty. From thee also have I gathered critical instruction and learned to speak and write. . . ."

In his last two novels, Brown made a valiant attempt to redeem Richardson from his genteel imitators, to create, by casting aside the seduction theme, a Richardsonian novel of sentimental analysis in a domestic setting, stripped of tragic and melodramatic elements alike. Had he succeeded, he might have become our own improbable Jane Austen, from whose similar attempt there developed in England the psychological-domestic novel of love and marriage that leads through George Eliot to Henry James. But Brown lacked the wit and irony as well as the talent for structure of Jane Austen —so that, aiming at modesty, he created dullness; and avoiding the spectacular, he fell into the inane. Certainly, what quiet triumphs his books achieved went unnoticed in his own day.

Clara Howard and *Jane Talbot,* both of which appeared in 1801, indicate by their very titles Brown's desire to return to the woman-centered novel with which Richardson began. His earlier books, all of which had failed to win popularity, are called by the names of their male protagonists: *Wieland, Arthur Mervyn, Ormond,* and *Edgar Huntly;* and the experience with which they deal is filtered through the perceptions of those protagonists. The later books, however, portray a world of female interests regarded through female eyes, perhaps partly as a bid for the alluring female audience that had already made Mrs. Rowson's fortune. In *Clara Howard,* the epistolary method of Richardson is used to tell the unspectacular tale of the difficulties that lie in the way of Clara's marriage to Philip Stanley, who is engaged (without love) to another woman. It is not a question of whom he will marry, but of who (both women are bolder than he) will marry him. Stanley's first love has disappeared, and Clara, though she is fond of him, dutifully sends him out to search for her.

Such minor misfortunes as slander, fraud, disease, and especially mental anguish befall all three members of this conscientious triangle before their problems are resolved (the lost Mary found engaged to someone else, etc.) and the wedding with which the book must end can take place. The plot is trivial, perfunctory both in its development and resolution, the study of the "heart" (particularly of the motives of a woman emotionally unwilling to part with the man she is morally unable to accept) everything. For the seduction archetype, Brown has substituted the more ancient New Comedy archetype of boy-gets-girl-loses-girl-gets-girl; but he is handicapped by his own lack of belief in the kind of romantic love which alone can justify that standard plot. Quite early in life, he had gone on record as deploring the fact that "the languishing and sighing lover is an object to which the errors of mankind have annexed a certain degree of importance"; and must have been embarrassed to find himself the author of a novel whose sub-title is "The Enthusiasm of Love."

Brown seems further to have been unaware that the New Comedy plot, being a comic version of the Oedipus conflict, demands that the initial check to love come from parental opposition, preferably the intervention of an unsympathetic father, whom the son can finally defeat in taking possession of the contested girl. The competing self-sacrifice of two women in love with the same man is hardly a satisfactory substitute. The popular mind demanded then, as it demands now, a villain, whether father or seducer, some dark projection of id or super-ego to be symbolically defeated; but Brown's book had no villain at all.

Brown had earlier employed seducers in his books; fathers scarcely exist at all in his work. His world (a little like that of Mark Twain) is one of mothers and sisters; mamas in particular are everywhere, even the sweethearts of his rather childlike, dependent men being addressed on occasion as "my dear mama"; but papas are at a premium. In *Jane Talbot,* however, there is at least the dramatic tension provided by the Bad Mother, Jane's adopted mother, Mrs. Fielder, who has forced her into one loveless marriage, and, even after the death of Jane's first husband, refuses to let her marry her first love, Henry Colden.

Colden, who, like many of Brown's young men, thinks of marriage as a way of finding a mother and a source of income at once, would not consider marrying Jane if she were disinherited; and so her mother's opposition is critical. "I cannot labor for bread," he tells Jane with astonishing candor, "I cannot work to live. . . . Hence it is, that if by marriage you should become wholly dependent on me it could never take place." But Colden's principles include others beside the resolve not to "labor for bread." He is, indeed, a committed radical, a follower of Godwin; and Mrs. Fielder rejects him as a prospective son-in-law because she believes him to be "the advocate of suicide; a scoffer at promises; the despiser of revelation, of Providence and a future state; an opponent of marriage, and . . . one who denied (shocking!) that anything but mere habit and positive law stood in the way of marriage, nay, of intercourse without marriage, between brother and sister, parent and child."

Here is Lovelace returned to life ("an opponent of marriage"), with Werther ("the advocate of suicide"), Chesterfield ("a scoffer at promises") and Diderot ("one who denied, etc., etc.") thrown in to complete the composite portrait of a villainous "libertine." To be sure, Colden only *appears* to be such a villain; but at least he provides momentarily a defining opposite to Jane, with his shadow sets off the whiteness of her virtue. Without a Lovelace there can be no Clarissa; and without Colden, Jane would have seemed as incomplete as Clara Howard. It is no tragic opposition, however, which they provide one another, but rather an educational one. Each learns from the other: Jane to make her piety more rational, Henry to make his rationalism more pious. But the exchange is by no means equal, Colden being much overmatched in moral energy by Jane Talbot. He is only a *theoretical* seducer, in need of money, an adolescent libertine, whose maturity is indistinguishable from his defeat, which is to say, his marriage. Converted at last to a belief in the "Divine Parent and Judge," he goes like a happy victim to the altar. So denatured a version of the clash between the Pure Maiden (Jane is not even a virgin) and the libertine (Henry is doubtless more virgin than she) provides no archetypal thrill, no drama deeper than words.

Earlier, in *Ormond: or The Secret Witness* (1799), Brown had created a more vivid and convincing Lovelace figure. Ormond is not really, despite the title, the central character of the story—though he comes closer than any male protagonist in Brown to being the equal of the woman he confronts. Constantia Dudley is the name of the non-Christian Clarissa to whom he acts the Lovelace, a woman who, Brown tells us, "formed her estimate of good and evil on nothing but terrestrial and visible consequences." It is perhaps the anti-clerical nature of this middle-class Great Goddess that made her so favorite a figure for Shelley, though there is something chilling about her reasonable approach to problems of matrimony. "To marry in extreme youth," she has told herself, "would be proof of pernicious and opprobrious temerity"; and one scarcely wonders at such cool wisdom from the daughter of a father who, "instead of familiarizing her with the amorous effusions of Petrarch and Racine . . . made her thoroughly conversant with Tacitus and Milton."

The softer and more romantic qualities of womanhood are reflected by the other female characters with whom Constantia is surrounded, especially by Helena Cleves, type of the sentimental, soft-headed woman made to be seduced. Through this gallery of females strides Ormond, armed and fully phallic; he has just returned from a military career which has ended on the barricades in France and possesses as a mistress the soft Helena, who commits suicide when he deserts her to woo Constantia. Toward him, as a projection of himself, Brown has all the ambivalence of a Goethe or Rousseau contemplating the Artist-Seducer; for Brown is aware that the principles which inspire Ormond are the revolutionary, enlightened ones which moved his own youthful enthusiasm. In Ormond, however, they have gone wrong, the Dream of Reason turned monstrous: "considerations of justice and pity were made, by a fatal perverseness of reasoning, champions and bulwarks of his most atrocious mistakes."

Ormond is, indeed, the mirror image of Henry Colden, Colden seen in reverse: at first, apparently an attractive though fanatically radical young man, he is revealed at last as a rapist and murderer. Colden, on the other hand, begins by seeming a thoroughgoing scoundrel, but turns out to be no more than the headstrong exponent of abstract nonconformism. For the latter, there is the reward of marriage and financial security, salvation by the female; for the former, death at the hands of his beloved, destruction by the female. In her father's neo-classic retreat at Perth Amboy, as chaste in its marble dress as the "temple" of Mrs. Rowson's *Lucy,* Constantia stabs Ormond with her penknife, swoons beside him and the bloody body of a man he has killed, preparing for her rape.

Ormond is surely the most passionate of Brown's books, but there is little erotic passion displayed between the men and women in it. Ormond pursues Constantia out of some dark need to symbolize in her violation his triumph over the female principle; while she is drawn to him largely by a curiosity much like his own. The book's sole marriage, offered as a sop to sentimental readers, perhaps, joins Constantia's friend, Sophia, through whom the story is chiefly told, to a certain Courtland. But for Courtland we are scarcely prepared; he remains a strangely unintegrated character, left over, apparently, from an incomplete work, *Jessica*, and used to give to the volume the slight note of conventional good cheer with which it closes. The tone with which Sophia describes the affection that leads to their marriage is oddly cool:

> Sufficient opportunity was afforded us, in an unrestrained and domestic intercourse of three months, . . . to gain a knowledge of each other. There was that conformity of tastes and views between us which could scarcely fail, at an age and in a situation like ours, to give birth to tenderness. . . . He had offered to be my companion [on a voyage to America], but this offer my regard to his interest obliged me to decline; but I was willing to compensate him for this denial, as well as to gratify my own heart, by an immediate marriage.

No sooner has she married him, however, than she leaves him in Europe while she sets sail for the United States in search of her beloved Constantia. How different the tone in which their reunion after long absence is described:

> I could not bear to withdraw my eyes from her countenance. If they wandered for a moment, I fell into doubt and perplexity, and again fixed them upon her, to assure myself of her existence.
> The succeeding three days were spent in a state of dizziness and intoxication. The ordinary functions of nature were disturbed. The appetite for sleep and for food were confounded and lost amidst the impetuosities of a master-passion. . . . I would not part from her side, but ate and slept, walked and mused and read, with my arm locked in hers, and with her breath fanning my cheek. . . .
> O precious inebriation of the heart! O pre-eminent love! . . . surely thy sanction is divine, thy boon is happiness!

Which seems an ecstatic rhapsody on passion, which the description of friendship? What were contemporary readers to make of such a perverse reversal of the expected terms of affection? Certainly, they were not looking for such homoerotic tenderness at the sentimental climax of a story of seduction. Love between the Pure Maiden and the most brutal Seducer they could understand and respond to, but not that between the Maiden and an old girl friend.

Surely they could not have interpreted their girlish reunion as a grand passion, purest form of the "precious inebriation of the heart." Like a more recent critic, the contemporary reader must have murmured to himself at the point where Sophia departs in the midst of her own honeymoon: "this circumstance is an added argument in favor of what has already been said that Brown did not understand the workings of the human mind. . . ." And that reader would have concluded with another commentator, "Love and friendship . . . are excluded from his bosom." For better or worse, the buyers of best-sellers had no need of Brown; everything that they meant by love had been defined for them by the clichés of female Richardsonianism, which had passed into their very lives and their own patterns of courtship and marriage.

In this light, Brown's failure at dealing with the love between men and women seems as symptomatic as the successes in the market-place of Mrs. Rowson's sentimental travesties—so deeply had the formulae of degraded Richardsonianism impressed themselves on the American imagination, that in the United States, well up into the twentieth century, no novelists, however committed and talented, could treat the relations of the sexes without falling prey to their influence. Only by bypassing normal heterosexual love as a subject could such writers preserve themselves from sentimentality and falsehood. Brown had failed in his direct attempt to recapture passion from the "female scribblers"; but in other works, he adapted to America the uses of terror, discovered a rival passion which could fill the vacuum left by the failure of love. He is the father of American gothic, and the initiator—as we shall see in Chapter 6—of a truly fertile line of development for the serious novel in the United States.

5

THE BEGINNINGS OF THE ANTI-BOURGEOIS SENTIMENTAL NOVEL IN AMERICA

NOT ONLY THE FEMALE SCRIBBLER recreated the seducer in the image of the intellectual and the artist; for quite opposite reasons, certain anti-bourgeois novelists had made the same transformation, in books which asked the reader to identify not with the female victim but with her male betrayer—thus introducing a note of moral ambiguity baffling to the simple-minded sentimentalist. Such novels provided models and prototypes for writers of fiction eager to break out of the trap of female Richardsonianism. Oddly enough, it was Richardson himself who provided hints for such writers. Like his eminent contemporary and fellow carrier of the torch to the back of the cave, Mesmer, Richardson founded two traditions at once: from the former via Phineas Quimby there evolved the Christian Science of Mrs. Eddy and via Charcot the psychoanalysis of Sigmund Freud; from the latter via Mrs. Rowson came *The Wide, Wide World* and via Rousseau Proust's *Remembrance of Things Past.*

By the time Mrs. Trollope made her well-advertised visit, the names of Rousseau and of Voltaire may have been indeed, as she reports, known to Americans "more as dirty words than as great names," but this certainly was not the case in the earliest days of our history. Before any native novelists had appeared, Rousseau's fiction was immensely popular with our readers, his chief novel, translated in England as the *New Eloisa,* becoming between 1761, when it was published, and 1764, when Horace Walpole's *The*

Castle of Otranto appeared to supplant it, the most widely read novel in the colonies.

Goethe was even more widely read. His *Werther* had to wait for American publication only five years after the successful British edition of 1779; and thus appeared in the United States well before the first American novel, William Hill Brown's Werther-like *The Power of Sympathy.* The hero of that book is found dead at the action's end, a suicide, "a letter . . . unsealed upon the table, and *The Sorrows of Werther* . . . lying by its side." Indeed, by the time Brown's book was in circulation, there had been seven American editions of *Werther;* and a series of poems and dramas on the theme, as well as adaptations and apocryphal continuations, had tried to take advantage of its popular appeal.

It is hard to distinguish the influence of Richardson himself on the "masculine" Rousseau-Goethe strain within the sentimental novel from that of his near-contemporary, the French novelist Prévost; and students of the matter have debated acrimoniously their relative weight in the development of what can only be called the anti-bourgeois novel. The bulk of the Abbé Prévost's important work had already been done before the appearance of *Pamela; The Man of Quality* was completed by 1731, *Cleveland* by 1739, *Le Doyen de Killerine* by 1740, and English editions had appeared almost simultaneously. Indeed, Richardson himself reached the continent chiefly in the translation made by Prévost (Rousseau, for instance, knew *Clarissa* only in Prévost's French), a translation in which Prévost admits that he "changed or suppressed" what he found unsuitable for the genius of his own tongue.

Even more importantly, perhaps, Prévost in his earlier novels had discovered, almost invented, England as a fact of the French imagination and consequently of the imagination of Europe. This imaginary Protestant (in fact a Benedictine, who, after various sentimental and ideological difficulties, settled back into the monastery), after some years of exile in England, peopled his works almost exclusively with Protestant characters and returned almost compulsively to his semi-mythicized English scene, the Protestant homeland. The sensibility that produced the novel is as we have seen essentially a Protestant one, and Prévost is its interpreter to Catholic Europe. If the triumph of the novel on the continent in the mid-eighteenth century meant also that England became the second fatherland of European intellectuals, the credit must go to A. F. Prévost d'Exiles, who continued in his periodical, *Le pour et le contre,* the task he had begun in his books: to prepare Europe for the impact of Richardson.

Prévost was the lesser writer in many ways, the author of untidy, sprawling books whose development is dependent on the passionate whim of their picaresque protagonists, and which wander, therefore, quite in the manner of the obsolescent romances, over the face of a largely legendary world. That Prévost calls his settings "England" or "America" rather than Arcadia makes finally little difference. He achieved one minor success, by the way as it were, in *Manon Lescaut,* originally an appendix to *The Man of Quality;* but he hit upon neither the bourgeois setting nor the seduction theme, which were necessary to give life to the modern novel. In addition, he lacked the sharp focus of the epistolary form, primitive examples of which existed in European literature but which did not become the prevailing novelistic form until Richardson arrived on the scene.

In organization and narrative technique, certainly, the *Werther* of Goethe, like the *Nouvelle Héloïse* of Rousseau, depends directly on the model provided by *Clarissa,* whose superiority to his own work Prévost frankly acknowledges in the introductory note to his translation. When the full impact of Prévost was felt, it contributed in both England and France to a reversion to that "improbable and marvelous" which Richardson had abjured, to the rebirth of the romance in the revolutionary, sadist, highbrow form of the gothic novel; but where it existed balanced against the domestic and puritanical realism of Richardson, it helped to produce the anti-bourgeois sentimental novel of Goethe and Rousseau.

From Richardson, both Goethe and Rousseau learned the basic lesson that the subject of the novel is the "human heart," which is to say, the psyche in all its complexities and dark self-deceits, but especially in the moment of love. In them, the novel remains both psychological and erotic, dedicated not to the unwinding of an action replete with sharp reversals and recognitions, but to the exploration of a moral choice. The setting remains ordinary bourgeois life, for them "provincial" life, a world remote from the court and the great centers. Richardson could conceive without difficulty a simple domestic scene in the midst of London; his continental successors felt the need of a bucolic background, defined with that compromise between pastoral and genteelly realistic which came to be called Biedermeier. In both, there is the desire still to avoid all extravagances of action, to relate ordinary occurrences, which offer their readers, in a language as simple and un-distinguished as their own, "tableaus of the objects that surround them, of duties within their grasps, of the pleasures of their own conditions. . . ."

In their search for the normal and the insipid, they go beyond their master himself. Rousseau puts it quite bluntly in the mouth of an interlocutor in his second preface: "As for interest, it is for everybody, it is nothing. Not an evil action, not a wicked man making the good ones tremble; events so natural, so simple, that they are too much so; nothing unforeseen, no *coup de théâtre;* everything is expected well in advance, everything happens as expected." This is not really, of course, the whole story; for the underplaying of action is made up for by an overplaying of feel-ing, an exploitation of sentiment and sensibility that approaches the pathological; and over the whole account, for all its domesticity, hangs the shadow of suicide, the allure of death felt as a final, dark titillation. Death of course belongs to the Clarissa archetype from the beginning. She is "absolute for death" from the point of her violation on; and her elaborate preparations for a pious and decorous end become almost obscene. Rousseau, however, taking a cue from Prévost, turns death from the hope of the ruined virgin into the secret longing of the melancholy protagonist, the male hero.

The whole drift of the anti-bourgeois tradition is in the direction of substituting a male mind for the female one at the center of the novel. Rousseau represents a transitional phase; he calls his book still, in the proper Richardsonian way, by the simple first name of his heroine, *Julie, ou la Nouvelle Héloïse.* This is only proper, for it is she who keeps the action moving forward and who, in her death, only somewhat less orthodox than Clarissa's, "edifies a pastor and converts an atheist." Rousseau is using his fable, after all, to plead a fundamentally feminist case, and thus to win for himself the feminine audience. Young girls, to be sure, he warns off in an introductory note, or at least pretends to; but to experi-enced ladies he promises to demonstrate, what they are, of course, already more than willing to believe, that "the cause of their un-ruliness is less in themselves than in our evil institutions," prima-rily in forced marriages dictated by "the avarice and vanity of parents."

Yet Saint-Preux is regarded with a particular tenderness and re-mains the mouthpiece of his author, as Lovelace is *not,* of course, the mouthpiece of Richardson; for Rousseau is bound to his seducer by an evident autobiographical tie, which is by no means the link binding the earlier novelist to his unequivocal villain. Already in Rousseau's fiction, Lovelace has been crossed with those melancholy outcasts into whom Prévost projected his own plight: Cleveland or Patrice; and though the inherited Don Juan figure does not cease to be a seducer (at least in intent), he blurs into the exiled, sensitive soul. Juan and Faust melt into a single romanticized figure, the exponent of freedom and death. On the one hand, such protagonists are thought of as being accursed, possessed by the *mal anglais,* the longing for self-destruction; on the other hand, they are considered *chosen* out of mankind for a terrible privilege. "I do not pretend that all of mankind should immolate itself by general agreement nor make a vast sepulchre of the world," writes Rousseau through his surrogate Saint-Preux. "There are those unfortunates too privileged to follow the common way, and for whom despair and bitter sufferings are the passport of Nature."

But suicide remains incidental in *Julie,* a rejected temptation; and the novel's male protagonist cannot really hold the center of the stage. Julie, whom he seduces but is forbidden to marry because of their difference in rank and fortune, becomes in the second part of the book a full-fledged Clarissa-character. She is Clarissa as housewife and mother, all the more Clarissa for attaining the age and status from which the violation of Lovelace cut off her prototype; for Julie's devirgination does not send her quite to the grave. She is married by Wolmar, *philosophe* and atheist, who invites her former lover back into their household as a tutor for their children, deliberately planning this improbable *ménage à trois* to discover whether or not his wife's virtue has survived her first fall. In this icily contrived ordeal, Julie triumphs; the passion of Saint-Preux, still smoldering despite a therapeutic trip around the world, is turned into holy adoration; and when she finally attains for herself that death which Saint-Preux has longed for but failed to claim through suicide, she begins the conversion of her husband to a belief in God and the immortality of the soul.

Trying to rescue one of her children who has fallen into the water, Julie contracts pneumonia, and dies in the midst of pious discourses. Her death, however, is the goal to which she has all along aspired, her release to a world where she will be able to await a guiltless embrace with her first lover; and when she has finally died, her sanctification is complete. A veil of gold embroidered with pearls is thrown over her already decaying face by her friend Claire, and so veiled she is put into the earth. The last word and the last tear belong to her friend rather than to her lover, as her sanctified end seals her into the pantheon of female saviors. Saint-Preux, having failed to achieve the death that redeems his mistress (though he sought it once by kissing her suppurating hand in an attempt to share her smallpox), must live on with her children and her husband, to complete the works of piety and salvation she has begun.

Werther is at last granted the accolade of death which Saint-Preux could not wrest from Julie, who had inherited it by matri-archal right from Clarissa herself; but he gives up in return for that reward even the brief physical consummation which the French lover had attained with his mistress. Though he wears the very uniform of Saint-Preux, buff and blue, and celebrates the same religion of sensibility, Goethe's protagonist is denied not only marriage but any carnal union on earth; for him death becomes finally, what it is in the process of becoming in *La Nouvelle Hé-loïse,* the only bridal bed. "Yes, Charlotte, thou art mine," he writes before his death by his own hand, to the woman who has (sanely enough) chosen his rival Albert, the practical man over the visionary. "I only go before thee to my father—to thy father . . . then will I claim thee as my own, and in the presence of the Eter-nal be united with thee from everlasting to everlasting!"

In the *Nouvelle Héloïse,* it is Julie who confides to a last letter a similarly dangerous sentiment: "Shall my soul exist without you? Without you, what bliss shall I taste? No, I do not leave you, I go to wait for you. The virtue which separates us on earth shall join us in our heavenly home." Clarissa could not even conceive of, much less accept, the extraordinary doctrine of sanctified posthu-mous adultery which informs both *Julie* and *Werther.* In the two later works, the *Liebestod* theme as well as the concept of the grand passion as necessarily adulterous return again into the conscious-ness of Europe, from the repressed depths of the collective mind where they had bided ever since the death of the codes of courtly love. In Rousseau and Goethe, the Tristan and Isolde story stirs again, blends with the Clarissa-Lovelace archetype.

Had Charlotte married Werther, Goethe makes clear without explicit statement, she would have turned him into an Albert (but this, not long before, was called "saving him"); rejecting him as a lover, without casting him off completely, she drives him toward death. To make the point clear, she is shown as actually sending him the pistols with which he will eventually destroy himself, even dusting them off like a good little housewife! She knows really at this point that Werther must die, and, however hesitantly, accepts the only climax which can preserve the (technical) integrity of her marriage and the innocence of her extra-marital relation. Her complicity in this regard Werther recognizes and hails: "Your hands have grasped these pistols . . . you have wiped them for me! . . . those hands from which I have long earnestly wished to receive my fate!" Here is the final twist—not a travesty but a sentimental reversal—of the theme of the redeeming Maiden. Woman who was the angel of redemption becomes the angel of death; but for Werther, death *is* redemption, the only salvation he can use.

By the time *Werther* was written the anti-bourgeois sentimental novel had become, in its most extreme form, the anti-type, the mirror image of the bourgeois sentimental novel. The two types are not, however, always clearly separated; they share the same thematic material and, can, indeed, cohabit within the covers of the same book, as in the case Rousseau's *Nouvelle Héloïse,* the first part of which belongs to the anti-bourgeois kind, though the second part subscribes to bourgeois orthodoxy. The traditions employ a common setting and a common technique; they both relate domestic events against a bourgeois, Protestant family background; both dedicate themselves to the commonplace; and both use the letter form of narration. In each, changes are rung on the expected topics of seduction, suicide, sentiment, and (occasionally) incest; and appropriately enough, reverence is paid to Richardson, though there is for each a different Richardson.

For the anti-bourgeois writer, incest, which Richardson himself completely avoided but which most even of his pious followers took up out of Prévost and the very air of the declining eighteenth century, became more than an added spice or even (as for the genteel moralists) a dramatic testimony to the continuing ill effects of seduction upon succeeding generations. For them it became, especially in terms of brother-sister incest, a challenge to the most sacred of bourgeois taboos. Unwitting attractions of this kind, the "power of sympathy" which drew together children of the same father unaware of their kinship, they took as a sign of the "triumph of nature" over social conventions and attempts at concealment; while the deliberate turning to the sister as preferred mistress they interpreted as a revolutionary gesture of contempt for middle-class custom and law. Those thinkers who had fallen under the spell of the Encyclopedists took a cue from Diderot in the *Supplement to the Voyages of Bougainville,* contending that any ban on a sexual union between brother and sister was irrational and maddening. The advocacy of mother-incest was avoided, not so much because—as Diderot cynically observed—no sane man of twenty would prefer a woman of forty to a girl of eighteen, but because it was *too* audacious, challenged the rule of the father too brutally.

Insofar as the anti-bourgeois novel took up the cause of passion against prudence, of nature against "habit and positive law," it was led to defend such unions. The threat of the father to the daughter (a favorite theme of Prévost, who likes to identify father and seducer) came to stand for the tyranny of the past, the blighting restraint exercised by inherited authority, while the joining of brother and sister, in however ambiguous an alliance, against the corrupt parent became the very symbol of justified revolution—and, indeed, a give-away of the Oedipal aspects of all eighteenth-century revolutionary thought. In light of this, it is easy to understand why the story of the Cenci and the image of the father-slaying Beatrice Cenci in particular haunt the Romantic imagination which gradually disengages itself from the sentimental one. Before full Romanticism emerges, however, the incest motif will have broken out of the shell of the sentimental-domestic tradition altogether. There is in it something too outrageous, too atrocious to be contained in a genre that disavows the improbable; and we shall see how it finds freer expression in the gothic tradition which makes the outrageous its *raison d'être.*

Suicide is, as a symbol of protest, more manageable within the limits of Richardsonian sensibility, more at home in the context of familiar realism and observation of contemporary manners. Death, even in a form as shocking to Christian orthodoxy as self-murder, offends the bourgeois mind less than sex. In an argument between Werther and Albert the challenge which killing oneself posed for bourgeois morality is dramatically summed up. For Werther, suicide is the noblest of all actions, a revolutionary gesture; for Albert, a man who would shoot himself is quite simply "the worst of lunatics." Werther demands that at the very least suicide be treated as *problematic;* Albert apparently feels that to yield even so far would mean giving away the belief in the goodness and reasonableness of life. Albert, however, is the bourgeois embodiment of Reason (beyond him lies only the final travesty of Flaubert's Homais), the natural enemy of the anti-bourgeois man of feeling. Imperceptibly, the sentimental plea to understand the poor, seduced, and abandoned girl who seeks death when there is no other way out ("Her lover," says Werther, commenting on just such a case, "is faithless, perjured!—he forsakes her . . . dark envelops her—. . . . Thus blinded . . . she plunges into the merciless deep, and sinks to rise no more!") blends into a defense of the deliberate rebel not only against the tyranny of convention, but against maturity, responsibility, life itself. ("In this picture, Albert, is portrayed the history of many men. . . .")

The defense of suicide may seem to Albert an act of madness, but it is inevitable corollary to the worship of feeling, to the religion of sentiment of which Richardson is the high priest. Some historians of the novel have distinguished between the two kinds of novels here classified as bourgeois and anti-bourgeois in terms of "sentiment" and "sensibility"; they attribute to the direct influence of Richardson the novel of sentiment but credit to the example of Prévost and Sterne the rise of the novel of sensibility. Those terms fade into each other, however, for they describe degrees in the cult of feeling: a resolve, on the one hand, to exploit emotion for its own sake, and on the other, to do so out of a sense that true goodness is to be found primarily there. For both Richardson and Sterne to weep was to be saved, and it was Richardson who insisted, "Sensibility is the principal glory of human nature." Yet tears do become for some writers not a kind of wordless prayer but a prelude to an abandonment (in despite of conventional morality) to the promptings of passion.

"A flood of tears," Goethe writes, "streamed from the eyes of Charlotte. . . . Werther threw down the paper, grasped her hand, and bedewed it with his tears. Charlotte . . . held her handkerchief to her eyes—their agitation was mutual and extreme . . . the sorrow she felt almost deprived her of the use of reason: she affectionately folded her hands in his, pressed them to her bosom . . . her glowing cheek sank on his . . . they were insensible to everything but mutual love." Richardson's conviction that true feeling is more akin to religious devotion than to animal impulse has been oddly transformed via Rousseau into the assumption which underlies this scene: the belief that passion justifies all, or at least dissolves all resistance to believing that it does. No longer is the religion of feeling sustained by the Bible and the "virgin pages" of *Clarissa* alone;

there has flowed into it not only the *Schwärmerei* of Jean-Jacques Rousseau but also that mystique of the natural and the primitive derived by the eighteenth century from the pages of Homer, *Ossian,* and Shakespeare and from the newly recovered folk ballads. Once grant to Richardson that the "goodness of the Heart" is "much preferable to the Head alone," and the way is open to the shameless glorification of the heart alone over the head: to a celebration of passion as superior to all institutions—state, church, the marriage ceremony itself.

The Pure Maiden of Richardson survives relatively unchanged in the period of readjustment between Richardson and Goethe; she is only debased a little, not destroyed—becomes Gretchen, which is to say a symbol of piety still, though weak and simple and utterly passive. Her lover meanwhile has become Faust, Goethe's Faust, which is to say a portrait of the artist as an unconventional young man. The pathos of the seduction story remains all the same; the traduced and deserted girl still compels the sympathy of the rebel, even as she has that of the bourgeois woman. The seducer himself, however, has become a man of the heart rather than of the head; and the fabulous encounter which in the images of Lovelace and Clarissa had symbolized the conflict of pious feeling with cynical reason, stands now for the clash of feeling with feeling—a timid sensibility confronting a bolder one. Saint-Preux is given an aristocratic name, evoking at once the departed glories of feudalism and the Church, but he is an aristocrat only in terms of an utterly new set of standards, an aristocrat of the spirit, ennobled by sensibility alone. Werther is the heir to his title, a Don Juan who, forced to drop his sword, has picked up instead the pen, the painter's brush—the tear-stained copy of *Ossian.*

Reason meanwhile has been split off, committed to a third character without an exact prototype in the original Richardsonian fable: the dull and philistine suitor (blending with the comic figure of the unwanted old man Soames who woos Clary at her family's behest), finally the husband, as the Clarissa-Lovelace archetype reverts to the mythic pattern of courtly love (where it does not more daringly set up a love-conflict of father-sister-brother), to the first European triangle of husband-wife-poet lover.

Yet the actors in this triangle have changed profoundly between the twelfth century and the early nineteenth. No longer is the husband a cruel tyrant forcing his unfaithful wife to eat the heart of her beloved; now he is pre-eminently the man of Reason: Rousseau's coolly understanding *philosophe,* Wolmar, or Goethe's patient and only too level-headed bourgeois, Albert. Meanwhile, the courtly lover, neurotically swooning and pining away, has been turned into the figure of the anti-bourgeois artist caught between bravado and self-hatred. Goethe provides in his life's work a whole gallery of such perfunctorily disguised self-portraits, from the completely slimy Weislinger in *Götz von Berlichingen* through the equivocal Werther to the essentially heroic Faust of Part I.

As the novel becomes in the hands of the anti-bourgeois writer more lyrical and more autobiographical than the Richardsonian prototype, seduction and adultery (unconsummated in life but fulfilled in the grave) turn into symbols not of a struggle between established and rising classes, but between the exceptional individual and conventional society. In this struggle, the woman comes to stand both for the seducer's reward and his temptation to compromise; while the seducer himself is more and more closely identified with the author, a projection of his self-pity and self-loathing. The self-conscious artist of the new age feels himself at once of the middle class and estranged from it, the son of a bourgeois committed to oppose everything in which the bourgeoisie believes. By the very act of becoming a writer, he has (he cannot help feeling) betrayed his father, abandoned the male world of consciousness and action for a dark flirtation with the unconscious, out of which he has emerged as from the womb of his mother. The girls who symbolize this betrayal of the paternal principle must be, less equivocally even than Clarissa, images of the Great Mother; they must be discovered first by their lovers like Charlotte surrounded by "six lovely children," at last like Julie on her deathbed reaching out to her children; or even seen in the midst of life as the living symbol of eternal motherhood, like Hawthorne's Hester, half avatar, half travesty of "that sacred image of sinless motherhood, whose infant was to redeem the world."

No wonder that the seducer-artist, secret lover of his forbidden Mother and eternally unsure that what seems for him life-fulfillment is not also sin and death, is doomed to impotence and despair. Out of the odd mating of Richardson's debased Don Juan and Prévost's melancholy exile, Cleveland, was born the archetype of the Outsider, the alienated artist, which was to persist in the mind of the West well into our own time. Variously figured forth in literature, the myth becomes flesh, passes from art to life in the shape of those great "dandies" Poe and Byron and Baudelaire.

With the figure of the seducer as intellectual invented by bourgeois women to terrify themselves and declare their contempt for culture, the rebellious artist identifies himself in perverse pride; and his role has ever after been confused, in his own mind and that of the society he battles, with the role of the fictional figure he emulates. Thanks to the sentimental novel, the artist came quite soon to be thought of not as one who makes things, a man with a talent or a skill, but as one who feels them, a quivering sensibility; and it has been possible for a long time to conceive of a poet who has never written a poem—only developed the life style proper to one who aspires to writing poetry.

This is the heritage bequeathed by the age of sensibility to that of Romanticism, this image of the *poète maudit,* the taboo figure whose blessing is his curse, the sensitive young man too good for a world he never made. In 1850, he is called Ishmael, in 1940 Shem the Penman; but he does not die. He cannot, for he is the projection of everyone in the modern world, artist or not. Where the last great communal myth system begins to collapse and the individual finds himself unprotected against the inruption of the id, unsure of his relationship to the ego-ideals left him by the past, he becomes aware of himself as everywhere alone. Only the artist, however, dares to confess this fact even to himself; and thus, especially when he is young, he is likely to think of himself as alone in the loneliness which is actually his bond with the rest of the world. Particularly in America, where a nation of rootless men confronts not the vestiges of older cultures, but the wilderness, this loneliness is most deeply felt and (by many) most hysterically denied. And here the artist, sole aristocrat in a world that has denied the aristocratic principle, must play out against great odds the role of Werther and Don Juan, the part of Faust.

II

Advertised as the first American novel, *The Power of Sympathy: or, The Triumph of Nature,* which appeared in Boston in 1789, represents a serious bid to enter the lists of literature. The strategies (and presumably the motives) of the author are a little confusing: the title page declares his book no mere fiction but an account "founded on truth," while the pair of couplets immediately below insist that the book's aim is to "win the Mind to Sentiment and Truth"; and the elegant dedication that follows more specifically explains that the author's intent is "to represent the specious CAUSES, and to expose the fatal CONSEQUENCE of SEDUCTION" for the benefit of "the young ladies of United Columbia."

Yet the work was published anonymously, as if the writer were not quite convinced that he was engaged in an honorable enterprise; and the frontispiece has nothing to do with the main story, illustrating neither "the power of sympathy" or "nature" triumphant, but portraying the climax of a rather unconvincingly interpolated episode based on a contemporary scandal involving adultery and suicide. The bow to piety and truth combines oddly with the attempt to cash in on current notoriety afflicting a respectable family; and the sanctimonious dedication turns disturbingly into an appeal to the most light-headed of all novel-readers, though apparently the chief consumers of the form, "the young Ladies," or, as the author describes them elsewhere, the "tender youth." The one young lady who appears in the book, however, a "Miss" of fourteen much worried about the dictates of taste "in the centre of politeness and fashion," affects to despise the kind of sentimental book in which she is a character. "The bettermost genii," she asserts, "never read any sentimental books—so you see sentiment is out of date."

The author of *The Power of Sympathy,* who is believed now to have been William Hill Brown, had a strong sense of writing an old-fashioned book, one without chic or current appeal. "Why my dear . . . ," the same young lady insists further, "I abominate everything that is sentimental—it is so unfashionable too." Oppressed, on the one hand, by a feeling that he is out of date in his literary ambitions, Brown is plagued, on the other, by a distrust of the very form of the novel—or at least by a sense that he must pretend to distrust that form. He comments in one place on the "many fine girls ruined by reading novels," though he hastens to make clear that he means specifically novels "not regulated by the chaste principles of true friendship, rational love and connubial duty." But there is, alas, little enough of such friendship, love, or duty in his book; only much talk about them.

There is a thick sententiousness about the book, borrowed from Richardson and outdoing the master in this one regard; but Richardson's name is not invoked in defense of sentiment. The much less respectable Sterne is instead called upon to testify and is in return defended. "Alas! poor *Yorick,*" Brown writes. "May thy pages never be soiled by the fingers of prejudice." Even the most solid and respectable of his male characters, called with obvious aptness "Worthy," blasts the "anti-sentimentalists" who object to Sterne. "Eyes have *they*," he thunders in Biblical terms, "but they see not—ears have *they,* but they hear not. . . ." Brown's own exclamatory style, all dashes, italics, and exclamation marks, is derived from the master invoked—though it has survived to our own day chiefly in the letters of schoolgirls. Brown, indeed, seems convinced that the future of the sentimental literature he loves, a literature which defends the "man of sense" (needless to say, "sense" here means "sensibility" and not reason) against the "Chesterfieldian" coxcomb, depends upon female writers as well as readers; and he issues a plea for more American novels "from the pens of ladies." In part, perhaps, because of this feminist plea, he was for a long time thought to be a woman, a certain Mrs. Morton, poet and sister to the dying lady in the scandalous frontispiece of his book.

At the heart of Brown's book, there presides the figure of the wise and widowed Mrs. Holmes, a "serious sentimentalist," flanked by an even more prolix and pious sage, her father-in-law, with whom she dispenses *"Mentor*-like lessons of instruction" to the novel's other characters. "The idiosyncratic feature of the American conscience," Geoffrey Gorer aptly remarks, "is that it is predominantly feminine. . . . Duty and Right Conduct become feminine figures." Mr. Gorer goes on to note (and it is worth pausing to take account of such future developments at the point where the super-ego in female form first enters our fiction) that "the fact that the rules for moral conduct are felt to emanate from a feminine source is a source of considerable confusion to American men. They tend to resent such interference in their own behavior, and yet are unable to ignore it, since the insistent maternal conscience is a part of their personality. . . . A second result . . . is that . . . modesty, politeness, neatness, cleanliness—come to be regarded as concessions to feminine demands, and . . . as such they are sloughed off—with relief but not without guilt—whenever a suitable occasion presents itself . . . the stag poker game, the fishing trip, the convention. . . ."

The semi-mythicized figure of Mrs. Holmes is set, appropriately enough, in a semi-mythicized rococo landscape, the first Great Good Place of our literature: the "dear groves" of *Belleview*. It is here in the midst of nature, that she conducts her "amiable conversations"—and it is for the natural world as opposed to the heartless social world of the city that Belleview stands. But Brown's is a neo-classical, a sentimental Nature, a world in which the contrary demands of Nature and Reason are served at once—the equivalent in terms of landscape of the concept of "rational love," or of the blend of "sentiment and truth" invoked in the superscription of the book. The lady of such a place can be neither illiterate or a prude. If, on the one hand, Mrs. Holmes advises her female correspondents to pretend deafness to any remarks directed against the clergy, she advocates the same reception for slurs cast on "Mechanicks." She is a democrat as well as a convinced churchgoer, and a defender of women's rights as well as a spokesman for their duties. She speaks out in favor of the "learned lady," and she defends such semi-respectable writers as Sterne and La Rochefoucauld. She even joins boldly in an attack on "poetic justice" in literature, protesting the invariable rewarding of the innocent as a false representation of life—and recommends the cynical maxims of the French philosopher as a proper antidote. She is in no grim sense a Puritan, but subscribes to her father-in-law's advocacy of charity for fallen women and to his belief in a God ever ready to forgive those who weep. Hers is a world not completely set against passion, though aware of its dangers, but rather one committed to the notion that "Love softens and refines the manners—mends the heart—makes us better men—gives the fainthearted strength. . . ."

Even this sentimental-enlightened view of life, in which Reason and Nature correspond as in an elegant dance, is finally brought into question, for it proves incapable of coming to terms with the revelation of seduction and the threat of incest or with the fact of suicide. Into the very heart of the Garden intrude death and deflowering; and from the Garden itself, from the very hands of Mrs. Holmes, comes the news that precipitates the black climax of the book. Seduction for Brown finally becomes the symbol of the uncontrollable demonic element in life, which lays waste the civilized but natural haven of Belleview. The book opens under the aegis of Mrs. Holmes, but closes under the influence of Werther. In its early pages, the "serious sentimentalist" has quoted the optimistic injunction of Goethe: "REVERENCE THYSELF!"; in the final pages, the hero, turning to literature for comfort, opens a book and reads the following words: "the time of my fading is near, and the blast that shall scatter my leaves. Tomorrow shall the traveller come, he that saw me in my beauty shall come; his eyes shall search the field, but they will not find me." The quotation is from *Ossian,* but surely the book in which Harrington found it was *The Sorrows of Young Werther;* for it is while reading these final verses in his own translation, that Werther is overcome by a prescience of his doom and flings himself at the feet of Charlotte, "insensible to everything but mutual love." Certainly, when Harrington is dead, that dangerous book is found by his side.

Like Werther, too, he condemns society as a conspiracy against the individual. "I despise its opinion—*Independency of spirit* is my motto—I think for myself." And he is led to reject its value and codes as entirely conventional. Finally, he consigns to God and the kingdom of Heaven, quite in the manner of Goethe and Rousseau, the task of righting the wrongs perpetrated in their names by society on earth. Suicide itself, Harrington hopes, can be redeemed by the sentimental baptism of tears. "Let tears of sorrow blot out my guilt from the book of thy wrath," he prays hopefully, and foresees himself not only ultimately forgiven but joined to the woman forbidden him on earth. "In heaven—there alone is happiness—there shall I meet her—there our love will not be a crime. . . ."

It is not, however, adultery, achieved or unconsummated, which the American writer is justifying in terms so like those of his European forerunners; this time it is unconsummated incest, and the villain is (in good American style) not the husband but the father. The Oedipus triangle based on the family romance may be translated from father-mother-son to husband-wife-lover in its European forms, courtly and anti-bourgeois sentimental; but in America it more dangerously takes the form father-sister-brother—though that form can be connected back through the generations with the familiar seduction theme in its "safe" Richardsonian version. Incest may be the secret horror toward which *The Power of Sympathy* tends, but seduction is its more openly elaborated motif.

From the dedication "to the young Ladies of United Columbia . . . to expose the fatal CONSEQUENCES of SEDUCTION," through the preface which repeats it almost word for word, to the body of the book, the theme is worked out in an exhausting series of variations. We learn that seduction "opens the door to a train of miseries," that "there is no human vice of so black a die . . . or which causes a more general calamity." It becomes at last the very image of original sin, and each of the two volumes, into which the book was originally divided, contains an allegory in which the terror of seduction is projected in religious terms. Four times the theme of sexual violation is taken up in *The Power of Sympathy,* first in "the story of Miss Whitman,'" a quite factual account of the famous seduction later worked by Hannah Foster into *The Coquette.* William Hill Brown entrusts to a paragraph spoken by old Mr. Holmes and to a long footnote of his own this tale of a woman betrayed by too much reading and a plausible love. Once pregnant, she tries in vain to buy herself a husband, then produces a dead child and herself dies of puerperal fever. Brown's account is eked out by an extract from one of Miss Whitman's letters and her own verse Elegy, in which, presumably at the point of death, she invokes her faithless lover under the ironic name of Fidelio. That same name in its female form is bestowed on another example of "the fatal CONSEQUENCES of SEDUCTION." Fidelia is a mad peasant girl dressed in flowing white, out of Shakespeare by way of Goethe, who had been "carried off by a ruffian" a few days before her intended marriage. Her true lover had committed suicide in despair, leaving her to a life of Ophelia-like insanity. Obviously a European peasant, she wanders quite improbably on the outskirts of Belleview, the sacred domain of Mrs. Holmes, casting a shadow even on that refuge.

The name of Ophelia, denied her closest counterpart in the novel, is reserved for the lady whose death graces the frontispiece, beneath which are inscribed her last words, "O Fatal! Fatal Poison!" Hers is not a conventional seduction story at all, but rather one of adultery. It is with her brother-in-law that Ophelia falls in love, while living in her sister's house; and their affair ("incestuous," Brown calls it) is revealed by "symptoms which rendered it necessary for Ophelia to remove into the country." The brother-in-law, who had promised to get a divorce and marry the dishonored Ophelia, is so annoyed by the interference of Ophelia's father that his love turns to hate, and Ophelia in despair drinks poison and dies. The story is awkwardly introduced and remains the only subplot not linked somehow to Belleview, which is the book's real center. It would be possible to believe it quite simply prompted by a desire to boost sales by exploiting fresh gossip, though in actuality it backfired, causing the partial suppression of the book; but it does at least foreshadow the subthemes of incest and suicide, and especially "the severe use of paternal power," elsewhere so important in the scheme of the novel.

The main plot begins with young Harrington playing the typical role of the seducer. He has seen a girl called Harriot and he desires her; but his father has forbidden an early marriage, and he is, in any case, "not such a Republican," he confides to his friend Worthy, "as to marry a poor girl. . . ." He has even prepared arguments to overwhelm her virtue, but never quite gets around to urging her to "obey the dictates of nature," for he is really more moralist than "amoroso." With astonishing speed he is converted to more democratic attitudes and to a decision to marry when confronted with "the dignity of *conscious* virtue" in Harriot, who, though penniless and ignorant of her own origins, is able to reverence herself in precisely the manner recommended by Mrs. Holmes.

There is, however, a second turn in the logic of the plot; for no sooner has Harrington been converted from would-be seducer to conventional suitor than the voice of Mrs. Holmes is raised in warning: "I HAVE A TALE TO UNFOLD!" Harrington is about to marry his sister! Harriot is the daughter of a certain Marcia Fawcett and Harrington's father, the fruit of her mother's fall from virtue; and it was to Belleview that her mother had come to die, when cast off by the older Harrington for the sake of the woman he married. Though the betrayed woman had won the love and charity of the senior Mr. Holmes, the forgiveness of God was another matter: He had pursued her sin (or was it the sin of her seducer?) even to the second generation, bringing to the verge of an incestuous union two sensitive creatures who could not accept life without each other. Faced with this consequence of the sin of others, Harriot goes into a rapid decline and dies (her passion still alive despite the knowledge that her lover is her brother), while Harrington commits suicide. The more liberal Christian or sentimental theories of forgiveness crumble before the mystery of the endless effects of iniquity; and the happy theory that love "mends the heart and makes us better men" buckles before the puzzle of the incest taboo and the unwillingness of passion to accept its limits.

The Power of Sympathy: or, The Triumph of Nature becomes finally (or rather, wants to, *tries* to become) what its title declares it: more a psychological, even a metaphysical essay than a lurid story told to shock and amuse. Like *Werther* itself, Brown's book threatens to turn into a study of the ambiguity of Nature; and like Goethe's later *Wahlverwandschaften,* whose title almost translates its own, it studies the strange, sometimes fatal attractions which move us beyond the power of will to resist or reason to control. In the first volume of *The Power of Sympathy,* the term Nature is used quite simply to describe a realm of peace and pleasure, symbolized by Belleview in all its rural charm. "Nature is everywhere liberal in dispensing her beauties and her variety—and I pity those who look round and declare they see neither," Mrs. Holmes writes.

Even into the earlier portions of Part II, the same view persists; Harrington can conceive of no higher name for his God than the good Deist term "Author of Nature." "Author of Nature!" he cries out in ecstasy. "From thee . . . floweth this tide of affection and SYMPATHY!" Here, on the same optimistic note, enters the second key term of the work; yet within three pages, Mrs. Holmes is writing, "Great God! of what materials hast thou compounded the hearts of thy creatures; Admire, o my friend! the operation of NATURE—and the power of SYMPATHY!—" For the lovers, who are brother and sister, have been fatally attracted to each other by the very force that makes their union impossible, by "the link of Nature." Indeed, the terrible climax of their double death is described as "the triumph of Nature," and Harrington is called "the dupe of Nature." But God, after all, is "the Author of Nature"—and the book trembles on the verge of blasphemy.

If Nature has brought Harrington and Harriot to their impasse and Nature is the handmaiden of God, in what sense is it possible to blame them for whatever they may do? The ideal represented by Mrs. Holmes's garden, the utopian dream of "rational love" proves to be an illusion; love and reason only accidentally coincide; the head and the heart are by no means always allies. "The head and the heart are at variance, but when Nature pleads, how feeble is the voice of Reason. . . ." "Allied by birth, and in mind . . . ," Harriot writes to her lover-brother, "the sympathy which bound our souls together, at first sight, is less extraordinary. . . . Shall we strive to oppose the *link of nature* that draws us to each other?"

With the temerity of passion, she ends using the very argument of Nature to justify incest which Harrington finally had not dared plead to justify simple fornication. The temptation to believe her argument and act on it, Harriot's death conveniently removes from them both; but another peril remains. "Reason is taken from the helm of life—" writes Worthy, Harrington's confidant, "and Nature—helpless, debilitated Nature . . . splits upon the rocks. . . ." What, then, is Brown's attitude to the suicide of Harrington, left to the mercy of what his friend calls "helpless, debilitated Nature"? Harrington's father has prophetically beheld him in a vision in hell among the other self-murderers; but Harrington himself foresees an ascension to Heaven as a reward for his long suffering and looks forward to a reunion with Harriot there. "Sympathy unites whom Fate divides," "in death they sleep undivided," we are told; but does the common burial signify an eternal union in heaven, where their "love will be no crime"?

The book finally equivocates in a way not untypical of the later American novel, hanging onto not the best but the worst of two possible worlds: the smugness of liberal gentility and the factitious sensationalism of anti-bourgeois sentimentality. When read at all, *The Power of Sympathy* has seemed to the respectable a suspect work, described, for instance, in a history of the novel published in 1952 as "a morbid, nasty book." At the same time, it has struck others as merely "a good domestic story calculated to impart unmistakeable impressions to the young." Its fundamental seriousness is the one quality both descriptions fail to take into account; but that seriousness cannot be ignored without falsifying the book altogether, for it is a literate book according to the standards of its own time, and an ambitious one.

It is, however, marred by an annoying thinness of realization throughout; Brown could not or would not take the pains to specify solidly the reactions of his characters, though he had in the letter form he borrowed from Richardson an admirable instrument for detailed psychological analysis. His people not only float in a scarcely defined space (he is interested in settings only when they are symbolic like the summerhouse of Mrs. Holmes), they act out of scarcely defined personalities. What bulk his novel finally possesses is attained not by working out the implications of action, motive, or theme but by working in extra sub-plots and extended homilies. Our earliest books are astonishingly slim in a time when Europe abounded with examples of the thick book, as if the mere effort of imagining a creative work on this side of the ocean exhausted the energy of the author; and the scant realization of *The Power of Sympathy* cannot, therefore, have been the cause of its unpopularity. Certainly it attracted little attention. What the partially effective efforts at suppression by the Apthorp family (relatives of "Ophelia") had begun, public indifference completed. The novel seems to have been mentioned in print only seven times from the date of its publication to 1850; and what recognition it has now is almost completely a function of the impulse toward exhaustive scholarship rather than of renewed critical interest.

Even less well read and remembered is Brown's *Ira and Isabella,* in which he returned once more to the theme of incest. This time he produced neither a tragedy of incest, like his own *The Power of Sympathy,* nor a *comédie larmoyante,* like Mrs. Rowson's *Lucy,* but a howling travesty—endowed with a "happy ending" capable of dissolving in laughter the whole obsessive concern with "the fatal CONSEQUENCES of SEDUCTION." One hopes the burlesque is deliberate, but it is hard to be sure. At any rate, in *Ira and Isabella,* the protagonists, who learn that their intended marriage cannot take place because Isabella is the illegitimate daughter of Ira's father, then discover that Ira, too, is illegitimate, not the son of that presumed father at all; and bastards both, they are blissfully united.

Though William Hill Brown's second book is an equivocal travesty and his first the mere skeleton of a novel, he remains a considerable figure. *The Power of Sympathy* may be finally only a sketch, but it is the sketch of a serious book; and it is probable that its failure is more the product of its virtues than of its faults. A mere accident of history determined that the first American novel be (despite its equivocations and uncertainty) fundamentally anti-bourgeois; the necessities of American character, particularly that of the largest reading public, made it impossible that from such a book a successful literature could take its cue.

6

CHARLES BROCKDEN BROWN AND THE INVENTION OF THE AMERICAN GOTHIC

THE GOTHIC, WHOSE EXAMPLE spurred on those serious American writers whom the example of the sentimental had only galled, is a sub-genre of the novel, invented in England, though it was adapted in Germany quite early by writers like E. T. A. Hoffmann, and reached our own novelists in both its British and German forms. Its first practitioner was Horace Walpole, who published, on Christmas Eve of 1764, *The Castle of Otranto*. Toward this improbable account of flight and pursuit in a pseudo-medieval setting and toward its hero-villain Manfred, Walpole's attitude was double. On the one hand, he concealed his authorship behind an Italian pen name and shrugged off the whole enterprise by remarking that "it is not everybody in this country may play the fool with impunity"; on the other, he boasted in a foreword of having freed "great resources of fancy" that had been unfortunately "dammed up by common life."

All the major themes and symbols of the gothic were present in Walpole's book, but it did not prove capable of starting a new fashion in fiction; the European imagination was not yet ready for it, would not be ready until that imagination had been modified by the Revolution and the Terror. Before 1789, *The Castle of Otranto* seemed merely a sport, the eccentric product of a literary antiquarian; after 1790, it was revealed as the lonely forerunner of an attempt at creating "the modern novel"—a term used by the Marquis de Sade (surely for the first time) in his *Idées sur les romans* to characterize the gothic romance. It was through the works not of Walpole but of two other English novelists that the gothic became the prevailing European mode in the years when William Hill Brown and Mrs. Rowson were still trying in the United States to revive the sentimental.

Just as the Richardsonian novel soon became the contested heritage of two conflicting parties, philistine and anti-bourgeois, so the gothic novel was fought for. But even as the sentimental novel seems essentially genteel, and is only exploited against the grain for anti-philistine ends, so the gothic romance is fundamentally anti-bourgeois and can only with difficulty be adapted to the needs of the sentimental middle classes. Nonetheless, it was a "female scribbler," Ann Radcliffe, celebrated by her bourgeois admirers as the "Shakespeare of the Romance writers," who first managed to make a success of gothic fiction. Her books, which appeared between 1789 and 1797, are all much alike, variations on the archetypal theme which she found in Walpole and made her own.

Through a dream landscape, usually called by the name of some actual Italian place, a girl flees in terror and alone amid crumbling castles, antique dungeons, and ghosts who are never really ghosts. She nearly escapes her terrible persecutors, who seek her out of lust and greed, but is caught; escapes again and is caught; escapes once more and is caught (the middle of Mrs. Radcliffe's books seem in their compulsive repetitiveness a self-duplicating nightmare from which it is impossible to wake); finally breaks free altogether and is married to the virtuous lover who has all along worked (and suffered equally with her) to save her. In the end, all the ghosts that have terrorized her are explained as wax-works or living men in disguise, the supernatural appearances that have made her enemies seem more than human revealed as mere mechanical devices, etc.

Mrs. Radcliffe's most successful version of her single theme is found in *The Italian,* which appeared in 1797; and, indeed, it is Italy, the Mediterranean South with its overtones of papistry and lust, that is the true ghost, never quite exorcized by the fables of the more genteel gothicists. That symbolic Italy represents only one of their debts to Restoration drama, from whose stock of sensational effects the gothic novelists rifled whatever seemed to them of use. If the gothic romance seems in certain regards more theatrical than the sentimental novel, whose beginnings after all were model letter books for the uncultured, this is because many of its devices were to begin with stage properties, and Walpole himself the author of *The Mysterious Mother* as well as *The Castle of Otranto*—in Byron's words, of "the last tragedy" as well as the "first Romance" of European literature. The basic fable of the gothic novel, however, at least as defined by Mrs. Radcliffe, seems actually derived from such books as *Clarissa*. Schedoni, the sinister male protagonist of *The Italian,* pursues his victim, just as Lovelace once pursued Clarissa; and at the center of the story appears that girl on the run, the Persecuted Maiden who, under one name or another, had been fleeing violation ever since Angelica took off at high speed through the pages of *Orlando Furioso*. There are, nonetheless, notable differences between the Richardsonian and Radcliffean treatments of the pursuit of the Maiden.

First of all, there is the matter of setting. The flight of Clarissa, however mythic in its implications, takes place in society—in a real, contemporaneous world of fashion, friends, parents, parties, and business. The flight of the gothic heroine is out of the known world into a dark region of make-believe, past the magical landscapes of a legendary Italy, along the shadowy corridors of the haunted castle, which is to say, through a world of ancestral and infantile fears projected in dreams. The sentimental heroine confronts the dangers of the present, that is, of life as recorded in the newspaper; the gothic heroine evades the perils of the past, that is, of life as recorded in history.

There is, moreover, a question of tone and emphasis. However melodramatic or even tragic the implications of the sentimental fable, its intent is to reveal the power of light and redemption, to insist that virtue if not invariably successful is at least always triumphant. The gothic fable, on the other hand, though it may (in its more genteel examples) permit the happy ending, is committed to portraying the power of darkness. Perhaps another way to say this is that the fully developed gothic centers not in the heroine (the persecuted principle of salvation) but in the villain (the persecuting principle of damnation). The villain-hero is, indeed, an invention of the gothic form, while his temptation and suffering, the beauty and terror of his bondage to evil are among its major themes.

Finally, there is the matter of the archetypal function of the basic gothic story; for such a function it must have or it could not have persisted as it did. The Clarissa-Lovelace archetype expresses, as we have seen, the sense of their own innocence possessed by the classes for whom the novel was produced. The myth of *The Castle* of Otranto, on the other hand, projects a sense of guilt and anxiety, the guilt of the Break-through, as dimly perceived by the bourgeoisie—and especially by the intellectuals who were its sons. "What is this secret sin; this untold tale, that art cannot extract, nor penance cleanse?" asks the question quoted from Walpole's The Mysterious Mother by Mrs. Radcliffe in The Italian. The answer in the original play is incest—incest of brother and sister-daughter bred out of an original incest of mother and son—the breach of the primal taboo and the offense against the father! In more general terms, the guilt which underlies the gothic and motivates its plots is the guilt of the revolutionary haunted by the (paternal) past which he has been striving to destroy; and the fear that possesses the gothic and motivates its tone is the fear that in destroying the old ego-ideals of Church and State, the West has opened a way for the inruption of darkness: for insanity and the disintegration of the self. Through the pages of the gothic romance, the soul of Europe flees its own darker impulses.

These deeper implications are barely perceptible in the gently spooky fiction of Mrs. Radcliffe, in which terror is allayed by the final pages, all inruptions of the irrational rationally explained away. Indeed, so polite does horror become in her novels, that it seems to a modern palate insipid. But in the single volume of another gothic fictionist, the Walpolean fable takes on a significance that evaded Mrs. Radcliffe's total body of work; and all its absurdity, its outrageous violence is released. That writer is the enfant terrible Matthew Gregory Lewis, who at the age of twenty wrote in three weeks the four hundred pages of The Monk, by which name he insisted on being called forever after ("a two-fold barbarity, Madam"). It is a fantastic, amusing, horrifying book, this shrill tour de force produced at top speed by an English boy to support his deserted mother. Actually composed in Weimar, it benefits perhaps by approaching the tradition of The Castle of Otranto as developed in German horror fiction rather than in the novels of English gentlewomen.

At any rate, the appearance of The Monk in 1796 made its author a showpiece at all the literary parties of that London season, though it also shocked the official guardians of morality so deeply that for perhaps a hundred years it remained bootleg reading. "A romance, which if a parent saw it in the hands of a son or daughter, he might reasonably turn pale," one of its shocked readers called it; "a poison for youth and a provocative for the debauchés." One considerate bookseller was reported to have underlined all "the worst parts for a sixteen year old subscriber, so that she might skip them!" And it was, perhaps, in a similarly marked copy that Byron browsed among its more scandalous passages, emerging with the horrified (and somewhat improbable) comment that they represented the "philtered ideas of a jaded voluptuary." The book seems inoffensive enough nowadays, though occasionally melodramatic to the point of howling absurdity; but it was obviously intended to offend and disturb the right-minded bourgeoisie, which in its own day rose satisfactorily to the bait.

A summary of its double plot gives some sense of the provocative nature of the novel, though shorn of the sensationally emphatic style, much of its force (and a little of its ridiculousness) is lost. The sub-plot is conventionally Radcliffean, dealing with two lovers, Agnes and Raymond, who are separated in the midst of complications involving, among other horrors, the bleeding ghost of a nun. Agnes is first imprisoned in a nunnery, then denounced by Ambrosio (the hero-villain of the main plot) and condemned to perpetual incarceration among rotting corpses in the vaults beneath the convent. She is, however, rescued in time for a reunion with her lover by a search party which discovers, at a critical moment of his villainy, Ambrosio and his Satanic mistress, Matilda.

Ambrosio, "Abbot of the Capuchins," is first presented as a much-admired preacher, an ostensible saint; but he is readily enough corrupted by the woman Matilda, who gains access to his cell disguised as a young novice; indeed, by the time she appears Ambrosio has already been inflamed by contemplating her portrait in the guise of the Virgin. Soon after they have become lovers, Ambrosio wearies of her and begins to dream of possessing Antonia, fifteen-year-old daughter of Elvira, a noble lady to whom he is confessor. With the aid of Matilda, who calls up the Devil to further his plans, he gets into the bedroom of Antonia, but is interrupted as he assaults her by Elvira, whom he kills.

He gives a sleeping potion to the terrified girl, who is taken for dead and consigned to a tomb, where he at last successfully rapes her among the rotting dead. When she screams, he murders her, fearing discovery; but he is captured all the same by the soldiers of the Inquisition, from whose prison he manages to escape by selling his soul to the Devil. He is, however, immediately transported by demons to the top of a mountain peak, from which, after being told that Elvira (whom he murdered) was his mother and

Antonia (whom he violated, then killed) his sister, he is cast to his terrified death.

By the time Lewis is through with this sadist farrago, the major symbols of the gothic have been established, and the major meanings of the form made clear. In general, those symbols and meanings depend on an awareness of the spiritual isolation of the individual in a society where all communal systems of value have collapsed or have been turned into meaningless clichés. There is a basic ambivalence in the attitude of the gothic writers to the alienation which they perceive. On the one hand, their fiction projects a fear of the solitude which is the price of freedom; and on the other hand, an almost hysterical attack on all institutions which might inhibit that freedom or mitigate the solitude it breeds. Chief of the gothic symbols is, of course, the Maiden in flight—understood in the spirit of *The Monk* as representing the uprooted soul of the artist, the spirit of the man who has lost his moral home. Not the violation or death which sets such a flight in motion, but the flight itself figures forth the essential meaning of the anti-bourgeois gothic, for which the girl on the run and her pursuer become only alternate versions of the same plight. Neither can come to rest before the other—for each is the projection of his opposite—*anima* and *animus,* actors in a drama which depends on both for its significance. Reinforcing the meaning of the haunted victim and the haunted persecutor (each the other's obsession) is the haunted countryside, and especially the haunted castle or abbey which rises in its midst, and in whose dark passages and cavernous apartments the chase reaches its climax. Symbols of authority, secular or ecclesiastic, in ruin—memorials to a decaying past—such crumbling edifices project the world of collapsed ego-ideals through which eighteenth-century man was groping his proud and terrified way. If he permitted himself a certain relish in the contemplation of those ruins, this was because they were safely cast down, and he could indulge in nostalgia without risk. If he was terrified of them, dreamed supernatural enemies lurking in their shadows, it was because he suspected that the past, even dead, *especially* dead, could continue to work harm. Even as late as Henry James, an American writer deeply influenced by gothic modes was able to imagine the *malaria,* the miasma which arises from decaying ruins, striking down Daisy Miller as she romantically stands at midnight in the Coliseum.

One of the most popular middlebrow derivatives of the gothic romance is the ghost story; and, indeed, from the start ghosts arise everywhere in the gothic's pages: pale symbols (parodies of the immortal soul in which men had begun to lose faith) of what persists after death. In the eighteenth century, the experience of rationalism had made it easier to believe that a noxious influence, an after-image which chilled the blood, outlasted physical decay, than that some integrating principle of good eternally survived. Similarly, the Devil lived on in the imagination after the death of God, men who would not have gone to church celebrating black masses or finding in the tale of terror some vestigial religious awe. Children of an age which had killed kings and bishops, cast down the holy places of their fathers, found it hard to convince themselves that specters did not walk with rattling chains, or that ancestral pictures did not bleed.

Beneath the haunted castle lies the dungeon keep: the womb from whose darkness the ego first emerged, the tomb to which it knows it must return at last. Beneath the crumbling shell of paternal authority, lies the maternal blackness, imagined by the gothic writer as a prison, a torture chamber—from which the cries of the kidnaped *anima* cannot even be heard. The upper and the lower levels of the ruined castle or abbey represent the contradictory fears at the heart of gothic terror: the dread of the super-ego, whose splendid battlements have been battered but not quite cast down —and of the id, whose buried darkness abounds in dark visions no stormer of the castle had even touched.

Most variously developed of all the gothic symbols is the Shadow, the villain who pursues the Maiden and presides over turrets and dungeon keep alike. He is apt to take the shape (in a genre which, like the sentimental novel, is both Protestant and bourgeois)- of the devious Inquisitor, the concupiscent priest, the corrupt nobleman—or, with almost equal appropriateness, the depraved abbess or the lascivious lady of the manor. And yet there is a sense in which the evil principle is mythically male, the female at best an accessory; for deep in the middle-class mind persist the equations of the Sentimental Love Religion.

Certainly, it is the Shadow projected as male which most impresses itself upon the imagination, becomes standard to the form; and the hero-villain of the tale of terror turns out to be a descendant of Lovelace, after all, though of a Lovelace regarded with tenderness rather than contempt. Like his sentimental prototype, the Manfred figure stands for the *animus*, that masculine archetype in which the feminine psyche projects all it has denied. But he is the *animus* regarded as forgivable victim of passion and circumstance, as admirable sufferer. His brow furrowed, his face frozen in the grimace of pain, his eyes burning with repressed fury, his mind tormented with unspeakable blasphemies (ancestor of Byron's Giaour, of Ahab, Heathcliffe, Rochester, and a thousand other "ungodly, godlike" men), he is proposed as another symbol of alienation twinned with the Maiden he pursues, a jailer no less lonely than his prisoner.

To define this aspect of the gothic hero-villain, the Lovelace archetype is blended with that of the Wandering Jew, Ahasuerus or Cartaphilus doomed to stalk the earth in hopeless pain until the Second Coming; but especially he is fused with the image of Faust. Don Juan and Faust alike are former villains of the orthodox mind made heroes in an age of unorthodoxy, Promethean or Satanic figures; and both come to stand for the lonely individual (the writer himself!) challenging the mores of bourgeois society, making patent to all men the ill-kept secret that the codes by which they live are archaic survivals without point or power.

Often the two archetypes are blended in a single literary character, as in the lover-scientist Goethe calls by the name of Faust. But there is a real difference between the rebel whose life style is cued by passion and the one whose life style is compounded out of pride and terror—between the seducer and the black magician. Faust challenges the limitations set upon experience not in the name of pleasure but of knowledge; he seeks not to taste life without restraint but to control it fully; and his essential crime (or glory!) is, therefore, not seduction but the Satanic bargain: to sell one's soul to the Devil. But what does it mean to sell one's soul? The symbol is immensely complex, its significances multiple; they can be summed up, however, in the single phrase *to choose to be damned,* whatever damnation is. Not to fall into error out of a passionate loss of self-control, not even to choose to sin at a risk of damnation; but to commit oneself to it with absolute certainty for "as long as forever is."

Damnation itself means various things to men of varying belief: a commitment to the vagaries of the unconscious; an abandonment of the comforts of social life—of marriage and the family, wealth and recognition; a rejection of all bonds of love and sympathy, of humanity itself; a deliberate plunge into insanity; and acceptance of eternal torment for the soul. When Huck Finn cries out, "All

right, I'll *go* to Hell," and Ahab, "From hell's heart I stab at thee!";
when Hester Prynne tears off her scarlet letter, they are Faustian
heroes. Anyone who, in full consciousness, surrenders the hope of
heaven (what everyone says heaven is) for the endurance of hell
(what everyone knows hell to be) has entered into a pact with
Satan; and the very act, therefore, of writing a gothic novel rather
than a sentimental one, of devoting a long fiction to terror rather
than love, is itself a Faustian commitment. The gothic novel was
not fully itself until it had discovered and made its center the diabolic bargain; this is as essential to its total significance as seduction to the Richardsonian novel.

The primary meaning of the gothic romance, then, lies in its substitution of terror for love as a central theme of fiction. The titillation of sex denied, it offers its readers a vicarious participation in
a flirtation with death—approach and retreat, approach and retreat, the fatal orgasm eternally mounting and eternally checked.
More than that, however, the gothic is the product of an implicit
aesthetic that replaces the classic concept of nothing-in-excess with
the revolutionary doctrine that nothing succeeds like excess. Aristotle's guides for achieving the tragic without falling into "the
abominable" are stood on their heads, "the abominable" itself
being made the touchstone of effective art. Dedicated to producing
nausea, to transcending the limits of taste and endurance, the
gothic novelist is driven to seek more and more atrocious crimes to
satisfy the hunger for "too-much" on which he trades.

It is not enough that his protagonist commit rape; he must commit it upon his mother or sister; and/ if he himself is a cleric,
pledged to celibacy, his victim a nun, dedicated to God, all the
better! Similarly, if he commits murder, it must be his father who
is his victim; and the crime must take place in darkness, among the
decaying bodies of his ancestors, on hallowed ground. It is as if
such romancers were pursuing some ideal of absolute atrocity
which they cannot quite flog their reluctant imaginations into conceiving. For the abominable, to be truly effective, must remain literally unspeakable; and where—as in the case of *The Monk*—it
has adapted itself to the censor and the mode, become respectable
and chic, it ends by seeming ridiculous. The abominable as an
absolute leads to either sickness or silliness, betraying the man who
is obsessed by the horror he evokes or the one who plays at it
merely to shock and succeed.

Some would say, indeed, that the whole tradition of the gothic is a pathological symptom rather than a proper literary movement, a reversion to the childish game of scaring oneself in the dark, or a plunge into sadist fantasy, masturbatory horror. For Wordsworth, for instance, heir of the genteel sentimentality of the eighteenth century, gothic sensationalism seemed merely a response (compounding the ill to which it responded) to the decay of sensibility in an industrialized and brutalized world—in which men had grown so callous that only shock treatments of increasing intensity could move them to react. Yet there is more than this even to *The Monk.* If Lewis writes in one sense what he must and in another what he hopes will sell, he also writes for a more conscious and respectable end: to shake the philistines out of their self-satisfied torpor. *Épater la bourgeoisie:* this is the secret slogan of the tale of terror; and it remains into our own time a not-so-secret slogan of much highbrow literature, particularly of such spectacular bourgeois-baiting movements as Dada, Surrealism, and Pop Art.

When the Beatniks emerge from their own retreats, bearded and blue-shaded and bagel in hand, to mock the "squares" of San Francisco with the monstrous disorder of life as they imagine and live it, they are playing the latest version of the game invented by "Monk" Lewis. Despite its early adoption by Mrs. Radcliffe, the gothic is an avant-garde genre, perhaps the first avant-garde art in the modern sense of the term. A pursuit, half serious enterprise, half fashionable vice, of the intellectuals of the end of the eighteenth century, it remained highbrow enough to tempt the Shelleys and Byron, for instance, to try their hands at it. The popular success of *Frankenstein,* perpetuated still in movies and known in its essence to children in the street, has obscured the fact that it was launched as an advanced book; and that it belongs to a kind, one of whose functions was to shock the bourgeoisie into an awareness of what a chamber of horrors its own smugly regarded world really was.

But the gothic represents also an attempt to redeem "the improbable and marvelous," the stuff of the fancy which Richardson had presumably banned from the new novel. It was, in short, an anti-realistic protest, a rebellion of the imagination against confining fiction to an analysis of contemporary manners and modes. It is not, on the other hand, a reactionary literary movement; for the fantastic world to which it turns is altogether different from the fictional setting of the baroque proto-novel, against whose "pomp and pageantry" Richardson had revolted. The tone of the *Astrée,* for instance, is nostalgic, its fables devised to feed the pastoral reveries of an upper class turned toward the past. The gothic re-assertion of *"sortilège et fantasmagorie,"* on the other hand, is sinister and disturbing, more like a nightmare than a dream; and its fables represent the hopes and fears of a group of intellectuals turned toward the future at a moment of revolutionary readjustment.

The Marquis de Sade in his essay on the "new novel" (as important for an understanding of the gothic as Diderot's *Éloge de Richardson* for an understanding of the sentimental) points out precisely what is at stake. Such books, he explains, are "the inevitable fruit of the revolutionary shocks felt by all of Europe. . . . For those who knew all the miseries with which scoundrels can oppress men, the novel became as hard to write as it was monotonous to read. . . . It was necessary to call hell to the rescue . . . and to find in the world of nightmare" images adequate to "the history of man in this Iron Age."

The key words are "nightmare" and "hell," revealing how consciously, on the one hand, some gothic writers turned to the night side of life, the irrational world of sleep, for themes and symbols appropriate to the terrors bred by the Age of Reason; and how, on the other hand, they saw their own role as Satanic, their kind of literature as a kind of half-playful black mass, an evocation of the Evil One, in whom, of course they were no longer prepared to confess believing. Gothicism is the Satanism of those to whom (officially at least) Satan has become a figure of speech. And yet the gothic writers insist upon using the traditional terminology for the diabolic, betraying a certain vestigial doubt (even perhaps hope) that there may be in the old legends a kind of truth.

Beside the good old word "hell," however, is placed the newer word "history," equally important to an understanding of the form; for behind the gothic lies a theory of history, a particular sense of the past. The tale of terror is a kind of historical novel which existed before the historical novel (the invention of Walter Scott) came into being. The Richardsonian novel of contemporary life had discovered the present for fiction, made time a medium in which characters moved. The social meanings of the Lovelace-Clarissa story assume a clear-cut conception of a differing Then and Now. Richardson claimed for his own province the Now, in which a servant could marry her employer's son; but by implication he has already defined a Then, in which that son would have taken such a girl whenever he desired her and on whatever terms his own whim prompted. This Then, the gothic novel claimed for its province, making of the past an essential subject of fiction for the first time. Shakespeare had, to be sure, written historical plays; but how ahistorical they, in fact, were: assuming a past indistinguishable from the present in all things (in costume, in speech, in moral attitudes) except for certain recorded events which happened to have happened then instead of now.

The gothic felt for the first time the *pastness* of the past; and though it did not, like the later novels of Manzoni and Scott, attempt with scholarly accuracy to document that difference, it tried to give some sense of it: the sense of something lapsed or outlived or irremediably changed. It is no accident that Horace Walpole was an "antiquary," a researcher into ancient modes and styles, who lived in a reconstructed "gothic" villa. The very adjective, which gave to both the home he designed and the fictional tradition he founded a name, implies a certain attitude toward the past. Originally "gothic" was a thoroughly pejorative word, applied not only to whatever belonged in fact to rude "medieval" times, i.e., any period before the sixteenth century, but also to any surviving mode of speech or behavior considered unworthy of enlightened modernity. Dueling, for instance, is referred to by one eighteenth-century critic as a "gothic custom," while another makes a fictional character condemn "husband" as a "gothic word." Rousseau, on the other hand, modestly describes his own novel, *La Nouvelle Héloïse,* as "gothic," meaning presumably that it possesses a certain antique simplicity and an unsophisticated style.

By and large, however, the writers of gothic novels looked on the "gothic" times with which they dealt (and by which, despite themselves, they were fascinated) as corrupt and detestable. Their vision of that past was bitterly critical, and they evoked the olden days not to sentimentalize but to condemn them. Most gothicists were not only avant-garde in their literary aspirations, but radical in their politics; they were, that is to say, anti-aristocratic, anti-Catholic, anti-nostalgic. They liked to think that if their work abounded in ghosts, omens, portents and signs, this was not because they themselves were superstitious, but because they were engaged in exposing "that superstition which debilitates the mind, that ignorance which propagates error, and that dread of invisible agency which makes inquiry criminal." Beneath the spectacular events of the tale of terror, the melodramatic psychology and theatrical horror, rings the cry, *"Écrasez l'infâme!"* The spirit of Voltaire broods over the haunted castle; and ghosts squeak eerily that they do not exist.

Yet the authors of gothic novels, followers of Voltaire though they were and exponents of the Enlightenment, were plagued by a hunger for the inexplicable, a need of the marvelous which they could neither confess nor escape. At a moment when everywhere rationalism had triumphed in theory and madness reigned in fact, they were especially baffled; and they ended by compounding the hypocrisy of their times with a corresponding hypocrisy of their own. In the name of optimism, they exploited melancholy; in the name of light, they paid tribute to darkness; in the name of history, they yielded themselves up to fancy.

Their attitude toward Catholicism is a case in point. Like most other classic forms of the novel, the gothic romance is Protestant in its ethos; indeed, it is the most blatantly anti-Catholic of all, projecting in its fables a consistent image of the Church as the Enemy; we have already noticed how standard and expected were the characters of the depraved monk, the suborned Inquisitor, the malicious abbess. Yet the gothic imagination feeds on what its principles abhor, the ritual and glitter, the politics and pageantry of the Roman Church. The ideal of celibacy and its abuses particularly intrigue the more prurient gothic fictionists, as do the mysteries of the confessional, where for ages—into the ear of God knows what lustful priest—was whispered "this secret sin, this untold tale," which they had made the subject of their art. Sixty years after *The Monk,* Nathaniel Hawthorne was still playing fast and loose with Catholicism, sending his Puritan protagonists into the very heart of Saint Peter's, into the confessional booth itself—only to withdraw them at the last possible moment, resolutely anti-Papist after all. The conversion of Hawthorne's own daughter to Catholicism and her entry into a convent mark a final consummation (achieved by history in despite of art) of the gothicists' long, absurd flirtation with the Church they presumably abhorred.

The contradictions between the liberal uses and demonic implications, the enlightened principles and reactionary nostalgia of the tale of terror by no means exhaust the ambiguities at its heart. A further conflict arises out of an attempt to solve the earlier ones by passing off the machinery of horror essential to the form as mere "play," "good theater," which demands not credence but the simplest suspension of adult disbelief. Far from satisfying the gothic writers, this device leaves them with the annoying sense that the kind of novel they produce presumably for high-minded ends is really no more than a lowbrow amusement, a literary vice (like the detective story and science fiction which are its heirs). Why, they are driven to ask themselves, do they indulge in the child's game of make-believe unless to titillate their own jaded sensations and those of their readers? But to *play* with horror, no matter what one's declared intent, is to pander to the lowest, darkest impulses of the mind.

Certain devices are built into the gothic from the start to help resolve its contradictions. There is, for instance, the convention of treating magic as science and thus reclaiming it for respectability in the Age of Reason; the magician Faust in his black robes becomes the scientist in his white coat (Dr. Frankenstein is a transitional figure on the way), and no good reader of newspapers cavils at him as improbable or outmoded. At first the sciences favored by the gothic romancers are those of the gothic past, astrology and alchemy; and such ancient symbolical dreams as the universal solvent and the elixir of life (in the works of Hawthorne, for instance, and those of E. T. A. Hoffmann) possess the imagination. Later, these are replaced or reinforced by the bourgeois pseudo-sciences of mesmerism, phrenology, ventrilocution (in the novels of Charles Brockden Brown and, once more, those of Hawthorne); and finally, in our own age, they are largely abandoned for popularized versions of modern physics.

Much more important in the early stages of the gothic was the convention of the "explained supernatural," invented first by Mrs. Radcliffe to assure her readers that nothing was really wrong with God's good world, though it might for a time seem so in the pages of her latest romance. Some anti-bourgeois, avant-garde gothicists found it convenient, too, to pretend that there were at last no ghosts, only wax images behind translucent black curtains; for they were, after all, as committed to an optimistic view of life by their rationalism as any lady entertainer of the bourgeoisie by her sentimental Christianity. The device of the explained supernatural is as useful for the reader as for the writer, enabling him to get his thrills and keep his self-respect; but it does more than that. It embodies in the very technique of fiction a view of the world which insists that though fear is real, its causes are delusive; that daylight reveals to us the essential goodness of a universe to which the shadows of night had given a false aspect of evil.

Like other self-protective devices of the gothic, the explained supernatural poses new problems as it solves old ones, leaving some readers at least with the sense of having been shamefully hoaxed, betrayed into responding with pity and terror to a mere bag of tricks. What is the point of horror that is not in some sense real? Only Hawthorne, of all writers who insist on casting a new light in their final pages on what they have all along presented in quite another, manages to leave us satisfied and unashamed; for he developed in his novels and tales a method of "alternative explanations" that permits us at the end of an action to throw back over it the interpretation that suits our temperament best. He gives us the choice of many readings: magical, mechanical, psychological; and even allows us not to make a choice at all, but like him to endure them all, to emerge from his story not with some assured insight into the causes of human depravity but only with a confirmed sense of the ambiguity of life.

Implicit in the gothic novel from the beginning is a final way of redeeming it that is precisely opposite in its implications to the device of the explained supernatural, a way of proving not that its terror is less true than it seems but more true. There *is* a place in men's lives where pictures do in fact bleed, ghosts gibber and shriek, maidens run forever through mysterious landscapes from nameless foes; that place is, of course, the world of dreams and of the repressed guilts and fears that motivate them. This world the dogmatic optimism and shallow psychology of the Age of Reason had denied; and yet this world it is the final, perhaps the essential, purpose of the gothic romance to assert.

The point was to find a means for expressing it; and that task was improbably entrusted to the gothic novel, whether its authors were aware of it or not. For that purpose they had to contrive a vocabulary of symbol and myth capable of bootlegging past the guardians of Reason perceptions of the irrationality of experience and life itself. The half-playful, half-pathological evocation of half-believed-in monsters remained for almost a hundred years the West's chief method for dealing with the night-time impulses of the psyche. What was essentially psychology and symbolism pretended, even sometimes to itself, to be horror pornography.

From the time of Richardson, the chief end of the novel had

been made clear: "to carry the torch to the back of the cave," to reveal the "hideous Moor" who lurks in its furthest reaches. The methods of Richardson are analytic, psychological; but the terms which occur to Diderot to explain them are melodramatic and symbolic—in short, "gothic." In *Clarissa,* the "cave" of the heart is concealed beneath the exterior actions of a girl and a man living ordinary lives in contemporary society; while the "hideous Moor" is no more than the sum total of the unconfessed, ambiguous motives prompting those actions, for which of course the actors give quite other, more laudable explanations. One can imagine, however, a kind of fiction in which the depths of the mind are represented in the text itself as a cave before whose mouth a bewildered girl stands paralyzed with fright; while the hideous Moor in fact leaps from its darkness, his black skin glistering, his white eyeballs bulging, his sinewy arms reached out to clasp and destroy. In such projective or symbolic fiction, character, setting, and incident alike are "true," not in their own right but as they symbolize in outward terms an inward reality.

In the history of the novel, the two modes, analytic and projective, have both flourished, the analytic developing through Flaubert and James to Virginia Woolf, Proust, and Joyce, the projective moving on through Poe and the Surrealists to a modern climax in Kafka. In many writers, however (in Melville for instance, and Dostoevski, in Dickens and Balzac and Faulkner), projective and analytic modes are mingled often confusedly; for such authors are the heirs of a confusion at the heart of the gothic about its own method and meaning. Precisely because the early practitioners of the tale of terror were only half aware of the symbolic nature of the genre, they did not know what kind of credence to ask for their protagonists—presenting them sometimes as fully motivated characters in the analytic sense, and at others, as mere projections of unconscious guilt or fear. Such an heir of the gothicists, for instance, as Melville was betrayed into giving to his symbolic Captain Ahab (who stands for "sultanic" hybris, i.e., for one aspect of the mind) a mind of his own; though the Parsee, who plays Satan to Ahab's Faust, is treated as a simple projection with an inner logic rather than a psychology.

II

Particularly in the tradition of the American novel, this confusion of modes and levels of credibility becomes a vexing problem; because of all the fiction of the West, our own is most deeply influenced by the gothic, is almost essentially a gothic one. In general, the European gothic reaches the level of important art only in poetry or drama, not in fiction; in America quite the opposite is the case.

Certainly the three novels granted by general consensus to be our greatest works are gothic in theme and atmosphere alike. It is not merely a question of certain trappings of terror: the delirious visions of Huck's father, the body dragged at midnight from the grave, the signs and portents of impending disaster discovered in howling dogs and slaughtered snakes, the ghostly visions through the fog of *Huckleberry Finn;* or the Spirit-Spout, the silent rising from the deep of the Great White Squid, the Saint Elmo's fire, the eerie Parsee who appears out of no place with his "tiger-like" crew, the baptism in pagan blood of *Moby Dick;* the Indian warlocks and Puritan witches, the yellow ruff and the memories of Anne Turner, the Black Man and his book, the letter A written in the heavens of *The Scarlet Letter.* Even more importantly, in each book, the Faustian bargain stands at the focus of action: Hester and Dimmesdale alike symbolically inscribe themselves as the Black Man's followers; Ahab, having entered into some unspeakable pact with Fedallah, strikes from hell's heart at the whale; Huck resolves to go to hell rather than restore a slave to its rightful owner. The Yankee skipper, the seduced woman, the motherless boy all play the role of Faust in our fiction, sometimes openly and in terror, sometimes secretly and as if it were a joke.

Not only in their major books, but elsewhere, too, our greatest writers sought out gothic themes: Melville most notably in *Pierre,* Hawthorne in *The Marble Faun,* Twain in *Tom Sawyer Detective* and *Pudd'nhead Wilson;* while the tale of terror in a thousand forms, as the story of slavery and black revolt, of Indian warfare, of urban violence, of quiet despair in the world of the freak and the invert and the maimed persists as a reigning genre among minor novelists, too. From Edgar Poe to Truman Capote, from Brockden Brown through George Lippard to Paul Bowles and Carson McCullers, from *The Monster* of Stephen Crane to *The Cannibal* of

John Hawkes, the images of alienation, flight, and abysmal fear possess our fiction. Until the gothic had been discovered, the serious American novel could not begin; and as long as that novel lasts, the gothic cannot die.

But why, one is driven to ask, *why* has the tale of terror so special an appeal to Americans? Surely its success must be derived in part from the failure of love in our fiction. Our novelists, deprived of the subject that sustained Stendhal or Constant, Flaubert or Proust, that seemed indeed to them *the* subject of the novel, turned to fables of loneliness and terror.

Moreover, in the United States, certain special guilts awaited projection in the gothic form. A dream of innocence had sent Europeans across the ocean to build a new society immune to the compounded evil of the past from which no one in Europe could ever feel himself free. But the slaughter of the Indians, who would not yield their lands to the carriers of utopia, and the abominations of the slave trade, in which the black man, rum, and money were inextricably entwined in a knot of guilt, provided new evidence that evil did not remain with the world that had been left behind.

How could one tell where the American dream ended and the Faustian nightmare began; they held in common the hope of breaking through all limits and restraints, of reaching a place of total freedom where one could with impunity deny the Fall, live as if innocence rather than guilt were the birthright of all men. In Huck's blithe assertion, "All right, I'll *go* to Hell," is betrayed a significant undermeaning of the Faustian *amor fati,* at least in its "boyish" American form: the secret belief that damnation is not all it is cracked up to be. In a strange way, the naturalized Faust legend becomes in the United States a way of denying hell in the act of seeming to accept it, of suggesting that it is merely a scary word, a bugaboo, a forbidding description of freedom itself! At any rate, Americans from the beginning responded passionately to the myth itself; even in the 1680's, before the invention of the main tradition of the novel, one Boston bookseller sold in the Colonies sixty-six copies of *The History of the Damnable Life and Deserved Death of Dr. John Faustus.* It was, needless to say, a record unapproached in those times by any other "light literature."

When the gothic novel appeared, then, it was greeted with great enthusiasm by Americans, who passed quite quickly from importing and reading its prototypes to attempting to emulate them. In this case, only ten years elapsed between the publication of the novels of Mrs. Radcliffe and Lewis and the first American gothic romances. Yet the gothic mode proved difficult to adapt to the demands of the American audience and the deeper meanings of American experience, for the generation of Jefferson was pledged to be done with ghosts and shadows, committed to live a life of yea-saying in a sunlit, neo-classical world. From the bourgeois ladies to the Deist intellectuals, the country was united in a disavowal of the "morbid" and the "nasty." No wonder the American pioneer in gothic fiction, despite the acclaim he won abroad, was driven first to abandon the gothic for the sentimental, then to give up novel writing completely.

If it had been only a matter of finding a reading public for the gothic, the situation would not have been really critical—only unprofitable; but there were other problems. The gothic, after all, had been invented to deal with the past and with history from a typically Protestant and enlightened point of view; but what could one do with the form in a country which, however Protestant and enlightened, had (certainly at the end of the eighteenth century!) neither a proper past nor a history? It was easy enough for the American writer to borrow certain elements, both of cast and setting, from the tale of terror; the Maiden in flight, for instance, was readily adaptable, and the hero-villain viable at least as a visual image—his burning eyes and furrowed brow transplanted themselves without difficulty. But what was to be done about the social status of such hero-villains? With what native classes or groups could they be identified? Traditionally aristocrats, monks, servants of the Inquisition, members of secret societies like the Illuminati, how could they be convincingly introduced on the American scene?

Similarly, it was not hard to provide the American equivalents of the moors, hills, and forests through which the bedeviled maidens of the gothic romances were accustomed to flee. But what of the haunted castle, the ruined abbey, the dungeons of the Inquisition? In America, such crumbling piles, architecturally and symbolically so satisfying to the eighteenth-century reader and writer, are more than a little improbable. Yet on them, not only the atmosphere, but an important part of the meaning of the tale of terror depended. An early American gothicist like the I. Mitchell who in 1811 published *The Asylum; or, Alonzo and Melissa* was able to imagine a gothic country house on Long Island; but such a structure in such a place remains not merely unconvincing but meaningless. The haunted castle of the European gothic is an apt symbol for a particular body of attitudes toward the past which was a chief concern of the genre. The counterpart of such a castle fifty miles from New York City has lost all point.

The problem of the gothic romance in this regard is analogous to that of the sentimental novel. Both had arisen out of a need of the bourgeoisie, fighting for cultural autonomy in a class society, to find archetypal characters and situations to embody their conflict with the older ruling classes. Just as the sentimental archetype had projected the struggle of the middle classes with established secular power, portrayed as a menace to their purity, so the gothic projected the struggle of those classes with ecclesiastical authority, portrayed as a threat to their freedom. In America, which possesses neither inherited aristocratic privilege nor an established Church, the anti-aristocratic impulse of the seduction theme is, as we have said, translated into feminism and anti-intellectualism; while the impatience with the past implicit in the gothic fable undergoes an even more complex metamorphosis. Charles Brockden Brown, single-handed and almost unsustained, solved the key problems of adaptation, and though by no means a popular success, determined, through his influence on Poe and Hawthorne, the future of the gothic novel in America.

If Brown deserved no other credit, he should be remembered at least as the inventor of the American writer, for he not only lived that role but turned it into a myth, later developed by almost everyone who wrote about his career. That he tried the impossible and that he failed; that he had disavowed his own art before his untimely death of tuberculosis at the age of thirty-nine; that he hardened from a wild disciple of the Enlightenment, a flagrant Godwinian ("Godwin came and all was light!") into a pious conservative; that he drew his inspiration from loneliness and male companionship, and that he ceased to be a creative writer when he married; that over his whole frantic, doomed career, the blight of melancholy presides. In a sense, Brown invented Edgar Allan Poe —all, that is to say, that the American writer came to seem to the mind of Europe and the sensibility of Romanticism—before Poe had ever written a line. Actually the latter poet was one year old when Brown died.

From the beginning, at any rate, it has been hard to describe Charles Brockden Brown without seeming to compose a poem on a symbolic subject. The portrait painter Sully, who saw him just before his death, has left the following account:

It was in the month of November,—our Indian summer,—when the air is full of smoke. Passing a window one day I was caught by the sight of a man, with remarkable physiognomy, writing at a table in a dark room. The sun shone directly upon his head. I shall never forget it. The dead leaves were falling then. It was Charles Brockden Brown.

If this seems less the product of observation than of Romantic fancy, it is no more fanciful than Brown's own description of himself to his dearest friend, Elihu Hubbard Smith, as "The child of passion and inconstancy, the slave of desires that cannot be justified . . ."; and it is considerably more restrained and faithful to fact than the account of his death, wracked by poverty and disease, imagined half a century later by his fellow Philadelphian and gothic heir, George Lippard. "The Heart Broken" is the title of Lippard's piece, by which he hoped, apparently, to do for Brown what Baudelaire was to do for Poe; but Lippard was unable to preserve the image of Brown as the victim of American philistinism after he had ceased to seem a figure of first literary importance.

To this very day, however, it is hard to rescue the man from the myth, to discover, for instance, even so simple a matter of record (one would assume) as what Brown looked like. According to one standard biography his hair was straight and "black as death," his complexion pale, sallow, and strange, accented by the "melancholy, broken-hearted look of his eyes." Another account describes him as "short and dumpy, with light eyes and hair inclining to be sandy, while the expression on his face reflected ill health rather than intellect. . . . Yet vividly in his countenance glowed the light of benevolence." Which is the truer portrait, the legendary delineation of what he hoped to seem or the more scholarly account with its overtone of debunking? Which is the *real* Charles Brockden Brown, the Brown who proved capable of bringing the American novel to birth?

The established facts of his brief career give some clues to the answer. He was born in Philadelphia in 1771 (the year in which Goethe published *Götz von Berlichingen*), and lived all his life in that city and in New York. He came from Quaker stock, which may have had some influence on his meditative habits, otherwise encouraged by his frail constitution and life-long sickliness. He is reported to have been a prodigy and to have received from the start a schooling worthy of his talents; but he was, despite the

praise that later came to his work, much of it from the best qualified sources, irremediably melancholy. Intellectual energy and
gloom complemented each other in his personality. Though he
never ceased proposing to himself the most ambitious cultural
schemes, he complained (or boasted—the tone is ambiguous) that
he was incapable not only of real happiness but even of the "lively
apprehension of misfortune."

What especially plagued him at the start was a conflict between
the commitment to a career in the law, into which his family had
urged him, and his own literary schemes, which he dreamed would
distinguish both him and his country. At the age of sixteen, for
example, he had already laid out plans for glorifying America (and
Charles Brockden Brown!) with three epics, on Columbus, Pizzaro,
and Cortez. New and radical ideas, derived ultimately from the
Encyclopedists and more directly from Godwin and Mary Wollstonecraft, tilted the balance against his proposed career as a lawyer; and put him into even sharper opposition to the society in
which he lived. To promulgate notions of social justice and to write
novels, to revolutionize American life and to achieve literary fame:
this double ambition he came to feel as a single impulse, not unlike
certain young radical writers in the United States of the 1930's.
The literary form which eminently suited both such political allegiances and such literary aspirations was at the moment he began
to write (the 1790's were almost gone) the "new novel," which is
to say, the gothic romance in its doctrinaire Godwinian form. "To
equal *Caleb Williams*" was the best Brown could hope for himself.

If there was a contradiction between the dream of a rational
Commonwealth and the hectic exploitation of horror in the gothic,
Brown did not feel it. His friend Smith, more consistent advocate
of the Enlightenment, might admonish him, "The man of Truth,
Charles, the pupil of Reason has no mysteries," but Brown could
turn with equanimity from the works of Diderot to *The Horrid
Mysteries* of the Marquis of Grosse. As a writer, he proposed both
to produce books with a "moral tendency" (enlightened, of
course) and to "ravish the souls" of his readers with "roaring passions." The essential human passion to which he hoped to appeal
in his examination of society, as well as by his exploration of terror, was curiosity: that curiosity of the sentimentalizing eighteenth
century, clues to which the Marquis de Sade was convinced he had
discovered in Richardson. "If you tell me," Brockden Brown once
wrote, "that you are one of those who would rather travel into the

mind of a ploughman than the interior of Africa, I confess myself of your way of thinking."

After publishing a dialogue on woman's rights called *Alcuin*— a preliminary concession to his doctrinal commitments—Brown plunged into a feverish bout of creative activity which saw the publication within two years (from September of 1798 to November of 1799) of his four best novels, *Wieland, Ormond, Arthur Mervyn* (Part I), and *Edgar Huntly;* and which left him with the uncompleted fragments of as many more. *Wieland,* which many readers value above all the rest, he completed within a month. This frantic outburst of energy seems to have been cued by two events, one internal, one external: first, his abandonment of the law and his decision to stake everything on his talent as a writer; and second, the death of his friend Elihu Hubbard Smith, who fell victim to yellow fever just as *Wieland* was coming off the press.

Brown had already lived through one epidemic in Philadelphia in 1793, but it was his second experience with the pestilence in the New York epidemic of 1798 that took possession of his imagination. Images of this disaster crept into the pages of *Ormond* and *Arthur Mervyn,* becoming for Brown symbols of all that is monstrous and inexplicable in life. Like Defoe before him and Manzoni and Camus afterward, he found in the plight of the city under a plague an archetypal representation of man's fate. For Brown, moreover, the general calamity was given added poignancy by the death of his friend, who, being a doctor, had not been able to flee its ravages. Despite the fact that he stayed with Smith throughout, actually falling ill himself though not critically, Brown apparently felt guilt as well as dismay at his friend's early death. He may even have suspected (who knows?) that he had infected Smith, carried the principle of infection which destroyed him.

It is possible that the character of Sarsefield, who appears first in *Ormond,* then in *Edgar Huntly,* with no explanation of the duplication, and who represents in each case the protagonist's closest friend, may play in the dreamlike plots of those two books the role of Smith. In *Ormond,* Sarsefield is slain by Turks, and is revenged in the best Achilles-Patroclus fashion by Ormond, who gallops from the field, five bloody heads of his opponents dangling from his saddle. In *Edgar Huntly,* the fantasy becomes even more ambiguously sinister, with Edgar shooting once at Sarsefield, Sarsefield once at him, though they are bound to each other by mutual love and the special bond between protector and protégé.

Brown's first four completed novels, combining as they do the appeals of the gothic and the sentimental, and written with a vigor unprecedented in American fiction, might have been expected to win a substantial audience for their author; but though they were critically well received, they didn't sell. The records show much praise, but no second printings. Partly in despair at not achieving popular success, partly out of a loss of faith in the radical principles which had been his motive force, Brown began to disengage himself from his commitment to fiction. As early as 1799, he had become the editor of a new magazine, and gradually the journalist, the man of letters took over from the poet, the mythopoeic writer. The process passed through two stages: first, a disavowal of the tale of terror, with its melancholy and pursuit of the outrageous; then a total rejection of the novel. The year 1800 saw the completion of the second part of *Arthur Mervyn* and the exhaustion of Brown's first spasm of creative energy. At this point he made a public pledge to abandon "the doleful tone and assume a cheery one," to substitute "moral causes and daily incidents in the place of the prodigious and the singular"—that is, to leave the gothic and take up the domestic sentimental.

But there had already been an undeclared shift in his attitudes between *Wieland* and *Ormond* on the one hand and *Edgar Huntly* and *Arthur Mervyn* on the other. The character of Carwin in *Wieland* (further developed in an unfinished work called *Carwin the Biloquist*) combines, in the style of Goethe, qualities of Don Juan and Faust. Carwin at one point declares to Clara, the suffering heroine of *Wieland* whom he stalks with Lovelace-like singlemindedness through the novel, "Even if I execute my purpose, what injury is done. Your prejudices will call it by that name, but it merits it not." He is the Richardsonian seducer, refusing even to grant that the dishonor which he threatens is real; all his formidable talents, even the mysterious gift of ventriloquism (which Brown calls "biloquism") are devoted to separating Clara from her true lover, maneuvering her into a position where she will have no protection against his assault.

Carwin, however, does not *look* like Don Juan: "His cheeks were pallid and lank, his eyes sunken, his forehead overshadowed by coarse, straggling hairs . . . his chin discoloured by a tetter. . . . And yet his forehead . . . his eyes lustrously black, and possessing, in the midst of haggardness, a radiance inexpressibly serene and potent . . . served to betoken a mind of the highest order. . . ." It is the face, of course, of the gothic hero-villain, of Mrs. Radcliffe's Schedoni or M. G. Lewis' Ambrosio: the ravaged aspect and hypnotic eye of one driven by a Faustian "thirst of knowledge," which was "augmented as it was supplied with gratification." "Curiosity," a Godwinian term, is the name Brown prefers for the Faustian lust to know; and Carwin even pleads in self-defense, after his activities have helped push Wieland, the brother of Clara, over the edge of religious insanity, that his "only crime was curiosity."

On this plea, Brown seems quite willing to acquit his hero-villain of any final guilt; for "curiosity" was his own reigning passion and Carwin is the projection of himself: insatiable seeker and man of many voices. "To excite and baffle curiosity," Brown once wrote about his own purpose as a novelist, "without shocking belief, is the end to be contemplated." In the end, Carwin is permitted to leave the pages of *Wieland* unpunished, though without any rewards—to take up once more his role of Wandering Jew, a tabooed figure incapable of finding rest or love. The true villain of the piece is not the doctrinaire revolutionary, the skeptical Carwin, but the religious fanatic, the believing Christian, Wieland, who ends by murdering his wife and threatening the life of his sister.

Through Wieland, Brown manages to project at once his distrust of religiosity and his obsession with the destructive aspects of the brother-sister relationship. *Geschwisterinzest* is everywhere in our literature (from William Hill Brown to Hawthorne, from Poe to William Faulkner) associated with death; only Brockden Brown, however, is willing to portray it as naked aggression. The tender alliance of brother and sister, so beloved of the Romantics, becomes in his works a brutal conflict; his brothers rob, cheat, and harry their sisters, yet are bound to them so closely that (as in *Edgar Huntly*) each feels his own life and death mysteriously linked to the fate of the other. At the climax of *Wieland,* Clara, threatened with death by her now maniacal brother, seems forced to choose between her own life and his. Brown relents a little, however, managing (through the intervention, this time beneficent, of Carwin) to contrive a resolution in which Wieland, taking up the knife Clara has dropped, stabs himself. The weapon is the sister's, but the hand which wields it the brother's own.

In *Ormond,* to whose sentimental aspects we have alluded earlier, the deed that is only threatened in the earlier book occurs. The Persecuted Maiden strikes back in self-defense; Constantia, Brown's second version of the Clarissa character he first sketched as Clara, kills her attacker, Ormond. Constantia, however, is not the sister of Ormond; and he is, therefore, permitted—the censor taken off guard—to approach her not in madness but in simple lust. Nevertheless, a point is made of Constantia's extraordinary resemblance to the actual sister of Ormond, as if to alert us to the fact that we are being presented with a case of attempted incest and fratricide once removed, though neither of these crimes, of course, could be proved in court.

There is, however, another significance to the murder of Ormond by Constantia, and this meaning Brown establishes with satisfactory clarity. By permitting his new Clarissa (however churchless he makes her out of respect to Godwin or Mary Wollstonecraft) to stab Lovelace-Faust, he symbolically disowns whatever in himself corresponds to the "curiosity," dedication to passion, and contempt for ordinary morality symbolized by the latter figure. After this, neither the Seducer nor the Faustian man is permitted to occupy the center of Brown's fiction; and even the love-combat of brother and sister is pushed to the periphery. He abandoned *Carwin the Biloquist* in mid-course and turned to *Arthur Mervyn* with its new kind of hero.

The yellow fever epidemic determines this unconfessed dividing line in his work: on the one hand, breaking up the group of New York intellectuals of which Smith had been the leading figure; and on the other hand, suggesting a new image for human misery, which cast doubt on man's ability to cope with it successfully. "The evils of pestilence by which this city has lately been afflicted will probably form an era in its history," Brown writes in the preface to *Arthur Mervyn*. "The schemes of reformation and improvement to which they will give birth, or, if no efforts of human wisdom can avail to avert the periodical calamity, the change in manners and population . . . will be, in the highest degree, memorable." The key phrase, of course, is "if no efforts of human wisdom can avail," reflecting the first shadow of the doubt which will eventually black out in the heart of Brown his youthful faith in "schemes of reformation and improvement."

From this point forward, at any rate, Brown's protagonists are dependent boys in search of motherly wives, rather than phallic aggressors in quest of virgins to sully. Victimized by cruel masters, images of the Bad Father, such protagonists wander about the world buffeted and misunderstood, until some understanding female, rich and mature and sexually experienced, provides them a haven. In them, "curiosity" still prevails, but it is no longer the fanatic passion of a Faust to know everything, only the nagging need of an ignorant boy to discover the adult secrets of the locked chamber, the forbidden room, the sealed chest. The Bluebeard myth replaces that of the Satanic bargain; and "curiosity" leads not to selling one's soul to the Devil, but to braving the taboo imposed by a cruel and irrational master. Having peeped through the key-hole at the forbidden mysteries, the curious boy is thenceforth persecuted, not for his guilt, but because of his knowledge of another's.

Finally, however, he is forgiven or rescued and adopted into marriage. So Arthur Mervyn is taken in hand by Mrs. Achsa Fielding ("she is six years older than you . . . she has been a wife and a mother already"), after a final nightmare in which he imagines the dead husband-father arising to shoot him through the heart. "My heart had nothing in it but reverence and admiration," he cries, protesting the innocence of his affection; but some guilt (some buried sense of the incest taboo broken) haunts him all the same. "Was she not the substitute of my lost mama? Would I not have clasped that beloved shade?"

The fact that Arthur Mervyn finally prefers the maternal widow, Mrs. Fielding, to Eliza Hadwin, a girl of fifteen, just the "age of delicate fervor, of inartificial love," infuriated Shelley, who, for all his admiration of Brown, could never forgive him for marrying off his hero to a sedate and wealthy Jewess instead of a poor "peasant-girl." There is, indeed, something symbolic in the choice at which Shelley, granted his point of view, had a right to rebel. For as surely as the death of Ormond had signified Brown's rejection of the demonic, his abandonment of Eliza represented his turning away from a Romantic commitment to art to an acceptance of the responsibilities of bourgeois life.

Clara Howard and *Jane Talbot,* those attempts at creating a sentimental novel without seduction, mark (as we have noticed) an effort at winning the great female audience; but more than that, they are further steps toward silence. In them, even the Bluebeard archetype has been surrendered and with it all desire to titillate curiosity or stir the darker passions. Brown is ready for the final disavowals, the surrender of his remaining liberal views ("From visionary schemes of Utopian systems of government and manners," his first biographer wrote, "Mr. Brown, like many others, became a sober recorder of things as they are") and of his career as an author ("Book-making, as you observe," Brown commented to his brother in 1800, "is the dullest of all trades, and the utmost any American can look for, in his native country, is to be reimbursed his unavoidable expenses").

With this brother and another, he went into the commission-merchant business; and, to set a final seal upon his capitulation, in 1804 married. But failure dogged his business efforts, compelling him at one point to sell "pots and pans over the counter," and tuberculosis brought suffering to his private life. What creative energies he had left, he devoted in these final years to *The Literary Magazine and American Register,* a periodical pledged always to keep in mind that "Christian piety is the highest excellence of human beings" and committed to printing material "free from sensuality and voluptuousness," which, "whether seconded or not by genius and knowledge, will . . . aim at the promotion of public and private virtues." Of his fiction, which came to seem to him as much an error as his early political activity, he wrote in 1803:

> I am far from wishing, however, that my reader should judge of my exertions by my former ones. I have written much, but take much blame to myself . . . and . . . no praise for any thing. I should enjoy a larger share of my own respect, at the present moment, if nothing had ever flowed from my pen, the production of which could be traced to me.

Myth (perhaps acted out by Brown himself as fact) has it that his last attempt at a tragedy he burned, keeping the ashes in a snuff-box on his desk until his death of tuberculosis in 1810.

I I I

Brown's achievement as a novelist is hard to assess. On only one thing do recent writers who discuss him agree, that his reputation is still moot and that it is somehow important for us now to come to terms with him. Brown remains in an odd way a living writer, because of the polemical tone which a discussion of his work necessarily still assumes. To define his rank and status involves an attempt at redefining the whole tradition of the American novel. Where he is placed depends upon, and in turn determines, the total shape of the literary hierarchy in which he is situated. A conventional "enlightened" attitude toward his work is expressed by

Parrington, who believed that though Brockden Brown was possessed of considerable technical skill, his example was "unfortunate" in so far as it represented an adaptation to American uses of the "blood-pudding school" of England. For Parrington, Brown's most admirable feature was his Godwinian politics, which led him to challenge the belief (held by "gentlemen who profited by social wrong") that injustice was "inherent in human nature"; and to insist that the source of that wrong "be sought in institutions rather than in the nature of man." The early American public, however —or at least so Parrington believed—ignored Brown's social theories in favor of his "gross Romanticism," so that his final influence was chiefly harmful.

More recently, George Snell has argued quite oppositely that although Brown is technically inept (Snell finds *Edgar Huntly*, for instance, "utterly incredible"), he was the founder of the "demonic, macabre, apocalyptic" school, which flourishes throughout the history of our literature and reaches a climax in Faulkner's *Absalom, Absalom!* It is certainly true, at any rate, that Cooper borrowed shamelessly from Brown; that Poe, who profited by his example, apparently esteemed him highly; and that Hawthorne not only placed him in his Hall of Fantasy (along with Homer, Shakespeare, Fielding, and Scott) but more generally observed that "no American writer enjoys a more classic reputation on this side of the water." Among his more eminent admirers who had gone on record by that time were Shelley (who ranked his gothic romances with Schiller's *Robbers* and Goethe's *Faust*), Keats, Hazlitt, and Godwin himself, who had returned Brown's admiration with enthusiasm on his own part. Certainly, it is utterly false to say, with a recent Parringtonian critic, that Brown is "liked only by the Professors who are taken in easily by the 'hollow men' of literature."

The problem is somewhat more complex than that. Those who find it difficult to take Brown seriously are, on the one hand, "realists" and, on the other, "formalists." Brown inevitably seems an incompetent and irrelevant writer to anyone who reads the history of our novel as a melodrama with a happy dénouement in which a virtuous but harried realistic tradition, after resisting the blandishments of fantasy, romance, and allegory, was recognized as the true heir to the patrimony. Brown, however, is an anti-realist in almost all respects, moving his irresolute and inconsistent protagonists through a time and space carelessly defined and bearing only a fitful, largely accidental resemblance to the facts of history or geography.

No more is Brown a formalist. He proves, indeed, especially disappointing to the critic who believes, or pretends to, that the novel is at best a skillful and sophisticated arrangement of words, a pleasantly intricate web of sensibility, which is judged good or bad in terms of how complex and various, though finally unified, is its abstract pattern. Brown is a writer careless to the point of shamelessness. He is likely to introduce a character into the action and let him wander about for pages before telling the reader where he comes from, what he is after, or even what his name is. Brown's resolutions are willful, hasty, often a little absurd, depending on broad coincidences hard to credit. Since he wrote four of his novels (plus the fragments of others) at the same time, he sometimes switches incidents or characters or simply names back and forth among them in a bewildering way. Often he will detach an episode for independent expansion or use elsewhere, leaving quite inexplicable vestiges in the original book. He is especially fond of attaching almost identical incidents to different characters in the same book, or of suggesting confusing resemblances between unrelated people without ever troubling to justify or exploit those deliberately planted resemblances.

The world through which his characters move is given local names (Philadelphia, for instance, or New York or Perth Amboy), but his scenes have little in common with the places they presumably represent. Only when he describes something monstrous and extraordinary like a city under a pestilence, do his descriptions approach the "reality" of the realists. Only when the real world itself, that is to say, comes to seem a symbolic nightmare does it accommodate itself to the sensibility and dreamlike style of Brown. That is why the set-piece of the anthologies, exempted from blame by his severest critics, is the description of the yellow fever epidemic in *Arthur Mervyn*.

For better or worse, then, Brown established in the American novel a tradition of dealing with the exaggerated and the grotesque, not as they are verifiable in any external landscape or sociological observation of manners and men, but as they correspond in quality to our deepest fears and guilts as projected in our dreams or lived through in "extreme situations." Realistic milieu and consistent character alike are dissolved in such projective fictions, giving way to the symbolic landscape and the symbolic action, which are the hallmarks of the mythopoeic novel. Simply to acknowledge the existence and importance of such a tradition is embarrassing to some readers; for it means, on the one hand, a questioning of the sufficiency of realism, which justifies art by correlating it with science; and on the other, it suggests a disturbing relationship between our highest art and such lowbrow forms of horror pornography as the detective story, the pulp thriller, and the Superman comic book, all of which are also heirs of the gothic.

To understand more specifically, however, the role of Brown in the definition of the American novel, it is necessary to look closely at *Edgar Huntly,* the most successful and characteristic of his gothic romances. *Wieland,* usually preferred to it, is convincing only here and there, being the victim of confusions that Brown could not assimilate (as he did those of *Edgar Huntly*) to the meanings of his story. The plot of the latter book can be summarized with relative simplicity, for a book of Brown. Searching for the murderer of Waldegrave, brother of his fiancée, Huntly discovers Clithero Edny who, beneath the elm under which Waldegrave had been murdered, comes at midnight to dig a pit in which he sits and sobs. Clithero is, it turns out, sleepwalking, tormented by various guilts which do *not* include that for the murder of which Huntly has suspected him. Rather he has (back in Ireland) killed the brother of his protector, Mrs. Lorimer, in a misguided effort at preserving her from that brother's irrational malice. Mrs. Lorimer, however, feels that she is doomed by her protégé's act, since she believes her own life tied by mystic bonds to that of her brother, who was her twin. In anguish over her delusion and the guilt which it imputes to him, Clithero goes mad and attempts to kill his mistress, thus helping to spare her the painful anticipation of her end.

Having told this improbable story to Huntly, Clithero disappears into the Pennsylvania wilderness, through which Huntly (prey of curiosity still) attempts to track him down, only to fall prey to somnambulism himself and to wake one day at the bottom of a pit. As Huntly at this stage of the novel has almost blurred into his alter ego Clithero, so the hole dug by the obsessed Irishman has mysteriously become the vast trap in which Huntly finds himself, confronted with a panther, a tomahawk mysteriously close to hand. The panther killed, then eaten raw and his flesh vomited up again (the whole episode comes to seem a rite of initiation which will prepare Huntly for later demands on his manhood), Huntly succeeds in finding a way out. He is led, however, through subterranean passages to a cave in which Indians hold captive a girl—strange to the main action of the story and quite unintegrated into what follows.

Huntly delivers her from the Indians, but is wounded in the struggle and left for dead; he is reborn again, however (surely he is the most often reborn of heroes), and begins a wilderness trek in which he shoots at and is shot at by unrecognized friends. Absolutely alone at last, with even those who love him turned unwitting foes, he nevertheless manages to return to civilization, where he learns that Waldegrave has been murdered by Indians, perhaps the very ones involved in his own adventure. This information when it comes seems utterly anticlimactic, irrelevant to what has become the real theme of the book. More important for the resolution is the further information that Sarsefield, Huntly's own benefactor, had been the first lover of Mrs. Lorimer. They are married, her husband having meanwhile died as well as her brother, who had hated Sarsefield; but Clithero reappears once more, frightening Mrs. Sarsefield into a miscarriage. He flees again and finally drowns himself to avoid being committed as insane, leaving Huntly free to complete their identification by wooing the daughter of Mrs. Lorimer, with whom Clithero had been in love.

It is a charmingly, a maddeningly disorganized book, not so much written as dreamed, but it convinces the reader, once he has been caught up in the fable, of its most utter improbabilities; for its magic is not the hocus-pocus of make-believe, but the irrational reality of the id. "The miracles of poetry, the transitions of enchantment," Edgar Huntly boasts, "are beggarly and mean compared with those I had experienced. Passage into new forms, overleaping the bars of time and space, reversal of the laws of inanimate and intelligent existence had been mine to perform and witness." Yet all these "perils and wonders" Brown has managed to present without invoking specifically supernatural agencies; not a breach of natural law, justifiable in terms of necromancy or sorcery, but only human madness and especially somnambulism, diseases explicable by medical science, lie at the root of the "marvelous" in *Edgar Huntly*.

Brown's novel is an initiation story, the account of a young man who begins by looking for guilt in others and ends finding it in himself; who starts out in search of answers but is finally satisfied with having defined a deeper riddle than those he attempted to solve. "What light has burst upon my knowledge of myself and mankind . . . ," Edgar Huntly cries. "How . . . enormous the transition from uncertainty to knowledge. . . ." But what has he learned really at the close of this odd murder mystery? That the Indians killed his friend is a piece of information which does not thrill the reader and could not have stirred him to so ecstatic a response. It is more general wisdom that Huntly acquires, discovering that "the crime originated in those limitations which nature has imposed on human faculties." This applies not only to the crime of Clithero of which it is specifically said; it is applicable to all human evil. "How little cognizance have men over the actions and motives of each other. How total is our blindness in regard to our own performances." Any man may wake to find himself at the bottom of a pit. *We are all sleepwalkers!*

But if we walk in our sleep, we also run in our dreams. Life is a nightmare through which we pursue or are pursued in a wilderness where the unexpected and the absurd, the irrelevance of what comes before to what comes after are the basic facts of existence. In *Edgar Huntly,* for instance, the boundaries between person and person are abrogated; people are always turning into each other. Clithero raises his hand to kill Mrs. Lorimer and discovers he is really assaulting his beloved, Clarice. Huntly comes upon a total stranger, a sleepwalker, only to find that he is a sleepwalker, too, and to end under the protection of the same foster-mother, engaged to the same sister-bride.

In this world of transformation, not only do unlikes turn into likes, but things themselves become their own opposites. The best motives lead to the worst ends: attempting to protect Mrs. Lorimer, Clithero kills her brother, almost kills her. The dead prove to be alive; Sarsefield, protector of Huntly, and Wiatte, brother of Mrs. Lorimer, "start to life at the same moment"; while Huntly, as we have seen, is himself apparently dead twice, rises twice to life. Friends become enemies, the protector the destroyer; Sarsefield almost kills Edgar even as Edgar tries to kill him. Through such an unstable world one must flee continually from foes known and unknown: from the lunatic and the brother inexplicably dedicated to evil, from the panther and the Indian and the unwittingly hostile friend—finally, from the principle of destruction in the very self. The image of flight with which the gothic began is in *Edgar Huntly* raised to its highest power, revealed as the image of life itself.

Brown, however, seems to have thought of *Edgar Huntly* as performing in the first instance a specifically American task. In a prefatory note, he speaks not only of his resolve to employ for the ends of wonder pathology rather than black magic, "to exhibit a series of adventures . . . connected with one of the most common and wonderful diseases of the human frame," but also of his desire to naturalize gothic terror by presenting it in terms of an action "growing out of the condition of our country." "New springs of action," he insists, "and new motives to curiosity should operate . . . ," since the institutions of our society "differ essentially from Europe." There is a little chauvinism in his plea, a little of the provincial's eagerness to strike a bold cultural pose; but there is also a sense of how unviable (as we have already observed) are the myths and meanings of the European gothic romance in a classless, historyless country. Had some early writer as self-consciously considered the problem of seduction in our literature, the role of love in American fiction might have been far different.

"One merit the writer may at least claim," Brown continues in the preface to *Edgar Huntly,* "that of calling forth the passions and engaging the sympathy of the reader, by means hitherto unemployed by preceding authors. Puerile superstition, and exploded manners; Gothic castles and chimeras, are the materials usually employed for this end. The incidents of Indian hostility,* and the perils of the western wilderness are far more suitable; and, for a native of America to overlook these, would admit of no apology." There is something so natural, so inevitable about Brown's proposed substitutions of American for European symbols that it is hard to appreciate, after the fact, how revolutionary a leap of the imagination his project demanded. The very success of his adaptive devices makes it hard to appreciate them yet testifies to how deeply they responded to our imaginative and mythic needs.

For the corrupt Inquisitor and the lustful nobleman, he has

---

* It is worth noting at this date when the Indian character is making such a spectacular comeback in serious fiction (in such books as Ken Kesey's *One Flew over the Cuckoo's Nest,* for instance) that the archetypal colored man of the American imagination is the redskin. Mythologically speaking, the Negro is a late comer to our literature, who has had to be adapted to the already existing image of the original Noble Savage. Our greatest Negro characters, including Nigger Jim, are, at their most moving moments, red men in blackface.

substituted the Indian, who broods over the perils of Brown's fictional world in an absolute dumbness that intensifies his terror. Brown's aboriginal shadows do not even speak. They merely threaten by their very presence, their "gigantic forms," "huge limbs," and "fantastic ornaments" representing visually the threat they embody. "I never looked upon or called up the image of a savage," Edgar Huntly says, "without shuddering." There is some sense in Brown of the historic "Indian problem," of the appropriation of their lands by white colonists and their futile dreams of revenge; but "Queen Mab," the spokesman for their cause, though prepared for at some length, does not finally appear in the book. It is not the Indian as social victim that appeals to Brown's imagination, but the Indian as projection of natural evil and the id; his red men are therefore treated essentially as animals, living extensions of the threat of the wilderness, like the panthers with whom they are associated.

For the haunted castle and the dungeon, Brown substitutes the haunted forest (in which nothing is what it seems) and the cave, the natural pit or abyss from which man struggles against great odds to emerge. These are ancient, almost instinctive symbols, the *selva oscura* going back to Dante and beyond, while the cave as a metaphor for the mysteries of the human heart is perhaps as old as literature itself. Brown tries quite consciously to identify the pit in which Edgar Huntly awakes with the terrible womb-tomb dungeons of Mrs. Radcliffe and Monk Lewis. "Methought I was the victim," Huntly says at the moment he becomes aware of where he is, "of some tyrant who had thrust me into a dungeon."

It should be noticed that the shift from the ruined castle of the European prototypes to the forest and cave of Brown involves a shift not just in the manner of saying what the author is after. *The change of myth involves a profound change of meaning.* In the American gothic, that is to say, the heathen, unredeemed wilderness and not the decaying monuments of a dying class, nature and not society becomes the symbol of evil. Similarly not the aristocrat but the Indian, not the dandified courtier but the savage colored man is postulated as the embodiment of villainy. Our novel of terror, that is to say (even before its founder has consciously shifted his political allegiances), is well on the way to becoming a Calvinist exposé of natural human corruption rather than an enlightened attack on a debased ruling class or entrenched superstition. The European gothic identified blackness with the super-ego and was therefore revolutionary in its implications; the American gothic (at least as it followed the example of Brown) identified evil with the id and was therefore conservative at its deepest level of implication, whatever the intent of its authors.

In so far, then, as our response to these natural symbols is determined by the native gothic tradition, we are conditioned to regard them, and the life of the unconscious for which they stand, as destructive. There is, however, a counter-tradition, Rousseauistic perhaps in its origins, for which forest, cave, and savage, Nature itself, and the instinctive aspects of the psyche they represent are read as beneficent, taken to symbolize a principle of salvation. The dialogue between these two views has continued, basically unresolved, in American life and art until our own time. But it could not even begin until the attitudes of Rousseau had been translated into an American language of myth and symbol, just as the attitudes of the gothic were so translated by Brown. This second great act of translation was achieved in James Fenimore Cooper's naturalization of the historical romance, to an examination of which we must turn next.

7

JAMES FENIMORE COOPER

AND

THE HISTORICAL ROMANCE

THE HISTORICAL ROMANCE shares with the gothic a concern with the past and desire to restore to prose fiction "the improbable and marvelous," which the sentimental novel of contemporary life had disavowed. It can be argued, as a matter of fact, that the historical romance is nothing more than a development—more masculine, more "scientific," and more genteel—of the middle-brow or Radcliffean branch of the tale of terror. One gothic sub-tradition, that is to say, is assumed into black Romanticism (which culminates in the *Fleurs du mal*), the other into white (which reaches a climax with Wordsworth's *Prelude*).

Like black or anti-bourgeois Romanticism, the white or philistine variety is based on a belief in the superiority of feeling to to intellect, the heart to the head; though for it, the heart is carefully distinguished from the viscera or the genitals, whose existence is scarcely admitted at all. The white Romantic is as concerned as his more melancholy opposite number with the picturesque and the exotic, with whatever is different from everyday middle-class life; and like him, he seeks in ballad material, fairy tales, and folk epic a source of strength not readily available to the sophisticated writer in a complex society. For the white Romantic, however, the primitive remains something clean and heroic, immune to the darkness and the demonic; Homer not *Ossian* is his model, and he identifies the Homeric with the cheerful and hopeful note required in his own work. To him melancholy is treason, the true faith an acceptance of the universe, which he confuses a little with the bourgeois culture of his own time. If he has any reservations about the world he lives in, they lead him toward nostalgia rather than rebellion.

White Romanticism is, then, closely related to the genteel Sentimentalism we have already had occasion to notice. Both, certainly, have a peculiar affinity for the middle-class, Anglo-Saxon mind, and both reject tragedy and sexual passion. The historical romance is, therefore, not merely a "male" counterpart to the Richardsonian ladies' novel, it is also a predestined best-seller; and, indeed, its most eminent producers were, like the "female scribblers" with whom they competed, merchant-authors, no less sensitive to the demands of the market-place than to those of art. For their mass audience, these entrepreneurs of fiction preserved such popular aspects of the gothic romance as the harried heroine and the motif of flight, sensing that Europe was not yet ready (if it ever would be) to let the Persecuted Maiden come to rest. In Scott, not only does she run still but the hero runs, too: side by side with his beloved, or toward her, or away—it scarcely matters, so long as they are both in motion. Indeed, one of Scott's favorite names for the novelist is the "master of motion."

Flight in the historical novel is, however, no longer archetypal in its implications. Hero and heroine flee not projections of their feared inner selves but real enemies, genuine conspiracies, external dangers. Action itself becomes the end, the evasion of ennui sought through a constant change of tempo and place. Though certain landscapes of the white Romantic fictionists come to have symbolic overtones, they are chiefly prized as examples of hitherto unexploited settings, glimpses of the unknown. Vicarious tourism draws the reader on, as he pursues the breathless hero to the mountain fastnesses of Scotland or the shores of Lake Otsego, to which in a little while he will come in person, guidebook in hand. The historical Romance (and its companion form, the Romantic narrative poem as practiced by Byron) represents the sight-seeing of the middle classes before cheap and speedy transportation had made it possible for them to do it in the flesh. The devotees of the genre are, unlike Brockden Brown's ideal reader, more interested in penetrating the interior of Africa than that of a ploughman's mind. It is precisely Africa they want, mapped, documented, and in detail; and it is Africa they get.

The Cook's tour of the historical romance extends, moreover, not only through space but time. Even as such fiction discovers

geography for the middlebrow imagination, it discovers history—
real history as distinguished from legend or myth. The gothicists
had plunged already into the "dark backward and abysm of time,"
but the haunted castle was a work of the imagination, not archae-
ology, and its inhabitants truer to the memories of nightmare than
to the findings of anthropology. The writers of the historical
romance, however, were pledged "to represent, by means of an
invented action, the state of mankind in a past, historic epoch"
(the definition is Manzoni's); and they felt more and more the
need to shore up their vision of how life had been at a certain moment with documents, statistics, and quotations out of the record.
That is why the novels of both Manzoni and Scott are eked out
with appendices that contain the raw fruits of their research, testi-
monies to their skill as historians and to the 'truth" which underlies
their fictions.

It is a thoroughly absurd idea, the notion that the truth of a
work of art is capable of documentary proof; and it becomes eventually an excuse for throwing overboard the elementary principles
of inner consistency, psychological conviction, and faithfulness to
the quality of experience, upon which the authority of a novel
really depends. Yet it was Scott himself who set all the West on
this false scent, being, for all his Romantic commitments, enough
the bourgeois of his time to believe in "positive science" and "positive truth." If we read him still, it is because he created a myth of
the past which cannot (whether we respond to it still with enthusiasm or not) ever die; but he prided himself on being the exponent
of a science of the past, naively convinced that it was his understanding of an earlier epoch that was immortal.

The myth of the past of which Scott is the master builder is
quite different from that created by the tale of terror, for the latter
is sentimentally radical, the former nostalgically conservative. The
young Charles Brockden Brown takes off from Diderot and the
assumptions of the Age of Reason, the middle-aged Sir Walter
Scott leads into the Oxford Movement and the revival of Catholicism. Cardinal Newman thought so, at least, observing that Scott
had served "by his words, in prose and verse, to prepare men for
some closer and more practical approximation to Catholic truth."
It would have surprised Scott (certainly a good Protestant in his
own eyes) to realize that his glorification of the past, his flirtation
with medievalism, his celebration of a glamour which had passed
away—commercially viable attitudes, all of them—could develop

into ideological forces leading to dramatic apostasies and strange conversions. He seemed sometimes merely to play at his own conservatism, acting the Jacobite much as Fenimore Cooper did the Tory—in part, because he was sure nothing could really come of it; and he found the safest of thrills in pledging allegiance to a cause securely lost! The historical romance is by definition not serious; indeed, the unconscious longing of the gothic romancers for the past they consciously vilify is a more genuine tribute than the *Ivanhoe* kind of pageant celebration.

Scott would not, of course, have wanted to leave Abbotsford for a medieval castle or a Highland hide-away, any more than Cooper would have wanted to abandon his Westchester County home or his Paris hotel for a wigwam; they felt free to create fantasies of flight from civilized comfort to primitive simplicity because they were sure that no one would believe them any more than they believed themselves. That is one advantage of being a businessman writing for other businessmen and their wives. They did not, however, defend their falsifications of the past in such frank terms; Cooper, for instance, was accustomed to present his own versions of the *beau idéal* of frontier life as if they were history; and only when driven to the wall would he admit the legendary quality (he preferred to think of it as "idealization") of his books. The supermyth of the theoretically anti-mythic historical romance is that its myth is History.

The early historical romance represents, in general, the tribute that philistinism pays to the instinctive, the civilized to the "natural," the moderate to the outrageous; for the past which it celebrates is characterized not only by its distance in time but by its presumable freedom from restraint and prudence, its absurd commitment to honor and courage. The "heroism" of the heroic age celebrated by the historical romances turns out to mean nothing more than the sum total of its differences from settled bourgeois life in the second and third decades of the nineteenth century.

Rob Roy or Natty Bumppo, Robin Hood or Chingachgook project the bourgeois's own slight margin of resentment against the safe, commercial way of life he has desired, and for which, indeed, he would fight. The white Romantic's outlaw or Indian is neither a demonic nor a disturbing figure by the time he has been naturalized in popular literature, though his prototype, appearing on the outskirts of the city, would have been hunted down by posse or police. Such tame Outsiders represent the impulsive and the irrational only as a passing temptation (appealing chiefly to unsettled youth) not as a profound threat; and when the historical romancer follows his creations into the wildwood, everyone knows that he is only kidding; that he is, in fact, sitting in a warm, well-furnished study, worrying—between bouts of composition—about his copyrights or income tax.

The Faust of the gothicists can find no place in such anti-demonic fables, with their reluctance to face the ambiguous or the problematic. Robin Hood or Daniel Boone move into the mythic center; the unsophisticated rebel-victim or half-civilized refugee from society. The historical romance permits no hero-villains. The hero is the man who receives the rewards (comes into the inheritance, marries the girl he loves, wins the approval of the reader); and the man who receives the rewards is the hero—life is as simple as that. The villain, conversely, is the one who is baffled and exposed, frustrated in his schemes and revealed as devoid of honor, finally rejected by the reader. He may even be a seducer, if his actual crime is delicately enough suggested, and if his victim is a lower-class girl. Even Scott, his reputation already established, was forced to expurgate an upper-class seduction from *St. Ronan's Well.*

The essential fable of the historical romance (more stereotype, perhaps, then archetype) ritually assures its readers of the triumph of good over evil—and to make this point with sufficient clarity, there can be no confusion between virtue and vice. Initially confused about his own ambitions or the true identity and character of those who surround him, often himself maligned and misrepresented, the hero is forced to flee—usually into the midst of some famous historic conflict just then conveniently approaching its climax. The heroine meanwhile has been abducted or is off on some private evasion of her own, for reasons only revealed in the final pages. The two are kept apart as long as possible, but are finally joined by the intervention of either some noble figure out of history or some notorious outlaw fresh from the greenwood (if possible, of both). By the same agency, their problems are resolved, their enemies discomfited, all confusions cleared up. The good is revealed as good—and triumphant; the evil as evil—and defeated. There is no suggestion that good and evil may be bound to each other by any link but chance, or that the confusions of life may be rooted in moral ambiguity rather than in temporary ignorance or deliberate deceit.

The historical novelists provide many satisfactions and delights:

comedy and intrigue, adventure and conflict and suspense. At their best, they are masters of pace, compelling the reader's breathless commitment to the unfolding of an action, and masters of illusion, convincing the reader that it terribly matters whether a ninny of a boy and a pale shadow of a girl end up in each other's arms. They are skilled at the evocation of a scene, especially in a natural setting, and at transition from scene to scene; they can even make plausible the development of less complicated varieties of hatred and love. But they are powerless to suggest the complexities of human motivation, the discrepancy between will and action, the immense possibilities of self-deceit, the "mystery of iniquity." The novel moved toward the nineteenth century as the potential heir to the tragic view of life, with which the stage seemed no longer able to come to terms; but the historical romance refused to fulfill the obligation that possibility imposed; it had no means for confessing that the tragic is real.

Twice in the history of the English novel, tragic prototypes had appeared, and twice they had been rejected, before the second decade of the nineteenth century was over. The example of *Clarissa* proved viable only on the continent; in England itself, it was, as we have seen, debased and bowdlerized by the genteel female novelists, who, with uncanny precision, initiated everything in it that was false or readily falsified. The gothic strain, which in America had fed the fancy of C. B. Brown and was to inspire Poe, and which in Germany had become an essential ingredient of the First Part of *Faust*, progressed in England no further than the extravagances of *The Monk*. The tragic elements of the Faustian theme, implicit from the first, remained undeveloped or travestied, until they were utterly rejected by the genteel male novelists who founded the historical romance. These founding fathers turned back, not inappropriately, to the example of Fielding, who had at the very start of the bourgeois novel provided (first in *Joseph Andrews*, then more spectacularly in *Tom Jones*) an anti-tragic alternative to Richardsonianism.

Fielding's example cues first of all a literature of masculine protest, an attempt to rescue prose fiction from the bourgeois ladies, who were in fact Richardson's chief, though by no means only, readers. For the heroine, Fielding proposed to substitute the hero; for the boudoir, the out-of-doors; for an obsessive concern with seduction and marriage, a more varied interest in social relations of all kinds; for what he took to be Richardson's hypocritical prurience, an easy tolerance of promiscuity and a general candor in dealing with sex. Fielding, however, went further than this, identifying as feminine—and therefore to be avoided—not only conventional Christian piety, but sensibility itself, and, indeed, any analytic concern with the "heart." The fear of not seeming manly enough haunts him everywhere, inhibiting reflection and delicacy and subtlety alike; and leading to that exaggerated heartiness, bluffness, and downright crudity of manner, required in a society where the male has continually to prove that he is one of the boys.

The conventional womanly tearfulness of the sentimental novel Fielding did not clearly distinguish from its underlying tragic view of existence, rejecting both in favor of a presumably more masculine comic view of life. His comedy depends upon a fundamental assumption that goodheartedness—a quality apparently to be found almost universally in personable, wild young men—will prove a sufficient defense against malice and misfortune; and that there is a principle of simple justice at work in the world. "Comic epic" is the term Fielding himself preferred for his work; and by "epic" he apparently intended to suggest both the rich, rolling expansiveness of his fictional world, and his narrative method, which (allowing for auctorical asides) aims rather at spinning a yarn than analyzing motives. Fielding's method is in fact more dramatic than epic, as befits one who began as a dramatist, and Shakespeare is his model rather than Homer; though his, it must be understood, was a far different "Shakespeare" from the one we have inherited from the later Romantics.

Through the later eighteenth and earlier nineteenth centuries, the illusion of the pseudo-Shakespearean novel lured on writers and critics alike, the name of Shakespeare being rather promiscuously bestowed on novelists of varying abilities and types. With the coming of Scott, however, the title was bestowed, as it were, finally; and the other contenders retired from the field. But what did the title *mean*? There were, to be sure, certain attributes of Shakespearean drama directly translated into the novel of masculine protest: the sense of swarming life, for instance, and the broad social range of the dramatis personae, with characters high and low carefully distinguished by levels of speech; and in these respects Scott was Shakespearean above all the rest. But essentially the word "Shakespeare" was used as an honorific to make popular writers seem of more than current interest, to redeem the best-seller for literature. It described especially the writer who was "healthy," which is to say, unaware of or unwilling to admit the importance of the problematical and the demonic.

Broad bawdry, turbulent action, horseplay and honest male sentiment—these come to be the hallmarks of pseudo-Shakespearean art. That these characteristics inadequately represent the Shakespeare we think we read is beside the point; they are the essential characteristics of the Anglo-Saxon, male middlebrow—and Shakespeare is the one artist about whom he considers it manly to have no doubts.

The pseudo-Shakespearean novel is, however, not merely middlebrow; it is also theatrical. An age which, for a while, had to content itself with reading plays, was tempted into writing fiction as if it were stage drama for closet reading, into shifting the center of interest from character to plot, from analysis to action. The limitations of inwardness imposed by the conventions of the stage, against which the greatest dramatists have always struggled, were welcomed by the exponents of anti-sensibility as a principle of the novel. Those larger-than-life gestures, so necessary in the theater, where the distance between spectator and actor cannot be varied or controlled, were transplanted into prose fiction. More specifically, New Comedy in its late domestic, sentimental form became the model for the structure of the novel. The rigid, theatrical plot, with its clearly marked reversals and recognitions, imposed on prose narrative its mechanical patterns; the revelation (of true parentage, of innocence or guilt, of concealed identity) with its attendant moment of surprise and relaxed tension, came to be thought of as the point of the novel—which had, at this point, utterly forgotten its torch-carrying function.

But the New-Comic love affair replaced the love-combat between seducer and virgin, hero-villain and terrified fugitive. Henceforward love in middle-class fiction would mean almost exclusively the adventure of a featureless juvenile and ingenue, separated by purely external circumstances and united at the close to no one's real surprise; and from Scott through Dickens, even the most serious British novelists found themselves absurdly committed to investing scores of pages, thousands of words in a theme which might have little to do with their essential plots or their own views of life. This tribute paid, however, they were granted a surprising degree of freedom in the remainder of their books, providing always that nothing elsewhere cancelled out the possibility of the final embrace or cast doubt on its importance in the eternal scheme of things.

The pseudo-Shakespearean novel had from the first inhibited inwardness and tragedy; but at the moment that it was bred with the Romantic myth of the past to produce the historical romance, it was further expurgated. Gentility had spread insidiously from the female audience to the male, forbidding, on the one hand, the candor and sexual horseplay of Fielding, and, on the other, the horror-pornography of the tale of terror. The historical romance is the "cleanest" of all sub-genres of the novel thus far, the creation of a self-conscious attempt to redeem fiction at once for respectability and masculinity. The acclaim which greeted Scott is surely due in part to a sense in the bourgeois community that the novel in his hands at long last had become fully acceptable, not merely "pure" but patriotic, too. Opening Scott's last volume, one could look forward to communing with a "healthy" soul engaged in an examination of the historic past which had helped determine contemporary society, and finding in it heroic and eccentric types able to make one glad to be alive.

I I

Though attempts to write fiction based on historic events and involving historic characters had been made well before the beginning of the nineteenth century, the historical romance as we have defined it is the invention of one man, Sir Walter Scott; and the genre did not exist until the appearance of his *Waverley* in 1814. Before he became a novelist, Scott had collaborated in the publication of a collection of Border ballads, *The Minstrelsy of the Scottish Border,* and had written poems of his own, derived in theme and manner from those ballads. Some of them were included in the *Minstrelsy* itself; and it is hard, indeed, to tell where his editorial reconstructions end and his own pieces begin. Scott started his career as a writer by adapting, almost counterfeiting the folk literature of an earlier age—out of motives both antiquarian and patriotic, motives which persist into his later fiction and help give it its typical form.

Cues for such a nationalist, historical approach to literature, Scott had found earlier in the work of German poets like Bürger, whose "Lenore" he had translated, and Goethe, whose *Götz von Berlichingen* he had also put into English. In German *Sturm und Drang,* he had come upon the exploitation of terror as well as the mystique of the folk and the quest for a native tradition; and to such terror he had pledged himself as a young man, decorating his room with a skull and striking all the proper gothic poses. His interest in German culture had led to a meeting with "Monk" Lewis, to whose *Tales of Wonder* he contributed some of his early verse. The titles of the two anthologies to which the young Scott entrusted his first work mark the double inspiration with which he began: the evocation of wonder and the revival of minstrelsy. Had he become a novelist at this stage, he might have been a full-blown gothic romancer.

Indeed, he appends to *Waverley* two fragmentary ventures into prose fiction, the first of which is the Walpoleian *Thomas the Rhymer,* and the second *The Lord of Ennerdale,* a novel in the manner of Mrs. Radcliffe. In the General Preface to the *Waverley Novels,* Scott describes his first attempt: "I had nourished the ambitious desire of composing a tale of chivalry, which was to be in the style of the Castle of Otranto, with plenty of Border characters, and supernatural incident." But that "ambitious desire" had remained unfulfilled for fifteen years; and the book, which might have been published in the same year as *Edgar Huntly,* managed to see the light as a "curious" fragment, representing outlived aspirations, thirteen years after Brockden Brown had given up fiction and four years after his death. It must be remembered that Scott began as a middle-aged novelist; born in the same year as Brown, he did not publish his first romance until he was forty-three!

Not only Scott but the world he lived in had lost its youthful fire in the years between the French Revolution and the rise and fall of Napoleon; both he and it were ready for the voice of moderation, weary of shrillness and horror. Yet Scott never surrendered completely his own taste for the gothic; he acted as the literary sponsor of Maturin, perhaps the most talented of all purely gothic authors in England, and defended *Frankenstein* against other bourgeois critics. In only two of his novels does Scott manage to dispense with the supernatural, disavowing the use of all portents, ghosts, witches, and prophecies; and so self-conscious is he about the gesture, that he goes out of his way to boast of eschewing "the mystic, and the magical." "The mystic, and the magical" an audience brought up on the tale of terror demanded, and Scott strove to please, without permitting the gothic to dominate his plots or cast its dismal pall over the "healthy" vigor of which he was proud.

The trappings of the gothic seemed to him part of the popular author's stock in trade; the meanings of the gothic were alien to him.

Only once did Scott produce a book of sheer terror, an essentially gothic tale in which love and death are blended to produce the authentic sadist shudder; but this novel was rather the creation of his illness than of his will. In such pain from a gallstone attack that he could not even write, Scott dictated *The Bride of Lammermoor,* a novel of which he later remarked that "he did not recollect a single incident, character or conversation." After he had, with some trepidation, read it through, he found it "monstrous, gross and grotesque," but (fortunately, he thought) comical, too. "Still the worst of it," he commented, "made me laugh, and I trusted the good-natured public would not be less indulgent." To take horror too seriously, he felt, was to confuse life with delirium, to become like Coleridge too murky and opaque, or like C. B. Brown unhealthy. Scott did, indeed, believe Brown to have possessed "wonderful powers," but to have wasted them on the gothic mode, which was old-fashioned and not even "wholesome."

Scott's fundamental conception of the function of the novel was too modest to sustain the Faustian pose; his one "hell-fired" book he, quite unlike Hawthorne, regarded not as a triumph but as a mistake. That the novel might "instruct the youthful mind" or even "sometimes awaken the better feelings and sympathies," he was prepared to grant; but basically he thought fiction "a mere elegance, a luxury contrived for the amusement of polished life." The novelist was for him not prophet or oracle or teacher, only an elegant entertainer, a puppet master; and the outcome of the plots he contrived had nothing finally to do with the values by which men lived: "whether the Devil flies away with Punch, or Punch strangles the Devil, forms no real argument as to the comparative power of either one or the other, but only indicates the especial pleasure of the master of motion."

The real point is that Scott was an amateur, a novelist not because this seemed an important vocation, but because authorship was one of the things that befell him in a busy life, and because by it he had won fame and even wealth. The writing of fiction, which he first attempted before the turn of the century, he put aside until 1805, when he made a start on the book that was finally to appear as *Waverley.* But this romance of 1745 he decided, on the advice of a friend, to leave incomplete, like his earlier efforts. He was unwilling, he tells us, to risk the reputation he had built up as a poet (particularly for *The Lady of the Lake*) by throwing on the market an untried commodity bearing the name of the old firm. One day, however, searching for some fishing tackle, Scott found his abandoned manuscript among the lines and flies! The year was 1814 and his poetry beginning to run a poor second to Byron's, so that the discovery seemed to him a sign, an indication of a new way to woo his old audience. For a while he continued to produce both verse and prose until the failure of "The Lord of the Isles" convinced him that his poetry was no longer commercially viable. "Well, well, James . . . ," he told his publisher, "since one line has failed, we must stick to something else."

From that point on, he was a novelist, though for a long time only by way of an avocation. Quite as importantly in his own eyes, he was a lawyer, sheriff, sportsman, and antiquarian, and most importantly of all, the Laird of Abbotsford. Only financial disaster made him a writer of novels before all else, driving him to produce between his forty-third and sixty-first years more than twenty-five books. He wrote at immense speed and under the terrible pressure of a need to owe no one anything, until his body buckled under the strain; yet he earned in some quarters more contempt than pity. "Wretched trash," Coleridge wrote in 1827 of the books Scott had been publishing just before that year, and added coldly that Scott's collapse was the proper reward for an "attempt to unite the Poet and the Worldling."

Certainly, there is more than a little truth in the final charge. Into Scott's work went not only the lawyer's respect for institutions and precedents, but also the entrepreneur's view of business as the high chivalry of the modern world; while his view of himself as an amateur did not preclude him from making money out of his books, but only from taking himself seriously as an artist. And though the personal bitterness of a Coleridge (who thought of Scott as his literary heir turned philistine) now seems irrelevant, his more general view still prevails among some critics; E. M. Forster, for instance, after telling us that Scott has "neither artistic detachment nor passion" ("he only has a temperate heart and gentlemanly feelings, and an intelligent affection for the countryside"), goes on to say: "And his integrity—that is worse than nothing, for it was a purely moral and commercial integrity . . . he never dreamt that another sort of loyalty exists."

Yet it is not fair to say merely that Scott is the creator of the male middlebrow audience and of the "healthy" best-seller; for besides a "temperate heart," "gentlemanly feeling," etc., he possesses mythopoeic powers to an extraordinary degree. It is hard—and a little discomfiting—for critics to remember that the novel may function on the level of myth as well as that of literature. As an artist, Scott is deficient in moral intelligence, clumsy in style, inadequate in characterization (except for the flat "clown," who passes from Shakespeare through him to the contemporary stage), untidy in form; as a maker of legends, however, he possesses authenticity and greatness. It is this nonliterary greatness which enabled him to stir the imagination of Europe and make the past of Scotland seem the mythic past of a whole continent. There is something a little absurd about Italian sopranos and tenors shrilling romantic phrases at each other in the cardboard Highlands of *Lucia di Lammermoor;* and the Russian court ladies who came draped in tartans on a pilgrimage to Abbotsford are ridiculous enough. Nevertheless both anomalies represent the awareness of half the world that Scott's genteel projections of lost causes and lapsed allegiances along the Border respond to a psychic need felt in Italy and Russia as well as in the British Isles.

The classic formulation of Scott's white Romantic myth is to be found in *Rob Roy,* whose seeds are already in *Waverley.* In his introductory note to the latter book, Scott tells us that it was the product of improvisation, a romance which had largely written itself:

> The whole adventures of Waverley, in his movements up and down the country with the highland cateran Bean Lean, are managed without skill. It suited me best, however, the road I wanted to travel, and permitted me to introduce some description of scenery and manners. . . .

Though couched as an apology, this is actually a summary of the essential archetypes of the Scott plot. The "movements up and down the country" represent the motif of flight and pursuit; the "scenery" stands for the mythicized Highland landscape; and the "highland cateran Bean Lean" is typical of those id-figures who emerge from the primitive wilderness and project the irresponsible yearnings of Scott's finally responsible protagonists. Even more important in *Waverley,* though not mentioned here, is the more beneficent spokesman for life outside the law, Fergus McIvor. Waverley himself typifies those young men whom Scott, in a review of his own work, called "amiable and very insipid," one of whom in each of his books represents the author and his ideal reader. The true heart of the adventures of such a young man, which is what most of Scott's fables boil down to, is not the love interest (in *Waverley* the choice between those symbolic posies, the wild Flora and the domesticated Rose) but the *road* which leads across the Border from England to the Lowlands and the Highlands, winding back and forth through space and time between "a civilized age and country" and one more "favourable for romance."

In *Rob Roy,* Scott is more than usually conscious of this purpose, and for that reason calls his book for once (he informs us at the suggestion of his publisher) by the name of the Highland character who embodies the theme of cultural contrast on which he trades. "It is this strong contrast," he writes in an introduction, "betwixt the civilized and cultivated mode of life on one side of the Highland line, and the wild and lawless adventures which were habitually undertaken and achieved by one who dwelt on the opposite side of that ideal boundary, which creates the interest attached to his name." Scott's sentence is neither elegant nor entirely lucid, but it makes its main point, defining symbolically "the Highland line," "that ideal boundary," across which a young man, this time English and called Frank Osbaldistone, shuttles in search of himself, and indicating why the title of the book is the name of a character whose affairs occupy so small a proportion of its total bulk.

Scott is somehow aware that the nominal themes of the book do not represent its deepest source of appeal. The question of whether Frank will save his father's threatened business, outwit the villain Rashleigh and marry Diana Vernon are mere *plot* concerns, as conclusively foregone as the outcome of the events of 1715, which provide the historical background for the action. What is really at stake throughout is the question of where the final allegiance of Frank will go: to his father (whose point of view is seconded by "the Bailie") or to Rob Roy. In the Bailie and Rob are projected the two paternal images which divided the soul of the Scottish author proud of his double descent: from the lowlander, the prudent, middle-class merchant, pledged to profits, security, Protestantism, and the English King; and from the wild Highland brigand, dedicated to honor, mad adventure, Catholicism, and the Jacobite cause. On an even deeper level, they represent the principles of obedience and subversion, the controlled life of the super-ego and the impulsive life of the id. The darker aspects of the latter way of life are projected by the villain Rashleigh, stock Seducer and gothic persecutor, who possesses all the characteristics of Rob Roy (he, too, is a Jacobite, an enemy of the state, a disturber of the peace) except honor; and they are displayed in harsher colors, too, in Helen McGregor, wife of Rob, a black Hecate figure, blood-stained, fanatic, and immune to mercy.

Whatever these two represent in its demonic form, Rob embodies in all its allure; he is the very spirit of risk and of the wilderness which he inhabits, a natural man and embodiment of the romantic North. He is a thoroughly mythical character (for all of Scott's attempts to prove his historical truth through most of an introduction, five appendices and a "Post-script"), linked backward through his name, with its overtone of despoiling the king, to Robin Hood and Robin Goodfellow—those greenwood gods of the folk. Both analogies were surely in Scott's mind, for he mentions the former semi-mythic character by name, attributing the fame of Rob Roy to his having played "such pranks in the beginning of the 18th century, as are usually ascribed to Robin Hood. . . ." And the word "pranks" seems more reminiscent of Robin Goodfellow himself than of the quasi-historical namesake. Rob Roy is not merely on another side from Frank Osbaldistone's father; he is in another world, belongs to another race. Scott describes him as possessing the "wild virtues . . . and unrestrained license of an American Indian," and characterizes his ideas of morality as "those of an Arab chief. . . ."

Rob Roy is more than a greenwood spirit and Noble Savage, however; he is in a real sense the Muse of young Frank, the embodiment in life of all that the Romantic writer seeks in art. At one place in *Rob Roy,* Scott makes the point that there is a "natural taste" which belongs to mountaineers, and that Highlanders in particular possess feelings "allied with the romantic and poetical." Frank was at twenty (he tells his own story backward in the novel, from the viewpoint of a successful middle-aged man) convinced that he was a poet, impatient with everything except "literature and manly exercises." From the lofty vantage of his art, he especially looked down on business. The sense in which the businessman could be understood as an "ambitious conqueror," or in which "he resembled a sailor whose confidence rises on the eve of tempest or battle" Frank could not then perceive. No more could he understand his father's (and Scott's) belief that commerce connects "nation with nation, relieves the wants, and contributes to the wealth of all."

To that father, who felt obliged to despise poets not only as a businessman but also as a member of a dissenting sect, Frank seemed merely to insist on idling away his life like a boy when he should have been earning a living like a man. Scott stacks the cards against poor Frank and against the cause of art as well by attributing to Frank an absurd poem and an incompetent translation of *Orlando Furioso*. The latter effort, merely mentioned in Chapter II at the point of Frank's break with his father, is actually read aloud to Diana Vernon in Chapter XVI, at the climax of the action. Far from greeting it with sympathy or praise, Diana makes it the occasion for a tirade against Frank for wasting his time on verse when he should be concerned with his father's property as well as his and hers. Turning on him in the name of mercantile and bourgeois notions of morality, she is, ironically enough, described by Scott as "resembling one of those heroines of the age of chivalry."

Over and over again the blunt, philistine point is hammered home: not poetry but business is the end of life and, indeed, the chivalry of the modern world. Frank, however, learns this dispiriting lesson almost too late for it to be of any use, having first left his father's home and counting house in pride and obduracy. "But it was too late . . . and Heaven had decreed that my sin should be my punishment, though not to the extent which my transgression merited." From this point on, he is plunged into a series of adventures which threaten to bring ruin to the family firm, poverty and even death to him; but the original sin, it should be noted, the first Fall of the bourgeois-Protestant world is *the refusal to go into the father's business*. Not even for so dire a transgression, however, does Scott permit the truly tragic to enter his fictional world. Frank escapes (sinner though he is) the devious plots of the enemies of his father and his kind, largely through the aid of Rob Roy, the Highland rebel who loves him as a son yet must yield him up at the end to Lowland prudence and accommodation.

The demands of the happy ending require that Frank be reconciled with his father and give up both poetry and Rob Roy, who is last seen "astride a rock with his long gun, waving tartans, and the single plume in his cap." But the same exigencies also require that in return for Frank's sacrifice of his "inclinations" to the needs of the firm, old Mr. Osbaldistone permit him to marry Diana Vernon, a Roman Catholic and daughter of a leading Jacobite. Diana is, indeed, an alter ego of Rob himself, another spirit of the wildwood, whose first appearance is as a huntress (like the goddess whom her name recalls), riding a jet-black horse, her own jet-black hair streaming in the wind. "Wild gaiety" and "romance" are the association she evokes in the mind of Frank; while for Andrew Fairservice, comic version of the dissenting Lowland viewpoint, she is the essence of paganism itself: "a daft queen they ca' Diana Vernon (weel I wot they might ca' her Diana of the Ephesians, for she's little better than a heathen—better? she's waur. . . .)"

Yet she is not the Great Dark Goddess she seems, only the Good Bad Girl, that stock character of popular fiction, who despite appearances and circumstances, proves virtuous in the end. Did she not dissuade Frank from the pursuit of poetry, sending him back to protect his father's interests? Everyone is permitted to have his cake and eat it, too, in the imaginary world of Scott. Symbolic figures representing irreconcilable allegiances seal their parting with a kiss, the Bailie and the outlaw (kinsmen, of course) embracing each other and promising mutual service, each in his kind. Frank has had to give up the art of literature, though he married an embodiment of the "romantic." But Scott can practice the art his hero surrenders, for he knows how to make it not the rival but the co-adjutor of commerce. Thus his readers are permitted at one and the some time to despise literature and to enjoy a novel, aware that it is "a mere elegance, a luxury contrived for the amusement of polished life."

In terms of the fable itself, Rob Roy, surrogate for the primitive and the poetical, has been dismissed to his Highland fastness, left to eke out his remaining days in a struggle for a lost cause, and to be no more a protector and a guide but only a bitter-sweet memory. It is his own youth which the bourgeois artist is dismissing, though he confuses it with the youth of his society. Yet finally the name of Rob Roy names the book and sells it ("the germ of popularity," Scott calls his title); and he is invoked in its final words: "Old Andrew Fairservice used to say, that 'There were many things ower bad for blessing, and ower gude for banning, like ROB ROY.' " It is the final tribute of the white Romantic to the world of untamed nature and the id, which he can bring himself neither to live by nor disown; and the Rob Roy-Robin Hood archetype projects this ambivalence. The bourgeois world could not afford to let so apt a symbol of its divided heart die out of the literature while that division lived on; and in America in particular it throve especially, both in the form Scott gave it and in the adaptation of James Fenimore Cooper.

III

Cooper is eminent among the followers of Scott; only Manzoni rivals him, and Manzoni was limited by the fact that the sole Noble Savages of his world were peasants. But Cooper was in a favorable position for taking up the master's suggestion that Robin Hood and the Indian are one; and he ended by creating a middlebrow image of the primitive as heroic which displaced even the Highlander in the mind of the West. Cooper's red men had an initial advantage in their dusky skins, for in the dreams of Caucasians forbidden impulses are typically projected in dark-skinned figures. Moreover, his primitives resemble more closely than the wild clansmen of Scott the version of the Noble Savage proposed by the rudimentary anthropology of the Encyclopedists, which already existed in the imagination and awaited only a fable, an archetype as apt as Scott's, to become a staple of the bourgeois novel.

That fable was created in a series of five novels by James Fenimore Cooper, who had learned from Scott to invest his projections of the primitive with the pathos of the lost cause, and to play out his action on the "ideal boundary" between two cultures, one "civilized and cultivated," the other "wild and lawless." The American name for that "ideal boundary" is, of course, the "frontier"; and on a continent which provided almost limitless possibilities for moving such a frontier westward, there was not one "Highland line" but many. For Scott's romantic North, Cooper substituted his own romantic West and the end is not yet in sight. It is taking no final credit from Cooper, justly irked throughout his life at being tagged "the American Scott," to say that he learned much from (not imitated!) the author of *Rob Roy,* any more than it is uncomplimentary for him to insist that he is indebted to Brockden Brown for the suggestion that "the incidents of Indian hostility, and the perils of the Western wilderness are far more suitable" for the American writer than "castles and chimeras."

Merely to have conceived of joining the materials of Brown to the modes of Scott, of blending the American highbrow and the

European middlebrow, is a creative act; to have by that act redeemed the American past for the imagination is an even greater
achievement; yet Cooper performed, as we shall see, more even
than this. Unlike Scott, Cooper was not willing to be a mass entertainer of polite society; his books were to him weapons in a battle
against the abuses of society. With a courage unsurpassed by any
American writer since, he engaged in a quarrel with his own country and people, his own time and place, marked by all the ferocity
of baffled love. Yet like Scott, he desired deeply, too, to be a *success,* commercially as well as critically. "A good, wholesome, prof-
itable and continued pecuniary support," he wrote, "is the applause
talent most craves." Indeed, before excoriating the mass American
audience, Cooper had won it; so that he found himself in the almost unparalleled position of being listened to by those who really
represented all he most detested in American life.

Finally (though not before supporting himself by his pen for
twenty years), Cooper managed to lose the public he roundly
abused yet expected to sympathize with him and subsidize his attacks. Most of his books (he wrote some forty-five, fiction and
non-fiction) have not survived the fluctuations of his reputation or
the issues which prompted them. His talent for invective and his
moral intelligence were greater than his psychological insight or
poetic skill, and his collected works are monumental in their cumu-
lative dullness. Particularly unreadable are the novels of his later
years, when his invective had turned to hysteria and his intelligence
was stifled by his piety. To the student of ideas, he is endlessly
fascinating; and a history of his times could be (and, indeed, has
been) mined from the body of his fiction. But to the reader of
novels he is, except for a handful of books, a tantalizing, an ultimately disappointing case.

He himself foresaw his fate, writing in 1850, "If anything from
the pen of this writer . . . is at all to outlive himself, it is, unquestionably, the series of 'The Leather-Stocking Tales.' " But this does
not quite manage to state the whole irony of the situation. Out of
his immense production, the bulk of it serious to the point of di-
dactic deadliness, the handful of books still read with pleasure by
any number of Americans are entertainments, the most Scott-like
of all his romances. Moreover, we read them in large print and
embellished with pictures, remember them, if at all, as children's
books, exciting and incredibly boring by turns. And to realize that
in all likelihood *The Last of the Mohicans* has been throughout the

world the most widely read of all American novels only chills us the more.

It is true that in the past eminent European novelists like Balzac and D. H. Lawrence have been moved to exclaim over certain works of Cooper, "beautiful . . . grand . . . a masterpiece . . ." or "a crescendo of beauty"; and Melville himself once said in formal tribute, "The man, though dead, is still as living to me as ever. . . . He was a great, robust-souled man, all whose merits are not yet fully appreciated." But Lawrence's enthusiasm was directed to the Leatherstocking Tales, Balzac's to *The Pathfinder* in particular; and, indeed, around these few books whatever vital controversy still rages is centered. Twain's famous attack, "Fenimore Cooper's Literary Offenses," like Lawrence's great defense in *Studies in Classic American Literature,* is based on that handful of texts; while in Melville's short eulogy the disquieting note is struck, ". . . his works are among the earliest I remember, as in my boyhood producing a vivid and awakening power upon my mind." "As in my boyhood"—there is the fatal phrase. Let us not avoid it, but take it as a clue to the very essence of Cooper's appeal.

In what novels of his survive, Cooper is a writer for children, more specifically for boys. In this respect his Leatherstocking Tales share a single fate with the first two parts of *Gulliver's Travels, Robinson Crusoe,* at least some of the romances of his master Scott —particularly, perhaps, *Ivanhoe*—and such books of Dickens as *Oliver Twist,* as well as Stevenson's *Treasure Island* and *David Balfour.* All of these books (the examples which occur are inevitably Anglo-Saxon) have certain characteristics in common; all of them have male protagonists, adult or juvenile; all involve adventure and isolation plus an escape at one point or another, or a flight from society to an island, a woods, the underworld, a mountain fastness—some place at least where mothers do not come; most all of them involve, too, a male companion, who is the spirit of the alien place, and who is presented with varying degrees of ambiguity as helpmate and threat: Friday, Alan Breck Stewart, Long John Silver, Fagin, Robin Hood. The relation between the protagonists takes various forms: servant and master, foster-father (good or bad) and foster-son, lover and beloved. It is always opposed, at least implicitly, to the "stickier" and more sentimental kinds of relationships involving women, whether that of mother and child, husband and wife, or passionate wooer and mistress. When endearments are permitted between such male pairs (as between Oliver and Fagin, for instance, or Long John Silver and Jim Hawkins), they are typically presented as blandishments concealing a threat; for such love always threatens to develop into sexuality and sexuality would turn the pure anti-female romance into the travesty of inversion and would frighten off the child reader.

Found here and there in British literature, scarcely at all in other traditions, this "boyish" theme recurs with especial regularity in American fiction, most notably in the two greatest novels ever written in the United States, *Moby Dick* and *Huckleberry Finn,* but elsewhere, of course, in Twain and Melville, as well as in Dana, Stephen Crane, Henry James, Hemingway, Faulkner, and Sherwood Anderson, among others. There is obviously something in the American character that responds to its appeal—or perhaps, conversely, the theme itself through our great books has served to create in its own image what we call the American character.

It is Cooper who first dreams the American version of this theme, converting a peripheral European archetype into the central myth of our culture. The consignment of his work, then, to the world of children is not, in a child-centered world, a sign of failure but of success; and precisely because he is the first writer in the United States of boys' books, he is the first truly American writer to have appeared. To understand the Leatherstocking series is, therefore, to understand the most deeply underlying image of ourselves; and to begin that understanding we must examine the career of James Fenimore Cooper, try to see clearly his actual relationship to the wilderness which he made the setting of his most successful books. There is some difficulty in dealing with the life of a man, who, though he lived much in the public eye, guarded many details of his existence from public scrutiny. He rather despised Scott for having taken pains to provide his biographer with documents and information, and forbade his own family to permit the publication of any authorized life. Yet in his novels and in the press, in his letters and his non-fiction, the record has been made.

I V

He was born in 1789, the year of the publication of *The Power of Sympathy,* in Burlington, New Jersey, but moved as an infant to the town which now bears his name, near Lake Otsego in New York state. His childhood home was on the edge of the forest in space, on the further margin of Indian-fighting days in time. The actual savages had long since departed westward and the real woodsmen had followed them; but a semi-Christianized, usually drunken stray of an Indian could occasionally be seen on the streets of his home town, or some old trapper, bewildered and offended by the inroads of civilization. It is important to realize how close Cooper was to and how far from the material he was to make his own. It is perhaps this particular degree of remoteness which determines the oddly abstract existence of the forest in his work—as if he had never walked through it (or on the other hand certainly not *studied* it) but only dreamed it. Cooper can, when he wants to, reel off lists of native American trees; but ordinarily his characters flee or pursue through woods which contain not oaks or beeches or maples, only unnamed archetypal trees, the tree-ish, conceptual trees children draw.

The simple fact seems to have been that Cooper had no especial affection for the American woods, in particular, or the American landscape in general, any more than he had for the American weather or seasons, about which he complains in his later, non-mythical books. Only the symbolic or, as he might have said, the "ideal" forest appealed to him; of the actual one, which he made but did not find romantic, he remarks in *Wyandotté,* "There is a wide-spread error on the subject of American scenery . . . the world has come to attach to it an idea of grandeur, a word that is in nearly every case misapplied. The scenery of that portion of the American continent which has fallen to the share of the Anglo-Saxon race very seldom rises to a scale that merits this term. . . ." Cooper, in any case, after a long career of mythicizing that landscape, declared his preference for the "sublimity of the Alps," the "wild grandeur" of the Italian lakes, the "noble witchery" of the Mediterranean coast.

Cooper's own family was made up of well-to-do landowners, men who by wise investments and speculation had grown rich on the lands opened up by the pioneers—and which had, of course, been first of all robbed from the Indians. Apparently, no direct connection of Cooper had acquired his land by force rather than purchase, and he did not, therefore, have the appropriator's need to vilify the expropriated, or the inherited guilt (of a Hawthorne, for instance) which plagues the descendants of such appropriators. Indeed, as economic depression depleted his own financial resources (like Scott he ended by writing under financial pressures), and as agitation began against the old patroon system, Cooper began to feel himself one of the dispossessed. It was easy for him to identify himself, too, in terms of his distinguished ancestors, great white chiefs all of them, with the ancestral nobility of the Indian tribes—and to identify the agitators calling for the breaking up of inherited estates with the crude squatters and despoilers who had first driven the red man from forest and plain.

It must be remembered that Cooper asks of his reader not sympathy for the Indian people in general but for the Indian chief, the aristocrat at the end of his line. He is the most class-conscious of all American writers (to him Scott seemed not gentleman enough!), class-conscious the way only a provincial New York aristocrat could be; and his Jacksonianism was based on agrarian sympathies and especially a violent opposition to Whiggery: the philosophy of the new mercantile middle class. In his works, the American Revolution is presented as an unfortunate incident in the lives of men bound together by class interests, who divide temporarily in their allegiances but return again to their estates and their customary social intercourse after the war. He even goes out of his way to be kind to George III; and, indeed, until later experiences soured him, was mildly Anglophile in a typically upper-class way, even pretending to be English when he wrote his first book—though that device, indeed, may have been a cynical one, prompted by what he knew of the general public's provincial unwillingness to admire native efforts in the arts.

Cooper's religious affiliations reflect both his class position and his sense of continuity with Anglo-Saxon tradition; unlike that unchurched Universalist (trained by Moravians) Natty Bumppo, he was an Anglican, though he was not confirmed until the very end of his life. He had been a warden of Christ Church in Cooperstown long before he received his confirmation from his wife's brother, an Episcopal bishop. With Natty, Cooper shared an immunity to Calvinism and its vestigial influences rare among American writers; between them, they represent the beginning of an anti-Puritan strain in our literature that sustains the credo of original innocence. There are, to be sure, occasional Puritans among the characters of Cooper's books, but they are cruelly caricatured (the Reverend Meek Wolfe in *The Wept of Wish-ton-Wish* is a typical example, his name in itself a summary of Cooper's views), and the author rejects them without a trace of real ambivalence.

The residual secular Puritanism which gives to the anti-Puritanism of Hawthorne or the anti-Presbyterianism of Melville its special complexity and depth is totally lacking in Cooper. It is perhaps because the doctrine of original sin has lost for him, with the loss of its Calvinist underpinnings, all effective force that his novels fail finally to achieve a tragic dimension. Melville writing on Hawthorne was to observe that the "blackness, ten times black" against which tragedy is defined in American writers derives from vestiges of New England theology, and there is real truth in the observation. Certainly Cooper, lacking that religious background, lacks also the philosophical denseness and moral richness of the greatest American fiction of the nineteenth century. There is nothing in his basic attitudes to counter the sentimental piety of genteel Protestantism except a certain eighteenth-century faith in progress and civilization; but this does not set up a tension favorable to serious art. Evil is finally as unreal to Cooper as to that oddly Whiggish Tory, Scott.

What chiefly determined the shape of his career, however, was his marriage, a happy and apparently placid one, to the daughter of a rich and distinguished family. To Susan De Lancey he surrendered the direction of his domestic life, making her his social arbiter in a way typically American. His submission (whatever reservations he had were buried deep and could express themselves only in literature) he granted cheerfully to his wife and four daughters, following whose whims and needs he changed his home to a place closer to the city, then plunged into a seven years' tour of Europe in search of the refinements of civilization. When his family finances collapsed, he wrote furiously for thirty years to provide his wife and daughters with the comforts he thought of as the proper tribute of the male to the superior virtue of the female.

The notion of the sacredness of womanhood and the sanctity of every member of the sex, the supreme creed of the female sentimentalists, he accepted as literal truth, ritually portraying all upperclass, white, Anglo-Saxon women as without sin. If he ever groaned beneath the weight of this intolerable burden of an eternally confessed moral inferiority, he never groaned openly and would have been appalled to think his wooden ingenues were in fact his revenge upon the sex; just as his dream of an idyllic union with the red man was his inner escape from a world of blameless, sexless females. Only the Indian in him, which is to say the unconscious, is allowed to blaspheme against the pale-face virgin. Whittal, the halfwit pseudo-savage of *The Wept of Wish-ton-Wish,* says of Faith, the blue-eyed, blue-veined, blondest of all possible Snow Maidens,

" 'tis a woman of the pale-faces, and, I warrant me, one that will never be satisfied till she hath all the furs of America on her back, and all the venison of the woods in her kitchen. . . ."

After his marriage, Cooper was apparently set to live the eventless, busy life of a gentleman, but two events, one a national disaster, the other a casual challenge, turned him into a writer. In 1820, at the age of thirty, he wrote his first book, *Persuasion,* apparently in order to win a bet from his wife, who had taken him up on a casual remark that he could produce a book as good as the piece of female fiction she had annoyed him by praising. Yet his first book is no burlesque (as were Fielding's and Cervantes' under somewhat similar circumstances), not an anti-novel at all, but a quite serious, somewhat plodding, Jane Austen-ish study of the problem of marriage—indistinguishable, one imagines, from the novel he had begun by emulating.

Scott had started his career as a writer by trying to counterfeit the folk style of the Border ballads; Cooper began his imitating an English gentlewoman entertaining and edifying her peers. It is disconcerting to find him impersonating a female (as late as 1823 he was continuing in this vein, publishing two short stories under the name of "Jane Morgan"), but even more so to discover him betraying the American's provincial hunger for counterfeiting European civilization. Cooper was soon forced, however, both by his own sense of the inadequacy of his first venture and by the critics' adverse comments on his failure to use the native scene, to an even more devious act of dissimulation. In *The Spy* he produced an American imitation of the kind of book written by Europeans for whom the United States is a symbol of primitivism and anti-culture. Here, indeed, is the secret of his success on the continent, for he is above all others the kind of "American romancer" Europeans dream and need; or at least, in a few of his many books, he managed to seem so. For Americans his appeal is somewhat more complicated. To his earliest native readers, his evocation of a way of life not so far from theirs in time (in *The Spy* he recounted events not fifty years past), or even in its quality, provided an illusion of remoteness. The indulgence in nostalgia for past simplicity is a final assurance of present sophistication.

At any rate, *The Spy,* which appeared in 1821 and was immediately successful, is the most Scott-like of all Cooper's novels, based on historical documents throughout, even Harvey Birch, the protagonist referred to by the title, being derived from an actual prototype. More importantly, Cooper has chosen the American Revolution as a setting because it provides just such an "ideal boundary" as Scott loved, across which the protagonists (a young Loyalist officer in disguise plays the role of the pursued juvenile, though his sister is the genteel heroine and is married off to a major in the Colonial forces) move between safety and danger, as well as between competing ways of life and codes of behavior. Most striking of all is the resemblance of Cooper's paired mysterious figures, upper-class and lower, Washington and Harvey Birch, to their counterparts in Scott's *Ivanhoe,* Richard Coeur de Lion and Robin Hood.

Yet *The Spy* fails to capture the archetypal appeal of its model. It is as moving as *Ivanhoe,* perhaps, on the mythical level, but cannot approach in this respect those Scott fictions which make the Highlands and Highlanders their theme. Cooper's fated Highlands is the forest, his predestined wild Highlander the Indian and the woodsman, his inevitable "ideal boundary" the frontier. These are all pre-existing concepts ready to live the life of legends in the American mind, awaiting only the word that will release them; that word Cooper finally speaks, though almost inadvertently, in *The Pioneers,* which was published in 1823. Reaching back in search of his own beginnings and those of his family, he discovers beneath that half-remembered, half-invented world one even more archaic: the childhood of America, which does not indeed really exist until he first embodies it.

The Pioneers was the first written of the Leatherstocking Tales; and though Leatherstocking himself is kept firmly in his place (he is a standard lower-class comic character, allowed to compete in pathos but not in importance with the provincial aristocrats who are Cooper's mythicization of his own family) and the Noble Savage appears only as the lost and drunken Old John Mohegan, the presence of these two characters was enough to assure the novel's success. Great analytic or poetic works, depending for their acceptance on an intimacy with language and structure which may seem at a first reading strange or even obscure, often have to wait long for their popularity; but the mythic work is likely to be greeted by instant acclaim. Certainly, the American public responded with enthusiasm to the first authentic romance by the dreamer of its national dream, for 3,500 copies of *The Pioneers* sold before noon of the day of publication.

Cooper was committed for the rest of his life to the promulgation of a myth; and though toward the end of his career, he came to understand the sense in which this was his essential function, for a long time he remained confused. The myth-maker and the man of letters were uneasily combined in him, and both were joined, after the collapse of his fortune prevented his living out a gentlemanly life of leisure, by the businessman, the canny exploiter of his own talent. He was an irascible man, driven by internal demons as well as external need, and he maintained the most difficult sort of relationship with his public, storming at his readers, scolding his critics, hysterically defending his own most trivial private activities in thick pseudo-fictions. What baffled him most, however, beneath all the minor contretemps in which he invested so much energy, was the contrast between his ability, as a half-conscious framer of legends, to satisfy deeply the mass audience, and his inability, as a fully conscious moralist and polemical social critic, to win its approval.

After *The Pioneers,* at any rate, he knew that he was destined to spend the rest of his life as an author of one sort or another; and, having moved to the suburbs of New York City (not only for his daughters' sake, but also to be closer to his publishers) he set about writing a sea story, which was to beat Scott at his own game. Proud of his own knowledge of seamanship and a little contemptuous of Scott's, he fell into Scott's own trap of identifying the truth of a novel with the faithfulness to fact of its details. If Cooper never managed to write a romance of the sea as satisfactory as his romances of the forest, it was because he knew the sea too well, approached it not as a dreamer but as an expert. Nevertheless, in *The Pilot* (and in at least one other of his several tales of the sea, *The Red Rover*), he produced one of the few books of his that can still be read with pleasure by the casual reader. The appearance of *The Last of the Mohicans* in 1826, however, marked his final discovery of his true vein; and from this point on, the true history of Fenimore Cooper becomes the fictional history of Natty Bumppo.

As Cooper moved in his imagination deeper and deeper into the American wilderness, he was in fact withdrawing farther and farther from it. His fancy continued on a pious pilgrimage westward —across the Mississippi to the Great Plains, even as he and his family made a cultural pilgrimage eastward—across the Atlantic to France and Italy. He finished *The Prairie,* most Western in its setting of all the Leatherstocking Tales, in Paris in 1827. It was presumably the end of the series (which Cooper was never to finish; actually, he wrote two more novels for it in the '40's and planned a third just before his death), for in it, Natty, having penetrated the territory of the Pawnee and the Sioux, dies, an old man, facing into the sunset. From 1826 to 1833, the Coopers remained in Europe, chiefly around the fashionable center of Paris; though Italy, with its indolence and gentle pride, seems to have pleased Fenimore Cooper best. It was not yet common in those days to speak of expatriation; and, indeed, Cooper left the United States not as one going into exile but as befitted his class and literary reputation, with a nominal consular post. Even when he had resigned this position, he continued to act the part of an unpaid but official representative of his country. In the midst of attending receptions, visiting celebrities, seeing sights and being lionized, he managed to find time for writing, for he depended upon the sale of his books to foot the bill.

He had been warned before he left that any American who stayed abroad more than five years ran the risk of never returning, and he stayed for seven and a half—in spirit never did go home again. He and America had drifted apart in the period of his absence; and though while abroad he had defended American culture against European attacks, he himself joined the assault on his return. Like many Americans in Europe, he had confused the nostalgic memory of his country with its fact, and coming back, he found it guilty of betraying both the memory and his defense of it based on the memory. He had already begun to fall into disfavor even before his return, for quite nonliterary reasons, his odd combination of Tory principles and democratic action proving especially infuriating to the Whigs; and he compounded the animosity after his repatriation. He had apparently toyed with the idea of giving up writing in 1833, but the seeming triumph of the "dollar-dollar set" depressed him, as did the disappearance of the older ruling classes of which he considered himself a member. "Where is the Gentry?" he cried, and lashed out at the financiers who had taken its place. Unfortunately, he was a man with little sense of proportion, and his larger quarrel with his country was soon almost lost in a petty quarrel with his fellow townsmen over picnicking rights on his Lake Otsego property. Certainly, this picayune issue bulks too large in his *Home as Found*, published in 1838, which otherwise might have formulated the first major statement in our fiction of the Europe-America theme.

For better or worse, Cooper plunged into a round of libel suits, statements to the press, endless wrangles about everything from the accuracy of his own naval history to women's property rights, the jury system, and universal suffrage. First of all American writers to take on the role of public accuser and nay-sayer, he still found time to complete his mythical account of that American past which he felt his enemies betrayed. In *The Pathfinder,* which appeared in 1840, and *The Deerslayer,* which came out a year later, Cooper turned back from the end of Natty Bumppo's life to his youth, to a time as distant as possible from the contemporary era which so irked him. Meanwhile, he had become more and more religious, committing himself, when all visible institutions failed his hopes (despite his increasing bitterness, neither hopelessness nor tragic acceptance were possible for him), to a pious trust in Providence. In *Oak Openings,* which was published in 1848 and which represents, therefore, his very latest thought, Cooper denied in the name of his newly confirmed faith the demonic, pre-Christian voice of the New World, which had spoken through him in his mythic books.

In the words of a converted Indian, once Scalping Peter and at the end just Pete, Cooper rejects the "Injin" in himself. " 'Tell me you make a book,' he said. 'In dat book tell trut! You see me poor old Injin. . . . I was great chief but we was children . . . t'ink tomahawk and warpath and rifle bess t'ings in whole world. . . . Stranger, love God. B'lieve his Blessed Son, who pray for dem dat kill Him. Injin don't do dat. Injin not strong enough to do such a t'ing. . . . I have spoken. Let dem dat read your book understand.' " After such a declaration, Cooper could not really return again to the Great Serpent or Long Rifle who had stood so long beside him, could not be as a child with the children of his pagan imagination. Just past sixty, he weakened quite suddenly and without previous warning, and in a little over a year he was dead. Daniel Webster was called upon to deliver an official eulogy at the memorial services, to render the thanks of a nation to the first maker of its myths; but he spoke out of ignorance of Cooper's works—a last, not untypical indignity: "As far as I am acquainted with the writings of Mr. Cooper, they uphold good sentiments, sustain good morals, and maintain just taste."

Though obviously spoken at a venture, these words do, alas, characterize much of Cooper's work; for they are intended to describe the sort of literature a gentleman might write, and Cooper was, whenever he wrote self-consciously, above all things a gentleman. Only his intelligence is slighted by Webster's summary, and the mythopoeic power which, in a handful of books, delivered him from the limitations of his class and his time. That handful of books we must be content (taking Cooper's own word for it) to consider the sole *living* part of his achievement. That he naturalized the sea story to the new world or first realized how shipboard society could be used to portray microcosmically a whole culture; even that he invented, in Eve Effingham, James's American girl before the fact, are matters of *historical* interest only.

Yet it is well to remember that Cooper invented not only the "Western," the prototype of all cowboy-and-Indian romances, the first embodiment of the ritual drama played out to this day in television fantasies called *Gunsmoke* or *Wyatt Earp,* but that he is also the first American author to project an alternative formulation of the theme which, in Hawthorne and Henry James, Fitzgerald and Hemingway, is played out in terms of a confrontation of Europe and America. This Europe and this America are, however, no more facts of geography than Cooper's Indians and whites are facts of ethnography; the place-names stand for corruption and innocence, sophistication and naïveté, aesthetics and morality.

The gentlemanly Cooper not only dreamed Tom Mix and Gary Cooper before the nineteenth century was half over; he also projected Lambert Strether, and all the other ambassadors without portfolio who, like Cooper himself, go to Paris to discover America and their own souls. Yet though the America-Europe theme and the Indian-white archetype go back to a common Romantic source, the former, in an odd way, turns the latter on its head. What does the damage is the suggestion that not naïveté and simple virtue but sophistication and elegance are lost with the passage of time and the march of progress. In the end, the study of the American abroad debouches into ambiguities which baffle popular understanding even as they shock popular morality. The "ambassadorial" novel can never like the Western win the mass audience; it must function as art rather than myth, depend on craftsmanship rather than intuition. It is for this reason that Cooper, who never solved the problems of language or form, could only project and not construct successful fictions on the Jamesian theme; books like *Home as Found* remain theoretical, concepts rather than realizations. Cooper had, alas, all the qualifications for a great American writer except the simple ability to write.

The Western, on the other hand, requires no "writing," for it is truly mythic, a substantial part of its meaning contained in the bare plot, transcending the limitations of language and surviving even in children's cut editions, television or movie versions and comic books. Precisely because the Leatherstocking Tales are the world's first Westerns, they have come to possess the imagination of the world—which is a satisfactory enough joke on the most self-consciously civilized and gentlemanly of all our writers, *"le grand écrivain Américain,"* whose image of himself so infuriated the ungentlemanly D. H. Lawrence. It no longer really matters whether one has actually read Cooper's books or not; he is possessed by them all the same, and just as Dumas in nineteenth-century France could call a work *Les Mohicans de Paris,* Bernard Malamud in twentieth-century America can entitle a story "The Last Mohican." Neither has to doubt that he will be understood, for the title of Cooper's romance has become a part of the common symbolic language of the western world.

V

Two mythic figures have detached themselves from the texts of Cooper's books and have entered the free domain of our dreams: Natty Bumppo, the hunter and enemy of cities; and Chingachgook, nature's nobleman and Vanishing American. But these two between them postulate a third myth, an archetypal relationship which also haunts the American psyche: two lonely men, one dark-skinned, one white, bend together over a carefully guarded fire in the virgin heart of the American wilderness; they have forsaken all others for the sake of the austere, almost inarticulate, but unquestioned love which binds them to each other and to the world of nature which they have preferred to civilization. To understand these figures and their relationship, we must first understand the order of the genesis of their myth: the sequence of the novels in which they appear, both as Cooper wrote them and in terms of the dates of their actions.

Though *The Pioneers* appeared in 1823, it is set in 1793, when Natty is over seventy; and though *The Deerslayer,* the last of the novels to be published, came out in 1841, the events it describes belong to the years between 1740 and 1745, when Natty is not yet twenty-five. Between the first and last written of the Leatherstocking Tales, the protagonist grows backward in time from old age to youth, from experience to innocence, from a world which Cooper could still, though barely, remember (in 1793, he would have been four years old) to an era before his father was born, a completely imaginary past. But Natty also moves through time from a moment when the United States had won its independence and had established a Constitution to a period when its separate existence had not yet been imagined.

But it is not quite as simple as all that; for if, on the one hand, Cooper between 1823 and 1840 re-imagined Leatherstocking from an "old and helpless man" to a youth not yet initiated into a career of killing, on the other hand, by 1827 he had also moved him *forward* some ten years, converting him from a pathetic-comic oldster with one tooth, haunting the margins of the settlements he despises—to a magnificent old patriarch who has come to die in ultimate loneliness in the ultimate West. After *The Pioneers,* that is to say, there are two separate pairs of books: one pair, *The Last of the Mohicans* and *The Prairie,* appearing in 1826 and 1827, the other, *The Pathfinder* and *The Deerslayer,* being published in 1840 and 1841. In the first book of each pair, Natty is placed in middle life (in *The Last of the Mohicans,* he is just the age of his author at the moment of writing the book); then he is either pushed forward into a mythical old age, or back to a legendary youth. In each of the later books of the pairs, he stands on the verge of a critical transition: in *The Deerslayer,* he is initiated into manhood; in *The Prairie,* inducted through death into whatever lies beyond. Each romance celebrates, as it were, a *rite de passage.*

In both cases, Natty is transfigured by a confrontation with death; in one, with that of his first victim, in the other, with his own. But in both, he is mythicized, transformed from the mundane reality of *The Pioneers* to another order of being. In that first novel, he is an old outcast, by turns noble and absurd, the kind of peripheral character who in a play by Shakespeare would have talked in prose. In Cooper, he talks by fits and starts a semi-comic American dialect which sets him off from the gentle characters who talk like an English novel for ladies. Natty is an ambiguous type at this stage, a kind of cross between Huck Finn and his Pap, alternately fleeing and defying the law for dubious reasons, and in the end, "lighting out for the Territory." Attending him and reinforcing his meanings is Old John Mohegan (the *first* last of the Mohicans), an Indian as old as he or older, who has been con-

verted both to the white man's religion and the white man's fire-
water. Twin symbols of dispossession, of all that cannot survive
the inevitable and desirable (providential, says pious Mr. Cooper)
march of civilization, they are not only doomed, but degraded.
Yet the one is capable of setting out once more to pursue the
retreating West, and the other of destroying himself in a symbolic
holocaust. In that flight and from those ashes, they are reborn,
stripped by youth or age of their accidental comic attributes (the
dripping nose, the rags, the lone tooth-stump) until they are revealed in all their mythic purity: the Christian Noble Savage
and the pagan Noble Savage, confronting each other across the
"ideal boundary," the fleeting historical moment at which, both
harried by the civilization that will ultimately destroy them, they
meet. In the end, one is a little paganized, the other a little Chris-
tianized—their respective nobilities both augmented in the process.

Natty is an oddly elusive character, almost anonymous. He apparently shuns his baptismal name and is finally buried under a
mere initial. Almost as if he were an Indian, he earns not inherits
his name, and is known variously as Deerslayer, Hawkeye, Pathfinder, Long Rifle, Leatherstocking, the Trapper. He is overtly
pious, meek, chaste (of course!), sententious—often a bore, a Protestant Noble Savage, worshiping in the Universalist Church of the
Woods; and yet he is also a dangerous symbol of Cooper's secret
protest against the gentle tyranny of home and woman. A white
man, who knows the "gifts" of his color and will not take a scalp
or be rude to a lady, a man without caste, who knows his place
and recognizes all officers and gentlemen as his superiors, he is
still a law unto himself: judge and executioner, the man with the
gun, the killer—however reluctant. He is the prototype of all
pioneers, trappers, cowboys, and other innocently destructive children of nature, which is to say, of the Westerner, quick on the
draw and immune to guilt.

In some ways, Leatherstocking seems a Faust in buckskins.
Faustian man, however, knows even as he acts that he is damned;
that his enterprise is ambiguous at the very least, and that he
must pay in suffering for the freedom he demands. Though he
defines himself by denying the Calvinist or Catholic theology of his
world, the Faustian man needs that theology to create the tensions
of his life; he is a blasphemer, and blasphemy is the sign of the
secret though tormented believer. The Westerner, on the other
hand, knows that what he does is blessed; that God and nature are

one; that man, even in solitude, is good. Faust without sin is Natty Bumppo.

And the Devil who is his companion, when genteel Christianity has denied the ultimate reality of the demonic, is Chingachgook, the Great Serpent, as he is called by one to whom the Serpent is no longer the eternal Adversary. The Indian represents to Cooper whatever in the American psyche has been starved to death, whatever genteel Anglo-Saxondom has most ferociously repressed, whatever he himself had stifled to be worthy of his wife and daughters; but the Indian also stands for himself, which is to say, for a people dispossessed in the name of a God they do not know and whose claims they will not grant. The charge of General Lewis Cass and other literal-minded critics of Cooper that his Indians have "no living prototypes in our forest," that they are "of the school of Mr. Heckewelder and not of the school of nature," is quite beside the point, though no more than Cooper deserves for his own insistence on the historical truth of his "narratives."

Cooper tells precisely the same sort of truth about the Indian that Mrs. Stowe was to tell about the Negro; in each it is guilt that speaks, the guilt of a whole community. Cooper's own boyhood was passed after the last Indian inruptions into his part of the world were over, after the Anglo-Saxons had triumphed not only over the savages but over their allies, the French, too—dark aliens who had once unleashed the primitive terror. Yet when he was a child, the nightmare of the red uprising still haunted his home town, and at one point the militia was organized to stand off a raid that never materialized. It is a little like the Southerners' uneasy dream of the black insurrection, almost as much a wish as a fear. To exorcise that self-punishing bad dream, Cooper returns, through the long story it took him nearly twenty years to tell, to the good dream which is its complement and antidote: the dream of primeval innocence and the companionship of red man and white. Ironically enough, he situates that dream in a time when the Indian menace was still real, had not yet been transformed from a daylight threat to a nighttime shadow troubling the *yengsees'* sleep.

Though the Leatherstocking romances are, first of all, entertainments, they are also propitiatory offerings. There is in all of them, at one point or another, a reflection of Cooper's quarrel with himself (with the "Indian" deep within him): the sound of an inner voice explaining, justifying, endlessly hashing over the appropriation of the land, on which Cooper's own wealth and status so directly depended. His first means of coming to terms with his guilt-feelings is by identifying himself with the injured party, dissociating himself from the exploiters. In reading his romances, the American boy becomes for a little while the Indian, the trapper; and returning later to his memories or to the books themselves, finds it easy to think of himself as somehow really expropriated and dispossessed, driven from the Great Good Place of the wilderness by pressures of maturity and conformism.

However seriously Cooper may have wanted to be taken on the level of ethnology or political history, he could not avoid projecting in the "natural man" and the "natural scene" a myth, an archetypal embodiment of psychological truth, which was opposite in all its implication to that of Charles Brockden Brown. As the latter is responsible for giving to the gothic myth its standard American form, so Cooper is responsible for the naturalization of the Rousseauistic myth. In each, the dark-skinned savage is used to represent the unconscious mind, what the age itself liked to call the "heart," and between the two is created a total picture of the ambivalence of the American sentimentalist toward the id and its promptings. From the beginnings of our literature, the question has been posed: Is the "natural" a source of spontaneous goodness, instinctive nobility, untutored piety? Or is it the breeding ground of a black, demonic, destructive force hostile to our salvation? Or is it the common spring of two conflicting impulses, one positive, one negative?

Needless to say, the American mind has wavered on the subject, not only in instances of author combating author, but often in terms of a single author arguing with himself, one impulse of his own mind evoking the counter-impulse. In Melville's *Moby Dick,* for instance, the sinister natural figure of Fedallah is set against the virtuous natural figure of Queequeg, while in the works of Twain, Nigger Jim confronts Injun Joe, the dark-skinned protector contrasted with the dark-skinned aggressor. Even in Mrs. Stowe, the primitive piety of Uncle Tom is balanced by the unredeemed natural mischief of the demonic Topsy. Cooper seems at first glance committed to a single side, or at least, so it is easy to remember him. We perhaps recall the eulogy of the good forest in *The Deerslayer,* spoken by Natty, who has just refused like a proper American to marry the Fallen Woman, Judith Hutter. And we recall by way of contrast the haunted black forest of Brown, think perhaps of what Hawthorne is to say later of the "dark inscrutable forest," "where the wildness of her nature [Hester Prynne's] might assimilate itself with a people alien from the law. . . ." Hawthorne can imagine the Faustian man in the American woods, but cannot conceive of the innocent Westerner.

There are, therefore, no Noble Savages in Hawthorne, any more than there are in Brown, no dusky Apollos, no wildwood gentlemen—only warlocks and bestial assassins, demi-devils and demi-brutes. But there are in Cooper himself counter-Indians, as it were, savages almost as ignoble as any of theirs. Bland and un-Puritan as he was, Cooper was forced still to admit that even in the wilderness there was violence and terror, even in the natural something dangerous to the progress of mankind. Certainly he was prepared to grant the reality of the bad Indian, deriving from a clue in Heckewelder, the Moravian missionary whose study of Indian life had so influenced him, his famous theory of the Two Tribes: Mohegan and Mingo, Pawnee and Sioux. Sometimes there is a suggestion that bad Indians are the product of interbreeding; the Mingoes, for instance, are less pure of blood than the Mohicans. Cooper certainly shares, and to some extent has helped perpetuate, the popular American belief that the breed is hopelessly evil. Yet there is a counter-suggestion in his work that the bad Indian is a false Indian, not really an Indian at all: and in *The Redskins* he makes a distinction (indicated in his subtitle, "Indian and Injin") between real redskins, who respect property and ancestral rights, and leveling white men, disguised as savages to hide their depredations against the landholders. In any case, Cooper manages to propagate both aspects of the American ambivalence toward the Indians: the Easterner's or missionary's sentimentalizing of the Vanishing American, and the Westerner's or Indian fighter's cynical contempt for the savage. Cooper's bad Indians, it must be understood, are neither the unredeemed pagans of Hawthorne nor the undeveloped animals of Brockden Brown; they are Elizabethan stage villains.

Throughout *The Last of the Mohicans,* there are chapter headings which identify the villain of that book with Shylock, Cooper's bad Indian with Shakespeare's Machiavel. But the key passage ("Cursed be my tribe/If I forgive him . . .") suggests the further identification of the whole Indian people with that other exiled race, the Jews. The worst the Indian does, Cooper implies by the comparison, is an act of vengeance for compounded ancient wrongs; and the malice of the bad Indian demands as complicated a response as that of Shylock. However sanctioned by Providence, the European persecution of the pagan Indian has bred monsters, just as the earlier European exclusion of the "perfidious Jew" had created usurers. It is a stroke of genius, this uniting of the images of the usurer and the scalper (of the rejected super-ego and the offended id), each with a knife in his hand, each dedicated to a terrible revenge. Yet in *The Last of the Mohicans,* the point is made in appended quotations rather than in the story itself, as if Cooper were not quite ready to let it become a central theme.

He takes it up again, however, this time more centrally, in one of the strangest of his books, that pious last testament to which we have already alluded, *The Oak Openings*. In this novel, Cooper writes for the last time a romance of Indian life (the date is 1812, the setting Michigan); but he is interested no longer in pursuit and escape. This time he is concerned with the problem of conversion: the conversion to Christianity of the Indian, Scalping Peter, whose dreams of an Indian uprising help bring about the murder of Parson Amen, a missionary to the red men. Parson Amen begins as a comic character, like David Gamut in *The Last of the Mohicans,* a weaponless man in a world of weapon-bearers, utterly ignorant of the conditions of life in the world he enters or of the elementary skills required for survival in it. He is revealed finally as a Holy Fool, however, his failure to come to terms with a world of violence his greatest virtue; and even his madness assumes in the course of the book the semblance of symbolic truth. He believes obsessively that the Indians are the Lost Tribes of Israel, and this provides at first numerous occasions for Cooper's typically heavy-handed humor.

But out of the misunderstandings that arise between him and the baffled Indians, to whom he insists on preaching this disconcerting doctrine, arise certain key questions on which the meanings of the novel depend: Are the Indians, indeed, lost—and is their casting away a mystery like that of the Jews? Or is it the *yengsees,* the whites, who are, as the Indians assert in rebuttal, really lost—turned toward the setting rather than the rising sun which points the way to their proper home? After all, the English are the "Jews" who have betrayed not only Christ but their Indian brethren; while the Indians are, in their own eyes at least, guiltless of that primeval crime, the Crucifixion, which has cursed the

Christian world with the evil spirits of rootlessness and aggression. Yet in the course of Cooper's fable, the Indians commit precisely the sin against a redeemer of which they have declared themselves innocent: they kill the missionary even as he prays for them, forgives them; and the hapless Peter, their conscience (though, like his namesake, not bold enough in the moment of crisis), ends repentant, asking forgiveness of the whites.

It is a dazzling piece of sleight-of-hand, which solves the problem of white guilt (from which Cooper began) by insisting on the deeper guilt of the Indian, who not only fails to *practice* forgiveness, but will not even pretend to honor it. Not with arms can the Indian avenge his expropriation (Peter, who preaches the great Indian revolt, ends by saving the whites from those he has inflamed), only with prayer accept it. In return, the repentant redskin is granted the privilege of being told by some ineffectual, pale-face maiden that the Indians have in fact a better right to America than the whites, or of being assured by a half-mad preacher that he and his people are, like the Jews, chosen. "They have been, and are still, the chosen people of the Great Spirit, and will one day be received back to his favor. Would that I were one of them, only enlightened by the words of the New Testament!"

If the good-bad Indian come to wisdom sounds a little like Uncle Tom, it is because Cooper and Mrs. Stowe were genteel sentimentalists together, the one no more capable than the other of tragic ambivalence or radical protest.

The Uncle Tom resolution of the Indian problem only comes, however, when Cooper has exhausted the vein of the Leatherstocking Tales. In that series itself, Cooper never combines a good Indian and a bad in a single skin, for this would make him human and require that he be treated as a psychological entity instead of an allegory; he is content to display projections of the beneficent and malevolent primitive in action side by side, portraying the one as the ally of Natty Bumppo, the other as his foe. The happy ending assures us that the principle of natural evil goes inevitably down to defeat and death; while the pathetic ending, with which it is intertwined, reminds us that the principle of natural good also (though more heroically) perishes from our world. The primitive, good or evil, Cooper never lets us forget is past history and a present dream.

Read against the factual background of Cooper's own life as

well as the lives of most of his readers, the Leatherstocking romances seem the simplest kind of wish-fulfillment fantasies. D. H. Lawrence, in his immensely illuminating study of Cooper, lists the obvious contrasts between reality and myth set up in the series: The Wigwam vs. My Hotel—Chingachgook vs. My Wife—Natty Bumppo vs. My Humble Self; and he underlines the particular pathos of the final contrast by quoting from one of Cooper's letters describing his social activities in Europe: "In short, we were at the table two counts, one monsignore, an English Lord, an ambassador and my humble *self.*" It all seems pat enough, this turning from (a relished yet somehow resented) real life in society to a dream life in nature: a kind of Walter Mitty story with Walter Mitty offstage as author—and therefore a Walter Mitty story told without irony. But it is more complex than this; for deeply implicated in the boyish reverie that turns the harried husband and breadwinner into the man in the woods with a gun, modest and potent at once, are disturbing sexual overtones, which combine with and are reinforced by an uneasy ambivalence toward the problem of race relations.

VI

In order to see clearly what is involved, we will have to look more closely at *The Last of the Mohicans.* It was not Cooper's own favorite in the series (he preferred *The Deerslayer*), but it has always been the world's, because in it there is defined almost perfectly the basic myth of Leatherstocking. Not merely are elements scattered through the other four romances here gathered together: the good Indian and the bad, the dark Maiden and the fair, the genteel lover and the stern, tender-hearted father, the comic tenderfoot and the noble red patriarch; these elements are presented in their pure essences. Natty is nowhere more super-eminently his sententious, cool, resourceful self, Chingachgook nowhere more noble or terrifyingly at home in the woods (and his archetypal meanings are here reinforced by Uncas, Cooper's third mythical character, who makes here his only appearance); while Magua is so essentially the bad Indian, "reptile," "fury," "Devil," and Shylock in one, that beside him Cooper's other villains seem scarcely to exist. Cora and Alice (the names themselves are almost mythical), the passionate brunette and the sinless blonde, make once and for all the pattern of female Dark and Light that is to become the standard form in which American writers project their ambivalence toward women.

No chases are more thrilling and absurd, no movements into danger less credibly motivated, no rescues more hair-raisingly ridiculous, no climaxes more operatic than those of *The Last of the Mohicans*. The scenery is almost totally abstract, archetypal; among unnamed trees, two women and their protectors flee before a sinister purusit, twice resumed, which takes them to the mythic cave of Charles Brockden Brown, behind a rocky waterfall worthy of Scott, and eventually onto the bosom of a wooded lake (Cooper's very own!), the image of which haunts our dreams but can never be discovered by picnicker or fisherman. And in all the magic woods (sometimes more like those of Shakespeare's *A Midsummer Night's Dream* than any native forest), no mosquito bites, no ant crawls; the charmed underbrush itself relents and will not tear the clothes or mar the looks of the two girls who without soap or comb or brush must maintain their symbolic beauty, light and dark, unblemished. Were one of the actors once to sweat or belch or retire to the bushes to relieve himself, the spell would be broken; we would know that all of them were merely flesh. But nothing gives the game away. The Indians talk like mythic Celts out of *Ossian,* the gentry like Fenimore Cooper remembering the genteel British novel, Natty himself like an improbable blend of stage provincial, backwoods preacher, and instinctive sage. The novel is so all of a piece that reality does not intrude.

The "history" of the French and Indian Wars, into which the fable is set, belongs in our minds to the pre-history of America, an archaic world in which anything is possible; and for all his occasional concern to get the facts right, his title-page vaunt that he is writing a historical "narrative," Cooper cannot persuade us that the victims of the historic massacre described at the center of his book really bleed. It is a dream "dreamt among the trees," a Midsummer Night's dream. From the play of that name, indeed, Cooper derives almost as many chapter headings as he does from *The Merchant of Venice;* and truly *The Last of the Mohicans,* too, presents us with a world subject to magical transformations. Not only does the threat of death turn in an instant to the promise of life, the darkest danger to the most glorious delivery; but men are changed into beavers, bears revealed as men.

The reader's problem is finally how to take the romance at all seriously, to find in it more than amusement, a Midsummer Night's entertainment. "The 'pure' adventure story is deliberately superficial," James Grossman tells us in an otherwise insightful book on Cooper; "It has no serious concern with the outside world which it uses as a decoration and aid to action." Yet it is incredible that a book which has moved the world for more than a hundred years should have "no serious concern" with that world. The so-called literature of escape is always at its depths religious, a ritual statement of what its audience prays the world might be or even hopes it is. If Cooper, for once, had not planted explicit meanings in his fable, such meanings might well have been implicit in the theme he imagined. But there is evidence that he was attempting quite consciously to grapple, in the midst of scenes of adventure, with a serious subject, indicated by the quotation (from *The Merchant of Venice,* once more) on the title page: "Mislike me not for my complexion. . . ." *

It is an odd (and ambitious) novel that tries to be at once the dark Shakespearean comedy and the light, a farcical presentation of metamorphosis and romantic love—and a somewhat melancholy, bitter-sweet examination of the problems of race and color. Yet this is precisely what Cooper has tried; and it is misleading for Grossman to insist that *"The Last of the Mohicans* uses race as a painter might use coloring arbitrarily for effect." It should be remembered that *The Last of the Mohicans* (1826) was written just after *Lionel Lincoln* (1825) and was followed by *The Prairie* (1827), *The Red Rover* (1828), and *The Wept of Wish-ton-Wish* (1829). These books frame the beginning, in 1826, of Cooper's seven-year expatriation, and bear directly on certain feelings stirred up in him by the desire to leave, for a while at least, his own country. The novels in this group revolve in large part around two themes: the relations of white America to white Europe, and those of white America to red America. More profoundly, they are concerned with the sense of guilt felt by Americans over the Revolution against the mother country and the expropriation of the Indians.

Lionel Lincoln is one of the darkest of Cooper's books, the nearest thing perhaps to a true gothic romance that he ever pro-

---

* The line is, of course, spoken in Shakespeare by a Moor, i.e., a Black Man—and here Cooper anticipates the mythological adaptation, so important in later American books, of the Negro character to the myth of the Indian.

duced. Against a background of mysterious events, it tells the story of Lionel, an officer in the British Army though a native of America, who is nearly converted to the Colonial cause. At the last minute, however, he discovers that the wise old patriot who had nearly convinced him is an escaped lunatic—for whom authority means the keeper, and freedom an opportunity to indulge his delusions. Whatever Cooper's conscious opinions of the justice of the American War of Independence, his unconscious doubts are here clearly enough portrayed! And they are further illuminated by his ambivalence toward the protagonist of *The Red Rover*, a Revolutionary pirate who has taken to a career of crime because the commander of a British ship on which he was serving had insulted America. Buccaneer and madman, these are the images which occur to him for the revolutionist, the founding father or first fighter for the Republic. But his quest for the beginnings of the American character takes him back beyond the period of our Revolutionary War, back to the conflict of *yengsee* and Indian, to the original struggle for the American land. In *The Last of the Mohicans*, he seemed to find the moment he sought in the French and Indian War; and in *The Prairie*, which he completed in Europe, he killed off Natty Bumppo, as if to indicate that he was through with the theme.

Cooper had, however, stirred up in *The Last of the Mohicans* and ignored in *The Prairie* a problem more complicated even than that of the struggle for a continent—the question of the relations between men of different races in the New World; and to that problem he returned in *The Wept of Wish-ton-Wish*, which is his attempt to deal nonmythically (i.e., without the presence of Natty Bumppo) with the problem of miscegenation, in terms of the question: Has the flight from Europe and the expropriation of the Indians bound white man and red in such an inextricable knot of mutual interest and guilt that they must eventually blend into one (accursed!) race?

In *The Wept* an Indian boy, Conanchet, captured by whites, is recaptured by an Indian raiding party, who take along with him a girl child of the family which has kept him in captivity. When they are both grown, he makes the white girl, who presumably loves him, his squaw; but when he discovers that her parents are still alive he surrenders her to them, and gives himself up to his Indian enemies, dying by the hand of Uncas, remote ancestor of the handsome young brave of *The Last of the Mohicans*. It is

Conanchet, however, who plays the true Uncas role in this novel, being described as "the last sachem of the broken and dispersed tribes of the Narragansett."

The contrast of color between him and his wife, whom he calls Narra-mattah, Cooper emphasizes with all the ambivalent relish of one savoring the nightmare of miscegenation, never letting us forget that it is a "dark glittering eye" and "dark visage" which daily approached the "golden hair and azure eyes" of the kidnaped pale maiden. There is something close to obscenity in his lingering descriptions of Narra-mattah's white, white skin with its "delicate tracery of veins." Conanchet, who shares Cooper's primitive horror of the mixing of blood, finally turns away his beloved white squaw with her papoose, "an offspring with an Indian cross of blood." "Conanchet is a tall and straight hemlock," he firmly tells the clinging, protesting woman, "and the father of Narramattah is a tree of the clearing, that bears red fruit. The Great Spirit was angry when they grew together. . . . Let the mind . . . forget the dream among the trees." He can be persuaded only to grant her the hope of reunion in heaven, a sop for her sentimental unwillingness to accept the terrible boundary between race and race: "they say that one just man died for all color. . . . If this be true he [Conanchet] will look for his woman and boy in the happy hunting-grounds."

Conanchet is good Indian enough to disavow the mingling of alien bloods and the mixture of cultures, Christian and pagan, for which it stands. His foil in the book is the imaginary bad Indian, Whittal-Nipset, a half-wit white boy, who has also been captured by the Indians and has emerged from his stay among them convinced that he is a redskin warrior: "Whittal is a warrior on his path. . . . Nipset hath a mother in her wigwam. . . ." Not only does he parody the hope of acculturation elsewhere favorably embodied in Natty Bumppo, but he travesties, too, the Indian case against the white world, elsewhere nobly presented by patriarchs like Tamenund or pled with heroic malice by such villains as Magua. In the mouth of the pseudo-Nipset, all the charges of the Indians, their boasts of virtue and long-suffering become absurdities, the fantasies of a deranged child. Like the half-idiot boy in *Lionel Lincoln,* who seconds the patriotic escaped madman, Whittal caricatures cruelly whatever he advocates; and the dream of "going native," the dream "dreamt among the trees," which Cooper himself to some degree has sponsored, is here finally denied. There is no escaping the march of civilization or the obligation of one's innate "gifts." In any case, *The Wept of Wish-ton-Wish* must be read as the first anti-miscegenation novel in our literature; and *The Last of the Mohicans* must be re-read in its light. Miscegenation is the secret theme of the world's favorite story of adventure, the secret theme of the Leatherstocking Tales as a whole.

The plot of *The Last of the Mohicans* is essentially the New-Comic fable which Scott had made standard in the historical romance, decorated with American-gothic trimmings out of Charles Brockden Brown. Against a background of Indian terror, there are played out an abduction, a rescue, a final duel (involving the death of the villain), and a plighted troth to indicate the restoration of order and innocence. Everything, however, has been strangely doubled, so that the novel finally contains *two* full romantic plots, separated by the "historic" description of the massacre at Fort Henry, "a Narrative of 1757." A pair of girls, Cora and Alice Munro, attempt (for reasons never made quite convincing) to join their father, the commanding colonel at Fort William Henry, though that stronghold is being besieged by Montcalm and his Indian allies. They are provided with one heroic escort, Major Heyward; and are accompanied by one comic traveling companion, a wandering psalmist called David Gamut. Gamut is typical of those Cooper figures, whose final avatar is Parson Amen, representing the absurdity and pathos in the wilderness of men who will not touch a gun but take quite literally the Christian injunction to return good for evil. "Praised be God," David Gamut says, "I have never had occasion to meddle with murderous implements." On the way to the fort the girls and their escort are betrayed to their enemies by a treacherous Indian guide, Magua, but are rescued by Natty, Chingachgook, and Uncas. The massacre intervenes; the two girls are again captured by Magua, are once more rescued by Natty and company; and, after various complications, are finally delivered by a struggle in which one girl, one good Indian, and several bad Indians die.

It all seems fair enough—two plots, two chases, and two deliveries being just twice as good as one; and, in any case, it all fits quite nicely the required two-volume form in which Cooper's novels appeared. But there is a deeper duplicity at stake. Why, for instance, two girls? They are paired off, light against dark, for

what one might call with Mr. Grossman "decorative" purposes,
just as in Rousseau and even in Richardson, before him, there
had been, for contrast and balance, a female companion to the
heroine. But the relationship of Cooper's two girls is so close
(they have a father in common) and their appearances so strikingly different, that one suspects the author of some deeper intention. Alice, the "most juvenile" of the "two females," has a
"dazzling complexion, fair golden hair and bright blue eyes." The
developing action shows, too, that she is not gifted with the
firmness of her sister Cora, whose "tresses . . . were shiny and
black like the plumage of a raven," while "her complexion was not
brown, but it rather appeared charged with the color of the rich
blood, that seemed ready to burst its bounds." Yet Cora, for all
her bursting blood, envies the more pallid Alice. "She is fair!
Oh surpassingly fair!" Cora sighs. "Her soul is pure and spotless
as her skin."

The point is clear: one is "spotless," which is to say, sexless;
the other charged with blood and ready to break through all
bounds: a passionate woman, who appeals to the instinctual Indians and who in turn responds to their dark, primitive beauty.
"Who that looks at this creature of nature," she exclaims in
admiration, beholding Uncas, "remembers the shade of his skin";
or again, this time of Magua, "Shall we distrust a man because
his manners are not our manners and that his skin is dark?" Yet
"noble, melancholy" Cora is not merely a woman capable of
stirring and responding to passion. She is corrupted woman,
stained even before birth with the blackness of the primitive and
passional, her mother having been "a lady . . . descended, remotely, from that unfortunate class . . . so basely enslaved. . . ."
(Cooper cannot bring himself to say the word "Negro"!) She
represents, in short—though rather in what she is, than what she
does—all that early nineteenth-century male gentility privately
lusted for in a female, but publicly denied, would not marry.

It is for this reason that Major Heyward will not have Cora;
though we know that she loves him and suspect that he responds
a little. He was, after all, to confound matters even further, "born
at the south, where those unfortunate beings are considered of a
race inferior. . . ." Major Heyward will not, however, admit the
charge of Cora's father, "You scorn to mingle the blood of the
Heywards with one so degraded," preferring to attribute his reluctance to the power exerted on him by "the sweetness, the

beauty, the witchery" of the Snow Maiden, Alice. She is, conveniently enough, no daughter of a dark-skinned mother, but fit offspring of the Scottish "suffering angel," who had waited in her cold North for twenty years in perfect celibacy, until her husband's first wife had died. When Heyward proposes at last to the pure Alice, she responds, not with the proud warmth of Cora, but trembles and almost faints as is "common to her sex."

Not only is the ingenue doubled in *The Last of the Mohicans,* but doubled, too, are the savages, good Indian and bad, Uncas and Magua, paired lovers of Cora. How much these two are alike and yet how different they are! Uncas leaps into sight at one critical moment, "fresh and bloodstained" from his heroic efforts, while Magua (whom Cora has first beheld with pity and admiration as well as horror) holds up his "reeking hand" to boast, "It is real but comes from white veins." The redskin killer as deliverer and aggressor, they are both finally destroyed by their love for the "noble, melancholy" maiden; though Uncas is first advanced by that love on the evolutionary scale "centuries ahead" of his race, while Magua is degraded by it almost to an animal level. Cooper will not attribute the threat of rape even to Magua, taking pains to deny that Indians ever practice such a crime, though he will not permit himself to use the word. He portrays Magua as proposing only a loveless, a forced marriage. "Let the daughter of the English chief follow and live in his wigwam forever," and, at the baffled climax, threatening her with death: "Woman, choose; the wigwam or the knife of Le Subtil."

In the end, the two dark lovers of the dark Cora struggle to destroy each other. She is killed by a follower of Magua; that follower in turn killed by Uncas, who is stabbed to death by Magua. It is Natty Bumppo who finally shoots the bad Indian, hanging to a cliff in vain attempt at escape. Though Cooper's own contemporaries urged him to let Cora and Uncas be joined in marriage, his horror of miscegenation led him to forbid even the not-quite white offspring of one unnatural marriage to enter into another alliance that crossed race lines. The last of the Mohicans is portrayed as the last, the Vanishing American shown to have vanished because (so Cooper at least believed) the color line is eternal and God-given. It is a fantastically ahistorical note.

At the funeral of Cora, the Indian girls who strew her body with flowers sing of her union in the Happy Hunting Grounds with the gallant warrior who had preferred her because "she was of a blood purer and richer than the rest of her nation." But Natty will not permit their pious hope, shaking his head "like one who knew the error of their simple creed"; and when Colonel Munro, broken by his bereavement, urges the Scout to tell the female mourners that "the time shall not be distant when we may assemble around His throne without distinction of sex, rank or color," he refuses. " 'To tell them this,' he said, 'would be to tell them that the snows come not in the winter, or that the sun shines fiercest when the trees are stripped of their leaves.' " Even beyond death, the ferocity of Cooper's dread of miscegenation will not yield. With Magua he seems to believe (though his relative ranking of the races would have been different) that the Great Spirit has made men of different colors as unlike as the different species of the animal world: the Negroes black as bears and condemned to work forever like the beavers; the whites pale as ermine and destined to be traders, though also dogs to their women and wolves to their slaves; the Indians redder and brighter than the sun, chosen to represent the image of God and to live a fully human life.

It is clear finally that the doubling of the women and Indians in Cooper's novel not only reflects his ambivalence toward the instinctual life in sex and nature, but also permits him to double the plots and themes which they embody. In one fable, the bad Indian and the soldier struggle for the Maid without Spot, who is at last won by the hero and married; in the other, the good Indian and the bad contest the possession of the Dark Lady, to whom the victor is united only in a *Liebestod*. In the world of Grace, true happiness is possible; but in the world of Nature, all lies under a curse. "Cursed be my tribe/if I forgive him . . ." says Shylock-Magua; but cursed also is the tribe which does not forgive—which is to say, all imperfect mankind. Civilization and submission, however incomplete, to Christianity mitigate the curse, which is therefore virulently effective only on the dark-skinned and primitive peoples of the world. Various characters in *The Last of the Mohicans* speak variously of the curse. For Munro, it is slavery itself: "a curse entailed upon Scotland by her unnatural union with a foreign and trading people"—miscegenation between the Scottish noble savages and the mercantile pale-faces to their south! For Cora, the curse is a mystery. To the ancient Indian, Tamenund, she declares, with "burning" blushes, "Like thee and thine, venerable chief . . . the curse of my ancestors has fallen heavily on their child"; but when asked why grace has been shown to the whites and only rigorous justice to the colored peoples, her sole answer is an evasion: "but why—it is not permitted to inquire." In his own final words, Tamenund can only echo her, "Men of the Lenape! . . . the face of the Manitou is behind a cloud! . . . You see him not; yet his judgments are before you." It is a tautology with which we are left: one is cursed for not being white by the fact of not being white.

VII

There is real tragic potential in the theme of miscegenation as a curse and punishment for a curse, potential to be realized in the fiction of William Faulkner; but neither in *The Last of the Mohicans* nor *The Wept of Wish-ton-Wish* does Cooper succeed in releasing its power either as poetry or action. The New-Comic theme is even more perfunctorily handled, a gesture by Cooper to the *Zeitgeist* rather than a concession to his own deepest needs. We are aware of the implicit tragic theme as a somber undertone, of the nominal New-Comic theme chiefly as an annoyance; but there is a third theme, not yet fully explicated, on which the life of the novel in the world's imagination largely depends. The third theme is closely linked, of course, to the extraneous hero, Natty Bumppo. In the earliest novel in which he appeared, Natty was scarcely integrated into the main plot and therefore posed no difficult questions; but once he had been promoted from his status as a supernumerary, moved to the center of the continuing series, he became an embarrassment. In an age of Romance, what can one do with the hero who, *in essence and by definition, cannot get the girl?*

In order to answer this, it is necessary to understand first of all *why* Natty can never marry; and it is doubtful whether Cooper himself ever consciously or clearly saw this, though instinctively he remained faithful to the limitation, the uncomprehended taboo. In *The Prairie*, as in *The Last of the Mohicans*, Natty is the deliverer, the rescuer, the man who arrives in the nick of time— but only to deliver the ingenue into the arms of someone else, a stuffy and genteel young man of the proper station in life to marry the kind of young lady Cooper considers worthy of being a heroine. It is partly his class origins which make it impossible for Natty, after he has killed Magua, to be rewarded with Alice.

"Now, I come of a humble stock," he says, knowing his own place in the scale of things like all "good" men in Cooper, "though we have white gifts and a white natur'." But even when Cooper goes out of his way to provide Natty with girls of his own caste—Mabel Dunham, the Sergeant's daughter in *The Pathfinder,* or Judith Hutter, the bastard foster-daughter of Floating Tom in *The Deerslayer*—Natty cannot take the final step. Either, as in the former case, we are told that the girl he loves loves someone else; or, as in the latter, that the girl loves him, but is too "stained" for his native nobility, the fallen daughter of a fallen mother, betrayed by aspirations above her station to the officer-seducers of the nearby garrison.

The truth is that Natty is barred from marriage and the family by a prior commitment to a lonely life in a state of nature. "Moral hermaphrodite" that he is (the term is Balzac's), he can only enter into an abstract and fruitless union with the wilderness itself; his true Bride is, as he tries to tell Judith Hutter, the forest, or more precisely the Spirit that inhabits it: "She's in the forest, Judith— hanging from the boughs of the trees in a soft rain. . . ." And when asked if he has ever found it pleasant to listen to a girl's laughter, he answers, "Lord bless you, gal—to me there is no music so sweet as the sighing of the wind in the treetops and the rippling of a stream . . . unless, indeed, it be the open mouth of a certain hound, when I'm on the trail of a fat buck." An obvious choice for Natty would seem to be an Indian girl, brought up to the world he loves and, in a sense, its very personification; but Natty is, as we have begun to see, a fanatical exponent of racial purity. Magua may speak of him (he intends a grudging compliment) as "one whose skin is neither red nor pale," but Natty insists with almost maddening repetitiousness throughout *The Last of the Mohicans* that he is "a white man without a cross," that the has "no taint of Indian blood." "I am white," he is still maintaining in *The Deerslayer,* "have a white heart, and can't in reason, love a red-skinned maiden," though he is willing to grant when pressed that he is "a little red-skin in feelin's and habits." When he is offered an Indian bride in that later book, she is old and ugly, the whole episode a degrading travesty, monstrous enough to justify Deerslayer's comment, "I've known them that would prefer death to such a captivity."

The entire incident represents an attempt not only to caricature Indian-white relations but to parody marriage itself, as the word "captivity" reveals. The union with a squaw means to Natty not only the mingling into an unthinkable hybrid of gifts intended by God to be distinct; it also stands for the loss of freedom involved in any permanent connection with a woman, red or white. It would have meant in short a kind of *emasculation,* since the virility of Natty is not genital but heroic and cannot survive in the marriage bed any more than beside the hearth. Insofar as Natty projected the marginal discontent of Cooper (and his America) with the kind of life which in the main he loved, he was doomed to remain unattached to Woman, who symbolized that life. "I may never marry," Natty says at one point, "most likely Providence [which is to say, James Fenimore Cooper], in putting me up here in the woods, has intended I should live single and without a lodge of my own."

Yet there is a relationship which symbolically joins the white man to nature and his own unconscious, without a sacrifice of his "gifts"; and binds him in life-long loyalty to a help-meet, without the sacrifice of his freedom. This is the pure marriage of males—sexless and holy, a kind of counter-matrimony, in which the white refugee from society and the dark-skinned primitive are joined till death do them part. Natty himself in *The Last of the Mohicans* contrasts the love which links him to Uncas (and his father, the Sagamore) with the sentiment which has sent Heyward in pursuit of Alice: "I have heard . . . that there is a feeling in youth which binds man to woman closer than the father is to the son— It may be so. I have seldom been where women of my color dwell; but such may be the gifts of nature in the settlements." It is an odd enough notion that tender heterosexual love is a possession only of men in settlements, and that in its place the forest breeds an equally tender passion between males who "winters and summers, nights and days, have . . . roved the wilderness in company, eating of the same dish, one sleeping while the other watched. . . ." Uncas, to be sure, dies at the end of the action, but Chingachgook is left; and it is with him that Natty shares a common grief even as Uncas and Cora share a common death, Major Heyward and Alice a common marriage bed. "No, no," cries Hawkeye, gazing yearningly at the rigid features of his friend, who has been bewailing his loneliness, "no, Sagamore, not alone. The gifts of our colors may be different, but God hath so placed us as to journey in the same path. I have no kin, and I may also say, like you, no people. . . . The boy has left us for a time; but Sagamore, you are not alone."

The man without a cross and almost without a country clasps hands with the dispossessed savage, who has outlived his race—expropriator and expropriated, united by their tears; and we learn not only that they will remain faithful until Chingachgook has leaped into the flames (this we have known since the first romance of the series), but also that not even death will part the twain. The union in heaven that Natty will not grant the man and woman—between whom passion made the bar eternal—he grants himself and his Indian friends, for they yearn to join not flesh but souls. "Depend on it, boy, whether there be one heaven or two, there is a path in the other world by which honest men may come together again," he says in *The Last of the Mohicans;* and in the later *Deerslayer,* he makes an even stronger case. "But of all doctrines, Sarpent," he insists, "that which disturbs me . . . most, is the one that teaches us to think a pale-face goes to one heaven and a red-skin to another; it may separate in death them which lived much together, and loved each other well in life."

Yet the passion that joins male to male in Cooper is not in its implications as innocent as he wants to think. Why, if there is no sense of a lurking danger in such a relation, has he made the beloved Chingachgook not merely dusky (a natural sign of the forbidden), but marked him with a death's head for a totem, and called him the Great Serpent. The "sarpent," who is the special enemy of woman, is also, and by the same token, the symbol of temptation; and of this Cooper is dimly aware. "Now I'm naturally avarse to sarpents and I hate even the word," Natty remarks, "On account of a certain sarpent at the creation of the 'arth, that outwitted the first woman; yet, ever since Chingachgook earned the title he bears, why the sound is as pleasant to me as the whistle of the whip-poor-will of a calm evening." The clue is here, the revelation that the very end of the pure love of male for male is to *outwit* woman, that is, to keep her from trapping the male through marriage into civilization and Christianity. The wilderness Eros is, in short, not merely an anti-cultural, but an anti-Christian, a Satanic Eros; and yet it is proffered by Cooper (barring such an occasional slip as we have just examined) and accepted by his readers as innocent. To believe this one must become as a boy, to whom neither sex nor violence is real, and to whom mother is the secret enemy, to be evaded even as she is loved.

That is why Cooper is so fond of presenting his anti-female alliance of outcast and savage in an atmosphere of make-believe, of "playing Indians." Even in *The Wept of Wish-ton-Wish,* for instance, there is a mock-marriage of Indian and white used to underline by contrast the horror of the real mating of Conanchet and Narra-mattah. That pure union joins "the last of the Narragansetts" to Submission, a mysterious white man, who declares of himself: "Though of white blood and of Christian origins, I can almost say that my heart is Indian." Conanchet's final words to his wife, which are aimed only at preparing her for his death and her abandonment, urge her to give up the dream "dreamt among the trees," and to return to the settlements of her people. But Submission, presumable killer of his king and man without a last name, Conanchet leaves safe in the woods, perched in one of the trees that define the dream. He has declared already that their lives "are one," and he goes to his own death, leading a war-party of hostile Indians away from his "brother."

The passion which joins together the men of races forbidden to mingle in marriage is everywhere in Cooper, appearing finally in *The Chainbearer,* in which Mordaunt Littlepage falls in love at first sight with the old Indian known variously as Susquesus, Sureflint, and Trackless. The passage is quite remarkable. Sureflint advances with the customary declaration of loneliness, "No tribe—no squaw—no papoose"; and Littlepage comments, comparing the red-skin with the pale-face girl his family are urging him to marry, "Priscilla Bayard herself, however lovely, graceful, winning and feminine, had not created a feeling so strong and animated, as that which was awakened within me in behalf of old Sureflint." This quite extraordinary reaction is paralleled, as James Grossman points out, by Natty Bumppo's declaration to Jasper, his presumable rival for Mabel Dunham in *The Pathfinder:* "if I had to marry you, boy, I should give myself no consarn about my being well looked upon . . . ," though this time, for once, the beloved boy is white.

The final give-away comes, however, as Grossman is again acute enough to see, in *Jack Tier,* a sea story published toward the end of Cooper's writing career. In this novel, there is sketched an erotic relationship between two males—old buddies they seem at first glance, though one has forgotten or pretends to have forgotten the other—so complicated in its blend of love and hate, loyalty and rejection, that it is rivaled only by such Melvillean sinister homoerotic relationships as those of Redburn and Jackson, Billy Budd and Claggart. Cooper seems on the very verge of treating candidly the kind of feeling that, romanticized and idealized, had lent an attractive ambiguity to the companionship of Chingachgook and Natty Bumppo; but at the very last minute, he loses his nerve and "reveals" that the evil Captain Spike's strange friend, Jack Tier—is really a woman, Spike's wife, Molly Swash! By 1848, however, there was little Cooper could do to undercut his own creation; his version of a love between males, more enduring and purer than any heterosexual passion, had become an undying myth as had Natty and Chingachgook, perhaps the only two characters in American literature endowed with the kind of archetypal life otherwise lived by Don Juan, Don Quixote, Falstaff, and Robinson Crusoe.

ACHIEVEMENT
AND
FRUSTRATION

8

CLARISSA IN AMERICA:

TOWARD

MARJORIE MORNINGSTAR

NONE OF THE FORMS of the novel adapted from European prototypes has influenced American fiction more profoundly than the
sentimental tale of seduction. First of all, the seduction story
proper has never for long ceased to be written or read in the
United States; dismissed as old-fashioned, exhausted, intolerable,
it reappears not only as the best-seller but even as the advanced,
the New Novel. In the second place, the heroine of the seduction
struggle, the Protestant Virgin and redeemer first called Clarissa,
has continued to impose herself on American life and fiction alike,
outliving even the abandonment of the fable in which she confronted the Seducer. Third, and most important of all, the long
uncontested reign in America of sentimental archetypes and
clichés has made it almost impossible for our novelists to portray
adult sexual passion or a fully passionate woman.

On the most popular level, of course, the combat of the pure
woman and the seducer-rapist has never been abandoned, though
it seems for a while to have been exiled to the drama and from
there to have passed to the moving pictures. The earliest cinema
assimilated the fallen archetypes of seduction along with many
others; and in one sub-form of the lowbrow Western, the traditional sex combat is played out to the present moment, the white-
hatted hero intervening just before the black-hatted villain manages to violate the rancher's blond daughter. Even the old class
distinctions are dimly maintained, the seducer being given often
the status of dude, gambler, or banker, and wearing, until quite

217

recently, not only the black mufti of civilian life, but also an "Eastern," upper-class mustache. The horse-opera version of the seduction fable represents a male kidnaping of an originally female theme: the projection of an erotic daydream in which the Fair Maiden is first (almost) raped, then rescued to be legally possessed, but *cannot save herself.*

Both hero and villain of the latter-day sentimental story are, as we observed earlier, created by splitting the Lovelace figure into two components, whatever is truly masculine and cleanly attractive being identified with the "good," and whatever is grossly phallic or unduly polished being identified with the "bad." The nonrepentant Lovelace, who wants merely to enjoy Clarissa sexually, is made one man; and the repentant Lovelace, who wants to marry her, is made another. Sometimes, indeed, the white-hatted Lovelace is permitted a genital past, symbolized by a previous connection with some dark, preferably Mexican, prostitute, in which he has burned away all lust, purified himself for the blond Maiden. On the basis of such hints, or of none at all, the audience puts Humpty-Dumpty together again, joins in its own consciousness the halves of the fragmented hero-villain. The spectator tears the dress from the pale shoulder and breast of the struggling girl in the lonely cabin, and at the same time pounds toward the cabin on his lathered white horse to save her. His better and worse instincts simultaneously gratified, he cheers as the bunkhouse Clarissa, still safe though charmingly ruffled, learns that her virginity does not save but must be saved by the male deliverer, who will extort it from her (legally, legally!) as the price of her delivery.

Neither shifts in official morality, nor literary manifestos proclaiming sexual freedom, nor even actual changes in social behavior appear to have shaken the mystique of virginity on which our response to the threat of rape and seduction depends. It is our least rational attitudes toward sex to which the seduction story appeals; and on that level, the responses of men and women are sharply distinguished from each other. Women, at least, seem to find little archetypal satisfaction in the sub-variety of the Western which makes the heroine a contested pawn. Yet in the latter half of the nineteenth century, the female audience, pledgd to an almost intolerable gentility, no longer could relish without feelings of guilt the old fantasy in which the figures with which they identified were first ravished, then succeeded by their humility in castrating their ravishers. In its place, there appeared a mythic proto-literature in which women eternally suffer not from sexual assault but from the general failure of males—not, that is to say, from men's potency but from their weakness: their cowardice, lack of moral firmness, insufficient intelligence, proneness to get drunk or ill, or to die when most needed, The popular line of Richardsonianism ends in the seduction story without seduction!

Its history in the more serious novel is almost equally duplicitous. Cooper, like Scott, had accepted the decision of the genteel audience that ladies could no longer be seduced, at least in the pages of books; but like his Scotch predecessor, he felt free to permit lower-class characters to endure that ungenteel indignity, even to the point of becoming pregnant. Against Cora and Alice, he would not, as we have noticed, allow the threat of sexual violation to be raised, only that of a forced marriage and consignment to a wigwam; but Judith Hutter in *The Deerslayer* is far enough removed from the upper ranks of society to be portrayed as doubly involved in the seduction tangle. Cooper is desperately polite in his language, reticent to the point of obscurity; but it is clear that Judith is herself the offspring of a mother seduced or abandoned, and that her coquetry and her refusal to accept her station in life have, if not deprived her of her virginity, at least so compromised her honor that she is not a fit bride for Deerslayer. It is typical of Cooper—who reverses in this respect the meanings implicit in the seduction theme—that he makes of Judith's indiscreet involvement with the officers in the British garrison an occasion for a sermon not against the effrontery of upper-class seducers, but against the shamelessness of female social climbers, willing to barter their virtue for a rise in status.

Nonetheless, Cooper did not seem really at home with the seduction story, using it only this once and then quite peripherally; indeed, his major themes afforded him no scope for developing the deeper meanings of the Clarissa archetype. William Gilmore Simms, on the other hand, who is perhaps Cooper's most successful follower both in tales of Indian warfare and of the American Revolution, was attracted to the seduction fable in one of its most popular forms. In two novels, he succeeded in giving fictional form to the famous "Kentucky tragedy" which, occurring first as fact, passed almost immediately into literature, and has ever since continued to haunt the imagination of American writers. In *Charlemont,* which was published in 1856, and *Beauchampe,* actually a sequel to the first novel though it appeared in 1842, Simms tells a tale which had already served as the kernel of *Greyslear* (1840) by Charles Fenno Hoffman and an unfinished play by Edgar Allan Poe called *Politian* (1835-36). The account of how Anna Cooke persuaded a certain Jeroboam Beauchamp to kill for her sake a prominent Kentucky politician and attorney, Solomon P. Sharp, who had in her girlhood seduced her, and how the accomplices, after being sentenced to be hanged, committed suicide, makes a choice melodrama; the very embodiment of a Romantic era, which that era itself could not forbear turning into a myth. Not only Poe and Hoffman and Simms, but the playwrights Charlotte Barnes, John Savage, and T. H. Chivers took up the theme; and in *World Enough and Time* (1950), Robert Penn Warren returned to it once more, seeking in its mythic substance clues to the meanings of justice and honor in an age when Byronism had inflated those concepts with passionate rhetoric. The popular success of Warren's novel indicates how, under whatever aegis, the seduction story continues to stir the popular mind; and its uncomfortable rejection by many highbrow critics, who had until the appearance of this novel considered Warren one of their own, is a sign of how baffled the merely literary man may be by such archetypal material.

For Simms, some twenty years after the actual episode, the story offered the spectacular possibilities inherent in gossip about prominent personalities (he scarcely changed the real names of his protagonists), as well as the gothic appeal of dark violence and shrill melodrama. He was a writer with a truly operatic taste for posturing and high-flown language, so that when his heroine, called first Margaret Cooper, then Anna Cooke, cries out, "War always with my foe—war to the knife—war to the last!" we almost fancy we are hearing it sung. The terrific moments are all mercilessly exploited: the dying murderers in each other's arms; the stabbing of the cowardly Solomon Sharp by Beauchamp, who cannot provoke him to a duel; the desperate whispering of Sharp that he could not have been the father of Anna's child, since it was born black! Simms is, of course, a Southerner, who ended estranged from much of his audience over slavery and the Civil War, and the merest *hint* of miscegenation is about all he can manage, though in other matters he is so brutally explicit that Poe himself found him "revolting." " 'It was not mine!' " Simms has Sharp say of Anna's baby, " 'and to say whose it was is scarce so easy a matter, but—' and he drew nigh and whispered the rest of the sentence, some three syllables, into the ears of the husband."

Those three syllables the prurient, race-haunted imagination of the Southerner presumably had no difficulty in supplying.

Yet Simms was not interested only in the horror to be wrested from his material. Good Sentimentalist as well as belated gothicist, he extorts the tear as well as the shudder. Primarily, however, Simms thinks of himself as a historian, a sociologist; and he finds the roots of the double crime of passion and revenge in the social conditions of the border: that leading edge of the westward movement, that margin which symbolizes the yearning for innocence and its inevitable defeat. (It is an aspect of the story which particularly intrigues Warren later on.) "The population of a frontier country . . . scattered over a large territory," Simms writes in the "Advertisement" to *Charlemont,* "and meeting infrequently, feels the lack of social intercourse; and this tends to break down most of the barriers which a strict convention usually establishes for the protection . . . of sex and caste. . . . It follows, naturally, that they are frequently wronged and outraged, and just as naturally that their resentments are keen, eager and vindictive." It is an acute enough observation of the genesis of the "code of the West," a type of insight available to one who, born in Charleston, South Carolina, lived for some time as a young man under frontier conditions in Mississippi.

But Simms is not content to attribute the fall of Anna and her excessive lust for vengeance simply to "conditions." The very nature of the fable, in which the seduced girl does not immediately forgive and die, but lives long enough to strike back through a male avenger, who is merely the extension of her will; in which she does not convert and redeem by Christian example, but destroys by a border code of honor—contains an implicit condemnation of that girl for betraying her archetypal role. Simms's two-volume work is the first protest in our literature against woman's refusal in life to act out the humble, long-suffering part assigned her by the Richardsonian myth.

Simms is quite explicit on this score in the same "Advertisement." "Her character and career will illustrate most of the mistakes which are made by that ambitious class, among the gentle sex, who are now seeking so earnestly to pass out from that province of humiliation to which the sex has been circumscribed from the first moment of recorded history." And he goes out of his way to point out, as a warning to those not yet utterly lost, that the "proposed change in her condition threatens fatally some of

her own and the best securities of humanity." Like a good Richardsonian Sentimentalist aware of living in an unfavorable age,
he reminds the Anna Cookes of his time of what every Clarissa
once knew, that her essential function is to typify the heart ("Her
very influence over man lies in her sensibilities"), not to usurp
the function of the head ("It will be a perilous fall . . . when . . .
in the extreme development of the mere intellect, she shall forfeit
a single one of those securities of her sex").

Simms is not, to be sure, a distinguished writer, as he himself
well knew; he is only a symptomatic one. "Here lies one," he
wrote in a modest epitaph composed for himself, "who, after a
reasonably long life, distinguished by unceasing labors, has left
all his better work undone." Yet once in his career he hit upon
an archetypal theme and saw through to its meanings, which others
had fumbled away. Unlike Poe or Mrs. Bragaldi, who transposed
an essentially American and nineteenth-century fable to seventeenth-century Rome or fifteenth-century Milan, or C. F. Hoffman,
who moved it back to Revolutionary days—watering the seduction
down to a mere abduction—Simms kept his tale at that precise
point in time when the American woman was sloughing off one
role, known in all its possibilities, for another, dangerously unexplored. That he succeeded in adapting the seduction archetype
to the inner needs of women and the inner fears of men in his
own time is a tribute both to his own acuity and to the resiliency
of the myth with which he worked.

II

Hawthorne was engaged in a similar venture at just about the same
time, portraying first in Hester in *The Scarlet Letter,* then in Zenobia in *The Blithedale Romance,* the spirit of impatience with
their status that moved women in his world. There is something
a little unconvincing in his projection of feminism back into the
seventeenth century. He can attribute prophetic anticipations of
female discontent to Hester, but there is nothing for her to *do*
with them inside the scene Hawthorne has imagined for her, since
they are portrayed by Hawthorne not as the causes of her seduction but as its consequence, irresponsible conceptions of a mind
which has been condemned to live outside the law and society
itself. Yet Hawthorne's description of Hester's theories makes

them sound like the notions Simms attributes to Anna Cooke:

> Indeed, the same dark question often rose into her mind, with reference to the whole race of womanhood. Was existence worth accepting, even to the happiest among them? . . . As a first step, the whole system of society is to be torn down and built up anew. Then, the very nature of the opposite sex, or its long hereditary habit, which has become like nature, is to be essentially modified, before woman can be allowed to assume what seems a fair and suitable position. Finally, all other difficulties being obviated, woman cannot take advantage of these preliminary reforms, until she herself shall have undergone a still mightier change; in which, perhaps, the ethereal essence, wherein she has her truest life, will be found to have evaporated.

Though he has earlier denied to females of Hester's era the "ethereal" quality of their later descendants, Hawthorne has at this point forgotten which world he is in. His quarrel is not with Hester but, through her, with the emancipated ladies of his own time.

It is for their sake that he has Hester finally disavow the temptation to become the deliverer of her sex, has her confess herself too "stained with sin, bowed down with shame" to perform a task which demands an "angel and apostle . . . lofty, pure and beautiful." By her submission, Hester saves herself from the fate of Zenobia, in whom feminism is real, contemporary, and unrepented (she is suspected of being a portrait of Margaret Fuller), and who is visited with a final fate more vindictively stage-managed than any other doom in Hawthorne. Described as "Woman, bruising herself against the narrow limitations of her sex," Zenobia is actually bruised against the ambivalent hostility of Miles Coverdale, the narrator of the novel in which she appears, and of Hawthorne, who speaks almost directly through the mask of Coverdale. It is hard to know which infuriates Hawthorne more, Zenobia's impassioned cry, "If I live another year, I will lift up my own voice in behalf of woman's wider liberty!" or her abject surrender to the brutally masculine reformer, Hollingsworth, who shouts down her plea for women's rights: ". . . if there were a chance of their attaining the end which these petticoated monstrosities have in view, I would call upon my own sex to use its physical force, that unmistakeable evidence of sovereignty, to scourge them back within their proper bounds!"

The impotent, failed poet Coverdale in some sense must mean his assurance that he would love to kneel before a woman ruler, bow in adoration to a Protestant Virgin; though he is convinced, too, that only a broken heart makes women reformers rather than passive lovers, that feminism is the result of ill-regulated or ill-bestowed passion. Perhaps, most of all, he distrusts Zenobia not for being an emancipated woman but for being a fully sexual one, for having forced him, at their first meeting, to imagine her naked ("in Eve's earliest garments," he delicately puts it), to respond to what in her is rich, warm, and dangerous. For having sinned in the flesh with men more masculine than he, and for having survived in all the opulence of that flesh to pollute his imagination, Zenobia must—in Coverdale's telling of the tale—die, the victim of her own despair. Hawthorne-Coverdale's portrait of the drowned Zenobia, fished up after her suicide, is a masterpiece of sadistic horror, pregnant with all the nuances proper not to her life but to the nauseating dream which betrays a shameful, unconfessed wish.

It is not only with the seduction of the corrupted woman, "high-spirited" or "headstrong," that Hawthorne deals, but also with that of the pale, the "ethereal'" Maiden; though he cannot find it in his heart—or more precisely, perhaps, within the limits of the decorum he shared with his age—to portray the actual ruin of any innocent. His "weakly maidens," eternally threatened, eternally escape; and even his full-blown passionate females are only *postulated* as sexually experienced. His reticence extends to describing the actual fall even of those indecorous females to whom the loss of chastity comes in part as a consequence of their own refusal to believe in its importance. It is notorious that *The Scarlet Letter* is a seduction story without a seduction, a parable of the Fall with the Fall offstage and before the action proper begins. Similarly, the hinted-at but never quite defined original sin of Zenobia or of Miriam in *The Marble Faun* must be taken on faith. Certain women move onto Hawthorne's fictional stage already deflowered; no woman is deflowered in his fictional present.

Hawthorne is the only American novelist of classic stature who deals centrally in his most important works with the seduction theme; yet there is no seduction scene (even the devirgination of Donatello, which is of a man by a woman, is accomplished in the outer darkness between chapters and could not be proved in court) in any of his works! Perhaps it is just as well that he never tried one, since the American conventions for describing such scenes were vulgar and false to a degree that defied redemption. How much more moving and even sexually exciting is Hawthorne's description of Hester's symbolic letting down of her hair before her lover in the forest clearing ("By another impulse, she took off the formal cap that confined her hair; and down it fell upon her shoulders, dark and rich, with at once a shadow and a light in its abundance . . .") than Simms's intendedly passionate evocation of Margaret-Anna's surrender in another forest (". . . and there they lingered! He, fond, artful, persuasive; she, trembling with the dangerous sweetness of wild, unbidden emotions. Ah! why did she not go? . . . The moon rose until she hung in the zenith . . . the rivulet ran along, still prattling through the groves . . . but they no longer heard the prattle of the rivulet . . . and it was only when they were about to depart, that poor Margaret discovered that the moon had all the while been looking down upon them . . .").

Yet from his very first novel on, Hawthorne had attempted to deal with the seduction theme, evoking in *Fanshawe* stereotypes right out of the stock of the genteel sentimental novel: the depraved Seducer, the virtuous Maiden, the brave young lover—Lovelace and Clarissa, plus the supernumerary male rescuer made necessary by the latter-day failure of nerve before the prospect of letting any real young lady get raped.

Any of the "d——d female scribblers," whom Hawthorne thought of as his rivals, could have done as well with the sentimental New-Comic plot: a virgin is tricked by a scoundrel with a forged letter, purportedly from her father, and led off into a lonely valley where she is on the point of being violated when she is rescued by her true lover. This absurdly conventional action is rendered in the style of the female epigones of Richardson, with no real inwardness, almost none of the sustained, almost painfully detailed psychological probing which is the forte of their master.

Sentiment seems, for all his choice of theme, to concern Hawthorne as little in *Fanshawe* as does psychology. He capitalizes scandalously little upon the sentimental possibilities of his story, milking for the proper quota of tears only the episode of a criminal at his mother's deathbed, and the scene in which the girl praying for her virtue dares call upon that criminal in the name of that abandoned mother. "I have thought of my mother . . . ," Hawthorne has him answer; "I remember the neglect, the wrong . . . that she received at my hands . . . by those words you have turned my heart to stone." Perhaps the lonely young man who had long lived in a widowed mother's house knew more about the feelings involved in the inevitable betrayals of mothers by sons than of the passion of a rapist. Beyond this hidden allusion to his own home life, Hawthorne is no more deeply involved in the pathos of abused innocence and the terror of hardened criminality than he is in the female satisfactions of a matrimonial happy ending. Neither emotional aspect of his ill-chosen fable accords with his need to project at the beginning of his writing career the self-distrust and self-pity which, under his irony and reserve, were to remain the hallmarks of his fiction. The dread of social, artistic, and sexual failure is imposed on the uncongenial theme, bends it toward the pathetic at least, if not the tragic. By a simple doubling of the heroic male protagonist, Hawthorne adopts the stereotypes of seduction to his own deepest personal exigencies.

His heroine, Ellen Langton, that is to say, has not the customary one, but two true lovers: Edward Walcott, who is handsome, vigorous, full of natural grace and forgivable "boyish" excesses; and Fanshawe, who is slight, pale, melancholy—afflicted by some mysterious "blight ere maturity." The latter is, in short, a Werther-like portrait of the scholar-artist as a doomed young man, a type to whom Hawthorne elsewhere in his early work gives the name "Oberon" to indicate that he is not of this world. The Oberon character can by definition neither get the girl or live to full maturity, yet in *Fanshawe* he is permitted to beat his healthier competitor to the struggling maiden, actually to save her by his intervention. It is a concession to self-pity, the last kindness of the defeated artist to his own image; yet Hawthorne, even in so melting a mood, refuses to imagine Oberon-Fanshawe in actual physical combat with the forces of evil. His melancholy hero merely tosses a stone into the ravine where Ellen is pleading with her abductor, distracts that abductor from his purpose, and watches as the attacker, eager to destroy all witnesses to his crime, climbs the steep side of a cliff, slips and falls to his death.

After Ellen is thus saved, however, Fanshawe does not claim her hand; only in the moment of her swoon, when she seems more charming corpse than menacing live female, can he achieve a sort of consummation. "He lifted the motionless form of Ellen in his arms, and . . . gazed on her cheek of lily paleness with a joy, a triumph, that rose almost to madness. . . . He bent over her, and pressed a kiss—the first, and he knew it would be the last—on her pale lips. . . ." It is a way of *not* eating your cake and having it, too.

It is clear from the logic of Fanshawe's character as Hawthorne has conceived it that he cannot have the girl, any girl, that he is psychologically impotent; but Hawthorne prefers to have him disavow her, deliberately reject the salvation she offers, choosing instead an early grave, after which Ellen is free to marry Edward Walcott, whom her patience and faithfulness save from roistering and other "passions and pursuits that would have interfered with domestic felicity."

Fanshawe is finally an unsuccessful novel, but in it Hawthorne finds the pattern and invents the protagonists that inform almost all the rest of his work. In *The Blithedale Romance,* for instance, his next-to-the-last completed novel, the personae of *Fanshawe* reappear in a more richly worked out social context, and with a more complex kind of inwardness as well as a more consistent symbolic significance. Fanshawe has become Miles Coverdale, peeping Tom and unsuccessful artist, who is not permitted this time the luxury of saving anyone or even of dying, but only of confessing at the end that he has all along loved the girl he could not win for himself. Hollingsworth, who corresponds to Edward Walcott, aggressive, phallic, desired by women though in minor ways sadly astray, is once more allowed the marriage which is his salvation. This time, however, he is humbled even as he is saved, spiritually castrated, since in his case the "passions and pursuits that would have interfered with domestic felicity" are his ideas for social reform, the "philanthropy" which has been the vital core of his life. Poor, lucky Hollingsworth totters, almost crawls to the happy ending; it is Hawthorne-Oberon-Coverdale's secret revenge.

Between *Fanshawe* and *The Blithedale Romance,* the Oberon character, who embodies Hawthorne's earliest view of the function and fate of the artist, is variously transformed. In *The Scarlet Letter,* he becomes Dimmesdale, the artist as hypocrite, the man whose power over words and souls is based on an unconfessable guilt; and his secret sin is identified as seduction. Certainly, *The Scarlet Letter* is the only eminent American book before the modern period to have made—or to have seemed to make—passionate love its center, and it was this which moved the scandalized critics to talk about the beginnings of "a French era" in our chaste literature. Actually, Howthorne's short novel is not as much against the American grain as it superficially appears to be. Master of duplicity, he is especially duplicitous in this regard, refusing, for instance, even to mention in his text the word "adultery," though the "A" which symbolizes it glows at the center of almost every scene. The little Puritan children of the seventeenth century, franker than adults of the nineteenth, are permitted "the utterance of the word that had no distinct purport to their own minds, but was more than terrible to her [Hester] . . ."; but the reader is not permitted to overhear it. As a matter of fact, little children in more recent generations, taking the book off the shelves in the children's library, where it has been permitted to stay by the most high-minded librarians, have doubtless been puzzled over what the mysterious letter does stand for, since no word for Hester's crime that is familiar to them begins with that chaste letter.

Though sex is centrally present in *The Scarlet Letter* as it is not in our other great novels, it is there rendered reticently, incomprehensibly enough to seem, though not innocent, perhaps, as good as innocent. To understand just how shadowy and sterilized its treatment of passion really is, it is only necessary to compare Hawthorne's novella with a real example of the continental novel, with Rousseau's *Nouvelle Héloïse,* for instance. We know he regarded that novel highly all his life, first reading it because it was forbidden, and describing it as "admirable" in a list of books which he prepared for himself at the age of sixteen. More importantly, he returned to it just when he was ready to produce *The Scarlet Letter,* bogging down this time, but reviving in himself a sense of that forbidden and secretly relished work. In the course of a pilgrimage to the Rousseau country in 1859, he wrote:

In Switzerland, I found myself more affected by Clarens, the scene of the love of St. Preux and Julia, than I have often been by the scenes of romance and poetry. I read Rousseau's romance with great sympathy when I was hardly more than a boy; ten years ago or more I tried to read it again, without success; but from my feeling of yesterday I think it still retains its hold on my imagination.

It is possible to exaggerate the parallels between the book that moved Hawthorne in his youth and the one he wrote in his middle age, yet certain general similarities are really there. The three characters of Julie, Saint-Preux, and Wolmar correspond illuminatingly with Hester, Dimmesdale, and Chillingworth; and the basic pattern of the *Nouvelle Héloïse* is repeated in *The Scarlet Letter:* a second temptation after a first fall, ending in an unnatural triangle perpetuated under strange circumstances. The differences, however, are more striking and more significant, especially the expurgation in Hawthorne's book of all direct reference to the physical aspects of passion. From Hawthorne's imagination, fired in adolescence, Rousseau's fable must pass through his conscience, created in solitude and confirmed in his marriage to a good woman; and it emerges finally much transformed. The dangerous doctrines that passion justifies all and that adulterous love renounced on earth will be recognized in heaven survive in Hawthorne not as articles of faith, but as problematical convictions, temptations to Faustian pride. Moreover, passion is rendered in *The Scarlet Letter* not as lived, but as remembered or proposed. The reality of the flesh, which in Rousseau provides a counterbalance to his excessive sentimentality, tends to disappear in Hawthorne.

The anti-rhetoric of Hawthorne, which defends him against sentimentality, also prevents him from rendering sensuality, dissolves all ecstasies in ironies. Everywhere in his work a peculiar tension is created between the passionate analogues he evokes and the dispassionate quality of his actual text. Behind Dimmesdale and Hester, we are aware not only of Saint-Preux and Julie, but of the original Abelard and Héloïse, castrated priest and his beloved, and of David and Bathsheba, whose love is portrayed in the tapestries of Dimmesdale's house. Again and again in the text, references are made to the infamous Overbury case, Chillingworth being identified with the Dr. Forman who was its chief villain. But the filth involved in that case: the suggestions of homosexuality, the aphrodisiacs, the poison enemas, the wax mommets with a "thorn thrust through the privity"—all these are transmuted into abstract evocations of evil and concupiscence.

In the end, we are left with the sense that surely something more terrible than mere adultery is at stake behind all the reticences and taboos, that Hawthorne may be dealing, half-consciously at least, with the sin of incest, for which his mother's family, the Mannings, had once been publicly disgraced. So at least

one commentator (Vernon Loggins in *The Hawthornes*) has suggested, and this Hawthorne's life-long preoccupation with the
theme, as well as the moment at which he composed his greatest
novel, would seem to confirm. *Felt's Annals,* referred to in the
"Custom-House Introduction," records the unsavory case of the
Mannings; and the pictures it evokes jibe with the key images of
The Scarlet Letter: two girls in the market-place, each with an "I"
in her cap; and their beloved brother fleeing through the lawless
wilderness! Brother-sister incest: it is the kind of love, as we have
seen, proper to the gothic tale, of which *The Scarlet Letter* is the
supreme example in our fiction; but in that book, it has been
translated down to a less terrible crime, which itself has been
reduced to its own mere initial. Historically, a woman found guilty
of adultery would have been condemned to wear the two letters
"AD"; but this seems to Hawthorne not abstract enough, and he
substitutes the single "A," that represents the beginning of all
things, and that, in the primers of New England, stood for *Adam's
Fall*—in which we (quite unspecifically) sinned all!

The carnal act upon which adultery depends is not merely unnamed in *The Scarlet Letter;* it is further deprived of reality by
being displaced in time, postulated rather than described. So displaced, that act becomes in the psychologist's sense, prehistoric;
affects us much as the spied-upon primal scene (mother and father
intertwined in bed), blurred by the amnesia of guilt. It is an original sin, more an "emblem" or a "type," in Hawthorne's terms,
than a deed. "Ye that wronged me are not sinful," Chillingworth
says to his wife and her lover, "save in a kind of typical illusion."
In one sense, the postulated original sin seems merely a convenient
explanatory device. Certainly, it accounts naturalistically for the
existence of Pearl, the illegitimate daughter of Hester. But Pearl
seems less a real child than an allegorical representation of the
fruits of sin; and we are offered, as if jestingly, the alternative
explanation that she is a by-blow of the Devil. In addition, Hester
must be from the very beginning a mother, though she appears
among men who are, within the time of the story itself, rendered
as impotent. The impotence of Dimmesdale, however, must be felt
as a punishment, the typical self-castration of the seducer, celebrated in the American novel from the time of *Charlotte Temple;*
and we are, therefore, asked to believe that at some point before
the action begins he traduced Hester's innocence, thus unmanning
himself. Actually, he is portrayed as one for whom sex is a re-

membered nightmare or a futilely longed-for hope; and he does not even kiss Hester at his moment of Satanic exhilaration in the forest.

If it is finally hard for us to believe *on a literal level* in the original adultery of Hester and Dimmesdale, this is because their whole prehistory remains shadowy and vague. Hawthorne's gestures at indicating the social backgrounds and historical contexts of his characters are half-hearted and unconvincing, a bow toward realism. And his book is finally dream-like rather than documentary, not at all the historical novel it has been often called—evoking the past as nightmare rather than fact. It is, therefore, easier to believe in the diabolical transportation of Chillingworth from Germany than in any more rational theory of his arrival on the scene; just as it is easier to imagine Pearl plucked from a rosebush than carried for nine months within her mother. All the characters come into existence when the book begins and do not survive. Hester is simply not there until the prison doors open; and at that moment Chillingworth drops from the air. So born they must die with the action's close—contrary to the traditions of the Victorian novel. For all his desire to end his book like his contemporaries, Hawthorne finds it difficult to say simply that Pearl left the country and married well. He is much more comfortable with the end of Chillingworth, who withered away, as is quite proper for a protagonist regarded by his author as a "shadowy figure," one of a "tribe of unrealities," who cease to exist when he stops thinking of them.

Actors in a dark hallucination, Hawthorne's protagonists are aptly moved by a guilt as hallucinatory as themselves: a crime as vaguely defined, though as inescapable in its consequences, as the unknowable transgression in Kafka's *The Trial*. It is enough for Hawthorne to suggest the Oedipus situation: an equivocal mother, an evil father—and between them, Dimmesdale, who is described as first as "child-like" and at last as "childish." The whole action moves toward the climactic moment, when, after years of cowardly silence and a momentary temptation to flee, that child-figure totters into the noonday public square to confess his fault before the whole community. At that point, Oedipus-Dimmesdale blends with the image of Doctor Johnson standing in the Uttoxeter market-place to make public amends for an offense against his father. It is a story which obsessed Hawthorne all his life, which he wrote out as an exemplary tale for children and told himself in his diary, a story obviously representing to him some buried guilt of his own.

That guilt the prehistoric fall of *The Scarlet Letter* explains, too, in encoded form. It is incarnate in Hester, most "gorgeous" of his Dark Ladies; for "gorgeous" is to Hawthorne a dirty word—a token of pollution. But why is gorgeousness a trap and love a crime, why beauty forbidden and joy banned to the nineteenth-century American? There was, *The Scarlet Letter* suggests, another fall in the Eden of the New World at precisely the moment at which the book unfolds, a communal fall to match Hester's private one. The very first page tells us that "whatever Utopia of human virtue and happiness" men may imagine in whatever land, they find it necessary "to allot a portion of the virgin soil as a cemetery, and another portion as the site of a prison." Before such a prison, Hawthorne's tale begins, and in such a cemetery, it comes to a close; and between, he attempts to explain how sin and death, for whose sake they exist, have come into the Puritan Common-wealth. Yet it is, finally, his own crisis of conscience that Haw-thorne translates into a mythical history of America, his own ex-perience of womanhood that he projects in Hester.

Sitting day after day beside the bed of his dying mother, con-fronted by his wife of whom she did not approve, and watching through the window his daughter Una playing the death scene to which she must eventually come—Hawthorne must have become aware with special poignancy of the web of femaleness in which we are involved from cradle to grave. But what this glimpse into the maternal mysteries did to him we do not know, except for the fact that he wept once when his mother died, again when he had fin-ished the "hell-fired" book which is her memorial; and that some-where between these two public betrayals of emotion, he suffered from what his family called "brain-fever."

The incest theme, however, even in its disguise of adultery, be-longs primarily to the pre-plot of *The Scarlet Letter;* its plot is concerned with a second, quite different fall: a second temptation, in the face of which his characters, postulated as having been powerless before the "dark necessity" of their original fall, are portrayed as capable of free choice. Yet their freedom is ironic, for what they must learn freely to accept is the notion that free-dom is the recognition of necessity. *The Scarlet Letter* is the most utopian of American books: not the Paradise Regained it seems at first, but only an Eden Revisited.

In the seeming Eden of the New World, a man and woman, who are still essentially the old Adam and Eve, deceive themselves for a moment into believing that they can escape the consequences of sin. The woman has served a prison term and bears on her breast the sign of her shame, and the man, who was the occasion of that shame, has lived secretly with his guilt and powerless remorse; yet in their deluded hope, they meet in the forest, plot a flight from the world of law and religion. For an instant, that hope seems to transfigure not only them, but the dark wood into which they have strayed. When Hester flings aside the scarlet letter and lets down her hair, the forest glows to life: "Such was the sympathy of . . . wild, heathen Nature . . . never subjugated by law, nor illumined by higher truth with the bliss of these two spirits. Love . . . must always create a sunshine that overflows upon the natural world."

Yet Hawthorne cannot grant these lovers even the mitigated bliss he earlier permitted the May King and Queen in "The Maypole of Merry Mount"; for between them lies the taboo of adultery, as real to him as to his ancestors. Hawthorne does not accept without qualification the judgment of his ancestors, though he condemns Hester's proposal of flight even as they would have, uses to describe it the Faustian metaphor. He is, after all, a modern, secular thinker, for whom nothing is self-evident, everything problematical; and he is being tempted as he writes to make a retreat from his own community very like Hester's. Yet, for all his quarrel with Puritanism and its persecuting zeal, he knows that no American can really leave behind the America which the Puritans have once and for all defined.

America represents for Hawthorne not only the marginal settlement, set between corrupt civilization and unredeemed nature, but also the rule of moral law in the place of self-justifying passion or cynical gallantry. In *The Scarlet Letter,* passion justifies nothing, while its denial redeems all. The fallen Eden of this world remains fallen; but the sinful priest purges himself by public confession, becomes worthy of his sole remaining way to salvation, death. Even Hester, though sin and suffering have made her an almost magical figure, a polluted but still terrible goddess, must finally accept loneliness and self-restraint instead of the love and freedom she dreamed. She cannot become the greater Ann Hutchinson she might have been had she remained unfallen, cannot redeem her sex from the indignities against which she once raged and plotted in secret. Passion has opened up for her no new possibilities, only closed off older ones.

The relationship of Hester and Dimmesdale is not, however, the only passionate connection in the novel. Through the five years covered by the book's action (the unwritten pre-plot takes up two more, from the marriage with Chillingworth to the birth of Pearl, thus adding up to the mystic seven), one relationship grows in intimacy, depth, and terror. In it, Dimmesdale plays a key role once more, though this time a passive, feminine one, his tremulous hand laid to his heart. Between him and Chillingworth, grows an intense, destructive emotion (a "dark passion," Hawthorne calls it), compounded of the intolerable intimacy of doctor and patient, analyst and analysand, husband and wife, father and son, cuckold and cuckolder. It is a bond like that which elsewhere in American literature joins together Simon Legree and Uncle Tom, Claggart and Billy Budd, Babo and Benito Cereno.

Both earlier and later in Hawthorne's own work, such connections exist between the sexes: father and daughter, as in "Rappaccini's Daughter"; husband and wife, as in "The Birthmark"; mesmerist and female subject, as in *The Blithedale Romance;* or lover and beloved, as in "Ethan Brand." In the last work, Hawthorne describes Esther as "the girl whom, with such cold and remorseless purpose, Ethan Brand had made the subject of a psychological experiment, and wasted, absorbed and perhaps annihilated her soul in the process." It is a pattern as old in our fiction as Brockden Brown's *Wieland;* and the prototype of the destructive lover is Carwin, in whom the seducer is merged (following Goethe's example) with the scientist, Don Juan with Faust. In Brown, however, as in Hawthorne everywhere else, the dark passion exists between a man and a woman. Chillingworth, however, is as much a devil as a man; while Dimmesdale is, of course, male: a one-time seducer reduced by unconfessed guilt to feminine passivity. And their relationship seems an odd combination of the tie between Faust and Gretchen, on the one hand, with that between Faust and Mephistopheles on the other.

The terms used to define the nature of their union are significant: "a kind of intimacy," a "paternal and reverential love," described by Dimmesdale's parishioners as the "best possible measure . . . unless he had selected some one of the many blooming damsels to become his devoted wife." Hester, who has been the wife of one and the mistress of the other, yet never as close to either as they are to each other, says reproachfully to Chillingworth: "no man is so near to him as you. . . . You are beside him, sleeping and waking. . . . You burrow and rankle in his heart. Your clutch is on his life." "Burrow" is the key word for Chillingworth's penetration of Dimmesdale's heart: "burrow into his intimacy . . . deep into the patient's bosom . . . delving . . . probing . . . in a dark cavern." The climax comes with the exposure of the secret of Dimmesdale's bosom, his own scarlet letter, embossed (perhaps!) in the very flesh. "He laid his hand on his bosom, and thrust aside the vestment," Hawthorne says at the moment of revelation, portraying Chillingworth in an ecstasy, leaping into the air. He knows at last the ultimate secret of his dearest enemy; and knowing it, has possessed him, accomplished a rape of the spirit beyond any penetration of the flesh. "He has violated," Hester comments, echoing Hawthorne's description of Ethan Brand, "the sanctity of the human heart."

Hawthorne is not content, however, to leave the last word with Hester, answering her in his own voice, his own typically hypothetical manner:

It is a curious subject of observation and inquiry, whether hatred and love be not the same thing at bottom. Each, in its utmost development, supposes a high degree of intimacy and heart knowledge; each renders one individual dependent for the food . . . of his spiritual life upon another. . . . In the spiritual world, the old physician and the minister—may, unawares, have found their earthly stock of hatred and antipathy transmuted into golden love.

Out of the ambivalence of love and hatred, the constitutionally double-dealing Hawthorne has distilled an equivocation which undercuts, at the last moment, the whole suggested meaning of his book. He has not, to be sure, committed himself finally; but his last qualification for the passion of Chillingworth and Dimmesdale is favorable, while his last word on that of Hester and Dimmesdale is quite the opposite. Though earlier Hester has boasted, "What we did had a consecration of its own," the only proof of her assertion she could offer was, "We felt it so! We said so to each other!" Dimmesdale does not demur in the forest, where he is temporarily mad; but he answers Hester in the market-place, at his moment of greatest insight: "It may be that we forgot our God—when we violated our reverence for each other's soul. . . ."

As one bucket goes up, the other goes down; and we are left with the disturbing paradox (mitigated, to be sure, by Hawthorne's customary, pussyfooting subjunctives: "may have found," "may be that we forgot") that love may conceal a destructive impulse and work for ill, while hatred may be only a disguised form of love and eventuate in good. If on the one hand, *The Scarlet Letter* leads toward a Goethe-like justification of diabolism as an instrument of salvation, on the other hand, it insists, in a very American way, upon the dangers of passion. It is certainly true, in terms of the plot, that Chillingworth drives the minister toward confession and penance, while Hester would have lured him to evasion and flight. But this means, for all of Hawthorne's equivocations, that the eternal feminine does not draw us on toward grace, rather that the woman promises only madness and damnation. It is the eternal demonic—personified in the wronged husband—which leads Dimmesdale on; and saved by his personal Serpent, he can in turn save his Eve—his apparent weakness deliver her apparent strength.

There is, however, a turn of the screw even beyond this; for though Hester works, perhaps unwittingly, to destroy Dimmesdale, saps his courage and brings him to the verge of selling his soul, it is to her that he must turn for support. Morally, he is finally stronger than she, but physically he depends upon her as a child upon its mother. It is on her arm that he ascends the scaffold, on her breast that he rests his trembling head. "Is she angel or devil?" Hawthorne's wife had asked him of Beatrice Rappaccini, when he was in the process of creating that prototype of Hester; and his answer was that he did not know! With Hester herself, he is still equivocal; she is the female temptress of Puritan mythology, but also, though sullied, the secular madonna of sentimental Protestantism, a true descendant, via Julie, of Clarissa.

Similarly, Dimmesdale is a descendant of Lovelace via Saint-Preux; though he is further transformed, as we have noted, following the example of Mrs. Rowson's Montraville. There is, in Hawthorne, a certain irony in the treatment of the unmanned seducer who represents, if not himself, an important aspect of that self; yet not even Montraville staggers to his end as feebly as Dimmesdale. His final reduction makes explicit the relationship in which the man and woman, who in the book's pre-history played Lovelace and

Clarissa, now stand: "It was hardly a man with life in him that tottered on his path so nervelessly. . . . He still walked onward, if that movement could be so described, which rather resembled the wavering effort of an infant with its mother's arms in view. . . ." Such motherly arms do, indeed, wait to receive him, the arms of Hester, of whom earlier Hawthorne has written: "Had there been a Papist among the crowd of Puritans . . . he might have seen in this beautiful woman . . . the image of Divine Maternity. . . ." The guilty lovers' consummation plotted in the forest between the minister and the outcast does not take place; but that minister, become a child, embraces innocently that outcast, sanctified by motherhood. "They beheld the minister, leaning on Hester's shoulder and supported by his arm around him. . . . Hester partly raised him, and supported his head against her bosom. . . ." At the last moment of his life, Dimmesdale, the eternal son, has found his way back to the breast, no longer barred to him by law or taboo. The qualified happy ending comes this time not from *Paradise Lost* but *Paradise Regained:* "Home to his Mother's house private return'd." It is the most suitable of endings for a book produced out of the anguish of personal failure and the death of a mother.

The Scarlet Letter is, then, our only classic book which makes passion a central theme. Born into an age and a class pledged to gentility, Hawthorne was denied a vocabulary adequate to his subject, driven back on duplicity and cunning; and in the end, he seems to adorn that subject rather than present it, conceal it with fancy needlework, "so that the Capital A might have been thought to mean . . . anything other than Adulteress." Indeed, the phrase from "Endicott and the Red Cross," written some thirteen years before *The Scarlet Letter,* suggests that from the first the cryptic "A" may have represented to Hawthorne not only "Adultery" but "Art." Certainly, he regarded his own art as involving precisely that adornment of guilt by craft which he attributes to Hester's prototype: "sporting with her infamy, the lost and desperate creature had embroidered the fatal token with golden thread and the nicest art of needlework. . . ."

Unable to break through the limitations of his era or to repress the shame he felt at trifling with them, Hawthorne ended by writing in the form of a love story an elegiac treatise on the death of love. *The Scarlet Letter* is, in one of its major aspects, a portrayal of the attenuation of sex in America, the shrinking on our shores from

Brobdingnagian parents to Lilliputian children. In a note in his journal, Hawthorne reminds himself that Brobdingnag, where Gulliver once sat astride the nipples of gross, lusty girls, was located on the coast of North America, home of the mid-nineteenth-century fleshless bluestocking! *The Scarlet Letter* is concerned not only with passion but also with America (another possible signification of Hester's letter), that is to say, it attempts to find in the story of Hester and Dimmesdale a paradigm of the fall of love in the New World. The Puritans who move through Hawthorne's pages belong to a first-generation community, which, despite its revolt against the paternal figures of kings and bishops, has not itself lost "the quality of reverence" or contracted "the disease of sadness, which almost all children in these latter days inherit along with the scrofula. . . ." The inhabitants of Hawthorne's seventeenth-century world still live in the Elizabethan afterglow; "for they were the offspring of sires . . . who had known how to be merry. . . ." It is the generation which succeeds them that made gaiety a "forgotten art" by darkening American life with "the blackest shade of Puritanism."

Hawthorne recreates these first ancestors not merely as merry rebels, but as mythical progenitors. Twice over he describes them as they pass ceremonially, a "procession of majestic and venerable fathers," among them his own ultimate "dim and dusky grandsire . . . grave, bearded, sable-cloaked and steeple-crowned. . . ." And the mothers who inhabit Hawthorne's dream are scarcely less overwhelming. "The women . . . stood within less than half a century of the period when Elizabeth had been the not altogether unsuitable representative of her sex. . . . The bright morning sun, therefore, shone on broad shoulders and well-developed busts, and on round and ruddy cheeks, that . . . had hardly grown paler and thinner in the atmosphere of New England." Hawthorne is, to be sure, somewhat ambivalent about the abundant fleshliness of these mothers of his race, suggesting that their "moral diet was not a bit more refined" than the beef and ale with which they satisfied their bellies. Yet there is something nostalgic, even rueful about his acknowledgment that since those early days "every successive mother has transmitted to her child a fainter bloom, a more delicate and briefer beauty, and a slighter physical frame. . . ."

To the world of such lush and substantial women, Hester unquestionably belongs. She is not an "ethereal" latter-day invalid like Sophia Hawthorne, but "lady-like . . . after the manner . . . of those days; characterized by a certain state and dignity, rather than by the delicate, evanescent and indescribable grace, which is now recognized as its indication." Dimmesdale, however, is no father, no mythic progenitor at all; after his love affair, at least (in which surely he was more seduced than seducing), he has been shrunken to Lilliputian size—seems a modern, alienated, anguished artist, transported into a more heroic age. He is not a Puritan, but a child of the Puritans, their diminished offspring, inheritor of melancholy, and the prototype of Hawthorne's own fallen generation. His fall from potency and his return to the maternal embrace just before death constitute an "emblem" of the fate of the American male. And when he is reborn, he becomes first Clifford Pyncheon in *The House of the Seven Gables* and then the impotent, estranged Coverdale, whose very name re-echoes his own. Beyond this, there is, among Hawthorne's finished works, only *The Marble Faun,* in which Hawthorne insisted on marrying off his alienated artist (this time a sculptor called Kenyon) to a good woman—as pallidly Anglo-Saxon, as improbable in the marriage bed as himself.

Most ambiguous of all the avatars of Oberon-Fanshawe is Clifford Pyncheon, who is, indeed, oddly out of place in the cheery, middlebrow pages of *The House of the Seven Gables.* Symbol of the estranged artist, he seems in the book's philistine context a demi-idiot: half withered old man and half child, the passive victim of the world's brutality. He is finally more than this, however —a portrait of Oberon as the ghostly surviver of a world that has ceased to exist. The thirty years he has passed in the prison which the world prepares for such "sybarites" have left him broken, a quivering sensibility without will or passion. With no ethical commitment to temper it, the "necessity for the beautiful" has turned Clifford into a monster, who weeps because an organ-grinder's monkey is ugly, and turns from the face of his own loving but unlovely sister.

Against his decaying impotence is set the strength of the daguerreotypist and rebel, Holgrave, who is often confusingly referred to in the text as "the artist." He is not, however, in Clifford's way an "artist of the beautiful," but rather an artist of the practical: a man of the people, self-taught, a little vulgar. Half technician and half creator, he is what would be called in our time a producer of "mass culture"—and he is, appropriately enough, identified as a latter-day magician, a descendant of mesmerists.

Both he and Clifford long for the novel's ingenue, the good girl Phoebe, who is described at one point as "a religion in herself." But there is, of course, really no contest; Clifford wants finally only to ogle a little, and this favor Phoebe brings herself to grant him with no loss to her virginal *mana*.

The only question to be resolved by the action is whether Holgrave will ravish Phoebe or permit her to be his savior, whether he will play the part of *Fanshawe's* rapist or of its more virile half-hero. In the end, with a single gesture he disavows his youthful radicalism and his male aggressiveness, commits himself to marriage. "It will be far otherwise than you forebode," he reassures Phoebe, who is hesitating over his proposal. "The world owes all its onward impulse to men ill at ease. The happy man inevitably confines himself within limits. I have a presentiment that, hereafter, it will be my lot . . . to conform myself to laws, and the peaceful practice of society." For this avowal, he receives the reward promised in the genteel Love Religion to the male who rejects the Lovelace role. "The bliss which makes all things true, beautiful and holy shone around this youth and maiden. They were conscious of nothing sad or old. They transfigured the earth and made it Eden again, and themselves the first two dwellers in it." So man is restored to the Garden by the love of a good woman and not by utopian social schemes for remaking the world. No wonder that more sentimental critics never weary of insisting that the thematic resolution of *The House of the Seven Gables* "may well justify preference for it over *The Scarlet Letter*." Such readers do not note, perhaps, the faint sigh of doubt with which Hawthorne qualifies the domesticated Edenic vision, "But how soon the heavy earth dream settled down again!" They remember only the Dickensian lightness of tone, the sunshine, the small boy buying sweets, the comic Old Venner—and are happy to recall that Hawthorne felt (or at least said he felt) *The House of the Seven Gables* a book "more proper and natural for me to write."

In *The Blithedale Romance,* the sunshine begins to dim, the pathos implicit in Hawthorne's four-sided triangle to reassert itself; and though in *The Marble Faun* Oberon-Kenyon manages to find a bride, the cheerfulness of *The House of the Seven Gables* is not recaptured. Toward the end of his life, Hawthorne finds himself once more confronting in all their original ambiguity and disorder the symbolic protagonists on whom briefly he had succeeded in imposing his sentimental will. One of the three unfinished novels with which he was wrestling before he died is *Septimius Felton;* and in the contradictory manuscript versions of that book which survive, Ellen and Fanshawe and Edward Walcott return to haunt him.

Septimius-Fanshawe, a pale, scholarly youth, competes for the hand of Rose Garfield, the ultimate Ellen, against the hearty Robert Hagburn, last embodiment of Edward Walcott. But even deeper imaginative elements arise and escape from the author's conscious control. A third lover, a British officer called Cyril Norton, enters the scene, attempts to kiss Rose and is killed in a duel by Septimius. He has brought with him, however, the incestuous ambiguities of Hawthorne's early story, "Alice Doane's Appeal," and the very names of the protagonists shift eerily as if trying to establish a meaning of which Hawthorne is not quite aware. At one point Rose Garfield is called Alice; and at another Robert Hagburn becomes Robert Garfield as if he were her brother, while Septimius is suddenly called Norton as if to indicate some blood relationship to the man he has killed. Finally, although Rose and Septimius have already become engaged, Hawthorne decides that these two at least *are* in fact half-brother and sister.

Meanwhile, symbolic figures of darkness move through the world of the more realistic protagonists: an *anima*-character called Sybil, identified with a bloody flower that grows from graves; a magician-Bad Father, whose companion and emblem is a gigantic spider. At the close of his career, Hawthorne loses himself in a *Walpurgisnacht* dream of father-hatred and incest, guilt and Faustian aspiration, quite like that from which he began in "Alice Doane's Appeal." The seduction theme has been restored to the gothic envelope in which his initial fear of sexuality had encysted it.

It is so encysted, of course, in Melville's sole attempt at a sentimental novel, *Pierre*. Like most of Melville's books—like *all* of them, Melville himself would have said—*Pierre* is finally a "botch" because it is the product of contradictory ambitions. Melville had been betrayed by the success of his earliest novels, pseudo-documentaries of escape from bourgeois life, into believing that it would be some day possible for him to earn his living as a writer; and in none of the works written at the peak of his powers is he innocent of some attempt to adapt them to the market. "Dollars damn me," he said quite frankly of his situation. Of all his novels, however, *Pierre* is the most deliberately aimed, in its opening pages at least, at the largest potential audience, which is to say, the female one.

Certainly, he declares his intentions concerning *Pierre* clearly enough in a letter to Mrs. Hawthorne: "But, My Dear Lady, I shall not again send you a bowl of salt water. The next chalice I shall commend, will be a rural bowl of milk." *Moby Dick* was written for Hawthorne, for the discriminating male reader; *Pierre,* for the wife of that reader, for a second-best audience. Its very style declares that it represents not only a shift of scene from ocean to countryside, but a change of tone appropriate to one who now addresses "My Dear Ladies": "There are some strange summer mornings in the country, when he who is but a sojourner from the city shall early walk forth . . . and be wonder-smitten with the trance-like aspect of the green and golden world." When into this Edenic world of green and gold, Melville introduces two fair, bright-eyed lovers ("Lucy!" "Pierre!"), and sets to preside over it no paternal Thunderer, but the Great Mother herself, the Queen of Heaven as aristocratic American lady—called Maria, of course —what more could a female reader ask? It is milk for milk that Melville offers: a return of nourishing warmth to the warm nourisher who had borne him.

The theme itself seems orthodox and womanly enough, too, the traditional subject of genteel literature since the beginnings of the novel in the United States: "the fatal Consequences of Seduction." For in a little while, the third avatar of the Great Goddess appears to stand beside Maria and Lucy—Pierre's half-sister Isabel, in whom Hecate joins Ceres and Kore; the trinity is complete: the mother, the promised bride, and the layer-out of the dead. Isabel is, however, no mere allegorical figure; for like Lucy in *Lucy Temple,* and Harriot in *The Power of Sympathy,* she is the standard bastard daughter of the father—revelation of his secret sin and bait in the trap of retributory incest. Working with such material, Melville must have felt justified in writing to his publisher, who had begun to grow uneasy over the lagging sales of *Moby Dick,* that his new effort, "a regular romance, with a mysterious plot to it & strong passions," was surely "very much more calculated for popularity than anything you have yet published of mine." Indeed, Melville thought that they might as well make a fresh start with so fresh a novel, and suggested, in order not to prejudice the possible new public, that they put on the flyleaf the name "Guy Winthrop" or simply *"By a Vermonter."*

Yet all along he knew that he had other ambitions for the book. "So now let us add Moby Dick to our blessing, and step from that," Melville wrote to Hawthorne. "Leviathan is not the biggest fish;—I have heard of Krakens." Surely, *Pierre* represents an attempt to haul some such ultimate monster of the deeps to the surface. Was Melville fooling only his publisher or himself, too— really convinced that he could conceal his Kraken in a bowl of milk? His critics and his audience were not deceived when the book appeared, raising charges of incoherence and indecency, even protesting against the time-honored incest theme, so remote had gentility grown from its own roots by the mid-nineteenth century. "Belongs to the German school," one reviewer, perspicacious as well as indignant, observed. "Yes! '*Pierre*' is a species of New York Werther, having all the absurdities and none of the beauties of Goethe's juvenile indiscretion."

III

Had he been willing to eschew all hopes of reaching the genteel female audience, or to give up the dream of pleasing the official arbiters of taste, Melville might have had the kind of quasi-respectable success attained by George Lippard, whose *The Quaker City; or, The Monks of Monk Hall,* first published in 1844, sold 60,000 copies the first year (compared with the 283 copies of *Pierre* sold ten months after publication) and which was still apparently being bought at the rate of 30,000 a year when Lippard died in 1854, not yet quite thirty-two years old. It is not necessary to believe the author's boast on the title page of *The Quaker City* that "No American novel has ever commanded so wide-spread an interest, as this work," or to credit completely the claim of the 1845 edition to represent a twenty-seventh printing; but one must take seriously the report of a Philadelphia newspaper at the time of Lippard's death that "He was the author of a number of novels, which have been read probably as extensively as those of any other writer in the country. . . ." It was not easy, certainly, to earn three or four thousand dollars a year by writing in Lippard's time; but this he managed to do, appealing to the lower middlebrow audience, which otherwise would have had to subsist on such imported fare as the novels of Eugene Sue, whose compound of gothicism and sentimental eroticism gave him the sweet-smelling savor of "dirtiness."

It is hard to know exactly what the nature of Lippard's audience was or precisely what satisfactions they sought in his books. He thought of himself as the inheritor of the tradition of Charles Brockden Brown, his fellow Philadelphian, about whom he wrote a touching magazine piece and to whom he dedicated *The Quaker City*. The combination of sex, horror, and advanced social thought that had once been the specialty of Brown Lippard provided, too —though on a slap-dash literary level considerably below that of his predecessor. He had, however, Brown's capacity for yielding up the imagination to a frenetic vision, out of which the author makes a book not so much by composing a fiction as by recording an uncensored nightmare. In such a novel as *The Quaker City*, the archetypal bugaboos of the popular mind—malicious hunchbacks, sinister Jews, hulking deaf-and-dumb Negroes, corrupt clergymen, and bloated bankers—murder, rape, carouse, and collapse finally into drunken stupors inside or beneath a gothic whorehouse, whose lowest level is a stagnant sewer. Unfaithful wives are poisoned, the skulls of old women bashed in, the virginity of sobbing young girls violated; but nothing is presented as gratuitous horror, the staple of the less pretentious dime novels; all is offered as a true revelation of *what really goes on inside*. In Lippard, pornography is justified as muckraking.

Gangster and banker, clergyman and bawd, lawyer and doctor —these are presumably the real rulers of society caught off guard; and the nightmarish evocations of the book a literal description of how the rich and their henchmen amuse themselves with the money they have sweated from the laboring man. This is the populist vision of upper-class life and the economic system which maintains it translated directly from private fantasy to fiction, without emendation or expurgation, but it is a religious fantasy as well as a political one, a poor man's apocalypse. In the small-town Protestant mind, the Big City is Sodom; and "Woe unto Sodom!" says the title-page illustration of Lippard's novel, evoking all the prurience associated with urban centers of iniquity by a thousand revival meetings.

Lippard himself was a pre-Marxian socialist, always armed under his Byronic cloak against the possibility of an attack by a hired assassin of the masters of society, and the founder of a secret order to fight back against them: the "Brotherhood of the Union," of which he was "Supreme Washington." His program was unequivocally revolutionary; "When Labor has tried all other means in vain—. . . . then we advise Labor to go to War . . . War with the Rifle, Sword and Knife!" He thought of his novels, stories, and pamphlets (he published twenty-three books in some twelve years) as weapons in the holy war of labor. Long before the Communist theory of art as a weapon had been developed, Lippard had anticipated it: "LITERATURE merely considered as an ART is a despicable thing. . . . A literature which does not work practically, for the advancement of social reform, or which is too dignified or too good to picture the great wrongs of the great mass of humanity, is just good for nothing at all."

It is not, however, literature in general that Lippard has to justify as a social weapon, but horror pornography in particular. Psychologically, of course, popular radicalism has always taken advantage of the tendency of relatively naive and uneducated people to project on the upper classes which they despise the erotic and sadist fantasies of which they are ashamed, thus providing themselves with the luxury of at once indulging and disavowing their own most shamefully masturbatory dreams. An ambitious, half-starved orphan boy just past twenty, knowing nothing of political reality except what his fancy suggests, makes an admirable spokesman for such a group. And just such a boy was George Lippard, near enough culturally to his readers to share their darkest fantasies, but far enough from them to articulate what they could only feel.

Understandably enough, it is seduction, the seduction of a poor girl by a pampered gentleman, which furnishes Lippard the key image for satisfying both the social and sexual demands of his audience; and in him, for the first time in America, perhaps, the Richardsonian theme takes on a fully conscious significance as a symbol of class war. "We'll be seduced no more!" the readers of *Pamela* had cried; and Lippard's readers echo more crudely, "You can't rape us!" The immediate occasion for *The Monks of Monk Hall* was an actual incident in which a Philadelphian who had killed the seducer of his sister, aboard the Camden ferry, was held in a New Jersey prison, tried in a New Jersey court, and then—to the relief and joy of his fellow citizens—acquitted by New Jersey justice. The sentimental popular acclaim that followed the release of the murderer led to the writing of the novel, which itself apparently helped swell an upsurge of public opinion that resulted in the passage of an anti-seduction law in the state of New York in 1849. It is a prime example of art as social action!

Lippard is eager to leave no doubt that seduction is the central theme of his crowded and complex "Romance of Philadelphia Life, Mystery and Crime." In his preface to one of the later editions, he writes, "I determined to write a book founded upon the following idea: *That the seduction of a poor and innocent girl, is a deed altogether as criminal as murder . . . the assassin of chastity and maidenhood is worthy of death by the hands of any man, and in any place.*" At the end of the main action of the book, editorial is translated into dithyramb, a song of triumph sung by a brother who has just avenged, with "the life current of the Libertine," the seduction of his sister: "Is that the murmur of a brook . . . is that the song of a bird? No, no, but still it is music—that gushing of the Wronger's Blood! . . . I would dance. Yes, Yes, I would dance over the Corse! . . . in sight of God and his angels, I would dance over the corse, while a wild song of joy fill the heavens. A song— huzza—a song! . . . This, this is the vengeance of a Brother!' "

It is by all odds the most false and forced passage in a novel not seldom false and forced, Lippard's amends for having lingered so lasciviously over the details of the rape, and for having encouraged the reader to relish those details with him. The fall of the seduction theme from gentility had freed it from the old restraints and reticences that had hedged it in; and Lippard profited to the full from this new freedom. At the level of Melville's *Pierre,* a charge of immorality meant the loss of sales and a blow to his quest for popularity; but at the level of *The Quaker City,* to be charged with having produced "the most immoral work of the age" meant to be even more widely read. Lippard cites the accusation against his morals proudly, taking it as a testimony to the truth and social efficacy of his novel; and he is not averse to exploiting it for sales. Like the very earliest American novelists, he boasts that he has torn the veils of delicacy aside in the interests of exposing the seducer; but unlike his predecessors, he lets us look our fill at the scandals behind the veil:

The left hand of Lorimer, gently stealing round her form, rested with a faint pressure upon the folds of her night-robe, over her bosom, which now came heaving tremulously into light. . . . Closer and more close, the hand of Lorimer pressed against the heaving bosom, with but the slight folds of the night-robe between. . . . Brighter grew the glow on her cheek, close pressed the hand on her bosom, warmer and higher arose that bosom in the light. . . . In a moment, Mary raised her glowing countenance from his breast. . . . Her breath came thick and gaspingly. Her cheeks were all a-glow, her blue eyes swam in a hazy dimness. She felt as though she was about to fall swooning on the floor . . . the languor came deeper and more mellow over her limbs; her bosom rose no longer quick and gaspingly, but in long pulsations, that urged the full Globes in all their virgin beauty, softly and slowly into view . . . and her parted lips deepened into a rich vermillion tint. 'She is mine!'

I V

Fifty years before *Sister Carrie*, Lippard had worked out a combination of sex and social protest in a style very like Dreiser's compound of conventional sentimental diction and colloquial speech. Whether or not Dreiser himself read Lippard's brutal exposé of Life in the Great City is hard to know; but certainly their books, making due allowance for changes in taste, are strikingly similar— parallel manifestations of a need in the nongenteel sub-audience for a revival of the seduction archetype, a hunger that even the endless reprintings of *Charlotte Temple* could not assuage. It was in the '90's, after a half-century in which gentility had apparently triumphed over passion, that the "fatal consequences of seduction" began once more to assert themselves as a compelling theme of serious literature. In 1893, a twenty-one-year-old writer called Stephen Crane published *Maggie—A Girl of the Streets;* in 1894, Mark Twain's *Pudd'nhead Wilson* appeared; and in 1899, Theodore Dreiser, at the summer home of his closest friend Arthur Henry ("If he had been a girl, I would have married him, of course"), wrote down on a blank page the words "Sister Carrie" —and wondered what they were intended to mean.

In plot, Crane's book is the most faithful of all to the stereotypes of the theme: an innocent girl is seduced, made pregnant, cast out by her family, and ends committing suicide, while her seducer is being victimized by the evil woman for whom he has left her. It is not even a Lady whom Crane has portrayed, but—in unconscious submission to bourgeois taboos—a girl of the people, an operator in a sweatshop, who lives on the Bowery. Crane's intention, described in an inscription in a gift copy as making "room in heaven for all sorts of souls, notably an occasional street girl, who are not confidently expected to be there by many excellent people," is surely not uncongenial to the great bleeding heart of sentimental America. Yet his book was a commercial failure; no respectable publisher could be persuaded to issue it, and the privately printed edition signed "Johnston Smith" remained unsold, despite Crane's attempt to promote it by having four men sit in front of the El all day reading it. The book provided no titillation at all—the physical seduction going undescribed—only a great, gray brutality of language (no "dirty" words, to be sure, though much profanity) and a constant play of irony, sometimes subtle, more often obvious. The violent, drunken mother acting out her expected indignation over the fall of her daughter, and the stupid, brutalized brother going through the standard motions of vengeance are travesties. Such parody of the "vengeance of a Brother" no ordinary reader could forgive, any more than he could forgive the literary pretensions of the novel: the tight form and the poetic language of the descriptive passages, which pull away from, when they do not condescend to, the characters described. *Maggie* is a good book neither in the critics' nor the great audience's sense; it is only the book of a good writer.

Twain's *Pudd'nhead Wilson* provides even fewer archetypal satisfactions. His fallen woman, Roxana, is a Negress, about whose seduction by a white man (accomplished before the action proper of the book begins) Twain himself refuses to be incensed; it is postulated in the book as a fact of life or an act of God, something that just happens to black wenches, useful for beginning a plot. A much lesser novelist, Albion W. Tourgée, had in his first novel *'Toinette* (1876) pictured the revolt of a slave girl, who after the Civil War demands marriage of the Southern gentleman who has been her lover and is the father of her child. Though she has only the slightest trace of Negro blood, her lover refuses in horror, and she leaves him. This issue Twain scarcely seems to know exists; what moral indignation he feels is directly against slavery as an institution and especially against sons who betray their mothers, rather than against Virginia gentlemen who betray slave girls. Neither in his respectable nor in his bootleg fiction is Twain really interested in the traditional meanings of the seduction theme.

It is only Dreiser who proves capable of reviving that theme for serious literature, for he takes it seriously: finding in the impregnation and abandonment of helpless women no mere occasions for melodrama (as in Twain) or for exercises in irony and contrasting style (as in Crane). Dreiser is qualified first of all by his essentially sentimental response to the plight of the oppressed, by what he himself calls—attributing the feeling to one of his characters—an "uncritical upswelling of grief for the weak and the helpless." There is in him none of the detachment and cynicism of Crane, none of the utter blackness and pessimism of Twain; he is as "positive" through his tears as any female scribbler. Even his famous determinism is essentially sentimental at root, amounting effectively to little more than the sob of exculpation: "Nobody's fault! Nobody's fault!" Much is made by his friendlier critics of the fact that just before the beginning of his writing career Dreiser discovered Balzac; much more should be made of the fact that long before that encounter, his imagination had already been formed by Ouida and Laura Jean Libby. If, on the one hand, the daughters of the non-Anglo-Saxon American poor find in him a voice, on the other, the stickier writers for women through him achieve literary respectability.

It is no accident that for several years he was able to edit successfully the Butterick magazines, purveyors of fashion, fiction, and useful articles ("What to Do When Diphtheria Comes") to lower-middlebrow women; nor was his writing for such an audience an unfortunate interruption in his career, a prostitution of his talent. Nobody, as many writers have learned to their grief through both success and failure, can deceive such an audience for very long; one hint of condescension gives the game away. If Dreiser managed to please such a group of readers, it was because *at the deepest level, he shared their values;* and the friends who worked so hard to save him from the deleterious effect of such "hack work," and finally persuaded him to abandon it—understood nothing. When Dreiser in " 'The Genius' " describes the youg artist, Eugene Witla (his barely disguised self-portrait), as beginning with a love of the the painting of that insufferable anti-artist Bouguereau, this is not just a revelation of the author's insufficient culture; it is also a revelation of his fundamental taste. For better or worse, Dreiser is bound in weakness and in strength to the values of the sentimental lower middle class.

When he wrote on rejection slips sent to contributors to *The Delineator,* "We like realism, but it must be tinged with sufficient idealism to make it all of a truly uplifting character. . . . The fine side of things—the idealistic—is the answer for us . . ." he was not merely playing with a straight face the part for which he had been hired. To his good friend H. L. Mencken, to whom surely he could speak frankly, he wrote in quite the same vein that he would like for another of his magazines (this one presumably freer from outside control), *The Bohemian,* no "tainted fiction," but stories that testified to their authors' "knowledge of life *as it is,* broad, simple, good-natured." If there is a fundamental flaw in Dreiser, it resides neither in his stylistic clumsiness, which for strength's sake is easily forgiven, nor in his tritely elegant literary vocabulary, the *kitsch* interior-decorating with which he cannot forbear touching up his scenes, but in the fact that his novels are in fact "uplifting" —which is to say, sentimental rather than tragic.

How, then, did Dreiser come to be, as one of his publishers was later to put it, "the one man to have first created an audience for daring books," the defendant in obscenity trials which came to seem to his contemporaries forums at which the cause of a new, frank literature could be advocated? It is hard now to see the sense in which Dreiser's books, whatever their other merits, are daring at all. Certainly, they do not describe the sexual act or its more passionate preliminaries with a frankness or pornographic intensity comparable to George Lippard's. Dreiser came of the kind of people who copulate in the dark and live out their lives without ever seeing their sexual partners nude; and he was brought up on the kind of book which made it impossible for him to write convincingly about the act of love; his subject was, like theirs, when erotic at all, the traditional "consequences of seduction."

His notion of a passionate interchange between lovers involves such "poetic" apostrophes as, "Oh, Flower Face! Oh, Silver Feet! Oh, Myrtle Bloom!" The erotic, that is to say, demanded for him a veneer of the poetic; and his concept of poetry is perhaps best indicated by the metrical chapter titles in *Sister Carrie:* "And This is Not Elf Land: What Gold Will Not Buy," "The Way of the Beaten: A Harp in the Wind." It is all a little like what his brother, Paul Dresser (also the champion of the fallen woman in "My Gal Sal"), was doing in the popular song. There is power in Dreiser, to be sure; no one gives better the sense of the dazzled entry of the small-town girl into the big city; no one renders better the seedy milieu of the status-hungry on their way up or down; but no American writer is more the victim of the sentimental wound, less capable of dealing with passion. When he resists the impulse to poeticize, Dreiser does love scenes like this: "Carrie rose up as if to step away, he holding her hand. Now he slipped his arm about her and she struggled, but in vain. He held her quite close. Instantly there flared up in his body the all-compelling desire. His affection took an ardent form. . . . She found him lifting her head and looking into her eyes. What magnetism there was she could never know. His many sins, however, were for the moment all forgotten." It is banality raised to the power of evasion, an implicit denial of the reality of passion.

He could never portray, for all his own later hectic career as a lover, any woman except the traditional seduced working girl of sentimental melodrama. Yet because the deceived woman, the seduced virgin are for Dreiser the images through which he understands America and himself, he stumbles into scandal. The man who makes good and the girl who goes bad, these stereotypes of the folk (occasionally reversed, for variety, to the girl who rises and the man who falls) are the sole symbols that move him to write, and it is with the fallen girl that he begins his career. He is in fact the avenging brother that earlier writers only imagine; and Sister Carrie, like Jennie Gerhardt after her, is a household image, one of those sisters of his own, who were always getting into trouble: running off with married men or embezzlers, coming home pregnant. The phrase which came unbidden into his mind was not a simple girl's name, as in the typical woman's book, but "Sister Carrie," and in the novel itself he tries to justify the first word in various ways. Meeting her married sister in Chicago at the beginning of the book, Caroline Meeber is hailed by that full title, "half affectionately" bestowed on her, Dreiser tells us, by her family; and by the end of the story, when she is translated into a kind of unchurched nun, celibate, lonely, and dedicated to charity, it seems even more appropriate. Surely, the quasi-religious pun is intended; and yet, first of all, Carrie is not the sister of her fictional family or even a Little Sister of the Poor, but one of Dreiser's own sisters, redeemed from the shabby failures of her actual life. If not a brother's vengeance, Sister Carrie is his amends.

Why, then, did it irk and shock so many readers? How, to begin with, could so conventional an account of a small-town girl, seduced first by the flashy drummer, Drouet, then talked into a bigamous marriage with the repentant embezzler, Hurstwood, so horrify the wife of Dreiser's publisher? Legend at least tells us that she was so dismayed that she persuaded her husband not to promote the book which he had already contracted to print. There is no apparent moral ambiguity in Dreiser's presentation. Both Hurstwood's robbery and Carrie's love affairs are called evil, and

Hurstwood is quite satisfactorily punished, degraded to the level of a skid-row panhandler, left about to commit suicide in a flophouse. Before that, he has been harried from failure to failure, his pride and virility broken until he crawls in the slush, begs a few dollars from the woman he has wronged. Not even Montraville or Hollingsworth had been so degraded for their offenses! Even Carrie, though she has the kind of success denied her seducer, and achieves the material comforts of which she once scarcely knew how to dream, cannot find happiness in her career as an actress or in herself. To make the point clear, Dreiser lingers almost tearfully over Carrie's melancholy figure at the end, pauses to apostrophize her: "Oh, Carrie, Carrie! . . . know, then, that for you is neither surfeit or content. In your rocking chair, by your window dreaming, shall you long alone. In your rocking chair, by your window, shall you dream such a happiness as you may never feel." It is the lyrics of a popular song again—"Old Rocking Chair's Got Me," *obligato*. What more did Mr. and Mrs. Doubleday want? Blood? The death of the girl who had fallen? Crane had already provided that in a book which no one would print, which sold even fewer than the 650 copies of *Sister Carrie* that went out of the one thousand printed. Dreiser, with an instinct for self-dramatization, liked to speak of the "suppression" of his first book, but in fact it did as well as Melville's *Pierre*.

It is true that Dreiser lapsed at this point into ten years of silence, which is to say, a decade of editing, and writing articles and short stories, but no novels; yet this seems to have been less a lock-out on the part of the publishers (actually he was given an advance during this period on a book which he never finished) than some deep, psychological slow-down within him. Carrie had represented more than an expurgated version of his unfortunate sister (when he emended life it was always in favor of that "sufficient idealism" which he had urged on his contributors); she had been, in a way, a disguised portrait of himself: a Portrait of the Artist as a Girl Gone Wrong. "Thus in life there is ever . . . the mind that reasons, and the mind that feels," Dreiser had written in *Sister Carrie,* thinking of himself. "Of the one come the men of action . . . of the other, poets and dreamers—artists all. As harps in the wind, the latter respond to every breath of fancy, voicing in their moods all the ebb and flow of the ideal. Man has not yet comprehended the dreamer any more than he has the ideal. For him the laws and morals of the world are unduly severe. Ever

hearkening to the sound of beauty, striving for the flash of its distant wings, he watches to follow. . . . So watched Carrie, so followed. . . ." In this respect, too, she is a sister to her author, also
a "harp in the wind"; and it is perhaps precisely the bovarysim
revealed in such a passage, the *Weltschmerz* and self-pity, the half-
secret caviling at moral restraints which put off the popular reader.

In *Jennie Gerhardt*, Dreiser did not again make the mistake of
portraying the anti-bourgeois, sentimental artist in the girl who
goes bad. This time he draws a portrait of his mother as reflected
in the experience of his sisters, his poor suffering mother, whom he
could never forget holding up to him as a child her shabby shoes
and saying, "See poor mother's shoes? See the hole there?" He was
the mama's boy par excellence, dreaming always of that figure
"potent and alive," who had—despite the ogre papa—made their
home seem "like Fairyland." In the novel, the mother-sister figure
is identified not only with Jennie, but with all of "the distraught
and helpless poor," while the figure of the father is fractured into
the religious tyrant Mr. Gerhardt; Senator Brander, Jennie's first
lover, who wants to marry her but dies too soon; and Lester Kane,
son of a rich family, who deserts Jennie when he is threatened
with disinheritance. None of the three, however, though each makes
Jennie suffer in some way, can finally qualify as a villain, not even
old Gerhardt. They are finally all melted down in the universal
solvent of Dreiser's pity for victims—revealed as not the rejecting
fathers they first seemed, but weak sons, pleading forgiveness from
the eternally offended Jennie-Mother. It is only the abstract "system," which is the really Bad Father; and if the seduction novel in
Dreiser's hands takes on social meanings once more, those meanings are not translatable into any conventional theory of the class
struggle. In his books, humanity as a whole struggles against the
inhuman nature of things as they are. Seducer and victim are
equally betrayed, equally to be pitied: Lester Kane is condemned
by his own weakness to die apart from his love, and Jennie for all
her strength can only look through the iron grille of the cemetery
at his coffin being lowered into the earth.

The fictional world of Dreiser is the *absolutely* sentimental
world, in which morality itself has finally been dissolved in pity;
and in such a world, Charlotte Temple is quite appropriately reborn. No theme but seduction can contain the meanings Dreiser is
trying to express, no catastrophe but deflowering start his heroines
on their way toward total alienation. But any allusion to deflower-

ing had become in Dreiser's time taboo; and even the once-stand-
ard description of an unmarried mother's affection for her illegitimate child, a sympathetic rendering of her refusal to consider it
unclean, had come to seem in bourgeois circles a flaunting of decency itself. To the anti-bourgeois camp in the literary world of
the early twentieth century, Dreiser's orthodox sentimental plea for
sympathy rather than scorn for the fallen woman seemed, therefore, a revolutionary manifesto, an emancipation proclamation!
And in the context of the developing struggle, in the courts and in
the magazines, he did, indeed, become the spokesman for the
forces combating genteel censorship, winning in the end a freedom
in the handling of sex which he himself was incapable of exploiting.

Meanwhile, his theme had become more and more explicitly the
denial of personal moral responsibility, the assertion that the individual who was to be pitied could not be blamed. After a while, he
was scarcely distinguishable from his friend Clarence Darrow, making a tearful, mechanistic courtroom plea for a criminal facing the
sentence of death. It is appropriate, therefore, that the novel in
which Dreiser gives full-dress treatment to the contention that
nothing is anybody's fault should take place largely in the courtroom, quote extensive sections of an actual court record. In *An
American Tragedy,* which was published in 1925, a poor boy on
the make in society (his prototype in real life came from a fairly
comfortable family) lets drown (his prototype deliberately plotted
and executed the crime) a factory girl whom he has got pregnant,
and who stands in the way of his marriage to a rich debutante.
Even in the columns of the newspapers, Dreiser can only find new
instances of what early reading and experience have made for him
an obsessive theme. Whatever he thinks he is trying to prove, he
must prove it by setting in motion the Seducer and the Seduced,
the passionate or vain young man indulging his desire for power
and the baffled girl, lonely and eager to be fed well, dressed well,
inducted into the mysteries of beauty. What makes *An American
Tragedy* particularly American is the fact that Clarissa falls prey
not to Lovelace but to Horatio Alger!

For his services in reviving a myth as old as the bourgeois novel
itself, Dreiser was identified as a "naturalist," a term of contempt
to the genteel, and a rallying cry for those who were engaged in
the struggle against gentility. And the battle which he fought inadvertently at first he engaged in quite consciously after a while; by
those who hailed him as a great emancipator, he was persuaded

that it had been his aim all along to release Americans in life and art for the pursuit of passion; and especially in *The Genius* he abandoned his more essential seduction theme to plead the cause of Don Juan. It is partly Dreiser's own fault, therefore, if he has come to seem part of the Lawrentian sexual revolution of the '20's, otherwise carried forward by that homegrown D. H. Lawrence, Sherwood Anderson; though perhaps most of the responsibility lies with such champions of his work as Dorothy Dudley. In her study of Dreiser's impact on America, Miss Dudley reports the following astonishing conversation between Dreiser and herself on the subject of his mother. " 'Was she really so alive, so "pagan" as you call her? Was your father enough for her then, or did she find others?' 'She did if she wanted to, I'm certain of that. She had a way of doing what she wanted to do without disturbing the rest of us. But I was too young, I don't know about that.' 'Well, maybe she did. Maybe your father was not your father. How do you know?' " This fondest fantasy of the erotic sentimentalism of the '20's—illegitimacy or putting one over on Father—Dreiser disavows. His mother's "paganism" he would apparently like to keep spiritual, abstract, and he shies at adultery, which is not, in any case, a main subject of his essentially American books. The new mystique of passion Dreiser never really embraced—not retroactively for his mother anyhow; but the older mystique of virginity he had left behind. And this defection perhaps cut him off from the kind of middlebrow popularity which, granted his gifts and limitations, he should have enjoyed.

That popularity Herman Wouk, profiting by the collapse of hyper-genteel taboos in the bourgeoisie itself, has managed to attain. The struggle of writers like Dreiser, ironically enough, made it possible to write in 1955 the pure bourgeois novel of seduction as originally created by the female Richardsonians. Only one fundamental revision has been made in the mythos of seduction between *Charlotte Temple* and *Marjorie Morningstar* (their very titles indicate their kinship): the newer genteel Sentimentalism will not let the fallen woman die. That Marjorie in losing her virginity has been permanently maimed, incapacitated for the full enjoyment of marriage, Mr. Wouk does not doubt; yet he insists on marrying her off into a bitter-sweet happy ending. The twentieth-century Clarissa no longer is condemned to end her life by suicide or a broken heart, when her honor is lost; she is granted the partial redemption of marriage to an athletic lawyer, ends not in the wretched hovel where Charlotte came to die, but in the split-level house beautiful of exurban New York. Perhaps this is why she can no longer save anyone but herself, though she is still capable of damning the man who devirginates her. Something of the old mythic power still clings to her, some last trace of the aura of Clarissa, that secular savior, whose piety and sexuality were felt, for all their absurdly conventional dress, as real and terrible. But Marjorie has followed the downward path of travesty already foreshadowed in Charlotte, seems finally only a silly girl who turns into a dull suburban lady, the ghost (dead she would have been more alive) of the Protestant virgin, oddly turned Jew.

Between Richardson and Wouk, falls the shadow of Flaubert, who has taught Wouk. Wouk, however, will not confess this truth, which even the facts of his own fable substantiate, but attempts to exorcise it by editorial comment and implicit moralizing, trying to lift our hearts high above such earthbound reflections. The voice which, despite his censorship, keeps whispering to him and his readers alike, "Clarissa is Bovary, Marjorie is Bovary, you are Bovary," he identifies with the voice of the Seducer, against whose wiles it is his function to warn the bourgeois American world.

Who is the Seducer in Wouk's novel, the modern counterpart of the irresistible Lovelace, whose struggle with the immovable Clarissa all Europe once followed through a million words? He is called Noel Airman, which is to say, *Luftmensch,* the impractical schemer who never touches the ground, though he was born Ehrman, which is to say, man of honor. Denying his Jewish birthright, Wouk apparently means to tell us, by denying his Jewish name, Noel also denies virtue; and we are not surprised to discover that he is not only an actor, pianist, and playwright, but also a valueless bohemian and, especially, Don Giovanni once more!

Airman, like Lovelace before him, is both seducer and freethinker, besides being possessed of a grace alongside of which bourgeois manners and morality seem grubbily and unpleasantly safe and sane. Lovelace, however, was an aristocrat, survivor of the class just then blending (as Richardson shows by the possibility of his wooing Clarissa) into the mercantile bourgeoisie; Airman is not sure where he belongs. He is intended to be a member of a self-appointed aristocracy of culture, a highbrow (miserable imitation of Noel Coward that he actually is): the equivalent to the middlebrow imagination of the Dandy and the *poète maudit.* And this finally is the true subject of Wouk's book, its underground theme. The bourgeoisie has won its fight against the old nobility, the last item on its agenda having been the Freedom from Seduction. But suddenly, from among its own sons, a new enemy appears to cry that there is no seduction, that all is permitted, that the values for which their fathers fought against the old nobility are lies.

There is some justification, after all, for recasting Lovelace as Airman, since, as we have seen, it was on the model of the former that Rousseau created his Saint-Preux, on whom in turn Goethe modeled Werther; and from Werther have stemmed all the portraits of the artist as a young seducer down to our own time. It is Wouk's unique contribution to American letters to have identified this bugaboo of middle-class ladies with the "Jewish intellectual," trading on a stereotype of such highbrows as cynical, bohemian, neurotic, negative, much given to idle talk about obscure books and Sigmund Freud. To the fear of the Jewish intellectual as seducer, which troubles the sleep of lower-middlebrow Anglo-Saxon maidens, he has finally given genteel literary expression. But beside his bad Jew, Wouk is careful to set good ones: soft-hearted, handball-playing professional men; kindly, old, ridiculous uncles; warm, expansive mamas—but especially Marjorie herself.

From the earliest moment, Jewish heroines have been viable in American novels; the rich widow, Mrs. Achsa Fielding, whom Arthur Mervyn marries in Brockden Brown's romance, is a Jewess, as is Hawthorne's Miriam in *The Marble Faun*. They soon become, however, forbidden exotics—dark, alien types whom the hero, after Brown, is not permitted to marry—for lurking behind and beside them is the Jewish villain, the Smiler with a Knife. Shylock and Jessica, Isaac and Rebecca: these are the prototypical pairs reflected in such American works as Melville's *Clarel* and *Mrs. Peixada* by "Sidney Luska," though it is Scott's model rather than Shakespeare's which our writers follow; since in their imaginations to marry the Jew's daughter does not cease to be a sin even if she is converted, whatever Shakespeare may once have believed. In *The Yoke of the Torah*, "Sidney Luska" de-mythicizes the Jew's daughter at last, portrays her as a dull, bourgeois girl whose marriage to the sensitive hero of the novel means his spiritual and moral death.

Marjorie is the end-product of this de-mythicizing process, by which Scott's Rebecca becomes Luska's Tillie (" 'Oh my daughter,

she works like a horse. . . . And such a *good* girl. Only nineteen
years old and earns more than a hundred dollars a month. . . .
She's grand. She's an angel' "), but she is Tillie mythicized again,
Tillie as Clarissa—out of the fire into the frying pan! However,
there is a further, an essential difference. Marjorie is, first of all,
detached from the melodrama of the encounter with the gentile,
allowed to choose only between the Jewish intellectual and the
Jewish bourgeois. The effect of putting her into so totally Jewish a
context is to make her seem scarcely Jewish at all (though much
is made of her difficulties with religion), hardly distinguishable
from the Sweetheart of Sigma Chi. In another sense, Wouk's novel
represents the entry of the newest shibboleth of sentimental liberalism into the sentimental novel of seduction, the assimilation of
anti-anti-Semitism into the kind of book which had already assimilated abolitionism, Christian socialism, woman's rights, temperance,
etc., etc.

Marjorie Morningstar is, in this respect, the first fictional celebration of the mid-twentieth-century *détente* between the Jews and
middle-class America; and the movie which has followed, the *Time*
story and the *Time* cover picture are, in effect, public acknowledgments of that fact. Among the enlightened minority audience of the
arts, the transformation of the Jew from bugaboo to culture hero is
as old as Kafka and James Joyce. In the high literature of Europe
and, more slowly, in that of the United States, gentile and Jew have
joined forces to portray the Jewish character as a figure representing man's fate in the modern, urbanized world. In general, the
point of such portrayals is to suggest that we live in an age of rootlessness, alienation, and terror, in which the exiled condition so
long thought peculiar to the Jew comes to seem the common
human lot. This is neither a cheery nor a reassuring view; and it
is therefore incumbent on the lower-middlebrow novelist, Wouk, to
suggest a counter-view: the contention that the Jew was never (or
is, at least, no longer) the rootless dissenter, the stranger which
legend has made him, but rather the very paragon of the happy
citizen at home, loyal, chaste, thrifty, pious, and moderately successful—in short, not Noel Airman but Marjorie Morningstar,
which is to say, Charlotte Temple given a second chance.

9

GOOD GOOD GIRLS AND
GOOD BAD BOYS:
CLARISSA AS A JUVENILE

THERE WAS, HOWEVER, a period of thirty years or more (from the end of the '50's until the '90's had begun) when the seduction story was excluded from female middlebrow fiction—a period in which women, grown too genteel for sex, cast about for new fables to feed their fantasy. And in a certain kind of Western they found some satisfaction at least.

Owen Wister's *The Virginian* first made respectably popular the mythic romance of the cowboy and the schoolmarm and the ethical clash which nearly frustrates their love. The cowboy's commitment to honor, to the surviving code of the duel, and the schoolmarm's commitment to Christian forgiveness and nonviolence force an inevitable crisis, that nearly disrupts the marriage with which the novel has all along promised to end. On their wedding day, the Virginian and Mary Wood quarrel over whether he shall answer or evade the challenge of the villain, Trampas; and when he goes out, after all, to fight, Mary swears she will not marry him. His opponent killed, however, the Virginian returns, redolent with the sweet smell of gunpowder, virility, and success, to find his bride (her motivation scarcely examined) ready to embrace him. The Sermon on the Mount has yielded to the code of the West with only the most perfunctory of struggles. *The Virginian* is a fable, cloying and false, which projects at once the self-hatred of the genteel eastern sophisticate confronted with the primitive, and his dream of a world where "men are men," i.e., walk with smoking guns into the arms of women who cheerfully abdicate their roles as guardians of morality. The enduring appeal of this slight, slick novel (until recently required reading in many American high schools) is testified to by the unacknowledged plagiarism of its theme in the recent movie *High Noon,* in which Gary Cooper, in whom myth after myth has become flesh, incarnates the Virginian, too.*

Such a story did not, however, finally satisfy female readers, who even in the mid-nineteenth century yearned to see women portrayed as abused and suffering, and the male as crushed and submissive in the end. Though such readers joined the campaign to excise passion from the novel, they were not really happy either with the kind of literature that campaign produced in the later works of Harriet Beecher Stowe or in the whole body of fiction by William Dean Howells. The latter novelist is, indeed, the embodiment of the writer an age demanded and did not really want: the author of flawlessly polite, high-minded, well-written studies of untragic, essentially eventless life in New England—the antiseptic upper-middlebrow romance. Yet his forty books, in which there are no seductions and only rare moments of violence, are too restrictedly "realistic" to do justice to the reality of dream and nightmare, fantasy and fear. Only in *A Modern Instance,* written in 1882, does Howells deal for once with a radically unhappy marriage; and here he adapts the genteel-sentimental pattern which had substituted the bad husband (his Bartley Hubbard has "no more moral nature than a baseball") for the Seducer, the long-suffering wife for the Persecuted Maiden or fallen woman.

It is the theme Melville and Hawthorne had fumbled back and forth in the unwritten Agatha story, and which J. W. DeForest had written in *Miss Ravenel's Conversion.* In this study of the conflict of loyalties and love against a Civil War background (the book appeared in 1867), Lillie Ravenel turns down Edward Colbourne, obviously more worthy of her, for the "magnetic" Lieutenant-Colonel Carter. High-colored, with flashing black eyes and an ability to speak French—unlike the more plodding "good" protagonist—Carter would have been the Seducer in a franker time. But though he compares Carter to the "hideous apes with carnivorous appetites, whose desire it was to devour the approaching stranger," even the boldly realistic DeForest is victim enough of

* In an unforeseen reversal of the original plot, Arthur Miller has in *The Misfits* written a movie about the triumph of female values of love over the death-centered values of the code. To do this, however, he has had to transform the school teacher of the legend into the semblance of Marilyn Monroe.

the genteel mode to make his character no more than an embezzling, unfaithful spouse. Passionate and immoral, he still wants only, however unworthily, to marry Lillie.

Even in *St. Elmo* (1866), the pseudo-gothic villain-hero of Augusta Wilson's all-time best-seller who gives his name to the book is never permitted to threaten assault, ends by offering marriage to the persecuted orphan girl, Edna Earl. When it becomes too great a strain on credulity to believe in St. Elmo's self-control, he is shipped off on a long sea voyage, and the reader can turn with relief to the heroine in her now quite unexceptionable struggles. When he gets back into the fictional scene, St. Elmo has not only reformed but has become a clergyman, whose offer of marriage Edna cannot refuse. The unworthy wooer competes with the unworthy husband for the place of Lovelace in the sentimental fable; but even their unworthiness is sometimes tempered by the tenderness or squeamishness of the lady authors. The rejected suitor may be, as in Maria Cummins' *The Lamplighter* (on whose prose style Joyce's Gertie McDowell, thirty years later, still bases the rhetoric of her erotic daydreams), merely in appearance unworthy. He was not, it turns out, really flirting with the most notorious coquette in Saratoga Springs, only pleading with her to take better care of her sick mother!

Such perfunctory explanations or reconciliations seem often less important than the tear-extorting episodes of unmerited female suffering which precede them, and which lend to the wives and maidens of the sexless sentimental romances of the '60's an aura of martyrdom—equal almost to Clarissa's own. The double feat demanded of the respectable writer of the era is to create a Clarissa who is not raped (she turns out to be a debased Jane Eyre), and a Lovelace who is not a rapist (he is invariably a vulgarized Rochester). In this they must have succeeded, for they were read with fantastic avidity. *The Lamplighter* sold 40,000 copies in eight weeks, and one "limited" edition out of the scores in which *St. Elmo* was printed totaled 100,000 copies! Yet the successes of the purely commercial purveyors of domestic sentiment are unimportant except as they cast light on the contemporary failures of more serious writers.

Howells, who inhabits the quietest, upper-middlebrow levels of the genteel world, hangs on his wall the embroidered motto of Mrs. Hentz and Mrs. Wilson: "Keep it Clean!"—but he refuses to set up beneath it the ikon of the Suffering Woman, the idol of the secret religion of the sentimental lady writers. No more could he set up the image of any secular Aphrodite; in the niche of the White Goddess, a fully clothed, upper-class, middle-aged Anglo-Saxon lady sits holding a cup of tea and making conversation, moderate, gracious, and witty. This is why his books possess neither passionate nor "religious" overtones, but take up again the failed gambit of Brockden Brown's *Clara Howard* or Cooper's *Persuasion:* a tradition which William Gilmore Simms called "a very inferior school of writing, known as the social life novel." This literature of evasion, Howells, resolutely cheerful, progressive, and sane, considered both "scientific" and Anglo-Saxon. In his *Heroines of Fiction,* he insists that English and American readers are quite willing to permit the writer to handle "such relations of men and women as George Eliot treats in *Adam Bede"* (typically, he will not say the word "adultery"), if only the writer agrees to maintain "scientific decorum." And though he can adduce only one American book as an example, he argues that Anglo-Saxon literature has not really evaded the treatment of passion.

> It is quite false or quite mistaken to suppose our novels have left untouched these most important realities of life. They have only not made them their stock in trade; they have kept a true perspective in regard to them; they have relegated them in their pictures of life to the space and place they occupy in life itself, as we know it in England and America.

Yet whatever "space and place" sex may have occupied in Anglo-American life as observed by a self-made gentleman like Howells, it certainly once occupied most of the fictional "space and place" of the novel; and the diminution of its allotted area, according to the "true perspective" of gentility, left a vacuum into which new sentimental material immediately rushed. One source of such material is the spirit of social protest and the causes with which that movement occupied itself. Many critics have pointed out, detachedly or in anger, that the withdrawal of sexual passion from art leads to an increase of horror and sadism; it has not been similarly noted that such a withdrawal leads also to the disguised masochism of the "protest" novel.

To this very day, in such writers as John Hersey, Irwin Shaw, and James Michener, the sentimental novel of social protest survives, dedicating itself to such latter-day issues as anti-Semitism, racial discrimination, the atom bomb, McCarthyism, etc., etc., eternally searching for new examples among the abused "little people" to set in the position of the Persecuted Maiden. One result of the eternal search of the reformer-sentimentalists for new causes is that the old ones wear out, come to seem ridiculous. Nothing, for instance, seems to the enlightened of today more absurd than the teetotal or the anti-tobacco campaigns (except possibly the drive against sexual vulgarity); yet it was with such causes that the socially conscious novel began. The campaign against liquor is, of all reforming movements, the one most easily adapted to the demands of traditional Sentimentalism and the image of the Suffering Woman. Even in such sophisticated works as *Miss Ravenel's Conversion* and *A Modern Instance,* drunkenness is used as a chief symbol for the husband's betrayal of the wife; in the latter, indeed, it is a substitute for the kind of sexual defection Howells is squeamish about handling.

The saloon, of course, was for a long time felt as the anti-type of the home, a refuge for escaping males nearly as archetypal as the wilderness and the sea. Ever since *Rip Van Winkle,* the image of a bust with the boys has stood for the flight from the shrew. Some deep sense of this surely is in all anti-saloon literature; and it is not surprising to learn that Timothy Arthur, author of the comically stereotypical *Ten Nights in a Bar-Room* (1854), was a man who devoted most of his career to fictional studies of the break-up of marriage, by liquor, card-playing, and other causes too complex to win for him the fame he achieved by exploiting the simpler anti-domestic vices. The abused woman, beaten or neglected by the drunken bully, has become so standard a fixture in the sentimental melodrama of life in America, that we can scarcely believe it to have been invented at any given moment. Surely, the child has bent under the swinging doors to cry "Is my father in there?" from the beginning of time.

Walt Whitman was perhaps not the inventor of the form; but he had in 1842 written in *Franklin Evans or The Inebriate* one of the earliest temperance novels, a book he himself considered the first in the field. It would be lovely to believe that the poet later called "the dirtiest beast of the age" was also the creator of so philistine a literary kind. *Franklin Evans* is, in any case, a deeply earnest plea for total abstinence, though Whitman later tried to pass it off as a mere potboiler, a joke on its readers. Periodically throughout his life, Whitman was to swear off liquor, dedicate himself to health and pure cold water; and whatever guilt prompted those vain pledges of abstinence is projected in *Franklin Evans,* through images sentimental (the hopeless drunk loses his job, watches his wife fade and die) and gothic (from a bout of drunken euphoria, the victim awakes to find himself married to an octoroon). The volume ends, after piling up example after example of the fatal consequences of drink, with an impassioned plea to the reader to join the ranks of the reformers, who are about to march on the "musical Saloons" in an effort to crush the "Red Fiend" and deliver the youth of America from those poisonous dens "where the mind and the body are both rendered effeminate together."

The greatest of all novels of sentimental protest is, however, dedicated not to the problem of drink but to that of slavery, though its author was a total abstainer, who would appear at literary luncheons only if promised that no wine would be served. The novel, of course, is Harriet Beecher Stowe's *Uncle Tom's Cabin,* which she read in installments to her children as she composed it in 1851 and 1852. They wept as they listened; and she wept, too, returned to each installment at such a pitch of frenzy that she began after a while to feel as if the volume were being dictated rather than invented. "The Lord himself wrote it!" she insisted later; and if He had, indeed, written and autographed it, it could not have sold better—some 300,000 copies in the very first year of publication, and millions in the following years, perhaps outstripping even *The Last of the Mohicans.* It is an astonishingly various and complex book, simplified in the folk mind, which has remembered in its place the dramatic version in which Mrs. Stowe had no hand and which she saw, secretly, only once.

In *Uncle Tom's Cabin,* there are two contrasting studies of marriage: one between an opportunistic, morally lax husband and an enduring Christian wife; another between a hypochondriacal, self-pitying shrew—an acute but cruel caricature of the Southern lady—and a gentle, enduring husband. The latter relationship between the St. Clares, who are mother and father to Little Eva, is from a purely novelistic point of view the most skillfully executed section of the book; but it is scarcely remembered by *Uncle Tom's* admirers. No more do the really erotic episodes stick in the collective memory of America: neither Legree's passionate relationship with the half-mad slave girl, Cassy, nor his breathless, ultimately frustrated attempt to violate the fifteen-year-old quadroon, Emmeline.

The story of the decline of Cassy from a protected Creole childhood, in which she is scarcely aware that she is a Negro, through her lush bondage to a chivalrous white New Orleans lover, in which she is scarcely aware she is a slave, to the point where she is pawed publicly in the slave market and degraded to the level of becoming Legree's unwilling mistress is fictional material of real interest; merely sketched in by Mrs. Stowe, it has recently been worked out in great detail by R. P. Warren in *Band of Angels*. Yet it fades from the mind even just after we have read *Uncle Tom*. It is not essential to the book which became part of our childhood. Of the complex novel created by Mrs. Stowe (or God!), America has chosen to preserve only the child's book.

Though we *know* Emmeline and Cassy are cowering in the attic at the moment that Quimbo and Sambo under Legree's direction are beating Uncle Tom to death, it is only the latter scene which we *feel*. We respond to the suffering and the triumph and the distressingly tearful arrival, just too late, of Marse George, the boy who has loved and remembered Tom and who is our surrogate in the book. All the conventional loves and romances of the book slip away, precisely because they are conventional, but also because they are irrelevant: the boy-girl all-white love of Eva and her cousin Henrique; and even, though it is a unifying thread joining the first volume of the novel to the second, the separation, the individual flights, and the joyous reunion in Canada of Eliza and George. We remember Eliza and the bloodhound, Eliza on the ice; we have to check the text to discover what happened to her after she left the floes behind, to remember that with her husband she emigrated to Liberia! Poor George—his existence is fictional only, not mythic. Unlettered Negroes to this day will speak of a pious compromiser of their own race, who urges Christian forbearance rather than militancy, as a "Tom" or "Uncle Tom"; it has become a standard term of contempt. But no one speaks of the advocate of force who challenges him as a "George," though Mrs. Stowe's protagonist of that name was a very model for the righteous use of force against force.

Only Uncle Tom and Topsy and Little Eva have archetypal stature; only the loves of the black man for the little white girl, of the white girl for the black, of the white boy for the slave live the lives of myths. Mrs. Stowe's laudable effort to establish a counter-stereotype to the image of the black rapist that haunts the mind of the South was a failure. We do not remember the turncoat puritan

Legree squeezing the virginal breast of Emmeline, eyeing her lust-fully; he is frozen forever, the last enduring myth of the book, in his role of slave-driver, at his purest moment of passion, himself the slave of his need to destroy the Christian slave Tom: "There was one hesitating pause, one irresolute relenting thrill, and the spirit of evil came back with sevenfold vehemence; and Legree, foaming with rage, smote his victim to the ground." It is at this moment that Legree seems the archetypal Seducer, ready for the final violation which the reader has all along feared and awaited with equal fervor.

For all the false rhetoric of Mrs. Stowe's description, that blow has an impact as wide in its significance as the assault of Lovelace, the attack of Cain; in it, the white man seals his guilt against the black, confesses his complicity in an act at once predestined and free. This is the moment that stays with us always, balanced against the counter-moment in which George grasps the hand of the dying Tom—*too late,* for Mrs. Stowe cannot help telling the truth—and weeps. The fact of brutality, the hope of forgiveness and mutual love: these are the twin images of guilt and reconciliation that represent for the popular mind of America the truth of slavery. How oddly they undercut the scenes of separated families, of baffled mother-love, at which Mrs. Stowe worked so hard—feeling perhaps that to her bourgeois readers slavery would stand condemned only if it were proved an offense against the sacred family and the suffering mother.

The chief pleasures of *Uncle Tom's Cabin* are, however, rooted not in the moral indignation of the reformer but in the more devious titillations of the sadist; not love but death is Mrs. Stowe's true Muse. For its potential readers, the death of Uncle Tom, the death of Little Eva, the almost-death of Eliza are the big scenes of *Uncle Tom's Cabin,* for they find in the fact and in the threat of death the thrill once provided by the fact or threat of sexual violation. Death is the supreme rapist who threatens when all other Seducers have been banished to the semi-pornographic pulps. And it is the sexless child who comes to seem his proper victim, after the nubile Maiden is considered too ambiguous and dangerous a subject for polite literature. The aroma of sexuality clings to this Maiden, innocent as she may be; and Eliza, for instance, caught by her pursuers, might easily become the object not of bloodlust, which is considered safe, but of quite specific sexual desire. Mrs. Stowe was Puritan enough not to flinch from such problems, but most of her readers were not; and they selected from her gallery of abused females the sexless child to remember and revere.

Little Eva seemed the answer to a particularly vexing genteel dilemma. To save the female for polite readers who wanted women but not sex was not an easy matter. The only safe woman is a dead woman; but even she, if young and beautiful, is only half safe, as any American knows, recalling the necrophilia of Edgar Allan Poe. The only *safe,* safe female is a pre-adolescent girl dying or dead. But this, of course, is Little Eva, the pre-pubescent corpse as heroine, model for all the protagonists of a literature at once juvenile and genteelly gothic.

Though the essential theme of the novel is, as we have come to see, love, it has never been forbidden the spice of death; and in its beginnings, it presented both in one, though both in terms of a fully adult world. In the earliest bourgeois fiction, we remember, the reader was permitted to assist at the last moments of the betrayed woman, no more excluded from the deathbed than from the marriage bed or the couch of sexual betrayal. In the later, more genteel stages of the novel, however, when it was no longer considered permissible to witness female sexual immorality, the reader was banned from the bedrooms of mature women even at the moment of their deaths. He had to content himself with the spectacle of the immaculate child winning her father to God by her courage in the face of a premature end.

Little Eva is the classic case in America, melting the obdurate though kindly St. Clare from skepticism to faith. What an orgy of approved pathos such scenes provided in the hands of a master like Harriet Beecher Stowe, or the later Louisa May Alcott, who in *Little Women* reworked the prototype of Mrs. Stowe into a kind of fiction specifically directed at young girls! Here is the *locus classicus* from *Uncle Tom's Cabin*.

"Dear papa," said the child, with a last effort, throwing her arms about his neck. In a moment they dropped again; and, as St. Clare raised his head, he saw a spasm of mortal agony pass over the face—she struggled for breath, and threw up her little hands.

"O God, this is dreadful," he said, turning away in agony, and wringing Tom's hand. . . . "O, Tom, my boy, it is killing me!" . . .

The child lay panting on her pillows, as one exhausted—the

large clear eyes rolled up and fixed. Ah, what said those eyes, that spoke so much of heaven? Earth was past, and earthly pain; but so solemn, so mysterious, was the triumphant brightness of that face, that it checked even the sobs of sorrow. . . .

The bed was draped in white; and there, beneath the drooping angel-figure, lay a little sleeping form—sleeping never to waken!

If there seems something grotesque in such a rigging of the scene, so naked a relish of the stiffening white body between the whiter sheets; if we find an especially queasy voyeurism in this insistence on entering the boudoirs of immature girls, it is perhaps the fault of our post-Freudian imaginations, incapable of responding sentimentally rather than analytically to such images. The bed we know is the place of deflowering as well as dying, and in the bridal bed, a young girl, still virgin, dies to be replaced by the woman, mourning forever the white thing she once was. At least, so an age of innocence dreamed the event; they did not have to *understand* what they dreamed. With no sense of indecorum, they penetrated, behind Mrs. Stowe, the bedroom of the Pure Young Thing and participated in the kill. To be allowed (vicariously) to murder the deflowered Clarissa of the earlier novel is, perhaps, satisfactory enough, since the appeasement of guilt, the hatred of sin lies at its root; but to murder (just as vicariously) the pre-adolescent Virgin is to be granted the supreme privilege of assaulting innocence, appeasing the hatred of virtue, which must surely have stirred uneasily before such atrociously immaculate examples. And it is all done without recourse to "sex," as sex was then quite narrowly defined—*cleanly* sadistic to an age in which no one suspected that the shadow of the Marquis de Sade might fall upon the social reformer. All was permitted the writer capable of combining such erotic evocations of death with attacks on slavery or demands for the reorganization of debtors' prisons, boys' schools, and almshouses.

The notion that Mrs. Stowe (whose blend of morality and prurience led her to expose the love life of Byron and his sister, when she had run out of material closer to home) might be a pornographer was as unthinkable to the great audience of her age as the fact that Dickens, her teacher in this regard, drew all his life on his own odd taste for pre-nubile girls. That Dickens' Little Nell is the model for Little Eva seems probable enough; though, indeed, the atmosphere of the era makes the simultaneous emergence of such archetypal small girls far from unlikely. It is Dickens, however, who first provides in *The Old Curiosity Shop* (1842) the iconography of the Holy Family of the genteel Protestant bourgeoisie. Not the Divine Boy but the Good Good Girl is imagined, cuddled not in the arms of the mother but in those of the father, and not at the moment of birth but at that of death. When *The Old Curiosity Shop* first appeared, critics spoke of the affiliation of Little Nell to Cordelia; and indeed, the final scenes of *King Lear* must have suggested to Dickens the form of what has been called the Protestant *Pietà:* the white-clad daughter, dying or dead, in the arms of the old man, tearful papa or grandfather or (in America) the woolly-haired slave.

It is the unendurable happy ending, as the white slip of a thing too good for this world prepares to leave it for the next, while readers and parents, lovers all, sob into their handkerchiefs. The Good Good Girl, blond, asexual goddess of nursery or orphanage or old plantation house ("Always dressed in white," Mrs. Stowe writes of Eva, "she seemed to move like a shadow through all sorts of places, without contracting spot or stain; and there was not a corner or nook . . . where those fairy footsteps had not glided, and that visionary golden head, with its deep blue eyes, fleeted along"), must die not only so we may weep—and tears are, for the sentimentalist, the true baptism of the heart—but also because there is nothing else for her to do. There lies before the Little Evas of the world no course of action which would not sully them; allowed to grow up, Little Eva could only become—since she is forbidden the nunnery by the Protestant ethos and the role of the old maid is in our culture hopelessly comic—wife, mother, or widow, tinged no matter how slightly with the stain of sexuality, *suffered* perhaps rather than sought, but, in any case, *there!*

I I

Only the girl-child seems, however, a sufficiently spotless savior to the imagination of America, which boggles at the notion of a pure boy. In Dickens, the pale dwarfish monsters of piety include not only Little Nells but boys, too: Tiny Tim and Paul Dombey and Oliver Twist, who though he does not ever quite die is constantly flirting with that final consummation. In the United States, however, such figures seem alien. Little Lord Fauntleroy is an import once much admired by Europeanizing females, but always scorned by nativists no matter how sentimental. He seems in our context the "little gentleman," miniature version of the polished, foreign seducer: an outsider who wears his Sunday clothes on weekdays and would rather walk shod than run barefoot. Sometimes he is called scornfully a "mamma's boy" but this term must be analyzed carefully, since *all* American boys belong to mother— even Tom Sawyer, traditional enemy of all "little gentlemen." Tom, indeed, has no father at all, his only parent that Aunt Polly whom he would die for rather than betray.

To betray the mother—to deny her like the young rogue in *The Prince and the Pauper*—this is the unforgivable sin. What then is the difference between the Good Good Boy and the Good Bad Boy, between Sid Sawyer, let us say, and Tom? The Good Good Boy does what his mother must pretend that she wants him to do: obey, conform; the Good Bad Boy does what she really wants him to do: deceive, break her heart a little, be forgiven. For a long time the Good Bad Boy was called the "bad boy" without qualification, since his goodness needed no adjective to declare itself to those who really knew him; and the very epithet was enough to insure a best-seller: *Confessions of a Bad Boy, Peck's Bad Boy,* etc. How much longer it took for a book to be called *Bad Girl* and how different the connotations of the title! "Oh, Tom, you bad boy!" Becky Thatcher cries to Tom and we take it as an endearment. It is the fate of the Good Good Girl (who must suffer, too, like the more mature savior-figures before her) to love such boys precisely because they play hooky, cuss, steal in a mild sort of a way, dream of violence. Where taboos forbid the expression of sexuality such delinquency is a declaration of maleness.

The Good Bad Boy is, of course, America's vision of itself, crude and unruly in his beginnings, but endowed by his creator with an instinctive sense of what is right. Sexually as pure as any milky maiden, he is a roughneck all the same, at once potent and submissive, made to be reformed by the right woman. No wonder our greatest book is about a boy and that boy "bad"! The book is, of course, *Huckleberry Finn* (with its extension back into *Tom Sawyer*), an astonishingly complicated novel, containing not one image of the boy but a series of interlocking ones. Tom Sawyer exists as the projection of all that Sid Sawyer, pious Good Good Boy, presumably yearns for and denies; but Huck Finn

in turn stands for what Tom is not quite rebel enough to represent; and Nigger Jim (remade from boy to adult between the
two books) embodies a world of instinct and primal terror beyond
what even the outcast white boy projects.

In our national imagination, two freckle-faced boys, arm in arm,
fishing poles over their shoulders, walk toward the river; or one
alone floats peacefully on its waters, a runaway Negro by his
side. They are on the lam, we know, from Aunt Polly and Aunt
Sally and the widow Douglas and Miss Watson, from golden-
haired Becky Thatcher, too—from all the reduplicated female
symbols of "sivilization" It is these images of boyhood which the
popular imagination further debases step by step via Penrod and
Sam or O. Henry's "Red Chief" to Henry Aldrich on the radio
or the insufferable Archie of the teen-age comic books. Such
figures become constantly more false in their naïveté, in their
hostility to culture in general and schoolteachers in particular;
and it scarcely matters whether they are kept in the traditional
costume of overalls or are permitted jeans and sweaters decorated
with high-school letters.

Twain is surely not responsible for all the vulgar metamorphoses of his images of boyhood; but in one respect he is a conscious accomplice of the genteel kidnapers of Huck and Jim.
Since not only in his avowed children's books, but almost everywhere in his work, Twain writes as a boy for a world accustomed
to regarding the relations of the sexes in terms of the tie that
binds mother to son. Not only does he disavow physical passion,
refusing the Don Juan role traditional for European writers; but
he downgrades even the Faustian role incumbent on American
authors. In him, the diabolic outcast becomes the "little devil,"
not only comical but cute, a child who will outgrow his mischief,
or an imperfect adult male, who needs the "dusting off" of marriage to a good woman. It was in the fading '60's that Twain's
typical fictional devices were contrived, in the '70's that they were
perfected—at a time, that is to say, when everywhere in the
popular American novel the archetypes were being reduced to
juveniles. As Clarissa becomes a small girl in *The Wide, Wide
World,* so Werther becomes a child in Twain's total work, turns
into the boy-author Mark Twain; and not only the American
women who made Susan Warner's book a best-seller approve,
but their husbands, too, who laughed at their wives' taste—just
as Twain had at his wife's before being challenged to write *The*

Gilded Age. Even dirty, tired, adult Europe approves, finds no offense in *The Innocents Abroad* itself, since Twain was playing a role that European self-hatred and condescension to the United States demanded, acting the Good Bad Boy of Western culture. For everyone, male and female, European and American, he represents the id subverting tired ego-ideals, not in terror and anarchy, but in horseplay, pranks, and irreverent jests.

There is notoriously a price for assuming a mask, indeed, always a suspicion that what the mask hides is no face at all! And certainly one senses in Twain the need to act out for public laughter the aspects of himself which he feared might evoke private snickers. His buffoonery is obviously a camouflage for insecurity, the insecurity of a man with genteel ideas and bad manners, with pretensions to aristocratic origins and no formal education. Yet all along, he seems to have believed that somewhere beneath the high-jinks of Twain, there was a real and quite serious Sam Clemens: with serious ideas, too dangerous to utter; and serious ambitions, too lofty to risk in the market-place—even a serious vein of bawdry, too masculine and broad for the general reader. But his serious ideas eventuate in the sophomoric cynicism of "What is Man," his serious aesthetics in the sentimental banalities of *Joan of Arc,* his serious bawdry in the pseudo-archaic smutty jokes of *1601.*

Finally, Twain is betrayed not by his contempt for culture, which is involved, ironical, and sometimes wickedly witty, but by his pretensions to culture. He was a man fitfully intelligent when he did not know he was thinking, a spottily skillful stylist when he was not aware he was writing artistically; but he lacked critical judgment completely (his notion of criticism was a hunt for boners in the Leatherstocking Tales), and was tormented by an urge toward self-parody that verged on self-punishment. He is, therefore, an embarrassment to admiring critics, who tend either to swallow whole his dishearteningly uneven achievement; or to admire him only for the bitter wisdom presumably concealed from the vulgar beneath the hilarious surfaces of his work. There are corresponding traps for dissenting critics, who may find Twain the beneficiary of a cult of native humor finally more deadly than the cult of museums which he exposed; or cry out that his "philosophy" is the product of a childish mind, and his dissembling of it for popularity's sake shameful.

To make of Twain either a cult or a case, however, is finally to lose the sense of him as a poet, the possessor of deep and special mythopoeic powers, whose childhood was contemporaneous with a nation's; and who, remembering himself before the fall of puberty, remembered his country before the fall of the Civil War. The myth which Twain creates is a myth of childhood, rural, sexless, yet blessed in its natural Eden by the promise of innocent love, and troubled by the shadow of bloody death. The world in which his myth unfolds is one in which passion is less real than witchcraft, ghosts more common than adulterers; but it is also one in which a pure love between males, colored and white, triumphs over witches and ghosts and death itself. It is, of course, a world already dreamed in the fiction of Cooper and Poe, Dana and Melville, but never before labeled: "For Children Only!" And if we remember Twain's quite serious predecessors rather than his more sentimental followers (Stephen Crane, Booth Tarkington, etc.), we can understand how his novels define a boundary between myth and bathos, the highbrow Western and the boys' book.

It is hard to say whether the fear of sex, a strange blindness to the daily manifestations of sex, or the attenuation of sexuality itself drove the American novel back over the lintel of puberty in the declining years of the nineteenth century. Twain himself seems to have believed, not unlike Hawthorne before him, that it was the last; certainly, he had no sense of being *forbidden* to talk about a kind of passion which burgeoned everywhere in his society. In *1601*, at least, he seems to believe, though the conviction is offered in the guise of a joke, that genitality itself had withered to the vanishing point in America: "Then spake ye damned wyndmill, Sir Walter, of a people in ye uttermost parts of America that copulate not until they be five-and-thirty years of age, ye women being eight-and-twenty, and doe it then but once in seven yeares." In the mouth of "ye damned wyndmill," this is spoken contemptuously, but in his own voice, Twain (who did not in fact marry until he was past thirty) makes a similar assertion about the young people of his childhood community, this time with a certain amount of pride.

Chastity. There was the utmost liberty among young people—but no young girl was ever insulted, or seduced, or even scandalously gossiped about. Such things were not even dreamed of in a society, much less spoken of and referred to as possibilities.

The dream which Twain dreamed, at any rate, did not include such possibilities; and *his* memories of the past, at least, were duly expurgated, though just once in *Tom Sawyer* his censorship relaxes. For a single moment, we see Becky caught out peeking at the dirty picture in the teacher's anatomy book, and for that moment we are reminded of the living flesh beneath the pinafores and roundabouts. But it does not finally matter; for Twain will not let his protagonists, not Becky or Tom or Huck, over the borderline of adolescence, playing such games with their ages that the reader cannot tell from page to page whether they are barely out of kindergarten (in *Tom Sawyer,* Tom is just losing his baby teeth) or on the verge of manhood (in *Huckleberry Finn,* one summer later, Huck, Tom's apparent co-eval, is fourteen). Yet Twain's dream of boyhood begins with a dream of love in a sexless world; and, indeed, the "Boy's Manuscript," which he wrote in 1870, and which is the seed of all the later books about Huck and Tom, is an account of a love affair between eight- or nine-year-olds—involving flirtation, jealousy, and reconciliation, though not, of course, passion.

Yet for all its sexual purity, Tom's childhood world is intimately acquainted with death. Violence is omnipresent, yet somehow is never considered to impugn innocence, so long as it does not involve concupiscence. The plan of Injun Joe in *Tom Sawyer* to take revenge on the Widow Douglas was apparently based on an actual case involving the threat of rape, which Twain bowdlerized to a mere slitting of the nostrils and notching of the ears—thus apparently making it suitable for child readers.

There is the sense everywhere in Twain that *violence doesn't count,* the muting of sensitivity before aggression which is always demanded by slapstick and the more brutal forms of farce; and it is this which the one favorable review of *Huckleberry Finn* applauds as "a total absence of morbidness in the book," a proof that "the *mal du siècle* has not yet reached Arkansas." Twain's treatment of the Grangerford-Shepherdson feud strikes the reviewer as a prime example: "described only as it would appear to a semi-civilized boy of fourteen, without the slightest condemnation or surprise. . . ." But this is scarcely the whole story; for concurrent with such a brutalized acceptance of terror in Twain, is a guilt-ridden obsession with it, an inability to let it alone. Twain's attitude toward violence is finally as complicated, subtle, and deliberately ambiguous as his attitude toward sex is naive, sentimentalized, and hopelessly evasive. He is not only the creator of childhood idylls but a great poet of violence; and, indeed, even his humor depends upon a world in which there is neither a stable order nor civil peace.

His hope for order and peace he invested in the genteel Atlantic seaboard society into which he married, after years of drifting from job to job through West and East and South, looking for these qualities especially in his wife, whom he drafted as a super-ego, a living conscience. "I would . . . quit wearing socks if she thought them immoral," he said of his Livy, of whom he asked that she regularly "dust him off," make him worthy of the civilization she represented. He never chafed at Livy's demands, though he occasionally evaded them like the Good Bad Boy he never ceased to be, perhaps even regretted that she forbade too little; it would have made life more interesting if she *had* declared socks immoral! The society which had bred him, made him the untidy, disorderly boor he always felt before his wife, he recalled as a world of violence and horror. It seemed to him a chaotic middle ground between the South (with its no longer viable patriarchal ideals and its obsession with Sir Walter Scott), which his family had left behind just before his birth, and the true Western frontier (with its denial of all hierarchy and tradition), which had moved on ahead. Missouri he remembered as a slothful sub-frontier, in which the fathers no longer had any authority, and the mothers sought in vain to assert certain simple-minded standards of piety and decorum. Certainly, his own father had died in Twain's childhood, crying despairingly, "Let me die!"; while his mother had pleaded with him at the deathbed, "Only promise me to be a better boy. Promise not to break my heart."

Yet to Twain, Missouri was also a world of innocence and freedom and joy, a world in which *he,* at least, had been innocent and free and joyous, a naked boy, swimming and fishing and smoking on Jackson's Island. To the idyllic era of his childhood, Twain's mature mind reverted over and over, only to discover that the era had been lived out in a society marred by disorder and violence and slavery. It was the violence which he especially recalled: the dead man he had discovered after breaking into his father's office; the vagabond shot down in the street and gasping for breath beneath the heavy Bible laid on his chest; the hellish storm that had broken the night Injun Joe died, and had left him whimpering for the salvation of his soul; the tramp who had burned himself to death in the local jail, setting himself on fire (perhaps!) with matches the boy Twain had smuggled to him. Each terror brought with it the shadow of guilt: he should not have been sneaking into his father's office after dark; he should have been good enough to regard the crash of thunder with equanimity; he should have protested against laying so heavy and pious a burden on a dying man's chest; he should not have passed contraband through the bars.

Twain began to feel after a while that he carried with him the infection of death, out of the world he had left into the new world in which he sought peace. The death of his father, perhaps, and certainly that of his brother, Henry (whom he pilloried later as Sid all the same), he felt as somehow his responsibility; but these at least belonged to the life he had led before meeting Livy. When his son died, however, after an act of carelessness on his part, his favorite daughter, Susy, while he was absent in Europe ("died where she had spent all her life till my crimes made her a pauper and an exile"); when his daughter Jean developed epilepsy, and his wife ailed, he was more than ever ridden by a guilt which he could not allay, except by trying to persuade himself that death was a final good. "She has found," he said of Susy, "the richest gift the world can offer." Yet the books in which he tried, toward the end of his own life, to express his dark despair are flat and unconvincing or shrill and sophomoric. When Hannibal becomes Eseldorf, and Tom Sawyer is excluded from the final version of *The Mysterious Stranger,* all tension and ambiguity depart from Twain's work and with it his special charm.

His most profoundly sad books are the most mad and idyllic, his wisest those he wrote dreaming not thinking: dreaming the golden dream that threatens momentarily to turn into nightmare: and the wisest and saddest of them all, as it is also the craziest and most euphoric, is, of course, *Huckleberry Finn.* Indeed, to turn from *Huckleberry Finn* to the rest of Twain's work is disheartening; for there are only portions of other books which approach it; most of the first part of *Life on the Mississippi,* a good deal of *Pudd'nhead Wilson;* and to a lesser degree, *The Innocents Abroad, A Connecticut Yankee in King Arthur's Court, Tom Sawyer.* Beyond this, there is much that is merely occasional, even trivial; much that is without passion or point; much that is highfalutin or absurdly noble; much that is terrifyingly unfunny and empty. After a while, the reader who has made the mistake of reading too much Twain begins to feel that even the books he has liked cannot possibly be as good as he has thought them; that what Twain has left behind is not so much a real *oeuvre* as a bag of tricks: the accoutrements of a role, whose meaning has been lost to us with the death of its performer and a change in taste.

And then one reads *Huckleberry Finn* again, hears—intermittently at least—a voice which is neither Clemens' nor Twain's but genuinely Huck's, which is to say, not the voice of a genteel sentimentalist or a clown in full make-up, but of a boy-Ishmael: "the juvenile pariah of the village . . . idle, and lawless, and vulgar, and bad. . . ." The phrase is out of *Tom Sawyer,* of course, and it is with that earlier book that any discussion of *Huckleberry Finn* must begin; for it is Tom who discovers Huck, after his own book has begun, and discovering him, almost inadvertently, discovers also a great mythic theme. That theme succeeds in time in overwhelming the love story of Tom and Becky, which was the first inspiration of the book, and even thrusts aside the kind of genre picture ("Whitewashing the Fence"—the illustrator's dream!) which was its second. Of Tom Blankenship, the original of Huck, Twain writes in *The Autobiography:* "He was the only really independent person—boy or man—in the community . . ."; and in *Tom Sawyer,* adds that all the children, at least, "wished they dared be like him." The memory of "all the boy" Twain was or dreamed himself afterward is Tom; the memory of all he was not and only wished he dared aspire to be is Huck; and it is fitting that they be companions, the books named after each, sequels.

"Mark Twain's next book will bear the title of 'Huckleberry Finn, A Sequel to Tom Sawyer,' " a puff in *The Dial* for February, 1884, announced; and when the book actually appeared, it was called *Adventures of Huckleberry Finn* (*Tom Sawyer's Comrade*), but Twain was unwilling to depend on advertising and the title page alone to make his point. "You don't know about me," the first sentence of the new novel reads, "without you have read a book by the name of *The Adventures of Tom Sawyer. . . .*" And it is well, for once, to take Twain at his word, though there intervened between the publication of the first book (in 1876) and the second eight years, nearly seven of which Twain spent bogged down and unable to write a line, once his first impetus had taken him through the fifteenth chapter of the book as it presently stands. He did not know what to do when the raft had been taken out from under him and his characters! The point was, though it took Twain seven years to find it out, that his new book had ceased to be a continuation of the old, developing a much more complex relationship to it than that of a mere sequel.

Though *Huckleberry Finn* begins in the same long, idyllic summer of which *Tom Sawyer* had already consumed more than the normal number of weeks, and comes to a close in the following year, both boys have grown older by perhaps five or six years. And the author, too, has matured, is only *playing* now at producing an entertainment for children. If *Tom Sawyer* was always a boy's book, even when Twain thought he was writing for adults, *Huckleberry Finn* is from the start, on one of its levels at least, not merely an adult but a subversive novel, as the board of the Concord Public Library should have been congratulated for seeing. From time to time, Huck regresses to the age he was in the earlier book, chiefly when he comes face to face with a nubile, attractive girl, as in the Wilks episode—throughout which he is portrayed as feeling for the nineteen-year-old, red-haired Mary Ann the kind of nine-year-old passion little Billy Rogers had felt for a girl of the same age in the "Boy's Manuscript"; "I've seen the girl that is my doom. . . . Oh, she is *so* lovely! And she loves me. I know it. I could see it easy. She's nineteen years old Christmas. I never, never, never will part with *this* one! NEVER!" But such strategic retreats in time cannot conceal the basic change in Twain's conception of Huck, who has ceased to be merely a clownish foil to Tom, essentially *stupid* though good of heart. There is no mention in *Huckleberry Finn* of "Huck's slow mind," no condescending references to his efforts at thought as "a mental struggle."

It is, of course, Huck who tells the second tale with an apparent artlessness that touches true poetry, a kind of speech which characterizes him better than his author can. But the switch into first-person narrative does not in itself insure the new view of Huck. Twain attempts twice more to let Huck speak for himself, in *Tom Sawyer Abroad* and *Tom Sawyer Detective;* but in each case Huck lapses back into the role of obtuse oaf, his conversation sprinkled with burlesque boners: "diseased" for "deceased," "prostitution" for "prosecution," or "the solar sister" for "the solar system." Even in *Huckleberry Finn,* the first comic substitution has been smuggled (anything for a laugh!) into the Wilks episode, which is, in all respects, the falsest part of the book. And in *Huckleberry Finn*, too, Huck has been permitted occasionally to gush over the loneliness of life on the Mississippi in a schoolgirl style, which betrays his unsuspected affiliation to the female orphans of Susan Warner and Maria Cummins. Nothing in that book, however, descends to the level of *Tom Sawyer Abroad*, in which Huck hails a new bit of scenery as "the darlingest place there is" or improbably explains that "there was a dear little temple" between the paws of the Sphinx.

The language of Huck is a function of Twain's understanding of his character and role, and varies in authenticity with the author's sense of what both he and his character are doing. In all three Tom Sawyer stories, Huck is Tom's Noble Savage, a sentimentalized id-figure (and in this respect Jim is his double), representing the Good Bad Boy's dream of how bully life might be without parents, clothing or school; and in those books, Huck is even more condescended to than admired. In *Huckleberry Finn*, however, Huck does the condescending toward Tom, who represents in that book his misguided ego-ideal, the embodiment of a "literary" style which he cannot really afford. When he is truest to himself, Huck respects, in the teeth of all he has been taught, Nigger Jim, which is to say, an even more ultimate id-figure; in his weaker moments, he joins Tom in relegating the surrogate for the instinctive life to the world of make-believe, which is also a prison.

In general, the two boys represent to each other the writer's conception of "experience" and the nonreader's conception of "art." It would be pleasant to say that they fuse finally into a single figure: but even in the terms of Twain, they represent not so much two aspects of the same man as that man's sense of what he has become, opposed to what he has escaped becoming. In American life as a whole, the two are notoriously disjoined: the artist and the naïf, the man who has made it and the man who never knew it was there to be made. It is all very well to tell us that Huck's original ended as "a good citizen and greatly respected." This, we know, is not true of the fictional Huck, who is finally lost to Tom and respectability alike. Though in boyhood, Mark-Tom and Tom-Huck (surely, the inversion of the names is a deliberate joke!) were permitted to play hooky together; it is clear that once Mark-Tom decides to be good, to marry Livy, he will never again answer Tom-Huck's meow. Only in fantasy will he slide down the lightning rod again; but even his fantasy will end on a note of separation, not really belied by the desperate attempts, published and unpublished, to continue beyond *Huckleberry Finn* his childhood alliance with the village pariah.

If we think of the two books not as sequels but as alternative versions of the same themes (hopelessly concealed from the author himself in *Tom Sawyer,* more consciously developed in *Huckleberry Finn*), those themes will become clearer to us, reveal themselves in their mythic significance. Stripped of incidental ornaments, *Tom Sawyer* and *Huckleberry Finn* are seen as the same dream dreamed twice over, the second time as nightmare; though, to be sure, the terror of the second dream is already at work in the first, whose euphoria persists strangely into the second. In both books, there is a pretended, a quasi-ritual death to the community and its moral codes; though in *Tom Sawyer* that "death" is a lark, undertaken in childish pique, while in *Huckleberry Finn* it is a last desperate evasion, an act of self-defense. In both, there is a consequent spying on the community from cover to watch the effects of that death, the aftermath of regret: the childish dream of the suicide, who longs to be present at his own discovery, come true. In the one case, however, the spying is a prelude to a triumphant return, a revelation, in the other, to a further flight and concealment.

In both, there is an escape to an island, indeed, to the same island, on which the refugee lives, for a little while, with his good companions and in the bosom of nature, fishing, swimming, smoking the pipe forbidden by mothers. But in the one case, the natural Eden is purely a boys' paradise, from which one returns home as from a picnic; in the other, it is a temporary asylum not only from "sivilization" but from pursuit, enslavement, and death; and leaving it, the refugee plunges into further flight. The good companions, in the one case, are other boys, homesick almost from the start; in the other, the sole companion is a run-away slave, whose home is nowhere. In both, there is a night-journey across the river back into the abandoned world of obligations and restraints, a scouting foray into what has become enemy country; but in the one case, the scouting prepares for a return, in the other, a more desperate withdrawal.

In both, the escapee and presumed ghost watches from a place of concealment (how much in both books is peeked at, witnessed, overheard!) a sentimental *Pietà,* the sorrow of the "mother" over her mischievous and presumably lost boy. But how different is Huck's witnessing of Aunt Sally's tears, which are not even shed for him, from Tom's watching Aunt Polly cry. Though the descriptions are not unlike ("And twice I . . . see her setting there . . . with her eyes toward the road and tears in them. . . . And third time I waked up at dawn . . . and she was there yet . . . and her old grey head was resting on her hands, and she was asleep." "He had to keep still long after she went to bed, for she kept making broken-hearted ejaculations . . . and turning over. But at last she was still, only moaning a little in her sleep"), Tom is already prepared for his reconciliation with the offended mother while Huck is already incubating his great refusal. In Tom's pocket all the time is the message, *"We ain't dead—we are only off being pirates"*; while Huck is preparing inwardly for the moment when he will declare: "But I reckon I got to light out for the territory ahead of the rest, because Aunt Sally she's going to adopt me and civilize me, and I can't stand it."

In both books, there is a terrorized flight from a threatening Satanic figure, who also stands outside of the comunity from which the boy-protagonist tries to escape in earnest or in play; and in each case, the outlaw figure represents a grotesque travesty of the boy himself, his innocence distorted into an image of guilt. Tom plays the robber, the pirate, which Injun Joe is in fact; Huck yearns in Widow Douglas' house for the life of ignorance and sloth, which his Pap actually lives. But in *Tom Sawyer*, the shadow of the protagonist is represented as utterly alien, a melodramatic half-breed out of a dime novel; in *Huckleberry Finn*, Huck's shadow is his own father: no creature of melodrama, but the town drunk—a vision of what he himself may well become! Pap Finn had, indeed, been cast for the role of Muff Potter in an early version of *Tom Sawyer*, but he was too real a terror for that theatrically gothic tale.

In both books, the shadow figure controls or threatens a treasure (the same "innocent" buried loot of dead murderers), which can be possessed in peace only after he has died; and in both, the plot involves a simultaneous revelation of that death and the protagonist's deliverance: his coming for the first time, or again, into a fortune. In both cases, the death of the demonic guardian of the hoard is rendered with special horror: Injun Joe at the cave's stony sill, a broken case-knife in his hand and the gnawed claws of bats beside him; Pap, naked and stabbed in the back, in the floating house of death, its walls scribbled with obscenities. But only in *Huckleberry Finn* is the full Oedipal significance of their deaths revealed, the terrible secret that the innocent treasure can be won only by the destruction of the Bad Father!

In both books, there is a good angel, too, a redemptive *anima* figure, contrasted with the threatening shadow. In *Tom Sawyer,* that figure appears in the form of Becky Thatcher, juvenile version of the snow maiden: "a lovely little blue-eyed creature with yellow hair plaited in two long tails, white summer frock." She is called, unequivocally enough, Tom's "new angel," and, for all her peeping at the forbidden picture in the teacher's book (what momentary demonic impulse prompted Twain to such a give-away?), will obviously grow up to be just such a good woman as Twain himself married and idolized. Meanwhile, she scarcely knows which she admires more in the Good Bad Boy Tom, his badness ("Oh, you bad thing!"), which it will give her pleasure to subdue, or his goodness ("Tom, how *could* you be so noble!"), which she calls forth and will sustain. It is of marriage with her that Tom dreams; for, as he explains to Huck, she is a "girl" not a "gal"! But marriage, to Huck, means only domestic strife and the abandonment of the world in which he is at home. Wistfully and a little jealously, he remarks, "Only if you get married I'll be more lonesomer than ever."

Yet Huck has his good angel, too, appropriately enough as black as Becky Thatcher is white: not a future good woman but a runaway slave, who represents his aspiration toward a deeper level of the primitive, even as Becky represents Tom's yearning for a "higher" level of civilization. Miss Watson's Jim is the Becky Thatcher of *Huckleberry Finn.* They cannot be present in the same book; Jim does not appear in *Tom Sawyer;* and when he enters the sequel Becky withdraws, making even her brief farewell bow under the name of Bessie Thatcher. With Jim, of course, Huck does not dream of any sexual relation, any more than Tom does with Becky; nor does he think of their union in terms of a marriage. Yet they pet and sustain each other in mutual love and trust: make on their raft an anti-family of two, with neither past nor future, only a transitory, perilous present of peace and joy.

Like Tom and Becky, Huck and Jim triumph over the petty pride that threatens to separate them in the midst of horror and pursuit, declare their affection without shame or fear of ridicule in the face of death; yet, like Tom and Becky, they seem to be already drifting apart after their moment of deliverance. For Huck and Jim, there is no possibility of a continuing love; Jim has a family, which will presumably claim him, and Huck must follow the centrifugal impulse which has made and will keep him the "only independent person . . . in the community." Moreover, he and Jim are separated not by the schoolyard code which forbids the fraternizing of boys and girls, but by the profound social gulf between black and white in ante-bellum Missouri. Huck himself knows that the talk of another lark involving Jim, the outing to the Indian territory will not really materialize, and that he will have to "light out . . . ahead of the rest." Twain could not ever quite manage to write anything publishable about the projected expedition, though he went to work on it almost immediately after finishing *Huckleberry Finn*. The prospect of "howling adventures amongst the Injuns" is merely another of Tom's artistic lies, a forecast as vain as his assurance in the earlier book that Huck will come and live with him after he and Becky are married.

Three's a crowd, whether the third be Becky or Jim, Tom's *anima* figure or Huck's; and after an unsuccessful try, in *Tom Sawyer Abroad,* to carry along both Huck and Jim on an adventure of Tom's (the two play scarcely distinguishable end-men to Tom's interlocutor), Twain settles in *Tom Sawyer Detective* for his original white pair. Jim presumably returns to his wife and children, whom Twain had temporarily forgotten; and, of course, Becky, in whom he never *quite* believed at all, makes no further appearance. Tom and Huck had, as a matter of fact, already stood alone at the close of both *Tom Sawyer* and *Huckleberry Finn;* for each book tries to end with a pact in which the Good Bad Boy and the juvenile pariah come to terms: the juvenile pariah agreeing to accept an adoptive mother, and the Good Bad Boy agreeing in return to accept the pariah into his world of make-believe—the robber gang or the expedition to the territory. Both the integration into the family and the playing of terror in the place of living it stand for a surrender of independence, since Tom, who thinks he wants to be like Huck, secretly wants Huck to be like him. In *Tom Sawyer,* the melancholy happy ending works; but *Huckleberry Finn,* which begins with the collapse of that first happy ending, closes with the hint it will not hold the second time either.

All of which means, finally, that *Huckleberry Finn* is a true book, *Tom Sawyer* only "mostly a true book" with "some stretchers," one of which is its ending. Huck can tell the truth about Tom, for though he lies by preference almost always, he *knows* when he is lying; but Tom is incapable of telling the truth about Huck, because he does not ever know when he is lying. At the point in *Huckleberry Finn* when Huck is about to disengage from the spell of Tom's long magical summer and plunge into his own, he sees quite clearly what Tom is like: "So then I judged that all that stuff was only just one of Tom Sawyer's lies. I reckoned he believed in the A-rabs and the elephants, but as for me I think different. It had all the marks of a Sunday-school." Toward the end of the book, however, when he has *become* Tom, Huck seems to lose this insight, and submits himself to the hoax of trying to steal Jim in fiction as he has already tried in fact; but at this point, the book has become Tom's, not his.

By and large, it is possible to say that *Tom Sawyer* is a fable of lost boyhood written by Tom, while *Huckleberry Finn* is that same fable transcribed by Huck. Somewhat misleadingly, Tom's version does not appear in first-person, though Twain considered telling it that way, and the "Boy's Manuscript," which is its germ, is actually written so. But its third-person narrative is finally even more right; for Tom is himself always an actor in a fiction of his own making, and, of course, he and Mark Twain are alternative sketches of the same character. Just as Tom speaks in a literary style compiled out of his favorite reading, so his book is a compound of genteel and gothic clichés, tempered with the condescension and humor which Twain considered proper in a book written for children. One of the chief functions of its style is to make the events it describes seem less real. The reality of the emotions it evokes is deliberately called into question by overwriting which verges on burlesque: "Life to him seemed hollow, and existence but a burden" or "He thought he loved her to distraction, he regarded his passion as adoration; and behold it was only a poor little innocent partiality." What we are asked to remember always is that the characters described so solemnly are eight- and nine-year-old kids!

Yet toward his own book as a whole, Twain adopts the same ironical tone, closing it with the words: "So endeth this chronicle. It being the history of a *boy,* it . . . could not go much further without becoming the history of a man." "So endeth this chronicle. . . ." It is at once a confession of falseness and an attempt to evade it, utterly different from the conclusion of *Huckleberry Finn:* "so there ain't nothing more to write about, and I am rotten glad of it. . . ." *Tom Sawyer* is the first of a long line of books intended to be read by a boy with his father looking over his shoulder, and thus to perpetuate for a new generation the legend of an older one. From it descends a tradition, which passes via Stephen Crane and Booth Tarkington to the creators of Henry Aldrich and the Good Bad Boys of contemporary comics: the ritual praise of good-badness as the true Americanism. "He warn't *bad,* so to say . . ." Aunt Polly insists, thinking Tom dead, "only misch*eev*ous. . . . *He* never meant any harm, and he was the best-hearted boy that ever was. . . ."

Huckleberry Finn, however, is not the progenitor of anything, because it is written neither by Tom nor Mark Twain, but by the evoked Huckleberry himself, who makes it quite clear at the end that he intends to write no more: "and if I'd 'a' knowed what trouble it was to make a book I´ wouldn't 'a' tackled it, and ain't a-going to no more." Nor could Twain himself make him change his mind, though he tried to call him up over and over for an encore. Only once did Huck really possess his presumable author, speak through him in his authentic voice. In the book called by his name, Huckleberry Finn exists, dictates his own style, his own moral judgments, his own meanings, which neither Twain nor the reader has to understand to experience. Tom Sawyer notoriously enters the book before it is finished, not letting Huck speak for himself again until the very last pages; but though he can counterfeit Huck's style, he cannot make him live, only move woodenly through the howling farce—which reveals the poverty of Tom's values and imagination, and exposes the falsity of his role. He is no more the "Tom" he claims to be than is Huck, but *really* Sid, the model boy whom he hates and whose name he assumes: Sid disguised as Robin Hood!

In one sense, *Huckleberry Finn* seems a circular book, ending as it began with a refused adoption and a projected flight; and certainly it has the effect of refusing the reader's imagination passage into the future. But there is a break-through in the last pages, especially in the terrible sentence which begins, "But I reckon I got to light out for the territory ahead of the rest. . . ." In these words, the end of childhood is clearly signaled; and we are forced to ask the question, which, duplicitously, the book refuses to answer: what will become of Huck if he persists in his refusal to return to the place where he has been before? It is easier to project Tom's future, and perhaps this is the best way to begin. Huck has been *forced,* in the course of the action, to become Tom; but Tom has eagerly taken on the role of Sid, and in doing so has given away the secret so well kept in *Tom Sawyer:* the Good Bad Boy and the Good Good Boy are not so different, after all—mother's boys, both of them. Tom will become a lawyer, a banker, a senator, at best—maintaining even into adulthood his permitted good-badness—a writer, which is to say, Mark Twain! Clemens did not deceive himself about the meaning of this, confessing to William Dean Howells: "If I went on now, and took him into manhood, he would just *lie,* like all the one-horse men in literature. . . ."

But what if Twain had taken "on into manhood" Huck Finn, who lies, to be sure, but never in any "one-horse" literary way? Having rejected the world of the mothers, Huck is condemned really to "go to Hell," to be lost in a sub-world of violence, a violence so universal that it is not judged but breathed like an atmosphere. It is a world in which one survives by his own wits and the stupidity of others: a world bounded on the one side by Pap, the corrupt victim; and on the other, by the Duke and the King, the feckless victimizers. When Huck catches his last glimpse of those two charming and vicious operators "astraddle of a rail," he expresses for them more pity than he finds to spare for anyone else in the book: "and I was sorry for them poor pitiful rascals, it seemed like I couldn't ever feel any hardness against them any more in the world."

One cannot help feeling that it is his own fate which Huck foresees in their plight, and that it is himself he weeps for. Even so he must end up, too, tarred and feathered, unless he dies like his father, stabbed in the back and set adrift on the river. When his father's fate is revealed to him by Jim at the novel's conclusion, Huck can find nothing to say. A happy ending is going on that Twain does not want to imperil; but had Huck been permitted to speak, one suspects that he might have paraphrased his own comment on the doomed crooks aboard the *Walter Scott:* "I felt a little bit heavy-hearted about Pap, but not much, for I reckoned if he could stand it I could." It is the only reaction really proper to the most lost of all American anti-heroes.

In his relationship to his lot, his final resolve to accept what is called these days his "terrible freedom," Huck seems the first Existentialist hero, the improbable ancestor of Camus's "stranger," or the protagonists of Jean-Paul Sartre, or the negative characters of the early Hemingway. But how contrived, literary, and abstract the others seem beside Huck! He is the product of no metaphysics, but of a terrible break-through of the undermind of America itself. In him, the obsessive American theme of loneliness reaches an ultimate level of expression, being accepted at last not as a blessing to be sought or a curse to be flaunted or fled, but quite simply as man's fate. There are mythic qualities in Ahab and even Dimmesdale; but Huck *is* a myth: not invented but discovered by one close enough to the popular mind to let it, this once at least, speak through him. Twain sometimes merely pandered to that popular mind, played the buffoon for it, but he was unalienated from it; and when he let it possess him, instead of pretending to condescend to it, he and the American people dreamed Huck—dreamed, that is to say, the anti-American American dream.

Yet this thoroughly horrifying book, whose morality is rejection and whose ambiance is terror, is a funny book, at last somehow a child's book after all; and the desperate story it tells is felt as joyous, an innocent experience. This ambiguity, this deep doubleness of *Huckleberry Finn* is its essential riddle. How can it be at once so terrible and so comfortable to read? It is, of course, a book which arises out of the part of the mind for which there are no problems, only experiences; and its terrors are those we know best how to live with, since our memories do not go back beyond the point where they had begun to haunt us. There is, moreover, the lyrical quality of much of the book, the colloquial poetry which celebrates the natural world and childhood as two aspects of a single thing. The historical moment to which Twain's child-centered imagination returned was the moment when America was passing out of a rural childhood into urban maturity; and the pattern of his own life seemed, therefore, the prototype of the national experience. As time has gone on, and for more and more Americans the world of nature has shrunk to the memory of faraway vacations and an occasional visit to the old folks; as even the river has been spanned and harnessed to industry, Twain's vanishing rural community has come to seem more and more mythic, strange, and beautiful. One of the troubling mysteries of our life is that we can only know as adults what we can only feel as children; and *Huckleberry Finn* manages to evoke the lost world of boyhood with all the horror and loveliness it once possessed for the child who lived it.

Besides, the book *is* funny; the Duke and the Dauphin as comical as they are unspeakable; the occasional quips riotous; the medley of burlesque and parody and understatement the performance of an old pro, a practiced and talented clown. Even the long ending, taken by itself, is a masterpiece of sustained farce hard to match in any literature. To deplore the ending has become one of the clichés of criticism; and it is true that it is worked out at so great length that it imperils the structure of the book; it is even apparently true that the gratuitous torturing of Jim is too brutal and painful a joke to seem really funny to the sensitive or enlightened or genteel. Regarded closely enough, Tom's scheme for stealing away a Negro whom he knows to be free is not only sadistic but thoroughly immoral, a confusion of literature and life, which leads to the infliction of artistic tortures upon a real human being!

And why do Jim and Huck, too simple and marginal to be taken in by Tom's affections, play along with his absurd plan? To them, the need to escape is urgent and every delay a threat, for they do not possess Tom's inside knowledge. In a way, of course, the horseplay is intended precisely to keep us from asking such questions, to confuse our sense of what is illusory, what real. But we have a right to demand answers all the same to questions which Twain has himself, however ambiguously, posed; and the answers are not hard to find. In the first place, the essential virtue of Huck and Jim is to endure whatever befalls them; and to them, moreover, there is nothing any more ridiculous about what Tom does than there is about what society inflicts on them every day. After all, what can a man, who all his life has known *he can be sold,* find more absurd than that. To Huck as well as Jim, all heroism and all suffering are equally "unreal," equally asinine; and the tomfoolery of "Marse Tom" seems to them no stranger than the vagaries of Judge Thatcher. Similarly, the pretended royalty of the two scoundrels strikes them as no more or less just and rational than that of the legitimate rulers of Europe. The seediness of the Duke and Dauphin undercuts the pretensions of all aristocrats, even those who smell much sweeter, just as Tom's absurdities (for which, after all, he is wounded!) show up the chivalry of the quite serious Grangerfords and Colonel Sherburn, mock even Huck's self-dramatization.

The burlesque tone of the finale manages to suggest such ideas, but at the same time keeps them in the realm of slapstick, where they do not appear either problematical or horrifying. The essential point of the ending is to reassert the duplicity of the book, to play out its moral issues as *jokes;* for if we were once to stop laughing, we would be betrayed out of the Neverland of childhood back into an actual world of maturity. The book must end just short of Huck's growing up, thus leaving us with the conviction that his gesture of total rejection and the brief, harried honeymoon which preceded it, are as endless as childhood's summers, really eternal. Believing this, we can believe, too, that whatever Huck's final decision may foreshadow or imply, his ending is, indeed, happy—the book which describes it a book about happiness.

If *Huckleberry Finn* is, finally, the greatest of all books about childhood, this is because it renders with a child's tough-mindedness and a child's desperate hilarity a double truth fumbled by most other books on the subject: how truly wonderful it is to remember our childhood; and yet how we cannot recall it without revealing to ourselves the roots of the very terror, which in adulthood has driven us nostalgically to evoke that past.

It is easy to exaggerate the difference that a few generations and the "sexual revolution" have made in the Good Bad Boy in literature. Even though he is allowed now a certain amount of good clean sex * (not as the basis of an adult relationship but as an exhibition of prowess) and forbidden in exchange an equivalent amount of good clean violence, his standard repertory of permitted indiscretions remains pretty much the same. Like Tom Sawyer and Huck before him, the Good Bad Boy begins his revolt by playing hooky, though in these times of prosperity and extended adolescence, he runs away (at least in the books of J. D. Salinger or the "Beat" writers) not from grade school but from prep school or college. Similarly, he is allowed still to "hook" things, though in these lusher days the ante has gone up from the few candles or the side of bacon which made up the loot of Twain's books. Salinger and Jack Kerouac alike attempt to project images of their own lost youth in the guise of Huckleberry Finn, though like most Americans, they have him confused with Tom Sawyer. Rural no longer in their memories or nostalgia, they yearn still for boyhood, and speak in their books through the boy's mask in a language as far removed from literate adult speech as was Huck's. Their prepschool or hipsterish sub-languages fail, however, to become the kind of poetry which Twain succeeded in making, at their worst seem self-parodies: "And I said to myself, Wham, listen to that, man. That's the West, here I am in the West. . . . Whooee, I told my soul, and the cowboy came back and off we went to Grand Island."

Whether on the upper-middlebrow level of Salinger or the bohemian-*kitsch* level of Kerouac, such writers echo not the tragic *Huckleberry Finn* but the sentimental book with which it is intertwined. In *Catcher in the Rye,* Holden Caulfield comes to the dead

* On the model of Henry Miller, who like his master Walt Whitman, succeeded in becoming a Good Bad Bay only in middle age, but who continues even in old age to be the Tom Sawyer of the current generation, crying at all the windows, "Come on out and play."

end of ineffectual revolt in a breakdown, out of which he is impelled to fight his way by the Good Good Girl in the guise of the pure little sister, from whose hands he passes directly into those of the psychiatrist. In *On the Road,* whose characters heal themselves as they go by play-therapy, the inevitable adjustment to society is only promised not delivered. In the book itself all the stigma of Tom Sawyer are already present except for the return to Aunt Polly; Paul Goodman, in a recent review, without specifically recalling the stereotype, has identified them precisely:

> One is stunned by how conventional and law-fearing these lonely middle-class fellows are. They dutifully get legal marriages and divorces. The hint of a "gang-bang" makes them impotent. They never masturbate or perform homosexual acts. . . . To disobey a cop is 'all hell.' Their idea of crime is the petty shoplifting of ten-year-olds stealing cigarettes or of teen-agers joyriding in other people's cars. . . . Their behavior is a conformity *plus royaliste que le roi.*

The fact that one is tempted, even impelled to speak of such a writer as Kerouac at over thirty-five as a "boy," the fact that he writes as one of the boys is as symptomatic as the fact that middle-aged ladies in their bridge clubs call themselves "the girls." The flight from sexuality led to a literature about children written for the consumption of adults; but the reading of that literature has turned those adults in their own inmost images of themselves into children. Indeed, the Good Bad Boyhood has not merely impinged upon adult life, it has become, like everything else in America, a "career." The age of Kerouac's protagonists is just as ambiguous as that of Mark Twain's, though for opposite reasons. Twain blurred adolescence back into boyhood to avoid confronting the problem of sex; the newer writers, accepting the confusion of childhood and youth, blur both into manhood to avoid yielding up to maturity the fine clean rapture of childish "making out." The protagonists of the hipsters have crossed the borderline of genital maturity, but in all other respects they have not left Jackson's Island. *Plus ça change, plus c'est la même chose*—which in American means, "Boys will be boys."

10

THE REVENGE ON WOMAN: FROM LUCY TO LOLITA

THE REIGN OF SENTIMENTALISM in the American novel not only made it exceedingly difficult for our writers to portray sexual passion, but prevented them as well from drawing convincing portraits of women. As late as 1901, we remember, William Dean Howells could find only *one* American fictionist before Henry James—Hawthorne—whose "heroines" seemed worthy of being ranked with those of Fannie Burney, Maria Edgeworth, Jane Austen, Miss Farrier, Mrs. Opie, and Mrs. Radcliffe! It should be remembered that Howells was not even looking for candor in the portrayal or vigor in the character; to him both Defoe and Richardson, for instance, seem outside the pale, living as they did in "the day before we began to dwell in decencies, before women began to read novels so much that the novel had to change the subject, or so limit its discussion that it came to the same thing."

For Howells, a proper literature ("There is nothing hurried or huddled in it, nothing confused or obscure, nothing excessive or inordinate"), in which proper women could flourish, begins with Goldsmith and is perfected by Jane Austen, both models of "the instinct of reticence . . . with its admirable limitations," and co-inventors of "the Heroine who was above all a Nice Girl . . ." Howells will in a pinch take the Nice Girl over the real girl (it is characteristic that he does not call her a "woman"), for he is himself a self-consciously cheerful adherent of Sentimentalism; yet he cannot find in our classic fiction heroines to satisfy even his bloodless taste. Our female entertainers are, by any standards, of small account even beside Mrs. Opie; and our serious male novelists are trapped hopelessly between certain genteel prejudices which they share with the mass audience and a secret reluctance to abide by those prejudices. The *double* falsity of many American heroines—of Cooper's, for instance, and of Melville's—arises out of the compounding of the inadequacy of the sentimental prototypes by the writer's lack of faith in them.

There is something perfunctory and forced about Cooper's cataloguing of the standard attributes of "the most juvenile" of the "two females" in *The Last of the Mohicans.* He provides her almost automatically with a "dazzling complexion, fair golden hair and bright blue eyes," and we do not doubt that she is a type he would *like* to admire; but the metaphors with which he feels obliged to adorn her portrait lie lifeless on the page: "The flush which still lingered above the pines in the western sky was not more bright nor delicate than the bloom on her cheek; nor was the opening day more dewy than the animated smile which she bestowed on the youth. . . ." A writer like Poe, on the other hand, can scarcely bring himself to do more than list the stereotyped data which indicate the Fair Lady, attaching them to a name which one would like to take for a joke but does not quite dare: "the fair-haired and blue-eyed Lady Rowena Trevanion, of Tremaine." Hawthorne, of all Americans, tries hardest to redeem the figure of the Nice Girl, and has left behind a gallery of such types: from the lower-class Phoebe of *The House of the Seven Gables* ("a cheerful little body," "as graceful as a bird . . . as pleasant about the house as a gleam of sunshine falling on the floor through a shadow of tinkling leaves") to the New England virgin, Hilda in *The Marble Faun* ("A fair, young girl dressed in white," "how like a dove . . . the fair, pure creature," "without suspicion or shadow upon the snowy whiteness of her form . . ."). Surely, these are portrayals prompted by a secret hate!

Occasionally, beneath Hawthorne's life-long, patient apotheosis of the pale-face American girl, an undercurrent of dis-ease heaves queasily, betrays its presence. The very image of the snow maiden, which is his special metaphor for the Nice Girl, can with the slightest shift of emphasis become an explicit reproach. "Pretty fancies of snow and moonlight," he condescendingly calls Hilda's paintings in *The Marble Faun,* likening them to "so many feminine achievements in literature"; but his own books are, insofar as they glorify the Phoebe-Priscilla-Hilda type, not so very different from those "feminine achievements," and the epithet rebounds on him and his heroines at once. This, indeed, he knows at some level, though he ιs incapable of saying so directly; instead he entrusts the heretical criticism to one of his bad women. Just after the first appearance of Priscilla, the gorgeous and depraved Zenobia refers to the pallid outcast as "this shadowy snow-maiden, who, precisely at the stroke of midnight, shall melt away at my feet in a pool of ice-cold water and give me my death with a pair of wet slippers." But it is Coverdale, which is to say, Hawthorne himself, who almost immediately catches a cold of which he nearly dies; and shivering in his bed, he sighs, "How cold an Arcadia was this!"

The Lucy of Melville's *Pierre,* whose symbolic name identifies her immediately, is another sexless White Lady, her color appropriate to the book which its author thought of as a "rural bowl of milk." The first symbol of her presence, seen before we catch sight of her, is a "snow-white glossy pillow"; and when Melville begins to catalogue her charms, whiteness sets the tone: "Her cheeks were tinted with the most delicate white and red, the white predominating. Her eyes some god brought down from heaven; her hair was Danae's, spangled with Jove's shower; her teeth were dived for in the Persian sea." In short, she is white and gold and blue, the conventional color scheme, though Melville has a hard time simply saying so. It is only, Melville assures us, "the angelical part of Lucy" which interests him anyhow; but how can a man marry, go to bed with an angel—how can an author, even in fancy, deflower her? "One husbandly embrace," he has Pierre reflect, would cause her spirit to evaporate; and he cries out, "By heaven, but marriage is an impious thing!"

As late as the time of Henry Adams, the figure of a woman refined to the point where copulation with her seems blasphemous possesses the imagination of the most sophisticated American writers. Adams was convinced that no writer of his own day was capable of portraying women fairly. "Howells," he observed, "cannot deal with gentlemen or ladies; he always slips up. James knows almost nothing of women but the mere outside; he never had a wife." Practically alone among nineteenth-century writers, Adams is willing to abandon the physical image of the American young lady as a blond Goddess; his Esther, for instance, "has a bad figure, which she makes answer for a good one. She is too slight, too thin; she looks fragile. . . . Her features are imperfect. Except her ears, her voice, her eyes, which have a sort of brown depth like a trout brook, she has no very good points." Nonetheless, he cannot imagine a truly sexual heroine; and, indeed, the young ladies of both *Democracy* (1871) and *Esther* (1884) end by rejecting their suitors and the very notion of marriage as an "impious thing." Only in the image of the Virgin could Adams find an ideal of womanhood to which he subscribed; but "marked American type" that he was, he insisted on imposing that divine ideal on actual ladies whom he knew, though when he died, there was discovered in his wallet the following litany which he had composed:

> Simple as when I asked your aid before;
> Humble as when I prayed for grace in vain
> Seven hundred years ago; weak, weary, sore
> In heart and hope, I ask your help again.

Before the twentieth century, only Mark Twain among all our novelists, popular or serious, seems to have mocked outright the blue-eyed Protestant Virgin, who pre-empted in our fiction the position real women might have filled. But he was a privileged jester, set apart by the blessing-curse of never being taken at his word. In "Those Extraordinary Twins" (1894) he tells the reader quite candidly that he had planned at first to have "a silly young miss for heroine," who would fall in love with the "good" half of a pair of Siamese twins. The "bad" half, however, was to break up the match by drinking so much that his weaker brother would get scandalously drunk. But "Those Extraordinary Twins" began quite rapidly to turn into *Pudd'nhead Wilson,* which, among other things, meant that "the lightweight heroine" Rowena was pushed out of the center by the developing tragic character of Roxana.

The first name of the "lightweight heroine" recalls not only Poe's incredible "Lady Rowena Trevanion, of Tremaine," but more deliberately, perhaps, the fair Rowena, bland blonde of Scott's *Ivanhoe;* while her last name, which is Cooper, evokes the author of the Leatherstocking Tales, whom Twain so brutally ridiculed in the much-reprinted essay "Fenimore Cooper's Literary Offenses." Scott he detested with an even purer hatred, believing that he had utterly corrupted the Southern imagination by dreams of chivalry and romance, which made it quite impossible for any Southern writer to face reality or describe an actual woman! In *Life on the Mississippi* (1883), Twain quotes the following extract from a New Orleans newspaper: "On Saturday, early in the morning, the beauty of the place graced our cabin, and proud of her freight the gallant little boat glided up the bayou"; then launches into an impassioned attack on the prose style and the notions which underlie it: "the trouble with the Southern reporter is Women: Women, supplemented by Walter Scott and his knights and beauty and chivalry, and so on. . . . A curious exemplification of the power of a single book for good or harm is shown in the effects wrought by *Don Quixote* and those wrought by *Ivanhoe*. The first swept the world's admiration for the medieval chivalry silliness out of existence; and the other restored it."

Yet Twain himself is not immune to the Scott-disease which he diagnoses; Westerner and Southerner at once, his divided self carries on an endless civil war. It is the chivalrous Twain who gallops to the defense of Harriet Shelley, in a sentimental essay defending wife and home, unrivaled in our literature except by Mrs. Stowe's similar apology for the wife of Byron, just as it is the chivalrous Twain who invents Becky Thatcher in *Tom Sawyer* only to forget her in *Huckleberry Finn,* where he absent-mindedly refers to her as "Bessie." But there is one chivalric idol, one legendary embodiment of pure womanhood, he could never forget: Joan of Arc. In her, Twain was able to invest the baffled virgin-worship of the Protestant American male—remaking her, in her suffering and tragic triumph, into the image of Clarissa Harlowe, of whom, to be sure, he may never have heard.

In an early essay, Twain praises Joan's "patient endurance, her steadfastness, her granite fortitude," characteristics one and all of the standard suffering female of genteel literature. He protests against paintings which portray Joan as a peasant, "a strapping, middle-aged fish-wife," for he knows she must really have looked like the American Good Good Girl, like Charlotte Temple: "a lithe young slender figure . . . dear and bonny and lovable, the face beautiful and transfigured. . . ." In his fat, two-volumed pseudo-fiction devoted to her life, Twain makes Joan into a full-fledged female savior, "girlishly fair and sweet and saintly in her long white robe," and burned for our sins.

For a good American like Twain, all offenses are offenses against the woman; to be born is to rack the mother with pain; to be married is to blaspheme against purity; to have a child is to set a seal on such blasphemy, publish it to the world. Simply to be a man is to be impure, to betray; and there is nothing to do but to kneel at the feet of the offended female and cry for forgiveness. Twain's study is more an act of expiation than a book; and for this reason he worked at it as he worked at no other work. It is, however, precisely the piety of *Joan of Arc* which makes it unreadable to all but the most grossly sentimental. When it appeared in 1896, it was already absurdly old-fashioned, a piece of romantic medievalism that out-Scotted Scott. Yet *Maggie—A Girl of the Streets* had already been published, and *Sister Carrie* was only three years off; and while such books did not destroy Sentimentalism by any means, they replaced the Good Good Girl with the Good Bad one —the sanctified virgin with the hoyden or the whore with a heart of gold.

I I

All through the history of our novel, there had appeared side by side with the Fair Maiden, the Dark Lady—sinister embodiment of the sexuality denied the snow maiden. The Indian, as we have seen, is divided into Mingo and Mohawk, Pawnee and Sioux— good Indian and bad; and similarly woman is bifurcated into Fair Virgin and Dark Lady, the glorious phantom at the mouth of the cave, and the hideous Moor who lurks within. In each case, the dark double represents the threat of both sex and death; the red Indian with his bloody scalping knife is also a rapist (however equivocal Cooper may pretend to be about it), just as the Dark Lady with her luxuriant flesh is a bearer of poison. In such a symbolic world, sex and death become one.

In the novel itself, however, the paired ladies, blonde and brunette, had come into existence for purely decorative purposes, before they were adapted to symbolic ones. As early as *Clarissa,* the suffering heroine was provided with a foil, a gay Miss Howe to complement a somber Clary; and in Rousseau, the contrasted girls of *La Nouvelle Héloïse* are a simple study in mood and coloring. Charles Brockden Brown in *Arthur Mervyn* seems on the verge of exploiting to the full the encounter of fair and black when he sets Eliza Hadwin against Mrs. Achsa Fielding and requires his hero to choose between the poor young country girl or the rich Jewish widow, "unsightly as a *night-hag,* tawny as a Moor, the eye of a gypsy, low in stature, contemptibly diminutive. . . ." But Arthur chooses to wed the "night-hag," presumably to live happily ever after; and nothing is made of the promised contrast between simple health and worn-out sophistication.

Perhaps more to the point is Scott's use of the black-hired Jewess Rebecca as a foil to the blond Anglo-Saxon Rowena in *Ivanhoe,* which must have deeply impressed the mind of an American public that has not yet relinquished the story as an entertainment commodity. Scott, however, scarcely differentiates his girls—and when Ivanhoe abandons Rebecca for Rowena, it proves nothing except a revulsion on his author's part from mixed marriages. If there is any literary antecedent for the special American use of the split heroine, any motive for it beyond the split psyche of American writers, it is probably to be found in the sonnet sequence of Shakespeare.

The puritanical sense of conflict in the black and white melodrama of the *Sonnets* must surely have appealed to the Shakespeare-soaked Romantic writers of the nineteenth century; and, though they ignored—at a loss—his contrast of homoerotic and hetereosexual love, they must have welcomed his metaphor of the "fair" love and the love "colour'd ill." The primeval terror of darkness, the northern fear of the swarthy southerner, the ingrained European habit of identifying evil with blackness: all these contribute to make the vision of the Dark Lady of the sonnets seem archetypally appealing: "For I have sworn thee fair, and thought thee bright/Who art as black as hell, as dark as night." Shakespeare's lusted-for and hated black woman blends, at any rate, with the Romantics' concept of the *Belle dame sans merci* into the figure of the American Dark Lady; and both are reinforced by the resurgence out of the Christian past of the archetypes of Lilith and Eve who brought sin into the world.

It is Cooper who first permits the contrast its symbolic significance, as we have already noticed, in his opposition of the blooming, bold Cora and her pallid, swooning sister Alice, or the corrupt, lovely Judith and her unearthly, pure, mad sister, Hettie. That the girls be sisters, thus secretly confessing their kinship, is Cooper's invention, a device taken up by Hawthorne in *The Blithedale Romance,* where he saves it for a revelation, a surprise. It is not, however, until Hawthorne develops the theme, that it comes fully into its own; what was for Cooper an idea entertained by the way is for him an obsession. Married himself to an ethereal ice-lady, Hawthorne excelled in imagining all his life dark figures which have the irreality and queasy appeal of masturbatory fancies. How exotic they are, how *gorgeous* (it is Hawthorne's ambivalent adjective), and how poisonous: non-Anglo-Saxons, all of them, Mediterraneans, Orientals, Jews—or at least given to an oriental lushness in dress and in the flesh, not considered quite decent in New England society.

The prototype of them all is Beatrice Rappaccini, who grows up in her father's deadly garden among his strange, dangerous blooms, which are in "their gorgeousness . . . fierce, passionate, and even unnatural." They are the product, Hawthorne tells us in a revealing choice of words, of "adultery," an illegitimate crossing of species. Behind the hocus-pocus of the story, the gothic mystification, it is clear what the secret weapon of Beatrice is, the poison that would have made her superhuman, "as terrible . . . as beautiful." It is, of course, the full magic of sex with which she is endowed, that primal power bred out of ladies by civilized life, but deliberately bred back into Beatrice by her magician father. "Wouldst thou then, have preferred the condition of a weak woman, exposed to all evil and capable of none?" her baffled father asks her, when she seems to be rejecting his gift. And drinking the antidote that kills her, denying her genital potency for the sake of a less potent young man whom she loves, Beatrice answers—Good Bad Girl at the last—"Yes!"

It is an answer repeated by Hawthorne's other Dark Ladies, who seem always to share his own puritan conscience: Zenobia dies of love because her kind of love has no place in the genteel American world; Miriam in *The Marble Faun* endures captivity and suffering, subdues her gorgeous power to the capacity of the weaker man she desires. Even Hester finally submits, accepts a life which is a kind of Protestant nunship, though her beloved must die to convince her that not the unleashing of her passion but its denial means salvation.

In general, Hawthorne's Dark Ladies are superior to their pale sisters not only in their symbolic resonance but even in their evocation of the reality of the flesh; in their portraits, Hawthorne alternates between the absurdest allegorical devices and a vivid projection of their sexual allure. Even Howells could never forget the passage in which Coverdale tells us of Zenobia, "She was dressed as simply as possible, in an American print (I think the dry goods people call it so), but with a silken handkerchief, between which and her gown there was a glimpse of a white shoulder.

It struck me as a great piece of good fortune that there should be just that glimpse." Here is a genuine and genial sensuality, the rendering of the actual feel of a woman, so exceedingly rare in American fiction; and for a moment the style neither evades nor overstates. For the instant at least, Zenobia is no mere projection of the fear of and longing for the flesh. But it is only an instant; in a sentence or two, we are back to the improbable hot-house flower in her hair, "an exotic of rare beauty . . . so brilliant, so rare, so costly . . . ," and we have left the real world of American dry goods for the fake world of theatrical properties out of gothic stock. Such momentary transformations from theater to flesh *never* occur, however, in Hawthorne's handling of his Good Good women, which is, perhaps, why his one book without a Dark Lady, *The House of the Seven Gables,* is his most sentimental and philistine; while his single novel without a snow maiden, *The Scarlet Letter,* is the truest and most tragic.

In *Pierre,* Melville, just then in the full flush of his enthusiasm for Hawthorne's work, attempted to project onto the kind of scene congenial to Hawthorne images of a metaphysical "blackness ten times black." The unfortunate Pierre gives up the daylight graces of the White Maiden Lucy, which he cannot abide desecrating in marriage, for the "nameless beauty," "the long-suffering, hopeless anguish" of the Dark Isabel. Unlike Hawthorne's Dark Ladies, however, Isabel is not sexually aggressive; her darkness is the shadow of the incest taboo, cast by the sins of the father on the generation which follows. Yet in the end, Pierre, Lucy, and Isabel end up in an emblematic *ménage à trois,* based presumably upon mutual self-sacrifice, but actually redolent of unconfessable ambivalent desires. Pierre attempts to hold to him at once the White Maiden and the Dark, the longing for life and lust for death, the visible embodiments of the centripetal and centrifugal urges of his own divided soul; but it is a vain and fatal effort.

Isabel herself, who prefers the language of Shakespeare to that of flowers, calls herself the Bad Angel, Lucy the Good. The sentimental conventions of the novel, she takes for the eternal symbolism of God, reading into her own brunette coloring her meaning and fated role. "Is Lucy Tartan the name? . . . she came, with her blue eyes turned beseechingly on me; she seemed as if persuading me from thee . . . methought she was that good angel, which some say, hovers over every human soul; and methought—oh, methought that I was thy other—thy other angel, Pierre—. . . . Say,

Pierre, doth not a funerealness invest me? Was ever hearse so plumed?—Oh, God; that I had been born with blue eyes, and fair hair! Those make the livery of heaven! Heard ye ever yet of a good angel with dark eyes, Pierre?—no, no, no—all blue, blue, blue. . . ." And Pierre's penultimate words later echo her, "Away! —Good Angel and Bad Angel both!—for Pierre is neuter now!" Yet he is not quite "neuter" even at the last; for death is a denial of the white Lucy, an acceptance of the black Isabel, who (in the book's final words) "fell upon Pierre's heart, and her long hair ran over him, and arbored him in ebon vines."

Beside Melville's lucid self-consciousness, other writers seem almost inadvertent in their uses of Dark and Fair Ladies. Oliver Wendell Holmes comes close to a deliberate exploitation of the contrast in *Elsie Venner* (1861), where he sets up with some care the customary opposition of a "dependent, frail, sensitive" blue-eyed lady (she is a schoolmarm of brahmin stock) and the dark-eyed "ophidian" girl, Elsie, but he does not permit them to enter into the archetypal contest for the soul of the hero. Elsie possesses all the gothic stigmata of the Dark Lady ("black hair twisted in heavy braids . . . diamond eyes"), plus the eerie characteristics of a snake-woman (she hisses when she talks, and is preternaturally cold to the touch); but she is intended, Holmes tells us, to represent only the prenatal influence of snake bite!

Critics of Holmes's own day talked of Undine and Lamia, but he brushed them aside, disclaiming all mythic intent; and he would have been, perhaps—though he was a doctor and something of a psychologist himself—even more dismayed at modern suggestions about "phallic women" and the *vagina dentata*. Holmes turns to psychology in his "psychological romance," not to reveal hidden impulses in the lower depths of the mind, but to combat the old theology with the new science; to challenge "the dogma of inherited guilt and its consequences." That Elsie is not responsible for the promptings of a nature conditioned before she was born by the bite of a serpent, Dr. Holmes is sure all his readers will understand; and he asks us, therefore, to consider her not a sinner but a patient.

In other writers, the symbolic contrast recurs as a cliché or a scarcely noticed convention: the blond, scatter-brained Rowena and the tragic mulatto Roxana in *Pudd'nhead Wilson;* or the seduced and avenging Laura Van Brunt and the Quaker Nice Girl, Ruth Bolton, in Twain's one "serious" novel *The Gilded Age;* or the death-ridden Creole Margaret and Mrs. Conway with "her light hair, blue eyes, and delicacy . . . of skin" who intrude so inappropriately upon Whitman's temperance novel, *Franklin Evans*. But surely the ultimate *reductio* of the theme is found in *Uncle Tom's Cabin* where the Pale Maiden as dying child, Little Eva, is paired off with the Dark Lady as pesky brat, Topsy. Just as, in more adult versions, the sexuality denied the pallid virgin is projected in the gorgeous brunette, so here the mischief and normal juvenile cussedness denied the little angel is projected in the figure of the little (black) devil. Mrs. Stowe lingers over their dramatic confrontation, making what symbolic capital she can of it.

> There stood the two children, representative of the two extremes of society. The fair, high-bred child, with her golden hair, deep eyes, her spiritual, noble brow and prince-like movements; and her black, keen, subtle, cringing yet acute neighbour. They stood the representatives of their races. The Saxon, born of ages of cultivation, command, education, physical and moral eminence. The African, born of ages of oppression, submission, ignorance, toil, and vice!

The moral polarity has become an ethnic one!

True enough, from the beginning, the Dark Lady had represented the hunger of the Protestant, Anglo-Saxon male not only for the rich sexuality, the dangerous warmth he had rejected as unworthy of his wife, but also for the religions which he had disowned in fear, the racial groups he had excluded and despised. The black woman is typically Catholic or Jew, Latin or Oriental or Negro. Wherever the Dark Lady plays a serious role in our literature, she is likely to represent either our relationship with the enslaved Africa in our midst or with the Mediterranean Europe from which our culture began; she is surrogate for all the Otherness against which an Anglo-Saxon world attempts to define itself and a Protestant one to justify its existence. The figure of the Creole woman especially possesses the imagination of the blond American, because she unites in one flesh the opposing European and African poles.

In Mrs. Achsa Fielding, Brockden Brown almost invented the first Dark Lady of our fiction—but he is not *afraid* enough either of her experience in passion or her connection with things European to imbue her with a sufficiently sinister allure. His Arthur Mervyn desires to become not innocent but mature; and the notion of cosmopolitanism strikes him as a fulfillment rather than a threat. Only when innocence and Americanism come to seem a single thing, do the Catholic, the European, the Jew, the devirginated woman fuse into an archetypal image of terror. It is Hawthorne who first creates in *The Marble Faun* the international romance, in which the Fair Maiden and Dark Lady come clearly to stand for American innocence and European experience. He moves his scene to a mythic Italy—half the cultural mecca of Baedeker, half the demi-hell of Mrs. Radcliffe—an appropriate setting for his dark-haired Miriam, who evokes at once the tyranny of the Vatican, the bloody tale of the Cenci, and the mystery of the eternally alienated Jew.

Yet Miriam remains in *The Marble Faun* merely a spectacle for Hawthorne's visiting Americans, just another tourist attraction for the snow maiden, Hilda, and the genteel artist, Kenyon. Both willingly surrender her to Europe and embrace each other at the end, America discovering America, timidity a matching timidity even in the heart of malaria-infested Rome.

III

Even Hawthorne, however, only tentatively approaches the theme; it is not until Henry James that the Dark Lady-Fair Girl archetype and the myth of the American in Europe are fused into a rich and unified subject. Nowhere is James more deeply indebted to Hawthorne than in this area, and nowhere is he more deeply involved in the main American tradition; yet commentators seem scarcely to have noticed his use of the Hawthorne patterns of dark female and light. F. O. Matthiessen comes close with the guarded observation on *The Wings of the Dove:* "It may be an accidental residue of romanticism that, as was the usual practice of Hawthorne and Melville, the innocent heroine is fair, and the dangerous worldly girl dark." As a matter of fact, the conventional moral color-scheme is everywhere in James's best books, an integral part of his deepest symbolism. Though the Nice American Girl, who appears variously in *Portrait of a Lady, The Wings of the Dove,* and *The Golden Bowl,* is derived, on the one hand, from James's cousin, Minny Temple, who died of tuberculosis at the age of twenty-four, on the other hand, she is a descendant of Hilda in *The Marble Faun,* Hawthorne's prototypical sketch of the American Girl abroad.

Hilda is, in that book, portrayed as the Lady of the Doves, a dove herself, and that image is quite directly borrowed to characterize Milly Theale in *The Wings of the Dove,* as the title itself attests; they are downy, white birds both of them, ready to fly from guilt to America or death. Maggie Verver in *The Golden Bowl* is even more profoundly linked to Hilda, when James says of her that she is one who "wasn't born to know evil," "must never know it," thus joining her to the strange breed of human whom Hawthorne had first imagined as blond and snow-white enough to be exempt from original sin. Of Hilda he had said (and we are told that he was making a spiritual portrait of his own wife!): "Her womanhood is of the ethereal type, and incompatible with any shadow of darkness or evil. . . . She would die of her first wrongdoing,—supposing for a moment that she could be capable of doing wrong." Both James and Hawthorne, that is to say, confused the symbolic figure of innocence, projected by Sentimentalism as a blond Maiden, with certain fair girls whom they actually knew; and joined in the genteel conspiracy to persuade those girls themselves of their immunity to evil. It is a fantastic heresy against both orthodoxy and fact, as well as a terrible burden that women themselves were finally to cast off in the great sexual revolution of the early twentieth century.

James, at least, never questioned the sentimental heresy, only added to it the necrophiliac titillation (otherwise exploited by Poe and Mrs. Stowe) by identifying the immaculate virgin with the girl dying or dead. This identification is made as early in his work as *Daisy Miller* (1879), though it does not reach a climax until *The Wings of the Dove* (1902), the working title of which was *La Mourante.* It is from the dead that James's truest, richest inspiration comes, from a fascination with and a love for the dead, for death itself; and it is no accident that his Muse and his America are both figured forth by the image of a girl who died at twenty-four.

In a certain sense, all of his stories are ghost stories—evocations of a tenuous past; and his most distinguished minor work is quite baldly cast in this rather vulgar, popular form. "The 'ghost story,'" he wrote in one of his prefaces, "as we for convenience call it, has ever been for me the most possible form of the fairy tale." But at a deeper level than he consciously sought in doing his intended stories of terror (he called, we remember, even *The Turn of the Screw* "a potboiler"), James was forever closing in on the real subject that haunted him always: the necrophilia that has always so oddly been an essential part of American romance. In his notebooks, James kept writing to himself suggestions for a story about a girl whose long-awaited husband "comes in the form of death," or of the artist whose long-planned achievement comes in the same form. In "The Altar of the Dead" (1895), the protagonist burning candles for a dead girl and dead friends in a service not somehow quite religious, almost finds love in a fellow necrophile, but dies himself at the moment of surrender. In *The Sense of the Past* (1910), a young man retreats through an old portrait, i.e., traditional art, into a world of ghosts, where he himself seems a ghost; and no consummation to any relationship is possible. He had been driven into his retreat, symptomatically enough, by dismay at the modern American girl, whose love for the native and the contemporary, James remarks scornfully, makes her fittest mate the *cowboy!* But "Maud-Evelyn" is his oddest fiction of all; in this disturbing story, the protagonist, humoring parents unwilling to admit the death of their daughter, is overwhelmed by their mad faith: lives through an imaginary love affair with a dead girl, wooing, being engaged, wedding, and at last mourning the woman he had never had. It is, in a sense, a giveaway, yet also a final consummation of the American asexual affair with the Pure Maiden—a willful derangement of the senses that makes possible cohabitation with a ghost.

Not all of James's Pure Maidens are so frankly corpses, however; some lead complex lives of suffering and renunciation in the flesh. Occasionally he is content to portray his dove girl as standing alone, confronting the dark experience which complements her innocence in the form of a male wooer only. Such, at any rate, is the pattern of *Daisy Miller,* the best-loved by the popular audience of all his works. More often, however, he provides for them foils like Madame Merle in *Portrait of a Lady,* Kate Croy in *The Wings of the Dove,* or Charlotte Stant in *The Golden Bowl,* who are distinguished from their ethereal opposites by the traditional thick, dark hair and dark eyes. Such dark counter-virgins circle nervously about their more passive opposites, their destined prey—drawn by an ambivalent love, much like the passion that joined and divided Hawthorne's Zenobia and Priscilla. In *The Wings of the Dove,* James made quite explicit the interplay of his contrasted heroines' paleness and darkness, rest and restlessness: "the angular, pale princess . . . merely seated, merely still. The upright lady, with thick dark braids . . . makes the whole circuit and makes it again. . . ." It is scene-design, to be sure, interior decoration; but it is also a moral emblem.

Representing innocence and experience, the Pale Maiden and Dark Lady also stand in James's personal mythology for the American and the European, or more precisely, the American girl who has remained true to her essential Niceness and the American lady who has fallen to the level of European cynicism and moral improvisation. In James's recasting, the conventional figure of the blond virgin takes on new dimensions through the mere addition of wealth to her definition—by augmenting the charm of chastity with the magic of money. There is something dazzling, almost magnificent about the Jamesian *Principessa Americana,* though she remains traditionally modest all the same, an Heiress of All the Ages who is yet a Nice Girl. He seems to have taken a cue from Hawthorne, who in a summary note at the end of *The Scarlet Letter* projects the image of the heiress for the first time: "Pearl—the elf-child,—the demon offspring . . . became the richest heiress of her day, in the New World." Like Pearl before them, James's heroines aspire not only to be American aristocrats, ennobled by wealth, but *real* princesses, too. They seek, that is to say, Old World titles that will grace their newly won eminence with ancient sanctions, even as Little Pearl had done before them: "Letters came [to Hester], with armorial seals upon them, though of bearings unknown to English heraldry."

In return for her recognition by Europe, the Pale Maiden offers her recognition of it—an exchange of ambassadors, in effect. But her recognition is also a redemption; and if she seems superficially intent only on carrying Europe home as loot, souvenirs, museum pieces, this is merely her way of symbolizing the bringing of a lost continent to the light. For the cultural goods she bears off, including a certain kind of husband, she is willing to pay in dollars, but *in no other currency.* Certainly, she will surrender no jot of American morality or even punctilio; and, indeed, James's insistence on this point led less friendly critics to describe his earlier work as long-drawn out studies of why an American girl does *not* marry an earl. The Nice Girl in her Jamesian form seeks a European husband—Merton Densher, Prince Amerigo, Osmond—not because she desires to escape the moral limitations of her own life but because she is eager to proselytize in its behalf: to naturalize her bridegroom to the American ethos, as Clarissa or Pamela had sought once to naturalize their lovers to the world of bourgeois values. The not-quite-nice American girl, on the other hand, seeks to yield herself up to Europe and its ways, as do Kate Croy or Charlotte or Madame Merle. To Henry James the Fair Maiden, the Good Good Girl is quite simply America itself—her whiteness the outward manifestation of our mysterious national immunity to guilt, which he feels as at once lovely, comic, and quite terrible.

Of all the European husbands in James, only Prince Amerigo understands this mystery in all its implications, which is why he is called after the man, his presumable ancestor, who first discovered the New World. Amerigo has learned about the pure American woman, who is, in the European sense, not a woman at all (what lust he has for female flesh and spirit is satisfied by Charlotte Stant) by reading one of those typical American books without women, Edgar Poe's *The Narrative of A. Gordon Pym*. And he knows, therefore, that in moving into the polar world of American morality, he is leaving behind the moral "blackness of darkness" to which as an Italian he has grown up, to confront "a dazzling curtain of light, concealing as darkness conceals, yet of the color of milk or snow. . . ." The reflections of the Prince echo almost directly the words of the close of *Gordon Pym:* "The darkness had materially increased, relieved only by the glare of the water thrown back from the white curtain before us." But the "shrouded human figure" which emerges from the curtain at the end of the world, and the hue of whose skin is "the perfect whiteness of the snow," blends into the figures of the other castrating White Ladies of our literature: the snow maiden Priscilla and milky Lucy. Maggie Verver is at once the embodiment of a country which dreams such virgins of milk and snow, and another example of the type; but she is also the portrait of the artist who makes such a maiden his Muse—a self-portrait of Henry James. Poe in *The Narrative of A. Gordon Pym* had been content to portray the woman not as one of flesh, by which the classic American novelists have been haunted, but merely as a "white mist," a magnet and a devouring whirlpool; James recreates of the same aboriginal mist the figure of Maggie: more Christ than woman, more angel of death than Christ.

There are ambiguous undertones in all of James's renderings of the conflict of Dark Lady and White Maiden; for though he never doubts the moral superiority of the ethos projected by the Nice American Girl, he yearns for the grace and cultured ease of the European life-style. Yet in only one of his novels, does he permit the representative of American values and Anglo-Saxon woman-hood to show at a real disadvantage. In *The Ambassadors*, all the delicacy and moral tact ordinarily represented by the Fair Maiden are embodied in the male figure of Lambert Strether, surely the most maidenly of all James's men. The American girl abroad is caricatured as Mamie Pocock; and the Europeanized American woman transfigured and redeemed as Maria Gostrey; but these oddly transformed and transvalued renderings of the Fair Girl and Dark Lady do not really stand at the center of the book or bear its symbolic weight. In *The Ambassadors*, the sexual allure of Europe is finally projected as a middle-aged French woman living in adultery; though, to be sure, she is an Aphrodite figure discreetly draped to avoid shocking James's genteel readers. "A goddess still partly engaged in a morning cloud," James himself calls his Madame de Vionnet, "a sea-nymph waist-high in a summer surge." If we know by inference what lies below the waist of Madame de Vionnet, we must thank our own experience, for James is reluctant to make explicit the genital facts of the case.

Yet the real sense of the book demands that we understand Strether as caught between the claim of America and the appeal of Europe, a world desexed and morally engaged opposed to one sexually potent and ethically lax. In *The Ambassadors*, however, the world of American values is no longer imagined in the form of the beautiful *mourante*, Minny Temple, fixed in an eternal youth by the fact of death but rather in the shape of what Minny might have become (what the American dream does indeed become) had she lived on, hardened and matured. It is Mrs. Newsome who projects the American female, the Heiress of All the Ages come to middle age, icy and imperious, the snow maiden turned into "some particularly large iceberg in a cool blue northern sea." In a wonderful stroke, James excludes her from the actual sense of the book; for she does not have to be present to be felt. The cold Atlantic winds that blow eastward from her immense frigidity represent her sufficiently. The sympathy of the aging, virginal hero (we are told he has been married before, has a son, but we do not believe it, scarcely remember it) goes this time quite unequivocally toward the adulterous woman, the Dark European Lady. The blue Iceberg has, however, in effect castrated him, and he cannot love what he approves; and so ends urging others to enjoy what he is incapable of possessing.

It is worth considering for a moment the fact that in the four novels of James now generally considered his best, the archetype of Dark Lady and Fair has arisen to possess him: to give his work not only technical authority and novelistic insight but a mythic dimension as well. Three of the four books, *Portrait of a Lady, The Wings of the Dove,* and *The Golden Bowl,* are successive attempts to work out the same pattern-story in which the deepest experiences of James's life cohere: his encounter with death in his cousin Minny's early end, his recognition of an authentic American art in the work of Hawthorne, the expansion of his moral horizon in his removal to Europe. It is worth noticing that in these works, too, he flirted with or actually faced the forbidden American theme, which he himself spoke of squeamishly as "the adulterine element in the subject." Yet no Nice American Girl could in James be guilty of adultery, which remained for him the European, the Mediterranean sin—quite understandable in citizens of a world where neither romance nor free choice entered into marriage, but utterly shocking in an American. One cannot imagine, for instance, James benignly desiring for the American Dark Lady Charlotte Stant the happiness he wishes, through Strether, for her French opposite number, Madame de Vionnet. There is a strange double standard for Europeans and Americans built into his particular version of the Fair-Dark polarity.

For James, certain women, who must be among other things Americans, are innocent by definition and forever; like Hawthorne he assumes a fundamental and ineradicable distinction between females born not to know evil and those born to endure the effects of sin. Melville in *Mardi* more dangerously suggests that the Fair Maiden once sexually possessed even in marriage, becomes—or is revealed as—the Dark Lady. *Mardi* is, however, a hectic and untidy book, in which Melville managed to find neither a satisfactory rhetoric nor a set of symbols; and his heretical suggestion is almost lost in a blur of contradictory intentions.

Mardi (1849) was apparently begun as a mock-documentary, an attempt to show up the critics who had caviled at the truth of *Typee* (1846) and *Omoo* (1847), books based in part on fact. Melville seems, however, to have rapidly abandoned his scheme "to see whether the fiction might not, possibly, be received for a verity; in some degree the reverse of my previous experience"; so that finally *Mardi* looks forward, toward his work to come, rather than backward to work already done. In one aspect a tentative approach to the style and themes of *Moby Dick,* in another it is the first version of the Fair Girl-Dark Lady archetype somewhat differently rendered in *Pierre.* In its earliest narrative pages, it bears a marked resemblance to *Gordon Pym,* which had appeared some ten years earlier, though Melville as far as we can tell never read Poe. Unlike Poe, however—and unlike his later self writing *Moby Dick* —Melville could not resist in *Mardi* the temptation to introduce a woman into his essential plot, an improbable Anglo-Saxon virgin who floats on a raft into his fable, disrupting utterly its probability and coherence.

The girl, who is kept prisoner by a Polynesian enchanter-priest and his three warrior sons, turns out to have blond hair, blue eyes, and milk-white skin, and must therefore be rescued from the emissaries of darkness by an onslaught which ends in the death of the old priest. Though ridden by guilt because of the murder which is her price, and unable to get from her any rational story of who she is, the protagonist settles down with the blond Maiden (she is called Yillah) on a convenient sub-tropical island. After a brief, rather unconvincing interlude in a South Seas bower of love, he wakes one morning to find his beloved gone. The purity represented by Yilliah is in Melville's treatment ambiguous from the start, for it makes its initial appearance in the hands of demonic agents, is won even temporarily only by the death of the old man, disappears upon possession, and is pursued at the risk of blasphemy, "the last, last crime." The desolate cry of Pierre, "By heaven, but marriage is an impious thing!" is already implicit in the theme.

As he trails Yillah through the archipelagos of the Pacific, Taji is "pursuer and pursued, over an endless sea," himself trailed by the three sons of the dead magician, the outraged "brothers" of the Fair Girl—even as he is lured on by three maidens, as dark as the three avengers, who bear him tokens from a swarthy enchantress called Hautia. Arrived at the womb-tomb sea-caverns of Hautia, Taji dives for the drowned image of his lost Yillah, which glimmers in their depths like a ghost side by side with the jewel of Hautia. He cannot manage, however, either to recover the ghost of innocence or to touch the bottom of experience, and is contemptuously dismissed, having learned only one thing: the dark-eyed handmaids of Hautia all somehow contain within them the vanished Yillahs of the world—and he can attain neither.

Mardi is, it must be remembered, a honeymoon book, the work into which Melville plunged almost immediately after his marriage; but in the single marriage ceremony described in the novel, the groom is pictured with a millstone attached to his neck, so disguised with flowers that he can scarcely recognize it. The fable itself, however, cuts deeper and more cruelly than any merely defensive male humor. Nothing less than the whole sentimental myth of redemption through marriage is challenged by Melville's suggestion that the milk-white bride is corrupted by the consummation of marriage. If the most husbandly embrace converts the Fair Maiden into her Dark opposite, reveals Clarissa as Circe— then man is doomed forever to choose between the blasphemous pursuit of an unattainable ideal and the self-destructive plunge into the gulf of sensuality. So at least *Mardi* seems to insist. Melville is reported to have read the installments of his work in progress regularly to his bride, and certainly, from time to time she helped him with the copying; but what she could have made of so disturbing a revelation of her husband's ambivalence toward women and sexual passion is hard to say. There is some evidence that mercifully she did not understand it at all; for in a letter to her mother she writes, "I suppose by this time you are deep in the 'fogs' of *Mardi*—if the mist ever does clear away, I should like to know what it reveals to *you*—" Indeed, it is doubtful that Melville himself knew quite what he was doing in a book which he tells us he wrote "Like a man walking in his sleep."

IV

In the nineteenth century at least, treasonable attacks on the cult of the Pure Woman are dreamed, not planned. Like James's unwitting revelation that the snow maiden is a corpse, Melville's exposure of her identity with the Dark Lady is invested in a kind of make-believe, an atmosphere of fantasy in which everything is permissible because nothing is proffered quite seriously. It is only when the stereotype of the Good Good Girl is challenged in "realistic" fiction, in novels which eschew the camouflage of gothicism and allegory, that the great audience is disturbed. The largest reading public, which is unaware of its vision of immaculate womanhood as a myth, does not rise to defend it as a myth; but cries out in horror when it is attacked on the level of fact—a simple truth about the wives, sisters, mothers, and daughters of America. This is why the same readers who were neither dismayed nor titillated by James's later conversion, via a "ghost story" or an offhand reference to the least-read work of Poe, of the Pale Maiden to a ghost, bought, eagerly read, and horrifiedly attacked James's portrait of the American Girl in *Daisy Miller*.

For better or worse, the popular James of his own times was the author of this little book; and it is chiefly in terms of their relationship to *Daisy Miller* that Howells describes the female readers of James: "to read him if for nothing but to condemn him is the high intellectual experience of the daughters of mothers whose indignant girlhood resented while it adored his portraits of American women." But what made such mothers indignant at and resentful of poor Daisy, with her unspeakable little brother, her shocked American admirer and her naïve resolve to consort with Italians just as she had with her "gentlemen friends" in Schenectady? That she be cut by her convention-bound compatriots in Rome seems probable enough; but that American editors should have rejected so American a book as somehow shocking is hard to believe.

As late as 1936, one historian of the American novel, though no longer prepared to describe Daisy as "an outrage on American girlhood," still found her a caricature and the product of a confusion. Any lady really endowed with "active innocence" and "personal daintiness," that critic argued, would not have acted like Daisy Miller because "she would not have cared to be conspicuous." It is a last, weak afterthrob of the spasm of fascinated revulsion with which the genteel female audience greeted *Daisy Miller* in 1879. The motives of that audience Howells, who managed to please it all his life, ticked off in his own impassioned apology for Daisy: "The American woman would none of Daisy Miller . . . because the American woman . . . was too jealous of her own perfection to allow that innocence might be reckless, and angels in their ignorance of evil might not behave as discreetly as worse people."

James is, however, careful to make it clear that Daisy is finally and unequivocally innocent. Though she went alone to the Colosseum with the Italian Giovanelli, and stood with him, unchaperoned and unobserved, in the moonlight until midnight, she remained quite intact. It is Giovanelli himself who says at her grave, " 'She was the most beautiful young lady I ever saw, and the most amiable,' and then he added, 'and she was the most innocent.' " Daisy is, in short, the prototype of all those young

American female tourists who continue to baffle their continental lovers with an innocence not at all impeached, though they have now taken to sleeping with their Giovanellis as well as standing with them in the moonlight. What the European male fails ever to understand is that the American Girl is innocent by definition, *mythically* innocent; and that her purity, therefore, depends upon nothing she does or says. But James's Daisy is also the Good Bad Girl, *only* the Good Bad Girl; and her creation impugns not at all the Clarissa-Charlotte Temple archetype.

She is an improbable sister to the hard-riding, hard-shooting sometimes cigar-smoking, heroines of the dime novel; for in serious literature and the popular paperback alike, the Good Bad Girl, with her heart of truest gold beneath the roughest of exteriors, survives to become a stock character of the movies, a living embodiment of the American faith that evil is appearance only. Model or waitress or dance-hall girl, the modern version of the falsely impugned Maiden is discovered staggering drunk in the roué's penthouse, watched climbing with overnight bag the gangplank to the philanderer's yacht, followed by the camera as she slips from table to table, embrace to embrace with a pert wiggle of her rear—only to be revealed at the dénouement as virginal though indiscreet. She represents an American, which is to say, an expurgated recasting of the continental image of the virtuous whore, a Grushenka with a maidenhead; and, indeed, in Dreiser the two images fade into one.

Yet Daisy is, in another sense a transitional figure, the hinge upon which the American adoration of pure womanhood swings over to reveal its underside of fear and contempt. The first notable anti-virgin of our fiction, the prototype of the blasphemous portraits of the Fair Goddess as bitch in which our twentieth-century fiction abounds, is quite deliberately called Daisy—after James's misunderstood American Girl. She is, of course, the Daisy Fay Buchanan of Scott Fitzgerald's *The Great Gatsby,* the girl who lures her lovers on, like America itself, with a "voice . . . full of money." More like James's Maggie Verver, perhaps, than Daisy Miller in the potency of her charm, she is yet another Heiress of All the Ages: great-great-granddaughter of that priceless Pearl, who got the best of the Old World and the New. She is an odd inversion of Clarissa-Charlotte Temple-Maggie Verver; no longer the abused woman, who only by her suffering and death castrates her betrayer, but the abusing woman, symbol of an imperialist rather than a colonial America. The phallic woman with a phallus of gold, she remains still somehow the magic princess James had imagined as the heroine of *The Golden Bowl:* "High in a white palace the king's daughter, the golden girl." To Fitzgerald, however, her fairy glamour is illusory, and once approached the White Maiden is revealed as a White Witch, the golden girl as a golden idol. On his palette, white and gold make a dirty color; for wealth is no longer innocent, America no longer innocent, the Girl who is the soul of both turned destructive and corrupt.

There is only one story that Fitzgerald knows how to tell, and no matter how he thrashes about, he must tell it over and over. The penniless knight, poor stupid Hans, caddy or bootlegger or medical student, goes out to seek his fortune and unluckily finds it. His reward is, just as in the fairy tales, the golden girl in the white palace; but quite differently from the fairy tales, that is not a happy ending at all. He finds in his bed not the white bride but the Dark Destroyer; indeed, there is no White Bride, since Dark Lady and Fair, witch and redeemer have fallen together. But it is more complicated even than this. Possessed of the power of wealth, Fitzgerald's women, like their wealthy male compeers, who seem their twins rather than their mates, are rapists and aggressors. Of both Daisy and her husband Tom, Fitzgerald tells us, "they smashed up things and creatures and then retreated back into their money." In a real sense, not Daisy but Jay Gatz, the Great Gatsby, is the true descendant of Daisy Miller: the naïf out of the West destined to shock the upholders of decorum and to die of a love for which there is no worthy object.

In Fitzgerald's world, the distinction between sexes is fluid and shifting, precisely because he has transposed the mythic roles and values of male and female, remaking Clarissa in Lovelace's image, Lovelace in Clarissa's. With no difficulty at all and only a minimum of rewriting, the boy Francis, who was to be a center of vision in *The World's Fair,* becomes the girl Rosemary as that proposed novel turned into *Tender Is the Night.* Thematically, archetypally even such chief male protagonists as Gatsby and Dick Diver are females; at least, they occupy in their stories the position of Henry James's Nice American Girls. It is they who embody innocence and the American dream, taking up the role the flapper had contemptuously abandoned for what was called in the '20's "freedom"; but they do not know this, projecting the dream which survives only in themselves upon the rich young ladies whom they desire. Early in *Tender Is the Night,* Dick Diver comes upon Nicole in Europe, and, dazzled by her "cream-colored dress . . . her very blonde hair . . . her face lighting up like an angel's," thinks of her as "a scarcely saved waif of disaster bringing him the essence of a continent. . . ." He reads into her, that is to say, the conventional meanings of the Good American Girl. But before his marriage with her has finally unmanned him, he comes to see her as an "evil-eyed" destroyer, and longs "to grind her grinning mask into jelly."

It is he, however, who is ground into jelly, crushed and driven from the imaginary sentimental paradise of married love to the lonely male refuge, the counter-paradise of mindless drunkenness. We see him last making the sign of the cross, a priest of Sentimental Love, who has arrived in the empty temple after the abdication of his goddess. Nicole, the goddess who failed, is postulated in the novel as a schizophrenic, in an attempt to explain her double role as Fair Lady and Dark, her two faces, angelic and diabolic, the melting and the grinning mask. But the schizophrenia is really in Diver, which is to say, in Fitzgerald, which is finally to say, in the American mind itself. There are not, in fact, two orders of women, good and bad, nor is there even one which seems for a little while bad, only to prove in the end utterly unravished and pure. There are only two sets of expectations and a single imperfect kind of woman caught between them: only actual incomplete females, looking in vain for a satisfactory definition of their role in a land of artists who insist on treating them as goddesses or bitches. The dream role and the nightmare role alike deny the humanity of women, who, baffled, switch from playing out one to acting out the other. Fitzgerald apparently never managed to accommodate to the fact that he lived at the moment of a great switch-over in roles, though he recorded that revolution in the body of his work. His outrage and self-pity constantly break through the pattern of his fiction, make even an ambitious attempt like *Tender Is the Night* finally too sentimental and whining to endure.

Only in *The Great Gatsby* does Fitzgerald manage to transmute his pattern into an objective form, evade the self-pity which corrodes the significance and the very shape of his other work—and this is perhaps because Gatsby is the most distant of all his protagonists from his real self. To Gatsby, Daisy appears in the customary semblance of the Fair Maiden, however; he finds her quite simply "the first 'nice' girl he had ever known." It is Howells' genteel epithet which occurs to him, though by Fitzgerald's time the capital letters are gone and the apologetic quotation marks have insidiously intruded. Daisy, rich and elegant and clean and sweet-smelling, represents to her status-hungry provincial lover, not the corruption and death she really embodies, but Success—which is to say, America itself. In Fitzgerald, the same fable that informs James is replayed, subtly transformed, for like James he has written an anti-Western, an "Eastern": a drama in which back-trailers reverse their westward drive to seek in the world which their ancestors abandoned the dream of riches and glory that has somehow evaded them. Fitzgerald's young men go east even as far as Europe; though unlike James's young women, they are in quest not of art and experience and the shudder of guilt, but of an even more ultimate innocence, an absolute America: a happy ending complete with new car, big house, money, and the girl.

In the symbolic geography of *The Great Gatsby,* the two halves of a nation are compressed into the two settlements on Long Island of West Egg and East Egg, from the first of which the not-quite arrived look yearningly across the water at those who are already *in,* Jay Gatsby at Daisy Buchanan. There is no need for a symbolic Europe to complete the scene; and, indeed, even in *Tender Is the Night,* Europe is only a place where the East Eggians go to play, a transatlantic extension of East Egg itself. In a concluding passage of great beauty and conviction, Fitzgerald manages to convey the whole world of aspiration which Daisy has represented to Gatsby, and transforms the book from a lament over the fall of the Fair Woman to an elegy for the lapsed American dream of innocent success:

And as the moon rose higher the inessential houses began to melt away until gradually I became aware of the old island here that flowered once for Dutch sailors' eyes—a fresh, green breast of the new world . . . the trees that had made way for Gatsby's house, had once pandered in whispers to the last and greatest of all human dreams; for a transitory enchanted moment man must have held his breath in the presence of this continent . . . face to face for the last time in history with something commensurate with his capacity for wonder.

And as I sat there brooding on the old, unknown world, I thought of Gatsby's wonder when he first picked out the green light at the end of Daisy's dock. He had come a long way to this blue lawn, and his dream must have seemed so close that he could hardly fail to grasp it. He did not know that it was already behind him, somewhere back in the vast obscurity beyond the city, where the dark fields of the republic rolled on under the night.

For Fitzgerald, "love" was essentially yearning and frustration; and there is consequently little consummated genital love in his novels, though he identified himself with that sexual revolution which the '20's thought of as their special subject. The adolescent's "kiss" is the only climax his imagination can really encompass; and despite his occasionally telling us that one or another of his charters has "taken" a woman, it is the only climax he ever realizes in a scene. In his insufferable early books, the American institution of *coitus interruptus,* from bundling to necking a favorite national pastime, finds at last a laureate; and even in his more mature works, his women move from the kiss to the kill with only the barest suggestion of copulation between. Hemingway, on the other hand, is much addicted to describing the sex act. It is the symbolic center of his work: a scene to which he recurs when nostalgically evoking his boyhood as "Up in Michigan"; illustrating the virtues of the sturdy poor as in *To Have and Have Not;* reflecting on civil strife and heroism as in *For Whom the Bell Tolls;* or projecting the fantasies of a man facing old age as in *Across the River and Into the Trees.* There are, however, no *women* in his books! In his earlier fictions, Hemingway's descriptions of the sexual encounter are intentionally brutal, in his later ones unintentionally comic; for in no case, can he quite succeed in making his females human, and coitus performed with an animal, a thing, or a wet dream is either horrible or ridiculous. If in *For Whom the Bell Tolls* Hemingway has written the most absurd love scene in the history of the American novel, this is not because he lost momentarily his skill and authority; it is a give-away—a moment which illuminates the whole erotic content of his fiction.

Hemingway is only really comfortable in dealing with "men without women." The relations of father to son, of battle-companions, friends on a fishing trip, fellow inmates in a hospital, a couple of waiters preparing to close up shop, a bullfighter and his manager, a boy and a gangster: these move him to simplicity and truth. Perhaps he is best of all with men who stand alone—in night-time scenes when the solitary individual sweats in his bed on the verge of nightmare, or arises to confront himself in the glass; though he is at home, too, with the Rip Van Winkle archetype, with men in flight from women. Certainly, he returns again and again to the fishing trip and the journey to the war—those two traditional evasions of domesticity and civil life. Yet he feels an obligation to introduce women into his more ambitious fictions, though he does not know what to do with them beyond taking them to bed. All his life, he has been haunted by a sense of how simple it all was once, when he could take his Indian girl into the clean-smelling woods, stretch out beside her on the pine-needles (her brother standing guard), and rise to no obligations at all. In a story called "Fathers and Sons," he writes a tribute to that prototypical, mindless, undemanding, scarcely human girl: "Could you say she did first what no one has ever done better and mention plump brown legs, flat belly, hard little breasts, well holding arms, quick searching tongue, the flat eyes, the good taste of mouth . . . and hemlock needles stuck against your belly. . . . Long time ago good. Now no good."

In Hemingway the rejection of the sentimental happy ending of marriage involves the acceptance of the sentimental happy beginning of innocent and inconsequential sex, and camouflages the rejection of maturity and of fatherhood itself. The only story in which he portrays a major protagonist as having a child is the one in which he remembers with nostalgia his little Trudy of the "well holding arms, quick searching tongue," and looks forward to the time when his son will have a gun and they can pop off to the forest like two boys together. More typically he aspires to be not Father but "Papa," the Old Man of the girl-child with whom he is temporarily sleeping; and surely there is no writer to whom childbirth more customarily presents itself as the essential catastrophe. At best he portrays it as a plaguey sort of accident which forces a man to leave his buddies behind at the moment of greatest pleasure as in "Cross Country Snow"; at worst, it becomes in his fiction that horror which drives the tender-hearted husband of "Indian Camp" to suicide, or which takes Catherine away from Lieutenant Henry in *A Farewell to Arms*.

Poor things, all they wanted was innocent orgasm after orgasm on an island of peace in a world at war, love-making without end in a scarcely real country to which neither owed life or allegiance.

But such a relationship can, of course, never last, as Hemingway-Nick Adams-Lieutenant Henry has always known: "They all ended the same. Long time ago good. Now no good." Only the dead woman becomes neither a bore nor a mother; and before Catherine can quite become either she must die, killed not by Hemingway, of course, but by childbirth! It is all quite sad and lovely at the end: the last kiss bestowed on what was a woman and is now a statue, the walk home through the rain. Poe himself could not have done better, though he was haunted not by the memory of a plump little Indian on the hemlock needles but a fantasy of a high-born maiden "loved with a love that was more than love" and carried away by death.

Had Catherine lived, she could only have turned into a bitch; for this is the fate in Hemingway's imagination of all Anglo-Saxon women. In him, the cliché of Dark Lady and Fair survives, but stood on its head, exactly reversed. The Dark Lady, who is neither wife nor mother, blends with the image of Fayaway, the exotic servant-consort reconstructed by Melville in *Typee* out of memories of an eight-year-old Polynesian girl-child. In Hemingway, such women are mindless, soft, subservient; painless devices for extracting seed without human engagement. The Fair Lady, on the other hand, who gets pregnant and wants a wedding, or uses her sexual allure to assert her power, is seen as a threat and a destroyer of men. But the seed-extractors are Indians or Latins, black-eyed and dusky in hue, while the castrators are at least Anglo-Saxon if not symbolically blond. Neither are permitted to be virgins; indeed, both are imagined as having been often possessed, though in the case of the Fair Woman promiscuity is used as a device for humiliating and unmanning the male foolish enough to have entered into a marriage with her. Through the Dark anti-virgin, on the other hand, a new lover enters into a blameless communion with the other uncommitted males who have possessed her and departed, as well as with those yet to come. It is a kind of homosexuality once-removed, the appeal of the whorehouse (Eden of the world of men without women) embodied in a single figure.

When Hemingway's bitches are Americans, they are hopeless and unmitigated bitches; symbols of Home and Mother as remembered by the boy who could never forgive Mama for having wantonly destroyed Papa's Indian collection! Mrs. Macomber, who, in "The Short Happy Life of Francis Macomber," kills her husband for having alienated the affections of the guide with whom she is having one of her spiteful little affairs, is a prime example of the type. And "the woman," in "The Snows of Kilimanjaro" another, who with her wealth has weaned her husband from all that sustained his virility, betrayed him to aimlessness and humiliation. Like Fitzgerald's betrayed men, he can choose only to die, swoon to the death he desires at the climax of a dream of escape.

The British bitch is for Hemingway only a demi-bitch, however, as the English are only, as it were, demi-Americans. Catherine is delivered from her doom by death; Brett Ashley in *The Sun Also Rises* (1926) is permitted, once at least, the gesture of herself rejecting her mythical role. But it is quite a feat at that, and Brett cannot leave off congratulating herself: "You know it makes one feel rather good deciding not to be a bitch." Yet Brett never becomes a woman really; she is mythicized rather than redeemed. And if she is the most satisfactory female character in all of Hemingway, this is because for once she is presented not as an animal or as a nightmare but quite audaciously as a goddess, the bitch-goddess with a boyish bob (Hemingway is rather fond of women who seem as much boy as girl), the Lilith of the '20's. No man embraces her without being in some sense castrated, except for Jake Barnes who is unmanned to begin with; no man approaches her without *wanting* to be castrated, except for Romero, who thinks naïvely that she is—or can easily become—a woman. Indeed, when Brett leaves that nineteen-year-old bullfighter, one suspects that, though she avows it is because she will not be "one of those bitches who ruins children," she is really running away because she thinks he might *make* her a woman. Certainly, Romero's insistence that she let her hair grow out has something to do with it: "He wanted me to grow my hair out. Me, with long hair. I'd look so like hell. . . . He said it would make me more womanly. I'd look a fright."

To yield up her cropped head would be to yield up her emancipation from female servitude, to become feminine rather than phallic; and this Brett cannot do. She thinks of herself as a flapper, though the word perhaps would not have occurred to her, as a member of the "Lost Generation"; but the Spaniards know her immediately as a terrible goddess, the avatar of an ancient archetype. She tries in vain to enter into the circle of Christian communion, but is always turned aside at the door; she changes her mind, she has forgotten her hat—the apparent reason never matters; she belongs to a world alien and prior to that of the Christian churches in which Jake finds a kind of peace. In Pamplona, Brett is surrounded by a group of *riau-riau* dancers, who desert a religious procession to follow her, set her up as a rival to Saint Fermin: "Some dancers formed a circle around Brett and started to dance. They wore big wreaths of white garlic around their necks. . . . They were all chanting. Brett wanted to dance but they did not want her to. They wanted her as an image to dance around." Incapable of love except as a moment in bed, Brett can bestow on her worshipers nothing more than the brief joy of a drunken ecstasy—followed by suffering and deprivation and regret. In the end, not only are her physical lovers unmanned and degraded, but even Jake, who is her priest and is protected by his terrible wound, is humiliated. For her service is a betrayal not only of his Catholic faith but of his pure passion for bullfighting and trout-fishing; and the priest of the bitch-goddess is, on the purely human level, a pimp.

v

In the work of William Faulkner, the fear of the castrating woman and the dis-ease with sexuality present in the novels of his contemporaries, Fitzgerald and Hemingway, attain their fullest and shrillest expression. Not content with merely projecting images of the anti-virgin, he insists upon editorializing against the woman he travesties in character and situation. No Jiggs and Maggie cliché of popular anti-feminism is too banal for him to use; he reminds us (again and again!) that men are helpless in the hands of their mothers, wives, and sisters; that females do not think but proceed from evidence to conclusions by paths too devious for males to follow; that they possess neither morality nor honor; that they are capable, therefore, of betrayal without qualm or quiver of guilt but also of inexplicable loyalty; that they enjoy an occasional beating at the hands of their men; that they are unforgiving and without charity to other members of their own sex; that they lose keys and other small useful articles with maddening regularity but are quite capable of finding things invisible to men; that they use their sexuality with cold calculation to achieve their inscrutable ends, etc., etc.

Until his last books, Faulkner treated with respect only females, white ladies or colored women, past the menopause. The elderly maiden or widowed aunt is the sole female figure in his fiction exempt from travesty and contempt. Up to the very verge of her climacteric, woman seems to Faulkner capable of the most shameless concupiscence, like Miss Burden in *Light in August,* cowering naked in the garden of the decaying house waiting to be captured and possessed in an obscene game of hide-and-seek. Faulkner sometimes gives the impression of the village misogynist swapping yarns with the boys at the bar in order to reveal a truth about women which shocks even himself. Like old Varner in *The Hamlet,* he keeps assuring his readers that he "cheerfully and robustly and undeviatingly" declines to accept "any such theory as female chastity other than as a myth to hoodwink young husbands. . . ." But there is little robust or cheerful about his attitudes, however undeviatingly he may assert them; he is less like Varner fundamentally than like Hightower, the scared and stinking refugee from life in *Light in August,* who cries out in despair that "the husband of a mother, whether he be the father or not is already a cuckold . . . what woman has ever suffered from any brute as men have suffered from good women?"

Pubescent or nubile women, for Faulkner, fall into two classes, roughly corresponding to those of Hemingway, though for the former both are terrifying: great, sluggish, mindless daughters of peasants, whose fertility and allure are scarcely distinguishable from those of a beast in heat; and the febrile, almost fleshless but sexually insatiable daughters of the aristocracy. Not the women he observes but those he dreams inhabit Faulkner's novels, myths of masculine protest: the peasant wench as earth goddess (Lena Grove in *Light in August,* Dewy Dell in *As I Lay Dying,* Eula Varner in *The Hamlet*), or the coed as nymphomaniac Venus (Cecily of *Soldiers' Pay,* Patricia in *Mosquitoes,* Temple Drake in *Sanctuary*). Their very names tend toward allegory, "Dewy Dell," for instance, suggesting both a natural setting and woman's sex, her sex as a fact of nature, while "Temple Drake" evokes both a ruined sanctuary and the sense of an unnatural usurpation: woman become a sexual aggressor—more drake than duck.

Unlike the natural women of Hemingway, Faulkner's dewiest dells turn out to be destroyers rather than redeemers, quicksands disguised as sacred groves. In his portrayal of Lena Grove, he relents for once into something like admiration; but his Eula Varner is more typical. Faulkner begins by describing Eula, the goddess who presides over the revels of *The Hamlet* and is married off in the end to its Devil, Flem Snopes, in terms of a pagan dithyramb to Aphrodite: "Her entire appearance suggested some symbology out of the old Dionysic Times, honey in sunlight and bursting grapes, the writhen bleeding of the crushed fecundated vine beneath the hard rapacious trampling goat-hoof." What begins as a pre-Christian eulogy to the inarticulate manifestation of sheer fertility imperceptibly slips over into a puritan cry of distress and distaste before unredeemed, burgeoning life.

When Faulkner abandons mythology for more direct physical description, his uneasiness before Eula's languor and inert lusciousness is even more clearly betrayed. "She simply did not move at all of her own volition, save to and from the table and to and from bed. She was late in learning to walk. . . . She remained in it [her perambulator] long after she had grown too large to straighten her legs out. . . . She did nothing. She might as well have been a foetus." If she is a foetus, however, Eula is an almost intolerably alluring one, a foetus-vampire, as it were; for hanging sluggishly in her mother's arms, she seems, Faulkner writes, even at the age of five or six, an "indisputably female burden like a bizarre and chaperoned Sabine rape." And after she begins to walk to school, men and boys gape, whistle, and howl in the unquenchable anguish and joy of pure desire. It is an absurd conceit, hysterical, a little mad—tolerable only because Faulkner so obviously believes in it, believes in the terror of mere inert female flesh not as a fact of life but as an article of faith!

Just as his Eula figures are all motionless, quivering, mammalian softness, Faulkner's Temple figures are sheer motion, a blur of dancing legs and wind-blown hair in a speeding car: "sexless yet somehow troubling." It is the assertion of femaleness which upsets him in Eula Varner; and it is its denial which disturbs him in Temple Drake. Temple is disconcertingly almost a man, almost phallic; and, indeed, at the moment of her rape by Popeye, it is difficult to tell which one is the phallus bearer, to whom the bloody corncob really belongs. "Then I thought about being a man," Temple says later, "and as soon as I thought it, it happened. . . . It made a kind of plopping sound, like blowing a little rubber tube wrong-side outward. . . . I could feel it, and I lay right still to keep from laughing about how surprised he was going to be . . ." In *Sanctuary*, Faulkner's revulsion from woman's betrayal of her traditionally submissive role reaches so shrill a pitch that, in simple self-defense, he has felt it necessary to disavow that novel as a pot-boiler; yet it is obviously written in earnest though at white heat, a nightmare

directly transcribed. Fortunately, it is not quite convincing enough
to be unbearable, though it possesses enough hallucinatory vividness to give it the baleful appeal of a Dickensian or Dostoevskian
grotesque. *Sanctuary* is, on the one hand, the darkest of all Faulkner's books, a brutal protest to the quality of American life written
in the pit of the Great Depression; but on the other hand, it is the
dirtiest of all the dirty jokes exchanged among men only at the
expense of the abdicating Anglo-Saxon Virgin.

Temple is not only a lady, but the very image of all those Fair
Ladies whose fall or resistance had been the central subject of genteel literature ever since *Charlotte Temple* was published in the
United States. That her name is an inversion of that of the prototypical American heroine is, perhaps, only an accident, one of the
more satisfactory jokes of history; and certainly Faulkner did not
know that the original of Maggie Verver was Henry James's cousin
Minny Temple, whose frailness, white skin, and red hair also distinguish Temple Drake. The title of his book, however, makes it
clear that Faulkner is fully aware that he is dealing not with a
mere change in mores but with the desecration of a cult object.
Out of the "high delicate head" of Faulkner's Temple, at any rate,
look eyes which are "cool, predatory, and discreet," but their discretion is belied by the "bold painted mouth." She fools no one;
the wife of a gangster into whose hideout she has stumbled sees
immediately that though Temple, like her illustrious prototypes, is
still the Girl on the Run, she no longer means to run quite fast
enough to get away. And even Gowan Stevens, Temple's escort
and male opposite number, is not too drunk to understand what
she really wants, though drunk enough not to be able to take advantage of his knowledge. "Don't think I don't see your name
where it's written on that lavatory wall!" he tells her in impotent
spite. It is the final degradation; the holy name on the lavatory
wall!

Before Faukner is through, we have been compelled to watch
the ex-snow maiden, the former golden girl, not only raped (which
is nothing new, of course, since she was born being raped, was
Clarissa before she was Maggie Verver), but begging to be had,
whimpering for the consummation she had once fled in terror. Beside Temple, pleading with Red, brutal thug and stud, to satisfy
her, even Daisy Buchanan seems in retrospect a quasi-lady, Brett
not really a bitch at all. Western literature before the coming of
Sentimentalism is rich in images of destructive women—Thaïs and

Cleopatra and Lilith herself; but Temple is more than a recrudescence of that rejected orthodox archetype. She represents a lust of the nerves rather than of the flesh, a *programmatic* concupiscence entered upon as a declaration of independence, is in short a queasy male image of the flapper—the New Woman of the 1920's. Not content to be violated, the woman becomes the violator and Faulkner responds with nausea:

> He came toward her. She did not move. Her eyes began to grow darker and darker, lifting into her skull above a half-moon of white, without a focus, with the blank rigidity of a statue's eyes. She began to say Ah-ah-ah-ah in an expiring voice, her body arching slowly backward as though forced by an exquisite torture. When he touched her she sprang like a bow, hurling herself upon him, her mouth gaped and ugly like that of a dying fish as she writhed her loins against him. . . . With her hips grinding against him, her mouth gaping in straining protrusion, bloodless, she began to speak. "Let's hurry. Anywhere. . . . Come on. What're you waiting for?" She strained her mouth toward him, dragging his head down, making a whimpering moan. "Please. Please. Please. Please. You've got to. I'm on fire, I tell you."

Toward the end of his life, Faulkner seems to have repented of his many blasphemies against woman and to have committed himself to redeeming one by one all his anti-virgins; but his attempts at redemption somehow do not touch the level of acceptance reached by his original travesties. In *Requiem for a Nun,* he portrays Temple as a mother, as married to Gowan Stevens, who once read her name on the lavatory wall. Insanely burning once more for a new Red, she is not permitted to abase herself again, but is redeemed by the self-sacrifice of a Negro girl, and is left at the play's end aching with a higher lust for religious belief, about to follow her husband home. In *The Town,* Faulkner carries Eula's refurbishing even further than he had Temple's, actually rewriting Eula's past history as he pretends to recapitulate it, and turning her into the very model of female courage and endurance. This time the former avatar of female corruption herself performs the act of self-sacrifice, dies to assure an honorable future for her daughter—an innocent young girl, who is left at the novel's end advancing, wide-eyed and pure, on Greenwich Village. The epitaph inscribed on Eula's grave by her impotent husband is, we are asked to believe, truer than that husband can guess or any decent citizen is prepared to grant:

EULA VARNER SNOPES
1889   1927
A Virtuous Wife is a Crown to her Husband
Her Children Rise and Call Her Blessed

And even this is not the end. In *The Long Hot Summer,* a film which lists Faulkner's name among the credits, Eula is de-mythicized as well as redeemed: made into the customary Holly-wood image of the sexy but sincere young wife, who begins wrig-gling like a taken fish in the arms of her new husband, while the boys wolf-call and wail in the stifling dusk. In the end, however, she helps to win that husband from weakness to strength, returns to his arms and legitimate bliss, when he has proved himself a true son to his father and a good citizen! Eula and Temple alike fade into the stereotype of the Good Bad Girl, who in turn gives birth to the sweet young thing, and the Protestant Virgin is restored to her shrine; but it makes no difference. Faulkner's art fails him when he turns from nausea and despair to sentimentality and maudlin pity; and even the popular mind rejects his attempts at converting his archetypes into the stereotypes of market-place culture.

Not only in Hemingway and Faulkner and Fitzgerald, but in John Held, Jr. and in the Anita Loos of *Gentlemen Prefer Blondes,* the archetype of the snow maiden as gold-digger, the bad blonde takes over. The vampire, symbol of sexual aggression as cannibal-ism, first formulated as a male, had been turned by the Romantic imagination into the Dark Lady, the "vamp" as she was called when Zenobia had become Theda Bara. During the '20's, however, in a second revolutionary shift, Mary Pickford and Theda Bara became one, America's Sweetheart and the vampire amalgamated into the bleached blonde. The notion that fair hair is the product of the peroxide bottle rather than of race or culture, a disguise rather than an outward and visible sign of an inward and invisible grace, becomes an article of cynical un-faith. A whole disillusioned generation eyeing the peroxide blonde (after a while "platinum" rather than golden, as if the old symbol of wealth were not opulent enough) remarks nastily, "Yes, but what color is she below the waist?" Jean Harlow is the first avatar of that new and blasphemous dream, first of the series that includes Marilyn Monroe and Jayne Mansfield. The movies, out of respect for the Hays office, must pretend that they are Good Bad Girls one and all—Good Girls who only appear bad for a little while; but the mass audience knows better, knows they are really Bad Good Girls—Bad Girls who pass themselves off as good by wearing the hair and skin and eyes that were once the sacred investiture of the Protestant Virgin.

It is fitting that the most memorable and terrible woman in an American novel of the '30's is a portrait of the blond movie actress, a kind of *ersatz* Jean Harlowe. She is, of course, the Faye Greener of Nathanael West's *Day of the Locust,* and her very name is a fitting climax to the series we have been tracing through the history of our fiction: Charlotte Temple to Temple Drake, Daisy Miller to Daisy Fay to Faye Greener.*

In West's earliest fiction, there are traces of queasiness before woman's surrender of her traditional role, her usurpation of male privileges which so disturbed Faulkner. In *The Dream Life of Balso Snell* (1931), this is projected as a fantasy in which the female turns, at the moment of possession, into something disturbingly like a male. "Throwing his arms about her, Balso interrupted her recitation by sticking his tongue into her mouth. But when he closed his eyes to heighten the fun, he felt that he was embracing tweed. He opened them and saw that what he held in his arms was a middleaged woman dressed in a mannish suit and wearing hornrimmed glasses." To such a betrayal, in which the erotic object becomes at once something mannish and schoolmarmish, there is only one answer: "By this time, Balso had gotten one of his hands free. He hit Miss McGeeney a terrific blow in the gut and hove her into the fountain."

The rest of West's fiction contains a series of precisely such blows in the female gut: travesties of the teasers and betrayers and lady rapists who assault and torment his male protagonists, baffle them in their search for a love which is more than desire. Even the most submissive of Good Girls only succeeds in enraging West, as the Betty of *Miss Lonelyhearts* enrages her lover. "She was like a kitten," he thinks, "whose soft helplessness makes one ache to hurt

* It seems odd that it did not occur to me earlier that her name suggests, too, how the grass is always greener on the other side—for West, the blond, gentile side.

it." And taking her nipple between his fingers, " 'Let me pluck this rose,' he said, giving a sharp tug. 'I want to wear it in my button-hole.' " It is in *A Cool Million,* however, that the Good Good Girl, again called Betty, gets her full comeuppance, raped with appalling regularity from the time she is twelve, pursued by mad dogs, bullies and corrupt politicians, she fulfills her destiny as the final adornment of the Colonial American Room of Wu Fong's whore-house, where she blends admirably into a background of "antimacassars, ships in bottles, carved whale bone, hooked rugs."

Betty is still the Good Good Girl, even as an unsuccessful prostitute, an American Justine, which is to say, a victim. But Faye Greener is the blond bitch in all her archetypal purity, a woman willing at last to take up the role that old Rappaccini had once vainly dreamed for his daughter: "to be endowed with marvellous gifts against which no power and strength could avail an enemy . . . to be as terrible as . . . beautiful." Like Temple Drake before her, Faye does her destroying on the run; pursued by everyone, possessed by anyone with the price, she is somehow unattainable still —certainly to the artist-narrator, Tod, who has seen her pawed by a seedy cowboy actor and a brutal Mexican hanger-on, but cannot quite bring himself to buy her. "If only he had the courage to throw himself on her. Nothing less violent than rape would do. The sensation he felt was like that he got when holding an egg in his hand. Not that she was fragile or even seemed fragile. It wasn't that. It was her completeness, her egg-like self-sufficiency, that made him want to touch her." But she cannot really be touched, for she is the dream dreamed by all of America, the dream of a love which is death; and in a strange sense she remains virginal as death is virginal: the immaculate, degraded *anima* of a nation, her realest existence on the screen.

It is because West's book is about Hollywood, and because he knows that Hollywood is where all America comes to die, that Faye is its proper center, dispensing what the bored hinterlanders do not quite know that they desire, as they press against the restraining ropes at a gala preview: a *Götterdämmerung,* an orgy of destruction. Precisely because she is a phantom bride, she is also a child, epitome of the quest for eternal youth which is the obverse of the lust for death: "Although she was seventeen, she was dressed like a child of twelve in a white cotton dress with a blue sailor collar. Her long legs were bare and she had blue sandals on her feet." The long legs are a further clue: those improbable legs which America has bred onto the naturally short-legged female form. "She was a tall girl," West tells us of Faye, "with wide, straight shoulders and long, sword-like legs." The rest is conventional enough: the long neck, the full face, the widely divided breasts, the platinum hair tied back with a blue ribbon, the sailor suit of a small girl; but it is the sword-legs which gave away the game.

"Her invitation wasn't to pleasure," West explains, "but to struggle, hard and sharp, closer to murder than to love. If you threw yourself on her, it would be like throwing yourself from the parapet of a skyscraper. You would do it with a scream. You wouldn't expect to rise again. Your teeth would be driven into your skull like nails into a pine board and your back would be broken. You wouldn't even have time to sweat or close your eyes." Only the fantasies of post-World War I Germany have reflected (in films like *The Blue Angel*) comparable excesses of male masochism; and Marlene Dietrich, who embodied the cruel woman of those fantasies, soon emigrated to the United States which appreciated even more than Germany the delicious threat of her million-dollar legs. But it is not male masochism alone which creates and acclaims images of the castrating bitch; there is a corresponding female sadism which greets such images and collaborates in their fabrication.

Though the long-suffering victim does not disappear from popular woman's literature, she is flanked in the mid-twentieth century by a new figure, the lady with the whip. Most often that newer figure is projected backward in time, cast as the heroine-villainess of a historical romance, as if to insist that the dangerous woman belongs to the there-and-then rather than to the here-and-now. The protagonists of such books are not possessed by their numerous lovers but possess them, use, exhaust, and abandon their men— leave them to defeat or death. "Avatars of the Bitch," Gershom Legman calls such villainous heroines in an indignant pamphlet called *Love and Death,* which is directed against the sadist travesties of women and the celebration of violence on all levels of our culture. *Gone With the Wind* draws his special wrath, though its bitch-lady, Scarlett O'Hara, seems mild enough beside the women of Faulkner or Nathanael West. As popular literature goes, Margaret Mitchell's novel is notably "clean," the sort of fat, traditional book on which high-school students make their "book reports" for the class, while they are busily reading *Peyton Place* outside.

Gone with the Wind's heroine, Scarlett O'Hara, is less the portrait of a woman than an embodiment of the Northern stereotypes of the suffering South (the really orthodox Daughters of the Confederacy walked out on her!): corrupt, vain, though at last more sinned against than sinning. The sentimentality of *Gone With the Wind* is chiefly political; but its politics is embodied in an erotic fable, whose heroine is permitted an act of violence beyond anything Brockden Brown allowed Constantia Dudley. She is allowed not merely to kill a would-be attacker, but to *enjoy* the act with a joy deeper, more organic than any she finds in love.

> Like lightning, she shoved her weapon over the banisters and into the startled bearded face. Before he could even fumble at his belt, she pulled the trigger. . . . The man crashed backwards to the floor. . . . Scarlett ran down the stairs and stood over him, gazing down into what was left of the face above the beard, a bloody pit where the nose had been, glazing eyes burned with powder. . . . Her eyes went to the stubby hairy hand on the floor so close to the sewing box and suddenly she was vitally alive again, vitally glad with a cool tigerish joy. She could have ground her heel into the gaping wound which had been his nose and taken sweet pleasure in the feel of his warm blood on her bare feet. She had struck a blow for Tara—and for Ellen.

For the old plantation and for the abused woman: these are the causes in whose name the New Woman strikes; and avenging the fallen Clarissas of the past, she becomes the bitch-killer.*

VI

Once the Good Good Girl has been exposed, no sentimental stereotype of womanhood is safe; first the mother and then the angel child are revealed as bitches, too. Quite early in the game, Melville had challenged the standard clichés of motherhood with the portrait of Mary Glendenning in *Pierre*. She is not, like Mrs. St. Clare in *Uncle Tom's Cabin*, a traditional Bad Mother—descendant of

---

* But turning killer, she becomes fair game herself; and the way is open for such male counter-fantasies as Norman Mailer's *An American Dream*, in which the Dark Lady, turned wife, is murdered by the sympathetic protagonist, who also buggers the Bad Blonde, revealed as a Nazi, while the Good Blonde is being snatched from him by the powers of darkness. And in the end, all male murderers and desecrators go scot free.

the stepmothers in Grimm—who loves herself more than her child, but a *Good* Mother, whose very goodness is revealed as a threat, a loving mother, whose love serves only to unman her son. The sickly-sweet entanglement between Pierre and his mother, who flirt and flatter like a pair of lovers, ends in mutual misunderstanding and alienation. In pharisaic pride, the mother casts out her son, when he once dares to reject her rule and her notions of respectable behavior: "Then erected all her haughtiness again, and stood before Pierre in incurious, unappeasable grief and scorn for him. . . . 'Beneath my roof, and at my table, he who was once Pierre Glendenning no more puts himself.' "

So intense is Melville's involvement in the crisis of rejection which he attempts to transcribe, that he can find no language for it, falls into a rhetoric impossible to believe and even difficult to follow; and we remember that on his own marriage certificate, his mother's name is written in the place of his bride's! Like Mark Twain, who was also obsessed by the theme of the divorce between mother and son, Melville cannot abide thinking of that rupture as final. Twain's Good Bad Boy, Tom Sawyer or Tom Canty in *The Prince and the Pauper,* merely seem to deny the mother, only play at running away from home, but return at last to be forgiven and redeemed. Huck, to be sure, rejects a whole series of surrogate mothers from the Widow Douglas to Aunt Sally, but he is an orphan—postulated as a "motherless boy"; and, no more than his author, does he dare deny the value of what he is somehow unable to accept. Melville's reconciliations with the mother, however, are invariably projected as symbolic rather than real. Pierre can never recover on earth his first innocent relationship with Mary Glendenning (between them falls the shadow of the incest taboo); though the "orphan" Ishmael has been picked up at the close of *Moby Dick* by "the devious-cruising *Rachel* . . . in her retracing search after her children," rescued by the ship which represents eternally-suffering motherhood.

Only in the twentieth century is the charge of betrayal unequivocally leveled against the mothers themselves, the counterattack begun. The key work on the subject was imagined in the '20's, though never quite written, in the book which Fitzgerald called at one point *The Boy Who Killed His Mother,* but which he gradually transformed into *Tender Is the Night,* by changing its boy-hero into a girl, who gets along reasonably well with *her* mother! It is Fitzgerald's friend Hemingway, who, though he stops short of portraying matricide, launches the full-scale assault: turning Mother into a monster of piety, who despises the great clean outdoors of rod and gun, and rises from her copy of *Science and Sanity* to destroy Father's collection of Indian artifacts while he is off teaching junior to shoot. There is no question about junior's allegiance; through Nick, the boy Hemingway always in some sense remained, the choice is made once and for all in a short story called "The Doctor and the Doctor's Wife": " 'Your mother wants you to come and see her,' the doctor said. 'I want to go with you,' Nick said."

In the gallery of anti-mothers, perhaps the Addie Bundren of Faulkner's *As I Lay Dying* (1930) is the most icy and terrible. Marriage to her had meant chiefly an escape from teaching school, and from the children in whom she had found pleasure only when beating them: "I looked forward to the times when they faulted, so I could whip them." And when, after her marriage, she finds herself with child, a rage gathers in her against her husband that only cuckolding him can satisfy. "And when I knew that I had Cash," she thinks in her last reverie, "I knew that living was terrible and that this was the answer to it. . . . When he was born I knew that motherhood was invented by someone who had to have a word for it because the ones that had the children didn't care whether there was a word for it or not." The image of the mother of bastards, who hates the life which painfully grows in her, is passed on from Faulkner to his disciple, Robert Penn Warren. The mother of Jack Burden in *All the King's Men* is the special heiress of the Faulknerian rage. To her grown son, she seems "a woman without heart, who loved merely power over men and the momentary satisfaction to vanity or flesh which they could give her," in short, the conventional bitch of contemporary American fiction. And at the climax of the novel's action, she reveals to that son that he is, indeed, a bastard, his presumed father really betrayed; though it is from this moment of truth that a new relationship between them grows possible, one based neither on the traditional notions of maternal purity and faithfulness nor on a revulsion from them which debouches in hate.

On the more popular levels, that stage of reconciliation is never reached. Once more a sentimental cliché heaves over sickeningly in the ooze at the bottom of the mass mind, reveals its underside of delusion and horror; the hackneyed tribute "I owe it all to Mother!" turns into a self-pitying whine which converts the same words to a condemnation. The emasculated display everywhere their attenuated private parts; the Oedipal captives hold up their silver chains to the light; and a nation of mama's boys kick and scream that it is all mama's fault. The age demands that the Devil-Mom replace the saint-Mom; but no one asks that real women replace allegorical lay figures in the maternal role. The new stereotype is redeemed for literature, however, the anti-mother made flesh in a single distinguished novel, Wright Morris' *Man and Boy* (1951).

This is an oddly dispassionate little study of a bird-watching, maniacally tidy housewife, who pares her toe-nails with a knife stolen from her husband, and is called universally "Mother"—though her only son died before the action begins. She has, in effect, killed him; driven "the Boy" before her merciless, unremitting, and unsympathetic love, first into the household refuge of the bathroom, then to the more universal sanctuary of the war, in which he has died a hero's death. Early in the game, she had wrested from the Boy the gun, given to him by his defeated father as a token of manhood; and having no other way of making a big bang, "the Boy" ended by blowing himself up. Nowhere in our literature is the castrating mother-wife, shaving her legs, getting into her girdle, spreading newspapers on the newly washed floor, studied with less hysteria or self-pity. As Mother moves through her Big Day (she has been asked to christen a destroyer which is being named after the Boy) to its climax, everything crumbles before her assurance: her husband's feeble attempt at conspiratorial revolt with a chance accomplice, a dwarfed soldier called Seymour Lipido; the conventions and procedures of the United States Navy; the insolence of the children of the poor.

Oblivious, magnificent, and terrible, she advances on the docks, presumably under the escort of a naval officer, but really under the sole protection of an immense, stupid cleaning lady, who holds over her a green parasol and alone knows her divinity. The bottle broken and the ship duly dubbed, Mother insists upon making a speech, utterly irrelevant to the occasion, before a cowed crowd of listeners; and Seymour Lipido (who has already been converted enough to yell, "Viva Mrs. Ormsby—nuts to the Navy!") makes the response on which the book ends. " 'Here she comes,' he cried, 'Here comes Mother!' and rose from his seat in such a manner that Mr. Ormsby, like a man on a springboard, rose with him. As one man they rose together, some of them, like Mr. Ormby, a little stunned, but all of them able, with the help of their wives, to get to their feet. Coming toward them, soberly, was Mother, her flanks protected by the U.S. Navy, with Mrs. Myrtle Dinardo still in full charge of the sky."

The image of the golden girl child dies the hardest death of all in the American psyche; but this, too, yields before the general onslaught on the concept of pure womanhood. To this very day, the juvenile version of the Good Good Girl survives—not only in children's books and comic strips like "Little Annie Rooney," but even in the work of so serious a middlebrow writer as J. D. Salinger. His Esmé in "For Esmé—with Love and Squalor," like Holden's kid sister in *The Catcher in the Rye,* redeems from madness a mind at the point of surrender; and if in "A Perfect Day for Bananafish," the child Sybil cannot save the life of Seymour Glass, at least she illuminates for him the world of adult corruption. Salinger is as addicted as any contemporary to portraying full-grown women as bitches, but he clings to the pure child as a foil. He proffers Seymour Glass's erotic trifling with the golden-haired little Sybil (he plays with her fingers, kisses her feet) not as one more neurotic symptom, but as an attempt to escape from sexual bondage to the freedom of love; in his work, in short, the child becomes the rival of the wife.

Before the turn of the century, however, Stephen Crane had, in his *Whilomville Stories,* begun the debunking of the little angel, revealing the golden-curled, pink-and-white girl-child as a source of mischief and deceit, though the prevailing tone of these tales is so sentimental and cute that it is hard to take him seriously. The game of calling little angels little devils is an old and respectable one—quite unexceptionable to a popular audience, as long as it is clear that the author is really only kidding. The Good Bad Small Girl of this type is related to the "tomboy" figure, the rebel against femininity, who, as every genteel reader knows, will be transformed at the moment that she steps out of her overalls into her first party dress and is revealed as worthy of love! The lesbian implications of this image were not apparent to the great audience of the past, which would have found in any hint of female homosexuality the really unforgivable blasphemy against the conventions of womanhood. But Carson McCullers has taken full advantage of those implications, projecting in her neo-tomboys, ambiguous and epicene, the homosexual's sense of exclusion from the family and his uneasiness before heterosexual passion. Indeed, nothing is more suitable for such ends than the child's bafflement at weddings and honeymoons and the mystery of copulation, which these rituals at once declare and conceal. With the collaboration of Julie Harris, Mrs. McCullers has made the boy-girl of *Member of the Wedding* familiar to all of America; so that we have come to accept the Good Bad Tomboy, Huck Finn as F. Jasmine Adams, as a standard form of our nostalgia for pre-sexual bliss.

It is Faulkner, however, who first attempts to portray not merely the small Good Bad Girl, but the (expected) Good Girl as (actually) bad. In *Absalom, Absalom!*, the young girl Judith is discovered, leaning over the edge of a loft and screaming with the bloodlust her brother does not share (he trembles, nauseated), while her father wrestles, naked and bloody, with one of his Negro field hands. Judith is not merely the tomboy contrasted with the sissy brother; she is, though only in embryo, the child witch, travesty of the good woman as well as the pure child; and she belongs quite properly in the company of the ghouls and ghosts who make *Absalom, Absalom!* the most gothic of Faulkner's books. Yet Faulkner somehow cannot manage to keep Judith alive after her first scene; for the plot pushes her to the periphery, and she blends with a Negro servant woman and her old-maid aunt into a composite creature, a symbol of featureless femininity: "It was as though we were one being, interchangeable and indiscriminate . . . the three of us, three women. . . ."

In *The Hamlet,* he tries again with the young Eula Varner, who is formulated, in a book more comic than gothic, rather as the girl bitch than the child witch. The scene in which the schoolmaster Labove, helpless with the desire that an eleven-year-old girl has stirred up in him and will not satisfy, chases her mindless quivering flesh round and round the classroom comes closer than anything in American literature to the horrific vision of *Death in Venice:* a revelation that the pursuit of childhood is not harmless nostalgia but decadence and the will to self-destruction. In Faulkner, however, it is, in all its unmitigated horror, played for the laughs, culminates in a pratfall rather than a tragic death. Eula knocks her schoolmaster-lover down and " 'Stop pawing me,' she said. 'You old headless horseman Ichabod Crane.' "

Eula is the *femme fatale* as a small, fat girl; but she destroys only as the blind, fertile thrust of nature destroys, without malice or intent. Quite different is the female protagonist of William March's *The Bad Seed* (1954), who consciously desires evil but wears in the presence of adults a mask of innocence, which she has learned to simulate reading *Elsie Dinsmore*. The avowed themes of March's book: the question of whether criminal traits can be inherited and the decision of a mother to kill her own child—are of secondary importance; what thrilled the great audience and made this novel March's only best-selling work is his revelation of the sweet young thing as sadist and killer. It is this motif which filled the theaters and movie-houses with middlebrow, middle-class communicants eager to participate in the defilement of their own sacred images. That defilement is carried even further in Vladimir Nabokov's *Lolita* (1958), whose subject is the seduction of a middle-aged man by a twelve-year-old girl; and which has already achieved the two supreme successes possible to heretical works: an initial banning and a subsequent life as a best-seller, despite its endorsement by eminently respectable professors.

Nabokov's theme involves multiple ironies; for in his novel, it is the naïve child, the female, the American who corrupts the sophisticated adult, the male, the European. In a single work, Richardson, Mrs. Stowe, and Henry James are all controverted, all customary symbols for the encounter of innocence and experience stood on their heads. *Lolita, or the Confession of a White Widowed Male* is the international novel moved to America along with the émigré who is its male protagonist. As full as *The Marble Faun* or *The Ambassadors* of guidebook observations, it devotes them not to châteaux or museums or the Church of the Capuchins but to highways and motels and roadside cafés; its America comes out of the AAA Tourguide and Duncan Hines, as surely as the Europe of Hawthorne out of the Baedeker. Nowhere in our recent literature is there so detailed and acute a picture of our landscape, topographical and moral, as in *Lolita*. But more profoundly than the scenery and the setting, Lolita herself is America—just as Daisy or Hilda or Maggie were America before her; and representing America to the mind of a European, she is even more Annabel Lee than Maggie Verver. Indeed, the book begins with an evocation of Poe's "Kingdom by the Sea"; and before it is through, the names of his girl-love and Nabokov's fade into each other, blur to a single entangled formula: "Annabel Haze, alias Dolores Lee, alias Loleeta. . . ." Annabel Lee as nymphomaniac, demonic rapist of the soul—such is the lithe, brown Campfire Girl, who loves her mummy but was devirginated at the age of twelve (like Justine before her, Nabokov reminds us)!

Into Lolita and her mummy, the bitch-girl and the semi-preserved suburban predator, the pure American female has been split and degraded; but the European confronts her in both her latter-day avatars as helplessly as when she was still whole and dazzling in her purity. Like Prince Amerigo in *The Golden Bowl*, Nabokov's Humbert Humbert is still engaged in the discovery of America through Poe and the American woman; but unlike the Prince he is not redeemed, merely fascinated, raped, driven to murder, and left to die of a heart attack in jail. At every turn of its complications, the perverse theme of *Lolita* parodies some myth of the Sentimental Love Religion and the cult of the child. And it is surely for this reason that the book was banned and then blessed with a popular success; for it is the final blasphemy against the mythical innocence of the woman and the child, more than sufficient unto a day haunted by the fear that there may, after all, have been such an innocence—that somewhere underground it may still persist.

11

THE FAILURE

OF SENTIMENT AND

THE EVASION OF LOVE

THE FAILURE of the Sentimental Love Religion and the rejection of the Protestant Virgin are the two most critical and baffling facts of the history of the novel in America. But that failure and that rejection are inevitable, granted the profound division in the American awareness of women, arising from an impossible demand that they represent at once the ruined and redeeming virgin-bride dreamed by Sentimentalism, and the forgiving mother, necessary to sustain an imaginary American commonwealth of boy-children, camerados at work and play.

Perhaps the clue to an essential difficulty is here. If marriage dismays the American writer, though his earlier European prototypes assured him it was salvation itself; and if lawless passion unnerves him, though his later European colleagues assure him that it "justifies all"—this is because both marriage and passion impugn the image of woman as mother, mean the abandonment of childhood. The keynote of our special sentimentality had been set even before the mid-nineteenth-century American renaissance by Nathaniel Parker Willis. Writing of that soon-forgotten figure some fifty years after his debut, Oliver Wendell Holmes remembered that in 1830 "Willis was by far the most prominent young American author"! He recalled his epicene grace, "something between a remembrance of the Count D'Orsay and an anticipation of Oscar Wilde," and compared him to a portrait of Hippolytus: "the beautiful young man who had kindled a passion in the heart of his wicked step-mother."

There could be no apter image to preside over the birth of our literature: the evocation of a delicate homosexuality, fleeing from gross female assault and haunted by the incest taboo. And even more to the point are the verses which Holmes quotes from Willis, written when he had already won the fame he desired, but was appalled to realize that he had swapped time for success, was over the sill of manhood:

> I'm twenty-two, I'm twenty-two,—
> They idly give me joy,
> As if I should be glad to know
> That I was less a boy.

It is maturity above all things that the American writer fears, and marriage seems to him its essential sign. For marriage stands traditionally not only for a reconciliation with the divided self, a truce between head and heart, but also for a compromise with society, an acceptance of responsibility and drudgery and dullness. To this ultimate surrender, the Young Werther had preferred death; and Werther, as we have noticed earlier, was the moral guide of the first hero of American fiction.

It is more complicated even than this, however; for marriage also means an acceptance of the status of a father: an abandonment of the quest to deliver the captive mother and an assumption of the role of the ogre who holds her in captivity. There is no authentic American who would not rather be Jack than the Giant, which is to say, who would not choose to be "one of the boys" to the very end. The ideal American postulates himself as the fatherless man, the eternal son of the mother.

He does not, of course, see himself as the swaggering son of the continental imagination, the adulterer who in every cuckolded husband humiliates his father and revenges his mother. Romantic adultery is regarded with horror by the American bourgeois and the classic American novelist alike, for it is hopelessly involved with a European class society abandoned forever; by most of our writers it is not really regarded at all, only ignored at the prompting of a largely unconscious self-censorship. To our writers, for whom courtly love is something learned about in school, extramarital passion seems not only an offense against the mother, but also, like marriage itself, a disclaimer of childhood: a way of smuggling adult responsibility and guilt in through the back door.

Only a temporary alliance with a savage maiden whose language one cannot understand: a mindless, speechless, brief encounter in some tropical Happy Valley appears to our traditional writers a possible image for a love which does not compromise freedom. But in the end, even this seems to them not quite safe.

There is finally no heterosexual solution which the American psyche finds completely satisfactory, no imagined or real consummation between man and woman found worthy of standing in our fiction for the healing of the breach between consciousness and unconsciousness, reason and impulse, society and nature. Yet in no nation in the world are those cleavages more deeply felt, declared, indeed, in the very pattern of historical life, visibly represented by the frontier. And in no nation is the need to heal such divisions more passionately recognized. The quest which has distinguished our fiction from Brockden Brown and Cooper, through Poe and Melville and Twain, to Faulkner and Hemingway is the search for an innocent substitute for adulterous passion and marriage alike. Is there not, our writers ask over and over, a sentimental relationship at once erotic and immaculate, a union which commits its participants neither to society nor sin—and yet one which is able to symbolize the union of the ego with the id, the thinking self with its rejected impulses?

We have already noticed that the first legend to seize the American imagination is the story of Rip Van Winkle, which has outlived the general reputation of its author, and which for years continued, as a popular drama, to reach the kind of audience to whom books remain forever a mystery. It is all a joke, of course, the jocular tale of a man who wakes up to find, when he has slept off his superhuman drunk, that he has also slept away the life of the shrew who bullied him, as well as that of George III, who had oppressed his country. Even as such a jest, however, the Rip archetype possesses surprising vitality, surviving to this day in the comic strip "Bringing Up Father," whose very title refers ironically to American woman's image of herself as a culture bearer, the civilizer of her spouse.

Though the Catskills for which Jiggs lights out is Dinty Moore's saloon, the alcoholic aroma of his escape remains the same as Rip's; and though Maggie takes opera lessons and aspires to "high society," she is still Mrs. Rip, a status-striving shrew. There is something already a little old-fashioned about "Bringing Up

Father," both in its up-from-the-working-class background and in the frankness with which it reveals the power struggle between husband and wife. The true Rip type—whether embodied in Jiggs or Major Hoople or the Uncle Willie of "Moon Mullins"—seems faintly archaic, a hangover from a more brutal age, before one spouse had agreed to put down the rolling pin or the other to bend the elbow no longer. The successor of Rip-Jiggs is Dagwood Bumstead, who goes to work every day and welcomes the tyranny of Blondie as quite what his own inadequacy demands and merits. On the most popular level, the image of the wife as shrew seems to be dying, abandoned to middlebrow novelists like Philip Wylie or quite serious calumniators of the female like Faulkner or Hemingway or Wright Morris. The disreputable figure of Rip himself dies harder, appearing with all his old scapegrace charm in, for instance, Faulkner's "Uncle Willy," where he is portrayed as the small boys' ally in their war against the mothers. "He wasn't anybody's uncle, but all of us, and grown people, too, called him . . . Uncle Willy." It is a hopeless war these days, the war against good women; and Uncle Willy, who cannot sleep away the lifetime of his opponents, is driven out of town.

Sometimes, in more serious books, Rip doffs his comic role and appears in new guises, less the clown but still essentially the man on the run from his wife. In the unwritten story of "Agatha," he teased the imaginations of Hawthorne and Melville in the form of the sailor, Robertson: that anti-Enoch Arden who returns from a long absence to find his former wife, not married again but still waiting—and flees again westward to a new escape. In *The Wonder Book*, Hawthorne through his alter ego Eustace Bright had already gone on record as refusing to re-tell the tale of Rip in its original version, though begged to by eager children. "Among those misty hills, he said, was a spot where some old Dutchmen were playing an everlasting game of nine-pins and where an idle fellow whose name was Rip Van Winkle had fallen asleep and slept away twenty years at a stretch." It is interesting to note how gun, dog and wife disappear from this discreet summary, to which Eustace Bright will add no more. "But the student replied that the story had been told once already, and better than it ever could be told again, and that nobody would have a right to alter a word of it until it should have grown as old as 'The Gorgon's Head.' . . ." "The Gorgon's Head"—it is an odd association, which evokes the missing wife at a symbolic remove, as the female face which turns the beholder to stone!

Despite his disclaimer, however, Hawthorne actually did rewrite Irving's tale, or at least embodied certain of its elements in the shadowy sketch which he called "Wakefield." It is not quite a story, this ironic little portrait of a man endowed with "a quiet selfishness . . . a peculiar sort of vanity . . . a disposition to craft," who one day steps out of his door and, for the legendary twenty years, remains away, merely as "a little joke . . . at his wife's expense," "a long whimwham." But the joke is finally at Wakefield's expense, since outside the purlieus of his own home, he becomes for Hawthorne a hopelessly alienated man: "the Outcast of the Universe." Hawthorne's story is racked, that is to say, by a guilt entirely absent in Irving's tale, in which there is no note of equivocation about the joyousness of Rip's deliverance: "there was one species of despotism under which he had long groaned and that was petticoat government. Happily that was at an end; he had got his neck out of the yoke of matrimony, and could go in and out whenever he pleased. . . ."

What is posed originally as an innocent lark soon becomes problematic; for the myth of Rip is more than just another example among the jollier fables of masculine protest; it is the definition, made once and for all—as Eustace Bright justly observes—of a fundamental American archetype. In some ways, it seems astonishingly prophetic: a forecast of today's fishing trip with the boys, tomorrow's escape to the ball park or the poker game. Henpecked and misunderstood at home, the natural man whistles for his dog, Wolf, picks up his gun and leaves the village for Nature—seeking in a day's outing what a long life at home has failed to provide him. It is hard to tell whether he is taking a vacation or making a revolution, whether his gesture is one of evasion or of subversion; but in any case, he seeks some ultimate Good symbolized by the keg of excellent Hollands and the male companions, who do not even talk (that is the province of his wife), merely indicate the liquor and continue with their game—their eternal playtime in the hills.

It is scarcely surprising that such a legend would have a special appeal for Melville, whose whole writing career represents, as it were, an escape to an inner Catskills, a Happy Valley of natural ease and male camaraderie, into which his imagination had translated the experience of his early manhood. To no one did marriage seem so utterly Paradise lost (as we have observed in looking at *Mardi*); to no one did bachelorhood appear so enviable a state. In "Benito Cereno," the innocent ship which Captain Delano leaves to plunge into a web of horror and intrigue is called *The Bachelor's Delight;* in *Moby Dick,* the last glimpse of joy and peace enjoyed by the crew of the *Pequod* comes in their encounter with another whaler named the *Bachelor;* while one of Melville's most intriguing short stories contrasts "The Tartarus of Maids" with "The Paradise of Bachelors." No wonder, then, that Melville turns at the end of his life to the most traditional of all American fables of anti-marriage. His idyllic tale, a composite of verse and prose, was intended as part of a volume he was preparing in his last years to dedicate to his wife. Like that other ambiguous tribute, *Mardi*, "Rip Van Winkle's Lilac" demands some knowledge of the language of flowers for a full understanding; but even to a cursory reader its essential meaning is clear. Melville's tale is an apology for the original Rip, put in the mouth of a bohemian painter, who prefers the shadow of the lilac tree reputed to have been planted by Rip's own hand to the shelter of the whitewashed church. The implication is that art is nurtured not by institutionalized religion but by the impulse which leads man to overthrow petticoat tyranny and head for the hills.

But why has Melville symbolized Rip's heritage by a lilac? For what precisely does it stand, this casual gift of the lazy reprobate to the American artist? We are told two things about it: first, that its blossoms have replaced Dame Van Winkle's pot of pinks and hollyhocks; and second, that its trunk stands in the place of a willow which endured as long as the house lasted and could not be cut down by Dame Van Winkle's ax. But pinks represent both boldness and woman's love, while hollyhocks stand for ambition and fecundity. Opposed to these symbols of aggressive, fertile femaleness, the lilac bloom betokens humility and the joy of youth —appropriate to the modest companionship of boys. The willow, of course, figures forth mourning, the blight that cannot be removed as long as hearth and home continue; while the lilac bush means joy, the rapture which arises when both have become dust. The gift book for Mrs. Melville, who in its code is called "Winnifred" (which means, appropriately enough "White Phantom"!), is entitled *Weeds and Wildings, with a Rose or Two.* What tender meanings roses had for Melville, we know from his portrait of that rosy and beloved boy Billy Budd; but Mrs. Melville, it is interesting to note, suffered from rose fever!

II

Though the myth of Rip Van Winkle embodies the sketch of an alternative to married life, in Irving's version, the mountain spree is tucked away in a few lines, Rip plunged unceremoniously into his Big Sleep—as if to suggest that the escape from the shrew can only be dreamed, not lived. Even on a more serious level, some American writers follow his lead, making not the search for an erotic substitute but the simple failure of married love their essential theme. Hawthorne, for instance, peoples his tales, as we have already seen, with a succession of Wakefieldian "outcasts," capable only of beholding love but not of sharing it. Disconcertingly, he offers such impotent Peeping Toms as prototypes of the American artist.

The metaphor of the trapped spectator is a kindlier one than that of the Peeping Tom, but it describes the same kind of peripheral observer, who is reborn in the form of James's Lambert Strether in *The Ambassadors*. Though the remote original of his character was William Dean Howells, James refused in the end to make him an artist, even a *poète manqué* like Coverdale. "I can't make him a novelist—too like W.D.H.," he wrote to himself. ". . . But I want him 'intellectual' . . . fine, clever, literary almost: it deepens the irony, the tragedy. The Editor of a Magazine—that would come nearest. . . ." A good deal of Howells remains, nonetheless, and even a judgment on Howells; for the "happy ending" of *The Ambassadors* is one of the saddest in all our literature, leaving us with the heartbreaking image of Strether as the man who *sees* everything but can do nothing, understands everything but can possess nothing.

James is not quite candid, however, insisting that Strether's choice of impotence is a willed, a moral act, and that his very voyeurism is insight and "vision." Miss Gostrey, however, is not deceived. When she asks Strether quite directly whether he will not remain in Europe, not take his reward, not, in effect, take her—Strether answers that to be right he must "not, not out of the whole affair . . . have got anything" for himself except "wonderful impressions," which is to say, thrilling peeps into reality. "It's you

who would make me wrong," he tells Maria Gostrey; but she protests, "It isn't so much your *being* 'right'—it's your horrible sharp
eye for what makes you so." But Strether is really nothing but that
"horrible sharp eye," which is his sole organ of morality; and, in
this sense at least, he is his own author: less Howells than Henry
James who began with "pedestrian gaping" along Broadway, and
remained always the big-eyed child, imagining "the probable taste
of the bright compound wistfully watched in the confectioner's
window, unattainable, impossible. . . ." It is this James who invents the technique of the "center of consciousness," i.e., a device
for making the peeper the focus of a work of art, and who insists
that "art deals with what we see." It is only in the work of art
that James, like Coverdale before him, can possess symbolically
what in reality he cannot touch; and of his very limitations he
makes the form and substance of his fiction, which is not, as he
liked to boast, "felt life" so much as *"seen"* life."

For all his subtlety and tact, James is basically, hopelessly innocent, an innocent voyeur, which is to say, a child! And he is, indeed, the first novelist to do in full consciousness what Twain in
Huckleberry Finn did just once unawares: present the complexities
of adult experience as perceived by a pre-adolescent mind. The
child character, made compulsory in our books by the restrictions
of gentility and the fear of sex, is first used in *What Maisie Knew*
to confront rather than evade experience. James's novel, like the
later books which follow its pattern, is a kind of initiation story,
though it deals not with a full-scale initiation from innocence to
maturity but with a quasi initiation that ends in a withdrawal. In
the Jamesian version of the Fall of Man, at any rate, there are four
actors, not three: the man, the woman, the serpent, and the child,
presumably watching from behind the tree.

The Peeping Child is only a junior version of the Peeping Tom
as pallid poet or aging editor of a magazine; but it has had a special appeal to the American imagination. In *What Maisie Knew,*
James not only invents the fable, but sets the technique for presenting it; and, indeed, the vicarious ocular initiation presupposes the
convention of controlled point of view. Once James has shown
how to do it, novelist after novelist sets himself to portraying the
corrupt world as reflected in the innocent eye. Eye to the crack in
the door, ear attuned from the bed where he presumably sleeps—
curious or at idle play, the innocent observer stumbles upon the

murderer bent over the corpse, the guilty lovers in each other's arms, the idolized jockey in a whorehouse, a slattern on his knee, and, like the boy in Sherwood Anderson's story, is left, crying, "What did he do it for? I want to know why."

The end of innocence via the ocular initiation is bafflement and nausea; beyond the cry of the kid at the window, it is hard to imagine a real acceptance of adult life and sexuality, hard to conceive of anything but continuing flight or self-destruction. This many American writers besides Anderson see quite clearly; Faulkner, for instance, presents a similar insight, though with a brutality and terror beside which Anderson's sentimentality is revealed in all its inadequacy. Quentin Compson, who has watched as a child an adult drama of passion and death in "That Evening Sun Go Down," relives it as an adolescent witness and peripheral actor in *The Sound and the Fury* and *Absalom, Absalom!;* then dies by his own hand on the verge of manhood, refusing to step over the mystic barrier of twenty-one. Joe Christmas, in *Light in August,* on the other hand, manages to reach the age of Christ at the crucifixion, even after his induction into nausea at the age of five. But at fourteen, he cruelly kicks the naked black girl upon whom he might have lost his virginity; and at thirty-three, decapitates the aging woman who has made him her lover, thus assuring his own eventual lynching. Impotence and sadist aggression, suicide direct or indirect; it is not only to Faulkner that these seem the choices for an American whose imagination is fixed forever on one of the two major crises of pre-adolescent emotional life. Yet it is around these crises that our literature compulsively circles: the stumbling on the primal scene, mother and father caught in the sexual act (or less dramatically, the inference of that scene from creaking springs and ambiguous cries); or the discovery of heterosexual "treachery" on the part of some crush, idolized in innocent homosexual adoration.

In our time, the subterfuges which have traditionally concealed from author and audience alike the true nature of the castrated peeper are no longer necessary. By 1926, it was possible for Hemingway in *The Sun Also Rises* (and thirty years later, even a movie version could make the point unequivocally—though not without some show of daring) to portray an emasculated Jake Barnes, all of whose desperate clutching of Brett creates between them a friction which only erodes, never sparks to life. To be sure, Hemingway tells us that it is "the War" which has afflicted

Jake with the absurd wound which he examines in the mirror of his lonely room; but "the War" is merely a convenient tag for the failure of values and faith which converted a generation of young American writers to self-hatred, bravado, and expatriation. The same forces, at any rate, which have "emancipated" Brett have unmanned Jake; forced him into the role not only of witness to Brett's love affairs, but of pimp as well—setter-up of scenes which, beheld or imagined, can only drive him to queasy despair. From the time of Hemingway, impotence has been a central symbol in our fiction, a felt clue to the quality of American life, erotic and spiritual.

Faulkner, who is Hemingway's contemporary and admirer, has exploited the same theme, conceiving as eunuchs both Flem Snopes, symbol of the new bourgeoisie, the sterile lover of money, and Popeye, the spawn of urban alleys, Prohibition, and the hysteria of the Great Depression. The self-pity, which in Hawthorne, James, and even Hemingway has softened the horror of the portrait of the American as impotent voyeur, the insistence that, for better or worse, he is an intellectual, "one of us"— disappears in *Sanctuary*. The dreadfully intelligent eye of Strether has become the absurd and moronic stare which the name Popeye implies; and it looks not out of the face of a gentleman, but from the rat's face (when he watches her in the barn, Popeye seems to Temple one of the smaller rodents) of a killer. He is the ultimate, as he is the most revolting, avatar of the desexed seducer, but he is also a terrible caricature of the child witness, not like Peter Pan one who chooses not to grow up, but one who cannot. "And he will never be a man properly speaking," a doctor says of Popeye when he is five, ". . . he will never be any older than he is now."

When Popeye leans over the bed in Madame Reba's whorehouse, watching Temple Drake perform the act of darkness of which he is incapable ("the two of them would be nekkid as two snakes, and Popeye hanging over the foot of the bed without even his hat off, making a kind of whinnying sound"), he is projecting a brutal travesty of the American artist, helpless and fascinated before the fact of genital love. Similarly, in that other central "love" scene, in which Popeye rapes Temple with the corncob, Faulkner is parodying his own blasphemy of the Pale Protestant Virgin—portraying the hysterical masculine protest of his time in the image of the maimed male, revenging himself on woman who has maimed him with the first instrument that comes to hand, a weapon in place of the phallus.

But he is revealing, too, the secret of the descendants of Natty Bumppo in popular literature: those cowboys, for instance, who ride off into the sunset leaving the girls they have rescued behind; and they have been postulated as virile without sexuality, their only weapons (like Popeye's) in their hands, for only thus can they be imagined as representing the innocence of the West. The taboo that separates them from the women they preserve is so unself-consciously accepted, so widely known, that a television comedian can set the nation to laughing with a quip about the unconventional cowboy who insisted on kissing the girl in the last scene and was trampled to death by his jealous horse.

But just as Natty became with the westward expansion a cow-puncher, with the retreat from the frontier, he was urbanized into the image of the private detective, called—in the language of that literature itself—the "private eye," the peeper institutionalized at last. Through the corrupt city, the innocent tough guy who finally sees all, though he is slugged, doped, sapped, shot at, and bribed on the way to his vision, moves on an immaculate journey. The undraped daughters of the rich, tight-breasted virgins and nympho-maniac night-club entertainers, tempt him with their proffered bodies; but he is faithful only to his buddies, and like Lambert Strether, to "what is right."

In a typical gesture, the shamus of *The Maltese Falcon* (1930) sends the sexually attractive woman who loves him off to jail; but even this rejection is finally not decisive enough. From Dashiell Hammett, the private eye is passed on to Raymond Chandler and from him to Mickey Spillane, who recreates him at last for the ultimate audience—the readers of pocket-books, who put down their quarters in millions in search of myths more appropriate to their lives than those of high literature. In Spillane's Mike Hammer, Faulkner's Popeye is reborn as a culture hero, a chevalier of the city streets, blasting down the female he never manages quite to possess, and who, dead in one book, rises up in the next, phallic and aggressive, deadly whether clothed or nude. "She was a beautiful evil goddess with a gun in her hand," he writes in *The Big Kill* of Marsha, who lies dead a moment later, shot by the kid she has spurned and wounded: "the tongue of flame that blasted from the muzzle seemed to lick out across the room with a horrible vengeance that ripped all evil from her face, turning it into a ghastly wet red mask that was really no face at all." The climax of *Vengeance Is Mine,* however, is really more satisfactory, since it is Mike Hammer himself who does the shooting, and he blasts not the face of the goddess but the naked body of a luscious blonde, making the only penetration possible to the cripple of love with the slug of a .45.

III

When the Hawthorne-James-Faulkner gambit is refused and the American writer does not make impotence itself his subject, he is left to choose between the two archetypes of innocent homosexuality and unconsummated incest: the love of comrades and that of brother and sister. From his trip to Europe, undertaken just after he had finished *Moby Dick,* Melville brought back with him not only the oleograph reproduction of Guido Reni's "Beatrice Cenci" mentioned earlier but also a life-long memory of the relief sculpture of Antinoüs, favorite boy of the Emperor Hadrian, a work of art ("head like moss-rose with curls and buds —rest all simplicity") then on display in the Villa Albani. He returned, that is to say, from his cultural pilgrimage with an icon of incest justified and of homosexuality glorified, in memory of which it is perhaps fair to call the themes we have been describing the Antinoüs archetype and the Cenci archetype.

Both themes are juvenile and regressive, that is, narcissistic; for where woman is felt to be a feared and forbidden other, the only legitimate beloved is the self. Pure narcissism cannot, however, provide the dream and tension proper to a novel; the mirror-image of the self is translated in the American novel either into the flesh of one's flesh, the sister as *anima;* or into the comrade of one's own sex, the buddy as *anima.* Certainly, Melville's greatest work is essentially an account, as he himself hints, of "Narcissus, who because he could not grasp the tormenting, mild image he saw in the fountain, plunged into it and was drowned": but the alter ego of Narcissus-Ishmael is projected as the Polynesian cannibal, Queequeg, in whom the seeker in quest of his own "tormenting, mild image" finds a genuine other. Marriage to a woman would have seemed to Melville's hero intolerable; only through a pure wedding of male to male could he project an engagement with life which did not betray the self.

This is an alternative deeply appealing to the American mind and essentially congenial to the American experience. If one considers the series of distinguished fictions which begins with Cooper's Leatherstocking Tales and passes through Poe's *Narrative of A. Gordon Pym* (as well as his abortive *Journal of Julius Rodman*), Dana's *Two Years Before the Mast,* Melville's whole body of work culminating in *Moby Dick,* Twain's *Huckleberry Finn* and Henry James's "The Great Good Place," and is refurbished in our own time in such works as Faulkner's "The Bear" as well as Hemingway's *The Sun Also Rises* and *The Old Man and the Sea,* it is evident that there is an archetype at work, a model story, appearing and reappearing in a score of guises, haunting almost all our major writers of fiction.

What is hard to understand at first is why middle-class readers were not appalled at the implications of the homoerotic* fable, opposed as it is to almost everything in which middle-class society pretends to believe. Only by assuming an unconscious marginal rejection of the values of that society on the part of all or most of its members can we come to terms with its glorification of a long line of heroes in flight from woman and home. Cooper's Natty flees the settlements and the prospect of marriage with squaw or pale-face maiden; Melville's Ishmael rejects his cruel stepmother and the whole world of security she represents; Poe's Gordon Pym deceives and defies his family to go to sea; Twain's Huck evades all the women who try, with rigor or gentleness, to redeem his orphaned state; James's Dane flees from his social commitments to ladies and ladies' luncheons. None of these protagonists, moreover, manages to disown all female ties without seeming to reject life itself. "Whenever it is a damp, drizzly November in my soul," Ishmael remarks, "then, I account it high time to get to sea as soon as I can. This is my substitute for pistol and ball. With a philosophical flourish Cato throws himself upon his sword; I quietly take to ship."

Yet for a man to love death is not nearly so suspect in bourgeois America as for him to love another man; and in all the classic American books we have been examining, there are hints of such

---

* "Homoerotic" is a word of which I was never very fond, and which I like even less now. But I wanted it to be quite clear that I was not attributing sodomy to certain literary characters or their authors, and so I avoided when I could the more disturbing word "homosexual." All my care has done little good, however, since what I have to say on this score has been at once the best remembered and most grossly misunderstood section of my book. *Ubi morbus, ibi digitus.*

a love: in some, buried deep beneath the ken of the authors themselves, in others moving just beneath a transparent surface. How could Antinoüs come to preside over the literature of the nineteenth-century United States, which is to say, at a time and in a place where homosexuality was regarded with a horror perhaps unmatched elsewhere and ever? Certainly, in the popular literature of the period, the "sissy," the effeminate boy, nearest thing to a fairy mentionable in polite books, was a target upon which the fury of a self-conscious masculinity vented itself with especial venom. In the long run, however, so violent a disavowal of male inversion fostered an ignorance of its true nature; the "sin" or "crime" of homosexuality was conceived only in the grossest physical terms, so that a love as abstract and unconsummated as Dante's for Beatrice (or Shakespeare's for his aristocratic boy!) seemed unexceptionable to the most genteel. Mothers, indeed, rejoiced at "harmless" romantic attachments between their sons, conceiving of them as protections against the lure of the flesh, which might lead to venereal diseases or the impregnation of quite undesirable lower-class girls. Even in the minds of women, that is to say, "evil love" could only be conceived of in connection with "evil women," and the relations of males seemed therefore healthy by definition. Indeed, to this very day, anyone who suggests that such relations are occasionally at least ambiguous is regarded as a disturber of the peace, a public enemy.

In our native mythology, the tie between male and male is not only considered innocent, it is taken for the very symbol of innocence itself; * for it is imagined as the only institutional bond in a paradisal world in which there are no (heterosexual) marriages or giving in marriage. Paradisal, however, means for hardheaded Americans not quite real; and there is, in fact, a certain sense of make-believe in almost all portrayals of the holy mar-

---

* Things have changed radically in this regard, however. When the traditional sentimental relationship of white man and colored is evoked these days, it is likely to be quite the opposite of innocent, as the following passage from James Purdy's *Cabot Wright Begins* spectacularly indicates: "Taking Winters Hart's left hand in his, Bernie held his friend's dark finger on which he wore a wedding-ring, and pressed the finger and the hand. Far from being annoyed at this liberty, Winters Hart was, to tell the truth, relieved and pleased. Isolation in a racial democracy, as he was to tell Bernie later that night, as they lay in Bernie's bed together, isolation, no thank you."

riage of males, set as they typically are in the past, the wilderness, or at sea—that is to say, in worlds familiar to most readers in dreams. After Mark Twain, one of the partners to such a union is typically conceived of as a child, thus inviting the reader to identify the Great Good Place where the union is consummated with his own childhood, a region more remote and less real to the grown man than the dimmest reaches of pre-history. It is Stephen Crane who finds the proper name for that Neverland, calling it "Whilomville," which is to say a town which never had an "is" but only a half-recalled, half-invented "was." Everywhere in our classic fiction—in Cooper's use of the historical past, in Melville's evocation of his own receding youth, in Twain's or Faulkner's reversion to a rural boyhood, there is implicit a suggestion that the Edenic affair is lived out in a Garden in the process of being destroyed. The sound of axes is heard; the trees fall; the ground is broken for factories and stores; and the reader feels that he is being asked to recreate in fantasy a place to which neither he nor the author can ever return—the "home" to which the American writer complains he cannot go back again.

In our classic fiction, the heroes of such attempts at evasion are shown, at their stories' close, remanded to the world of reality. Ishmael, "alone escaped alive," comes back to tell his tale, Gordon Pym to write down his authentic account of adventure, Huck Finn to take another whirl at being civilized. Though he is already speaking of his next escape, even the motherless boy is last presented at the moment of his restitution to the society of women. Henry James, too sophisticated to equivocate about the reality of the Great Good Place, portrays his hero as awaking from a simple dream, from a twelve-hour sleep. Natty alone is never portrayed outside the universe of fantasy; pursuing the elusive West to the very end, he makes of his death the ultimate escape, for which his later avatars yearn but which they can never seem quite to attain. Those others act out not a permanent removal from the society which irks them, but an outing, a long excursion. Tom Sawyer's career as a pirate parodies the dream to which his author subscribed, gives the whole game away: the vows of eternal alienation and the message to Aunt Polly concealed in a pocket all the time: "We ain't dead—we are only off being pirates."

Perhaps it is this sense of make-believe which redeems so

subversive a theme for the most genteel and diffident reader. It represents a projection, entertained *without final faith,* of a way of life hostile to the accepted standards of the American community: a counter-family that can only flourish in a world without women or churches or decency or hard work, living what one is tempted to call "life with father," or, more precisely, "life with foster-father." Such terms seem to hold up well enough, superficially at least, in describing the erotic tie at the heart of *Huckleberry Finn,* for instance, or those in fictions like Faulkner's "The Bear" and *Intruder in the Dust,* as well as in certain stories by Stephen Crane and Sherwood Anderson. In these fictions, a small boy is represented as turning to a colored foster-father in revulsion from a real father, felt as brutal or ineffectual or effete; or he is portrayed as seeking out the dark-skinned, outcast male in an attempt to escape the mothers of his world, who are wholly committed to respectable codes of piety and success.

Such a reading, however, only seems satisfactory if we set a book like Mark Twain's in the context of a popular tradition which falsifies him even as it derives from him: the vulgarized juvenile, which descends by way of Stephen Crane's *Whilomville Stories* to the heavy-handed cuteness of Booth Tarkington's *Penrod.* In that middlebrow line of descent, the filial relationship of Negro and child is transformed into the stereotype which William Lyon Phelps describes condescendingly in a foreword to Crane's tales of childhood: "Little children and big Africans make ideal companions, for the latter have the patience, inner sympathy, forbearance, and unfailing good humor necessary to such an association. Both Stephen Crane and Booth Tarkington have given us permanent drawings in black and white." Twain's treatment of Jim in *Huckleberry Finn* is, however, complex enough to preserve him from becoming a merely stereotypical darkie; and that very complexity makes it impossible to describe him as just a substitute father. Sometimes he seems more servant than father, sometimes more lover than servant, sometimes more mother than either! His relationship with Huck must be seen not against the later sentimental tradition of "little children and big Africans," but against an earlier tradition of more nearly coeval loving pairs like Natty and Chingachgook, Gordon Pym and Dirk Peters, Ishmael and Queequeg. In Jim, Huck finds the pure affection offered by Mary Jane without the threat of marriage; the escape from social obligations offered

by Pap without the threat of beatings; the protection and pet-
ting offered by his volunteer foster-mothers without the threat
of pious conformity; the male companionship offered by the
Grangerfords without the threat of the combat of honor; the
friendship offered by Tom without the everlasting rhetoric and
make-believe. Jim is all things to him: father and mother and
playmate and beloved, appearing naked and begowned and be-
whiskered and painted blue, and calling Huck by the names
appropriate to their multiform relationship: "Huck" or "honey"
or "chile" or "boss," and just once "white genlman."

It is an impossible society which they constitute, the outcast
boy and the Negro, who, even for Huck, does not really exist
as a person: a society in which, momentarily, the irreparable
breach between black and white seems healed by love. Huck,
who offends no one else, begins by playing in Tom's company
a stupid joke on the sleeping Jim; then almost kills him as the
result of another heartless stunt; teases him to the point of tears
about the reality of their perils on the river; and finally joins
with Tom once more to inflict on Jim a hundred pointless torments, even putting his life in unnecessary danger. And through
it all, Jim plays the role of Uncle Tom, enduring everything,
suffering everything, forgiving everything—finally risking a lynching to save "Marse Tom's" life. It is the Southerner's dream,
the American dream of guilt remitted by the abused Negro, who,
like the abused mother, opens his arms crying, "Lawsy, I's
mighty glad to git you back agin, honey."

Only on the unstable surface of the river and in the dark of
night, can such a relationship exist, and its proper home is the
raft, which floats on the surge of flood-time into the story, a gift
from the non-Christian powers of Nature. "There warn't no home
like a raft, after all . . . ," Huck reflects. "You feel mighty free
and easy and comfortable on a raft." But the very essence of life
on a raft is unreality. "The motion of the raft is gentle, and
gliding, and smooth, and noiseless . . . ," Twain writes in *A Tramp
Abroad;* "under its restful influence . . . existence becomes a
dream . . . a deep and tranquil ecstasy." Yet the dream of life
on the river always threatens to turn for Twain into a nightmare.
In 1906, he comments on a recurring dream in which he was once
more piloting a boat down the Mississippi:

It is never a pleasant dream, either. I love to think about those
days, but there's always something sickening about the thought

. . . and usually in my dream I am just about to start into a
black shadow without being able to tell whether it is Selma
Bluff, or Hat Island, or just a black wall of night.

The idyll of Huck and Jim is a dream at whose heart lurks a
nightmare. All about them on the lawless river, crime is plotted
and violence done, while the river itself is ever ready to mislead
and destroy with fog or storm or snag. Thieves and murderers
seek the same avenue of escape which Huck and Jim follow in
domestic peace. And at last, in the persons of the Duke and
Dauphin, the evil of river life invades the raft itself. The floating
island paradise becomes an occupied country, a place where
absurd and sodden scoundrels hatch deceit and seek to avoid
retribution. There is no way to escape evil forever, no absolute
raft; and once the home of Huck and Jim has been invaded, they
cannot manage to establish their little Eden again. For a moment
after the fiasco at the Wilks', it seems as if Huck and Jim are
about to recapture their first freedom: "it *did* seem so good to be
free again and all by ourselves on the big river, and nobody to
bother us." But the King and Duke appear at the last minute, and
Huck collapses into despair: "it was all I could do to keep from
crying."

If one moves from a literal to a symbolic level, the difficulties
involved in reading Jim and Huck as father and son become even
greater. It is hard to think of a figure, union with whom signifies
a coming to terms with the natural and impulsive, as finally
paternal; much more suitable is the metaphor of the spouse. Only
marriage is a relationship complicated enough to stand for so
complicated and ambiguous a cluster of meanings; the search for
a parent, a master, a slave, an equal, a companion, a soul—a
union with one's deepest self which is simultaneously a rejection
of the community to which one was born. This Melville, at least,
most canny and conscious of all exploiters of this common theme,
realized with great clarity, working out the metaphor of the holy
marriage in great detail in the pages of *Moby Dick,* to which we
must turn for clues to what elsewhere remains confusing and
confused.

Three elements are necessary for the *hierogamos:* the longed-
for spouse, the questing lover, and the sacred setting. The setting,
though it is, of course, only another projection of the world of

instinct represented by the desired spouse, is of great symbolic importance. It is an Eden, to be sure, which is to say, a place out of time and history, as well as beyond the bounds of society; but it is a natural Eden, nature as Eden. Only in the mind of Henry James is that Great Good Place portrayed as an ordered and cultivated garden, though even for him it provides a vantage point from which one can look out "over a long valley to a far horizon," like some "old Italian picture." More typically, it is portrayed as a camp-site in the wilderness, a raft floating down the river, an isolated valley on a South Sea island, a lonely wood sought as a refuge from combat, a ship on the open sea. What it cannot be is city or village, hearth or home; for isolation is the key, the non-presence of the customary—in the words of Henry James, "the absence of what he didn't want." And what "he" especially does not want is *women!*

In America, the earthly paradise for men only is associated, for obvious historical reasons, with the "West"; and it is possible to regard the classic works which he have been discussing, in this sense, as "Westerns." Despite certain superficial differences, they are, indeed, all closely related to the pulp stories, the comic-books, movies, and TV shows, in which the cowhand and his side-kick ride in silent communion through a wilderness of sagebrush, rocks, and tumbleweed. The Western, understood in this way, does not even require an American setting, being reborn, for instance, in Hemingway's *The Sun Also Rises* in the improbable environs of Paris and Burguete. One must not be confused by the exotica of expatriation: bullfights, French whores, and *thés dansants*. Like the American East, Paris in Hemingway's book stands for the world of women and work, for "civilization" with all its moral complexity, and it is presided over quite properly by the bitch-goddess Brett Ashley. The mountains of Spain, on the other hand, represent the West: a world of male companions and sport, an anti-civilization, simple and joyous, whose presiding genius is that scarcely articulate arch-buddy, "good, old Bill."

For Hemingway there are many Wests, from Switzerland to Africa; but the mountains of Spain are inextricably associated in his mind with the authentic American West, with Montana whose very name is the Spanish word for the mountains that make of both isolated fastnesses holy places. It is in the Hotel Montana that Lady Ashley ends up after her abortive romance with the bullfighter Romero; and it is from the University of Montana that

Robert Jordan, hero of *For Whom the Bell Tolls,* takes off to the Spanish Civil War. But it is not only a pun that binds together for Hemingway his two paradisal retreats; it is also the sacred sport of fishing. Though the monastery of Roncesvalles stands on a peak high above Jake's place of refuge, it serves only to remind Hemingway's characters of a religion now lapsed for them. "It's a remarkable place," one of them says of the monastery; but Bill, the good companion, observes mournfully, "It isn't the same as fishing, is it?"

It is in the trout stream of Burguete that Jake and Bill immerse themselves and are made whole again and clean; for that stream links back to the rivers of Hemingway's youth, the rivers of upper Michigan, whose mythical source is the Mississippi of Tom Sawyer and Huck Finn. "We stayed five days at Burguete and had good fishing. The nights were cold and the days were hot. . . . It was hot enough so that it felt good to wade in the cold stream, and the sun dried you when you came out. . . ." They are boys again, back on Jackson's Island, which is to say, safe in the Neverland of men without women. Jake is, in his quest for the Great Good Place, at one with almost all the other heroes of Hemingway; though somehow it is he who has managed to find again the magical stream of which the wounded, half-mad *tenente* in "Now I Lay Me" can only dream: "I would think of a trout stream I had fished along when I was a boy and fish its whole length carefully in my mind. . . . But some nights I could not fish, and on those nights I was cold-awake and said my prayers over and over. . . ."

In the double-barreled story, "Big Two-Hearted River," it is impossible to tell whether the hero (called Nick this time) is moving through reality or fantasy. We can know only that he has returned, or dreams he has returned, once more to the River that is always different and always the same; and that this time he fishes it inch by inch to the edge of the tragic swamp which he will not enter. This time there is no question of choosing between fishing and praying; fishing has become clearly a prayer, or at least a ritual, in the midst of which a disguised prayer is uttered in the guise of a childish epithet. "Chrise," Nick says at one point, when he knows he is at last really *there,* "Geezus Chrise," and Hemingway tells us he says it "happily." In the dreams of the River both in "Now I Lay Me" and "Big Two-Hearted River," however, the Hemingway hero imagines himself alone; in *The Sun Also Rises,* a second self is with him, a companion to share the inarticulate sentimentality that becomes finally too embarrassing to bear, bursting with pure masculine love. " 'Old Bill' I said. 'You bum!' " And when the time for parting comes, when the bluff, immaculate honeymoon is over, when the telegram arrives to announce that the outsiders are coming, Brett and Cohen, woman and Jew, it is a third fisherman, an Englishman called Harris, who blurts out in his drunkenness what neither Jake nor Bill can quite confess: "I've not had so much fun since the war. . . . We *have* had a good time."

What Hemingway's emphasis on the ritual murder of fish conceals is that it is not so much the sport as the occasion for immersion which is essential to the holy marriage of males. Water is the symbol of the barrier between the Great Good Place and the busy world of women; and everywhere in our fiction, the masculine paradise is laved by great rivers or the vast ocean, washed by the ripples of Lake Glimmerglass or the spume of Glens Falls, even— in Poe—drowned, swallowed up in a liquid white avalanche: "and now we rushed into the embraces of the cataract, where a chasm threw itself open to receive us." Not only in chronicles of shipwreck like *Gordon Pym* or *Moby Dick,* but even in so mild an account of masculine evasion as James's "The Great Good Place," the metaphor of a descent into the waters prevails; though to be sure, in the case of James we are reminded of the bathtub or hydrotherapy rather than a plunge into the maelstrom: "He didn't want, for a time, anything but just to *be* there, to steep in the bath. He was in the bath yet, the broad deep bath of stillness. They sat in it together now with the water up to their chins. . . . He had been sunk that way before, sunk . . . in another flood. . . . *This* was a curtain so slow and tepid that one floated practically without motion and without chill."

To descend into the charmed waters where one can float "practically without motion" is, in effect, to die; and the flight to the watery world is a kind of suicide, a quietus self-imposed. Melville, in whom much that is elsewhere implicit is made explicit, makes it clear that the land is the realm of the super-ego, the water that of the id; and he at least does not hesitate long between them. Like Bulkington, the supernumerary hero of *Moby Dick,* he turns his own back on the "leeward land": "The port would fain give succor; the port is pitiful; in the port is safety, comfort, hearthstone, supper, warm blankets, friends, all that's kind to our mortalities. . . . But in landlessness alone resides the highest truth, shoreless, indefinite as God—so better is it to perish in that howling infinite, than to be ingloriously dashed upon the lee, even if it were safety."

Better death than castration, articulate Melville cries; but he does not foresee death as inevitable for the man who plunges into the "all-subduing" element, the shoreless wastes of his own unconsciousness. What seems a suicide may be in the end a baptism and a transfiguration, an immersion and a resurrection. "Take heart, take heart, O Bulkington . . . ," Melville writes at the close of the "six-inch chapter" which he calls Bulkington's "stoneless grave"; "Up from the spray of thy ocean-perishing—straight up, leaps thy apotheosis!" So (in gentle parody) Tom Sawyer is resurrected after "drowning," while Huck, presumably slaughtered like a pig, takes the plunge and lives again; so Ishmael, drawn into the ocean whirlpool, or Gordon Pym, sucked into the chasm beneath the cataract, emerge unscathed to write gospel accounts of their survival. The picnic, the day's outing from which the male fugitive returns, is also a watery grave; and though, like the Ancient Mariner, the survivor lives on chiefly to tell his tale, he returns purged and guiltless.

In fact, only he is guiltless in our world; for—our classical novelists believe with Shakespeare—no man born of woman is innocent enough to combat evil without being converted into its image. Each must be born again, the second time not of the murky flood of blood, amniotic fluid, and milk which characterizes female gestation, but out of the immaculate flux of waters which characterizes a birth into the world of men without women. A new birth implies a new family, a wifeless and motherless one, in which the good companion is the spouse and nurse, the redeemed male the lover and child, each his own progenitor and offspring. The disgust of the American male at our original birth is most clearly and passionately expressed in Melville's sketch called "The Tartarus of Maids." In this extraordinary piece, Melville describes the processes of natural gestation (to him a mechanical and brutal function) from inside, as it were—in terms of a guided tour through a paper mill. Proceeding from a "large bespattered place, with two great round vats in it, full of a wet, weedy-looking stuff, not unlike the albuminous part of an egg" into a "room, stifling with a strange, blood-like, abdominal heat," he beholds at last the end product of a process which takes "nine minutes to the second": "suddenly, I saw a sort of paper-fall, not wholly unlike a water-fall; a scissory sound smote my ears, as of some cord being snapped; and down dropped an unfolded sheet of perfect foolscap, with my 'Cupid' half faded out of it, and still moist and warm . . . here was the end of the machine." To convert into "royal sheets" the "imperfect foolscap" produced by a female machine, which is powered by the fall of "Blood River" through what Melville calls the "Black Notch," is no easy task. They must either be reimmersed, as we have seen, in the waters of life which seem those of death, or else be dipped into an altogether alien bloodstream.

The alternative to immersion and rebirth is the baptism in the blood of a beast. Quite often, indeed, the holy marriage is sanctified by the ritual killing of a totem, the ram offered in the place of Isaac; though in the American version of the fable of sacrifice it is Isaac who kills the beast, becomes his own father at the moment of killing him, while the colored mother-midwife-beloved stands by as witness. From Natty Bumppo's first deer to the buck whose shooting by young Ike McCaslin is described in Faulkner's "Delta Autumn," such doomed animals play a leading role in American fiction. When Ike is smeared with the blood of his victim by Sam Fathers, half-Indian, half-Negro ("and Sam dipped his hands into the hot blood and marked his face forever while he stood trying not to tremble"), even the scarcely literate can understand the ritual that is being performed. Indeed, with the expulsion of sex from polite novels and the consequent demotion of the hero to childhood, such outdoor stories became a staple of middlebrow literature. In the forest rather than brothel or bedroom, through murder rather than sex, the child enters manhood, trembles with nausea over the broken bird or lifeless rabbit rather than the spread-eagled whore.

In our more serious fictions, from *Moby Dick* to Faulkner's "The Bear" or Hemingway's *The Old Man and the Sea,* such tales are redeemed from sentimentality by making of the animals involved not mere occasions for the loss of virginity but monstrous embodiments of the natural world in all its ambiguous and indestructible essence. Either, like Moby Dick, such totemic beasts are ubiquitous and immortal; or, like Big Ben, the bear of Faulkner's story, they cannot be destroyed until "the last day"; or, like the giant swordfish of *The Old Man and the Sea,* they cannot be brought back as trophies. They are sacred embodiments of power, taboo objects whose death is a blasphemy if it it not a rite. Behind all such tales echoes the reproach of God to Job: "Canst thou catch Leviathan with a hook!" and their guilt-ridden protagonists regret the violence they enact even as they enact it. It is the boast of the young Isaac McCaslin and his hunting companions that they go to the woods once a year "not to hunt bear and deer but to keep yearly rendezvous with the bear which they did not even intend to kill." Yet *finally* the bear dies as lesser bears have died before him, the whale is harpooned and stripped, the swordfish mounted above the fireplace, and (as was foretold) the innocent world ends; for Ishmael and Ike McCaslin live, after all, in America, where the way is opened for the rape of nature by the pioneers who come to it in love and in search of communion. At any moment, the pure huntsman may find himself transformed into his anti-image, the Faustian man—Captain Ahab, who thrusts at the unfallen world not in reverence but in rage.

But worse is yet to come—for after the tragic betrayal, the comic anti-climax follows fast. Natty Bumppo gives way to the bounty-hunter, to Buffalo Bill; and Buffalo Bill is followed by the dude with pack animal and guide and whisky bottle, playing Indian and fleeing his wife! The real end of the flight to the forest never changes, only the equipment and the ideological justification. Like the dude who emulates him, the hero did not go out alone to encounter the spirit of the wilderness—but traveled always with a companion and guide; and like the hero, the dude still hunts some excuse to justify the ideal community of buddies isolated from the world, pursues the "primitive area," in which alone such a community can survive.

IV

But who are these good companions in their archetypal reality, as dreamed by our greatest writers rather than travestied by our poor selves?

The questing lover is, in general, a surrogate for the artist, the articulate man (Natty, grandfather of them all, is garrulous to a fault), whose tale is presented typically in the form of a first-person narrative, journal, diary, or running reminiscence: "And I only am escaped alone to tell thee." He is the artist projected as a pariah, an Ishmael—not *le grand écrivain américain,* which was, on occasion at least, as we have noticed, Cooper's conscious self-image. In Poe, for instance, Julius Rodman, the hero of his incomplete Western, is obviously intended to suggest the author; dwarfed, hypochondriac, oddly Semitic in appearance ("He was . . . not more than five feet three or four inches high . . . with legs somewhat bowed. . . . His physiognomy was of a Jewish cast . . ."), Rodman anticipates the westward trek of Lewis and Clark "urged solely by a desire to seek in the bosom of the wilderness, that peace which his peculiar disposition would not suffer him to enjoy among men."

It is Melville, however, who most consciously works out the figure of the fugitive-lover artist and gives him his generic name. In his series of portraits of the artist as outcast, he blends the Old Testament archetype of Hagar's unwanted son (Redburn is already called a "sort of Ishmael") with the figure of the taboo wanderer, about whom he had learned something during his sojourn in the islands of the South Pacific. Sometimes the rejected son is a merely comic character in Melville, a *schlemiel* with an absurd name, a ridiculous jacket, an outlandish vocabulary, and pretensions to gentility; but he is always threatening to take on tragic overtones. And often, indeed, he is mythicized into an almost divine presence, at once accursed and a source of blessing, Prometheus himself. The "I" of *Typee* is incapable of taking seriously his own godhead, but he has been renamed Tommo and started on the long road toward apotheosis; while the very title of Melville's next book, *Omoo*, is a Polynesian word for the untouchable Wanderer. In *Mardi*, the protagonist is not merely called Taji, another name for the taboo man, but is transformed into that semi-mythical figure. *Redburn* and *White Jacket*, intended potboilers, return to the comic version of the theme, qualifying its serious implications with a playful irony; but in *Moby Dick*, Ishmael takes on once again the full stature of the alienated man, though he enters the novel as a rather absurd greenhorn, apparently fitter for gags and pratfalls than the tragic illumination toward which he really moves.

Everywhere the figure of the Stranger moves through Melville's work: as the rich boy turned writer in *Pierre*, as the early avatars of the Confidence Man, as the exiled Israel Potter, as the ultimately alienated protagonist of "Bartleby the Scrivener," condemned to prison and madness and death. Snob, greenhorn, madman, *schlemiel*, god and exile: the Outsider has a score of forms in Melville's fiction, but he remains, in his various masquerades, always the artist, society's rejected son with his "splintered heart

and maddened hand . . . turned against the wolfish world." Though
Outsider, he is not alien; invariably a native white American in
Melville, he remains so as Twain's Huck and Faulkner's Ike
McCaslin and Hemingway's Nick Adams or Jake Barnes: lonelier
and lonelier in a country overrun by other stocks; "Chinese and
African and Aryan and Jew, all breed and spawn together until
no man has time to say which one is which nor cares. . . ."

Typically white and Anglo-Saxon (even Poe's Rodman turns
out really to have been "a native of England where his relatives
were of excellent standing"), the artist surrogate in the homoerotic Western is a disaffected child of the reigning race and class.
He is no late arrival, no member of a dusky or non-Aryan race
(when Saul Bellow re-imagined Huck Finn as a young Chicago
Jew in *The Adventures of Augie March,* scarcely any of his readers recognized the affiliation), but a renegade from respectability
and belongingness. He has cut himself out of the community that
bred him in a desire to embrace some alien shadow-figure symbolizing the instinctive life despised by his white, Anglo-Saxon
parents and his fated white, Anglo-Saxon wife.

But who is the alien helpmeet for him? There are various versions of the shadow-spouse in our literature, fumblings in various
directions toward the definition of a type symbolically appropriate;
but they finally cohere in a single image.

In the remote prototype of Irving, there is no single good companion but an indefinite group of European ghosts out of which
a single voice speaks the only word Rip Van Winkle hears—his
own name! In Melville, there are several attempts at portraying
the appropriate mate, from Toby, who is the narrator's companion
in the valley of the Typees, to the various avatars of Jack Chase,
the Handsome Sailor who appears in person in *White Jacket* and
who haunted Melville until the end of his life. The Sailor is represented by Bulkington in *Moby Dick* ("full six feet in height,
with noble shoulders, and a chest like a cofferdam . . ."), and
finally by Billy himself in *Billy Budd,* whose dedication recalls
in Melville's last days his first love: "To Jack Chase . . . Wherever
that great heart may now be . . ." But Billy is Jack Chase recast
in the image of Antinoüs ("head like moss-rose with curls and
buds"), so "welkin-eyed," angelic and beautiful that he threatens
to quite give away the homosexual secret he embodies. The first
Jack Chase is the idol of White Jacket, but more usually the love
which the Handsome Sailor stirs is more ambiguous, verges on

hatred and destruction. It is as if something in Melville himself, aware of what is from the conventional point of view dangerous in his yearning for his six-foot, Anglo-Saxon beauties, drove him to portray that yearning chiefly in dark parody; the relationship of Billy Budd and Claggart, who could have loved Billy "but for fate and ban."

Even outside his treatment of the Handsome Sailor theme, Melville turned on occasion to descriptions of such murderous and passionate relations between males. Steeling himself to kill his cousin and boyhood friend, thus insuring his own eventual death, Pierre cries out, "Oh Glen! Oh Fred! most fraternally do I leap to your rib-crushing hugs! Oh, how I love ye two, that yet can make me lively hate. . . ." And even the utterly hostile cohabitation of Benito Cereno and the slave Babo is an obscene parody of the intimate bond of lovers.

Melville is, of course, not alone among American writers in portraying such sinister relationships; and one of the most notable examples is to be found in the work of Hawthorne, whose own relation to Melville turned from an initial deep affection to coldness and distrust. Surely no loving tie is closer than the one established between Chillingworth and Dimmesdale in *The Scarlet Letter,* as the cuckold penetrates in icy intimacy his cuckolder's psyche. Hester, Chillingworth, and Dimmesdale stand to each other in that odd relationship which European critics call the unnatural triangle, in which two men are bound to each other through the woman they jointly possess, as they cannot "for fate and ban" possess each other.

In our own time, the unnatural triangle recurs in Saul Bellow's *The Victim* (1947), where it assumes a peculiarly American mutilated form, being, in effect, a triangle without an apex or with only a hypothetical one, which is to say, a triangle without a woman! Indeed, the whole of Bellow's work is singularly lacking in real or vivid female characters; where women are introduced, they appear as nympholeptic fantasies, peculiarly unconvincing. His true world is a world of men in boarding houses, men whose wives are ill, or have left them, or have gone off on vacation; and the deepest emotions he evokes are those which simultaneously join together and separate father and son, brother and sister, conman and victim. This holds true throughout the body of his work, from *Dangling Man* to *Seize the Day,* and is even seen, in a bizarre context, in *Henderson the Rain King,* in which Bellow actually returns (three times over) to the convention of the dark companion.* But in no book does the involvement of mates quivering between poles of attraction and repulsion take on a more crucial importance than it has in *The Victim*. Asa Leventhal, the hero of that novel, finds his lover-enemy Kirby Allbee in his very bed, but finds him there not with his wife but a casual whore. What binds the two men together is not the ambivalent tie of the cuckold and the cuckolder but of the Jew and anti-Semite. Bourgeois and bohemian, secure citizen and self-torturing bum, Semite and Anglo-Saxon, recent immigrant and old American—they are bound together by their manifold contrasts. Nothing renders them more "dependent for the food of spiritual life" upon each other than Allbee's indecent need for Jews to define his existence by defining a difference, or Leventhal's secret hunger for a hatred that can mark off the boundaries of his identity.

It is this realization on Bellow's part which differentiates his book from the host of righteous, liberal tract-novels about the problem of anti-Semitism, makes it a complex study of the deeper levels of life, on which the erotic and political fuse into a single passion, baffling but human. That passion is founded in a terrible physical intimacy which Bellow renders in terms of sheer nausea. "Leventhal . . . was so conscious of Allbee, so certain he was being scrutinized, that he was able to see himself as if through a strange pair of eyes: the side of his face, the palpitation of his throat, the seams of his skin. . . . Changed in this way into his own observer, he was able to see Allbee, too . . . the weave of his coat, his raggedly overgrown neck . . . the color of the blood on his ear; he could even evoke the odor of his hair and skin. The acuteness and intimacy of it astounded him, oppressed and intoxicated him." And when Allbee begs to touch Leventhal's hair—that alien, wiry, Jewish hair—actually reaches out and takes it in hand, the gesture is like a sexual assault; "He fingered

---

* With the publication of *Herzog*, Bellow has simultaneously entered the lists of best-sellers and embraced the subject matter of popular ladies' fiction (my best friend betrayed me with my wife); but Madeleine, the wife, seems a nightmare projection bred by baffled malice rather than a realized woman; and Herzog's passionate involvement with her remains, therefore, unconvincing. The most moving and credible relationship in the book is that between Herzog and his faithless friend, Valentine Gershbach, who turns out to be the most vital and believable human being created in the book. Bellow remains the laureate of such disturbing and ambiguous encounters.

Leventhal's hair, and Leventhal found himself under his touch and felt incapable of doing anything. But then he pushed his hand away, crying 'Lay off!' " After this, there is no climax possible except the "rib-crushing hug." Leventhal, the physical spell broken, drives the shoddy parasite out of his apartment by brute force. "Allbee fell back a few steps and, seizing a heavy glass ashtray, he aimed it menacingly. . . . Leventhal made a rush at him. . . . Pinning his arms, he wheeled him around and ran him into the vestibule. . . . The door, as Leventhal jerked it open, hit Allbee in the face. He did not resist. . . ." It is the consummation: an orgasm of violence, entailing a separation.

It is a long way from *Billy Budd* to *The Victim;* and by Bellow's time the Anglo-Saxon beauty, seedy and corrupt, has become the tormentor, while his swarthy opponent has taken on the sympathetic role. Melville is not yet ready to dissolve in irony the contrast of good blonde and evil brunette; as a matter of fact, his Billy is simply the Fair Maiden translated in sex—too much the Anglo-Saxon Virgin still to represent the dangerous and forbidden Eros which the good companion must embody. A *white* anti-bride will not in the long run really do: not the Good Bad Boys who accompany Tom Sawyer to Jackson's Island or their grown-up equivalent, the "old Bill" of *The Sun Also Rises,* not certainly the "Brother" of Henry James's "The Great Good Place," "a man of his own age, tired distinguished modest kind. . . ." In *Gordon Pym,* one can watch Poe learning as he goes that the Anglo-Saxon alter ego is no fit partner in the holy marriage of males, see how he abandons Pym's white shipmate, Augustus Bernard, to clear the way for the half-breed Dirk Peters. But the prototype had already been established by Cooper in the dusky figures of the Last Mohicans, father and son.

In dreams of white men, psychologists tell us, the forbidden erotic object tends to be represented by a colored man, such a figure as the "black pagod of a fellow," the "grand sculptured bull," "so intensely black that he must needs have been . . . of the unadulterable blood of Ham" whom Melville evokes for a moment at the beginning of *Billy Budd.* So in the communal American dream of love (beneath which lurks, for all the idyllic surface, a sense of trifling with taboos), the spouse of the pariah is properly of another race, a race suppressed and denied, even as the promptings of the libido are suppressed and denied. In the

Leatherstocking Tales, the anti-wife is the dispossessed Indian; in *Gordon Pym,* the half-mad breed; in *Huckleberry Finn*, the Negro slave; in *Moby Dick,* the uprooted Polynesian (even as in *Two Years Before the Mast,* which may have given Melville his cue); in Faulkner's "The Bear," the old man, half Chickasaw and half Negro. In Sam Fathers, "son of a Negro slave and a Chickasaw chief," one meaning of the dark skin is made clear; for his coloredness is taken as an ensign of kinship with the wilderness and the beasts who inhabit it. "Because there was," Faulkner writes, "something running in Sam Fathers' veins which ran in the veins of the buck too. . . ." Edenic nature, the totem, and the dark spouse: these are three symbols for the same thing—for the primitive world which lies beyond the margins of cities and beneath the lintel of consciousness.

V

Whatever the symbolic necessities which demand that the male *hierogamos* be inter-racial as well as homoerotic, that marriage takes on, by virtue of crossing conventional color lines, a sociological significance as well as a psychological and metaphysical one.* The elopement of the good companians comes, therefore, to stand for the healing of the social conflicts which most irk us, and before which we feel most powerless and baffled. Such a sociological extension of meaning by no means cancels out but rather enriches other, more profound significances and gives to them their peculiarly American form.

There is, of course, in the European novel—and even the drama, epic, and romance which precede the emergence of that genre—a tradition of the pseudo-marriage of males, stretching from, say, Don Quixote and Sancho Panza through Leporello and Don Juan, Robinson Crusoe and Friday to Pickwick and Sam Weller. *Robinson Crusoe,* in particular, seems to embody an

---

* Recently, we have grown more and more aware of how in the Civil Rights Movement the aspirations of Negroes for full freedom and the struggle of homosexuals to be accepted are oddly intermingled. And it is no use protesting (as Ralph Ellison has done, for instance) that they should be kept separate and pure. For better or for worse, they are mythically one in our deepest imaginations, as, indeed, James Baldwin has tried to make manifest—however shrilly and ineptly—in *Another Country*.

archetype much like that which haunts our classic fiction; and this is proper enough for a novel so bourgeois and Protestant that one is tempted to think of it as an American novel before the fact. The protagonists are not only black and white, but they exist on the archetypal island, cut off from the home community by the estranging sea. Cannibal and castaway, man-eater and journal-keeper, they learn to adjust to each other and to domesticity, on what is surely the most meager and puritanic Eden in all literature.

In *Robinson Crusoe,* however, the male relationship, even after shipwreck and abandonment, is kept rigidly within the European class-patterns of master and man. Within this convention (the Shakespearean convention, one wants to call it, for it is part of the basic symbolic structure of Shakespeare's work) the advocacy of the "natural" way of life is entrusted to the servant, and by virtue of that fact, clearly identified as inferior. The servant is, by definition, a comic character, who can never be taken quite seriously, never really understood as an ideological rival to his master. He can be cowardly, greedy, and carnal without stirring anything in us but smug condescension (cf. the role of the lazy, fearful tom-catting darkie in the popular arts up to the very present); he can eat flesh on Friday or loose his bowels over his horse in a moment of terror like Sancho Panza, for *nothing is at stake.* The servant may represent the protest of the unconscious against the ego ideals for which his master stands, but there is no equivocation about their relative rank or importance. To side with Leporello against Don Juan, Caliban against Prospero is unthinkable; and even Robinson Crusoe, good bourgeois that he is, teaches Friday "master" as his first word!

In America, however, we are a nation of Calibans and Lepo-rellos and Sancho Panzas—of "fugitive slaves." Europe is the master from which we have all fled. It is hard therefore for even the most class-conscious writer to keep his characters in their traditional places; Cooper himself, Tory-democrat that he is, proves incapable of defining Natty and Chingachgook in terms of a strict hierarchical relationship either to each other or to the "ladies and gentlemen," those supernumeraries in the plot who are presumably their betters. Melville, Twain, Faulkner, even a homemade dandy like Poe, quite frankly abandon the attempt. Who is the better man, Gordon Pym or Dirk Peters, Isaac Mc-Caslin or Sam Fathers, Huck or Nigger Jim, Ishmael or Queequeg? Though Jim is presumably a slave and calls even Huck a "young gentleman," the whole point of the work is that Jim is "free as any cretur." The rapid mobility of American social life, as well as its establishment by masterless men, makes it only too easy to conceive the relationship of instinct and ego, white and black, not as a tie between servant and master but as a marriage of equals.

Yet there are forces in our life, almost as profound and aboriginal, which work against such a concept. The Northern European white, blue-eyed stock which originally settled the United States, shabby as it was in its origins, soon set itself up as a ruling class eager to protect its hegemony and its purity, a purity especially identified with its pale, genteel women busy in schools and churches. The drama of an equal meeting and mating of Caucasian and colored men was remanded quite early to a mythical *state of nature,* or at least to the nearest equivalent of that state, the frontier, where trapper and Indian guide bedded down together. In the settlements, such equality could scarcely survive beside the facts of social organization: the Negro confined to his ghettos, the Indian harried and driven continually westward, the Polynesian sailor restricted to the waterfront city of cheap saloons and brothels.

There is an almost hysterical note to our insistence that the love of male and male does not compete with heterosexual passion but complements it; that it is not homosexuality in any crude meaning of the word, but a passionless passion, simple, utterly satisfying, yet immune to lust—physical only as a handshake is physical, this side of copulation. And yet we can never shake off the nagging awareness that there is at the sentimental center of our novels, where we are accustomed to find in their European counterparts "platonic" love or adultery, seduction, rape, or long-drawn-out flirtation, nothing but the love of males! What awaits us are the fugitive slave and the no-account boy side by side on a raft borne by the endless river toward an impossible escape; or the pariah sailor waking in the tattooed arms of the brown harpooner on the verge of some impossible quest. To emphasize the purity of such unions, the fact that they join soul to soul rather than body to body, they are typically contrasted with mere heterosexual passion, the dubious desire which threatens always to end in miscegenation. Yet, though such confrontations seem only to contrast the homoerotic and heterosexual ways of joining white and black, they suggest disconcertingly a general superiority of the love of man for man over the ignoble lust of man for woman.

It is for this reason, perhaps, that the colored rival of the wife is presented typically with the stigmata of something dangerous and disgusting as well as forbidden. Chingachgook wears a death's-head on his chest and a scalp at his belt, while Queequeg is horridly tattooed and bears with him a phallic god and shrunken head; even Jim, who possesses no particularly repulsive characteristics, makes his first appearance with his head muffled in a blanket—scaring Huck half to death—and is dyed, before the voyage is over, a sickening blue. The most monstrous of all the dark companions is Poe's hybrid Dirk Peters, who assumes in the course of Poe's description of him not only a bestial aspect but something of the appearance of a gnome or kobold, which is to say, the surviving image in the mind of *homo sapiens* of the stunted proto-men that they destroyed, the first dispossessed people, whose memory survives to haunt our fairy tales and nightmares. But the Neanderthal gnome is also the model for popular notions of "devils" or "demons," quite properly assimilated to the primordial figure that symbolizes our broken link with the animal world. For better or worse, the love-affair with the "Black Man" carries with it diabolic implications, hints of a union with infernal forces, as well as salvational overtones, promises of psychic redemption. And in *Moby Dick* Melville attempts to embody both in the two dark-skinned characters, supernumeraries in the action, who represent the polar aspects of the id, beneficent and destructive. The first is the Polynesian harpooner, Queequeg, whose relationship to Ishmael threatens to take over the entire book in its first portion; and the second is the Parsee, Fedallah, who is yoked to Ahab by a link as passionate, though quite different from that which joins the first two. The Parsee and the Polynesian are associated with two other representatives of the primitive, also harpooners, the Indian, Tashtego, and the African, Dagoo. Yellow, brown, red, and black, they seem, considered together, rather emblems than characters, signifying the four quarters of the globe and the four elements as well, for Dagoo is carefully identified with the earth, Tashtego with the air, the Parsee with fire, and Queequeg with water. Only Queequeg and Fedallah *thematically* matter, however, since they alone are used to represent the basic conflict which lies at the heart of the book, the struggle between love and death. Queequeg stands for the redemptive baptism of water (or sperm), and around him the "Western" or sentimental story which is one half of *Moby Dick* develops; while Fedallah stands for the destructive baptism of fire (or blood), and around him the gothic or Faustian romance which is its other half unfolds. But it is Queequeg who wins, though the two never meet face to face, Eros which triumphs over Thanatos.

Moby Dick can be read then not only as an account of a whale-hunt, but also as a love story, perhaps the greatest love story in our fiction, cast in the peculiar American form of innocent homosexuality. During 1851, the year in which he completed *Moby Dick,* Melville scored and underscored two passages, which he had come on in his current reading, and which must have seemed to him confirmations of his own deepest feelings. The first is from the *Maid's Tragedie* and runs:

> For aught I know, all husbands are like me;
> And every one I talk with of his wife,
> Is but a well dissembler of his woes
> As I am; would I knew it, for the rareness afflicts me now . . .

The second is picked out of the tale of David and Jonathan in Samuel II: "Thy love to me was wonderful, passing the love of women." Taken together, they define clearly enough what sort of love Melville would choose, what avoid to represent the force which conquers death; but the first indicates as well his uneasiness over his convictions, his fear that he may stand alone in preferring to the comforts of marriage the sentimental companionship of males.

In *Moby Dick,* the redemptive love of man and man is represented by the tie which binds Ishmael to Queequeg, while the commitment to death is portrayed in the link which joins Ahab to Fedallah; but the two relationships are disturbingly alike: both between males, one white and one colored. Indeed, the very darkness of Queequeg betrays a doubt about the angelic companion, oddly confuses him with the Satanic one. Melville is more conscious than he seems at first glance of the ambiguous nature of the love which he celebrates in *Moby Dick,* and which, beginning with the encounter of Ishmael and Queequeg, grows ever more general and inclusive, but never less suspect, as the story unfolds.

In Chapter XCIV, which is called "A Squeeze of the Hand," Ishmael is granted a final vision of the nature of love while he is busy with his shipmates squeezing the sperm of Stubb's whale. Though Melville is deliberately playing from the start with the double meaning of the word "sperm" (he comments on how "in old times sperm was such a favorite cosmetic," knowing well enough that it was semen not blubber which the medieval cosmeticians prized), the passage seems for a while an idyllic prose poem: "As I bathed my hands among the soft, gentle globules of infiltrated tissue . . . as they richly broke to my fingers . . . as I snuffed up that uncontaminated aroma . . . I forgot all about our horrible oath; in that inexpressible sperm, I washed my hands and heart of it. . . . I felt divinely free from all ill will or petulance or malice of any sort whatever. . . ." In sperm, that is to say, Ishmael has washed himself clean of the pledge to destroy and pursue, his implication in the blasphemous quest of Ahab; it is a counter-baptism to that of fire.

But the passage moves on to even more explicit and embarrassing erotic images, until at last (surely, not without a certain sly humor) Ishmael calls upon the whole world to perform a similar service of love: "nay, let us all squeeze ourselves into each other; let us squeeze ourselves universally into the very milk and sperm of kindness." Beyond this there is only the comic vision of the "angels in paradise, each with his hands in a jar of spermaceti," and an encyclopedic interlude, which prepares us for the following frankly phallic chapter, "The Cassock." The Cassock itself turns out to be the foreskin of the whale, and represents only the first of a series of allusions and puns, which, running through the brief chapter, play off against each other Christianity and male sexuality, the religion Melville rejected and the improbable place to which he turned in search of another.

The "unaccountable cone,—longer than a Kentuckian is tall," which is all that remains of the whale's phallus is associated in what seems a casual phrase ("and jet-black as Yojo, the ebony idol of Queequeg") with the love of Ishmael and the Polynesian harpooner. And we remember that before that image, Ishmael had salaamed twice or thrice, even kissed its nose, in the course of celebrating his holy marriage with Queequeg. The convocation of the two idolatries is deliberate, and both are identified with an even more abominable original by Ishmael's reference to what is "darkly set forth in the fifteenth chapter of the first book of Kings." The Biblical text to which Ishmael sends the reader deals with the rites practiced by the wicked Queen Maachah before just such a phallic idol, and makes a specific connection between those rites and sodomy: "And he took away the sodomites out of the land, and removed all the idols that his fathers had made." There is a certain playful contempt in this allusion, an assumption that the reader will not search out the reference or finding it not understand—any more than he will understand the crude anti-ecclesiastical pun with which the chapter ends. Ishmael has described how a section of the whale's foreskin is made into a garment for the "mincer," who cuts up the horse-pieces of blubber for the pots; and he stands back admiringly to look at him: "Arrayed in decent black; occupying a conspicuous pulpit; intent on bible leaves; what a candidate for an archbishoprick . . . !" There is something a little childish finally about the camouflaged anti-clerical bravado.

It will not do to sentimentalize or Christianize Melville's pagan concept of love. It is not *caritas* which he celebrates; and his symbol for the redeeming passion is Priapus rather than the cross. Perhaps it is least misleading to think of the love which redeems Ishmael as Platonic, in the authentic historical sense of the word. Rising from the particular object to the universal, it remains suspect nonetheless; for like the ideal Eros of *The Symposium,* it is grounded in a relationship unequivally rejected by the Judaeo-Christian tradition. Genteel or orthodox advocates of love should look hard at Melville's text before deciding to applaud the conquest of death he celebrates in *Moby Dick.* Yet it is love in the fullest sense which that book makes its center; not a brutal or casual relationship, but one which develops on the pattern of a marriage: achieving in the course of a single voyage the shape of a whole lifetime shared, and symbolizing a spiritual education.

Ishmael, who begins as a comic character, somewhat green, more than a little pedantic, everybody's butt, plays in the account of his meeting with Queequeg the role of the sacred virgin. He seems quite improbably, to have no notions during his last days ashore of picking up a woman, visiting a brothel, even getting drunk. Indeed, he is something of a prohibitionist, prissy as well as timid; and it takes all of his energy and spirit simply to find a bed for the night. Ishmael reacts just as his joking landlord had foreseen at his first glimpse of the barbaric fellow with whom he must share his bed. Everything about Queequeg appalls him: his tattooing, the shrunken head he carries about for sale, the ugly, black idol—and especially his great, glowing tomahawk pipe, half symbol of peace, half weapon of assault: "this wild cannibal, tomahawk between his teeth, sprang into bed beside me. I sang out . . . and giving a grunt of astonishment he began feeling me . . ." It is an inauspicious enough beginning, and the maidenly Ishmael is terrified: "I rolled away from him against the wall and . . . conjured him . . . to keep quiet and let me up."

"Coffin, Angels! save me!" Ishmael cries, appealing to the landlord and to the powers above. He does not yet know (though Melville perhaps does) that Queequeg is his dark angel, and that on Queequeg's coffin he will escape death at the book's close. He sees only that his tattooed and savage bedmate, like an enlightened spouse, immediately ceases his attack, rolls over and away from him as much as to say—"I won't touch a leg of ye . . ."; and what began in fright ends in security: "I never slept better in my life." During Ishmael's peaceful sleep, matters have developed, however; and he awakens in the harpooner's embrace: "I found Queequeg's arm thrown over me in the most loving and affectionate manner. You had almost thought I had been his wife. . . ." It is worth noting that Ishmael tends to think of himself in the passive, the feminine role; but even more critical is his immediate sense of their relationship as a *marriage,* which is to say, a permanent commitment: the sort of indissoluble union, which he, as a detached wanderer, has presumably been fleeing. To be sure, it all seems quite comic and unreal, this bedroom scene with a Polynesian sailor— only a gross parody of marriage; and Ishmael reflects ironically on "the unbecomingness of hugging a male in that matrimonial style. . . ."

Yet he begins to grow a little disturbed, too, at the thought of being somewhat trapped. "For though I tried to . . . unlock his bridegroom clasp . . . he still hugged me tightly, as though naught but death should part us twain." The final words echo the marriage service, but in evoking the shadow of death, they also betray an access of panic, arising from an old association between sexual satisfaction and punishment. This suggestion is fortified by the recollection of a childhood nightmare, itself symbolic of rejection, paralysis, castration, and death. Somehow the pseudo-matrimonial aspects of his waking bring to Ishmael's mind memories of his stepmother: another unsuitable bedfellow, perhaps, who may once have "expostulated" with him on "the unbecomingness of hugging . . .

in that matrimonial style," when he crawled in beside her for night-
time or morning comfort. The actual context in which he recalls
her, however, has nothing to do with hugging; she is remembered
as a legendary stepmother, a Bad Mother "who was all the time
whipping me or sending me to bed supperless."

Oddly enough, this juvenile domestic tragedy of being misunderstood and rejected by mama is almost the only specific piece of
information offered, in what is surely the vaguest of Melville's
books, about Ishmael's past. We learn nothing of the adult indignities which have presumably set his "splintered heart and maddened hand against the wolfish world"; indeed, it is as if there were
nothing but a runaway boy behind the outwardly mature form of
the narrator of *Moby Dick*. It is tempting to read into Ishmael's
little anecdote of crime and punishment a sense of guilt and power-
lessness associated with the boy's special sin of masturbation. Certainly, it is the "hand" which plays a key role in the waking nightmare: "a phantom hand," "not daring to drag away my hand";
and in the larger pattern of Ishmael's experience, too, that word
recurs in sensitive places. Not only does he describe his estrange-
ment in terms of "his maddened hand" set against the "wolfish
world"; but his reconciliation comes, as we have seen, in a chapter
called "A Squeeze of the Hand," when he tells us that he has at
last "washed my hands and heart," and cries out his appeal:
"Come, let us squeeze hands all around. . . ."

In the childhood episode recalled in Queequeg's arms, the boy
Ishmael was not as usual slippered, though he begged for that customary punishment. He was forced, instead, to remain in bed all
through the longest day of the year: "sixteen entire hours must
elapse before I could hope for a resurrection." He was, in effect,
condemned to impotence and death; and to this condemnation his
own unconscious subscribed, calling up the phantom hand that
held him powerless, awake but involved still in nightmare terror.
In his own fantasy, the sentence of a single, endless day had been
extended through all eternity: never, never (in either sense) to rise
again! And for what crime had he presumably been punished—
"some caper or other," about which he claims not to be sure, but
which he thinks may have involved an attempt to climb up his
mother's chimney. It is a fantasy more than a fact; and its interpretation suggests itself immediately, casts light on the meaning of
chimneys for Melville in such a later story as "I and My Chimney."

Finding himself in a matrimonial deadlock with Queequeg, Ishmael feels again the old threat of impotence and death. But though he is in bed, in that forbidden hugging-place, he is not this time trying to crawl up his mother's chimney. He embraces no woman, no obvious surrogate for the banned mother, only another male, a figure patriarchal enough, in fact, to remind him of George Washington! Surely, the matrimonial hug of such a companion is innocent, only a joke, an accidental result of trying to find a room in an overcrowded town. And though the memory of the nightmare terror of childhood recurs, it recurs purged; for Ishmael has for-given himself and is free at last to rise: "take away that awful fear, and my sensations . . . were very similar." Actually, he is free for a reconciliation with the tabooed mother; but this he will not know until the book's end, when, an orphan, he is picked up by "the devious cruising *Rachel*." His long sentimental re-education has now just begun.

Its first stage is represented by the disappearance of Ishmael's fear of Queequeg's tomahawk. That "wild pipe of his" becomes now only a peace pipe, "regularly passing between us . . ."; and their alliance can be regularly solemnized: "he pressed his forehead against mine, clasped me around the waist, and said that hence-forth we were married." Ishmael hastens to add, of course, "mean-ing, in his country's phrase, that we were bosom friends"; for the innocence of their connection must be asserted continually. This is Platonism without sodomy, which is to say, marriage without copulation: the vain dream of genteel ladies fulfilled in a sailor's rooming-house by two men. Queequeg promises that "he would gladly die for me, if need should be"; and die he does, for there *is* need. Indeed, only by his self-sacrifice is Ishmael's sentence of death finally commuted; only in his symbolic body is Ishmael snatched from death.

But all this is not to be for a little while; more immediately, they divide between them Ishmael's worldly goods (Melville, who can-not resist overdetermining everything, makes it thirty pieces of silver) and discuss the counter-claims of their rival religions. It is a scene half broadly comic, half subtly satiric: as Melville, on the one hand, gently parodies the problem of church allegiance in mixed marriages, and on the other, reflects in the style of *Typee* and *Omoo* on the insularity and rigidity of Protestant Christianity. Its real climax comes, however, with the kissing of the grotesque phallic idol, a bowing down before the less savory aspects of the natural and impulsive world which, for all its horror, seems to Melville the only source of love. And the chapter ends in bed, on a simple note of peace, never attained again in the rest of the book: "There, then, in our hearts' honeymoon, lay I and Queequeg—a cosy, loving pair."

Though this is, in a sense, a happy ending, Melville does not abandon his lovers here. There follows an account of their waking, Queequeg's Ramadan, the signing together on the *Pequod* for a whaling voyage, a series of minor incidents, including a sightseeing tour. In the course of those incidents, we learn a good deal about Queequeg's early life and see a display of heroism on his part, begin to feel that Melville is preparing for some shipboard climax —which never comes. Queequeg is not abandoned once the voyage starts, as is Bulkington; but he passes from the center to the periphery of the action. What matters to the reader is his relationship to Ishmael, but their occasions for meeting once they are aboard are few. Queequeg becomes Starbuck's harpooner, but his association with the first mate remains purely formal, devoid of typical significance and passion alike; and for the sake of the book's symbolic coherence, Melville smuggles in an encounter or two between the sundered lovers. Together, for instance, they work at making a sword-mat, with Ishmael acting "the attendant or page of Queequeg," and they find themselves in the same boat whenever there is a launching; but the most crucial of the scenes involving them as a pair comes in the chapter called "The Monkey-Rope," which presents, in effect, a picture of married life after the honeymoon.

It is in this chapter, that Melville, apparently the only time in the whole book, makes a deliberate change in the facts of whaling procedure, describing how Ishmael and Queequeg are tied together during the process of cutting in, in which one man balances on the whale's back, while the other, leaning over the side, helps him keep his slippery balance. "It was a humorously perilous business for both of us . . . ," Ishmael observes, "for better or worse, we two, for the time, were wedded . . . my own individuality was now merged in a stock company of two . . . another's mistake or misfortune might plunge innocent me into unmerited disaster and death." "Nor," he comments further, "could I possibly forget that, do what I would, I only had the management of one end of it." As if even this were not enough to make his point, Melville adds a footnote which explains that "only in the *Pequod* . . . the monkey and his holder were ever tied together. This improvement . . . was introduced . . . in order to afford the imperilled harpooner the strongest possible guarantee for the faithfulness and vigilance of his monkey-rope holder." For an instant, Melville seems to be thinking of the relations of husbands and wives in general rather than of the ideal marriage of Ishmael and Queequeg; and he reverts to the wry derisive tone of his comment on matrimony in *Mardi*.

When Ahab enters the book, however, the theme of love and marriage is pushed into the background, from which it emerges (in the unforeseen posthumous consummation of the relationship between Ishmael and Queequeg) only after Ahab has destroyed himself and the whole shipboard world he has subverted. Ishmael himself has been bent temporarily to Ahab's will, totally committed to the fulfillment of his monomaniac quest until the moment of his sperm-squeezing conversion; but he can do nothing even at that point, remains still the spectator he has become from the moment of Ahab's ascendancy over him. But as a spectator and Ahab's man, he has no longer any use for Queequeg, who is also converted into an accomplice to the blasphemous hunt. Ishmael begins Chapter XXIV with the words, "As Queequeg and I are now fairly embarked on this business of whaling . . . ," but before the chapter is over, Queequeg has been relegated to a supernumerary role in the gothic drama that stars Captain Ahab; the sentimental romance is temporarily over.

Corresponding to the gothic mood of *Moby Dick* after the voyage has begun is another relationship between a white man and a colored one, a quite different projection of the commitment of the ego to a life of impulse and instinct. In Ishmael, the heart of Western white civilization reaches out to the uncorrupted sources of natural life; in Ahab, the head of Western man turns to the same sources in search of power and fear. Queequeg's counterpart is Fedallah, the Parsee, who becomes Ahab's harpooner. He and his crew, however, are not signed on to the *Pequod*, but smuggled aboard, bootlegged on a commercial voyage by a madman; and once the ship is at sea, they rise out of the hold like nightmares. The first hint of their existence has come from Elijah, who has asked Ishmael, "Did ye see anything looking like men going toward the ship a while ago?" This Ishmael takes as a "plain matter-of-fact question," though he is baffled when he tries to pursue it; and we do not hear again of the dusky figures he is not sure whether he has seen or not, until in the moonlight watch two sailors hear the muffled noises of "somebody down in the after-hold that has not yet been seen on deck."

It is not, however, until the first lowering that Fedallah and his tiger-yellow cohorts make a daylight appearance. "With a start all glared at dark Ahab, who was surrounded by five dusky phantoms that seemed fresh formed of air." The coyly noncommittal "seemed" reminds us of Hawthorne; but once the figure of Fedallah "tall and swart . . . with one white tooth evilly protruding from its steel-like lips" has hissed "Ready" to Ahab, he and his crew are handled in terms of peculiarly Melvillean melodrama:

> But what was it that inscrutable Ahab said to that tiger-yellow crew of his—these were words best omitted here; for you live under the blessed light of the evangelical land. Only the infidel sharks in the audacious sea may give ear to such words, when, with tornado brow, and eyes of red murder, and foam-glued lips, Ahab leaped after his prey.

The style, overstated, hysterical, a little ridiculous, dismays the modern reader, as do the stock descriptions of Ahab as the gothic hero-villain. Indeed, the whole relationship of Ahab to Fedallah is rendered in precisely so artificial and unconvincing a mode, from their first lowering to Ahab's last sight of the Parsee tangled in the harpoons on Moby Dick's back.

The most recent moving-picture version of the book quite simply cut him out, apparently because the director was convinced that not even a medium invented to make falsity credible could redeem such material from absurdity. Yet the Parsee stands at the center of the whole machinery of signs and portents and prophecies, which lend the book its characteristically Satanic tone. In him is made manifest the spirit of Ahab's quest, all that impels "the rushing *Pequod,* freighted with savages, and laden with fire, and burning a corpse, and plunging into that blackness of darkness," and makes her "the material counterpart of her monomanic commander's soul." It is the Parsee who prays blasphemously at the forging of Ahab's magical harpoon, that is tempered in the pagan blood of the barbaric harpooners: " 'Ego non baptizo te in nomine patris, sed in nomine diaboli,' deliriously howled Ahab, as the malignant iron scorchingly devoured the baptismal blood." But this moment, over which the Parsee presides, and at which is spoken the "secret motto" of *Moby Dick,* is the thematic center of the book—at least insofar as it is Ahab's.

Without the Parsee to make explicit his damnation, Ahab is merely crazy, *Moby Dick* meaningless. But Melville does not really know how to handle him; for he is not a "character" at all, in the sense that Ishmael is a character—or even Queequeg. He possesses not literal reality but representative truth, and should be understood as a conventional device for portraying inwardness, a projected nightmare. Even Ahab, with his Machiavellian posturing, his rhetoric half out of Byron, half out of the Elizabethans, is almost equally absurd when understood literally. Though in the purely novelistic scenes with Starbuck, he must be taken as a genuine protagonist, with a mind and a past, in his relationship with Fedallah, he has no more mind than Moby Dick; for, like the whale, he is a projection: an emblem of the head itself, cut off from the heart and driven toward its own destruction in its sultanic loneliness. But he is also Faust, as the Parsee is also the Devil, both of them archetypes as well as projections. Certainly, Ahab lives a Faustian life: a "godlike ungodly old man" pressing on beyond all limits to penetrate the ultimate mysteries in despite of God himself; and certainly, he dies a Faustian death, howling defiance to the end: "Oh, lonely death on lonely life! Oh, now I feel my topmost greatness lies in my topmost grief. . . . Towards thee I roll, thou all-destroying but unconquering whale, to the last I grapple with thee; from hell's heart I stab at thee; for hate's sake I spit my last breath at thee. . . ."

Such a life and such a death Melville can render, however rhetorically, at least without embarrassment; but the compact with the Devil upon which they both depend for their meanings, and for whose sake, indeed, he has invented Fedallah, he cannot bring himself to portray. Only obliquely through the comic comments of Stubb and Flask, do we come to suspect that the bargain which makes Ahab a Faust has already been struck: "Flask, I take that Fedallah to be the devil in disguise . . . the reason why you don't see his tail is because he tucks it up out of sight, carries it coiled away in his pocket, I guess . . ."; "the devil there is trying to come round him and get him to swap away his silver watch or his soul, or something of that sort, and he'll surrender Moby Dick. . . ." If the point of such evasions is not a simple failure of nerve, but a desire to undercut ironically the whole Faustian myth, why is Fedallah in the action to begin with, and why do his Macbethian predictions so precisely and tantalizingly come true? What sort of double game is Melville playing with the very myth which lies at the center of his work? The second American Faust, like the first, was written by a man who did not know whether he believed in the Devil, and was embarrassed by the machinery of gothicism, which he was unable to abandon. Yet finally *Moby Dick* triumphs over the shoddiness of its gothic devices, as it triumphs over the naïveté and parochialism of its "Western" love story by deeply mythicizing both its components, and thus liberating them from novelistic restrictions and the implicit judgment of realism: by becoming, in short, the most improbable of all epic poems.

In the latter part of *Moby Dick,* even Queequeg is gradually transformed from a character into a myth, though he never quite loses his status as a fully realized protagonist—never seems, like Fedallah, *merely* what he stands for. His erotic function we have already noticed, but his role as a tutelary spirit of midwifery remains still to be examined. Not only does he act as a cicerone in the Grand Armada episode, pointing out, in the midst of woe and death, the newborn whale still umbilically attached to his dam; but earlier he has played the actual obstetrician, himself bringing Tashtego out of the womb-tomb of the whale's head. The Indian, who, while "cutting in," had been trapped in that suddenly sinking head ("coffined, hearsed, and tombed in the secret inner chamber and santum sanctorum of the whale"), first presents a leg at the opening which Queequeg has cleaved to rescue him. But Queequeg refuses the unorthodox presentation, turning him about until "he came forth in the good old way—head first. . . . Thus through the courage and skill in obstetrics of Queequeg, the deliverance or rather the delivery of Tashtego, was successfully accomplished. . . ." It is not Queequeg's first underwater rescue (he had earlier fished out of the waters of New Bedford the bumpkin who had mocked him), but this time the rescue is presented clearly as a symbolic act of resurrection.

Controller of life and death, Queequeg's own existence is in his power; and indeed, he is shown at one point as simply refusing to die, though a fever has brought him almost to his "endless end." Recalling, Ishmael tells us, some uncompleted obligations, the harpooner returns to life, after everyone has given him up, but not before he has made his own coffin from "some heathenish . . . lumber . . . cut from the original groves of the Lackaday Islands." On this coffin, after his recovery, Queequeg spends long hours copying the signs from his body, which not only stand for his identity, but constitute as well "a mystical treatise on the art of attaining truth." For a little while, this wondrously engraved coffin serves as his sea-bag; then, at Queequeg's own hint, it is converted into a lifebuoy to replace one that has been lost. Upon its strange metamorphoses, Ahab himself comments in a Hamlet-like soliloquy which follows an exchange with the carpenter who refurbishes it. He teases himself for a moment with the question, which he considers himself too far gone on the "dark side of earth" to fully credit: "Can it be that in some spiritual sense the coffin is, after all, but an immortality preserver?"

Of all the ship's accoutrements, only the coffin-lifebuoy survives ("owing to its great buoyancy, rising with great force") after Moby Dick has rammed the *Pequod;* and graven with the symbols of Queequeg's identity, standing in Queequeg's stead, it rises to the hand of Ishmael, who alone among the crew has risen to the surface of the sea. "Buoyed up by that coffin, for almost one whole day and night, I floated on a soft and dirge-like main." It is as if the prayer which Ishmael did not understand when he uttered it, has been answered. "Coffin, Angels! save me!" The coffin-lifebuoy is not, however, the only symbolic analogue for Queequeg the savior in the complex pattern of the book. Wherever the choice is made, of a seeming death which is really life, a suicidal plunge which eventuates in a resurrection, the holy marriage with Queequeg is being analogically repeated. Queequeg, who represents Oceania, the watery area of the world, is equated with the sea and with the whale who inhabits its depths. This is, of course, to say, with *Ishmael's* sea and *Ishmael's* whale; for Ahab's version of both are quite different, and are associated with the Satanic Fedallah. The descent into either (as opposed to the assault upon either), like the love-union with the dark savage (as opposed to the pact with him), signifies a life-giving immersion in nature or the id, a death and rebirth. That is why such erotic terminology is used to describe both the innards of the whale and the depths of the sea: the vestibule of the whale called "the bridal chamber of his mouth"; the bottom of the sea referred to as "the very pelvis of the world."

In his mythical descent, Ishmael ceases to be the latest avatar of Natty Bumppo, one more instance of a peculiarly American prototype, and fades into an archetype much more ancient by far. The whole movement of the book is from land to sea, from time to timelessness; and Melville succeeds in converting all that is provincial in his subject into the universal by removing it from the landbound world of history back toward the oceanic, which is to say, an archaic, an "antemosaic" world of portents and monsters, unchanged since the days of creation. The romance of Ishmael (even as the tragedy of Ahab) is finally seen against a dream landscape, where time has not yet come into existence; and where the acts of men are motivated not by psychology but by mythic patterns, set thousands of years before America was discovered.

It is with Jonah that Melville identifies Ishmael, the archetypal runaway; but his name further complicates the identification, making him an Ishmael who is a Jonah: an outcast son who is cast into the depths and brought forth again by the God whom he is fleeing. What Ishmael saw in his plunge into the depths we are not directly told; but we assume that his experience must have been like that of Jonah, to whom wisdom came in the belly of the whale.

We do learn, however, what Ishmael saw looking down into the sea in the midst of the Grand Armada, following the pointing finger of Queequeg. At the heart of the pod of frightened and frightening whales, at the very center of "consternation and affrights," he discovers "dalliance and delight"—which is to say, birth and copulation but *no* death. And this he reads as a sign that there is within the human self a place in which the "eternal mildness of joy" prevails deep below "the ponderous planets of unwaning woe." Ishmael interprets his glimpse into the world of natural immortality, where life is endlessly renewed by physical generation, as a guarantee that there is a renewal of the spirit, too, in human "dalliance and delight," which is all the immortality man can ever achieve. For this natural renewal of the soul, the Holy Marriage of Males, immune to the spiritual death implicit in fleshly marriage with women, is an alternative symbol.

Against this accidental glimpse into the heart of living mysteries, which constitutes Ishmael's real descent into the whale, Melville counterposes an account of a royally-sponsored, priest-guided tour through a whale's skeleton in the Bower of the Arsacides. From the spout-hole of the King's dead and grounded whale, a perpetual stream of vapor ascends, a presumable token that there is no death; but it is a fake, an "artificial smoke" manufactured by the priests to compel belief. Deep within the whitening skeleton, to which Ishmael penetrates like a man threading a maze, there is simply nothing: "no living thing; naught was there but bones." For Melville, this sterile showplace of prepared illusions represents all organized religion, especially the Presbyterianism to which he himself was raised; and he has Ishmael cry out in revulsion, "Only in the heart of the quickest perils . . . only in the profound unbounded sea, can the fully invested whale be truly and livingly found out."

To find out "the fully invested whale" is the end of Ishmael's quest, from which he was temporarily diverted by Ahab's magnetic charm; and wherever he dives deep he is faithful to that goal: in his acceptance of Queequeg's embrace; in his penetration of the Grand Armada; in his final descent toward the "button-like black bubble," the "vital center" of the vortex left by the sinking *Pequod*. All of these symbolize the life-giving immersion represented elsewhere in the book by Father Mapple, who first invokes the myth of Jonah, and who himself seems "kneeling and praying at the bottom of the sea"; by Bulkington, who is buried and resurrected in a single chapter: "Up from the spray of thy ocean perishing—straight up leaps thy apotheosis!"; by Pip, abandoned and rescued by those who never understand what he has seen; by Tashtego, whose thrashing arm above the sea seems an "arm thrust forth from the grass over the grave." Understood as a series of linked analogies, organized not as in a novel but as in a poem, *Moby Dick* displays an unsuspected unity. Even the cetological passages, those apparent digressions with their endless and apparently impertinent documentation, are revealed as a final Ishmael-Queequeg analogue: one more descent into the whale, this time a scholarly exploration, inch by inch, from skin to sex. "Have a care how you seize the privilege of Jonah," Ishmael warns himself, as he girds up his loins for the plunge into Leviathan.

Infinitely rich in significance, the descent into the depths is a theme in the oldest epic literature of our civilization; but it represents only one half of the archetypal adventures of the epic hero, who must not only disappear into the sea and rise again, but must also slay the dragon of the deep. Ishmael is, then, but one part of the split epic hero (and surely his splitting is a sign in itself of the divided state of the psyche in modern life), whose other part is Ahab. In the case of the latter, too, there is a tension established between the primary suggestion of the name Ahab, a wicked king whose blood was licked by dogs, and the secondary mythical association with Perseus and St. George: deliverers both and slayers of monsters. Ahab, however, saves no one, not even himself. He is the hero who is lost, even as Ishmael is the coward who is saved; for in Melville's scheme, the warrior who attacks the ravening beast goes down to death, while the prophet who runs away is preserved alive. Though like Ishmael Ahab seeks the whale "in the heart of quickest perils," he seeks him not to plunge into his jaws and be swallowed up but to attack and destroy him.

The one is a would-be murderer, the other a symbolic suicide. Ishmael goes to sea "as a substitute for pistol and ball"; Ahab embarks to "strike through the mask." But it is Ahab who must die, precisely because he has sought the death of the Other rather than of himself; for *Moby Dick* is based on the fundamental paradoxes which outlive in the Western mind the religion that once sustained them. Not only does the chant of the cheating witches of *Macbeth* ring through the book: "Fair is Foul and Foul is Fair!" but also the older assertion, more promise than threat, that Death is Life and Life Death. In Father Mapple's sermon, which appears quite early in the book, the fundamental proposition is asserted: "But what then? Methinks we have hugely mistaken this matter of Life and Death. Methinks that what we call my shadow here on earth is my true substance. . . ." Such paradoxes are worked out in great detail: Queequeg's coffin is, as we have noticed, a lifebuoy, while the great ship, which images forth the living world, is revealed as a hearse; Ahab, who only half-jestingly calls himself immortal ("I am immortal then on land or sea"), dies forever; but Ishmael, who considers himself already dead ("a quiet ghost with a clean conscience"), is reborn.

But why is Ahab doomed, the once heroic act of Perseus become in him an analogue of the Faustian bargain with the Devil? What does it mean to kill the monster anyway? As rich in significance as the baptismal descent, the battle with the dragon can be interpreted as the victory of light over storm and darkness; an attack of

12

THE BLACKNESS

OF DARKNESS:

EDGAR ALLAN POE

AND THE DEVELOPMENT

OF THE GOTHIC

IN HIS HARRIED CAREER as a journalist, book-reviewer, short-story writer, poet, and critic, Edgar Allan Poe tried twice to write a full-length novel, reworking each time chronicles of American exploration on sea and land. Both *The Narrative of A. Gordon Pym* (1837-38) and *The Journal of Julius Rodman* (1840) strike us as improbable books for Poe to have attempted, concerned as they are with the American scene and the great outdoors. The former is based upon accounts of pioneering expeditions to the South Seas, and especially a South Polar expedition projected by an acquaintance of Poe called J. N. Reynolds; while the second borrows heavily from the journals of Lewis and Clark, purporting to describe a trip across the Rockies which had preceded theirs.

There is little doubt that Poe was trying to cash in on contemporary interest in the remote and the unexplored, exploited, on the one hand, by such popular histories as Washington Irving's *Astoria* or *Adventures of Captain Bonneville,* and, on the other, by the Indian novels of James Fenimore Cooper. In the course of a review of the latter's *Wyandotté,* written in 1843, Poe reflects on the Leatherstocking Tales and remarks a little ruefully:

> . . . we mean to suggest that this theme—life in the Wilderness —is one of intrinsic and universal interest, appealing to the heart of man in all phases; a theme, like that of life upon the ocean, so unfailingly omniprevalent in its power of arresting and absorbing attention, that while success or popularity is, with

such a subject, expected as a matter of course, a failure might be properly regarded as conclusive evidence of imbecility on the part of the author. . . .

He goes on to add, however, that "the two theses in question," that is, the wilderness and life upon the ocean, are subjects to be avoided by the "man of genius . . . more interested in fame than popularity," for they belong to the lesser of the "two great classes of fiction," the "popular division" at whose head Cooper stands. Of this category, Poe remarks that "the author is lost or forgotten; or remembered, if at all, with something very nearly akin to contempt." He considers his own fiction in general part of the other great class, which includes the work of "Mr. Brockden Brown, Mr. John Neal, Mr. Simms, Mr. Hawthorne," of whom it can be said that "even when the works perish, the man survives."

Yet in *Gordon Pym* and *Julius Rodman,* Poe tried his hand at the two popular themes, attempting, for the first time perhaps, to treat the sort of legendary material which had appeared in Leatherstocking Tales with the scrupulous documentation of Irving's nonfictional accounts. The kind of book at which Poe aimed Melville was to produce with eminent success, beginning less than a decade later with the best-selling *Typee* (1846) and *Omoo* (1847), and raising the genre to unexpected power in *Moby Dick.* Poe is considerably less successful, failing completely in the case of the unfinished *Julius Rodman* to lend fictional life to borrowed documents; and achieving in *Gordon Pym* a work so hopelessly unpopular (in America at least), that only within the last very few years has a major attempt to redeem it been undertaken. Poe himself, some time after its appearance, was willing to write off *Gordon Pym* as a "silly book"; and certainly from the first he had considered it, or pretended to consider it, a shameless bid for popular success.

The whole apparatus which surrounds the anonymous final form of *Gordon Pym* is apologetic: an involved attempt on Poe's part to convince himself that his primary purpose in publishing the tale was to perpetrate a hoax on the reader. But this is an almost compulsive aspect of Poe's art in general, arising from a dark necessity, which dogged not only him among American writers, of remaining in ignorance about his own deepest aims and drives. Just so Cooper was obligated to believe that he was mocking his wife's literary taste before he could become an author, while Melville eternally persuaded himself that he was on the verge of producing as a wedding ring!). Though they are captured at the end, they have learned to love each other with a love pure enough to transcend their mutual prejudices and bitterness. The white man, wounded by an evil woman who would have separated the two good companions and feels no love, only a lust that does not even demand to know the name of the phallus-bearer who satisfies it, ends up lying in the arms of the colored man, who sings to him like a mother to a child; and still together, more than ever together, they are borne off to jail. As the old myth sinks deeper and deeper into the national mind, intertwined with nostalgic memories of books that we have read as children, like our fathers before us and theirs before them, it comes to seem truer than the reality of headlines. At the psychic levels, from which works of art proceed and to which they seek to return, not Little Rock but Hannibal is the place where black and white confront each other; not Eniwetok but the *Pequod* is the meeting-ground of the Kanaka and the American sailor.

Since the locus of our deepest response to the conflict of races is legend, we find it easy to believe that our dark-skinned beloved will rescue us from the confusion and limitations of a society which excludes him. Certainly, our classic writers assure us that when we have been cut off or have cut ourselves off from the instinctive sources of life, he will receive us without rancor or the insult of forgiveness. He will fold us in his arms saying "honey" or "Aikane"; he will comfort us, as if he knew our offense against him were only symbolic—an offense against that in ourselves which he represents—never truly *real*. And yet our novelists can never quite let us forget our guilt; the fictions which embody the myth of the *hierogamos* dramatize compulsively not only the role of the colored man as bugaboo but also as victim. The Polynesian sailor Hope in Dana's *Two Years Before the Mast* is shown dying of the white man's syphilis; Queequeg is wracked by a fever caught crawling in the hold on the white man's business; Crane's Negro is disfigured by the slow drip of acid in a burning house where he blindly attempts to rescue a white man's son; Cooper's Indian smolders in a drunken old age, victim of the white man's whisky; Jim is portrayed burdened with chains and weakened by a score of foolish torments imagined by Tom in the name of a white man's notion of "bulliness"; Lucas Beauchamp is hunted and chivvied, almost lynched in the name of the white man's justice.

The immense barrier of guilt between white man and dark man is no more mitigated in our classic fiction than is the gulf of color and culture itself; both, indeed, are emphasized to the point of melodrama, so that the final reconciliation may seem more tender and miraculous. The archeteype makes no attempt to deny the facts of outrage or guilt; it is nurtured by them. It merely portrays them as meaningless in the face of a passion immune to what Melville calls "that climax which is so fatal to ordinary love." "It's too good for true, honey," Jim says to Huck. "It's too good for true."

now threw affectionate arms around his stubborn neck; and did seem to joyously sob over him, as if over one, that however wilful and erring, she could yet find it in her heart to save and to bless.

Earlier, Ahab has appealed to the demonic Father God, in his blustering and bullying way, for just such a revelation: "My sweet mother, I know not. Oh, cruel! what hast thou done with her?" But when he has his answer, learns that the "sweet mother" resides still in the beauty of the natural world (it is precisely what was revealed to Ishmael in the midst of the Grand Armada), he will not listen. In the end, he proves not really interested in the reconciliation with the Mother, wanting nothing less than to grapple with the "fiery Father" himself, to be joined to him in an assault which is also an embrace: "I leap with thee; I burn with thee; would fain be welded with thee. . . ." He seeks madly to identify himself with the castrating power shadowed forth in the whale: the power that has scarred and maimed him and made his wife a widow, though they are scarcely wed. But the desire to be one with the forbidding fire is merely another version of the Faustian temptation, to be as a god; and all this is figured forth in Ahab's relationship with the Parsee, fire-worshiper and Devil, presiding genius of the infernal baptism.

Yet Ishmael, too, we remember, has temporarily at least lost faith in water and subscribed to fire, lent his voice to the pledge of the maddened crew to pursue the abominable quest. He, too, has dreamed of catching Leviathan with a hook, thus confirming his unity with Ahab in a common mythical identification. Though the one is Jonah, the one Perseus, both are Job: Job as Jonah, Job as Perseus. "Give not thyself up, then, to fire," Ishmael warns the reader in "The Tryworks," "lest it invert thee, deaden thee, as for a time it did me. There is a wisdom that is woe; but there is a woe that is madness." Multiple ambiguities undercut the simple polarity which the book superficially suggests. Even Queequeg, good angel and representative of the baptism to life, gives his blood along with Tashtego's and Dagoo's for the Satanic tempering of Ahab's harpoon; while the very sperm in which Ishmael washes himself clean of hate comes from a whale struck by the infuriated hunters, the very whale whose death meant the casting away of his alter ego, Pip.

Yet there is an irony beyond all of these. If Queequeg dies for

Ishmael, so does Ahab; though, to be sure, the one dies in deliberate self-sacrifice, the other in blind hybris. It is, however, Ahab's destruction which ransoms Ishmael's life, the playing out of Ahab's fury which instructs Ishmael in love. If, as Ishmael asserts at one point, a whaling ship was his Harvard and Yale College, Ahab was his major professor. The head, driven by woe past woe to sacrilege and murder, burns itself out in a terror by which the heart is purified: left alone in the sea of the unlimited, clinging to the symbolic body of the dark beloved, who seemed death and was really life. Only thus is the Father of Fury appeased. The sea rolls again in primeval calm, "as it rolled five thousand years ago," which is to say, before man had committed the primal offense. The instruments of rage are put away: the beaks of the hawks, which snatched violently at Ahab's hat, "sheathed"; the sharks' mouths, which gnawed hungrily at Ahab's oars, "padlocked."

The outcast son is buoyed up on the charmed sea, preserved until discovered by the cruising *Rachel,* that is, the Mother, whom he thought of as rejecting him, but who all along has wept for her children, refusing to be comforted. But the return to the Mother is a return also to God, to the numinous felt as maternal, to what Melville knew enough of Hebrew mysticism, even at the time of writing *Mardi,* to call the *Shekhinah:* "an awful glory. Sphere in sphere it burned:—the one Shekinah! The air was flaked with fire; deep in which, fell . . . tears . . ." The *Shekhinah* is the presence of God in the natural world, his spirit which he has sent into exile with all his outcasts, and which there weeps for them. "I have written a wicked book," Melville wrote to Hawthorne, "and feel spotless as the lamb." It is the final expression of the profound duplicity and unity of *Moby Dick:* I have written a wicked book (boasts Ahab-Melville), and feel spotless as the lamb (Ishmael-Melville rejoins).

Such a happy ending, however qualified, is more and more desperately insisted upon these days in the face of the contradictions between the relationships we dream and the relationships we live. In the motion picture *The Defiant Ones,* the old story is told again: Huck and Jim run from their pursuers through field and swamp once more—though this time they are escapees from a chain gang; and to emphasize their terrible bond they are chained together (the link that binds them is referred to wryly at one point the son against the father; a destruction of whatever is dark, repressive, and authoritarian in the psyche itself; a combat with the Devil or with God or with an inscrutable being who may be either; an assault on the irrational in nature and an attempt to resolve the world's mysteries by liquidating them. For Melville, such an onslaught is suspect in several ways. Not only does he sense a kind of Oedipal guilt in Ahab's frenzy against the "fiery father," in whose despite he seeks to hunt down the whale, but perceives that in him the struggle against the monstrous becomes the struggle against a Calvinist God, whom Ahab confuses with the traditional figure of the Devil!

Is not Moby Dick, after all, identified with Leviathan himself; and is not Leviathan the immortal symbol of the inscrutability of the created world, a mystery not to be resolved until the end of days? Is not that lower inscrutability, moreover, a type of the higher, of the ultimate mystery of the divine? Melville, for whom in *Moby Dick* the precepts of the New Testament are irrelevant, and who put in Christ's place a Polynesian harpooner, could not close his ears to the Old Testament challenge: "Canst thou catch Leviathan with a hook?" And does not the man who tries, does not Ahab become, in his alienation, his sultanism, his pride, blasphemy, and diabolism, finally more monstrous than the beast he hunts? When, on the last day, they confront each other, which is the Monster, Moby Dick in his "gentle joyousness," his "mighty mildness of repose," or Ahab screaming his mad defiance?

In complete contempt of the three-thousand-year-old pattern of myth, Melville permits the dragon-slayer to be slain, the dragon to escape alive; but it is hard to tell whether he really stands the legend on its head, allows evil to survive and heroism to perish. Only Ahab believes that the whale represents evil, and Ahab is both crazy and damned. Yet no child can abide the ending as it stands—in the book which parents and librarians alike expect them to enjoy; and in the comic-book version, revised for their special benefit, Moby Dick goes down with Ahab, whose death becomes merely the heroic price he pays for victory. For simple minds, the salvation of Ishmael is not enough; they cannot project their dreams of glory upon so passive a sufferer: the fugitive from life cast upon after a three-day chase, which both represents and parodies the immersion of Jonah as a type of Christ's burial and resurrection.

Ahab lost and Ishmael saved, the destroyer destroyed and the lover preserved by the symbolic body of his beloved: it is not finally quite so obvious and pat. Though Ahab and Ishmael are opposites, they are also one—two halves of a single epic hero; and only in their essential unity is the final unity of the book to be found. What Melville disjoined, in a typically American stratagem of duplicity, the reader must re-unite. In *Moby Dick,* the king-god-culture hero, who kills and is redeemed, is split into an active older brother and a passive younger, different sons of the same terrible father, who move, as it were, through separate works of art: the first through a belated horror tragedy, the latter through a nineteenth-century *Bildungsroman.* Yet though the agent in the first is projected as a finally rejected "he," and the witness in the second as a beloved "I," even structurally their two actions become one. The tragic play is encysted, enclosed in a comic narrative frame, on a model suggested, perhaps, by the Book of Job; though in Job, the chief protagonist is the same in the drama and frame-story. In *Moby Dick,* the protagonist of the frame-story is Ishmael, who becomes the trapped spectator of the drama of Ahab's fall, experiencing the catharsis of which Ahab is incapable. The heart, that is to say, witnessing the mad self-destruction of the head is itself purged and redeemed.

Heart and head, however, Ishmael and Ahab begin by confronting the same problem; for they are both described as rejected sons. The stepmother motif, first suggested by Ishmael's nightmare reminiscence in Queequeg's arms, is taken up again, toward the close of the book, in a chapter called "The Symphony." It opens on a moment just before the final three-day chase of Moby Dick and the catastrophe, which at this point seems inevitable; yet in that moment, all the world except for Ahab seems to relent. The two great principles, maternal and paternal, which divide the world and the minds of men, which make Ahab Ahab and Ishmael Ishmael, "the gentle . . . feminine air" and the "strong, troubled, murderous . . . masculine sea"—seem for once at peace with each other. "Those two seemed one; it was only the sex, as it were, that distinguished them." And at this point, even the stepmother, who had symbolically condemned Ishmael to death, symbolically returns to promise Ahab life:

That glad, happy air, that winsome sky, did at last stroke and caress him; the step-mother world, so long cruel—forbidding—

Negroes, those black "rascals" or "scamps," named pompously "Jupiter" or "Pompey," who lend a minstrel-show note to Poe's lighter tales. Woolly-pated and bow-legged, these characters play the role of mischievous, cowardly, stupid and faithful dependents, good always for a laugh when they say "soldiers" for "shoulders" or "clause" for "cause." The dark hordes of Too-Wit project the image of what the Southerner privately fears the Negro may be; just as the comic body-servant of Poe's other fiction projects the image of what the anti-abolitionist publicly claims he is. It is the darker image, however, which is true to Poe's memories of his boyhood and youth in the Allen household; while the lighter belongs only to certain patriarchal legends, to which he learned to subscribe during his days on *The Southern Literary Messenger*. In the single reference to the Negro in his correspondence, Poe complains to his step-father (the date is 1827): "You suffer me to be subjected to the whim & caprice, not only of your white family, but to the complete authority of the blacks."

At the climax of *Gordon Pym,* Poe dreams himself once more, though a grown man, subject to that nightmare authority; and the book projects his personal resentment and fear, as well as the guilty terror of a whole society in the face of those whom they can never quite believe they have the right to enslave. In Tsalal, blackness is no longer the livery of subjection but a sign of menace; so utterly black, that even the teeth concealed by their pendulous lips are black, the Antarctic savages inhabit a black land in which the vegetation and the animals, water itself are all subdued to the same dismal color. The voyage of Pym has transported him into the black belt, a black belt transformed from the level of sociology to that of myth, in whose midst the reigning Caucasian is overwhelmed by a sense of isolation and peril. Not even the glimmer of white teeth bared in a heartening smile cuts the gloom of this exclusive and excluding dark world, whose ultimate darkness is revealed in that final chasm in which Pym and Peters are trapped after the treacherous destruction of their white shipmates. "We alone had escaped from the tempest of that overwhelming destruction. We were the sole living white men upon the island." At this point, the darkness of "Nigger-town" merges at last into the darkness of the womb which is also a tomb, an intestinal chamber from which there is apparently no way of being born again into a realm of light.

How has Pym arrived here, in this place where whiteness itself is taboo, where even the flicker of a handkerchief, the flash of sunlight on taut sails, a little flour in the bottom of a pan stir terror, and doom the white man who feels at home in a world full of such pale symbols? Pym has sought a polar whiteness and has discovered instead a realm of the domination of black. It was (as Marie Bonaparte and other analytical critics have made clear) his mother whom Poe was pursuing in his disguise as Pym: that lost, pale mother, white with the whiteness of milk and the pallor of disease; and the imaginary voyage is a long regression to childhood. But hostilely guarding the last access to the White Goddess, stands the black killer, Too-Wit. In the ultimate reaches of his boyhood, where he had confidently looked for some image of maternal comfort and security, Poe-Pym finds *both* the white chasm and cascade and the black womb sealed off by black warriors.

I I

Down through the history of the minstrel show, a black-faced Sambo (smeared with burnt cork, whether Negro or white, into the grotesque semblance of the archetypal nigger) tries to exorcise with high-jinks and ritual jokes the threat of the black rebellion and the sense of guilt which secretly demands it as penance and purge. But our more serious writers return again and again to the theme: Melville, for instance, in "Benito Cereno" treating quite explicitly the tragic encounter between certain sentimental and comic stereotypes of the Negro and a historic instance of a slave mutiny. In that story, Captain Amasa Delano fails to recognize the rebellion on a Spanish slave-ship which he encounters, precisely because he is a good American. He is endowed, that is to say, with an "undistrustful good nature" and will not credit "the imputation of malign evil in man." This means in fact that he is quite willing to believe almost any evil of a European aristocrat, like the Don Benito who gives the tale its title; and is prepared to accept the most incredible behavior as the kind of "sullen inefficiency" to be expected of a Latin crew. On the other hand, he is incapable of believing a Negro, particularly a body servant, anything but a "faithful fellow."

It is just this phrase which occurs to Captain Delano as he watches Babo, a black slave who is actually holding his master prisoner, threatening death with the razor he presumably wields property of those writers whom he regards as "men of genius," the view of Brockden Brown and Hawthorne; and he quite consciously rejects the sentimentalizing of the savage which he finds in popularizers like Cooper. Indeed, Poe's aristocratic pretensions make it impossible for him to adopt such an attitude without the equivocations and soul-searching demanded of such liberal gothicists as the young Brockden Brown. His fictional world needs no good Indians because he believes in none; and try as he will, he cannot keep quite distinct the mutinous black cook, whom he calls a "perfect demon," from the "dusky, fiendish" figure of Dirk Peters. *Theoretically,* the tale of *Gordon Pym* projects through its Negroes the fear of black rebellion and of the white man's perverse lust for the Negro, while symbolizing in the red man an innocent and admirable yearning for the manly violence of the frontier; but in the working out of the plot, the two are confused.

It is true that the half-breed line-manager offers protection against the shipboard mutineers and the vicious natives of Tsalal; but his sheltering embrace is identified with the mortal hug of the grizzly bear, whose skin he wears to cover his bald pate. The figure of the black man blends ambiguously with that of the slave, while that of the red man blurs into that of the wild beast! The West, at any rate, was always for Poe only half real, a literary experience rather than a part of his life; but the South moved him at the deepest personal level. Insofar as *Gordon Pym* is finally a social document as well as a fantasy, its subject is slavery; and its scene, however disguised, is the section of America which was to destroy itself defending that institution. It is, indeed, to be expected that our first eminent Southern author discover that the proper subject for American gothic is the black man, from whose shadow we have not yet emerged.

Though the movement of *Gordon Pym* seems to bear us away from America, once Nantucket and New Bedford have been left behind, and to carry us through remoter and remoter seas toward the exotic Antarctic, it ends in a region quite unlike the actual polar regions. Heading toward an expected world of ice and snow, Pym finds instead a place of tepid waters and luxuriant growth; seeking a white world, he discovers, beside and within it, a black one. What has gone wrong? It is necessary for Poe to believe, in that blessed ignorance which frees forbidden fancies, that Pym's fictional voyage is bearing him toward the polar region, just as it was necessary for him to believe the whole story a delicious hoax;

but we, as latter-day readers, need not be the victims of either delusion. For all the carefully worked-up details about penguins, *biche de mer,* galapagos tortoises (bait for the audience which was later to subscribe to the *National Geographic*), Poe follows the footsteps not of Captain Cook but of his own first voyage in the arms of his mother, undertaken before his memory began, from New England to the South. In his deepest imagination, any flight from the North bears the voyager not toward but away from the snow—not to the South Pole, but to the American South.

Certainly, it grows not colder, but warmer and warmer, as Pym aboard the last ship to rescue him, the *Jane Gay,* pushes closer and closer to the Pole. "We had now advanced to the southward more than eight degrees farther than any previous navigators. We found . . . that the temperature of the air, and latterly of the water, became milder." Whatever pseudo-scientific explanations Poe may have believed would sustain this improbable notion of a luke-warm Antarctica, certain *symbolic* necessities were of more importance; he is being, in fact, carried back to Ole Virginny—as the color of the natives he meets on the Island of Tsalal (latitude 83° 20′, longitude 43° 5′ W.) clearly indicates. They are brawny, muscular, and jet black, with "thick and woolen hair," "thick and clumsy lips," these "wretches," whom Pym describes, after they have destroyed all the white men but him and Peters, as "the most wicked, hypocritical, vindictive, bloodthirsty, and altogether fiendish race of men upon the face of the globe." And he sets them in a world distinguished not only by blackness and warmth, but by a certain disturbing sexuality quite proper to Southern stereotypes of Negro life.* That sexuality can only be expressed obliquely by Poe, who was so squeamish about matters of this kind that the much franker Baudelaire was driven to remark, *"Dans l'oeuvre d'Edgar Poe, il n'y a jamais d'amour."* The phallicism of the island he, therefore, suggests not in human terms but by a reference to the islanders' chief crop, the *biche de mer*—a kind of sea-cucumber of which, Poe informs us, the authorities say that it "renews the exhausted system of the immoderate voluptuary."

The inhabitants of Tsalal are not, of course, the burlesque

---

* *Pym* represents the first serious attempt at introducing Negroes into our literature; and perhaps for that reason it is ignored (along with Melville's "Benito Cereno") by D. H. Lawrence in his *Studies in Classic American Literature.* Lawrence, at any rate, prefers his savages, Noble and Ignoble alike, Red rather than Black, and has written a history of our fiction with No Negroes Allowed.

Gordon Pym is presumably slain only to rise again, immersed and entombed only to be reborn—in his case, not once but over and over. Out of the coffin in the hold and out of a swoon that seems death itself, he is brought to life, but only to face mutiny and a new threat of destruction; and he emerges in the disguise of a ghost, his face coated with white chalk and blotched with blood, his clothes stuffed to resemble the bloated stomach of a swollen corpse. The threat of murder once again avoided, he is the victim of shipwreck; and almost dead once more (his life meagerly sustained by drinking the blood of a murdered shipmate), he is rescued by a passing ship, only to fall victim to a last catastrophe which leaves him buried alive just as in the beginning. A "living inhumation," Poe calls the state of life-in-death, to which his long circle brings him back; and he lingers almost sensuously over the details: "The blackness of darkness . . . the terrific oppression of the lungs, the stifling fumes from the damp earth . . . the allotted portion of *the dead.*" But even from this plight, Pym is rescued, this time by his blood-stained, demonic mate, Dirk Peters; and the two together approach the ultimate plunge into a white polar chasm, from which there is no reason to believe either can emerge. Indeed, it is precisely such an end which the pariah poet-sailor has prayed for, has loved in anticipation: "death or captivity among barbarian hordes . . . a lifetime dragged out in sorrow and tears, upon some grey and desolate rock."

Since Pym lusts for Gehenna rather than Eden, the companions he chooses on his quest embody not fertility or patient endurance but impotence and terror. Augustus Barnard, his first specter bridegroom, dies horribly, rots away visibly on a parody before-the-fact of Huck's raft: "His arm was completely black from the wrist to the shoulder, and his feet were like ice. . . . He was frightfully emaciated; so much so that . . . *he now did not weigh more than forty or fifty* [pounds] *at the farthest.* His eyes were . . . scarcely perceptible, and the skin of his cheeks hung so loosely as to prevent his masticating any food . . . without great difficulty." His painful death is not even sacrificial, merely another device to produce a shudder, especially at the point where his entire leg comes off in the hand of the man who is attempting to heave his rotten corpse into the sea!

Augustus' impromptu grave-digger is his successor; for it is Dirk Peters who tosses the first good companion over the side to the sharks who gather with gnashing teeth. But Peters is, as we have already noticed, a very ogre: such a monster, one of Poe's critics describes him, as children draw to scare themselves, a nightmare out of our racial beginnings. He is, in fact, as Marie Bonaparte suggests, the accursed hero who has destroyed the Father, taking on himself the guilt of the artist who only writes or dreams such horror. He protects the artist-surrogate of the plot with almost maternal tenderness, fights his battles like a big brother; and like a lover, holds him safe and warm when the defeated wanderer seeks his bloody embrace, impotent and whimpering. Yet the sought-for embrace is a rape and a betrayal, a prelude to certain death.

The climax of the relationship of Pym and Peters comes at the moment when the two are trapped on the Island of Tsalal, where all their companions have been killed by an artificial landslide contrived by the bloodthirsty black aborigines. The two survivors are trying to find their way out of a cleft in the earth that has providentially sheltered them; and Pym is suspended in fright on a sheer cliff wall.

For one moment my fingers clutched compulsively upon their hold, while, with the movement, the faintest possible idea of escape wandered, like a shadow, through my mind—in the next my whole soul was pervaded with a *longing to fall;* a desire, a yearning, a passion utterly uncontrollable. I let go at once my grasp upon the peg, and, turning half round from the precipice, remained tottering for an instant against its naked face. But now there came a spinning of the brain; a shrill-sounding and phantom voice screamed within my ears; a dusky, fiendish and filmy figure stood immediately beneath me; and, sighing, I sank down with a bursting heart, and plunged within its arms.

The "dusky, fiendish . . . figure" is, of course Peters, the half-breed; and the studied ambiguity of the passage, in which the language of horror becomes that of eroticism, the dying plunge becomes a climactic embrace, makes it clear that the *longing to fall* and the desire for the dark spouse are one, a single perverseness. Peters is not made an angelic representative of instinct and nature even at this critical instant; he remains still a fiend, even in the act of becoming a savior.

Poe espouses the view of instinctual life which is the common a best-seller, and Twain pretended he was a writer of books for boys.

The apologetic and playful preface to *Pym* has for us now chiefly biographical interest, illuminating the author but not the work. Whatever Poe's ostensible or concealed motives, he created in his only complete longer fiction not a trivial hoax but the archetypal American story, which would be recast in *Moby Dick* and *Huckleberry Finn*. Why, then, did Poe's book not achieve either the immediate acclaim accorded the latter or the slowly growing reputation won by the former? All the attributes of the highbrow Western are present in his novel: the rejection of the family and of the world of women, the secret evasion from home and the turning to the open sea. Only a bevy of black squaws and a few female corpses ("scattered about . . . in the last and most loathesome state of putrefaction") intrude into the world of pure male companionship which Poe imagines; and they provide no competition to the alliance of Pym either with his boyhood friend and Anglo-Saxon compeer, Augustus Barnard, or with his dusky demon, the "hybrid line-manager," Dirk Peters.

Rioting and shipwreck and rescue at sea do not break the rhythm of the flight that bears Pym farther and farther from civilization toward a primitive isolation, symbolized by the uncharted island and the lost valley, the derelict ship, and the small boat adrift at sea. Even Rip Van Winkle's initiatory draught, the alcoholic pledge to escape and forgetfulness, is represented in *Pym*. Buried in a coffin-like refuge in the black hull of a riot-torn ship, Gordon Pym finds at hand a bottle to console him; and later he and his companions fish up out of the flooded hold a flask of Madeira!

There are totemic beasts to spare in the pages of Poe's Western: a great white bear dramatically slaughtered, as well as legendary and exotic animals, compounded surrealistically out of incongruous familiar forms, and even stranger tabooed birds, who float lifelessly on a tepid and milky sea. And through it all, the outcast wanderer—equally in love with death and distance—seeks some absolute Elsewhere, though more in woe than wonder. Poe's realm of refuge and escape seems finally a place of death rather than one of love: the idyllic American dream turned nightmare as it is dreamed in its author's uneasy sleep. If the West means archetypically some ultimate innocence, there is no West in Poe's book at all—only an illusory hope that draws men toward inevitable disenchantment and betrayal. It is not merely that a gothic horror balances the quest for innocence in *Gordon Pym;* such a balance is the standard pattern of all highbrow Westerns. Only in Poe's novel, however, is the dark counterpoint permitted to drown out the *cantus firmus* of hopeful joy or to mar a final harmonic resolution.

Huckleberry Finn closes on a note of high euphoria, sustained by rescue and redemption and promises of new beginnings, which quite conceal from the ordinary reader the tragic implications of the conclusion; while *Moby Dick* ends with the promise of adoption, the symbolic salvation of the orphaned Ishmael by the crushing, motherly *Rachel.* Only at the close of *Gordon Pym* is the Great Mother identified with total destruction, a death without resurrection, a sterile, white womb from which there is no exit. "And now we rushed into the embraces of the cataract, where a chasm threw itself open to receive us. But there arose in our pathway a shrouded human figure, very far larger in its proportions than any dweller among men. And the hue of the skin of the figure was of the perfect whiteness of snow."

The book is finally an anti-Western disguised as the form it travesties; and this fact the great public, which will not in such matters be fooled, perceived—and perceiving, rejected the work. From the beginning, a perceptive reader of *Gordon Pym* is aware that every current sentimental platitude, every cliché of the fable of the holy marriage of males is being ironically exposed. Man's best friend, the dog, turns into a slavering monster ready to tear his master's throat to appease his hunger and thirst; a presumably loyal crew, led by the kind of standard black cook who plays the grinning and subservient comedian even in *Moby Dick,* mutinies; a bird flies through the pure blue air to drop "with a sullen splash" at the feet of a half-famished group of sailors "a portion of clotted and liverlike substance," a chunk of decayed human flesh; an approaching ship, hailed as a source of rescue, turns out to be a vessel loaded only with human carrion, from which issues "a smell, a stench, such as the whole world has no name for." Even the friendly bottle, traditional symbol of innocent male companionship, induces not joy but the D.T.'s, "an indescribable state of weakness and horror . . . a violent ague."

Most disconcerting of the parodies in *Pym* is that of the theme of resurrection itself, which later carries so much symbolic weight in both *Moby Dick* and *Huckleberry Finn.* Like Ishmael or Huck, men, or a man and a boy; the other suspect and impure, tries to join the disjoined in heterosexual passion, and its end is a catastrophe: a catastrophe symbolized by the "blackness" of the Negro, outward sign of an inward exclusion from grace.

At one level, Twain seems willing to accept the tragic position of the Negro as an inexplicable curse, crying out through the mouth of the pseudo-Tom in his moment of bafflement and despair, "What crime did the uncreated first nigger commit that the curse of birth was decreed for him. . . ." And certainly Roxy seems to share her master's assumption that blackness of the skin, the invisible taint of the blood carries with it an inevitable moral weakness. Her son's malice and cowardice, she is disconcertingly willing to attribute to the quantum of Negro blood which she has bequeathed him. "It's de nigger in you, dat's what it is," she screams at her son when he has refused to fight a duel; "Thirty-one parts o' you is white en on'y one part nigger, en dat po' little one part is yo' soul." Conversely, she has assured him at an earlier moment, after revealing to him the secret of his birth ("You's a *nigger—bawn* a nigger en a *slave!*"), that his white father at least had been a great man, who had been honored with "de bigges' funeral dis town ever seed." "Dey ain't another nigger in dis town dat's as high-bawn as you is . . . jus you hold yo' head up as high as you want to— you has de right. . . ."

This is, of course, a conventional kind of humor, and Twain is after the laughs which are easy enough to get by portraying one Negro calling another "nigger" in the proper dialect. But certain ironies proliferate disturbingly beneath the burlesque; and we are left baffled before the spectacle of slaves and outcasts accepting, as they insult each other, not only the offensive epithet "nigger," but all the assumptions implicit in that epithet. Insofar as Twain asks us to accept certain vaudeville gags as social history, we find his book and its meanings distasteful, an uncomfortable reminder of his own human failings; but we cannot help suspecting that behind the horseplay and grotesque melodrama of his plot, he may be attempting to translate an account of local prejudice into a fable revealing man's more universal implication in guilt and doom. If the false Tom is meant to represent not merely a Negro vainly pretending to be white, but the fruit of the betrayal and terror and profaned love which join all men, white and black, in our society —he must be made to embody the seeds of self-destruction which that relationship contains within it. He must therefore lie, steal, kill, and boast of his crimes, until, out of hybris, he reveals himself as a secret slave.

Though it is Pudd'nhead Wilson, local character, fingerprint expert and amateur detective, who presumably unmasks the impostor and wins the town's applause, it is really the false Tom himself who brings on his own downfall. Twain cannot resist a courtroom dénouement, a revelation and reversal sprung by some self-appointed sleuth at the darkest moment of a plot. Tom Sawyer, indeed, exists precisely to make such exposures not only in the books called by his name, but even in the one written in Huckleberry Finn's. Most readers will remember (and the reader of *Pudd'nhead Wilson* must to fully savor that book) how at the climax of *Huckleberry Finn*, Tom Sawyer, "his eyes hot, and his nostrils opening and shutting like gills," cries out of Jim: "They hain't no *right* to shut him up. . . . Turn him loose! He ain't no slave; he's as free as any cretur that walks this earth!" "As free as any cretur," the boy hero declares, blithely convinced that freedom is real, realer than the illusion of slavery; and, putting down that sanguine book, we believe him.

But a wry joke is already implicit in the phrase, which Twain no more sees than does Tom; and we as readers are not permitted to see it, as long as we remain within the spell of the happy ending. In *Pudd'nhead Wilson*, however, the protagonist, who is obviously Tom himself permitted at long last to grow up, rises to answer his own earlier courtroom cry, in just such a situation as he has always loved: " 'Valet de Chambre, Negro and slave . . . make upon the window the fingerprints that will hang you!" The double truth is in that instant complete: the seeming slave is free, but the free man is really a slave. It is an odd dénouement to a detective story enlivened by touches of farce: this revelation which condemns a hitherto free man to a life of servitude down the river, and leaves his mother sobbing on her knees, "De Lord have mercy on me, po' miserable sinner dat I is!" There is a happy ending this time for no one really except David Wilson (no longer called contemptuously "Pudd'nhead"), if one considers his acceptance by the philistine community really a blessing. To be sure, the same fingerprints which prove the presumed Tom a slave, establish the presumed Chambers as free; but his "curious fate" is equivocal if not actually tragic. Neither black nor white in his self-consciousness, he is the river. Twain makes clear that there is in the South no absolute distinction of black and white, merely an imaginary line—crossed and recrossed by the white man's lust—that makes one of two physically identical babies "by a fiction of law and custom a negro."

Once the "negro" Valet de Chambre has been dressed in a soft muslin robe and the "white" Thomas à Becket Driscoll in a tow-linen shirt, their roles are reversed and each plays the traditional role of his imagined race. The real Tom persists in protecting his "young master" despite the beatings he receives at his hands, and even saves him from drowning. But when, after his rescue, the white fellows of the false Tom tease him by calling his rescuer his "nigger pappy," the false Tom attempts to kill that rescuer. He cannot abide the suggestion that "he had a second birth into life, and that Chambers was the author of his new being," cannot assent to the American archetype embodied in Jim and Huck in *Huckleberry Finn*—and so drives a knife into his savior. No more can he abide being the son of a Negress, and ends by selling his mother down the river.

But it is not only the literally "false" Toms who betray their black mothers and play Cain to their Negro brothers; Twain's protagonists merely make melodramatically evident the fact that every mistreatment of a Negro, the simple continuance of slavery as an institution, is both a betrayal of the breast at which the Southerner who calls himself white has sucked, and of the brother he calls black, who has sucked at the breast beside him. In the mythical dénouement of Twain's book, it is suggested that all sons of the South, whether counted in the census as black or white, are symbolically the offspring of black mothers and white fathers, products of a spiritual miscegenation at the very least, which compounds the evil of slavery with an additional evil. The whitest aristocrat has nestled up to a black teat; the dullest slave may have been sired by some pure-blooded F. F. V. blade, discharging his blind lust upon a field wench or a house servant.

The family pattern of *Pudd'nhead Wilson* is opposite to that of *Huckleberry Finn*; for while the former is the portrait of a Southern, which is to say, a patriarchal society, the latter portrays a Western or matriarchal one. In the earlier book, the "sivilization" which Huck finally rejects is a world of mothers, that is, of what Christianity has become among the females who maintain it just behind the advancing frontier. It is a relatively simple-minded world, whose goal is virtue, which is defined as not cursing, stealing, smoking, or lying, but rather keeping clean, wearing shoes, and praying for spiritual gifts. In this world, the male principle is represented, if at all (Tom Sawyer has no father), by outcasts and scoundrels like Huck's unredeemable Pap—or some representative of nature and instinct like the runaway slave, Nigger Jim. In *Pudd'nhead Wilson,* on the other hand, it is the fathers who represent society, who are the defenders of a chivalric code which Twain elsewhere affects to despise, and the descendants of cavaliers. York Leicester Driscoll, Percy Northumberland Driscoll, Pembroke Howard, and Colonel Cecil Burleigh Essex: the names make the point perhaps too obviously. This is a world continuous with that of Renaissance England, a world in which "honor" is the sole code.

The patriarchal world of "honor" is also one of gallantry, of a kind of lustiness associated in Twain's mind with the court of Elizabeth, which for him represented a lost sexual Eden, contrasted (in his privately circulated *1601*) with a debilitated America, where men "copulate not until they be five-and-thirty years of age . . . and doe it then but once in seven yeeres." Though the men of Dawson's Landing, being Virginians, are potent still, their white women, who languish and retreat and die, are latter-day Americans, almost asexually genteel, so that only the Negress can match the vigor of the fathers with a corresponding fertility and power. Roxy is just such a Negress, and her union with Cecil Burleigh Essex represents not only a sociological but a symbolic truth. If the fathers of the South are Virginia gentlemen, the mothers are Negro girls, casually or callously taken in the parody of love, which is all that is possible when one partner to a sexual union is not even given the status of a person.

Twain's own judgment of sexual relations between black and white, slave and free is not explicitly stated; but there seems no doubt that he regarded the union between Roxy and Essex with a certain degree of horror, regarded it as a kind of fall—even in itself and a source of doom to all involved. There are two possible relations, two kinds of love between colored and white projected in our fiction, one of which is innocent, one guilty; one of which saves, one damns. The first provides a sentimental relation for the highbrow Western, the second a terrible one for the Southern gothic romance. The innocent relationship can exist only between of madness from the earthly paradise. In neither of these works, however, does Twain make it quite clear what has cast a shadow upon his idyllic world, what *particular* terror haunts his most nostalgic memories.

Only in *Pudd'nhead Wilson,* his most gothic book and an almost diagrammatic study in black and white, does he reveal that his specter is identical with Poe's and Don Benito's: "The negro." *Puddn'head Wilson* begins and ends in the village where *Huckleberry Finn* began and *Tom Sawyer* was played out, on the banks of the same symbolic river and in the same mythical pre-Civil War years. But between the "St. Petersburg" of the earlier books and the "Dawson's Landing" of the later one, there is a terrible difference. Pudd'nhead is represented as a mature and cynical stranger coming into the place at which Twain had never managed before to look from the outside. To his two boy heroes, it is so totally and entirely their world that they know it no more than their own faces. Only the outsider, the estranged adult Twain had become, rather than the unalienated child he remembered himself, offers an opportunity for perspective; and the opening of the novel pans slowly down on the village: its rose-clad houses, its cats, its sleepiness, and its fragrance—all preparing for the off-hand giveaway of the sentence beginning, "Dawson's Landing was a slave-holding town. . . ."

Striving to return as a grownup to the limit of a boy's memory, Twain arrives at the fact of slavery, once as imperceptible to him as the town itself. The Civil War is the watershed, in Twain's life, between childhood and manhood, innocence and experience, joy and despair; and this very fact insures that in his time of experience and despair he come to know that his innocence and joy, as well as the life that sustained them, were based on the labor and indignities of slaves. Yet the lost happiness, however based, was real; and Twain, whose dogmatic anti-Christianity can conceive no other paradise, cannot leave off returning to it in reminiscence and in art. All the same, he cannot deny the shamefulness of his plight, the pity of being forced to dream a boy's dream of freedom acted out in the world of slavery.

In *Tom Sawyer,* the paradox at the heart of Twain's essential myth is hushed up for nostalgia's sake and in the interests of writing a child's book; in *Huckleberry Finn,* it is present as a constant tension, though camouflaged by the poetry and high spirits of the text; in *Pudd'nhead Wilson,* it falls apart into horror and horseplay. In that novel, Hannibal is rendered from the very start not as a Western but as a Southern town. The river is no longer presented as a just-passed frontier, a defining limit between the realms of civilization and nature, a boundary which America touches and crosses on its way west; it is felt as a passageway into the deep South. "Down the river" is the phrase that gives a kind of musical unity to the work: a guilt-ridden, terrible motif repeated with variations, from the jesting taunts of its heroine, the Negress Roxana, to a fellow slave, "If you b'longed to me I'd sell you down the river 'fo' you git too fur gone . . ." to the bleak irony of the novel's final sentence, "The Governor . . . pardoned Tom at once, and the creditors sold him down the river."

The contrast with *Huckleberry Finn* inevitably suggests itself; for here the direction of the river Twain loved is regarded as pointing *only* into the ultimate Southern horror, the unmitigated terror of conscienceless and brutal slavery. The movement of the plot, the very shape of *Pudd'nhead Wilson* is determined by this symbolic motion toward the Gulf of Mexico—the movement of the Father of Waters toward a confluence with the great maternal sea; though here that symbolic motion represents no longer a dream of the flight to freedom, but only a nightmare of the passage into captivity. And at the center of the motion and the plot, stands the figure of the slave-girl Roxana, who has held at her breast both her own child and her master's, black and white milk-brothers. Roxana, however, defies all clichés; she is no gross, comfortable, placid source of warmth, all bosom and grin, but a passionate, complex, and beautiful mulatto, a truly living woman distinguished from the wooden images of virtue and bitchery that pass for females in most American novels. She is "black" only by definition, by social convention, though her actual appearance as described by Twain, "majestic . . . rosy . . . comely," so baffled the platitude-ridden illustrator of the official edition that he drew in her place a plump and comic Aunt Jemima!

Her own child, called Valet de Chambre, or Chambers, has been sired by Cecil Burleigh Essex, a white Virginia gentleman, and hence is even less the woolly-haired, swart, blubber-lipped caricature than she. Indeed he is scarcely distinguishable with his "blue eyes and flaxen curls" from his milk-brother, Thomas à Becket Driscoll, so that Roxana has no trouble switching the two in their cradles when Valet de Chambre is threatened with being sold down to shave him. " 'Faithful fellow!' cried Captain Delano, 'Don Benito, I envy you such a friend, slave I cannot call him.' " But Melville will not let it go, adding on his own behalf—in a tone less ironical than one would expect:

> Most negroes are natural valets and hairdressers. . . . There is . . . a smooth tact about them in this employment. . . . And above all is the great gift of good-humour . . . a certain easy cheerfulness . . . as though God had set the whole negro to some pleasant tune . . . to this is added the docility arising from the unaspiring contentment of a limited mind, and that susceptibility of bland attachment sometimes inhering in indisputable inferiors. . . . Like most men of a good, blithe heart, Captain Delano took to negroes . . . just as other men to Newfoundland dogs.

But Babo is, in fact, the leader of a black uprising that has already murdered his master's closest friend and bound his corpse to the prow; and Captain Delano in his unwillingness to imperil his fondness for Negroes, almost kills Don Benito when he makes a last, desperate attempt to escape. Still convinced that the true source of moral infection is to be found only in the decaying institutions of Europe, Captain Delano cannot understand why, even after the exposure of Babo, Benito Cereno continues to pine away and seems to long only for death.

Though the fact of slavery, out of which all the violence and deceit aboard the Spanish ship has been bred, remains a part of his own democratic world as well as Don Benito's aristocratic one, Amasa Delano is undismayed. Though only an incident has been dealt with and its deep causes left untouched, he finds in this no cause for despair, but demands that the Spaniard join with him in recognizing a happy ending. "You are saved . . . ," he cries to Don Benito; "You are saved: what has cast such a shadow upon you?" And he will not understand when the Spanish captain answers, "The negro." Indeed, Melville seems to share the bafflement of his American protagonist; a Northerner like Captain Delano, Melville finds the problem of slavery and the Negro a little exotic, a gothic horror in an almost theatrical sense of the word. Before his story is done, at any rate, he lets it lapse back into the language of the written record when he had to look for it in the first instance—quite unlike Poe who found this particular theme at the very center of his own experience.

In this regard, Mark Twain is much more like Poe than Melville. Whatever his conflicting allegiances, he was a Southerner in his roots and origin, who all his life long carried on a family quarrel with the part of the country in which he had long ceased to live. He had enlisted briefly on the side of the Confederacy, though he became finally a convert to the abolitionist cause and wrote in his finest book an attack on slavery; and he could never really disavow the Southern notion of "honor," though he mocked all his life Sir Walter Scott and the mad chivalric codes which the South had derived from Scott's books. The town in which Twain was born and to which his imagination compulsively returned existed on a boundary between South and West; and, indeed, his two youthful careers led him to turn first in one direction then in the other. As a riverboat pilot before the Civil War, he followed the Mississippi down to New Orleans, as a journalist and fortune-hunter after Abolition, he headed across that same river toward Nevada and California. Both worlds lured him, turn and turn about; and in his two most profound books, he faces first one way then the other, but reverses the actual order of his life.

Huckleberry Finn ends with Huck pointed west, ready to light out for the territory in search of a freedom he had deludedly and vainly sought with Jim by going down the Mississippi. Why, critics have asked ever since the book appeared, did Huck not cross the river to the Illinois side, go east to where freedom really existed as a political fact? But the East, though it claimed Twain at last, had no symbolic meaning for him; the motion toward childhood is for him a motion toward the South, down the river. It was, therefore, down to Arkansas that Twain moved the Missouri farm of his mother's sister and her husband, the Great Good Place of his earliest years, which is celebrated in the most moving and lyrical section of the *Autobiography,* and which had appeared earlier as a mythical refuge in *Huckleberry Finn* (1885) and *Tom Sawyer Detective* (1896). Like Poe, Twain thought of the trip home as a voyage south; but like the earlier writer, too, he felt that trip a descent into hell. Though Twain was always consciously more attracted than repelled by the ambivalent Eden of his boyhood, and in his memoirs tends to idealize its terror almost out of existence, his fiction tells quite another story. Huck Finn is able to reject Aunt Sally's utopia out of hand—for all the redolence of its good home cooking; and in *Tom Sawyer Detective,* it takes all of Tom's ingenuity to exorcise murder and the threat

In Poe the incest theme belongs to the private world of his own tortured psyche rather than the broader arena of social life in the South. Over and over, the writer, who married his scarcely nubile cousin and called her Sis, returns to the theme, particularly in that series of tales involving dark and terrible ladies, which is his most authentic and convincing achievement. The first of these stories is "Berenice" ("Berenice and I were cousins, and we grew up together in my paternal halls . . ."); and the line continues on through "Eleanora" ("She whom I loved in youth . . . was the sole daughter of the only sister of my mother long departed") to reach a climax in "The Fall of the House of Usher," in which the doomed beloved is at last identified as the protagonist's sister. Sometimes, as in "Morella" and "Ligeia," the dying succubus-bride is portrayed as not even being kin to her husband; but always she is clearly a dark projection of his psyche, as intimately related to him as his own image in the mirror. And always, too, she bears the stigmata of a tabooed figure: the dark eyes and hair, which mark her as the carrier of madness and death. She tends to become, indeed, the symbol of mortality, the figure of death itself—combining the characteristics of shadow and *anima*, as if intended to signify that the soul of a man and his death are one thing.

The uses of incest in sentimental and gothic fiction are, as we have already noticed, many; but in Poe, who deals customarily with problems of impotence rather than of power, the death-wish is always uppermost; and the desire to embrace the sister-bride means for him first of all a yearning to *fall*—a perverse longing to plunge into the destructive embrace of his own image in a dark tarn. The ending of "The Fall of the House of Usher" expresses directly the lust for a union with death which is Poe's ruling passion. Madeline, the sister of Usher, whom he has buried alive, returns from the grave to claim her brother just as he has, almost equally, feared and desired:

> Without those doors there DID stand the lofty and enshrouded figure of the Lady Madeline of Usher. There was blood upon her white robes, and the evidence of some bitter struggle upon every portion of her emaciated frame. For a moment she remained trembling and reeling to and fro upon the threshold,

then, with a low moaning cry, fell heavily inward upon the person of her brother, and in her violent and now final death agonies, bore him to the floor as a corpse. . . .

It is the most horrific of *Liebestods,* the ultimate expression of Poe's obsessive dream of being possessed by the dead, raped by a cadaverous sister-beloved, elsewhere projected in the story of Ligeia, who returns from death to take over the body of a second bride. But there is in Poe a complementary desire to possess the dead, to return embrace for embrace, violation for violation. At its mildest and most conventional, this longing is satisfied in fantasies of lovers joined as fellow ghosts beyond the grave or chatting cozily after the cataclysmic destruction of the world. In such tales, the erotic commerce of the specters is confined to speech, as in "The Colloquy of Monos and Una" or "The Conversations of Eiros and Charmion." Occasionally, however, Poe's necrophiliac heroes descend living into the tomb, like the protagonist of "Berenice," who returns with the bloody teeth of his beloved, or the narrator of "Ulalume," who scarcely knows why he has drifted back to the "dank tarn of Auber." Most frank of all Poe's celebrations of the union with a corpse is confided to the disarmingly sweet verses of "Annabel Lee":

> And so, all the night-tide, I lie down by the side
> Of my darling—my darling—my life and my bride,
> In the sepulchre there by the sea—
> In her tomb by the sounding sea.

The odd syndrome of child-love, necrophilia, and incest in Poe is too personal and pathological to shed much light on the general meaning of the latter theme in American literature and life. It is not without interest, however, to reflect that the tales of Poe have come to be thought of as a children's classic; and his fantasies—in which adults never copulate in the flesh, only rape each other's minds, at least as long as they are alive—are considered proper selections for classroom anthologies. In any case, he has had little direct influence on later serious American writers, until, perhaps, the time of Vladimir Nabokov, in whose *Lolita* the example of Poe is combined so oddly with that of Gogol. When gothic incest became a major theme in the mid-nineteenth century, it was embodied not in the figure of Madeline Usher but that of Beatrice Cenci.

to marry him. A charming and handsome Negro, who has "passed" without difficulty, he turns to the somewhat younger white man, who has adulated him and to whose sister he is engaged, deliberately evoking the vulgar taunt of the crudest Negro-baiters, "I'm the nigger that's going to sleep with your sister. Unless you stop me, Henry." And Henry, as he must, though only after long delay, shoots him.

Yet just before Bon speaks the words that doom him, Henry has cried to him, "You are my brother." Such brotherhood is more than a metaphor in *Absalom, Absalom!*, more even than the bond of having shared a single breast that links Twain's Tom to Chambers. In Faulkner's plot, the white man and the Negro who love and destroy each other are quite literally the sons of the same father, of Thomas Sutpen, the passionate, damned hero of the action. The younger, white son was born of a timid, genteel, rustic, puritanical creature, married for the sake of the status and respectability she could bestow; the older, black one was the offspring of a Haitian breed, foisted on an ignorant and ambitious young man by her unscrupulous parents. White and black, they find themselves locked finally in a terrible triangle, the two brothers more in love with each other than either with the sister (perhaps Bon loves no one, only wants to provoke his proud father into admitting the relationship from which he has fled), and the threat of incest over them all.

This is the final turn of the screw, the ultimate gothic horror which serves both to produce one more shock and to add one more level of symbolic relevance to the action: the man who screams in panic that some black buck is about to rape his sister is speaking of one who is, indeed, his brother, and whom secretly he loves. But the event of such love is only guilt and death and a retreat into a dark house, already sacked and gutted in a war fought to maintain the order which had bred the relationship itself. Sutpen and his Negro bride had already mated, already produced a child neither white nor black; and the frustration of a second incestuous match saves nothing. It serves only to prevent the grafting onto the narrow, Protestant provincialism of the rural South of a Catholic and urban grace, nurtured in Creole New Orleans. The adulterated Sutpen line eventuates not in the sensuous, elegant hybrid that might have been produced out of a mating of Charles Bon and Sutpen's white daughter, but in Jim Bond, mindless child of the offspring of

Bon's self-punishing marriage to an ignorant, ugly Negress: ". . . there was nothing left now, nothing out there now but that idiot boy to lurk around those ashes and those four gutted chimneys and howl until someone came and drove him away. They couldn't catch him and nobody ever seemed to make him go very far away, he just stopped howling for a little while."

Jim Bond (the name which meant "good" corrupted to one which means "slave") is not so much living flesh and blood as the terrible ghost that haunts the mind of such Southerners as Quentin Compson, who has been driven to uncover step by step the mystery of the Sutpens, and who represents the conscience of Faulkner himself. No wonder he grows frantic under his roommate's questioning: " 'Now I want you to tell me just one thing more. Why do you hate the South?' 'I dont hate it,' Quentin said, quickly, at once, immediately; 'I dont hate it,' he said. *I dont hate it* he thought, panting in the cold air, the iron New England dark; *I dont. I dont! I dont hate it! I dont hate it!"* These are the final words of the book; but they are followed by a genealogy, in which we read of Quentin Compson that he died in the very year in which he uncovered the secret of the death of Charles Bon, not yet twenty years old: a suicide, we learn in another place. It is the only possible ending to a novel in which the "Southern" as a genre reaches its final form. At the same time that *Absalom, Absalom!* solves the detective-story problem of who killed Charles Bon, it is answering another, profounder question, satisfying the Southerner's need to "know at last why God let us lose the war." The query is as desperate as that posed by Captain Delano: "What has cast such a shadow upon you?" And the answer is the same: "The Negro."

Yet the theme we have been examining does not exhaust the meanings of Faulkner's book. It represents only a single strand in an intricately constructed and immensely complex work, a showpiece of sustained rhetoric, whose total effect makes it at first bewildering, but which, in the long run, seems the most deeply moving of all American gothic fictions. In the history of that genre, *Absalom, Absalom!* is remarkable for having first joined to the theme of slavery and black revenge, which is the essential sociological theme of the American tale of terror, that of incest, which is its essential erotic theme.

It is not until *Band of Angels* (1955), however, that Warren, a Southerner himself and once involved in the Agrarian movement, turns to a full-scale treatment of the subject Twain had broached in *Pudd'nhead Wilson,* the plight of the white Negro. By turning the false Tom into a girl, however, Warren transforms the novel of miscegenation from the masculine murder mystery to the feminine bosom book, the erotic historical romance, creating a hybrid form whose strange pedigree would read: out of Margaret Mitchell by Mark Twain! Its fable deals with Amantha Starr, a young woman who discovers on her father's death that she is legally a slave and a Negro—and of her difficulty in deciding what, beneath "the fiction of law and custom," she really is.

The problem of identity is not for her as simple as it was for the exposed Valet de Chambre; what his mother confides in him and Pudd'nhead declares in open court, he himself believes. But Amantha does not know what to believe, for she has been sent as a child to an enlightened and pious college, where she has acquired a set of abolitionist clichés as useless to her in understanding the realities of slavery and being a Negro as are the opposite clichés of the Southern slaveholders. Nonetheless, an aura of miscegenation hangs over the series of love affairs which make up the history of Amantha, threatening to dissolve each embrace into a spasm of nausea or to convert it into a rape; yet she will not, she cannot bring herself to say, "I am a Negro!" No more capable of declaring herself white, she chooses to be nothing: an abstract victim without a particular identity. Like the hero of Ralph Ellison's *Invisible Man,* she fades from sight because she becomes nothing except her role; but in her case, the invisibility is willed. Her decision justifies her lovers in approaching her with disgust or condescension or pity— anything, that is to say, but love; and it is for that reason, that they are destroyed. Only when her white husband comes to realize that he, too, is a victim, she, too, a human ("The skin of every human being contains a slave" and its obverse), is he able to live with her not as a master or a benefactor, but as one weak and suffering being with another; and Amantha is at last free. It is a finally sentimental resolution, a retreat from the tragic blackness toward which Mark Twain had, however falteringly, moved.

To find a writer capable of accepting the darker implications of Twain's gothicism and pressing on to even more terrible resolutions, we must turn back to Warren's immediate master, William Faulkner. Faulkner instinctively begins with the realization, which we have discovered in Twain, that not murder only but miscegenation, too, must preside over the relations of black and white to produce the full gothic shiver. More shocking to the imagination of the South than the fantasy of a white man overwhelmed by a hostile black world is the fear that finally all distinctions will be blurred and black and white no longer exist. On what can the assurance of a God-given right to enslave Negroes or deprive them of rights be based, when no man can say with security who is the real Thomas à Becket Driscoll, who some black pretender? Precisely this prevision of total assimilation and chaos is entrusted to the young Canadian Shreve at the end of Faulkner's *Absalom, Absalom!* (1935):

> I think that in time the Jim Bonds are going to conquer the western hemisphere. Of course it won't be quite in our time and of course as they spread toward the poles they will bleach out again like the rabbits and birds do, so they won't show up so sharp against the snow. But it will still be Jim Bond; and so in a few thousand years, I who regard you will also have sprung from the loins of African kings.

But Jim Bond in the novel is an idiot, elusive as a ghost, a specter haunting the ravaged white family whose blood he shares.

In Faulkner's work, the threat of miscegenation is posed not only in terms of future racial contamination, but also in those of a present sexual threat. Out of the semi-obscene sub-literature of Southern racists, he captures and redeems the hysterical vision of the black rapist, the Negro who, by stealth or force (in Faulkner it is typically by stealth, which is to say, under the cover of a pseudo-white skin), possesses a white woman. The archetype answers precisely the abolitionist myth of the helpless Negro servant girl assaulted by her master. Against Roxana, pitifully proud of her relationship with the gentleman who leaves her pregnant with a flaxen-haired slave, is set the mother of Joe Christmas in *Light in August* (1932), trying to convince the doctor who attends her that the man who had fathered her bastard "was a Mexican. When old Doc Hines could see in his face the black curse of God Almighty." And against Simon Legree in *Uncle Tom's Cabin,* pursuing the terrified and virginal Emmeline, is balanced (in *Absalom, Absalom!*) the figure of Charles Bon, who has persuaded a white woman excluded by long conditioning from the world of upper-class society, and barred from the "solacing refuge" of the slave kitchens by the fact of his legal whiteness. Had he turned on his foster-brother at the moment of revelation, he could only have yelled what he earlier cried out to his presumed mother, "Yah-yah-yah! . . . Bofe of us is imitation *white*—dat's what we is. . . ." And what would he have made of Twain's afterthought, one of the final jottings in his journal, "the skin of every human being contains a slave"?

Certainly, Pudd'nhead Wilson, in his exhibitionist courtroom speech, when he rises to announce once more the old scandal that the son has killed his father (Twain somewhat timidly makes them only step-father and step-son), does not succeed in restoring to the community a sense of its own innocence by establishing the guilt of a single culprit. Yet this, as W. H. Auden convincingly argues, is the archetypal function of the detective story, to which genre *Pudd'nhead Wilson* seems to belong. It is, in fact, an *anti*-detective story, more like *The Brothers Karamazov* than *The Innocence of Father Brown,* its function to expose communal guilt: our moral bankruptcy, horror and shame, the stupidity of our definition of a Negro, and the hopeless trap of our relations with him. Wilson's disclosure of Roxy's hoax coalesces with Mark Twain's exposure to America of its own secret self. Each of Twain's chapters is headed by a quotation from "Pudd'nhead Wilson's Calendar," a collection of small-town dangerous thoughts; and at the head of the final chapter, under the rubric "Conclusion," he inscribes the following text: *"October 21, The Discovery.* It was wonderful to find America, but it would have been more wonderful to miss it." It is the most improbable of endings for a detective story, which depends precisely upon its readers' faith in discovery; but it is one appropriate enough for the anti-Western novel at the moment that it becomes anti-American in its revulsion from all clichés of innocent, new frontiers.

The assault upon the Western and its image of America did not, of course, die with Twain. In our time, it is most notably carried forward by Robert Penn Warren, a poet, critic, and pedagogue as well as a novelist, who has attempted the risky game of presenting to our largest audience the anti-Western in the guise of the Western, the anti-historical romance in the guise of that form itself. In this enterprise, he has followed the example of Twain himself, who pretended to be writing in *Pudd'nhead Wilson* a popular detective story even as he mocked the form; and who in "A Double-Barrelled Detective Story" carried the process even further, specifically parodying the methods of Conan Doyle. It is with historical fiction that Warren prefers to deal, seeing himself perhaps as the researcher (his first book dealt with the life of John Brown) just as Twain sees himself as the sleuth. In *World Enough and Time* (1952), at any rate, Warren attacks directly the myth of the West, using for his purposes the famous Beauchamp case, which had been treated earlier by Simms and Edgar Allan Poe. Warren, however, is not primarily interested in the fable of seduction and revenge, on which we have commented earlier; by shifting the point of interest from the Persecuted Maiden to her avenging lover, whom he calls Jeremiah Beaumont, he converts the tale from a study of the encounter of innocence and lust to a study of the encounter of romanticism and reality. Through all his attempts to substitute for life, or impose on life itself a sentimental dream of life, Beaumont has assumed the existence of a paradisal West, an unfallen Eden to which he can flee when all else fails him. In the end, Warren permits him to escape hanging (changing the facts of the original story for this purpose) and to seek out the wilderness of which he has so long dreamed. But that wilderness he finds to be no more than a festering swamp, in which he is ultimately murdered and his beloved, withered and haggard, commits suicide; and presiding over the travesty of the Great Good Place, no noble and immaculate Natty Bumppo, but a hump-backed monster dying in sensuality and filth: *la grande Bosse,* river pirate and nightmare made flesh, the visible shape of original sin which Beaumont's sentimental version of the West had denied.

In *Brother to Dragons* (1953), a long verse narrative, Warren continues his assault on the theory of original innocence, drafting Thomas Jefferson as a ghostly witness to a particularly brutal and meaningless crime committed by two of his nephews, who slaughter in a meat-house, for trivial reasons, a Negro—acting out ritually the guilt of the white man toward those he has enslaved.*

---

* The ghost of Merriwether Lewis haunts Warren's poem and has recently begun to haunt me, too—so blithe in his beginnings, so tragic in his end. He represents and his journals record an attempt to penetrate the American West erotically, joyously—to assimilate it in heterosexual love. But his death at thirty-five (murdered? a suicide?) marks the failure of that attempt as well as Lewis's personal defeat.

The most gothic books of both Hawthorne and Melville are presided over by the mythic face of this lady as painted by Guido Reni and adulated by two generations of American tourists. Over *The Marble Faun* of the one and the *Pierre* of the other, Beatrice Cenci casts a shadow of parricide and incest, suggests an added dimension of horror that Hawthorne at least was too cautious to specify in his own plot. It is important to remember that it was not really the original seventeenth-century painting of her in the Palazzo Barberini to which both Hawthorne and Melville made the obligatory pilgrimage; for both alike were possessed by a literary tradition which had grown up around the portrait, finally making it impossible to see past the myth of "a fallen angel," as Hilda calls her in *The Marble Faun,* "fallen, and yet sinless."

In response to the *myth* of the portrait, both American writers vibrated in accord; but about what it looked like they totally disagree. "With blue eyes and fair complexion, the Cenci's hair is golden," Melville writes; while Hawthorne informs us that from beneath Beatrice's turban "strayed a lock or two . . . of auburn hair. The eyes were large and brown. . . ." Since each had approached the picture as literature, each re-envisioned it in his own style. For Melville, the incest-stained innocent *must* be blond in order to make his symbolic point (elsewhere worked out in *Typee* and *Mardi*) that in some women the Fair Maiden and the Dark Lady are disturbingly confused:

> . . . physically . . . all is in strict, natural keeping: which, nevertheless, still the more intensifies the suggested anomaly of so *blonde* a being, being double-hooded, as it were by the black crape of the two more horrible crimes . . . possible to civilized humanity—incest and parricide.

It is, indeed, the blond Lucy of his own *Pierre* who, in that novel, stands before the portrait, which reflects the incest and terror that she has not recognized, not allowed herself to recognize in her closest companions, Isabel and Pierre.

Hawthorne goes even further by suggesting an actual resemblance between his Anglo-Saxon snow maiden and the mysterious portrait, that to him symbolizes not so much the ambiguity of light and dark as the mystery of alienation: "It was the saddest picture ever painted or conceived; it involved an unfathomable depth of sorrow . . . a sorrow that removed this beautiful girl out of the sphere of humanity, and set her in a far-off region, the remoteness of which . . . makes us shiver as at a spectre." In Hawthorne, the copy of Guido's Beatrice that plays a part in his own tale, is not the product—as in Melville—of an unknown hand, but has been lovingly painted by the Fair Girl herself, by his dove-like Hilda. Looking into her mirror, she fancies a similarity between her own expression and that of the Beatrice before whom she has sat so long. Hawthorne, however, hastens to make it clear that not her own sin but that of another had frightened Beatrice Cenci "into a remote and inaccessible region, where no sympathy would come," and that it is a similar fate which is shadowed on Hilda's face. Just as the earlier innocent had been crushed by a sense of her father's guilt, Hilda risks being crushed by an awareness of the crime of her friend, the Dark Lady, Miriam.

It is Miriam who is involved in a mysterious scandal which binds her to the sinister palace of the Cenci itself, Miaraim to whom Hawthorne's mouthpiece, Kenyon, says, "I shudder at the fatality that seems to haunt your footsteps, and throws a shadow of crime about your path, you being guiltless." But what precise crime has cast a shadow upon her, Hawthorne cannot bring himself to tell. It is connected, we know, with the hairy Model who dogs her footsteps, and who is bound to her, it is suggested, by blood as well as complicity, a man "so evil, so vile, and yet so strangely subtle, as could only be accounted for by the insanity which often develops itself in old, closekept races of men when long unmixed with newer blood." This suggestion of immemorial inbreeding, joined with the repeated allusions to Miriam's implication in "one of the most dreadful and mysterious events that have occurred within the present century," implies surely the sin of incest; but Hawthorne is at once too genteel and too fond of playful mystification to speak out that dread word.

Hawthorne had dealt openly with the subject of incest only in his early story "Alice Doane's Appeal," whose basic fable oddly resembles Faulkner's *Absalom, Absalom!* It opens with a murder whose solution involves the exposure of the feelings that bind together in an unnatural triangle a young man, his sister, and a stranger whom he suspects of being her lover, but who proves in the end brother to both. "He was my very counterpart," says Leonard Doane of Walter Broame; and this uncanny resemblance seems to him reason enough for his sister Alice to "inevitably love him . . . with all the strength of sisterly affection, added to that impure passion which alone engrosses all the heart." Driven half-mad by imaginings which project onto the stranger his own unconfessed desire for his sister, and infuriated further by that stranger's boasts of having conquered her, Leonard kills him. At the moment of death, however, he sees in the face of the man he has murdered "a likeness of my father."

As in Faulkner's novel, the brothers are as culturally unlike as they are physically the same; for just as in the twentieth-century fiction, one has been educated "in the cities of the old world" and one "in this rude wilderness." Cosmopolitan sybarite and rustic stalwart, they represent in their conflict not the struggle of Creole black and Puritan white brother, but the encounter of Old World and New World sons of the same fatherland, loyalist and colonial in a struggle for possession of the body of America. In the end, Hawthorne's fragmentary story threatens to become a parable of the American Revolution—a gothic treatment of the international theme, set back into the period when our national consciousness was in the process of being forged.

In the final years of his life, Hawthorne tried once more to create a substantial fiction dealing, beneath its spectacular machinery of bloody footsteps, ancestral curses, and lost wills, with the bloody confrontation of England and America. He achieved only a handful of fragmentary manuscripts in which the theme of incest struggles to assert itself, as it must in any fable treating a guilt-ridden fraternal relationship which begins in love and ends in murder.

In light of Hawthorne's life-long obsession with the subject, one is tempted to believe the contention of certain critics (finally unproven) that the incestuous Pierre of Melville's gothic romance is intended to be a portrait of Hawthorne; that the book was Melville's attempt to confess for his alienated friend the secret sin which presumably haunted him through all his years. Melville seems to have believed, at any rate, that he had penetrated the heart of Hawthorne's mystery; for when Hawthorne's son visited him in 1883, Melville told him—so Julian Hawthorne wrote later —"that there was some secret in my father's life which had never been revealed, and which accounted for the gloomy passages in his books." Julian was not much impressed, however, observing dryly, "It was characteristic of him to imagine so; there were many secrets untold in his own career." Whether, indeed, the "secret" revealed in *Pierre* is Melville's or Hawthorne's or neither's matters little; what is important is that it is the major underground concern of American gothicists in general, the erotic relationship proper to that form: brother-sister incest. *Pierre* represents the major attempt in the history of our fiction at making of that theme great art, at redeeming it from the stereotypes into which it had fallen, and wresting from it whatever symbolic meaning it had all along contained.

Even in the first chapters of *Pierre,* suggestions of a sickly incestuousness hover over the euphoric rustic scene. The young Pierre not merely flutters about his mother with the excessive gallantries of a courtly lover, tying her ribbon, her shoe-lace, but he addresses her as "Sister Mary"; and she, speaking of the blond Lucy who is to be Pierre's wife, refers to her as a "little sister." There is more than a trace of pride registered in the adjective, for Pierre's mother is securely aware of her sexual superiority to "little" Lucy, reflecting later that beside her son's fiancée she herself seems a quart decanter of port next to a pint decanter of pale sherry! But Pierre is not content just to *play* at incest with his mother, and marry—as an assurance of his fidelity to her—a girl who is clearly no sexual rival. Instead, he turns to a dark, alien figure, the complete denial of everything in his mother's milky, blue, pink, and gold idyllic world, but a reminder of what his wild father might have been before his marriage.

To complicate matters further, Isabel, the swart *anima*-figure who may be his sister, is half-mad and an outcast; so that to espouse her cause can be made to seem moral dedication and an attack on conformity. When Pierre decides finally to run off with Isabel, to pretend to the world that they are man and wife—so that he can at once protect her and not expose his father as a breeder of bastards—he is able to feel himself Christ-like, and his act a more than human self-sacrifice. Melville, however, refuses either him or the reader the privilege of living long with this illusion, pointing out that in attempting to transcend the codes of conventional society, Pierre has risked becoming a scandalous sinner rather than a moral hero. In the end, he is not the Christ or Titan he dreams himself, not even a Memnon or Hamlet, but a latter-day Widow of Ephesus. Like the woman of that legend, who, in dedicating herself to an impossible ideal of fidelity, ended by desecrating the grave of her husband in lust and hanging his body on a public gallows, Pierre invents for himself crimes beyond the ken of ordinary men, a dénouement almost as comic as it is terrible.

Even at the moment when he first confides to Isabel his decision to run off with her and accept the world's blame, conscious of his blamelessness, Pierre really knows what he is after. The secret motive of his ostensible sacrifice enters his awareness.

> He held her tremblingly; she bent toward him; his mouth wet her ear; he whispered it. . . . Over the face of Pierre there shot a terrible self-revelation; he imprinted repeated burning kisses upon her; pressed her hand; would not let go her sweet and awful passiveness.
>
> Then they changed; they coiled together, and entangledly stood mute.

The image of the serpent signals the presence of the serpentine horror of incest, already implicit in the pressure of a damp mouth at the ear; but there is a further fall to come. After Pierre has fled to the city, and has found there only failure and the torments of guilt, he comes to his dark sister to be consoled, to be held in her arms in "the peace of the twilight." But folded into that "sweet and awful passiveness" again, he leaps up in anguish, crying, "If to follow Virtue to her uttermost vista . . . if by that I take hold on hell, and if the uttermost virtue, after all, prove but a betraying pander to the monstrousest vice,—then close in and crush me, ye stony walls, and into one gulf let all things tumble together!"

It is pseudo-Shakespearean rant, the rhetoric of the cheapest gothic melodrama, a theatrical debasement of the pure Faustian cry of terror; but beneath its superficial falseness, there is at work an insidious attack on the platitudes of Romanticism, which had made of fraternal affection the symbol of an impossible purity. The gothic mode is essentially a form of parody, a way of assailing clichés by exaggerating them to the limit of grotesqueness; and in *Pierre,* Melville is mocking the banal tender plea, "Let me be a sister to you!", just as in *Absalom, Absalom!,* Faulkner was to mock the banal harsh taunt, "Would you want a nigger to sleep with your sister!" Yet there is rage in Melville, too, anguish at the thought that there cannot be an immaculate love of brother and sister; that this, too, is one of "The Ambiguities" referred to by the subtitle of his novel.

At this point, Pierre begins to rethink the evidence which has convinced him that Isabel was, indeed, his father's illegitimate daughter: her perhaps imagined resemblance to a portrait of his

father as a young man, her disordered memories, an initialed handkerchief. "Call me brother no more!" he cries in despair; and the
next moment he tries to argue away the concepts of virtue and vice,
even as he has argued away their blood relationship. Only the denial of one or the other can save him from confessing his utter
damnation, and he scarcely knows which to disavow first. He
brushes aside "these two shadows cast from one nothing" and goes
on to insist that "these, seems to me are Virtue and Vice. . . . It is
all a dream that we dreamed we dream. . . . From nothing proceeds nothing, Isabel! How can one sin in a dream." But when
Isabel, content with his dismissal of sin, unconcerned in her passivity, says simply, "Let us sit down again, my brother," Pierre is
driven to repeat his first denial, "I am Pierre." Isabel still unruffled
amends her request, "Let us sit down again, Pierre . . ." and together in the growing dark with no lamp lit, they fade into each
other in their fatal embrace.

Just as he sins (or perhaps does not) in the dream which is his
life, Pierre also dreams within that dream; and his dream within a
dream contains Melville's own reading of his book, a guide to future critics. The most analytic of novelists, Melville insisted always
on being the explicator of his own symbols and themes; and incest
was for him not a bedrock fact but a symbol, beyond which the
reader must go in search of total comprehension, a riddle to be
solved. Pierre sees in his dream a mountain shaped like a Promethean man, an outcropping of rock near his ancestral home, which
fades into the figure of Enceladus, the mutilated but "deathless son
of Terra"; and in turn this "American Enceladus," half-buried and
castrated ("Nature . . . performed an amputation, and left the
impotent Titan without one serviceable ball-and-socket above the
thigh"), fades into the image of Pierre: "but on the Titan's armless
trunk, his own duplicate face and features gleamed upon him with
prophetic discomfiture and woe."

When he awakes from "that ideal horror to all his actual grief,"
Pierre calls upon all his knowledge of myth and legend, hammers
away at the riddle like Moses at the rock, until he has made clear
to his own and Melville's satisfaction the meaning of his vision:

Old Titan's self was the son of incestuous Coelus and Terra, the
son of incestuous Heaven and Earth. And Titan married his
mother Terra, another and accumulatively incestuous match. So

Enceladus was both the son and grandson of an incest; and even thus, there had been born from the organic blended heavenliness and earthliness of Pierre, another mixed, uncertain, heaven-aspiring, but still not wholly earth-emancipated mood; which again, by its terrestrial taint held down to its terrestrial mother, generated there the present doubly incestuous Enceladus within him; so that the present mood of Pierre—that reckless sky-assaulting mood of his, was nevertheless on one side the grandson of the sky. For it is according to eternal fitness, that the precipitated Titan should still seek to regain his paternal birthright even by fierce escalade.

It seems almost more an evasion than an explanation; and certainly Melville permits himself to get trapped in the intricacies of his image, becoming as much its victim as its exploiter. What he seems to be saying on the simplest level is that in each individual there is a fundamental conflict of two principles, called variously earth and heaven, nature and spirit, id and super-ego; and that every human action is bred of a marriage of these principles, or of a union between one of them and some previous action bred of an earlier marriage. In Western civilization, these principles are typically identified with the mother and father, and any attempt to allegorize them produces, on the literal level, a story of incest. To become somehow one with the father—even at the risk of seeming to betray the mother or of threatening the sovereignty of the paternal principle itself—this is for Melville the meaning of Enceladus' escalade and of Pierre's elopement.

Whether or not this seems finally satisfactory as an explanation of the fable of Melville's book, it is, perhaps, the only example in our literature of a writer's conscious attempt to know what he is unconsciously meaning when he takes up the subject of incest. At the opposite pole from this is Poe, who was content simply to be possessed by his subjects (when pressed he could always pretend they were parodies or hoaxes, or disown them as "silly"), and whose works, therefore, seem in large part symptoms rather than achievements.

IV

Yet Poe produced, after all, one completely achieved work of art in his writing career, a character who belongs specifically to none of his stories though he is, in part, the creation of all of them—a composite of Julius Rodman, Gordon Pym, William Wilson, Roderick Usher, and all the other pale, tormented failures at aggression, exploration, and love, who are haunted, buried alive, or clasped in the arms of corpses. That character, who is, of course, Edgar Allan Poe (even the middle name is an invention, part of the legend), Poe not only wrote but *lived*—taking cues from Brockden Brown and Byron and Bulwer Lytton; and adding, where necessary, the appropriate lies. He told incompatible stories about his birth, falsified his age, claimed to have gone off to Greece to help in the fight for freedom; and when he died, bequeathed his life-long task of composing a Poe-image to a particularly hostile executor, Rufus Griswold. It was perhaps Poe's last hoax, a perverse joke on himself and his public; for Griswold, as Poe must have foreseen, proceeded to blacken Poe's reputation with all the aplomb of a self-consciously righteous man exposing a scoundrel. To make Poe seem an utterly irresponsible villain, Griswold was not above forging letters or lifting appropriate passages out of popular novels and fitting them into his account. Like Poe himself, that is to say, Griswold approached his subject's life as if it were a work of art.

So also did Baudelaire, that second and unforeseen collaborator in the posthumous rewriting of Poe, who was moved by a passion equal and opposite to Griswold's. In need of a hero, an alter ego, a model for his own version of the *poète maudit,* Baudelaire took up the still plastic image of Poe and made of it that French *symboliste* once-removed, the *Edgairpo* of the Europeans, which to this day baffles visitors from our side of the Atlantic. Baudelaire saw Poe simultaneously as the victim of America and as a second Christ whose cross was alcohol. Speaking from the first view, he says: "Some of the documents which I have seen persuade me that Poe found in the United States a large prison from which all his life he was making desperate efforts to escape"; and from the second, "I say without shame, because I feel that it springs from a profound sense of pity and affection, that I prefer Edgar Poe, drunk, poor, persecuted and a pariah, to a calm and virtuous Goethe or Walter

Scott. I should willingly say of him and of a special class of men what the catechism says of our Lord: 'He has suffered much for us!' "

It is easy enough to discount both statements of Baudelaire as examples of a new sentimentality, the sentimentality of the anti-bourgeois European poet, who tries to put art in the vacant place of God and America and mass society in that of the Devil. Poe was by no means the first or only writer in the United States to find himself at odds with his country. It is, indeed, the typical relationship between Americans and serious native writers of all kinds, even James Fenimore Cooper (who represented to Poe the antithesis of that to which he aspired) having found himself estranged from his fellow citizens, hostile to their way of life. But whatever quarrels Cooper may have had with the American public, he was never alienated from the deepest levels of the American mind. If, at his death, he was being read less and less, still his passing was felt as an occasion for national mourning, and Daniel Webster, the official spokesman of the era, called upon to pronounce his funeral oration. Poe, on the other hand, lay without a tombstone for twenty-six years, and when one was erected, the only notable American present was Walt Whitman. Yet it was not Cooper but Poe who became for the American imagination the eternal prototype of the American Writer. Cooper, who could make a nation's myths, could not himself become such a myth; while Poe, who created no archetypal figure to rival Natty Bumppo, himself became a legend. This is perhaps not quite what Poe meant when he referred in reviewing Cooper to two kinds of literature, in one of which "the books sometimes live, while the authors usually die"; while in the other, "even when the works perish the man survives"; but it is close enough to it to indicate that dimly he felt the nature of his own mythical role as well as that of the highbrow writer in general.

Poe represents, of course, the artist as outcast or outsider, surrogate for all in himself that the common reader secretly regrets having to reject in the name of morality or success; and as such, he is our own local instance of an almost universal archetype. Just before Poe's day, Byron (to whom Baudelaire compared Poe, calling the latter *"le Byron égaré dans le mauvais monde"*) had played that mythic role for all of Europe and America, composing his public figure by combining the image of Don Juan with that of the gothic hero-villain, whose ancestry we have traced back to Richardson and Prévost. The most ancient avatar of the alienated artist, however, is Euripides—that is to say, the legendary creature fabricated by Greek commentators and called by that tragedian's name. The pattern is typical in all respects: born of poor and disreputable parents, himself sullen and disagreeable, Euripides is portrayed as returning contempt for contempt, withdrawing to a seaside grotto to be alone with the books he prefers to men; and at the last, it is told, he is torn to pieces by dogs or, preferably, by enraged women!

The final apocryphal anecdote is, of course, drawn from the legend of Orpheus, a mythical being with whom the actual historical figure of the poet was hopelessly confused. But what does the Orpheus archetype, of which Poe was the improbable New World avatar, signify? It is intended, apparently, to express the dismay of the popular mind before the kind of poet who is no longer content to represent bardically the traditions of a closed society, but speaks in his own person—invents, as it were, personal consciousness. In such a poet, the community foresees its own imminent fall from the unity and peace of pre-conscious communal life, and they condemn him to death. But the spokesman for the ego is destroyed by representatives of the id—Maenads, the devotees of Dionysus, wild beasts—and in his moment of destruction is made divine, becomes one with Dionysus himself. Even at its most primitive level, the myth of the outcast poet does not end with his exclusion and death. He has had to suffer and be despised; yet he is loved, even apotheosized precisely for that suffering and despite.

In the nineteenth century, the alienated artist still functions as a scape-hero, though by this time he knows his own role in advance, collaborates in his life and work with the community who seek to impose the traditional role on him. Perhaps, he is a little too self-conscious of what he is doing, a little too much in love with his own pain and exclusion to ring quite true; but society needs him still, demanding of the poet that he enact in his life the rejected values of heedlessness, disorder, and madness—and also that he permit himself to be abused and rejected for enacting them; that he take upon himself both sin and punishment, and so free the community from the burden of its repressed longings and its secret guilt.

This poor Poe was, for his own good masochistic reasons, only too willing to do; and where he did not quite conform to the necessary pattern, Griswold amended the facts of his life, converting the dandy, the lonely aristocrat of the spirit, the lost Byron of the Western world into a willful drunkard, a dope addict, a feckless bohemian. Failing to understand the archetypal necessities of the case, certain respectable scholars of our own time have attempted to redeem Poe from his legend—perhaps because their own peace of mind depends on their proving that all the great writers of our past were as sane and orderly as any member of the Kiwanis Club, to which they themselves are likely to belong. One such critic writes, for instance, "One would like, for all time, to destroy fictions that Poe was a drunkard . . . ; he was not a dope fiend . . . : and he was not a rake. His life was, in fact, one of the dullest any figure of literary importance has lived in the past two hundred years." But Poe did, after all, marry a thirteen-year-old child and watch her die painfully over five years; did at least believe himself the victim of D.T.'s, and yet fling himself into frantic bouts of drinking when faced by sexual problems he could not solve; was at last picked up in the streets of Baltimore senseless, and turned over to a doctor, who wrote: "There is a gentleman, rather the worse for wear, at Ryan's 4th ward polls, who goes under the cognomen of Edgar A. Poe, and who appears in great distress . . ."; did die, four days later, of alcoholic poisoning. It is not quite as lively a death scene as that attributed by legend to Euripides, but it is surely not the dullest in the past two hundred years. And it haunts us still in the pages of Hart Crane's *The Bridge,* in which the poet fixes once and for all the truth no scholar can really desecrate:

> And when they dragged your retching flesh,
> Your trembling hands that night through Baltimore—
> That last night on the ballot rounds, did you
> Shaking, did you deny the ticket, Poe?

The image of Poe which for over a century has possessed the American mind is that image of failure and impotence so necessary to us in a world of success and power: an image of one who is the victim of society and of himself. But it is more specifically, perhaps essentially, the image of the *poet as drunkard,* the weak-stomached, will-less addict, forever swearing off and forever succumbing again. "For more than ten days I was totally deranged . . . ," Poe writes in a letter. "All was hallucination arising from an attack which I had never before experienced—an attack of mania-a-potu. May heaven grant that it prove a warning to me for the rest of my days. . . ." Mania-a-potu: it is the same somewhat unusual word Poe has used in *Gordon Pym* for *delirium tremens.* But D.T.'s are a part of American folklore, like drinking itself the source of an endless stream of uneasy jokes: "Close the windows; they're coming through the door!" The morning-after, the malfunctioning liver, the "shakes"—no jest will finally charm away the shadow which they throw over the idyllic dream of an innocent night at the bar with the boys.

In Poe's life, the fiction of "social drinking" is given the lie; for to him, even the first drink was a plunge toward dissolution, a kind of symbolic suicide. He plays in the American mind the role of an anti-Rip Van Winkle, projecting the fear that after the bust, one does not awake to a new and wifeless world, but continues to sleep the tormented sleep of the damned. If the figure of Poe in Baltimore refuses to be exorcised from the national imagination, it is because Poe's terrible death befell him in a moment of typically American evasion; not only did he fall drunken beside a balloting place (and to be drunk on Election Day is surely the most American of acts!), but his drunkenness was prompted by a flight from women and marriage. No wonder the folk mind never wearies of crying, "Let him die for the act we dream! Let him die the death we secretly desire!" It is in this sense, not Baudelaire's, that America was guilty of Poe's death—as it was guilty afterward of Scott Fitzgerald's and Hart Crane's and Dylan Thomas': those latter-day scape-heroes, who found not only sacrificial ends similar to Poe's but even Griswolds of their own to celebrate them.

The figures Poe created in his work were never as satisfactory, unfortunately, as the figure he composed with his life. Certainly Gordon Pym—though he moves into the first major scene "not a little intoxicated" and early confesses himself a member of the "numerous race of the melancholy"—does not ever come alive as a significant character, much less assume the tragic dimensions attained by Poe himself. Poe lacks as a writer a *sense of sin,* and therefore cannot raise his characters to the Faustian level which alone dignifies gothic fiction. When he tries to treat in his tales (in the "Duc de l'Omelette," for instance) the Satanic pact, he is embarrassed and seeks refuge in the heavy-handed horseplay he took for humor. The relations of Pym with Peters suggest from time to time the terrible bargain between Faust and Mephisto; but Poe will not permit Peters to become a real Devil, and Pym has obviously no soul to sell. Poe liked to boast that he had transformed the gothic from a "horror of Germany" to a "horror of the soul"; but by "soul" he seems to have meant only what we should call "sensibility." Certainly Pym, who in this respect resembles all of Poe's protagonists, responds even to torment aesthetically rather than morally; and for all his concern with evil, Poe provides only what Wallace Stevens would call an *Esthétique du mal*. If his own life seems to offer a more genuinely metaphysical shudder, this is thanks not to him but to the Puritan conscience of Griswold, which made of him a kind of vulgar Faust for the American market, just as Baudelaire made of him a *poète maudit* for the French one. If there seem to be even now two Poes, it is because he left a half-finished self that has been completed in one way for the American middlebrow audience, and in quite another for the highbrow French public.

13

THE POWER OF
BLACKNESS:
FAUSTIAN MAN AND
THE CULT OF VIOLENCE

IF EDGAR ALLAN POE fails finally to transform the gothic into the tragic, this is because he lacks that ultimate "power of blackness," which, as Melville observed, "derives its force from its appeal to that Calvinistic sense of Innate Depravity and Original Sin, from whose visitations, in some shape or other, no deeply thinking mind is always and wholly free." Scarcely any other of our classic writers, however, shares Poe's immunity to Calvinism; and it is, indeed, in their efforts to come to terms with a Puritan heritage, to render its insights in secular terms, that our chief nineteenth-century novelists reach the level of tragedy. By the nineteenth century, to be sure, American Puritanism had lost its original unity as well as its controlling position in American life, and had developed in two quite opposite directions toward two quite irreconcilable positions.

One wing had passed via eighteenth-century "enthusiasm" and Methodism toward a hysterical evangelism, which produced revivals like the Great Awakening of 1742, and which survives to this day in the meetings which fill for a moment otherwise empty movie houses up and down the land. This movement derives from the extreme Calvinist emphasis on Grace and on the personal nature of salvation; and ends by despising everything but Grace—rejecting learning and scholarship and intelligence itself. A hatred of all hallowed forms and a love for plainness in the church architecture and ritual is joined to an utter rejection of all "secondary goods." Inherent in their position is a fear of art that cuts as deep as the fear of sex; and there is, therefore, no possibility of literature developing out of their lowbrow, plebeian Puritanism, though of course a satirical literature attacking it has come regularly from the pens of rebels against it.

Middlebrow, middle-class Puritanism, on the other hand, preserves the respect for learning which made the original American Calvinists the founders of great universities. Its impetus carries it, by way of rationalism and religious liberalism, to Unitarianism and beyond to a series of post-Christian, syncretistic beliefs in which the notion of ecclesiastical "purification" is extended to a point where all ritual and dogma disappear, bearing away with them first the notions of the divinity of Christ and of original sin, and then of the necessity for an organized church. Religion is finally defined as a vague call to social service and "duty," and as anti-materialism, which is to say, a refusal to accept the body and its limitations (including death itself!) as real. Such a commitment to "spiritual" values leads, on the one hand, to a bland cosmic optimism, which denies "innate depravity" and considers evil an illusion or a mistake; and on the other hand, to a bloodless sort of asceticism, often combined with advanced social ideas.

The mid-nineteenth-century culmination of that faith is, of course, Transcendentalism: a creed constructed out of scraps of Carlyle, Swedenborg, German Idealist philosophy, and Hindu religion. More movement than system, Transcendentalism rests upon a series of assumptions sustained not by reason but by feeling and a homemade mythology. Some of the key assumptions are: that the real world is a world of ideas not apparent to the senses; that nature is beneficent and rational, and that man is, therefore, *at home* * in the universe; that, in fact, both man and Nature participate in God, who is not finally separate from either; that consequently the fittest church is unadorned Nature itself and the truest Bible the heart of the lonely thinker; that a man alone with himself is closest to perfection and that mass society tends to corrupt him; that there is no evil illusion and distrust of the self. Such beliefs urge upon man as his essential duty the act of saying "Yea!" to everything, of crying out "I accept the Universe!"

---

* Once more, Henry Miller comes to mind—though perhaps Benjamin Franklin, who easily and somewhat smugly believed the universe to be his home, is a better analogue than Emerson, who seems to have had always to strain a little in order to convince himself that he was really at ease in the cosmos.

The influence of Transcendentalism on the American essay and on American poetry through Emerson, Thoreau, Whitman, and their lesser disciples is marked, though not always fortunate; but in our classic fiction, the Transcendentalist appears chiefly as a comic character "cracked right across the brow," mocked by Hawthorne, for instance, in *The Blithedale Romance* and by Melville in both *Pierre* and *The Confidence Man*. Yet in their own time, Hawthorne and Melville alike were called "Transcendentalists" by book-reviewers (including Edgar Allan Poe), who handled that term with all the irresponsibility with which the word "existentialist" is now bandied about. These two writers represent, in fact, a third line of development from Puritanism, the only strain in which the rich paradoxes and tensions of Calvinism are not simplified in the interests of simple-minded orthodoxy or sentimental liberalism; and they engage in a common attempt to redeem the complex values of Puritanism from religion to art. It is hard to find a name for their view of the world; but perhaps the term "tragic Humanism" will do as well as any.

Among the assumptions of Melville and Hawthorne are the following: that the world of appearance is at once real and a mask through which we can dimly perceive more ultimate forces at work; that Nature is inscrutable, perhaps basically hostile to man, but certainly in some sense alien; that in man and Nature alike, there is a "diabolical" element, a "mystery of iniquity"; that it is impossible to know fully either God or ourselves, and that our only protection from destructive self-deceit is the pressure and presence of others; that to be alone is, therefore, to be lost; that evil is real, and that the thinking man breaks his heart trying to solve its compatibility with the existence of a good God or his own glimmering perceptions of goodness. From this it follows that the writer's duty is to say, "Nay!", to deny the easy affirmations by which most men live, and to expose the blackness of life most men try deliberately to ignore. For tragic Humanists, it is the function of art not to console or sustain, much less to entertain, but to *disturb* by telling a truth which is always unwelcome; and they consequently find it easy to view themselves in Faustian terms, to think of their dangerous vocations as a bargain with the Devil. It is for these reasons that they speak of their books not, like Poe, as hoaxes or burlesques, but as "hell-fired" and "wicked." Melville is not merely playing at Satanism when he confides to Hawthorne that the secret motto of *Moby Dick* is: *"Ego baptizo non in nomine patris, filii et spiritus sancti sed in nomine diaboli."* In 1850, the sole name for what we would call the unconscious was "hell"; and forays into that region were therefore regarded as courting damnation.

It is because they come to terms so frankly with the Faustian implications of their own enterprise that writers like Melville and Hawthorne (later Twain and Faulkner, too) are able to create Faustian characters, and to satisfy the dimly perceived need of many Americans to have their national existence projected in terms of a compact with the Devil. In Hawthorne, the scientist and the social reformer; in Melville, the ruthless exploiter of nature and the magnetic leader of men; in Twain, the refugee from culture, the young man who goes West; in Faulkner, the self-made man fighting for status and security—in each, some standard and respected American type is identified with the black magician who bartered away his soul. There is scarcely a heroic ideal of our native life which is not, in one or another of these writers' gothic books, illuminated by a weird and lurid light. Such ideals are not, it should be clear, merely travestied and debunked; they are rather revealed as equivocal, problematic—redeemed from easy sentimental acceptance and raised to a tragic power. It is Hawthorne who first opens up in our literature, as Melville himself explained, the tragic way; and the greatest of his gothic fictions, the first American tragedy is *The Scarlet Letter.* A "Puritan *Faust,*" it has been called, as if there could be in the United States any other sort of *Faust;* but it is important all the same to be aware that it was Hawthorne who set the diabolical pact in a Puritan context and cast upon the beginnings of life in America a gothic gloom that not even Longfellow's middlebrow idylls could relieve.

The Scarlet Letter is finally not essentially a love story at all; and though it is possible to gain some insights into its theme and tone by considering it an American, which is to say, a denatured and defleshed, *Nouvelle Héloïse,* it is more valuable to approach it as an American, which is to say, a less violent and hopeless, version of *The Monk.* Like Lewis' horror novel, Hawthorne's book deals with a man of God led by the desire for a woman to betray his religious commitment, and finally almost (Hawthorne repents at the last moment, as Lewis does not) to sell his soul to the Devil. Certainly, it makes more sense to compare the figure of Hester with that of the active Matilda, and Dimmesdale with the passive Ambrosio, who is seduced by her, than to try to find analogues for the American pair in Goethe's Gretchen and Faust. If Hawthorne's novella is, indeed, as has often been suggested, an American *Faust,* it is a *Faust* without a traduced maiden. Much less sentimental and Richardsonian than Goethe, Hawthorne is not concerned with the fall of innocence at the seducer's hand or with that seducer's salvation by the prayers of his victim.

The Faustianism of Hawthorne is the melodramatic Faustianism of the gothic romances: of Lewis, whom he read avidly, and of Maturin, from whose *Melmoth the Wanderer* he borrowed the name of a minor character in *Fanshawe.* Not only Lewis and Maturin, but Mrs. Radcliffe and Brockden Brown were favorite authors of the young Hawthorne; and from them he learned how to cast on events the lurid lights, the air of equivocal terror which gives *The Scarlet Letter* its "hell-fired" atmosphere. The very color scheme of the book, the black-and-whiteness of its world illuminated only by the baleful glow of the scarlet letter, come from the traditional gothic palette; but in Hawthorne's imagination, those colors are endowed with a moral significance. Black and white are not only the natural colors of the wintry forest settlement in which the events unfold, but stand, too, for that settlement's rigidly distinguished versions of virtue and vice; while red is the color of sexuality itself, the fear of which haunts the Puritan world like a bloody specter. The book opens with a description of "the black flower of civilized society, a prison" and closes on a gravestone, a "simple slab of slate," whose escutcheon is "sombre . . . and relieved only by one everglowing point of light gloomier than a shadow:—ON A FIELD SABLE, THE LETTER A, GULES."

It is the scarlet letter itself which is finally the chief gothic property of Hawthorne's tale, more significant than the portents and signs, the meteors in the midnight sky, or even "the noise of witches; whose voices, at that period, were often heard . . . as they rode with Satan through the air. . . ." Into that letter are compressed the meanings of all the demonic fires, scarlet blossoms, and red jewels which symbolize passion and danger in his earlier tales. It glows with a heat genital and Satanic at once—burning his fingers even centuries later, Hawthorne tells us in his introduction, like "red-hot iron"; and its "lurid gleam," the text declares, is derived "from the flames of the infernal pit." Its "bale-fire," at any rate, lights up the book with a flickering glare representing at once

Hester's awareness of guilt and Hawthorne's: his doubts over his plunge into the unconscious, and hers over her fall through passion into the lawless world of Nature.

What Hester inwardly perceives the book makes explicit: that the scarlet letter belongs not to her alone but to the whole community which has sought to exclude her. It is repeated everywhere: in the child she bears, who is the scarlet letter made flesh; in the heavens of secret midnight; on the tombstone which takes up her monitory role after she is dead; and especially in the secret sign on the breast of the minister, whom the community considers its special saint. In his dumb flesh is confessed what his articulate mouth cannot avow, not his transgression alone but that of all men who have cast the first stone. At the heart of the American past, in the parchment scroll which is our history, Hawthorne has discovered not an original innocence but a primal guilt—and he seeks to evoke that past not in nostalgia but terror.

It is on the frontier, the margin where law meets lawlessness, the community nature, that Hawthorne imagines his exemplary drama played out; but his primitive world is much more like Brockden Brown's than Cooper's. To him, the "dark inscrutable forest" seems rather the allegorical *selva oscura* of Dante than Natty Bumppo's living bride: the symbol of that moral wilderness into which man wanders along the byways of sin, and in which he loses himself forever. In its darkness, Hawthorne says of Hester at one point, "the wildness of her nature might assimilate itself with a people alien to the law. . . ." He projects no idyllic dream of finding in the forest the Noble Savage, only a nightmare of confronting the barbaric warrior and the Devil whom he serves; and the occasional Indian who emerges from his wilderness takes up a place not beside the pariah-artist but the black magician.

The virgin sea seems to him as unredeemed as the land, a second realm of gloomy lawlessness. For him sailors are ignoble savages, too: "the swarthy-cheeked wild men of the ocean, as the Indians were of the land. . . ." Neither Hawthorne's Indians nor seamen, however, play a critical part in the development of the action; they merely stand symbolically by, in their appropriate garb, speaking no word but watching "with countenance of inflexible gravity, beyond what even the Puritan aspect could attain." In the two important scenes at the foot of the scaffold, which so symmetrically open and close the book, there are red men in attendance, on the second occasion flanked by their even wilder confreres, the mariners "rough-looking desperadoes, with sun-blackened faces, and an immensity of beard." Yet neither the black desperadoes of the deep nor the swarthy and stolid Indians play the role in *The Scarlet Letter* entrusted to Cooper's Mingoes or the gothic savages of Brockden Brown.

The Magua of Hawthorne's novella is Chillingworth, the white doctor and man of science, so oddly at home in the alien world of the primitive. "By the Indian's side, and evidently sustaining a companionship with him, stood a white man, clad in a strange disarray of civilized and savage costume"; "old Roger Chillingworth, the physician, was seen to enter the market-place, in close and familiar talk with the commander of the questionable vessel." From his Indian captors and friends, Chillingworth has learned a darker "medicine" to complement his European science; but he has not ceased to be still "the misshapen scholar . . . eyes dim and bleared by lamplight," whose "scientific achievements were esteemed hardly less than supernatural." If on the one hand, Chillingworth is portrayed as the heir to the lore of the "savage priests," on the other, he is presented as a student of the black magic of "Doctor Forman, the famous old conjurer." To represent the horror of Europe, however, Chillingworth must be white, while to stand for that of America he must be colored; he is, in fact, a white man who grows black. Even the other protagonists notice his gradual metamorphosis ("his dark complexion seemed to have grown duskier . . .") into the very image of the Black Man, which is to say, Satan himself: "a striking evidence of man's faculty of transforming himself into a devil . . . if he only will . . . undertake a devil's office."

In general, one of the major problems involved in reading *The Scarlet Letter* is determining the ontological status of the characters, the sense in which we are being asked to believe in them. Caught between the analytic mode of the sentimental novel and the projective mode of the gothic, Hawthorne ends by rendering two of his five main characters (Hester and Dimmesdale) analytically, two ambiguously (Chillingworth and Pearl), and one projectively (Mistress Hibbins). Hester and Dimmesdale are exploited from time to time as "emblems" of psychological or moral states; but they remain rooted always in the world of reality. Chillingworth, on the other hand, makes so magical an entrance and exit that we find it hard to believe in him as merely an aging scholar, who has nearly destroyed himself by attempting to hold together a loveless marriage with a younger woman; while Pearl, though she is presented as the fruit of her mother's sin, seems hardly flesh and blood at all, and Mistress Hibbins is quite inexplicable in naturalistic terms, despite Hawthorne's perfunctory suggestion that she is simply insane.

The latter three are, perhaps, best understood as the "daemons" or "shadows" of the more actual protagonists. Chillingworth is clearly enough the shadow of Dimmesdale, a paternal image, the Bad Father who speaks with the voice of Dimmesdale's Calvinist heritage. He is a tormenting alter ego, capable of slipping past the barriers of cowardice and self-pity to touch the hidden truth. When Dimmesdale, hounded to penitence by his shadow, mounts the scaffold to expose his own long-hidden scarlet letter, Hawthorne offers us what seem alternative explanations of its genesis. It may be, he suggests, the result of some hideous self-inflicted torture, the psychosomatic effect of remorse, or the work, scientific or magical, of Chillingworth; but these we can see are only apparent alternatives, which properly translated reduce to a single statement: Dimmesdale and Chillingworth are one, as body and soul are one.

Certainly, Chillingworth cannot survive the minister's death, after which "he positively withered up, shrivelled away, almost vanished from sight." And when the process is complete, the old physician gone, leaving to the bastard child of his wife enough money to make her "the richest heiress of her day"—both that child and her mother disappear, too. From their refuge in the Old World, Hester returns alone to her place of shame and assumes again the burden of her guilt; for there is no longer any function for the "demon child" who was her shadow. From the first, Pearl has been projected as "a forcible type . . . of the moral agony which Hester Prynne had borne." Redeemed, however, by her father's last penance, and endowed with the wealth of his shadow, she vanishes, too, not out of the world but *into* it: "A spell was broken . . . and as her tears fell upon her father's cheek, they were the pledge that she would grow up amid human joy and sorrow, nor forever do battle with the world, but be a woman in it. Towards her mother, too, Pearl's errand . . . was all fulfilled."

Taken as a character constructed in psychological depth, Pearl is intolerable. Though she is the first child in American fiction whose characterization is based on painstaking observation of a real little girl (an astonishing number of details in her portrayal come from the notes Hawthorne took on his little daughter, Una), she is so distorted in the interests of her symbolic role that she seems by turns incredible and absurd. It is partly a question of the *tone* in which her actions are described, a tone sometimes sentimental and condescending (Hawthorne's son, Julian, interpreted the book as essentially a defense of bastards!), sometimes mystifying and heavily gothic. Daemonic Pearl certainly is, in her immunity to man-made law, her babbling in strange tongues, her uncanny insight into her mother's heart. But she is disconcertingly benign—as often compared to a blossom from a rosebush as to a witch! Her name is the clue to her essential nature, as surely as is Chillingworth's icy appellation; for she is "the gem of her mother's bosom," the Pearl of great price: not only Hester's torment, but also her salvation. "Thus early had this child saved her from Satan's snare. . . ."

Unaware of exactly what he is doing with his shadow characters: incapable of committing himself unreservedly to the gothic modes, but unable either to translate them into terms of psychological inwardness—Hawthorne tempers the daemonic in Chillingworth's case with melodrama, in Pearl's with sentimentality, and in Mistress Hibbins' with a kind of skeptical irony. The wizard Hawthorne can regard with horror, the elf-child with condescension; but to the full-blown witch, he responds with uneasy evasions, unwilling perhaps to grant reality to the nightmare which had aroused the persecuting zeal of his ancestors. Mistress Hibbins is, nonetheless, the third daemon of the book, the shadow of a sixth protagonist that we have not yet named: the Puritan community itself, which Hawthorne portrays as haunted by "the noise of witches; whose voices at that period, were often heard to pass over the settlements or lonely cottages, as they rode with Satan through the air."

The name of Mistress Hibbins is mentioned in Hawthorne's text before that of any of the other major characters of the book; and at four critical moments she appears on the scene. On her first appearance, she pleads with Hester to come with her to the forest and sign her name in the Black Man's book; on her second, she peers from her window into the darkness where the minister stands alone on the scaffold and cries out in anguish; on her third, she hails the minister as a fellow-communicant of Satan after he has met Hester in the forest and agreed to run off. The fourth scene is the longest, involving an interchange with Hester in which Mistress Hibbins claims fellowship not only with her and her lover, but impugns the whole community, for whose undermind of filth and fear she speaks: "Many a church-member saw I, walking behind the music, that has danced in the same measure with me when Somebody was fiddler, and, it might be, an Indian powwow or a

Lapland wizard changing hands with us!" Yet despite her critical role in the book, the dour-faced witch lady is rendered more as hallucination than fact. Her first entrance is hedged about with such phrases as: "it is averred" and "if we suppose this interview . . . to be authentic and not a parable . . ."; her second ends: "the old lady . . . vanished. Possibly, she went up among the clouds"; the third introduces the disturbing phrase, "and his encounter, if it were a real incident . . ." Only the fourth does not qualify its assertion of what happened with doubt, merely attributes Mistress Hibbins' diatribe to her "insanity, as we would term it."

Yet hedged about with doubts and characterized as mad, Magistrate Bellingham's sister is the mouthpiece through which the Faustian theme is introduced into the book. The Faustian theme, however, constitutes the very center of *The Scarlet Letter:* a profound crisis of the soul, for which Hawthorne was able to find no other image than one appropriate to the crazy dreams of a self-styled witch, or the blood-curdling story told to a child. Chapters XVI to XX, which make up the center of Hawthorne's tale, describe the encounter of Dimmesdale and Hester, the evocation of their old love, their momentary illusion of freedom, and the minister's moral collapse; but what begins as romance ends in gothic horror. It is Pearl who gives us the clue, asking her mother to tell the very story that she and her love have been acting out: "a story about the Black Man. . . . How he haunts this forest, and carries a book with him,—a big, heavy book, with iron clasps, and how this ugly Black Man offers his book and an iron pen to everybody that meets him here among the trees; and they are to write their names with their own blood. And then he sets his mark on their bosoms!" This is, indeed, the tale which Hawthorne tells in *The Scarlet Letter,* though for his characters the problem is not, as in the older versions of the story, whether they *shall* make such a pact, but whether they *have made* it; for in this new Faustian legend, one may enter into such an agreement unawares.

Over and over the essential question is asked. Pearl herself puts it to her mother just after her request for a gothic story, "Didst thou ever meet the Black Man, mother?" and Hester answers, "Once in my life I met the Black Man! . . . This scarlet letter is his mark!" Even earlier, Hester has inquired of Chillingworth, "Art thou like the Black Man that haunts the forest round about us? Hast thou enticed me into a bond that will prove the ruin of my soul?" But Chillingworth, smiling, has only evaded her query, "Not thy soul. . . . No, not thine!" It is Dimmesdale whom he implies he has lured into the infernal pact; and it is Dimmesdale who questions himself finally, though impelled by Hester's temptation rather than Chillingworth's torment, "Am I mad? or am I given over utterly to the fiend? Did I make a contract with him in the forest, and sign it with my blood?" This time it is Hawthorne himself who answers: "The wretched minister! He had made a bargain very like it! Tempted by a dream of happiness he had yielded himself with deliberate choice, as he had never done before, to what he knew was deadly sin."

For Hawthorne, the Faustian man is one who, unable to deny the definitions of right and wrong by which his community lives, chooses nonetheless to defy them. He is the individual, who, in pursuit of "knowledge" or "experience" or just "happiness" places himself outside the sanctions and protection of society. His loneliness and alienation are at once his crime and his punishment; for he commits a kind of suicide when he steps outside of society by deciding to live in unrepented sin; and he can only return to haunt the world of ordinary men like a ghost. Every major protagonist of *The Scarlet Letter* is such a specter. Of Hester, we are told that "she was as much alone as if she inhabited another sphere," and that "It was only the darkened house which could contain her. When sunshine came, she was not there." Dimmesdale asks of himself, "Then what was he?—a substance?—or the dimmest of shadows?"; and Hawthorne tells us of Chillingworth that "he chose . . . to vanish out of life as completely as if he indeed lay at the bottom of the ocean." Pearl, born of the original sin which has obliterated the substance of her elders, begins as "a born outcast of the infantile world. . . . Mother and daughter stood in the same circle of seclusion from human society."

Neither hate nor love can penetrate the spheres of unreality to which Hester, Dimmesdale, and Chillingworth have consigned themselves. The old physician proves incapable of believing himself a fiend or the two lovers sinners except in a "typical illusion"; and meeting after seven years, the minister and Hester "questioned one another's actual and bodily existence, and even doubted of their own. . . . Each a ghost, and awe-stricken at the other ghost!" Indeed, Hawthorne has the same trouble believing his characters real that they have themselves. "But to all these shadowy beings, so long our acquaintances," he says by way of valedictory, "we would fain be merciful." And we realize the sense in which he himself was, like Dimmesdale or Hester, alienated, removed to a sphere from which like some ghostly Paul Pry he peered down on the ghosts of his imagining. We have spoken of Hester and Dimmesdale as more actual than their shadows; but their actuality is a thin and tenuous thing, though the best at the command of a writer whom Poe advised, in critical impatience, to get a bottle of visible ink!

Not only alienation, however, defines Hawthorne's Faustian protagonists. They dream also of being *free*—uncommitted and unbound by history or moral responsibility. "Let us not look back," says Hester, playing the tempter to Dimmesdale, "the past is gone. . . . With this symbol, I undo it all. . . ." It is an American creed which she espouses, and like a good American, she looks to the world of nature for its consummation: "Doth the universe lie within the compass of yonder town. . . . Whither leads yonder forest track? Deeper it goes, and deeper, into the wilderness. There thou art free!" It is the dream already old by the time of Hawthorne of "lighting out for the territory," pursuing the endlessly retreating horizon of innocence into an inexhaustible West: the seed of a million Saturday matinees. "Begin all anew. . . . There is happiness to be enjoyed. There is good to be done. . . ." Really to believe this, however, is to leave behind the world of moral responsibility inhabited by Puritan saint and sinner alike, and to become a make-believe cowboy.

Here is the critical point at which the sons of Natty Bumppo part company with the descendants of Faust. The former cry out with their mythic progenitor in *The Deerslayer:* "When the colony's laws, or even the King's laws, seem agin the laws of God, they get to be onlawful and ought not to be obeyed." But who is qualified to say what God's laws are: a half-educated trapper without a cross in his blood, an unrepentant adulteress, an orphan boy on a raft with a stolen slave? *Vox dei, vox populi,* says the sentimental populist, and dissents in happy innocence; but the gothic rebel revolts against the will of God itself, saying a little naïvely with Huck, "All right, then, I'll *go* to Hell!" or shouting melodramatically with Ahab, "From hell's heart I strike at thee"; or, at least, insisting desperately with Dimmesdale, "But now,—since I am irrevocably doomed,—wherefore should I not snatch the solace allowed to the condemned culprit before his execution?"

Yet Dimmesdale is finally incapable of maintaining the Faustian stance. If *The Scarlet Letter* is, indeed, an American *Faust,* Dimmesdale is not really Faust himself but Gretchen, a secondary sinner lured on to destruction by a stronger one whom he loves, a tremulous victim led astray by daring arguments. It is true that in the end his weakness proves stronger than Hester's strength, leading him to repentance and public confession, while she dreams still of flight; but his is a Christian triumph, which cheats both the Devil who would damn him and the Faustian woman who considers that damnation bliss! Chillingworth is no more Faust than he, only a self-made Mephistopheles, the nearest thing to a real Devil Hawthorne could permit himself in his cautiously gothic tale; but he is a timid Devil at that. He and Dimmesdale are, at any rate, portrayed in one scene, ranging wide in terrible intimacy over the whole field of faith, and approaching the brink of apostasy: "It was as if a window were thrown open, admitting a freer atmosphere into the close and stifled study. . . . But the air was too fresh and chill. . . . So the minister, and the physician with him, withdrew within the limits of what their church defined as orthodoxy." Neither the Devil-doctor in his hate nor the guilty pastor in his ambivalent vanity dares throw himself into the uncertain depths of Faustian speculation or quarrel with the Calvinist God.

Hester, however, has no such scruples, but during her seven years of outward chastity and inward turmoil of the soul, leaves all limits behind: "she cast away the fragments of a broken chain. The world's law was no law for her mind." Ideas "as perilous as demons" became her familiars, persuading her to question the basic tenets of her faith, the place of woman, the very sanctity of life itself. "At times a fearful doubt strove to possess her soul, whether it were not better to send Pearl at once to heaven, and go herself to such futurity as Eternal Justice should provide." Met in the "vast and dismal forest" by the minister whom she has not confronted for seven years, except in his official role as defender of the religion against which they both have sinned, Hester greets him in the name of a rival, a pagan faith. He is at a loss in the "untamed forest," but she secure; for "her intellect and her heart had their home, as it were, in desert places, where she had roamed as freely as the Indian in his woods." How naturally the metaphor occurs to Hawthorne for whom the woods are haunted and the redskin a Satanic figure.

"She had wandered, without rule or guidance, in a moral wilderness," and consequently regarded "whatever priests or legislators had established . . . with hardly more reverence than the Indian would feel. . . ." It is a final satisfactory touch that a woman be not only the first Faust of classic American literature, but also the wildest Indian of them all!

There are finally no heroes in Hawthorne, for whom the illusion of heroism, the dream of transcending one's humanity, is the last diabolic temptation; neither man nor woman can break back into Eden, though man and woman together can momentarily restore Paradise on earth. That is to say, there are in his work no redeemed individuals, only redeemed *couples,* husband and wife, like the pair who, in "The Maypole of Merry Mount," accept expulsion from the Garden of irresponsible indulgence; or the one which goes out in "The Canterbury Pilgrims" from the Garden of icy abstinence; or the one which abandons at the end of "The Great Carbuncle" the Garden of unshareable bliss. Similarly, Holgrave and Phoebe in *The House of the Seven Gables,* Hollingsworth and Priscilla in *The Blithedale Romance,* both Kenyon and Hilda, Donatello and Miriam in *The Marble Faun,* by choosing marriage over passion and loneliness submit "to earth's doom of care and sorrow, and troubled joy. . . ." Hawthorne's muted, resigned conclusions reflect the final lines of Milton's *Paradise Lost* —the mitigated catastrophe of the seventeenth-century Puritan poet becoming unexpectedly the mitigated happy ending of the nineteenth-century Puritan fictionist:

> Some natural tears they drop't, but wip'd them soon;
> The World was all before them, where to choose
> Thir place of rest, and Providence thir guide:
> They hand in hand with wandring steps and slow,
> Through *Eden* took thir solitarie way.

In Hawthorne, this becomes more abstract and more sentimental. "As the moral gloom of the world overpowers all systematic gayety, even so was their home of wild mirth made desolate amid the sad forest. They returned to it no more. . . . They went heavenward, supporting each other along the difficult path which it was their lot to tread, and never wasted one regretful thought on the vanities of Merry Mount." Between Milton and Hawthorne lie nearly two hundred years of Sentimentalism, which sought to make of marriage another, better Eden, and of woman an innocent savior capable of restoring man to it. Hawthorne's fallen pairs, therefore, walk forth from their several false Gardens to a truer bliss; and his Gretchen-Eves sustain their trembling Adams, aware that, unlike their primal mother, they at least have not brought sin into the world.

"O felix culpa!" is the secret motto of all the novels of Hawthorne after The Scarlet Letter, novels in which he tries to relieve the gloom of the tragic vision of his greatest work. But unlike Augustine, Hawthorne comes to feel the fall of man a fortunate calamity not because it leads to the coming of Christ, but because it prepares the ground for marriage and the bourgeois family. It is a bathetic turn: a rejection of that "blackness ten times black" which Melville had discovered in Mosses from an Old Manse, in favor of the positive view of life, into which American writers are so often tempted after their first success—and which condemns them to subsequent failure. When Holgrave in The House of the Seven Gables chooses to become a husband rather than a magician, and will not play the mesmeric game of his Maule forebears, though another Pyncheon is within his power, he has made symbolically the great refusal which saps Hawthorne's later work of the tragic power that he fully tapped only once. After Holgrave finishes telling Phoebe the story of the strange control so dreadfully exerted by his ancestor over hers, he sees that her head is beginning to droop, her eyes to close:

> A veil was beginning to be muffled about her, in which she could only behold him and live in his thoughts and emotions. . . . It was evident that, with but one wave of his hand and a corresponding effort of his will, he could complete his mastery over Phoebe's free and virgin spirit. . . . To a disposition like Holgrave's, at once speculative and active, there is no temptation so great as the opportunity of acquiring empire over the human spirit. Let us, therefore . . . allow him integrity . . . since he forbade himself to twine that one link more which might have rendered his spell over Phoebe indissoluble.

Having refused the double temptation of Don Juan and Faust, the power to deflower a "virgin spirit" and to control another life, Holgrave is required also to surrender his reformer's dream that "the moss-grown and rotten Past is to be torn down, and lifeless institutions to be thrust out of the way, and their dead corpses, buried, and everything begin anew." In *The Blithedale Romance,* Hawthorne splits the single figure of Holgrave into two characters, the seducer-mesmerist Westervelt and the philanthropic reformer Hollingsworth, permitting the former to leave the scene unrepentant, while the latter capitulates to woman and marriage. In *The Marble Faun,* the scientific experimenter with souls is replaced by the alienated artist, who has bartered his place in humanity for a power over cold stone; but he, too, is finally led to the altar, while his alter ego (this time a jesuitical plotter and loathesome criminal) plunges to a bloody death. Only at the end of his life, Hawthorne seems to have tried again to find the tragic note that would redeem his gothic effects from triviality and theatricality; but he could not recover his pristine purity, so long compromised for the sake of Dickensian effects and concessions to genteel sentimentalism.

It is not for his saved protagonists but for his lost ones that modern readers remember Hawthorne, for his unreconstructed utopians and damned magicians—but especially for his lonely outcasts who prefigure the plight of modern, alienated man. In "Wakefield," he treats with irony the utopia of bachelorhood, which from the time of Washington Irving has had so special an appeal for American readers. In "The Man of Adamant," he deals with the utopia of absolute dissent, portraying a kind of *reductio ad absurdum* of Protestantism itself, which brings a man at last into so rigid and lonely an orthodoxy that he becomes the prisoner of himself, but chiefly he is concerned with the solitude of the artist in the utopia of his art, and his half-willful condemnation of himself to impotence and death.

In Hawthorne's imagination, the figure of the artist, whom he calls Oberon,* is always fading into that of the scientist, whose traditional name we know; for to him both seem men who, in the impassioned pursuit of a craft and the knowledge it yields, come to reject "brotherhood with man and reverence for God." To know, to create, to control, they are willing to step beyond all established bounds, suspend all customary moral standards and make them-

---

* A singularly suggestive choice of names, it occurs to me now; for in *A Midsumer Night's Dream,* Oberon is not only the master of illusion but also of his wife, whose essential passion he reveals as lust for a dumb beast, even as he wins from her the favors of the Ganymede-like boy for whose possession they contend.

selves alone the judges of the rightness of what they do. In Rappaccini and Aylmer and Ethan Brand, Hawthorne projects before the fact the dilemma of the atomic scientists in our time and predicts their essentially immoral stand. Aylmer in "The Birthmark" is the most utterly utopian of the crew; unable to abide the imperfections of mortality, the tiny scarlet hand of passion betrayed on the marble skin of his wife, he produces a perfection which is death —destroys what he loves. Ethan Brand is the coldest, the most detached researcher: a social scientist, really, who, seeking by mass interviews to discover the nature of the unpardonable sin, learns that it is "pure research." "He was now a cold observer, looking on mankind as the subject of his experiments, and, at length, converting man and woman to be his puppets, and pulling the wires that moved them to such degrees of crime as were demanded for his study." "Ethan Brand," however, has survived more as a fragment than a real tale. "A Chapter from an Abortive Romance" Hawthorne called it, yet—with the possible exception of "Young Goodman Brown"—it is his most explicit short treatment of the Satanic pact, and it ends on the proper melodramatic note of damnation. "O Mother earth," Ethan Brand cries just before casting himself into a lime-burner's furnace, "who art no more my Mother . . . O mankind, whose brotherhood I have cast off . . . O stars of heaven, that shone on me of old . . . farewell all, and forever. Come, deadly element of Fire,—henceforth my familiar friend! Embrace me, as I do thee!"

The intent is tragic, but the tone is false, and what began in terror ends in mere rant. "Young Goodman Brown," however, resists the impulse to inflated rhetoric and is finally the most successful, as it is the most subdued, of the Faustian tales. Committed to finding out beyond the limits to which human curiosity is permitted to penetrate, the real virtue of his neighbors, his ancestors, his wife, Brown commits himself to the Devil and is granted a vision of universal depravity and damnation. The whole community is revealed to him as hypocritical and evil: his grandfather proves indistinguishable from Satan himself; and even his wife, for all her freshness and fluttering pink ribbons, is discovered disporting herself at a witches' sabbath. But Brown's lonely vision in the heathen forest brings him no more security than peace; it cuts him off forever from his fellow men, fixes him in a terrible solitude, but it leaves him with no assurance that what he has seen is true. "Had Goodman Brown fallen asleep in the forest and only dreamed the dream of a witch-meeting?" Though he can never know the answer, never be sure whether the horror he experienced exists in the community or in the depths of his own foul heart, he can find no bliss in domesticity, no salvation in marriage. Confronted by his wife, who is called, of course, Faith, and who has slipped out eagerly to meet him on his return, he "looked sternly and sadly into her face, and passed on without a greeting. . . . And when he had lived long, and was borne to his grave a hoary corpse . . . they carved no hopeful verse upon his tombstone, for his dying hour was gloom." It is surely the most perfect in form and tone, as it is in import the most tragic of Hawthorne's tales, a piece of symbolic gothicism whose promise is fulfilled only in *The Scarlet Letter*.

Yet even in *The Scarlet Letter*, Hawthorne has begun to play the typically American game with damnation, to suggest that, after all, it is more menace than fact: an eternally unfulfilled threat, cheated of fulfillment at the last minute by divine mercy. Though all three of his major characters make the Faustian commitment, they are providentially tricked into Grace. Hester at first hampered by the holy burden of her child and later spared the last folly of flight by Dimmesdale's confession and death, remains in the place of her sin, attaching once more and forever to her breast the glorious badge of her shame. So earlier, Dimmesdale has, by penitence and self-immolation, transformed himself from a tormented victim of sin to "spirit sinking into deep repose," while Chillingworth—at that point more Devil than man—could only scream in rage, "Thou hast escaped me."

Of Chillingworth alone is Hawthorne willing to declare that "it only remained for the unhumanized mortal to betake himself whither his Master would find him tasks enough, and pay him his wages duly." But Chillingworth has ceased to be the ambiguous hero-villain who is Faust, becoming rather a simple embodiment of evil with which neither reader nor author is tempted to identify. Satan that he makes himself in the end, however, Chillingworth began at least as the wronged husband; and his final fate is mitigated as the doom of Hawthorne's succeeding melodramatic villains is not. Judge Pyncheon, latter-day Puritan turned businessman and pharisee, who has persecuted and robbed the innocents who share his blood, is dispatched from the pages of *The House of the Seven Gables* with all the stigmata of damnation upon him. In a chapter pat and moralistic enough to have become a classroom set-piece, Hawthorne consigns him to eternal darkness: "There is no face! An infinite, inscrutable blackness has annihilated sight! where is our universe? All crumbled away from us; and we, adrift in chaos, may hearken to the gusts of homeless wind, that go sighing and murmuring about, in quest of what was once a world!"

With the mesmerist Westervelt, the corresponding villain in *The Blithedale Romance,* Hawthorne manages to do little, dismissing him with a hasty parting curse put into the mouth of Miles Coverdale: "Heaven deal with Westervelt according to his nature and deserts!—that is to say, annihilate him." But Westervelt seems only a scapegoat, a conventional villain, whose unequivocal damnation serves chiefly to distract our attention from Hawthorne's unwillingness to face up to the problem of Zenobia's eternal fate. It is typical of Hawthorne that he can best imagine the Faustian role, in all its essential moral ambiguity, in terms of a woman: one of those Dark Ladies, whom Hester prefigures, and whom he has carefully excluded from his single sunny romance, *The House of the Seven Gables.* Whether Zenobia did, indeed, die unrepentant and presumably lost, he cannot persuade himself to decide. When her body is dragged up from the lake into which she has thrown herself in despair, she is found frozen into a position that projects the author's bewilderment before her fate. "She knelt as if in prayer . . ." he begins hopefully, then adds in quick qualification, "But her arms! They were bent before her, as if she struggled against Providence in never ending hostility." Yet this qualification in turn seems too unequivocal to leave without amendment, and he pushes it aside. "Away with the hideous thought. The flitting moment after Zenobia sank into the dark pool . . . was so long, in its capacity of God's infinite forgiveness, as the lifetime of the world."

His last female Faust is the somber, oriental Miriam of *The Marble Faun,* who, like her prototypes Hester and Zenobia, not only defies sexual taboos but thinks deep and dangerous thoughts, chafing at the limitations imposed on her sex by law and convention. With one terrible look, Miriam has caused the death of her persecutor and put in peril the soul of her beloved, who has followed the signal of her glance; but blood is not demanded for blood. Only that persecutor comes, in the course of the book, to a violent end; while both Miriam and Donatello, her lover, seem more nearly redeemed than lost in their consequent penance and sorrow. Miriam is disclosed finally, it is true, as a veiled and tragic penitent; but her own defense is left ringing in the reader's ears as she has passionately spoken it to the sculptor Kenyon: "Was the crime . . . was it a blessing in that disguise? Was it a means of education, bringing a simple nature to the point . . . which it could have reached under no other discipline? . . . The story of the fall of man! Is it not repeated in our romance of Monte Beni? . . . Was that very sin—into which Adam precipitated himself and all his race . . . the destined means by which, over a long pathway of toil and sorrow, we are to attain a higher, brighter and profounder happiness . . . ?"

It is a more complex and heretical version of the fortunate Fall than any of the sentimental reworkings, in the earlier tales, of the conclusion of Milton's *Paradise Lost*. But is it intended finally to mitigate the tragic nemesis of the Faustian legend, deprive us of the finale in which the hero-villain is dragged shrieking through a trap door to hell? Or is it supposed to represent only one more, the last and most treacherous of the Faustian temptations? And who is being tempted, Hawthorne or Miriam? The ambiguity of Hawthorne deliberately suspends such questions out of the reach of certainty; more bewilderingly than is his bewildering wont, he teases the reader first toward one conclusion, then another. Though the sculptor, who speaks for the author in the novel, has protested on first hearing Miriam's theory, "It is too dangerous, Miriam! I cannot follow you!", he ends by repeating her arguments to Hilda. "Is sin, then,—which we deem such a dreadful blackness in the universe, —is it, like sorrow, merely an element of human education. . . . Did Adam fall, that we might ultimately rise to a far loftier paradise than his?"

Put in Kenyon's blunt terms, the Faustian theory of the meaning of Faustian action only shocks the snow maiden Hilda, who cries, "Oh, hush! . . . This is terrible; and I could weep for you, if you indeed believe it." At her perhaps unexpectedly violent response, Kenyon hedges with quite Hawthorne-like adaptability, "Forgive me, Hilda! I never did believe it!" It is only loneliness, he explains —the artist's curse of solitude—which has led him to play with such perilous speculations, from which marriage to her, association with the "white wisdom" which she embodies, would save him once and for all. "O Hilda," he pleads abjectly, "guide me home!" But this is not the final word either; for Hawthorne is at last unwilling to rest on either an orthodox horror before heterodoxy or the intellectual's retreat toward domesticity and accommodation. Good Christian that she is, Hilda is more sentimental than strict, more genteel optimist than gloomy Calvinist; and when the question is asked, "What was Miriam's life to be?" the author can only defer, like Kenyon in the novel, to her "white wisdom." "But Hilda had a hopeful soul and saw sunlight on the mountain-tops."

Melville was truer, finally, to the vision of blackness, which he pretended to have discovered in Hawthorne, than was Hawthorne himself. The reality of damnation he never denied; but the *meaning* of it, for one committed to a skeptical and secular view, he questioned. Especially in his later works, he presented the "mystery of iniquity" in such complexly ironical contexts that the wariest of readers is occasionally baffled. Nevertheless, he kept faith throughout his fiction not only with the gothic vision in general, but with the Faustian theme; creating, along two main lines of descent, a notable series of gothic hero-villains, in each of whom a genuine Faust struggles to be born. The first line of descent begins with *Mardi,* whose hero, Taji or the Wanderer, none of the customary satisfactions of men can hold: not a union with the image of female purity (Yillah) or absolute passion (Hautia), or even with the *Shekhinah,* the personified presence of God, whom his companion, Mohi, perceives in a vision.

He presses on past the countries of the civilized world, allegorically represented by imaginary South Sea islands; and leaves behind even the utopian kingdom of Serenia, a kind of Unitarian Great Good Place, whose messengers bear the flower symbols of victory, immortality, and love, and whose citizens believe that Alma (Christ) and Right Reason are one. Even Taji's most faithful companions turn from him, when they realize he has left Serenia behind not temporarily but forever. "Nay, madman!" they cry by way of warning, "Serenia is our haven. Through yonder strait for thee perdition lies. And from the deep beyond, no voyager ever puts back." But this, of course, is precisely what Taji desires. "Let *me,* then, be the unreturning wanderer," he answers them; and ignoring their final plea, "Nay, Taji! commit not the last, last crime!" shouts his Satanic defiance: "Now, I am my soul's emperor; and my first act is abdication!" Maddened, he races seaward, still seeking the ungraspable spirit which has slipped from his honeymoon clasp, and still sought by three sons of the Old Man he killed to attain her: "Pursuers and pursued, over an endless sea."

It is an authentic, an unmitigated Faustian conclusion to a book which confronts directly the problem of the limits imposed by caution and convention on man's quest for knowledge and experience; but in *Mardi,* both the conclusion and the confrontation are hopelessly imbedded in matter which Melville's first readers found indigestible, "not only tedious but unreadable." Melville himself seems finally to have felt the impulse out of which he had produced *Mardi* as perilous if not downright diabolic; at any rate he determined to suppress the "unmanageable" element, which he held responsible for the book's failure, and to turn out next "a plain, straight forward, amusing narrative," "no metaphysics . . . nothing but cakes and ale." Those cakes-and-ale narratives are *Redburn* and *White Jacket,* the former of which he especially despised in retrospect, calling it "the beggarly *Redburn,*" and remarking that he had only written it to buy tobacco. Yet in both there are themes present, only half-consciously developed, out of which he was to create later some of his profoundest and most terrible effects. One such theme, which we have already examined from another point of view, is the love-conflict between the shipboard bully and the Handsome Sailor—a subject already stereotypical in popular fiction but handled by Melville in an extraordinary way.

Perhaps the most unforeseen consequence of his special handling of the theme is his transformation of the bully into a second version of the Faustian hero-villain—a version to which he was perhaps driven by the popular rejection of his sailor-*poète maudit,* but one to which he returned throughout his writing career. As late as *Billy Budd,* which he left unpublished, Melville was trying still to work out to his own satisfaction the meaning of the attraction-repulsion which drove the evil seaman and the innocent sailor to their mutual destruction. He had made in *Redburn* a first attempt, creating in Jackson an image of "natural depravity" capable of charming even those who saw through to his evil center. In his copy of *King Lear,* Melville, pondering the problem still, was to write some years later, "The infernal nature has a valor often denied to innocence"; and this valor, along with an extraordinary power over his shipmates, he bestows on Jackson. Though that utterly corrupt sailor "was as yellow as gamboge" and hairless to boot, though "his nose had brown down in the middle, and he squinted with one eye," nevertheless "one glance of his squinting eye was as good as a knockdown, for it was the most deep, subtle, infernal . . . eye . . . ever lodged in a human head."

Under its gaze, Jackson's fellows cringe, crawl to him, laugh at his sadistic jokes, do the work which he evades; while Redburn, whom Jackson inexplicably hates, becomes an Ishmael on the ship. It is quite simply the power of evil in Jackson, the sense of his damnation implicit in every gesture, which cows the crew like a superhuman mystery; the most unsubtle of seamen knows that "in truth, he carried about with him the traces of these things, and the mark of a fearful end nigh at hand. . . ." But what subdues everyone else, only exacerbates the rage of Jackson himself; his awareness that he "must die like a dog, in consequence of his sins" stirs in him a hatred for all mankind. He is presented as the victim not merely of the manifold diseases that rack his body, but of divine vengeance itself, "seamed and blasted by lightning." And he assumes as his end nears a kind of dark nobility, inextricably intertwined with the Faustian role he visibly plays: "The prospect of the speedy and unshunnable death now before him, seemed to exasperate his misanthropic soul into madness; and if he had indeed sold his soul to Satan, he seemed determined to die with a curse between his teeth."

The Satanic bargain is spoken of only hypothetically, but Jackson does, indeed, die with a blasphemy on his lips and a torrent of blood from his lungs spattering the sail, on which he is working as death strikes him down into the sea. It is of Tiberius, "the diabolical Tiberius at Caprae," that Melville, speaking through Redburn, is reminded; and he makes the proud vaunt: "I account this Yankee Jackson fully as dignified a personage as he. . . . Though he was a nameless vagabond without an epitaph, and none, but I, narrate what he was." It is the first stirring of an odd notion in Melville that in the classless world of democracy, aristocratic distinction is bestowed by entering into the diabolic compact; but he was not to be able to work it out explicitly until *Moby Dick*.

In *White Jacket*, he does not know what to do at all with the figure that demands to become Faust; unable to reject him utterly, he presents him as Bland, the master-at-arms, but cannot invent a fiction worthy of him. Melville does find his shipboard villain a new face this time, providing him with a mouth "somewhat small, Moorish-arched, and wickedly delicate" besides the customary "snaky black eye"; and before this "charming blackleg," White Jacket himself, the Ishmael of the later book, stands entranced: "I could not but abominate him when I thought of his conduct; but I pitied the continual gnawing, which under all his deftly donned disguises, I saw lying at the bottom of his soul. I admired his heroism. . . ." Yet Melville can find no real devil's work for him to do, only portray him as a petty smuggler broken in rank for a time, then restored to office.

There is in *White Jacket* a true Handsome Sailor, Jack Chase, who is Bland's ideal opponent in every sense, separated out from the *schlemiel*-hero with whom he is fused in *Redburn;* but he is never allowed to meet Bland head on. Melville may perhaps have felt, on one level of consciousness or another, that their relationship could not have been developed without suggesting the theme of overt homosexuality, which comes closer to the surface in this novel than in any other of his works, but is consigned to silence in a summary paragraph:

> The sins for which the cities of the plain were overthrown still linger in some of these wooden-walled Gomorrahs of the deep. . . . The landsman who has never read Walpole's *Mysterious Mother,* nor Sophocles' *Oedipus Tyrannus,* nor the Roman story of *Count Cenci,* dramatized by Shelley, let that landsman guardedly remain in his ignorance of even worse horrors than these, and forever abstain from seeking to draw aside this veil.

Like Jackson, a Yankee emperor, unsung except by Melville, Ahab is like him, too, "seamed and blasted" by lightning; like Bland, he is the victim of an inward "continual gnawing," and like both, is gifted with a "snaky eye" capable of cowing all opposition, enlisting the indifferent on an infernal quest. In Ahab's relationship with Fedallah, however, the Faustian bargain becomes explicit for the first time, pushing into the background the love-combat with the Handsome Sailor. There is such a sailor in *Moby Dick,* the beloved Bulkington, so carefully introduced and so abruptly, though apologetically, shuffled off the scene in Chapter XXIII. Surely, at some point in his writing of the novel, Melville must have imagined between Ahab and Bulkington the encounter that finally was yielded up to make place for Ahab's confrontation of the whale itself and of the power he attempted to strike at through the whale. The end, however, is the same; like Jackson, Ahab ends with blasphemy on his lips and damnation in his soul; though, much less equivocally, there is attributed to him the imperial dignity, proffered and then withdrawn from his prototype.

For all the magnificence of Ahab, Melville cannot even after *Moby Dick* surrender the Jackson prototype, or the theme with which he is associated from the start; but in the posthumous *Billy*

Budd, he tries once more. We recognize Claggart when he enters, though by this time there has been imposed on the face of evil the actual stone image of Tiberius, which Melville had finally seen in Rome in 1857, noting in his journal: "a look of sickly evil,—intellect without manliness and sadness without goodness." The uncanny, beardless yellow of Jackson's aspect has become almost marmoreal, "a pallor tinged with a faint shade of amber akin to the hue of time-tinted marbles of old"; but the same compelling eye still subdues all beholders with its dark glance, still stirs in Melville the old questions about the attractiveness of evil, and, even more disturbingly, about the mystery of its existence. "What was the matter with the master-at-arms?" he asks; and his answer (a Radcliffean answer, he tells us) is: "Natural Depravity: a depravity according to nature." To this natural depravity there corresponds a natural innocence, represented by Billy Budd, who is Jack Chase recast in the image of Antinoüs, even as Claggart is Bland recast in that of Tiberius.

In the Christian world, however, where the beauty of innocence cannot be made the minion to the lust of imperial evil, the encounter of the two is played out as passionate *hatred,* eventuates in melodrama. Claggart, who hates Billy with a helpless and ambivalent fury, accuses him to the captain of the ship on which they both serve, meanwhile fixing him with a "mesmeric glance"—"like the hungry lurch of a torpedo fish." Billy, falsely accused and unprepared for treachery, cannot speak but swings in exasperation at Claggart, killing him with a single blow; and over his sinewless body (more like "a dead snake" than a man), the captain can only exclaim, "Struck dead by an angel of God. Yet the angel must die." Not God himself this time but the instrument of God acted to destroy the blasphemer, and that instrument must bear—according to the laws of men—blood guilt and legal blame. The focus has shifted, with the shifting of Melville's concern and the burning out of his own diabolism, from the Faustian villain-hero to the innocent avenger; and with that shift, Melville's art has moved from the realm of the gothic to that of the sentimental. The abhorrence and pity for the "godlike, ungodly man," crucified on his own evil, kept in so desperate a balance in *Moby Dick,* has reverted again to the imbalance of *Redburn.* In *Billy Budd,* however, Claggart is not even permitted the Faustian death-speech of defiance and contempt; the only last words allowed are the submissive ones of Billy,

"God bless Captain Vere." That Devil, in whose name *Moby Dick* received its bloody baptism, has been disowned!

Between *Moby Dick* and *Billy Budd* come many works and many changes of heart, but, first of all, the astonishing, though finally unsuccessful experiment of *Pierre*. In this book, the Taji of *Mardi* is reborn, though he is removed from the sea which was the very symbol of his commitment to the unlimited. Pierre is the lonely spoiled child, the intellectual adventurer, the alienated artist in search of a devil to whom to sell his soul. Unlike Claggart or Jackson or Bland he is not evil by birth and definition, but by choice and vocation; he becomes the Devil's agent by rejecting the morality of the community in which he has lived at peace, ends by calling the concepts of vice and virtue which he cannot really deny the substance of a dream. He is the only hero of Melville who attempts to earn his living as a writer, a highbrow writer, who has determined (at the moment of his acutest financial need) to abandon the kind of literature that has made him a youthful success and write a work dedicated to nothing but truth. That this work turns out to be the very book in which he is a character is an illusionistic device by which Melville makes it clear that he and Pierre are symbolically one, and that the Faustian commitment of Pierre is indistinguishable from the creation of the work in which he exists.

Yet about Pierre's ultimate damnation, Melville does not equivocate. Pierre himself foresees his doom, as he must to make it fully terrible; and true to his Faustian role, he dies crying out that knowledge defiantly: "Now, 'tis merely hell in both worlds. Well, be it hell. I will mold a trumpet of the flames, and, with my breath of flame, breathe back my defiance." It is an acceptance, however, only of the fact of damnation but not of its justice—a little like Huck's cry from the heart, "All right, I'll *go* to Hell!" Melville does not cheat in the end like Twain, revealing that the "girl in Saddle Meadows" was not Pierre's sister after all (as Jim is revealed not to have been a slave), and Pierre therefore as innocent of incest as Huck of "nigger-stealing"; but there is an implicit protest all the same in Pierre's self-condemnation—a protest not against mistaken interpretation of God's law but against that law itself. Ahab himself had not questioned the price he was asked to pay, the just settlement of a bargain deliberately entered upon; but Pierre has acted in terms of charity not blasphemy, and that his end be damnation, too, that the end of love be hell seems to Melville to call in question the very meanings of "damnation" and "hell." "It is ambiguous still!" Pierre exclaims; and in this final word he is at one with his author.

The ambiguities of *Pierre* are further compounded in *The Confidence Man*, which is not a gothic romance at all, but an oddly wry and dry satire that never quite manages to explode into the release of laughter. Critics argue still about whether the multiformed hero of that book—who begins as the absolute Stranger, an "impostor from the East," and learns to be all things to all men—is Christ or Satan. Certainly, he begins in the guise of Christ (his first avatar is a deaf-and-dumb, submissive butt of the arrogant mob, dressed in white garments, which are the outer sign of his essential humility) and he preaches the orthodox gospel of Faith—or Confidence, Hope, and Charity. The question of whether the practice of those virtues leads mankind to loss or gain is, however, left tantalizingly open; and, in the end, we come to realize that we are being asked to consider not whether the Confidence Man is Saviour or Adversary, but *whether Christ is the Devil!* If this is, indeed, the case, then only Faustian doubt can deliver us from the ultimate con game, the trap of religious belief.

Melville's ironies are finally not unlike those at work in Mark Twain's equally skeptical but more avowedly Satanic story, *The Mysterious Stranger,* though in *The Confidence Man* neither those who have faith nor those who have doubt are rewarded. In Twain's book, on the other hand, the characters who enter into a pact with his amiable young Devil are favored above the pious Christians, granted insanity or early death, which—for Twain—are man's sole protections against suffering and vain regret. *The Mysterious Stranger* appears, to be sure, a little crude and sophomoric beside the subtleties of Melville's quietly mad novel; for, unlike Melville, Twain remained always a profoundly ignorant man, doomed to sound like the village atheist when he aspired to speak like Faust. There is a certain superficial resemblance between Pierre's Faustian assertion that "these two shadows cast from one nothing; these, seems to me, are Virtue and Vice. . . . I am a nothing. It is all a dream that we dreamed we dream . . ." and the statement of Twain's boy-demon that "there is no God, no universe, no human race, no earthly life, no hell. It is all a dream—a grotesque and foolish dream." The former avowal is, however, presented dramatically as the rationalization of a self-declared moral hero on the verge of incest; while the other is put forward as a final word of truth, a summary conclusion.

If Twain's status as a gothic writer depended only upon *The Mysterious Stranger,* he would not rank very high; for it is finally an obvious book, composed by one convinced that whatever shocked his genteel wife would make the foundations of organized Christianity tremble! Typically enough, the Faustian role in *The Mysterious Stranger* is shared by three youngsters (familiar pre-Civil War Hannibal types, disguised as late-sixteenth-century Austrians), who live in a town called Eseldorf, described as "a paradise for boys." It is the only kind of Paradise Twain could ever imagine; and the serpent who enters it is appropriately a juvenile demon, a kind of superhuman Huck Finn, who teaches his companions to amuse themselves by making *golems* and performing minor witchcraft in place of the less spectacular highjinks of the earlier novels. Before young Satan has inducted them into such higher make-believe, the Eseldorf boys have contented themselves with listening to ghost stories and learning to smoke from a servant in the village castle, called Felix Brandt though he is obviously Nigger Jim in whiteface.

It is perhaps because there are no Negro slaves in Eseldof, that Twain cannot evoke in its environs the full gothic horror which he attains in *Pudd'nhead Wilson.* Unable to play on the theme which evoked for him the essential shudder: "the skin of every man contains a slave," he is driven back on Pudd'nhead's second-best observation, his thought for April 1: "This is the day upon which we are reminded of what we are on the other three hundred and sixty-four." This amounts to an essentially banal observation about men, the stuff of comedy rather than of Faustian tragedy; and *The Mysterious Stranger* can never, therefore, seem quite serious to the adult mind. The boy Faust who is its narrator subscribes at the close to the Devil's doctrine ("He vanished and left me appalled, for I knew, and realized, that all he had said was true"); but it is harder to be moved at his words than at Huck's presumably comic decision to go to hell.

Huckleberry Finn is essentially a book about a marginal American type, who only wants to stay alive; but who does not find this very easy to do, being assailed on the one side by forces of violence, which begrudge him the little he asks, and on the other, by forces of benevolence, which insist that he ask for more. Against

the modesty and singleness of his purpose, everything else is meas-
ured and weighed: religion, the social order, other men. Huck
exists on a sub-moral level; for he cannot afford, in his minimal
economy, the luxury of living by the moral codes of the Widow
Douglases of his small-town world. Such codes assume a standard
of security, if not actual prosperity, to which he does not even
aspire: "She told me what she meant—I must help other people,
and do everything I could for other people and look out for them
all the time, and never think about myself. . . . I went out in the
woods and turned it over in my mind a long time, but I couldn't
see no advantage in it—except for the other people; so that at last
I reckoned I wouldn't worry about it any more, but just let it go."
Huck has not yet fallen, manages to live still without that "moral
sense," which his last avatar, the young devil in *The Mysterious
Stranger,* describes as the blight of mankind.

Yet Huck is not, of course, a devil or even a savage, only a
semi-barbarian; and having grown up on the edge of civilization,
he has always known, even before his brief indoctrination by Miss
Watson, the ethical precepts of her world. No more free-thinker
than savage, he not only knows, but, in an abstract way, believes
in these codes, by which he could not survive for an instant in the
lawless sub-society which he inhabits. There is, therefore, a constant disjunction in his mind (very like irony—and exploited by
Twain for irony's sake) between what he considers he *ought* to do,
and what he is aware that he *must* do; and it is this disjunction
which underlies the moral crisis of the book. Huck begins with
such minor crimes as lying and cussing, smoking and petty theft;
and, indeed, the first is so habitual a reflex that he scarcely knows
what to do at a point where apparently only telling the truth can
help him.

I reckon a body that ups and tells the truth when he is in a tight
place is taking considerable many resks, though I ain't had no
experience, and can't say for certain . . . and yet here's a case
where I'm blest if it don't look like the truth is better and actuly
safer than a lie. . . . I never seen nothing like it.

These lines are spoken by Huck in the Wilks episode, when
Twain's own reality-principle is being sold out to sentimentality;
but they reflect still the basic set which distinguishes the juvenile
pariah from the Good Bad Boy.

There is occasionally a certain bravado about Huck in his relationship to the world of morality, which he can neither abide nor disavow. When, for instance, Miss Watson (to whom "scrunching up" or yawning during lessons is a sin punishable in hell) tells Huck about the "bad place," he says he wishes he were there; and is considerably cheered to learn that Tom is likely to end up there, too. A moment later, however, he is in a state of depression and terror, imagining that he hears the voice of a ghost that "can't rest easy in its grave," seeing evil omens everywhere and performing his own rites of exorcism. "I got up and turned around in my tracks three times and crossed my heart every time." One must assume that he is beset by similar feelings of guilt and despair after his later nonchalant declaration: "Well, then, says I, what's the use you learning to do right when it's troublesome to do right and ain't no trouble to do wrong, and the wages is just the same? . . . So I reckoned I wouldn't bother no more about it, but after this always do whichever comes handiest at the time."

Huck had just made the first decisive move toward stealing Jim out of slavery, and feels that he has graduated at last from petty crimes to major ones. It never enters his head for a moment that protecting Jim against recapture is anything but *wrong;* for he has no abolitionist ideas and questions the justice of slavery no more than did Aristotle. He considers, however, that as an outcast he has little to lose; and is only overcome with horror when the Good Bad Boy Tom seems about to become his accomplice. His whole world of values is momentarily threatened, and only re-establishes itself when he learns that Jim has been all along free and Tom has known it: ". . . I couldn't ever understand before . . . how he could help a body set a nigger free with his bringing up." Huck believes in the equality of the races as little as he does in abolition; and when, after his long association with Jim, he is asked by Aunt Sally whether anyone was hurt in a steamboat accident, he answers blandly, "No'm, killed a nigger." There is no intended irony either in Huck's comment about Tom or in his response to Aunt Sally; Twain may *use* them ironically, but this must not mislead us. If Huck lies, runs, and hides for Jim's sake, even as he has lied, run, and hid for his own, this is not because he thinks he is acting in behalf of some higher moral code, but because he has extended his area of self-interest to a family of two. He loves Jim quite literally as himself, and is willing to go to hell for him, even as he was willing to go there for the sake of "scrunching" a little or cussing or smoking.

There is no irony, either, in the self-reproach, the acceptance of his own damnation which Huck finally speaks; whatever games Twain may be playing with his declaration, Huck quite simply believes it:

> . . . something inside of me kept saying, There was the Sunday-school, you could 'a' gone to it; and if you'd 'a' done it they'd 'a' learnt you there that people that acts as I'd been acting about that nigger goes to the everlasting fire.
>
> It made me shiver. And I about made up my mind to pray, and see if I couldn't try to quit being the kind of boy I was and be better . . . but deep down in me I knowed it was a lie, and He knowed it. You can't pray a lie—I found that out.

His attempted prayer a failure, Huck tries to write a letter to Miss Watson, telling her where Jim is, and thus putting things right with his conscience; but though doing it makes him feel "washed clean of sin for the first time," his love for Jim returns. He remembers not some abolitionist slogan or moral tag about the equal rights of all mankind, only how Jim "would always call me honey, and pet me, and do everything he could think of for me . . ." and he decides not to send the letter.

> . . . I studied a minute, sort of holding my breath, and then says to myself: "All right, then I'll *go* to Hell"—and tore it up.
>
> It was awful thoughts and awful words, but they was said. And I let them stay said; and never thought no more about re-forming. I shoved the whole thing out of my head, and said I would take up wickedness again, which was in my line, being brung up to it, and the other warn't.

At this point, the Faustian theme is improbably reborn in the midst of comedy and nostalgia. Lionel Trilling compares Huck at the moment of his decision to a courtly lover submitting to eternal torment for the sake of his beloved; but he seems more Faust than Lancelot: one with Ahab and Pierre and Hester and Ethan Brand. To be sure, Twain is toying with the theme, evading final responsibility; for he knows that the most genteel post-Civil-War reader, secure in a world without slavery, will see Huck, not as a Satanic and hybristic rebel, setting the promptings of his own ignorant heart over the law of the land and the teaching of his church—but as a moral hero. Yet in Huck, for an instant at least, the marginal loafer, the uncommitted idler is revealed as the American Faust; the dark side turned up of what *Huckleberry Finn's* first reviewer called "the ruffianism that is one result of the independence of Americans." Yet the revelation is made in so witty and charming and ambiguous a way, that the same reviewer has described Huck's terrible decision as "most instructive and amusing."

Twain has a further duplicitous device, which is quite simply to make his shiftless Faustian drifter a boy, a child with, he keeps assuring us, a truly virtuous heart. Not only does Twain shrug off the issues, social and moral, involved in a life based on lying and stealing with the implicit comment that "Boys will be boys!"; but he further confounds confusion by identifying his juvenile pariah with the sentimental stereotypes of the child as Noble Savage and the child as victim of society. Huck is, whatever his other faults, the most nonviolent of American fictional children, more like Oliver Twist than Tom Sawyer, who is his companion. Unlike Tom, he never fights with his fists; and though he takes up a rifle once against his delirious father, who has threatened him with a knife, he does not fire it. He never quite shoots even in self-defense; and during the Grangerford feud, for instance, finds a perch in a tree and merely watches, trembling, the foolish bravery of others. He runs, hides, equivocates, dodges, and, when he can do nothing else, suffers. Though admiring critics speak of him sometimes as "manly" or "courageous," he is actually timid almost to the point of burlesque—the anti-type of the foolhardy Tom. To be sure, aboard the *Walter Scott,* he whips up courage enough to eavesdrop on the quarreling crooks by reminding himself of what Tom Sawyer would have done ("and I says to myself, Tom Sawyer wouldn't back out now, and I won't either"); but more customarily, discretion is the whole of his valor. He is quite frank about his fears, telling us over and over: "I warn't feeling very brash, there warn't much sand in my craw"; "I was too scared"; "Well, I catched my breath and most fainted"; "It made me so sick I most fell out of the tree." And when the lynch mob, after which he has tagged along, breaks and runs before the defiance of Colonel Sherburn, Huck observes in self-mockery, "I could 'a' stayed if I wanted to, but I didn't want to."

He has, indeed, the right to be afraid, for he has no effective protectors. A "motherless boy," his father is his worst enemy; and he is, by the time he enters the scene, incapable of paying the price of membership in a respectable household, immune to "civilization." Moreover, his civilizers prove strangely unable to defend him; for when his own origins rise against him (he is, after all, the child of ignorance and drunkenness and violence), the polite community, disabled by sentimentality and a commitment to legal process, stands helplessly by. Not only do the half-world, which bred him, and the genteel community, which tried to adopt him, betray him; but Nature herself, to which he flees as a final refuge, proves a treacherous parent, offering, along with moments of joy and calm, times of terror in storm and fog. No wonder Huck is a strangely melancholy child—not only possessed of a sense of alienation ("lonesome" is almost his favorite adjective), but obsessed by, more than half in love with death.

From the first, the reader is made aware of Huck's dark preoccupations: "I felt so lonesome I most wished I was dead. . . . I heard an owl . . . who-whooing about somebody that was dead, and a whippoorwill and a dog crying about somebody who was going to die." And, indeed, he plays dead in order to survive, rigs a scene of murder to persuade his Pap (who has taken him for the angel of death!) and the world that he is beyond their reach: "They won't ever hunt the river for anything but my dead carcass. They'll soon get tired of that, and won't bother no more about me." Afterwards, he seems a ghost to everyone who knew him; and even at the moment just before what he calls his rebirth ("it was like being born again") at the Phelps farm, his original melancholia returns:

> there was them kind of faint dronings of bugs and flies in the air that makes it seem so lonesome and like everybody's dead and gone . . . it makes a body wish *he* was dead, too, and done with it all. . . . When I got a little ways I heard the dim hum of a spinning-wheel wailing along up and sinking along down again; and then I knowed for certain I wished I was dead—for that *is* the lonesomest sound in the whole world.

"Lonesome" and "dead": the two words are inextricably linked; and they rise in Huck's mind at the moment just before he leaves and just as he is about to re-enter the matriarchal world—which is all the civilization he knows.

"Hannibal" is Mark Twain's name for the world of belongingness and security, of school and home and church, presided over by the mothers. There are men on the upper levels of this respectable world (Judge Thatcher, for instance, self-important and pompous), but they are not, in *Huckleberry Finn,* presented as its rulers or its conscience. Tom, of course, has no father at all, is responsible only to Aunt Polly; while Huck is found at the book's start in the all-female household of the widow Douglas and the old maid, Miss Watson. "I never seen anybody but lied one time or another," Huck remarks at the outset, "without it was Aunt Polly, or the widow, or maybe Mary." These are the super-ego figures of the book, these husbandless mothers or fatherless daughters who cannot lie, only love. But the kindly widow is given a dour double in Miss Watson, as if to reveal the threat always lurking beneath matriarchal tenderness: the rigid piety, the petty discipline, the belief in soap—the love of money! Miss Watson, we remember, tempted by a slave-trader's generous offer, plans to sell her nigger, Jim, down the river and away from his family! The world of mothers, after all, believes not only in Providence and cleanliness and affection, but in slavery, too. Yet it is the best of all conceivable worlds to Mark Twain.

Into it all girls are inducted, apparently, simply by being born; for there are, in Mark Twain's Hannibal, no bad girls, only good ones, marriage with whom means an initiation into piety and conformity, the end of freedom. But as long as childhood lasts, Twain's boys are granted a special immunity from the codes of the mothers. Those mothers do not, of course, openly announce this privilege, only secretly hope that, against their avowed wishes, their sons will rebel, be properly "misch*ee*vous." The boy who conforms too soon, the Good Good Boy represented by Sid Sawyer, is despised a little by the mothers themselves, who prefer the Good Bad Boy, Tom—and long to convert into his image the juvenile pariah with the heart of gold, Huck Finn. There are no Bad Bad Boys in Twain's legendary town, no vicious delinquents beyond all hope of reform; such a thing is as impossible as a vicious woman! Even outside of his fiction, in personal reminiscence, Twain could not bring himself to grant that Huck's sisters had been prostitutes.

Evil he can imagine only in terms of a fully adult male, a Bad Father—like Injun Joe in *Tom Sawyer* or Pap in *Huckleberry Finn:*

His hair was long and tangled and greasy, and hung down, and you could see his eyes shining through like he was behind vines.

. . . There warn't no color in his face, where his face showed;
it was white; not like another man's white, but a white to make
a body sick, a white to make a body's flesh crawl—a tree-toad
white, a fish-belly white.

But sharing the same sub-world which Pap inhabits, the world of
those who will not accept or are not permitted to assume social
responsibility, is Nigger Jim, whose good blackness is ironically
contrasted with Pap's evil whiteness. Once Jim has run away, he
no longer really belongs to Hannibal at all, but to the river: symbol
of flight and the moral indifference of Nature. It is to the river that
Pap comes at the moment of his sordid death; on the river that the
crooks trapped aboard the *Walter Scott* die, too; the river that
the Duke and Dauphin seek in their eternal flight from the vengeance of the towns. And beyond the river is Indian territory, the
ultimate reach of alienation and anti-civilization.

This is the moral geography of the world in which Huck stands
poised just before the moment of adolescence, and his choices are
limited by the narrow possibilities of that world. Either he can accommodate like Tom or Sid, become the mothers' boy, after all; or
he can turn back into his father's sub-world, the tanyard, the hogs-
head, the wharves—accept a perpetual outsideness. He cannot, of
course, stay where he is in the no-man's land of boyhood, where
the two adult worlds meet, because the simple passage of time will
drive him out. For all his illusion of choice, he is not really free,
but imprisoned in his "independence"; for he is incapable of remaining inside the respectable community. There is, on the one
hand, too much of his father in him; and he is actually happy when
Pap carries him off: "It was pretty good times up in the woods
there, take it all around." On the other hand, there is too much
Miss Watson in all mothers: "a poor chap would stand considerable show with the widow's Providence, but if Miss Watson's got
him there warn't no help for him any more."

Huck's problem is, therefore, not to find his fate but to accept
it; and *Huckleberry Finn* is the history of his vain attempts to
escape that fate. He believes at first that he is running not from
himself but from his father and Miss Watson, from both limits of
the only society he knows. But he does not know to *what* he is
escaping, except into nothing: a mere anti-society, in which he is a
cipher, a ghost without a real name. "All I wanted was to go some-

wheres," he tells Miss Watson, "all I wanted was a change, I warn't particular." Huck is heading for no utopia, since he has heard of none; and so he ends up making flight itself his goal. He flees from the impermanence of boyhood to that of continual change; and, of course, it is a vain evasion except as it leads him to understand that *no* society can fulfill his destiny.

It is to the river that he turns, since the river is the only avenue of escape he knows; but the river betrays him, even as it betrays Jim in his complementary search for freedom. Bearing Huck toward the South, the river carries him from a matriarchal world to a patriarchal one, from one which believes in Providence to one which believes in honor ("Colonel Grangerford was a gentleman, you see. He was a gentleman all over . . ."); but for Huck, honor is a concept as unviable as good works or prayer. The chivalric world of the Grangerfords offers to take him in, to make him a little gentleman just as the Widow had wanted to make him a small Christian. There is even a patriarchal version of Tom Sawyer, young Buck, to be his companion and link to that world; but the end of chivalry is violence, for which Huck has even less taste than he has for telling the truth. And he stands at last, after the feud with the Shepherdsons has erupted into furious and wholesale slaughter, looking down at the dead bodies of two boys, who, unlike him, had been brought up to fight rather than run. "I covered up their faces, and got away as quick as I could. I cried a little when I was covering up Buck's face."

In the end, Huck has got out of the whole experience only a vague sense of guilt (he did carry the message which touched off the final combat), and another nightmare to add to his already full store. "I wished I hadn't ever come ashore that night to see such things, I ain't ever going to get shut of them—lots of times I dream about them." The episode of Colonel Sherburn does little to change his picture of life in the South, only adding a brutal murder (the shooting down for honor's sake of an unarmed, drunken lout, not very different from Huck's Pap) and a failed lynching, from which Huck turns away to go to a circus. The final condemnation of the South is spoken by Colonel Sherburn himself, who is the victim of its mad code of honor, but not of its hypocrisy: "If any real lynching's going to be done, it will be done in the dark, Southern fashion; and when they come they'll bring their masks. . . ."

The Wilks episode is transitional, still set in the patriarchal

world of the South, but centered, for Huck, around the figure of
Mary Jane, "most awful beautiful . . . her eyes . . . all lit up like
glory," on whom he develops a hopeless small-boy crush, seeming
suddenly five years younger. The whole section is unforgivably sentimental and melodramatic—a compound of sticky nobility and
stage gothicism, in the midst of which Huck's pure love is contrasted with the slobbering lustfulness of the Dauphin. At no point
in *Huckleberry Finn* is its protagonist so untrue to himself, or
Twain so near to yielding up the truth of his book to sentiment. Yet
finally Huck moves on past the temptation of puppy love, as he
has already passed through those of chivalry and courage. There is
no mock marriage, or even a dream of a future one, as in *Tom
Sawyer,* only a somewhat unconvincing touch of pathos, when the
only girl is left behind:

> I hain't ever seen her since that time that I see her go out of that
> door, no, I hain't ever seen her since, but I reckon I've thought
> of her many and many a million times, and her saying she would
> pray for me and if ever I'd 'a' thought it would do any good for
> me to pray for *her,* blamed if I wouldn't 'a' done it or bust.

Beyond this, there is Aunt Sally's farm, which looks at first
glance very like the Grangerfords'. There is the same double log
cabin, the same howling dogs to greet Huck; but his reception com-
mittee is quite different from the "three big men with guns pointed
at me," who welcomed "George Jackson" into the world of feuding
gentlemen. At the Phelpses', it is a Negro woman with a rolling pin
in her hand, then Aunt Sally herself, "her spinning stick in her
hand." We have moved from the world of gun-bearing fathers into
that of mothers, armed only with the symbols of domesticity. The
man of the house is the doddering, ineffective Hiram, scarcely real
beside his vivid wife. We are, in effect, back in Hannibal (Twain
in *The Autobiography* tells us that the original of the Phelps place
was in Missouri, but "I moved it down to Arkansas. It was all of
six hundred miles but it was no trouble"), and Huck is not
George Jackson, Sarah Williams, George Peters, or Adolphus; he
is, disconcertingly, Tom Sawyer! For a little while, he even thinks
like Tom, forgets the prescience of death that came over him with
the first sound of Aunt Sally's spinning wheel, and accepts her
house as if it were his Great Good Place, too. "It was a heavenly

place for a boy," Twain writes years later; but precisely for this reason it was no place for a boy who had chosen hell in its despite.

In Twain, indeed, only children are permitted to reject society and success; adults grow up into compromise and adjustment. Pudd'nhead Wilson represents, in a sense, Twain's version of Pierre, the alienated intellectual cast adrift in a community of philistines; and as Pierre confides his doubts about the world's morality to his unpopular novel, so Pudd'nhead sets his down in his "Calendar." Yet Pudd'nhead, unlike Pierre, has no consuming desire to publish his dangerous work; but shows it only to a single reader, resents it as a betrayal when that reader exposes it to the unappreciative public. Twain's own attitude toward the "Calendar" is more than a little disconcerting; reporting on the community's reaction to Puddn'head's satirical notes, Twain observes that "they read those playful trifles in the solidest earnest." But "playful trifle" seems hardly an adequate characterization of such a comment as: "Whoever has lived long enough to find out what life is, knows how deep a debt of gratitude we owe to Adam, the first great benefactor of the human race. He brought death into the world."

It is, perhaps, only a final twist of Twain's irony to pretend to dismiss such bitterness as trifling, but it is a protective irony, too, a defense of himself as well as Pudd'nhead. Indeed, though he distributed much of the "Calendar" through the novel in the form of chapter headings, he saved out a few that he considered too shocking, kept him in manuscript until his death. Wilson is, like his author, a man unsure of just when he is kidding himself, when the public; and his assumption of the role of humorist protects him against the day when he will be ready to change overnight from clownish Faust to eccentric detective, receive the full benefits of the happy ending which Twain has all along had in store for him. After his courtroom triumph, cheering crowds of citizens gather to acclaim Pudd'nhead, and match their praise of him with reproach of themselves. "His long fight against hard luck and prejudice was ended," Twain reports blandly; "he was a made man for good." If there is an undertone of irony in this, it is impossible to prove; and, indeed, there is scarcely room for it to exist in the minimal distance Twain has left between author and character. Like Pudd'nhead, Mark Twain, too, wants to have it both ways at once: to insult the society he lives in in the guise of tossing off "playful trifles," and to be hailed as a hero for discovering what no one really wants to know! If Pudd'nhead has seemed to play the role of Faust or Pierre, this is only because "hard luck and prejudice" have conspired to miscast him. His overwhelming desire for success (not alienation!) and the price he was willing to pay for it he has declared frankly enough in the epigraph to Chapter I: "Tell the truth or trump—but get the trick!"

II

From the time of Twain to that of Faulkner, it is hard to find a true Faustian character in American fiction. On the middlebrow level, that mythic figure is officially excluded by an orthodoxy of cheerfulness and acceptance. On the highbrow level, he is confused with the closely related archetype of the *poète maudit,* which descends ultimately from Werther and is influenced by French reworkings of Edgar Allan Poe. There is in such characters the Faustian potential, but most often their tragic possibilities are dissipated in posturing and self-pity. Their secret motto comes improbably from Emerson—not "to be great is to be damned," but "to be great is to be misunderstood." From the heroes of Henry Harland to those of Scott Fitzgerald, such not-quite tragic sufferers (they dream of expatriation rather than alienation, of going to Paris rather than hell!) continue to testify and perish, either on behalf of art alone or—more and more as the influence of Freud and Lawrence is felt—on behalf of sexual freedom, too. It is in the name of experience that they challenge the world, and it is against law that they chiefly chafe. But whether they are more innocent than their conforming fellow citizens or more guilty they cannot decide; and their authors write, therefore, books which are neither gothic nor Western, the kind of morally incoherent, sentimental works produced by Sherwood Anderson or Thomas Wolfe or Ross Lockridge.

World War I spurred the proliferation of such books; for in the minds of certain authors (the John Dos Passos of *Three Soldiers* is a key example), mass warfare came to seem essentially a conspiracy against the artistic sensibility, even more brutal than peacetime bourgeois life. The typical anti-war novel of the '20's is, therefore, more sentimental than political, rather like the "social" novels of Dickens, which judge society on the basis of how it treats the child —except that for writers like Dos Passos, not the child but the artist is the touchstone.* After World War II, the novelists, who succeeded in finding no new forms, revived once more the proto- types of twenty years before; and the American version of the *poète maudit* stalks again through the pages of Irwin Shaw's *The Young Lions,* a copy of Joyce's *Ulysses* under his bunk to make his affiliation clear. This time, however, he is permitted to fight back, to succeed rather than fail in the face of "hard luck and prejudice," to play Pudd'nhead Wilson—and thus to move even farther from the role of Faustian rebel. Successes or failures, however, such fig- ures can never blaspheme, only shally endlessly between with- drawal and accommodation, self-pity and self-congratulation; for they live in a world which has no name for sin.

Of all the avatars of self-pity who have possessed our literature for five decades, perhaps the only one to approach legendary di- mensions is Eugene Gant, who first appears in *Look Homeward Angel* and strives desperately to change and die in Wolfe's other thick, repetitious novels. Distinguished from our other innocent *poètes maudits* by his size, which has to match that of his author, Gant finally becomes neither heroic nor Gargantuan, but remains a great panting, blubbering hulk of an adolescent, who can age but not grow up. In a certain sense, he is more the successor to Huck Finn than to Stephen Dedalus, who was his immediate model. Joyce's Dedalus, both in *Portrait of the Artist as a Young Man* and *Ulysses,* broke out of the trap of self-pity and narcissism, pledging allegiance (while his detached and ironic author smiled) to the Satanic slogan: *Non serviam,* "I will not obey!" And he is harried into maturity, driven from home by the ghost of his mother, beside whose deathbed he had refused to kneel in prayer: "Silence, exile, and cunning," are the weapons he takes up in self-defense, weap- ons proper to the lonely Faustian man, who rejects in full aware- ness the pieties of family, church, and state. Gant's protective de- vices are nostalgia, *Weltschmerz,* and *Schwärmerei* (the German terms are inevitable in speaking of the single modern American author whom the Nazis found irresistible), the devices proper to the lonely child, who wants really only to recapture his lost, un- knowable Mother. "Naked and alone we came into exile. In her

---

* So also the anti-Hollywood novel (written and rewritten as late as Mailer's *The Deer Park*) and the anti-University novel (represented in the first part of Philip Roth's *Letting Go* and the whole of Bernard Malamud's *A New Life*) continue to charge those two institutions with the ultimate literary crime: betraying the writer, and thus proving them- selves no better than the War to End War itself.

dark womb we did not know our mother's face. . . . Which of us is not forever a stranger and alone? . . . O lost, and by the wind grieved, ghost, come back again." *Look Homeward Angel, You Can't Go Home Again:* the titles tell the story of the search and the frustration; and beyond them, the books reveal the love of that frustration and the seeking self: the little boy lost, for whom no world is real and satisfactory once mama's breast has been withdrawn, papa has died, and big brother has become a ghost endlessly mourned. There is no room for the Faustian passion where one is an outcast not because he has fallen but because he was born. And Wolfe's work finds its place, therefore, not even in the children's library, in which all terrible myths except those of passionate love can survive, but in the high school department, on the shelf of masturbatory dreams.

It is, perhaps, because in Faulkner's fiction alone, in the first half of the twentieth century, the Faustian figure persists as a living obsession, that Faulkner has come to seem our greatest contemporary novelist. What would strike us otherwise as mere hectic rhetoric and conventional gothic décor is transformed by this central concern into a tragic cry and an evocation of terror. In three of his major novels, Faulkner deliberately chooses the gothic mode, attempts to create the full-scale tale of terror, though everywhere he uses the devices of the form to invest with horror his vision of a chaotic and lost world. The first of these novels is *Sanctuary,* whose atrocities are presided over by Popeye, a two-dimensional, soulless machine of pure rapacity. The second is *Light in August,* whose Satanic segment unfolds under the aegis of Joe Christmas, the almost will-less offspring of a mating of black and white, possessed by the demons of rape and castration, murder and miscegenation. The third is *Absalom, Absalom!,* through which Thomas Sutpen, more ogre than man, stalks furiously toward his own destruction. It is only in the latter, however, that the authentic Faustian protagonist is created. *Sanctuary* is, on its more conscious levels at least, the least mythic of all Faulkner's works, and *Light in August* is, for all its bitterness and hysteria, a book about two saviors: Lena Grove, whom nothing can stop in her almost mindless quest of a father for her child, an inarticulate, unvirginal Mary in search of a Joseph; and Joe Christmas, in his inevitable crucifixion both Christ and anti-Christ. Born on Christmas Day without an acknowledged father, named at a venture "Christmas, the son of Joe," he dies, at the traditional age of thirty-three, nailed to the cross of his blood. And at the moment of his castration, which preludes his death even as the thrust of the lance into the side of Jesus, he seems to ascend to heaven on the spout of blood which the shocked reader realizes at that point has been shed for many:

> the pent black blood . . . seemed to rush out of his pale body like the rush of sparks from a rising rocket; upon that black blast the man seemed to rise soaring into their memories forever and ever. They are not to lose it, in whatever peaceful valleys, beside whatever placid and reassuring streams of old age, in the mirroring faces of whatever children they will contemplate old disasters and newer hopes. . . .

Only in Sutpen does Faulkner attempt the creation of the Faustian figure in whom the gothic achieves its thematic fulfillment. It is worth noting that he does not find his Faust among the humble peasants, black and white, who merely "endure"; nor does he discover him in the world of the aristocracy, of the Sartorises and their friends, in whom the old codes of honor of the South are remembered if not lived. Sutpen is a man without either honor or humility, only with a "grand design"; he is a poor white on the rise, the self-made man, whom Faulkner has elsewhere mocked and scorned, fighting his way toward acceptance and respectability. "He wasn't a gentleman," one of the narrators of *Absalom, Absalom!* insists, "he wasn't *even* a gentleman." A ragged and dirty boy, he is driven from a white man's house (whose owner rocks in a barrel-stave hammock, his leisure ensured by black sweat) by a Negro servant, though he has come in innocence to speak a helpful word; and he vows to make a secure place for himself in the world so that he need never again submit to such an indignity! For that secure place, he is willing to enter into whatever agreement hell may demand of him: "this Faustus, this demon, this Beelzebub fled hiding from some momentary flashing glare of his Creditor's outraged face . . . hiding, scuttling into respectability like a jackal into a rockpile. . . ." Yet though he is accused by Shreve (the Canadian roommate of Quentin Compson who speaks these words) of having made a compact with the Devil, Sutpen is not really credited with having a soul to sell. Commenting on Sutpen's coolness, the bravado which especially characterizes him, Shreve tries to write it off as "a part of the price he had got for whatever it was he had sold the Creditor, since according to the old dame he had never had a soul." In Shreve's irreverent account, the Satanic nature of Sutpen is treated with undergraduate levity. Not only does Shreve insist on referring to Sutpen's diabolic Master as "the Creditor" (apt enough metaphor in terms of the world of Sutpen who has ended by running a store), but he jokes about Sutpen's hiding his tail and horns "beneath human raiment and a beaver hat." It is not a new device for the American author embarrassed by the Faustian myth; indeed, it echoes quite directly the device by which Melville in *Moby Dick* lets jesting Stubb and Flask do most of the talking about Ahab's bargain with Fedallah.

Yet Shreve is surely not *only* making a dull joke over and over when he compulsively refers to Sutpen as "the demon." His epithet blends with those of the novel's other spokesmen: "fiend blackguard and devil," "ogre in an ogre-bourne with two phantom children," to create a common image more terrible and pathetic than comic or grotesque. Not only does Sutpen make his entrance into the story as the typical gothic hero-villain, emaciated and taciturn, his eyes "visionary and alert," guardedly watching out of a face baked black by some mysterious "oven's fever," but he grows in tragic stature as he struggles to achieve that grand design which brings only loneliness and madness and destruction to his children and himself. From the moment we see him first, naked and plastered with black mud, toiling in the virgin swamp beside his wild Negroes, to the point at which he falls beneath a scythe wielded by the father of a girl whom he has studded as if she were a beast, he becomes ever more monstrous and more admirable. In him, the very innocence that mitigates the Faustian guilt of other American heroes serves only to exacerbate that guilt; his invulnerable moral virginity merely increases the poignancy of the struggle, in which his "solitary despair" closes "in titan conflict with the lonely and foredoomed and indomitable iron spirit." Only the great mythic name is adequate to describe him; an old man selling calico to country girls in a tiny shack of a store, he is still somehow an "ancient and varicose and despairing Faustus . . . with the Creditor's hand already on his shoulder."

But Faulkner cannot sustain, from his ambivalent vantage-point, so tragic a view of the storekeeper, the status-hungry American on the make, the petty-bourgeois inheritor of a South that had belonged to his ancestors. Sutpen killed by Wash is revived as a Snopes, first as Ab, then as his son Flem. His past history is bestowed in some detail upon his successors; like Sutpen, the Snopeses also approach the grand house of a white man, still rocking in the same barrel-stave hammock, and are driven like him from the front door by a black servant. To be sure, Ab Snopes has approached not in innocent benevolence but with malice already in his heart, not inadvertently tracking mud onto the white porch, but deliberately walking through manure in order to sully the immaculate floors of the kind of man he despairingly and impotently hates.

The Snopeses, however, represent in Faulkner's mythology not only meanness of spirit and active malice; they are, by definition, clowns, who introduce into *Sanctuary* itself a note of sheer burlesque, when two of the tribe register in a whorehouse which they take for a hotel. When Flem Snopes makes his appearance in *The Hamlet* (1940), he is wearing a celluloid collar and a patent-leather bow tie, carrying a straw satchel; he is, in short, a comic character. It is as if Faulkner had in mind Marx's maxim about history repeating itself, the first time as tragedy, the second as comedy. For Flem is a second-generation figure, a post-Civil War representative of the demonic drive which earlier had propelled Sutpen toward his doom. This time, however, the Satanic social climber is distinguished not by the titanic despair and loneliness which compel pity and terror, but by a single-minded meanness of spirit against which laughter is the only defense.

Comic as he is, however, the Flem Snopes of *The Hamlet* is still a comic Faust. Though he moves through a world of the broadest farce, of back-country yarns, which swell and burgeon in the unreal atmosphere of tale-swapping in the gathering twilight of a summer's day, Flem becomes at last so genuinely sinister a figure that around him laughter dies to a chilled silence or rises to the pitch of hysteria. Only hell seems adequate to define his icy cunning, the cold aplomb with which he takes possession piece by piece of the whole crumbling world of the South. The voice of reason in the novel belongs to the sewing-machine salesman, Ratliffe, who speaks for Faulkner more directly than any other character in *The Hamlet;* but it is Ratliffe who dreams, or perhaps, more properly, has a vision of Flem's Descent into Hell. There is consternation among the minor devils at the point when he is ready to be "redeemed into eternal torment," for they cannot find his soul. Like Sutpen before him, he has none at all—only "a little kind of dried-up smear under one edge" of the asbestos box, where his most precious part has presumably been kept against the day of the running out of his contract. Worse, however, is to come; before the comedy is played out, it becomes clear that Flem has come to "the Creditor" not to submit to punishment but to take over hell itself. At the end, the Infernal Prince, scarcely knowing what has happened, discovers himself on his knees, looking up at Flem who sits calmly on his erstwhile throne. And he cries wildly, "Take Paradise!" while "the wind roars up and the dark roars down and the Prince scrabbling across the floor, clawing and scrabbling at the locked door, screaming. . . ." It is a simple-minded gag, really—not Faust but Satan begging for mercy at the last; but it is hard to laugh away.

That the South has remained through the last three decades our preferred literary arena of terror is, in great part, the achievement of Faulkner, a product of his mythopoeic genius; but it is also a product of the spirit of the times. As the dark-skinned peoples of the world stir uneasily, begin to make their bid for power, readers white and black turn to the imaginative record of the first large-scale encounter of the two races at close quarters, the struggle of Negro and white in the United States. Long before Little Rock, the attitudes of European intellectuals toward the American South and the American Negro were set by Faulkner's fiction; and, indeed, not only the white man's consciousness of the colored man but the colored man's own self-consciousness have been determined in large part by literary images, from Mrs. Stowe's Uncle Tom to Faulkner's Dilsey and Lucas Beauchamp. The European has un-fortunately tended to read Faulkner's gothic and symbolic distor-tion of life in Mississippi as literal sociological reporting; and Jean-Paul Sartre's *The Respectful Prostitute* provides a classic (and ridiculous) example of what happens when complex art is taken as simple fact. Only the American tradition of symbolic gothicism, which from Poe and Melville to Twain and Faulkner has never ceased to confront the problem of the Negro, has proved in an age of realism adequate to the complexities of life in the American South; and it is to Faulkner that young writers, Negro and white, continue to turn for clues to the "power of blackness" in our contemporary life.

Especially in Faulkner's early gothicism, succeeding novelists have discovered an example which has sustained them in their search for their own authentic themes and styles. One such line of development, which we have already noticed, is seen in the novels of Robert Penn Warren, the single long fiction of John Peale Bishop, *Act of Darkness,* and such novels of Erskine Caldwell as *Tobacco Road* and *God's Little Acre.* Caldwell, originally a short-story writer of considerable power, though always with a tendency toward melodrama, has deliberately vulgarized his themes, exaggerating the grotesquerie of Faulkner in the direction of the merely shocking, and creating a special brand of horror-pornography (grandpa eaten by the hogs, while brother is seducing sister in the splashing swill) that has made him one of the all-time best-sellers among the paperbacks. In him, the Faulknerian legend of the South reaches the wide audience capable only of the grossest responses and searching always for a violence capable of shaking their own torpor. Tough, tortured, and, at their best, determinedly intellectual, the masculine Faulknerians deal with the matter of the South not, like Caldwell, for its exoticism and suggestions of horror, nor even merely for the sake of atmosphere and tone, but because they are concerned with the complex moral and social problems at its heart, particularly those arising from the conflict and confluence of white and black.

Much more influential and varied, however, is a second Faulknerian line of descent in which women have rather consistently, though quite improbably, taken a leading part. Among the first generation of distaff Faulknerians are included such talented female fictionists as Katherine Anne Porter, Eudora Welty, and Carson McCullers; while in the succeeding generation Elizabeth Spencer and Flannery O'Connor have already achieved reputations. In the work of the earlier group, the obsessive concerns of Faulkner, and especially his vision of the South as a world of gothic terror disguised as historical fact, ceases to be the property of a single, eccentric author and becomes a living tradition; thanks to their transitional work, Mississippi has taken on for the imagination of the world the symbolic values attributed in the earliest years of the gothic to Italy. Against a background of miasmic swamps and sweating black skins, the Faulknerian syndrome of disease, death, defeat, mutilation, idiocy, and lust continues to evoke in the stories of these writers a shudder once compelled only by the supernatural. What tends to be dissipated in their fiction is the grossness, the sheer dirtiness, the farce and howling burlesque, all that keeps Faulkner from ever seeming precious, or, in any meaningful sense of the word, decadent. In Katherine Anne Porter, the grotesque tensions and masculine vigor of Faulkner still largely survive; in Eudora Welty, they tend to disappear among the more delicate nuances of sensibility; in Carson McCullers, especially after her first book, they have been quite subdued; and in Truman Capote, who is the heir of the feminizing Faulknerians, tone and style have been accommodated to notions of chic nurtured by such fashion magazines as *Harper's Bazaar*. In recent years, these journals have been remade in accordance with a new ideal of sensibility, defined by a taste for *haute couture,* classical ballet, baroque opera, certain more elegant rituals of the Church—and, above all, for the last, delicate distillation of Faulknerianism, a literature at once sensitive and Satanic.

Although (or perhaps because) this sensibility is quite frankly homosexual, it appeals to certain wealthy American women with cultural aspirations, and is, therefore, sponsored in their salons and published, with elegant taste, in magazines that cater to their other needs. The development of new markets for young writers who find themselves at home in those salons and magazines has gone hand in hand with the extension to America of the high bohemia which now includes New York as well as Venice or Ischia: a community hospitable to those who are internationalist and anti-bourgeois, so long as they are not sordid or sullen or bluntly political. The American writers who flourish best in this international society tend to be from the South; and, indeed, such a climate of expectation has been created in this regard, that aspirants to the chic audience are likely to pretend to Southern origins when they do not legitimately possess them.

In Faulkner, such writers find a ready-made *paysage moralisé,* through which to move their epicene protagonists, the landscape of the South already endowed with the proper symbolic values of decay and brooding evil. And in Faulkner, they find, too, a fear and distrust of women which they respond to according to their own lights. But it was not until the female intermediaries had begun the grafting of Jamesian sensibility onto the Southern gothic stem, that the true Magnolia Blossom or Southern homosexual style could be produced: pseudo-magical, pseudo-religious, pseudo-gothic.

Such fiction is often merely fashionable, for all its ostensible dedication to style and subtlety. Even Truman Capote, who from the beginning possessed considerable skill as a writer (it is impossible to imagine him writing anything as inept as Faulkner's *Mosquitoes*), has come more and more to play a part in print and out: to act for the benefit of his own limited world the elegant, sad androgyne—half reigning beauty and half freak. His promise has frittered away into journalism, as various magazines hasten to exploit him, send him on commissions to Russia, to Hollywood, etc. But even his novel, *Other Voices, Other Rooms,* already represents a falling away from the slight, authentic music of such an early story as "Children on their Birthdays." At the present moment, the queen has been replaced even in the superslicks by the beatnik;* but for perhaps ten years after World War II, the work of such fictionists as Capote and Carson McCullers profited by a *détente* in the middleclass, middlebrow war against homosexuality, just as the work of certain Jewish writers benefited by a similar relaxation on the anti-Semitic front. The new enlightenment according to psychoanalysis and intergroup tolerance has made it impossible for the right-minded to reject either fairy or Jew as subjects for our fiction, without self-reproach; and they have taken up the burden of *understanding* such deviants, often as their only remaining claim to liberalism.

In the lee of that understanding, certain writers, who only a generation or two ago would have had to produce semi-pornographic or encrypted books, have been able to make their ostensible subject what has so long been disguised or evaded in our classic fiction. Overt homosexuality carries with it, however, still the sense of taboo, and is almost always rendered, therefore, in gothic terms; though, as a covert theme, it informed the open-air Western mode. On the middlebrow and popular levels the new homosexuality is only now coming fully into its own. Capote (as artist rather than journalist) and Gore Vidal (as novelist rather than TV entertainer) have come to seem a little old hat, and even Paul Bowles begins to look like an enthusiasm of yesterday, while a serious new writer like Robert Phelps produces in *Heroes and Orators* (1958) a complex and troubling study of homosexual love that goes unnoticed; but Tennessee Williams and William Inge, moving from the stage to the screen, mold the imagination of our

---

* Both giving way in 1966 to that blend of beatnik and queer, the pop artist, whose camp style is at once a travesty and an emulation of the slicks themselves.

largest audience, and even in paperback detective stories, lesbian and queer become common properties.* Quite astonishingly, the gum-chewing popcorn-consuming hordes of the remotest hinterlands have accepted a new archetype of love (projected ideally by Anna Magnani and Marlon Brando) in which an aging, slovenly, aggressive woman—in a black slip—vainly assaults the innocence of a clean, incorruptible, beautiful young man—without a shirt. In ten thousand movie houses, the moment in which that infinitely desirable youth strips to the waist has come to represent the expected climax of the more arty film. His invert's strip tease takes place, of course, in a decaying clapboard house, outside of which the Spanish moss hangs ghostlike in the Southern night.

The child and the freak haunt such landscapes, too, images created out of the homosexual's conviction of the impossibility of love; and they move, not yet fallen into a world of acceptance and differentiated sex, through a society in which passion leads only to thralldom and suffering. Carson McCullers, in one book at least, manages to break through the parochialism and self-pity implicit in such a view of life, creating in *The Heart is a Lonely Hunter* an utterly convincing and terrible fiction. Written when she was only twenty-two, the book appeared in 1940, and is, in one sense, the last of the "proletarian novels," a true Depression book. Indeed, its success may be rooted precisely in the tension between public hysteria, proper to an age of social protest, and private anguish, proper to the sensibility of its author.

The Heart is a Lonely Hunter is a latter-day Southern love story, which is to say, a study of the failure of love, in this case the passion which unequally binds together two male deaf-mutes, one of them an almost bestial moron. That passion is rendered through the consciousness of one of those boy-girl adolescents shortly to become stereotypes; but in Mrs. McCullers' first novel, nothing is yet stereotypical. The melancholy Southern town, the deaf-and-dumb protagonists are completely satisfactory as fact and as symbol, fused into a single authentic vision suspended in the eye of a child, herself suspended at the verge of maturity. Mrs. McCullers' themes are common to the whole group to which she belongs: the impossibility of reciprocal love, the sadness of a

---

* The rise of Terry Sothern represents a later, analagous development—the passing of a kind of humor originally relished by audiences largely homosexual into the larger omni-sexual arena of popular culture—and its strange marriage with liberal anti-war protest in the best-selling movie, *Dr. Strangelove.*

world in which growing up means only learning that isolation is the lot of everyone. Mick (her very name makes the same point as her chopped-off hair) is the first of this writer's ambiguously boyish girls who stand outside of everything, even their own sex, feeling themselves freaks and seeking a society of freaks. But Mick is no Faust, even in the sense in which Huck was a Faust, and she becomes, in the course of her author's development, the Frankie of *Member of the Wedding,* a sentimental parody of herself, who exists to stir the easy tear at the pity of it all: a child victim, to be wept over condescendingly even as she weeps over a younger child victim, her cousin, or to be responded to with vague warmth as she cuddles in the arms of her black mammy—comes, oddly, back to the raft!

III

Not only the South, however, and the encounter of Negro and white have seemed to recent writers themes which literary modes based on reason and superficial observation must inevitably falsify. Modern war and the twentieth-century city have struck our novelists as phenomena more irrational and terrifying than the ghosts and haunted castles to which the gothic first addressed itself. Modes that once conveyed the shudder of man before the terror of the past as it persists into the present, come now to portray our horror before the evidences in contemporary society of a frightful future. The tale of terror seems more and more the most prophetic of all fictional genres: invented in the first surge of reaction to the Age of Reason, driven underground in a succeeding period of progress and civil peace, but again come into its own in an era of universal war, alienation from nature, failed revolutions, genocide, and ideological self-deception.

The modern war novel with its portrayal of incomprehensible violence, incoherent anguish, and ennui aspires toward the gothic form, but has been almost everywhere betrayed to sentimentality. Only in *The Enormous Room* of E. E. Cummings has a poet, already committed to hallucination and disjunction, proved capable of dealing with World War I in terms appropriate to its horror. Cummings' novel evokes a world in which reality slips fluidly in and out of focus in the rhythm of its protagonist's hysteria and despair, a world in which the real is haunted by itself. Other more "realistic" treatments of similar material, more popular at the moment of publication, have become now unreadable—seeming less adequate to the contemporary sense of what mass warfare is than Stephen Crane's impressionist *Red Badge of Courage,* which preceded them and was written by a man who had never seen combat.

Even Faulkner's *Soldiers' Pay,* not published until 1930, reflects still the standard disenchantment and self-pity of the middlebrow novel of anti-war protest; and *A Fable,* which he worked on up to 1954, represents his second try at making of the same materials, or profounder ones, something worthy of the experience of the A.E.F. It is a strangely moving effort to turn time back, to create after an uneasy period of peace and a second universal conflict, the book he and his contemporaries had failed to write the first time around. But *A Fable* is a dull, sentimental parable, tricked out with Faulkner's latter-day rhetoric, and projecting an intolerable backwoods Negro savior, who provides a second Christ-figure to balance the allegorical French corporal, who apparently bored Faulkner himself. Only in its occasional reversions to pure horror, its evocation, for instance, of the fetid atmosphere of a mass burial vault, does the book come to life. Not even the talent of Faulkner plus a commitment that brought him back again to the difficult subject has been able to break through the barrier that stands between the imagination of America and its experience in mass war. Travesties we have in great plenty, witting and unwitting entertainments, earnest tracts, anguished memoirs: all in the end defenses against that experience rather than illuminations of it.

If the novels written after World War I seem to become clichés even as they are committed to print, the novels of World War II are echoes of those clichés, products of minds so conditioned by the stereotypes of the earlier works that they seem never to have lived through the events of 1939-1945 at all. Only two recent books have risen above the dull slickness or sincerity of *The Young Lions* and *The Naked and the Dead.** Saul Bellow's *Dangling Man,* which deals with the pathetically comic nightmare of induction and stops just short of combat; and John Hawkes's incomprehensibly neglected *The Cannibal,* which deals with the comically pathetic nightmare of postwar occupation. Compounded

---

* Joseph Heller's *Catch-22* is a more recent exception—rendering with the techniques of the Black Vaudevillian a vision of war as ultimate burlesque, an event too farcical for tears.

of farce, fantasy, and macabre invention, his vision of the Europe left by two wars seems more appropriate to what we know than the inevitably rationalist falsifications of history. The rise and destruction of Nazism we have recorded in old newspapers and new textbooks as documented truth, actuality; but we have lived its course in our viscera and our nerves as a bad dream, in which, though we die for it, we cannot really believe.

Though the peculiar, wholesale horror of the great wars has eluded our greatest fictionists, and will exist for future ages only as a handful of clichés, the terror of the great Depression has fared better. The '30's thought of itself as a political period, and we have continued to think of it in a similar way, without being sufficiently aware that what it called politics was essentially apocalyptics: a commitment to revolution which is essentially a dedication to horror. Yet the typical fiction writer of the '30's would have been shocked to think himself a gothicist; if he were ideological enough not to mind being labeled, he would have called himself a "proletarian novelist."

The proletarian novel (sponsored in the first five years of the decade by the Communist critics, who had the sense of being the spokesmen for writers as different from themselves and each other as Dos Passos, Erskine Caldwell, and Hemingway) is not necessarily a book about proletarians. It is alternatively about poor farmers, members of the lower middle class, and, often enough, about intellectuals—specifically, about the intellectual's attempt to identify himself with the oppressed elements in society and with the movement which claimed to represent them. The proletarian novel was, theoretically, an attempt to glorify the Soviet Union and the Communist Party, and to prove that that Party was the consciousness of the working class in America. Yet the most characteristic aspect of such novels completely escapes all theories and definitions, for it is a product of the age as it worked on writers beneath the level of consciousness. This is the *tone* of the proletarian novel: the note of sustained and self-satisfied hysteria bred, on the one hand, of Depression years' despair and, on the other, of the sense of being selected as brands to be snatched from the fire.

From Marxism itself, the line of social thought which feeds into the proletarian novel had inherited a quasi-religious messianism. Two quite different sorts of feeling are involved, often confused with each other though logically separable: on the one hand, the desire that the good, clean, healthy workers of the future take over and destroy the whole heritage of the past, including the writer himself and his tradition; and on the other, the impulse of the writer to identify himself with the future, to feel himself strong and brutal enough to crush a world which has frustrated him. In the novel of the '30's, everything from sex to politics is assimilated into terror. It is, perhaps, the first fully self-conscious *secular* tale of terror, its object being to destroy not the phantoms of the past, but the institutions of the present, which are converted in its lurid light into ogres, as Wall Street is transformed into its haunted castle. All ghosts have been laid except "the specter" which, in 1848, Marx had announced was "haunting Europe," the specter of Communism. This means, in effect, a specter haunting a world of specters, horror confronting horror. And the proletarian novelists did, indeed, project violence in their fictions not only as that from which society was to be delivered, but also as the method of deliverance. In the shabby, gray days during which they wrote, the dream of violence possessed the American imagination like a promise of salvation. Politics was violent and a-politics equally so; whatever else a man publicly accepted or denied, he did not deny terror.

Obviously, the '30's did not invent terror and violence as fictional themes. They could find them not only in the picket-lines around them and in the Bonus Marchers, but in our classic novels as well. As far back as American books go, there are images of horror: the torn corpse stuffed up the chimney; the skull split by a tomahawk; the whale spouting blood. There are, however, two final transformations in the function and treatment of violence in fiction, which go even beyond the simple fact of its "neutralization"—its demotion from the world of the supernatural to that of everyday life. The first is the *urbanization of violence;* that is to say, violence is transferred from nature to society, from the given world that man must endure to the artificial world he has made, presumably to protect himself from the ravages of the first. There is, of course, a special horror in considering the law of fang and claw walled in but unmitigated in the brick and glass of the city-planners.

The city had been treated as a place of terror quite early in the nineteenth century by Dickens and by Baudelaire, who had variously transformed London and Paris into phantasmagoria of poverty and crime, lust and ennui; and behind both, there is the classic example of Dante, who at the very dawn of the modern city had already used his native Florence as a model for hell. In earlier American fiction, however, there are few instances of the gothic city, since most of our writers were pursuing memories of the frontier town, the colonial settlement in the clearing, when they were not simply escaping into the forest or out to sea. Brockden Brown, to be sure, had evoked the city under plague, a Philadelphia converted to a nightmare by disease and death; but Poe, who was, in a sense, his chief successor, abandoned, along with Brown's resolve to create horror without falling back on the supernatural, Brown's concern with American places. Poe surrenders the actual urban scene for unreal courts, the vaults beneath imaginary European towns, and especially lonely estates located on no maps. George Lippard, to be sure, returned to Philadelphia, which was his own native place as well as Brockden Brown's, and recreated it in his fantasy into a hellish sink.

The more sober and respectable writers of Lippard's own day, when they did not project their vision of the diabolical city back into the past, were likely to imagine it in the old world, like the Liverpool of Melville's *Redburn* or the Rome of Hawthorne's *The Marble Faun*. Even Twain, in his raucous populist way, and James, in more urbane fashion, played on the American ambivalence which regarded the European tour as at once a journey toward the culture of museums and guidebooks and a descent into hell. In *Pierre*, it is true, Melville tried his hand at creating a gothic version of New York: in the symbolic setting of that book, the city is the inferno into which the hero falls once he has excluded himself from the bucolic earthly paradise of Saddle Meadows. Over dark and merciless roads that leave the traveler bewildered and bruised, Pierre and Isabel come at night to the gloomy streets of Manhattan, where they find themselves at the mercy of the coachmen, "Charon ferry-men to corruption and death."

Yet it is, finally, not so much hell as Babylon into which Pierre brings his strange ménage, the "city of orgies" dreamed in the provinces by pious boys, whose visions of sin are derived from the Book of Proverbs and the Revelations of St. John; and the essential gothic tone is disrupted by sentimentality and melodrama.

"I say, my pretty one! Dear! Dear young man!! Oh, love, you are in a vast hurry, aren't you? Can't you stop a bit, now, my dear. . . ."

Pierre turned; and in the flashy, sinister, evil cross-lights of a druggist's window, his eye caught the person of a wonderfully beautifully-featured girl; scarlet-cheeked, glaringly arrayed, and of a figure all natural grace but unnatural vivacity. . . .

"My God!" shuddered Pierre, hurrying forward, "the town's first welcome to the youth!"

Precisely this provincial image, sentimental and lubricious, presides over the main line of American city novels from Whitman's *Franklin Evans,* through Crane's *Maggie,* up to the fiction of Dreiser and the "muckrakers"; and in its evocation, popular entertainer and serious "realist" are one, so long as both alike are young men from the midwest, making their tremulous way into the wicked Big Town, upon which they have projected all that their mothers and preachers have warned them of, and for which they ferociously long. Only in the '30's does the American city come at long last to seem, in the books of men born in those cities, not a latter-day reflection of Nineveh, but a horror in its own right—not less terrible but more so, since for such writers the city is quite simply all there is. The '30's mark the climax, too, of a second and even more critical change in the literary uses of violence: the *ennobling of violence* as "the midwife of history." Under the name of "the revolution," violence becomes not something to be fled, not the failing of otherwise admirable men, not a punishment for collective guilt— but the climax of social action. The process which had begun just after 1789 with the Terror, and had been hailed in the United States by the theoretically bloody-minded Jefferson, received in an age of mechanized warfare and mass production its final form. The lust for pain of Nietzsche and the hypostasizing of History by Hegel culminated in the twin horrors of Nazi and Soviet brutality; but a worse indignity had already been worked on the minds of the intellectuals, conditioned in advance to become apologists for one or the other system.

In light of this, it is easy to understand that questions of ideology are secondary, that it is the naked love-fear of violence which distinguished the novel of the '30's: a kind of passion not unlike that which moved the Germans before their final defeat, a desire for some utter cataclysm to end the dull dragging out of impotent suffering. Not only Communist-oriented writers produced urban horror literature in those days, but Southerners like Faulkner (in *Sanctuary*), John Peale Bishop (in *Act of Darkness*), or Robert

Penn Warren (in *At Heaven's Gate*). Where such writers had been already established or were to continue long careers, they produced books which seem in their total work eccentric, products of the age rather than of the men. Hemingway himself made an obeisance to the hectic mode in his oddly inept *To Have and Have Not;* and a mild, upper-middlebrow traditionalist like James Gould Cozzens produced, in *Castaway,* a novella uncharacteristically mad and, by that token, convincing beyond all his other books. It is a pity that his shrill parody of Robinson Crusoe, in which a castaway in a gothic department store can only discover his own footprint, has remained relatively unknown, while pointless critical disputes have raged over his fat failure, *By Love Possessed.*

The most admired novelists of the period itself, whose popularity has waned with the subsidence of the mood and sentiment which they helped define, are remembered now for their evocations of terror and despair—rather than for messages of hope or reform that they sometimes rather perfunctorily supplied in lieu of the more bourgeois happy endings. Not Steinbeck's advocacy of agricultural resettlement or the brotherhood of man but his rendering of the ambiguous terror of picket-line conflict in *In Dubious Battle;* not Dos Passos' dream of a redeemed U.S.A. but his bloody evocation of the lynched and castrated labor leader, Wesley Everest, hanging from a railroad bridge; not the May Day Parade in *Studs Lonigan,* but Farrell's picture of Studs lying in the gutter in his own vomit, contracting the pneumonia that is to kill him: these remain in the reader's mind—an exhibition of social horrors. In retrospect, the period of the '30's—at least during its first six or seven years, before Americans lost the awareness of living at the tail-end of a postwar period and began to feel themselves in a pre-war era—seems now a time in which new gothic forms were being created by writers who were determined not to know what they were doing.

If Nathanael West appears to us from our present vantage point the chief neglected talent of the age, this is largely because he was immune to the self-deceit which afflicted his contemporaries; he knew what he was doing. Despite his own left-wing political sympathies and the pressures of friends more committed than he, he refused to subscribe to the program for proletarian fiction laid down by the official theoreticians and critics of the Communist movement. And he turned unashamedly to the business of rendering the naked anguish he felt, rather than projecting the commitment to action and faith it was assumed he should feel. Even more importantly he rejected the concept of realism-naturalism, refused to play the game (variously connived at by Dos Passos and Steinbeck and Farrell) of pretending to create documents rather than poetry. He returned, despite the immediate example of three decades of falsely "scientific" writing, which sought to replace imagination with sociology, the symbol with the case report, to the instinctive realization of the classic American fictionists that literary truth is not synonymous with fact. West's novels are a deliberate assault on the common man's notion of reality; for violence is not only his subject matter, but also his technique.

His apprenticeship was served in Europe, in the world of the Left Bank, where from the Surrealists he learned (his finger-exercises are to be found in his first book, *The Dream Life of Balso Snell*) a kind of humor expressed almost entirely in terms of the grotesque, that is to say, on a perilous border-line between jest and horror. Yet his Surrealist-inspired techniques—the violent conjunctions; the discords at the sensitive places where squeamishness demands harmony; the atrocious belly-laughs that shade off into hysteria—are not very different, after all, from the devices of *Pudd'nhead Wilson* or *Gordon Pym*. West is, in a sense, then, only reclaiming our own; yet, in another, he is introducing into the main line of American fiction a kind of sophistication, a view of the nature of art, of which our literature was badly in need.

It is possible for an American, of course, to find in his native sources, his native scene and his American self cues for the special kind of horror-comedy which characterizes West's novels. The uneducated Twain once did precisely that, and the half-educated Faulkner has pretended at least to follow his example. Yet in Twain everywhere, and in Faulkner more and more as the years go by, there is evident a presumptuous, home-made quality, which mars their work whenever they pass from the realm of myth to that of ideas. Nothing is more bald and thin than the back-porch atheism of Twain's *The Mysterious Stranger,* except perhaps the red-neck Protestantism of Faulkner's *A Fable.*

The religious dimension which they failed to achieve, West attains in part because he is aware of a European tradition in thought and art, out of which Kafka, so like him in certain ways, had earlier emerged. It is not accidental that both these anguish-ridden comedians, as uncompromisingly secular as they are profoundly religious, should be Jews; for Jews seem not only peculiarly apt at projecting images of numinous power for the unchurched, but are skillful, too, at creating myths of urban alienation and terror. The '30's, not only in America (where Daniel Fuchs and Henry Roth—the latter in a single astonishing book, *Call It Sleep*—are outstanding figures) but everywhere, is a period especially favorable for the Jewish writer bent on universalizing his own experience into a symbol of life in the Western world. More and more it has seemed to such writers that what they in their exile and urbanization have long been, Western man in general is becoming. This is, presumably, the claim implicit in West's name (he was originally called Nathan Wallenstein Weinstein), his boast that he is an American Everyman; though surely to none does the epigram of C. M. Doughty apply more tellingly than to West, who quotes it in *Balso Snell:* "The Semites are like to a man sitting in a cloaca to the eyes, and whose brows touch heaven."

Yet West is a peculiarly American case, too. In one of his few published critical notes he declares: "In America violence is idiomatic, in America violence is daily." And it is possible to see him as just another of our professional tough guys, one of the "boys in the backroom" (the phrase is applied by Edmund Wilson, in a little study of our fiction, to West along with John O'Hara). This is not to deny, though West himself tried to, that West is, in some meaningful sense, a Jew. He is enough the child of a long tradition of nonviolence to be racked by guilt in the face of violence, shocked and tormented every day in a world where violence is, of course, daily and most men are not at all disturbed. In *Miss Lonelyhearts,* he creates the portrait of a character, all nerves and no skin, the fool of pity, whom the quite ordinary horror of ordinary life lacerates to the point of madness. His protagonist is given the job of answering "letters to the lovelorn" on a daily newspaper; and he finds in this job, a joke to others (he must pretend in his column to be a woman, for only women presumably suffer and sympathize), a revelation of human misery too acute for him to bear. It is the final modern turn of the gothic screw: the realization that not the supernatural, the extraordinary, but the ordinary, the everyday are the terrors that constrict the heart.

Dear Miss Lonelyhearts—

. . . I would like to have boy friends like other girls and go out on Saturday nites, but no boy will take me because I was born without a nose—although I am a good dancer and have a nice shape and my father buys me pretty clothes.

I sit and look at myself all day and cry. I have a big hole in the middle of my face that scares people even myself so I can't blame the boys for not wanting to take me out. . . .

What did I do to deserve such a terrible bad fate? I asked Papa and he says he doesnt know, but that maybe I did something in the other world before I was born or that maybe I was being punished for his sins. I dont believe that because he is a very nice man. Ought I commit suicide?

Sincerely yours,
Desperate

Miss Lonelyhearts is, finally, the comic butt who takes upon himself the sins of the world: the *schlemiel* as Everyman, the skeptical and unbelieved-in Christ of a faithless age. But such a role of absurd Christ is West's analogue for the function of the writer, whom he considers obliged unremittingly to regard a suffering he is too sensitive to abide; and in no writer is there so absolute a sense of the misery of being human, though he also believes that such misery is a more proper occasion for laughter than tears. He is child enough of his time to envision an apocalypse; but his apocalypse is a defeat for everyone. The protagonist of *Miss Lonelyhearts* is shot reaching out in love toward a man he has unwillingly offended; while the hero-*schlemiel* of the more deliberately farcical *A Cool Million: or The Dismantling of Lemuel Pitkin* (in theme and style a parody of Horatio Alger), staggers from one ridiculous, anti-heroic disaster to another, becoming after his death the idol of an American fascist movement. But the true horror-climax of his life and the book comes when, utterly maimed, he stands on the stage between two corny comedians, who wallop him with rolled-up newspapers in time to their jokes, until his wig comes off (he has been at one point scalped), his glass eye pops out, and his wooden leg falls away; after which, they provide him with new artificial aids and begin again.

It is not until *The Day of the Locust*, however, which is West's last book, and the only novel on Hollywood not somehow made trivial by its subject, that one gets the final version of the Apocalypse according to Nathanael West. At the end of the book, a painter, caught in a rioting mob of fans at a Hollywood première, dreams, as he is being crushed by the rioters, the phantasmagoric masterpiece he has never finished painting, "The Burning of Los Angeles." West does not seem finally a really achieved writer; certainly, no one of his books is thoroughly satisfactory, though there are astonishing local successes in all of them. His greatness lies like a promise just beyond his last novel, and is frustrated by his early death; but he is the inventor of a peculiar kind of book, in which the most fruitful strain of American fiction is joined to the European tradition of avant-garde, anti-bourgeois art, native symbolism to imported *symbolisme*. The Westian or neo-gothic novel has opened up possibilities, unavailable to both the naturalistic semi-documentary and the over-refined novel of sensibility, possibilities of capturing the quality of experience in a mass society—rather than retreating to the meaningless retailing of fact or the pointless elaboration of private responses to irrelevant sensations. Putting down a book by West, a reader is not sure whether he has been presented with a nightmare endowed with the conviction of actuality or with actuality distorted into the semblance of a nightmare; but in either case, he has the sense that he has been presented with a view of a world in which, incredibly, he lives.

Yet the importance of West's work was scarcely realized in his own day; and it would be misleading even now to speak of his general influence. Though his novels continued to move younger writers, and though the last few years have witnessed not only a growing critical acclaim, but attempts to extend his audience by stage adaptations and moving-picture versions, West is still more admired than directly emulated.* S. J. Perelman, who is West's brother-in-law and was a contributor to the little magazine *Contact,* which West helped edit, has been conducting a strange experiment, whose end is the transformation of Surrealist gallows humor into commercial entertainment. It is all part of an extraordinary process, which begins for literature in the columns of *The New Yorker,* and for art in the cartoons of the same magazine, as well as in certain shop-windows decorated by Salvador Dali—but whose end is not yet in sight. The avant-garde images of twenty-five years ago and

---

* Not so in 1966, when West's attitudes and devices have been assimilated into what already seems a new convention: that much-touted Black Humor, with which many of our latest writers seem perforce to begin, and the somewhat older practitioners of which (Bruce Jay Friedman, for example) have come to seem in a very few years established models and guides.

the grotesquerie which distinguished the short-lived *Contact* have become now the common property of gifte shoppes and greeting-card racks, fall as stereotypes from the lips of hip twelve-year-olds. "Hate cards" and ashtrays adorned with "Nebbishes" (the surreal, Jewish sad sack of West reduced to the level of *kitsch*) spread now the self-contempt, the anti-bourgeois virulence, the contempt for home, mother, birthdays, and Christmas, once the exclusive stock-in-trade of bohemians; and the "sick" joke popularizes the nause-ated giggle before violence, which not so long ago belonged only to books like *Miss Lonelyhearts.* "Can Johnny come out to play, Mrs. Jones?" "You know Johnny has no arms and legs!" "We don't want players. We need bases." *

It is not only a matter, however, of neo-gothicism becoming a prevailing mode on the level of popular culture; on more serious levels, too, the mode of West, if not his example, is evident. The alienated *schlemiel*-heroes of Saul Bellow surely owe something to West's protagonists, whose anguish never quite overbalances their absurdity; and everywhere in the Jewish American novelists of the last two decades, West's influence is felt, if only as a temptation toward sheer terror rejected in favor of sentimentality or some ab-stract espousal of love. Though lonely in his own time, West was not really alone in his attempt to redeem French horror for the American soul, as Poe had once redeemed that of Germany; Djuna Barnes (whom he probably did not even know) had made a simi-lar, even less popular assay in *Nightwood* (1937). The dislocated lyricism, hallucinated vision, and oddly skewed language of Miss Barnes's black little book were introduced to the United States by T. S. Eliot, with a rather unconvincing assurance of their ultimately religious import. In his preface, Eliot argues, at any rate, that the homosexual ambience of *Nightwood,* its ecstatic evocations of disease and death reflect a genuine concern with the problem of evil and not just an obsession with the properties of decadent gothi-cism. Linguistically, *Nightwood* is too complex, and thematically, it is too little concerned with the experience of America to achieve even the belated and limited success of West's work; it lives now chiefly in the minds of a limited number of admirers and in quota-

---

* The last and most winningly atrocious representative of sick jokery (the Jewish-heterosexual wing, of course, rather than the Southern-homo-sexual) is Lenny Bruce, in whom the distance between literature and enter-tainment, high art and low comedy threatens to disappear.

tions included in anthologies of modern verse, though it inspired in part the considerable achievement of Malcolm Lowry, whose cult threatens to overwhelm that of his predecessor.

Nonetheless, such a book as John Hawkes's *The Cannibal,* begun though it was before the author had ever read *Nightwood,* recalls its passionate commitment to extorting from terror a poetry that will not mitigate or deny that terror. Though it is in part the product of World War II, as we have observed earlier, Hawkes's novel is also the fruit of the impact of Surrealim on the American mind. Written when the author was only twenty-three, it manages to evoke the nightmare Germany of 1945 (super-imposed upon a persistent, ghost-like image of the same country during World War I), through which a lonely American soldier on a motor-bike rides frantically toward his inevitable death. Hawkes's Germany is a world in which the past haunts the present, the present the past; and both conspire to insure that the future (a nationalist German revolt is being plotted throughout the action, with the narrator as its chief, and succeeds as the book closes) will know itself also a ghost-ridden ghost as soon as it is born. In no official document or journalist's report is the "German problem" rendered so faithfully in terms of the monstrous unreality which is its essence. Certain scenes, minor incidents remain in the mind with a vividness hard to explain; and a glimpse, for instance, dreamed rather than observed, of a man dead two wars ago seems somehow an essential clue to a mystery at which historians nibble away in vain:

> There the Merchant, without thoughts of trade, dressed only in grey, still fat, had died on his first day at the front and was wedged, standing upright, between two beams, his face knocked backwards, angry, disturbed. In his open mouth there rested a large cocoon, protruding and white, which moved sometimes as if it were alive. The trousers, dropped about his ankles, were filled with rust and tufts of hair.

Not only Left Bank Surrealism, but the example of Kafka, too, has reinforced latter-day American gothicism, as Tieck and Hoffmann provided examples for Poe and Hawthorne a hundred years before. Translated by an Englishman and relished first of all by Americans, Kafka's books have in their posthumous career moved especially our writers and our critics, as seems only fair for an author who called one of his longer works *Amerika*. It is the most comic of his books, a tale which looks westward not only in its title but in its fable, the account of a flight to our shores; and it parodies throughout, by way of tribute, *Huckleberry Finn*. Kakfa is, moreover, though a Czech by birth and a German in language, an urban Jew in his deepest self-consciousness; and his most direct influence in the United States has been on certain second-generation American Jews, brought up in New York and Chicago, to whom his prophetic visions of a universal bureaucracy have seemed blueprints of the world into which they were born. Nathanael West, so much like Kafka in spirit, had never read him; but the Jewish writers of the '40's and after draw on him directly. Isaac Rosenfeld and Paul Goodman have recreated in their short stories a symbolism as shifty and evasive as Kafka's own, as well as a technique, half-essayistic, half-poetical, based on his example. They have, in addition, specified and expanded his Freudian insights, and made explicit the revolutionary implications of his vision, without losing the mad humor which is his essence. Though their stories have remained relatively unpopular, an unwitting travesty of their American adaptation of Kafka, "The Lottery" by Shirley Jackson, has become a standard middlebrow anthology piece, perhaps because it lacks the intelligence and wit of their best work.

Neither Rosenfeld (prematurely dead) nor Goodman has succeeded in creating a full-scale novel in the Kafkaesque mode,* which may be essentially too fragmentary and lyrical (Kafka himself finished none of his longer books) for the larger form. Their work is, moreover, too bound to their model to seem either quite authentic or really free—and too ideological to allow room for rich invention. Freer in his uses of Kafka and the whole Surrealist tradition is Bernard Malamud, whose first novel, *The Natural* (1952), was largely ignored, perhaps because the lively play of fancy, the trifling with illusion which characterize it disconcerted those who had picked it up expecting a "good baseball yarn." Actually it *is* a baseball story, disconcertingly out of Ring Lardner by T. S. Eliot: an account of the tragic career of a ball-player called Roy Hobbs, last hero of a culture which is not sure whether it needs more to

* Goodman has made a big try since, gathering together and augmenting some of his earlier short fictions. But *Empire City* is finally a disappointing work, and since its appearance Goodman seems to have turned entirely to the essay, hashing and rehashing his left-wing critique of American education.

cherish or to destroy its heroes. Out of the hectic atmosphere of the ball park (not specially set in Brooklyn, but reminiscent of that mythical place), the legends of the sports page, *The Natural* creates a magical universe—in which white witch and black witch struggle for the soul of a secular savior, who will restore the Waste Land to fertility, by winning the pennant for the home team. Naturally it is a pennant that cannot be won; and in the final scene, the hero is more Casey at the Bat than Grail Knight; but the humor only accents without destroying the tragic impact of the close. The special tone of *The Natural,* its lovely, absurd madness, tends to disappear from Malamud's later work, except in the title story of his short-story collection *The Magic Barrel;* and with that tone goes the poetic language that sustained it. In *The Assistant,* he turns back to the muted, drab world of the Depression as remembered two decades later, and the quality of his prose is adapted to the denial of the marvelous to which he has committed himself.

The gothic provides a way into not only the magical world inhabited by the baseball fan, and the child dreaming of King Arthur who still lives within that fan, but also into certain areas of our social life where nightmare violence and guilt actually exist. To discuss, for instance, in the light of pure reason the Negro problem in the United States is to falsify its essential mystery and unreality; it is a gothic horror of our daily lives. If Ralph Ellison's *Invisible Man* seems, as a novel written by a Negro about the Negro's plight, superior to any of the passionate, incoherent books of Richard Wright, this is because Ellison has bypassed all formulas of protest and self-pity and cast off the restrictions of mere realism. Only James Baldwin's *Go Tell It on the Mountain* has a comparable freshness and directness, but it lacks finally the madness which gives to *Invisible Man* a special kind of conviction. The whole middle of Ellison's book takes on a special quality of grotesqueness, because he begins and ends it with a Surrealist nightmare. The invisible man (invisible, of course, because he is black—and being black cannot be seen through a wall of clichés) crouches in a cellar retreat lighted by "exactly 1,369 lights." His electric power he steals from the Monopolated Light and Power, using it not only for illumination but also to keep his record-player going. On that player spins endlessly Louis Armstrong's "What Did I Do to Be So Black and Blue," to which the invisible man listens as he eats his favorite dessert of vanilla ice-cream and sloe gin.

Invisible Man is, like most neo-gothic fiction, a technical achievement as well as a statement of an important theme; indeed, its technique is keyed to the world of absurdity and violence which it projects, and its author rejects the last falsification of irrelevant or inert form. It is the special distinction of this kind of fiction that it neither fakes a concern with technique (like the *U.S.A.* of Dos Passos, all of whose *ersatz* experimentalism seems contrived to conceal a shallowness of characterization and a lack of over-all unity) or abandons all such concerns as beside the point (like much documentary fiction from Farrell to James Jones). The gothicist understands that it is the angle of perception which determines a novelist's meaning, reveals a world haunted and infernal, or subscribes to the illusion of one rational and dull. The gothic novel has been from the first experimental, not merely because it is pledged to the slogan, "Make it new!", but, much more importantly, because it sets itself the task of persuading skeptical readers to believe in ghosts or invisible men, to believe in themselves as ghosts or invisible men! This is, of course, ridiculous; and the gothicist must learn to be, as all American exponents of the mode since Poe have known, self-consciously funny, if he does not choose to be inadvertently silly. Beside the solemn experimentalist, there has existed in the United States the comic one, from the West of *Balso Snell* to the John Barth of *The Floating Opera;* and it is the latter who has seemed most often to suggest the deepest truth about our existence —which is always, in one way or another, absurd.

Perhaps the most distinguished of our recent, serious comic novelists is Wright Morris, who from *My Uncle Dudley* to *The Field of Vision* has been trying to convince his readers that Nebraska is the absurd hell we all inhabit. His commercial unsuccess, in spite of critical acclaim that for ten years has been greeting the amazing patience, ingenuity, wit, and tact of his work, is one of the puzzling cultural phenomena of our time. Perhaps his subject matter is a little too American for those who can appreciate the subtlety of his form;* the subtlety of his form a little baffling to those with a real taste for his provincial subject matter; his macabre humor at once too honest and too violent for anyone. He expresses a kind of

---

* John Barth, on the eve of his fourth novel, faces a similar problem, for what Nebraska is to Morris, Maryland has been to him. But *The Sotweed Factor* has won him wide critical acclaim; and perhaps his next work may yet win through to the big urban audience.

hopelessly American anti-Americanism unparalleled since Mark Twain; as is attested by the fact that his favorite enemy is Norman Rockwell. Other writers simply ignore Rockwell, though some of them recreate in *The New Yorker, Harper's,* or *The Hudson Review* the images which he more profitably and naïvely projects on the covers of *The Saturday Evening Post;* Morris insists on meeting him head-on on his own home ground. He contests with Rockwell, that is to say, the American inheritance, raises the critical question: to whom does the ball signed by Babe Ruth, Ty Cobb's glove really belong? To the easy affirmer or the man who says no? To Pudd'n-head Wilson or Huckleberry Finn?

There is no doubt about which side Morris is on. Like Ellison's invisible man, he declares over and over in all his books, "So I became ill of affirmation, of saying 'yes' against the nay-saying of my stomach—not to mention my brain"; but he does not consider this a surrender of his birthright, a prelude to expatriation or internal exile. On the contrary, he thinks of this (as he has attempted to demonstrate in his recent critical book, *The Territory Ahead*) as making him one with the great nay-sayers of our classical novel, with those who have, in revulsion from the life around them, penetrated even deeper into the only real America, "the territory ahead." Morris is not, however, in any sense a provincial in technique or form; he tells, with devices that depend on but do not imitate the experiments of European modernists, his native horror-story—and he tells it, like the Dadaists and Twain who anticipated them, for the laughs! Indeed, it is the balance of horror and comedy in his work which keeps it from turning, on the one hand, into mere farce and on the other into horror-pornography.

IV

From the time of Poe, two possibilities have been open to the gothic: the pursuit of genuine terror, "the hideous Moor" who lurks at the back of the cave; or the evocation of sham terror, the calling-up of ghosts in which no one believes. The one is a confrontation of the violence which is essential to our lives, the other an indulgence in it, a flirtation with horror for the sake of a shameful thrill. The popular audience has always demanded the pseudo-fiction of terror, which in all of its major forms Poe perfected for the American market-place: the ghost story, the detective story, and science fiction. The archetypal nature of such forms is indicated by the fact that their readers do not think of themselves as reading particular books or even the works of certain authors, but rather as seeking out and consuming the latest examples of the forms themselves. Though the three forms overlap somewhat in time, they really illustrate a sequence in the development of popular taste. The classic ghost story seems now an obsolescent subgenre, though as late as Henry James's *Turn of the Screw* or "The Jolly Corner," it could be used by a quite serious artist to project the frightfulness of secret concupiscence, or the encounter between what the ego has made of itself and the monstrous thing it might have become had certain repressed impulses been actuated. Since the full impact of Freudianism, however, ghosts have tended to seem metaphors rather than facts of experience—except in certain naïve works, in which they are evoked to thrill the kind of mind which otherwise finds satisfaction in shabby séances and table-tapping. An occasional ghost moves through the murky ambience of Truman Capote's stories, shouldering aside frail children and psychoanalysts; but, by and large, the form has fallen into the hands of middlebrow craftsmen like Lovecraft and Gerald Heard, who cater to the dated addictions of a rapidly shrinking audience.

After science has progressed to the point of explaining, or claiming at least to have explained, the under-soul, ghosts can be granted only the half-mocking credence accorded the Hallowe'en midnight show, at which the clichés of the oldest gothic tales: creaking doors, clutching hands, screams out of the dark (all explained in the last reel)—are taken once more out of stock. To be sure, certain favorite monsters return decade after decade: Dracula and the creature of Frankenstein; but they are classified these days as "fantasy," which tends to blur into science fiction. Science fiction denies, however, in its basic assumptions the belief upon which the ghost story properly depends: "There are more things in heaven and earth, etc." In its world, all haunting terrors are explicable; and there is nothing not dreamed of in the physics laboratory, or the classrooms where Dr. Rhine lectures on extra-sensory perception. But though science fiction had already begun with Poe's *Gordon Pym* (imitated by both Jules Verne and Conan Doyle) and his post-cataclysmic dialogues like *Eros* and *Charmion,* and though an essential protagonist of the form was created when Hawthorne imagined Aylmer, the conscienceless experimenter, science fiction as an official genre with a commonly accepted name had to wait for World War II and the explosion of the atomic bomb.

In the interim period, the detective story, or more properly the murder mystery (the first label pretends that the form is a kind of cool, clean puzzle-game, the second admits its obsession with death), has performed for the middlebrow reader the function of evoking and purging terror. Half artist, half scientist, Poe's C. Auguste Dupin imposes upon a world of irrational horror the semblance of order, proves over and over that the most grotesque nightmare (the mutilated bodies stuffed up a chimney in a room no one seems to have entered) can be understood, given acumen and a talent for analysis. The detective story in this form is based on an extension of the gothic device of the explained supernatural; but it is set in a frame, apparently invented by Poe himself, in which a narrator, more confused and terrified than the reader, watches the performance of a detective, more perspicuous and cool than that reader. The narrator is a somewhat duller than average man-in-the-street and the detective his version of the *poète maudit:* a lonely recluse who deigns to aid the society from which he has withdrawn. Such tales of detection, in the hands of serious writers, are used to project a pathetic image of the author himself as *socially useful,* however spurned and misunderstood.

Indeed, Poe himself was driven to dissolve completely the barriers between art and life, C. Auguste Dupin and Edgar Allan Poe, providing in *The Mystery of Marie Roget* a solution to an actual unsolved case of his own time, and in *Eureka* (where the mask of Dupin is dropped at last) the answer to the most baffling whodunit of them all, the solution to the case of Creation! But the detective story, in American literature at least, has always represented symbolically the *capitulation* of the recalcitrant artist to the bourgeois community—and is, moreover, itself such an act of capitulation. All of Poe's fictions represent a complex adjustment between his desire to mock his audience and to be accepted by it; but there is a wide range of difference in the degree of accommodation to popular taste, from the difficulty of *Gordon Pym* to the accessibility of the detective stories. The latter have been among the most widely admired of all his tales, even Abraham Lincoln, who, according to the best records, read no other fiction, having made an exception in their case. In the hands of mere hacks—and the form attracts the hack irresistibly—the detective story has continued to be the favorite off-hours reading of tired Presidents, as well as harried businessmen, novelists, professors, and other public figures in search of a minor vice with no unpleasant consequences.

Mark Twain, who mocked Sherlock Holmes in "A Double-Barrelled Detective Story," himself turned to the form over and over: in *Tom Sawyer Detective, Simon Wheeler, Detective* (attempted twice unsuccessfully, as a play and a novel), and *Pudd'nhead Wilson*. In the latter, he uses typically enough the moment of reversal and recognition, when Wilson, the amateur sleuth, reveals innocence and guilt in a single gesture, to mark the moment of his accommodation to the philistine community. Similarly, Faulkner's Gavin Stevens, another lawyer and amateur detective, who first appeared in a series of *Saturday Evening Post* stories (later collected as *Knight's Gambit*), represents Faulkner's own attempt to make peace with the South, America, and the world. Windbag and baffled lover, Stevens seems a mating of Senator Claghorn and J. Alfred Prufrock, an impotent revealer of the truth, pitifully proud of his own rhetoric and his Phi Beta Kappa key. The successive spokesmen for Faulkner in his books represent his successive images of himself, from Quentin Compson to Gavin Stevens, images of despair giving way to images of accommodation. The self-torturing and doomed Quentin, we remember, was a kind of detective, too, in *Absalom, Absalom!* moving doggedly toward the truth about the South that would destroy him. Stevens, on the other hand, though he also pursues ultimate questions of guilt and responsibility in *Intruder in the Dust* and *Requiem for a Nun,* heads not toward suicide but a middle-aged romance and the happy ending of marriage! It is Stevens who presides over Faulkner's retreat from horror toward sentimentality and easy affirmation; and it is fitting that he be Pudd'nhead Wilson reborn.

On the middlebrow level, the pseudo-scientific novel of detection is nearly dead in the United States; and, indeed, though invented in America, it has flourished chiefly in the form of British importations from Conan Doyle and Chesterton to Agatha Christie and Dorothy Sayers. After Dupin, we have produced no deductive amateur sleuths worthy of being set beside Holmes or Father Brown, Hercule Poirot or Lord Peter Wimsey, with the possible exception of S. S. Van Dine's Philo Vance; and Holmes himself pretended to despise even Dupin. Our essential contribution to the form in the twentieth century is a strange offshoot of the '30's novel of urban violence: a "realistic" exposé of corruption in the big city, presided over by the private eye. But the private eye is not the dandy turned sleuth; he is the cowboy adapted to life on the city streets, the embodiment of innocence moving untouched through universal guilt. As created by Dashiell Hammett, the blameless shamus is also the honest proletarian, illuminating by contrast the decadent society of the rich; and he speaks not with the pedantic condescension of Poe's Dupin but in the language of the people. The style of the urban mystery story, that is to say, descends from Hemingway via Dashiell Hammett and Raymond Chandler to Mickey Spillane, one of the great artificial styles of our time, the sophisticated counterfeit of simplicity turned cliché.

As it has descended the long way from Sam Spade to Mike Hammer, the proletarian thriller has come to treat the riddle of guilt and innocence more and more perfunctorily, as its occasion rather than its end. Though it has never abandoned violence and death, it has radically altered their impact by associating them ever more intimately with sex—that subject so pointedly ignored in the prototypical tales of Poe. Murder laced with lust, mayhem spiced with nymphomania: this is the formula for the chief surviving form of the murder mystery in America, though, indeed, that form has not surrendered its native birthright of anti-feminism.* It insists, however, on undressing its bitches, surveying them with a surly and concupiscent eye before punching, shooting, or consigning them to the gas-chamber. Not only in the cruder and more successful books of Mickey Spillane, but in the more pretentious ones of Raymond Chandler, the detective story has reverted to the kind of populist semi-pornography that once made George Lippard's *The Monks of Monk Hall* a black-market best-seller. Now, even as a hundred years ago, lower-middlebrow Americans find it possible to countenance bared breasts and bellies in their literature only when violence is threatening, or when somewhere in the outer darkness a gangster plots his kill. And now, even as a hundred years ago, such

---

* The recent triumphs of James Bond represent a new development of the thriller, in which, like Mailer's heroes, the Secret Agent triumphs over women not with the "equalizer" (which is to say, the deadly weapon) but the "avenger" (which is to say, the lively one). Ian Fleming is, to be sure, British, but he has learned from American prototypes; and it is the American mass audience which finds special satisfaction in his hero's sexual conquest of a Lesbian called Pussy Galore whose troop of fellow Lesbians from Harlem have been bleached white and turned approximately heterosexual in the movie version.

readers relish thinking that the sadist fantasies in which they find masturbatory pleasure are revelations of social disorder, first steps toward making a better world. "The realist in murder," Hammett writes of his own school, "writes of a world in which gangsters can rule nations and almost rule cities, in which hotels and apartment houses and celebrated restaurants are owned by men who made their money out of brothels, and in which a screen star can be the fingerman for a mob. . . ." And through this world, he continues, walks the private eye, the man of honor who is also the poor man, the common man. "If there were enough like him," Chandler concludes, "the world would be a safe place to live in. . . ."

The appeal of Chandler and Hammett has faded with the decline of Popular Front liberalism and their latest imitators provide more and more vulgar sensationalism without even the pretense of virtuous politics, quite losing the righteous middlebrow audience. That audience, particularly in its male segment, has turned to science fiction, which is to say, the gothicism of the future. The first wave of popular gothicism drew on the fear of the past, which haunted a revolutionary epoch on guard against counter-revolution and the restoration of old authority; and the last trace of this fear survives in the ghost story, which looks for terror only in the graveyard, from what is presumably dead and buried. The second wave of popular gothicism reflected a fear of the present, a need to be reassured that the recrudescence of violence and guilt in the vicarage, the country house, or on the old plantation could be controlled by the use of reason, the "scientific" discovery of the truth. This is the source of the classic detective story, and more remotely helps determine even the thrillers of Hammett and Chandler; though in their books not reason but only counter-violence can defeat decadence and corruption—counter-violence and dumb luck, which is to say, grace.

The third wave of popular gothicism appeals to the fear of the future, and is based on a fundamental ambivalence toward science, which is shaping that future. Yet it can appeal only to science itself to regulate its own dangerous course; and the fact that it calls its chief genre "science fiction" indicates the depth of its commitment to technology and the more "scientific" approaches to social problems. Its politics is reasonably liberal, which is to say, it generally favors strong social controls though only for the most unselfish ends; and its world-view is moderately secular, which is to say, it believes God is dead, but sees no reason for getting hysterical about it. For all their vaguely anti-capitalist commitment to planning, most of its writers are if not anti-utopian, at least suspicious of utopias; and in their deepest imagination, the physicist tends to turn in their imaginations into the magician, black or white. In their thoroughly rational universe, all the traditional feats of magic for which respectable scientific terms can be found are accepted as a matter of course: the passage of objects through unbroken barriers (teleportation), the calling-up of the dead (time-travel), the creation of *homunculi* (perfection of multipurpose robots with positronic brains), demonic possession (control of thought-centers by disembodied interplanetary wanderers).

Chiefly, however, it is the dissolution of the earth in fire, which so haunted Poe, a vision of the apocalypse, which obsesses the writers of science fiction, though in their language such ultimate events are referred to as the Third World War, the explosion of the cobalt bomb, etc. The ghost story deals with a terror that threatens to destroy the individual soul; the detective story with a hidden guilt that threatens to destroy the self-contained community, or, more contemporaneously, the social fabric of a city; science fiction evokes a cataclysmic horror that threatens the entire earth, the solar system, galaxy—or even the total universe. Science fiction, on its upper-middlebrow levels, at least, does not admit that it is essentially terror fiction; but with not untypical Anglo-Saxon self-righteousness (it is primarily an Anglo-Saxon form) insists that its ends are insight and morality. Its writers propagate, for instance, non-Aristotelian logic, engram psychology, interracial (even, in advance, interplanetary) tolerance, and, of course, the general cause of science. Yet simultaneously they pander to fantasies of flight, dreams of omnipotence—and, not least of all, the shameful pleasure of imagining the stench of burning bodies, the acrid dust of crumbling cities, the desolation of the man lost in space, the anguish of the oppressed in totalitarian utopias as yet unborn.

In the lowest-brow manifestations of the genre, in comic-books or movies made for adolescents, the theme of the bug-eyed monster predominates: the nightmare of the invasion from space, in which an audience of teen-agers (who otherwise daydream the invasion *of* space) watch on the screen their contemporaries being ingested by a shapeless and inexorable blob of hungry matter. But this is only the most vulgar projection of a more universal theme, implicit on all levels of science fiction: a loss of faith in the potentialities of humanity itself and a prevision of its destruction, a masochistic delight in imagining a future in which mutants, robots, extra-terrestrials, dogs, or simply *nothing* takes over. It is the hallucina-tory form of the fantasy of an American defeat in the next war, a victory for the Others—called simply Russia in the daily news-paper, but transformed into beings more alien and terrible in the depths of the unconscious. But it is also a reflection of the guilt of the scientists themselves, some of whom actually write science-fiction novels and all of whom presumably read solemn discussions of them in *The Bulletin of the Atomic Scientists*. The bomb, which is haunting not only those immediately concerned in its making, but all those committed to a faith in the scientific world-view somehow compromised in its production, plays in science fiction the role of the haunted castle in the earliest gothic romances. Yet on its sur-faces, in its intruded editorials, science fiction is often cheerful, looks forward to the space age and a new inexhaustible West among the stars. The hope on the surface and the terror beneath: it is a customary enough American pattern, not untrue fundamen-tally to the life we live; yet it has turned much science fiction into hypocritical horror-pornography, and stands in the way of its ever being converted into literature of real worth. Certainly, it is the only neo-gothic form which has never been used by a writer of the first rank to tell the kind of truth no middlebrow can confront.*

Yet not only science fiction, but gothic literature on all levels runs the risk of becoming horror-pornography: the extortion of a shudder for its own sake, the submission to reveries of violence for the sake of their voluptuous appeal. Even a writer of intendedly highbrow fictions like Paul Bowles, who served his apprenticeship writing for *transition* and has never abandoned the postures of the avant-garde, can end by providing for readers of the little maga-zines the same furtive, sadist satisfactions that ten-year-olds find in *Horror Comics:*

* William Golding's *Lord of the Flies* is no real exception to this, for though its modes are those of science fiction, its values are middlebrow. But Anthony Burgess's *Clockwork Orange* is, as are the novels of the French pataphysician, Boris Vian; and William Burroughs ever since *The Naked Lunch* has drawn more and more on the conventions of the Gothic of the Future, for ends that challenge the middle-class liberal. The early pages of *The Soft Machine* are, in fact, a masterpiece of the genre.

The man moved and surveyed the young body lying on the stones. He ran his finger along the razor's blade; a pleasant excitement took possession of him. He stepped over, looked down and saw the sex that sprouted from the base of the belly. Not entirely conscious of what he was doing, he took it in one hand and brought his other arm down with the motion of a reaper wielding a sickle. It was swiftly severed. A round, dark hole was left, flush with the skin; he stared a moment, blankly. Driss was screaming. The muscles all over his body stood out, moved.

It is only the beginning of a monstrous sequence, in which the author is palpably an accomplice, invites us to become accomplices, too; and at the end, a little ashamed, we cannot convince ourselves that the point has been to demonstrate "that violence arising out of the clash of the Westerner with the alien world of the East." Only a touch of humor, a conversion at the last moment of *volupté* to farce could have redeemed the scene from pornography to true gothicism; but it is all played straight-faced and breathless.

Still, this kind of travesty is a risk the gothicist *must* run, a danger to which most serious writers sooner or later expose themselves in America, where, for reasons we have indicated, the novelist tends to be defeated in his attempts to deal with love, sentimentally or analytically. In gothicism, the American novelist not only finds opportunities to render inward experience symbolically, to present the world which typically strikes him as a riddle in riddling terms: but in it, too, he discovers ways of mythicizing the brutality and terror endemic to our life. There is, moreover, incumbent on the American author an obligation to negativism, which the sentimental genres cannot fulfill and which realism converts to mere pamphleteering. All fictionists are committed, surely, whatever their other concerns, to revealing the inevitable discrepancy between what life at any moment is imagined and what it is, between what man dreams and what he achieves, between what he would like to believe and what he fears is true. But the "what he fears is true" is the subject par excellence of the gothic, when it is more than mere trifling and titillation.

Nowhere in the world does the writer feel more deeply than in the United States the secret appeal of the community at large that he deny their publicly asserted orthodoxies, expose their dearly preserved deceits. Nowhere is his nay-saying, his "treachery" more desperately needed. There is little temptation really for any American author to play too blatantly affirmative a role; he knows, from the moment he learns to read, that no one wants him to be the Good Good Boy, not even his mother who says so. The danger is not that he will become Sid Sawyer, but that he will learn to play the part of Tom, the Good Bad Boy, the pseudo-rebel with the note in his pocket assuring Aunt Polly of his undying love. To be Huck Finn he must be willing not to "light out for the territory" (Tom was prepared to take that Western outing, too!), but to "go to Hell," which becomes in modern terms, to be "unadjusted," "nihilistic," or "sterile." The words change, but the chorus of sympathetic and dismayed voices crying out in favor of "salvation" or "adjustment" or "commitment" or "love" never ceases: "Nay, Taji: commit not the last, last crime!" Against their allure, the writer has to fortify him chiefly his own sense of the failure of passion and skill in his fellow artists at precisely the point when they abandon blasphemy and turn back toward one or another Serenia. He knows, though high-minded critics occasionally try to obscure the fact, the fatal falling-off between *The Scarlet Letter* and *The House of the Seven Gables,* between *Absalom, Absalom!* and *A Fable, Moby Dick* and the first part of *Pierre* (Melville alone among American writers could plot but never carry through the betrayal of himself), *Huckleberry Finn* and *Joan of Arc*. And he recognizes that, in each case, the author has abandoned with the gothic mode and its negative message his truest self.

Our classic books are not, however, nakedly and openly nihilistic; despite their obsession with terror they provide endings moral and happy enough for any middlebrow reader. Indeed, their gothicism itself is part of their profound duplicity, for the gothic has always been a popular mode, since in a world where fewer and fewer men believe in the Devil, the diabolic stance can be passed off as an amusing sham. Not only the professional funny man, Mark Twain, but Hawthorne and Melville, even Faulkner disguise the diabolical bargains which are the centers of their great books with horseplay and self-conscious farce. Yet read properly that horseplay itself as well as the specious happy endings are revealed as final macabre ironies, blasphemous jokes at the expense of the unwary reader. "I have written a wicked book, and feel spotless as the lamb," Melville writes, giving away the secret; but he does not speak it aloud, only confides it in the ear of his fellow conspirator

Hawthorne, from whom he believed he had learned "the grand truth":

There is the grand truth about Nathaniel Hawthorne. He says No! in thunder; but the Devil himself cannot make him say *yes*. For all men who say *yes,* lie; and all men who say *no,*—why, they are in the happy condition of judicious, unencumbered travellers in Europe; they cross the frontiers into Eternity with nothing but a carpet bag,—that is to say, the Ego.

INDEX